ADVANCED DUNGEONS & DRAGONS™

SPECIAL REFERENCE WORK

DUNGEON MASTERS GUIDE

A COMPILED VOLUME OF INFORMATION PRIMARILY USED BY
ADVANCED DUNGEONS & DRAGONS™ GAME REFEREES, INCLUDING:
COMBAT TABLES; MONSTER LISTS AND ENCOUNTERS; TREASURE
AND MAGIC TABLES AND DESCRIPTIONS; RANDOM DUNGEON
GENERATION; RANDOM WILDERNESS TERRAIN GENERATION;
SUGGESTIONS ON GAMEMASTERING; AND MORE.

By Gary Gygax
© 1979 — TSR Games
All rights reserved
Illustrations by David C. Sutherland III
D. A. Trampier
Darlene Pekul
Will McLean
David S. La Force
Erol Otus
Cover by David C. Sutherland III

Distributed to the book trade in the United States by Random House, Inc. and in Canada by Random House of Canada, Ltd.

Inquiries regarding this work should be accompanied by a stamped return envelope and addressed to: AD&D Questions, TSR Games, POB 756, Lake Geneva, WI 53147.

Printed in the U.S.A.
Revised Edition — December, 1979
ISBN 0-935696-02-4

FOREWORD

Is Dungeon Mastering an art or a science? An interesting question!

If you consider the pure creative aspect of starting from scratch, the "personal touch" of individual flair that goes into preparing and running a unique campaign, or the particular style of moderating a game adventure, then Dungeon Mastering may indeed be thought of as an art.

If you consider the aspect of experimentation, the painstaking effort of preparation and attention to detail, and the continuing search for new ideas and approaches, then Dungeon Mastering is perhaps more like a science — not always exacting in a literal sense, but exacting in terms of what is required to do the job well.

Esoteric questions aside, one thing is for certain — Dungeon Mastering is, above all, a labor of love. It is demanding, time-consuming, and certainly not a task to be undertaken lightly (the sheer bulk of the book you hold in your hand will tell you that!). But, as all DM's know, the rewards are great — an endless challenge to the imagination and intellect, an enjoyable pastime to fill many hours with fantastic and often unpredictable happenings, and an opportunity to watch a story unfold and a grand idea to grow and flourish. The imagination knows no bounds, and the possibilities of the game of **ADVANCED DUNGEONS & DRAGONS** are just as limitless. Who can say what awaits each player, except a cornucopia of fantasy and heroic adventure? So much is waiting, indeed!

This book holds much in store for you as a DM — it is your primary tool in constructing your own "world", or milieu. It contains a wealth of material, and combined with the other works of **ADVANCED DUNGEONS & DRAGONS** (the **MONSTER MANUAL** and **PLAYERS HANDBOOK**) gives you all the information you need to play **AD&D**. But, as always, one more thing is needed — your imagination. Use the written material as your foundation and inspiration, then explore the creative possibilities you have in your own mind to make your game something special.

Dungeon Mastering itself is no easy undertaking, to be sure. But Dungeon Mastering well is doubly difficult. There are few gamemasters around who are so superb in their conduct of play that they could disdain the opportunity to improve themselves in some way. Fortunately, this work addresses the matter at length, and gives you plenty of suggestions on all aspects of Dungeon Mastering (as well as some of the finer points) in order to help you improve your own efforts. Take heed, and always endeavor to make the game the best it can be — and **all** that it can be!

Mike Carr
TSR Games & Rules Editor

16 May 1979

Cover: The book cover painting shows an encounter between three adventurers and an efreet on the Elemental Plane of Fire. The fabled City of Brass can be seen floating over a flame-swept sea of oil.

CONTENTS

TABLES AND CHARTS

PREFACE

What follows herein is strictly for the eyes of you, the campaign referee. As the creator and ultimate authority in your respective game, this work is written as one Dungeon Master equal to another. Pronouncements there may be, but they are not from "on high" as respects *your* game. Dictums are given for the sake of *the* game only, for if **ADVANCED DUNGEONS & DRAGONS** is to survive and grow, it must have some degree of uniformity, a familiarity of method and procedure from campaign to campaign within the whole. **ADVANCED D&D** is more than a framework around which individual DMs construct their respective milieux, it is above all a set of boundaries for all of the "worlds" devised by referees everywhere. These boundaries are broad and spacious, and there are numerous areas where they are so vague and amorphous as to make them nearly nonexistent, but they are there nonetheless.

When you build your campaign you will tailor it to suit your personal tastes. In the heat of play it will slowly evolve into a compound of your personality and those of your better participants, a superior alloy. And as long as your campaign remains viable, it will continue a slow process of change and growth. In this lies a great danger, however. The systems and parameters contained in the whole of **ADVANCED DUNGEONS & DRAGONS** are based on a great deal of knowledge, experience gained through discussion, play, testing, questioning, and (hopefully) personal insight.

Limitations, checks, balances, and all the rest are placed into the system in order to assure that what is based thereon will be a superior campaign, a campaign which offers the most interesting play possibilities to the greatest number of participants for the longest period of time possible. You, as referee, will have to devote countless hours of real effort in order to produce just a fledgling campaign, viz. a background for the whole, some small village or town, and a reasoned series of dungeon levels — the lot of which must be suitable for elaboration and expansion on a periodic basis. To obtain real satisfaction from such effort, you must have participants who will make use of your creations: players to learn the wonders and face the perils you have devised for them. If it is all too plain and too easy, the players will quickly lose interest, and your effort will prove to have been in vain. Likewise, if the campaign is too difficult, players will quickly become discouraged and lose interest in a game where they are always the butt; again your labors will have been for naught. These facts are of prime importance, for they underlie many rules.

Naturally, everything possible cannot be included in the whole of this work. As a participant in the game, I would not care to have anyone telling me exactly what must go into a campaign and how it must be handled; if so, why not play some game like chess? As the author I also realize that there are limits to my creativity and imagination. Others will think of things I didn't, and devise things beyond my capability. As an active Dungeon Master I kept a careful watch for things which would tend to complicate matters without improving them, systems devised seemingly to make the game drag for players, rules which lessened the fantastic and unexpected in favor of the mundane and ordinary. As if that were not enough hats to wear, I also wore that of a publisher, watching the work so as to make sure that it did not grow so large as to become unmanageable cost-wise. None of this was compromise, *per se*, but the process was most certainly a refining of what should logically be presented in the system.

Returning again to the framework aspect of **ADVANCED DUNGEONS & DRAGONS,** what is aimed at is a "universe" into which similar campaigns and parallel worlds can be placed. With certain uniformity of systems and "laws", players will be able to move from one campaign to another and know at least the elemental principles which govern the new milieu, for all milieux will have certain (but not necessarily the same) laws in common. Character races and classes will be nearly the same. Character ability scores will have the identical meaning — or nearly so. Magic spells will function in a certain manner regardless of which world the player is functioning in. Magic devices will certainly vary, but their principles will be similar. This uniformity will help not only players, it will enable DMs to carry on a meaningful dialogue and exchange of useful information. It might also eventually lead to grand tournaments wherein persons from any part of the U.S., or the world for that matter, can compete for accolades.

The danger of a mutable system is that you or your players will go too far in some undesirable direction and end up with a short-lived campaign. Participants will always be pushing for a game which allows them to become strong and powerful far too quickly. Each will attempt to take the game out of your hands and mold it to his or her own ends. To satisfy this natural desire is to issue a death warrant to a campaign, for it will either be a one-player affair or the players will desert *en masse* for something more challenging and equitable. Similarly, you must avoid the tendency to drift into areas foreign to the game as a whole. Such campaigns become so strange as to be no longer **"AD&D"**. They are isolated and will usually wither. Variation and difference are desirable, but both should be kept within the boundaries of the overall system. Imaginative and creative addition can most certainly be included; that is why nebulous areas have been built into the game. Keep such individuality in perspective by developing a unique and detailed world based on the rules of **ADVANCED D&D.** No two campaigns will ever be the same, but all will have the common ground necessary to maintaining the whole as a viable entity about which you and your players can communicate with the many thousands of others who also find swords & sorcery role playing gaming as an amusing and enjoyable pastime.

As this book is the exclusive precinct of the DM, you must view any non-DM player possessing it as something less than worthy of honorable death. Peeping players there will undoubtedly be, but they are simply lessening their own enjoyment of the game by taking away some of the sense of wonder that otherwise arises from a game which has rules hidden from partici- pants. It is in your interests, and in theirs, to discourage possession of this book by players. If any of your participants do read herein, it is suggested that you assess them a heavy fee for consulting "sages" and other sources of information not normally attainable by the inhabitants of your milieu. If they express knowledge which could only be garnered by consulting these pages, a magic item or two can be taken as payment — insufficient, but perhaps it will tend to discourage such actions.

I sincerely hope that you find this new system to your taste and enjoy it. The material is herein, but only you can construct the masterpiece from it, your personal campaign which will bring hundreds of hours of fun and excitement to many eager players. Masterful dungeoning to you!

CREDITS & ACKNOWLEDGMENTS

The following is an alphabetical list of all those persons who in some way contributed to the formation of this work. Naturally, each did not make an identical contribution, and those with whom I normally play **AD&D,** as well as those kind enough to review the initial manuscript, had more influence and engendered more ideas than did those others with whom I do not have the privilege of continued close association or contact. Nonetheless, all are herewith credited and thanked, trusting that each will know what his or her own contribution was! Peter Aronson, Brian Blume, Mike Carr, Sean Cleary, Jean-Louis Fiasson, Ernie (the well-known Barbarian) Gygax, Luke Gygax, Al Hammack, Neal Healey, Tom Holsinger, Harold Johnson, Timothy Jones, Tim Kask, Rick Krebs, Len Lakofka, Jeff Leason, Steve Marsh, Schar Niebling, Will Niebling, Jon Pickens, Gregory Rihn, John Sapienza, Lawrence Schick, Doug Schwegman, Dennis Sustare, Jack Vance, James M. Ward, Jean Wells, and Skip Williams.

Also to be thanked are those uncounted DMs and players who have been eager to improve adventure gaming and have spent their valuable time to give me the benefit of their thinking by letter or through personal contact at conventions. Your efforts to find ways to do things better, to point out ambiguities or flaws, and general desire to aid and encourage me are ap- preciated!

Bob Bledsaw of Judges Guild must also be given credit. He and his associates have certainly contributed to the overall improvement of fantasy adventure gaming, making the undertaking easier and encouraging still more interest in role playing.

Finally, no list of credits would be complete unless I especially thanked the artists who have been so much help with the entire compilation of **ADVANCED DUNGEONS & DRAGONS.** These artists are Dave Sutherland and Dave Trampier. Thank you, gentlemen!

If by any chance I have neglected anyone, please forgive me, as the task of finishing the **DUNGEON MASTERS GUIDE** has taken some two years; and during that time I have read hundreds of pages of suggestions, done thousands of pages of re- searching, and written about twelve hundred pages of manuscript. A job begun in 1976, often interrupted, has at last been completed. Notes made months or years ago have a way of getting lost in the last minute rush at the finish.

INTRODUCTION

The format of this book is simple and straightforward. The first sections pertain to material contained in the **PLAYERS HANDBOOK,** and each pertinent section is in corresponding order. Much information was purposely omitted from the latter work, as it is data which would not normally be known — at least initially — to a person of the nature which this game presupposes, i.e. an adventurer in a world of swords & sorcery. It is incumbent upon all DMs to be thoroughly conversant with the **PLAYERS HANDBOOK,** and at the same time you must also know the additional information which is given in this volume, for it rounds out and completes the whole. While players will know that they must decide upon an alignment, for example, you, the DM, will further know that each and every action they take will be mentally recorded by you; and at adventure's end you will secretly note any player character movement on the alignment graph.

After the material which pertains directly to the **PLAYERS HANDBOOK** comes the information which supplements and augments. There is a large section which lists and explains the numerous magical items. There are sections on the development of the campaign milieu, dungeon design, random creation of wilderness and dungeon levels, and the development of non-player characters. In fact, what I have attempted is to cram everything vital to the game into this book, so that you will be as completely equipped as possible to face the ravenous packs of players lurking in the shadows, waiting to pounce upon the unwary referee and devour him or her at the first opportunity.

Thus, besides the systems, I have made every effort to give the reasoning and justification for the game. Of course the ultimate reason and justification is a playable and interesting game, and how much rationalization can actually go into a fantasy game? There is some, at least, as you will see, for if the game is fantasy, there is a basis for much of what is contained herein, even though it be firmly grounded on worlds of make-believe. And while there are no optionals for the major systems of **ADVANCED D&D** (for uniformity of rules and procedures from game to game, campaign to campaign, is stressed), there are plenty of areas where your own creativity and imagination are not bounded by the parameters of the game system. These are sections where only a few hints and suggestions are given, and the rest left to the DM.

There is so much that could have been included herein that a major part of authoring this volume was deciding what would be omitted! The criterion was usefulness. First came material which was absolutely vital to play, then came the inclusion of what would be most helpful to you, and finally interesting items of broad appeal which tend to improve the flavor of a campaign were sifted into the work. Material included was written with an eye towards playability and expedition. The fun of the game is action and drama. The challenge of problem solving is secondary. Long and drawn out operations by the referee irritate the players. More "realistic" combat systems could certainly have been included here, but they have no real part in a game for a group of players having an exciting adventure. If you will do your best to keep the excitement level of your games at a peak, you will be doing yourself and your participants a favor which will be evident when players keep coming back for more.

The final word, then, is the game. Read how and why the system is as it is, follow the parameters, and then cut portions as needed to maintain excitement. For example, the rules call for wandering monsters, but these can be not only irritating — if not deadly — but the appearance of such can actually spoil a game by interfering with an orderly expedition. You have set up an area full of clever tricks and traps, populated it with well-thought-out creature complexes, given clues about it to pique players' interest, and the group has worked hard to supply themselves with everything by way of information and equipment they will need to face and overcome the imagined perils. They are gathered together and eager to spend an enjoyable evening playing their favorite game, with the expectation of going to a new, strange area and doing their best to triumph. They are willing to accept the hazards of the dice, be it loss of items, wounding, insanity, disease, death, as long as the process is exciting. But lo!, everytime you throw the "monster die" a wandering nasty is indicated, and the party's strength is spent trying to fight their way into the area. Spells expended, battered and wounded, the characters trek back to their base. Expectations have been dashed, and probably interest too, by random chance. Rather than spoil such an otherwise enjoyable time, omit the wandering monsters indicated by the die. No, don't allow the party to kill them easily or escape unnaturally, for that goes contrary to the major precepts of the game. Wandering monsters, however, are included for two

reasons, as is explained in the section about them. If a party deserves to have these beasties inflicted upon them, that is another matter, but in the example above it is assumed that they are doing everything possible to travel quickly and quietly to their planned destination. If your work as a DM has been sufficient, the players will have all they can handle upon arrival, so let them get there, give them a chance. The game is the thing, and certain rules can be distorted or disregarded altogether in favor of play.

Know the game systems, and you will know how and when to take upon yourself the ultimate power. To become the final arbiter, rather than the interpreter of the rules, can be a difficult and demanding task, and it cannot be undertaken lightly, for your players expect to play *this* game, not one made up on the spot. By the same token, they are playing the game the way *you*, their DM, imagines and creates it. Remembering that the game is greater than its parts, and knowing all of the parts, you will have overcome the greater part of the challenge of being a referee. Being a true DM requires cleverness and imagination which no set of rules books can bestow. Seeing that you were clever enough to buy this volume, and you have enough imagination to desire to become the maker of a fantasy world, you are almost there already! Read and become familiar with the contents of this work and the one written for players, learn your monsters, and spice things up with some pantheons of super-powerful beings. Then put your judging and refereeing ability into the creation of your own personal milieu, and you have donned the mantle of Dungeon Master. Welcome to the exalted ranks of the overworked and harrassed, whose cleverness and imagination are all too often unappreciated by cloddish characters whose only thought in life is to loot, pillage, slay, and who fail to appreciate the hours of preparation which went into the creation of what they aim to destroy as cheaply and quickly as possible. As a DM you must live by the immortal words of the sage who said: "Never give a sucker an even break." Also, don't be a sucker for your players, for you'd better be sure they follow sage advice too. As the DM, you have to prove in every game that you are still the best. This book is dedicated to helping to assure that you are.

THE GAME

APPROACHES TO PLAYING ADVANCED DUNGEONS & DRAGONS

A few brief words are necessary to insure that the reader has actually obtained a game form which he or she desires. Of the two approaches to hobby games today, one is best defined as the *realism-simulation* school and the other as the *game* school. **AD&D** is assuredly an adherent of the latter school. It does not stress any realism (in the author's opinion an absurd effort at best considering the topic!). It does little to attempt to simulate anything either. **ADVANCED DUNGEONS & DRAGONS** is first and foremost a game for the fun and enjoyment of those who seek to use imagination and creativity. This is not to say that where it does not interfere with the flow of the game that the highest degree of realism hasn't been attempted, but neither is a serious approach to play discouraged. In all cases, however, the reader should understand that **AD&D** is designed to be an amusing and diverting pastime, something which can fill a few hours or consume endless days, as the participants desire, but in no case something to be taken too seriously. For fun, excitement, and captivating fantasy, **AD&D** is unsurpassed. As a realistic simulation of things from the realm of make-believe, or even as a reflection of medieval or ancient warfare or culture or society, it can be deemed only a dismal failure. Readers who seek the latter must search elsewhere. Those who desire to create and populate imaginary worlds with larger-than-life heroes and villains, who seek relaxation with a fascinating game, and who generally believe games should be fun, not work, will hopefully find this system to their taste.

DICE

As the DM, the tools of your trade are dice — platonic solid-shaped or just about any other sort. The random numbers you generate by rolling dice determine the results based on the probabilities determined herein or those you have set forth on your own. In case you are not familiar with probability curves, there are two types which are determined by your dice: linear (straight line), which has equal probability of any given integer in the number group, and bell (ascending and descending line), which has greater probability towards the center of the group of numbers than at either end. The two curves are illustrated thus:

Linear curve

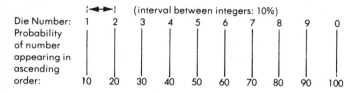

Linear probability develops a straight line of ascending probability when used as a cumulative probability as shown above.

Bell distribution, when used to delineate the probability of certain numbers appearing, develops a curved line like this:

Bell Curve (3d6)

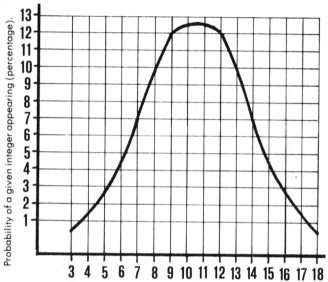

A single die, or multiple dice read in succession (such as three dice read as hundreds, tens and decimals) give linear probabilities. Two or more dice added together generate a bell-shaped probability curve.

Before any further discussion takes place, let us define the accepted abbreviations for the various dice. A die is symbolized by "d", and its number of sides is shown immediately thereafter. A six-sided die is therefore "d6", d8 is an eight-sided die, and so on. Two four-sided dice are expressed by 2d4, five eight-sided dice are 5d8, etc. Any additions to or subtractions from the die or dice are expressed after the identification, thus: d8 + 8 means a linear number grouping between 9 and 16, while 3d6 −2 means a bell-shaped progression from 1 to 16, with the greatest probability group in the middle (8, 9). This latter progression has the same median numbers as 2d6, but it has higher and lower ends and a greater probability of a median number than if 2d12 were used. When percentage dice are to be used, this is indicated by d%.

The d4 can be used to generate 25% incremental probabilities, random numbers from 1 to 4, with + 1 it generates a linear 2-5, etc. It can be used to get 1 or 2 (1 or 2 = 1, 3 or 4 = 2) or in conjunction with any other dice to get linear or bell-shaped probability curves. For example, 2d4 = 2-8, 3d4 = 3-12, d4 + d6 = 2-10, d4 + d20 (as d10) = 2-14. When rolled in conjunction with another die, the d4 can be used to determine linear number ranges twice that shown on the other die, thus: d4 reading 1 or 2 means that whatever is read on the other die is the number shown; but if the d4 reads 3 or 4, add the highest number on the second die to the number shown — so if d8 is the second die 1 to 16 can be generated, if a d12 is used 1 to 24 can be generated. If a d20 is used either 1-20 (assuming the use of a standard d20 which is numbered 0-9 twice without coloring one set of faces to indicate that those faces have 10 added to the number appearing) or 1-40 (assuming that one set of faces is colored) can be gotten by adding 0 if 1 or 2 is rolled on the d4 and 10 or 20 (depending on die type) if a 3 or 4 is rolled. Linear series above this are possible simply by varying the meaning of the d4 number; 1 always means add 0, but 2 can be interpreted as add the value (highest number) of the second die, 3 can be twice value, and 4 can be thrice value. Thus, a d4 reading 4 in conjunction with a d8 (linear curve 1-32) would mean 24 + d8, or 25-32.

What applies to d4 has similar application with regard to d6, d8, d12, and d20. The d6 has 16⅔% intervals, d8 has 12½% intervals, and d20 can have 10% or 5% intervals. A d6 is useful for getting a random number from 1 to 3 (1-2 = 1, 3-4 = 2, 5-6 = 3), while 1 to 5 can be easily read from a d20 (1-2 = 1, 3-4 = 2, 5-6 = 3, 7-8 = 4, 9-0 = 5).

The d20 is used often, both as d10 and d20. The bell-shaped probability curves typically range from 2-20 to 5-50, i.e., 2, 3, 4 or 5d20 added together. Also common is the reading as above with one decimal place added to the result to get 20-200, 30-300, etc. In the latter case, a roll of 3 on one die and 0 (read as 10) totals 13, plus one place, or 130.

Non-platonic solid-shaped dice are available in some places. The most common of these is a ten-sided die numbered 0-9. As with the d20, this can be used for many purposes, even replacing the d20 if a second die is used in conjunction to get 5% interval curves (1-20). Also, the die can give 0-9 linear curve random numbers, as the d20 can.

Other dice available are various forms of "averaging" dice. The most common of these has six faces which read: 2, 3, 3, 4, 4, 5. The median of the curve it generates is still 3.5, that of a normal d6, but the low and high numbers, 2 and 5, are only half as likely to appear as 3 or 4. There is a 33⅓% chance for either of the two latter numbers to be rolled, so the probabilities of absolutely average rolls are far greater. Other such dice have zeros on them, several low numbers, and so on. These sorts of dice, along with poker dice, "put & take" dice, or any other sort can be added in order to give you more flexibility or changing probabilities in random selection or event interpretation. For example:

The author has a d6 with the following faces: SPADE, CLUB, CLUB, DIAMOND, DIAMOND, HEART. If, during an encounter, players meet a character whose reaction is uncertain, the card suit die is rolled in conjunction with 3d6. Black suits mean dislike, with the SPADE equalling hate, while red equals like, the HEART being great favor. The 3d6 give a bell-shaped probability curve of 3-18, with 9-12 being the mean spread. SPADE 18 means absolute and unchangeable hate, while HEART 18 indicates the opposite. CLUBS or DIAMONDS can be altered by discourse, rewards, etc. Thus, CLUBS 12 could possibly be altered to CLUBS 3 by offer of a tribute or favor, CLUBS 3 changed to DIAMONDS 3 by a gift, etc.

In closing this discussion, simply keep in mind that the dice are your tools. Learn to use them properly, and they will serve you well.

USE OF MINIATURE FIGURES WITH THE GAME

The special figures cast for **ADVANCED DUNGEONS & DRAGONS** add color to play and make refereeing far easier. Each player might be required to furnish painted figures representing his or her player character and all henchmen and/or hirelings included in the game session. Such distinctively painted figures enable you to immediately recognize each individual involved. Figures can be placed so as to show their order of march, i.e., which characters are in the lead, which are in the middle, and which are bringing up the rear. Furthermore, players are more readily able to visualize their array and plan actions while seeing the reason for your restrictions on their actions. Monster figures are likewise most helpful, as many things become instantly apparent when a party is arrayed and their monster opponent(s) placed. Furnishing such monsters is probably best undertaken as a joint effort, the whole group contributing towards the purchase of such figurines on a regular basis. Be very careful to purchase castings which are in scale! Out of scale monsters are virtually worthless in many cases. As a rule of thumb, HO scale is 25 mm = 1 actual inch = 6' in scale height or length or breadth.

Figure bases are necessarily broad in order to assure that the figures will stand in the proper position and not constantly be falling over. Because of this, it is usually necessary to use a ground scale twice that of the actual scale for HO, and squares of about 1 actual inch per side are suggested. Each ground scale inch can then be equal to equal 3⅓ linear feet, so a 10' wide scale corridor is 3 actual inches in width and shown as 3 separate squares. This allows depiction of the typical array of three figures abreast, and also enables easy handling of such figures when they are moved. While you may not find it convenient to actually use such figures and floor plans to handle routine dungeon movement, having sheets of squares for encounter area depiction will probably be quite helpful. If you do so, be certain to remember that ground scale differs from figure scale, and when dealing with length, two man-sized figures per square is quite possible, as the space is actually 6 scale feet with respect to length. This is meaningful when attacking a snake, dragon, etc. if characters are able to attack the creature's body length. With respect to basically bipedal, erect opponents, scale will not be a factor.

Details of preparation and painting of miniature figures for the game are not germane to this work. Your hobby supplier will have an assortment of small brushes and paints for such purposes, and you may inquire there as to the best techniques of painting.

AIDS TO PLAYING ADVANCED DUNGEONS & DRAGONS

Various products such as modules, playing aids, and miniature figurines will be most helpful in establishing and maintaining an interesting and exciting campaign. There are so many such products available that it is not possible to detail each here, but some guidance can be given.

Paper products range from record sheets for characters and special screens for the DM, which contain frequently-consulted charts and tables on his or her side, to complete dungeon or world scenarios. TSR provides a broad selection of such goods, some of which are listed at the back of this work. You can obtain a complete list by writing to TSR at the address shown and asking for a current catalog. The only other source of approved and *official* **AD&D** material is Judges Guild, 1165 North University Ave., Decatur, IL 62526. Judges Guild publishes a large and continually expanding line of materials, and you should contact them for their current catalog. While there are many other works which appear to be useful in a campaign, only those bearing the **ADVANCED DUNGEONS & DRAGONS** logo and approval mark should be used.

Miniature figures used to represent characters and monsters add color and life to the game. They also make the task of refereeing action, particularly combat, easier too! In combination with a gridded surface, such as the DUNGEON FLOORPLANS (to be published by TSR in the near future), these miniatures will add a whole new dimension to your playing enjoyment. It is suggested that you urge your players to provide painted figures representing their characters, henchmen, and hirelings involved in play. The monsters can be furnished by you — possibly purchased through collection of small fees levied on each playing session. The **OFFICIAL ADVANCED DUNGEONS & DRAGONS** miniature figures will be released by Grenadier Models, POB 305, Springfield, PA 19064, about November 1979. These figures are the only ones which comply in all respects to **AD&D** specifications and the **AD&D MONSTER MANUAL**. Contact Grenadier for an up-to-date listing of available figures. Other approved lines of fantasy figures **APPROVED FOR USE WITH ADVANCED DUNGEONS & DRAGONS** will be offered by select manufacturers. Always look for the name, **ADVANCED DUNGEONS & DRAGONS**, and the TSR approval mark before purchasing figures for your campaign.

It is also very important to keep abreast of what is happening in the world of adventure gaming. You may do so by subscribing to such publications as THE DRAGON and WHITE DWARF — or you might find it convenient to purchase them from your favorite game supplier. For current frequency and costs, drop a card or letter to the address shown below, and ask for the latest information.

United States
TSR Periodicals
POB 110
Lake Geneva, WI 53147

Be certain to specify the names of the publications you are interested in.

Again, a word of warning. Many products might purport to be satisfactory for use with **ADVANCED DUNGEONS & DRAGONS**, but only those noted as OFFICIAL or *Authorized* **AD&D** items should be accepted. Do not settle for substitutes or second-rate material in your campaign; ask for approved **AD&D** products only!

CREATING THE PLAYER CHARACTER

GENERATION OF ABILITY SCORES

As **AD&D** is an ongoing game of fantasy adventuring, it is important to allow participants to generate a viable character of the race and profession which he or she desires. While it is possible to generate some fairly playable characters by rolling 3d6, there is often an extended period of

attempts at finding a suitable one due to quirks of the dice. Furthermore, these rather marginal characters tend to have short life expectancy — which tends to discourage new players, as does having to make do with some character of a race and/or class which he or she really can't or won't identify with. Character generation, then, is a serious matter, and it is recommended that the following systems be used. Four alternatives are offered for player characters:

Method I:

All scores are recorded and arranged in the order the player desires. 4d6 are rolled, and the lowest die (or one of the lower) is discarded.

Method II:

All scores are recorded and arranged as in Method I. 3d6 are rolled 12 times and the highest 6 scores are retained.

Method III:

Scores rolled are according to each ability category, in order, STRENGTH, INTELLIGENCE, WISDOM, DEXTERITY, CONSTITUTION, CHARISMA. 3d6 are rolled 6 times for each ability, and the highest score in each category is retained for that category.

Method IV:

3d6 are rolled sufficient times to generate the 6 ability scores, in order, for 12 characters. The player then selects the single set of scores which he or she finds most desirable and these scores are noted on the character record sheet.

NON-PLAYER CHARACTERS

Non-Player Characters: You should, of course, set the ability scores of those NPCs you will use as parts of the milieu, particularly those of high level and power. Scores for high level NPC's must be high — how else could these figures have risen so high? Determine the ability scores of other non-player characters as follows:

General Characters: Roll 3d6 for each ability as usual, but use *average* scoring by considering any 1 as a 3 and any 6 as a 4.

Special Characters, Including Henchmen: Roll 3d6 as for general characters, but allow the full range (3-18) except in the ability or abilities which are germane to his or her profession, i.e. strength for fighters, etc. For all such abilities either use one of the determination methods used for player characters or add +1 to each die of the 3 rolled which scores under 6.

THE EFFECT OF WISHES ON CHARACTER ABILITY SCORES

It is quite usual for players to use *wishes* (or *alter reality* spells found on scrolls) to increase their ability scores in desired areas, whatever the areas might be. It is strongly suggested that you place no restrictions upon such use of *wishes*. However, at some point it must be made more difficult to go up in ability, or else many characters will eventually be running around with several 18s (or even higher!). Therefore, when any ability score reaches 16, then it should be ruled a *wish* will have the effect of increasing the ability by only 1/10th of a point. Thus, by means of *wishes* (or *wishes* and/or *alter reality* spells) a *charisma* score of 16 can only be raised to 17 by use of 10 such *wishes*, the score going from 16 to 16.1 with the first *wish*, 16.2 with the second, and so on. This is not to say that magical books or devices can not raise scores of 16 or better a full point. The prohibition is only on *wishes*.

CHARACTERISTICS FOR PLAYER CHARACTERS

Use of the NPC personality traits and characteristics for player characters is NOT recommended. The purpose of **AD&D** is to allow participants to create and develop interesting player characters who will adventure and interact with their surroundings. If personality traits are forced upon PCs, then participants will be doing little more than moving automatons around while you, the DM, tell them how their characters react to situations. It is therefore absolutely necessary for you to allow each player the right to develop his or her character as he or she chooses!

This is not to say that some of the information used for development of NPCs cannot be used for PCs. If a player asks to have you make certain determinations for his or her character, you may do so if you believe that the player will be able to properly act the part as dictated by the dice rolls. Height and weight *should* be randomly determined for each PC, and the **HEIGHT AND WEIGHT TABLES** in the **PERSONAE OF NON-PLAYER CHARACTERS** section are useful in this regard. However, these tables do not actually give sufficient variation in upper limits of height and weight of humans, so you might find it necessary to allow the following height and weight variations for human player characters:

Human Male: Height — 2-20''; Weight — 10-200#

Human Female: Height — 2-12''; Weight — 10-120#

PLAYER CHARACTER NON-PROFESSIONAL SKILLS

When a player character selects a class, this profession is assumed to be that which the character has been following previously, virtually to the exclusion of all other activities. Thus the particular individual is at 1st level of ability. However, some minor knowledge of certain mundane skills might belong to the player character — information and training from early years or incidentally picked up while the individual was in apprenticeship learning his or her primary professional skills of clericism, fighting, etc. If your particular campaign is aimed at a level of play where secondary skills can be taken into account, then use the table below to assign them to player characters, or even to henchmen if you so desire.

Assign a skill randomly, or select according to the background of your campaign. To determine if a second skill is known, roll on the table, and if the dice indicate a result of TWO SKILLS, then assign a second, appropriate one.

SECONDARY SKILLS TABLE

Dice Score	Result
01-02	Armorer
03-04	Bowyer/fletcher
05-10	Farmer/gardener
11-14	Fisher (netting)
15-20	Forester
21-23	Gambler
24-27	Hunter/fisher (hook and line)
28-32	Husbandman (animal husbandry)
33-34	Jeweler/lapidary
35-37	Leather worker/tanner
38-39	Limner/painter
40-42	Mason/carpenter
43-44	Miner
45-46	Navigator (fresh or salt water)
47-49	Sailor (fresh or salt)
50-51	Shipwright (boats or ships)
52-54	Tailor/weaver
55-57	Teamster/freighter
58-60	Trader/barterer
61-64	Trapper/furrier
65-67	Woodworker/cabinetmaker
68-85	NO SKILL OF MEASURABLE WORTH
86-00	ROLL TWICE IGNORING THIS RESULT HEREAFTER

When secondary skills are used, it is up to the DM to create and/or adjudicate situations in which these skills are used or useful to the player character. As a general rule, having a skill will give the character the ability to determine the general worth and soundness of an item, the ability to find food, make small repairs, or actually construct (crude) items. For example, an individual with *armorer* skill could tell the quality of normal armor, repair chain links, or perhaps fashion certain weapons. To determine the extent of knowledge in question, simply assume the role of one of these skills, one that you know a little something about, and determine what could be done with this knowledge. Use this as a scale to weigh the relative ability of characters with secondary skills.

(See also **THE CAMPAIGN, SOCIAL CLASS & RANK IN AD&D.**)

STARTING LEVEL OF EXPERIENCE FOR PLAYER CHARACTERS

As a general rule the greatest thrill for any neophyte player will be the first adventure, when he or she doesn't have any real idea of what is happening, how powerful any encountered monster is, or what rewards will be gained from the adventure. This assumes survival, and you should gear

your dungeon to accommodate 1st level players. If your campaign has a mixture of experienced and inexperienced players, you should arrange for the two groups to adventure separately, possibly in separate dungeons, at first. Allow the novice players to learn for themselves, and give experienced players tougher situations to face, for they already understand most of what is happening — quite unlike true 1st level adventurers of the would-be sort, were such persons actually to exist.

If you have an existing campaign, with the majority of the players being already above 1st level, it might be better to allow the few newcomers to begin at 2nd level or even 3rd or 4th in order to give them a survival chance when the group sets off for some lower dungeon level. I do not personally favor granting unearned experience level(s) except in extreme circumstances such as just mentioned, for it tends to rob the new player of the real enjoyment he or she would normally feel upon actually gaining levels of experience by dint of cleverness, risk, and hard fighting.

It has been called to my attention that new players will sometimes become bored and discouraged with the struggle to advance in level of experience, for they do not have any actual comprehension of what it is like to be a powerful character of high level. In a well planned and well judged campaign this is not too likely to happen, for the superior DM will have just enough treasure to whet the appetite of players, while keeping them lean and hungry still, and always after that carrot just ahead. And one player's growing ennui can often be dissipated by rivalry, i.e., he or she fails to go on an adventure, and those who did play not only had an exciting time but brought back a rich haul as well. Thus, in my opinion, a challenging campaign and careful refereeing should obviate the need for immediate bestowal of levels of experience to maintain interest in the game. However, whatever the circumstances, if some problem such as this exists, it has been further suggested that allowing relatively new players to participate in a modular campaign game (assuring new players of characters of higher level) would often whet their appetites for continued play at lower level, for they can then grasp what it will be like should they actually succeed in attaining proficiency on their own by working up their original characters and gaining high levels of experience. This reasoning seems sound, and provided there is a separation of the two campaigns, and the one isn't begun until new players have had some number of expeditions as 1st level characters, it is not destructive to the game as a whole.

CHARACTER AGE, AGING, DISEASE, AND DEATH

CHARACTER AGE

At the onset of each and every character's creation it is necessary that you establish his or her age. For player characters and henchmen you must use the appropriate table. You may do the same for other characters, or you may assign age as you see fit in light of the milieu you have developed. There are two tables, one for non-human (the demi-humans, part humans, and the like) and one for humans.

Non-Human Characters Table:

Race	Cleric	Fighter	Magic-User	Thief
dwarf	250 + 2d20	40 + 5d4	—	75 + 3d6
elf	500 + 10d10	130 + 5d6	150 + 5d6	50 + 5d6
gnome	300 + 3d12	60 + 5d4	100 + 2d12	80 + 5d4
half-elf	40 + 2d4	22 + 3d4	30 + 2d8	22 + 3d8
halfling	—	20 + 3d4	—	40 + 2d4
half-orc	20 + 1d4	13 + 1d4	—	20 + 2d4

For multi-classed characters use the column which develops the highest age and use the greatest possible addition to the base age, i.e., do NOT generate the age variable by random die roll, but assign the maximum.

Humans Table:

Class	Age Plus Variable	Class	Age Plus Variable
cleric	18 + 1d4	magic-user	24 + 2d8
druid	18 + 1d4	illusionist	30 + 1d6
fighter	15 + 1d4	thief	18 + 1d4
paladin	17 + 1d4	assassin	20 + 1d4
ranger	20 + 1d4	monk	21 + 1d4

Bards begin at the age of the class in which they first begin.

Once character age is established, you must keep track of it from game year to game year. (Cf. **TIME IN THE CAMPAIGN.**) To normal game time years must be added any of the various unnatural causes of shortening life, i.e. *aging*. These effectively add years to the character's age. The effects of aging are given in the next section. The maximum age of any character is likewise explained.

AGING

In order to establish the overall effects of age, it is necessary to establish a number of standard age brackets for each race of characters. When age category is established, modify ability scores accordingly, making each change progressively from *young adulthood*, all additions and subtractions being cumulative. The only ability which may exceed 18 due to age effects (unless age restricts this) is *wisdom*. Most adjustments are in whole numbers, so that 18 strength drops to 17, even if it is from 18/00, as exceptional strength is not considered.

Age Categories:

Race	Young Adult	Mature	Middle Aged	Old	Venerable
dwarf	35-50	51-150	151-250	251-350	351-450
dwarf, mountain	40-60	61-175	176-275	276-400	401-525
elf, aquatic	75-150	151-450	451-700	701-1000	1001-1200
elf, Drow	50-100	101-400	401-600	601-800	801-1000
elf, gray	150-250	251-650	651-1000	1001-1500	1501-2000
elf, high	100-175	176-550	551-875	876-1200	1201-1600
elf, wood	75-150	151-500	501-800	801-1100	1101-1350
gnome	50-90	91-300	301-450	451-600	601-750
half-elf	24-40	41-100	101-175	176-250	251-325
halfling	22-33	34-68	69-101	102-144	145-199
half-orc	12-15	16-30	31-45	46-60	61-80
human	14-20	21-40	41-60	61-90	91-120

Young Adult: Subtract 1 point of *wisdom*, add 1 point of *constitution*.

Mature: Add 1 point of *strength*, add 1 point of *wisdom*.

Middle Aged: Subtract 1 point (or half *exceptional* rating) of *strength* and 1 point of *constitution*; add 1 point of *intelligence* and 1 point of *wisdom*.

Old: Subtract 2 points of *strength*, 2 points of *dexterity*, and 1 point of *constitution*; add 1 point of *wisdom*.

Venerable: Subtract 1 point of *strength*, 1 point of *dexterity*, and 1 point of *constitution*; add 1 point of *intelligence* and 1 point of *wisdom*.

It is important to remember that adjustments cannot exceed racial maximums nor can they be used if they cause abilities to exceed stated maximums. Likewise, any adjustments cannot lower any ability below racial or class minimums.

Unnatural Aging:

Certain creatures will cause unnatural aging, and in addition various magical factors can do so. The following magic causes loss of life span, aging the practitioner as indicated. See also **DISEASE** for other unnatural aging causes. (*Longevity* potions and possibly other magical means will offset such aging to some extent.)

Magical Aging Causes

casting *alter reality* spell	3 years
casting *gate* spell	5 years
casting *limited wish* spell	1 year
casting *restoration* spell	2 years
casting *resurrection* spell	3 years
casting *wish* spell	3 years
imbibing a *speed* potion	1 year
under a *haste* spell	1 year

Note: Reading one of the above spells from a scroll (or using the power from a ring or other device) does not cause unnatural aging, but placing such a spell upon the scroll in the first place will do so!

(Cf. **Death Due to Age** subsection of **DEATH.**)

DISEASE

As with poisons, this system does not attempt a specific treatment of a subject which is beyond its scope and purpose. What is done, however, is to give general categories of disease and maladies and their game effects, as well as the chance to contract an ailment according to the surroundings. Naturally, you will often have no need for any random determination of a disease, as the affliction will be specified, but even then you will find that the random determinants for *occurrence* and *severity* might be helpful.

Contraction of Disease:

Each game *month* you may wish to check each character to determine whether or not he or she has contracted a disease (or disorder). Check each *week* if conditions are particularly favorable:

> VERY HOT WEATHER OR HOT, MOIST WEATHER
> FILTHY, CROWDED CONDITIONS IN WARM WEATHER

Check *each and every time* the character is exposed to a carrier in a way which would allow the disease to be communicated. Note that disease carriers can be human, animal, insect, food, drink, vermin, dirt, filth, etc. As DM you must indicate any special disease circumstances applicable.

Contraction of Parasitic Infestation:

Each game *month* check for each character to determine if he or she has become infested with some form of parasite. Check each *week* if conditions are particularly favorable:

> FILTHY CONDITIONS AND WARM TEMPERATURE
> HOT, MOIST WEATHER

Check *each and every time* the character is exposed to a carrier of parasites. Carriers include humans, animals, dust, earth, manure, raw (or undercooked) meat, swamp water, etc.

CHECKS ARE MADE BY USING THE APPROPRIATE TABLES SHOWN HEREAFTER.

CHANCE OF CONTRACTING DISEASE

Base Chance	2%

Modifiers:

currently diseased or infested with parasites	+1%
crowding (city, encampment, shipboard)	+1%
filth (city, encampment, siege)	+1%
character is *old*	+2%
environment (marsh, swamp, jungle)	+2%
hot and moist climate (season or region)	+2%
character is *venerable*	+5%
exposure to carrier of communicable disease	+10%
cool weather or climate (high elevation, etc.)	−1%
cold weather, high mountains	−2%
shipboard after being at sea 2 weeks	−2%

Procedure: Adjust base chance of disease being contracted by applying modifiers. When the final percent chance to contract a disease is found, roll for each character concerned. If disease is indicated, go to the **DISEASE TABLE** below to determine what sort is contracted.

CHANCE OF PARASITIC INFESTATION

Base Chance	3%

Modifiers:

filth (garbage, manure, sewage, etc.)	+1%
improperly cooked meat	+2%
polluted water	+5%
swamp or jungle environment	+5%
cool weather or climate, desert climate	−1%
cold weather, high mountains, cool desert climate	−1%

Procedure: As for disease, and check **PARASITIC INFESTATION TABLE.**

DISEASE (OR DISORDER) TABLE

Dice Score	Area of Body Affected	Occurrence (d8) Acute	Chronic	Severity (d8) Mild	Severe	Terminal
01-03	blood/blood forming organs	1-3	4-8	1-2	3-5	6-8
04	bones	1	2-8	1	2-3	4-8
05	brain/nervous system	1-6	7-8	1-2	3-5	6-8
06-07	cardiovascular-renal	1-3	4-8	1-2	3-4	5-8
08-09	connective tissue	1	2-8	1	2-3	4-8
10-12	ears	1-7	8	1-6	7	8
13-18	eyes	1-7	8	1-5	6-7	8
19-40	gastro-intestinal	1-6	7-8	1-5	6-7	8
41-42	generative organs	1-2	3-8	1-3	4-7	8
43-48	joints	1-4	5-8	1-6	7-8	—
49-50	mucous membranes	1-7	8	1-6	7-8	—
51-52	muscles	1-5	6-8	1-5	6-7	8
53-65	nose-throat	1-6	7-8	1-6	7-8	—
66-85	respiratory system	1-6	7-8	1-5	6-7	8
86-96	skin	1-5	6-8	1-5	6-7	8
97-00	urinary system	1-6	7-8	1-5	6-7	8

PARASITIC INFESTATION TABLE

Dice Score	Parasites Infest	Severity (d8) Mild	Severe	Terminal
01-10	cardiovascular system	1-2	3-5	6-8
11-35	intestines	1-2	3-7	8
36-40	muscles	1	2-3	4-8
41-45	respiratory system	1	2-4	5-8
46-75	skin/hair	1-7	8	—
76-00	stomach	1-2	3-7	8

Occurrence determines whether the disease is a single *(acute)* attack or whether the disease will recur periodically once contracted *(chronic)*. Chronic maladies will affect the character periodically, and if they occur at the same time as any other malady (disease, disorder, or parasitic infestation), the severity of both will be increased. Thus, if two chronic maladies are contracted, the character is not likely to survive another disease attack.

Severity refers to the seriousness of the disease, disorder, or parasitic infestation and determines the period of disability (recovery time or length of illness which terminates in the character's demise) and the effects of the malady.

MILD: During the period of affliction the character is unable to perform strenuous activities and must rest. Some treatment must be determined by the DM to allow a shortening of the period of illness. A normal period is 1-3 weeks.

SEVERE: A severe malady will lower the character's hit points to 50% of normal and make him or her totally disabled for 1-2 weeks, plus a further 1-2 weeks of time during which the malady is in the *mild* state as the character recovers.

TERMINAL: The malady will cause death (or loss of the body part or function) in 1-12 days (longer periods are stated hereafter in the discussion of the various maladies).

Blood *et al.* afflictions will cause a loss of 1 point each of strength and constitution per week until totally cured. Thus, chronic problems here will slowly wear the character away. Terminal cases will take 1-12 weeks.

Bone afflictions are much the same as blood problems, and chronic cases and terminal afflictions can be treated in the same way.

Brain *et al.* problems will cause a loss of 1 point each of intelligence and dexterity per occurrence until totally cured, so chronic maladies will eventually be fatal. Terminal affliction takes only 1-12 hours for death to occur.

Cardiovascular-renal afflictions should be treated in the same manner as blood problems, except that terminal cases last only 1-12 days.

Connective tissue diseases (such as leprosy) permanently remove 1 point each of strength, dexterity, constitution, and charisma for each month of affliction — thus only an acute, mild attack will *not* cause such loss. Terminal cases will last until constitution is at 0, i.e. treat them as chronic, severe cases.

Ear afflictions which are terminal result in hearing loss in one ear.

Eye afflictions which are terminal result in blindness in one or both eyes (50%/50% chance for either case).

Gastro-intestinal problems of chronic nature cause the loss of 1 point each of strength and constitution per occurrence until cured, severe attacks causing such loss permanently. Terminal cases require 1-12 weeks for fatality.

Generative organ disorders cause no particular problems except spread of infection . . . . Terminal cases take 1-12 months.

Joint disorders of a chronic nature cause the loss of 1 point of dexterity, with each severe attack causing such loss on a permanent basis.

Mucous membrane problems of chronic nature cause the loss of 1 point of constitution, each severe attack causing such loss permanently.

Muscle disorders of chronic nature cause the loss of 1 point each of strength and dexterity, severe attacks having a 25% chance of causing such loss permanently. Terminal cases take 1-12 months.

Nose-throat afflictions of chronic nature have a 10% chance of causing a 1 point constitution loss each time a severe attack occurs.

Respiratory disorders of chronic, severe nature are 10% likely to cause the loss of 1 point each of strength and constitution (check separately for each). Terminal cases take from 1-12 months until fatality occurs.

Skin afflictions of severe nature are 10% likely to cause permanent loss of 1 point of charisma. Chronic, mild attacks are also 10% likely to cause such loss, while chronic, severe attacks will be 25% likely to cause such loss. Terminal cases will take 1-12 weeks for fatality.

Urinary system disorders of chronic, severe nature are 20% likely to cause the loss of 1 point each of dexterity and constitution per occurrence. Terminal cases will take 1-12 weeks.

ADJUSTMENTS TO OCCURRENCE AND SEVERITY DIE ROLLS*

constitution under 3	+2
constitution 3-5	+1
chronic disease or disorder	+1
severe parasitic infestation	+1
under 25% of normal hit point total	+1
constitution 10-12	−1
constitution 13-15	−2
constitution 16-17	−3
constitution 18	−4

Note: Die score of 0 or less on either roll indicates the character does not contract the disease.

* Not to be used for *parasitic infestation* determination.

DEATH

The character faces death in many forms. The most common, death due to combat, is no great matter in most cases, for the character can often be brought back by means of a clerical spell or an *alter reality* or *wish*. Of course, recovery of damage sustained might be a problem, but that is not insurmountable.

Death Due To Age:

This is a serious matter, for unless the lifespan can otherwise be prolonged, the character brought back from such death faces the prospect of soon dying again. Beyond the maximum age determined for the character in question, no form of magic which does not prolong life span will work. (Thus, some characters may become liches . . . .) Of course, multiple potions of *longevity*, *wishes*, and possibly magical devices will allow a greatly extended life span, but once a character dies due to old (venerable) age, then it is all over. If you make this clear, many participants will see the continuity of the family line as the way to achieve a sort of immortality.

Determination Of Maximum Age:

Unless the character dies of some other cause, he or she will live to *old* age. Use the following table to find the exact age at which a character will die of "natural" causes:

MAXIMUM CHARACTER AGE TABLE

Dice Score	Character Age Category	Variable*
01-10	old, lowest age	+ d8
11-25	old, highest age	− d4
26-60	venerable, lowest age	+ d6
61-90	venerable, highest age	− d10**
91-00	venerable, highest age	+ d20***

* Use the die to determine the addition or subtraction according to the span of years in the category:

UNDER 100	1 year intervals
100 to 250	10 year intervals (±d10**)
OVER 250	20 year intervals (±d20***)

** Treat a roll of 0 as naught rather than as 10, so in effect a random number between 0 and 9 is being generated.

*** Treat a die result of 20 as naught, so numbers between 0 and 19 are being generated.

Examples Of Maximum Age Determination:

The dice rolled indicate the *dwarf* character will live to *old* age, lowest figure, +d8. As the span considered is 100 years, d8 stands for decades, so the character will live for 251 years +10 to 80 years +0 to 9 years.

The same *dwarf* considered above is to live to *old* age, highest figure, −4. The variable is −10 to −40 years, −0 to 9 years.

The dice rolled for a *half-orc* character indicate that he will live to *venerable* age, highest figure, +d20. As the span considered is under 100 years, the character will live for 80 years +0 to 19 years, or 80 to 99 years, as a result of 20 equals 0 years added to maximum venerable age shown for the character race.

The dice show that a *high elf* character will live to venerable age, lowest figure, +d6. As the span of years for this character race is 400 years, the character will live to be 1201 +20 to 120 years, +0 to 19 years, or to an age of 1221 to 1340 years. Assume that the d6 shows 4, so 80 years are added (4 × 20 = 80) to bring life span to 1281 (1201 + 80), and then d20 is rolled and a 0 comes up, so total life span is 1281 years (1201 + 80 + 0 = 1281).

Death Due To Disease (Or Disorder) Or Parasitic Infestation:

Any character brought back from such a state will suffer the ravages of the disease or infestation — permanent losses in abilities, for example, until magically countered. Furthermore, such a character will be 90% likely to

still be suffering from the cause of death unless a *curative* is used. Even then, the character will have to spend time recovering as if from a severe illness. Ability losses which have been permanently sustained will *not* be corrected by a curative of any sort, including a *cure disease* spell. Magical corrections (*wishes*, *alter reality* spells, and magical devices) will certainly correct these deficiencies.

CHARACTER ABILITIES

EXPLANATION OF ABILITIES

Strength: The strength characteristic of a human or humanoid of any type, and of player-characters in particular, is more than a simple evaluation of the musculature of the body. Strength is a composite rating of physical power, endurance, and stamina. A rating of 3, for example, indicates that the creature in question has little of each of the three categories, a score of 10 or thereabouts shows that the creature has the norm for a human adult male (based on an assumed medieval standard where the typical individual was in "good shape" due to the necessity of hard labor), while a score of 18 means that the creature has a composite rating far above average in all respects. By way of comparison, kobolds will have an average strength rating of 9, goblins 10, orcs 12, hobgoblins 15, gnolls 16, bugbears 17, ogres 18, and trolls a strength rating of 18+. Gnomes have an average strength rating of 10, dwarves 14, elves 12, halflings 8, and giants 19 and up.

Exceptional Strength: Assume further that a strength of 18 indicates that the creature can lift weight equal to its own body weight, or 180 pounds, whichever is the greater, above its head. This rating is modified by a restriction that no creature of human/humanoid nature can lift more than twice its own body weight above its head. A human with an 18 strength and an additional percentile dice roll is able to lift 1 additional pound for every percentage point up to and including 50%, 4 pounds for every percentage point from 51% to 90%, and 8 pounds for each percentage point from 91% to 00%.

Intelligence: The intelligence rating roughly corresponds to our modern "IQ" scores. However, it assumes mnemonic, reasoning, and learning ability skills in additional areas outside the written word.

Wisdom: For game purposes wisdom ability subsumes the categories of willpower, judgment, wile, enlightenment, and intuitiveness. An example of the use of wisdom can be given by noting that while the intelligent character will know that smoking is harmful to him, he may well lack the wisdom to stop (this writer may well fall into this category).

Dexterity: The dexterity rating includes the following physical characteristics: hand-eye coordination, agility, reflex speed, precision, balance, and actual speed of movement in running. It would not be unreasonable to claim that a person with a low dexterity might well be quite agile, but have low reflex speed, poor precision, bad balance, and be slow of foot (but slippery in the grasp).

Constitution: This character ability rating is a general heading under which falls the character's physique, health, resistance, and fitness. An individual who catches cold if exposed to a slight draft has a constitution of 5 or less in all probability. Rasputin had an 18 constitution!

Charisma: Many persons have the sad misconception that charisma is merely physical attractiveness. This error is obvious to any person who considers the subject with perceptiveness. Charisma is a combination of physical appearance, persuasiveness, and personal magnetism. True charisma becomes evident when one considers such historic examples of Julius Caesar, Napoleon Bonaparte, and Adolf Hitler. Obviously, these individuals did not have an 18 score on physical beauty, so it is quite possible to assume that scores over 18 are possible, for any one of the named historical personalities would have had a higher charisma score — there can be no question that these individuals were 18's — if they would have had great attractiveness as well as commanding personal magnetism and superb persuasiveness.

CHARACTER RACES

PLAYER CHARACTER RACIAL TENDENCIES

As a general rule, the player will develop the personality and other characteristics of his or her personae in the campaign, and little or no DM interference is necessary in this regard. To find the general height and weight of a PC use the tables given for development of NPCs. Alignment must certainly affect, if not dictate, much of the actual behavior of each PC, and so it will affect characteristics as well. In this regard it is important for you to see that the particular characteristics of each persona meet with the overall character and alignment of the individual adventurer concerned. Racial characteristics can also be a factor. Consider the following guidelines.

Dwarves tend to be dour and taciturn. They are given to hard work and care little for most humor. They are strong and brave, but they also enjoy beer, ale, mead, and even stronger drink. Their chief love, however, is precious metal, particularly gold. They also enjoy gems, of course, particularly those of opaque nature (except pearls which they do not like) and diamonds. They like the earth and dislike the sea. Considering that their women tend to be bearded too, it is not surprising that some dwarves are somewhat forward in their behavior towards females not so adorned. If dwarves are a trifle suspicious and avaricious, they generally make up for such faults by their courage and tenacity.

Elves are often considered flighty or frivolous, and this is the case when they do not believe a matter to be of import. They concern themselves with the natural beauty around them, dancing and frolicking, playing and singing unless necessity dictates otherwise. Because elves love nature, they are not fond of ships or mines, but of growing things and the lands under the sky. They do not make friends easily, but friend or enemy is never forgotten. Their humor is clever, as are their songs and poetry. Elves are brave but never foolhardy. They feast, but eat sparingly, drink mead and wine, but seldom become drunk from excesses. While they find well-wrought jewelry a pleasure to behold, they are not overly interested in money or gain. Magic fascinates elves, however, and if they have a weakness it lies in this desire. If elves tend towards haughtiness and arrogance at times, they are not inclined to regard their friends and associates as anything other than equals.

Gnomes are most lively and full of humor — often on the black side or practical jokes. They enjoy eating and can drink as much as dwarves do. They are sly and furtive with those they do not know or trust, and even somewhat reserved with most bigger folk such as elves or humans. Gnomes love all sorts of precious stones, and they are masters of gem polishing and cutting. In most other respects they are not unlike dwarves, but they enjoy the open world of growing things almost as much as their mines and burrows.

Half-Elves are usually much like their elven parent in characteristics, although to somewhat lesser extent than a pure elf.

Halflings are quite similar to gnomes, although they eat more and drink less. They also are prone to favor natural beauty and the outdoors more than they do their burrows. They are not forward, but they are observant and conversational if in friendly company. Because they are more open and outgoing than either dwarves or elves, they get along with most other races far better than the former two do. Halflings see wealth as a means of gaining comforts only, for they love creature comforts. If they are not overly brave or ambitious, they are generally honest and hard-working when there is need. Halflings love stories and good jokes and are perhaps a trifle boring at times.

Half-Orcs are boors. They are rude, crude, crass, and generally obnoxious. Because most are cowardly they tend to be bullies and cruel to the weak, but they will quickly knuckle under to the stronger. This does not mean that all half-orcs are horrid, only most of them. It neither means that they are necessarily stupid nor incapable. They will always seek to gain the upper hand and dominate those around them so as to be able to exercise their natural tendencies; half-orcs are greedy too. They can, of course, favor their human parent more than their orcish one.

CHARACTER CLASSES

FOLLOWERS FOR UPPER LEVEL PLAYER CHARACTERS

Your players know that upon reaching certain levels and doing certain things (such as building a stronghold) they will be entitled to attract a body of followers. These followers might be fanatically loyal servants of the same deity (or deities) in the case of clerics, stalwart admirers of fighters, or whatever. Your players will eventually turn to you for information on who or what they gain — and, when the time actually comes they

have reached the level and done the right things, you will be able to quickly inform each and every one concerned of what fate has decreed by way of followers:

Clerics:

Roll for each category (all are 0 level men-at-arms).

2-8	heavy cavalry, plate mail & shield; lance, broad sword, and mace
3-12	medium cavalry, chain mail & shield; lance, flail and short sword
5-30	light cavalry, studded leather & shield; light crossbow and pick
5-20	heavy infantry, splint mail; battle axe and long sword
5-30	heavy infantry, chain mail; pole arm* and hand axe
5-30	heavy infantry, ring mail; heavy crossbow and short sword.
10-60	light infantry, padded armor & shield; spear and club

* Select type or types randomly or assign whichever you desire.

Fighters:

Roll once for leader type, once for troops/followers (all are 0 level men-at-arms).

Leader
01-40	5th level, plate mail & shield; +2 magic battle axe
41-75	6th level, plate mail & +1 shield; +1 magic spear and +1 dagger
76-95	6th level, +1 plate mail & shield; arms as above: lieutenant 3rd level, splint mail & shield; *crossbow of distance*
96-00	7th level, +1 plate mail & +1 shield; +2 magic sword (no special abilities); rides a heavy warhorse with *horseshoes of speed*

Troops/Followers
01-50	company of 20 light cavalry, ring mail & shield; 3 javelins, long sword, hand axe; and company of 100 heavy infantry, scale mail; pole arm* and club
51-75	company of 80 heavy infantry — 20 with splint mail, 60 with leather armor; 20 with morning star and hand axe, 60 with pike and short sword
76-90	company of 60 crossbowmen, chain mail; 40 with heavy crossbow and short sword, 20 with light crossbow and military fork
91-00	company of 60 cavalry — 10 with banded mail and shield, 20 with scale mail and shield, 30 with studded leather and shield; 10 with lance, bastard sword, and mace, 20 with lance, long sword and mace, 30 with lance and flail

* Select type or types randomly or assign whichever you desire.

Rangers:

Roll 2d12 to find the number of followers (or creatures attracted to service). When the number is generated, adjust the following percentile dice rolls as follows:

2d12 Result	Modify d% As Follows
2	add +25% to each roll
3	add +15% to each roll
4	add +10% to the first roll
5-6	add +5% to the first roll
7-9	no adjustment
10-12	deduct −5% from each roll
13-16	deduct −10% from each roll
17-20	deduct −20% from each roll
21-24	deduct −30% from each roll

If any addition or subtraction falls within a category no longer permissible, or if a subtraction results in a score under 01, *roll again.*

When the number of rolls the ranger player character is entitled to is discovered, and the adjustment necessary noted, determine the followers/creatures using the tables below. All scores over 70 are special, and the ranger is able to attract one follower/creature group only from each category, as noted.

Add all creatures of any sort to find total followers, demi-humans included.

Dice Score	Result
01-50	see HUMANS, TABLE I
51-70	see DEMI-HUMANS, TABLE II
71-80	see ANIMALS, TABLE III
81-90	see MOUNTS, TABLE IV
91-95	see CREATURES, TABLE V
96-00	see SPECIAL CREATURES, TABLE VI

HUMANS, TABLE I

Dice Score	Character Class	Level Range
01-15	cleric	1-4
16-40	druid	2-5
41-85	fighter	1-6
86-95	ranger	1-3
96-00	magic-user	1-3

DEMI-HUMANS, TABLE II

Dice Score	Character Race & Class	Level Range	Number
01-15	DWARF fighter	1-4	2
16-20	DWARF fighter/thief	1	1
21-40	ELF fighter	2-5	2
41-45	ELF fighter/magic-user	1	1
46-50	ELF fighter/magic-user/thief	1	1
51-60	GNOME fighter	1-3	3
61-65	GNOME fighter/illusionist	1	1
66-75	HALF-ELF cleric/ranger	1	1
76-80	HALF-ELF cleric/fighter/magic-user	1	1
81-85	HALF-ELF fighter/thief	1	1
86-95	HALFLING fighter	1-3	3
96-00	HALFLING fighter/thief	1	1

Note: Followers with the professed class of *thief* are always *neutral good*.

ANIMALS, TABLE III (One Roll Only On This Table)

Dice Score	Animal	Number
01-20	bear, black	1
21-55	bear, brown	1
56-65	blink dog	2
66-80	lynx, giant	2
81-00	owl, giant	2

MOUNTS, TABLE IV (One Roll Only On This Table)

Dice Score	Mount	Number
01-35	centaur	1-3
36-75	hippogriff	1
76-00	pegasus	1

CREATURES, TABLE V (One Roll Only On This Table)

Dice Score	Creature	Number
01-50	brownie	1-2
51-75	pixie	1-4
76-80	pseudo-dragon	1
81-90	satyr	1
91-00	sprite	2-4

SPECIAL CREATURES, TABLE VI (One Roll Only On This Table)

Dice Score	Special Creature	Number
01-05	copper dragon*	1
06-10	giant, storm	1
11-30	treant	2-5
31-75	werebear	1-2
76-00	weretiger	1-2

* Roll d4 + 1 to determine the age category of the dragon. It will, of course, possess no treasure.

Thieves:

Roll 4d6 to determine the number of lesser thieves which the character will attract. Determine race and level of each thereafter, modifying the d% roll for level as follows:

4d6 Result	Level Modifier Percent
4	add +20% to each roll
5-6	add +15% to each roll
7-9	add +5% to each roll
10-15	no adjustment
16-20	subtract −5% from each roll
21-24	subtract −10% from each roll

RACE OF THIEF

Dice Score	Race	Dice Score	Race
01-10	dwarven*	31-35	halfling*
11-20	elven*	36-55	half-orcish*
21-25	gnomish*	56-00	human
26-30	half-elven*		

LEVEL OF THIEF

Dice Score	Level	Dice Score	Level
01-20	1*	81-90	5
21-45	2	91-95	6
46-65	3	96-00	7
66-80	4		

* 1st level non-human (or part human) thieves have a 25% chance of being multi-classed. Use the table below if multi-class is indicated.

MULTI-CLASS THIEF FOLLOWER TABLE

Race	Other Profession (Roll d6 As Indicated)
dwarf	fighter
elf	fighter (1-3), magic-user (4-5), fighter/magic-user (6)
gnome	fighter (1-5), illusionist (6)
half-elf	same as elf above
halfling	fighter
half-orc	cleric (1-3), fighter (4-6)

Assassins:

Upon attaining Guildmaster/Guildmistress status, roll 7d4 to determine the number of lower level assassins in the local guild. You may adjust this result according to the population of the area if you deem it necessary. After determining this number, find the race and level (below) and then find which will stay (75% will desert the guild, as noted in the **PLAYERS HANDBOOK**). All new assassins coming to fill the ranks will be 1st level, but race must be determined on the **RACE OF ASSASSIN TABLE.**

RACE OF ASSASSIN TABLE

Dice Score	Race	Dice Score	Race
01-05	dwarven*	16-25	half-elven*
06-10	elven*	26-50	half-orcish*
11-15	gnomish*	51-00	human

LEVEL OF ASSASSIN

Dice Score	Level	Dice Score	Level
01-15	1*	66-75	5
16-30	2*	76-85	6
31-45	3	86-95	7
46-65	4	96-00	8

* 1st and 2nd level non-human (or part human) assassins have a 25% chance of being multi-classed. Use the table below if multi-class is indicated.

MULTI-CLASSED ASSASSIN TABLE

Race	Other Profession (Roll d6 As Indicated)
dwarf	no other class permitted
elf	no other class permitted
gnome	fighter (1-4), illusionist (5-6)
half-elf	no other class permitted
half-orc	fighter (1-2), cleric (3-6)

Grandfather/Grandmother of Assassins: The leader of all assassins (a nominal title at times . . .) will always have 28 followers of 2nd through 8th level as follows:

1 8th level, 2 7th level, 3 6th level, 4 5th level, 5 4th level, 6 3rd level, and 7 2nd level (= 28).

In addition, there will be from 4-16 1st level followers. Dice for race using the table above. It is recommended that you develop henchmen for the Grandfather/Grandmother after discovering the abilities of his or her followers. Mercenary fighters and men-at-arms should suit the circumstances, but in general they should be very well armed and equipped and include cavalry, infantry, and missile-armed troops as well. Naturally, should a NPC Grandfather/Grandmother of Assassins be displaced by a player character, followers will be 75% likely to leave, as usual, but the new leader will eventually attract a following of up to 44 (28 + 4-16) assassins, the newcomers being found as if they were attracted to a new Guildmaster of Assassins, i.e. 1st level newcomers.

Unless the followers are a body, they will not come at the same time. After the conditions for obtaining such a following have been met, generate a random number from 1 to 30 (d10 using d6 to determine 10's, 1-2 = no addition, 3-4 = add 10, 5-6 = add 20 to the score of the d10). The result is the day after completion of the requirements on which the first follower(s) will appear — in some cases, all of those coming. Thereafter, additional followers due the character will arrive at intervals of 1-8 days until all have arrived. If there is no one available to receive them they will wait from 1-4 days and then depart forever. In the latter case the character has lost that follower forever. It is permissible to allow some henchman or servant to care for followers if the character designates such duty.

The Paladin's Warhorse:

When the paladin reaches 4th or higher level, he or she will eventually call for a warhorse (as detailed in the **PLAYERS HANDBOOK**). It will magically appear, but not in actual physical form. The paladin will magically "see" his or her faithful destrier in whatever locale it is currently in, and it is thereafter up to the paladin to journey to the place and gain the steed. As a rule of thumb, this journey will not be beyond 7 days ride, and gaining the mount will not be an impossible task. The creature might be wild and necessitate capturing, or it might be guarded by an evil fighter of the same level as the paladin, and the latter will then have to overcome the former in mortal combat in order to win the warhorse. In short, the gaining of the destrier is a task of some small difficulty which will take a number of days, possibly 2 or more weeks, and will certainly test the mettle of the paladin. Once captured or won, the warhorse knows its ride and relationship to the paladin, and it will faithfully serve thereafter for 10 years. Thereafter, the paladin *must* seek another mount, as the former one will be too old to be useful.

The intelligence of a paladin's warhorse is 5-7 points. The number of hit points per hit die of the steed will never be fewer than 50% of the level of the paladin, i.e., a 4th level paladin means the warhorse he or she gains will have at least 2 hit points per hit die, excluding the additional bonus of +5, while a 16th level paladin's special steed will have maximum hit points (8) per die, of $5 \times 8 = 40 + 5$ (additional hit points) = 45 total hit points for 5 + 5 hit dice.

If the character loses paladinhood for any reason, there will be an immutable enmity between character and mount, and the former will not be able to ride the latter, while the steed will escape at first opportunity.

SPYING

In general most spies will be hired assassins, although it is likely that some regular spies will be employed by player characters from time to time. Most spying missions will fall into the following categories:

SIMPLE: Missions which require information regarding the general state of

defenses and numbers of troops or preparations for some activity. *Simple missions require only the observations of the spy acting in a non-critical role, i.e. just being around as one of many individuals in the place.*

DIFFICULT: Missions of this category require the spy to gain some secret information such as plans, documents, maps, etc. *Difficult missions require the spy to gain access to something or gain the confidence of someone, and so the spy must actively pursue his or her role in an outstanding manner.*

EXTRAORDINARY: Missions of long, complex, and hazardous nature which require insinuation of the spy into an organization or operation and the relay of detailed information on a continuing basis from the spy. *Extraordinary missions require long-term association of the spy with the spied-upon and the continuing acquisition of general and specific information of highly detailed and secret nature.*

In simple missions there is little risk of discovery, while risks become more likely in difficult missions, and very great in extraordinary missions. Where a player character is involved, spying missions are a matter of interaction according to the dictates of the player involved, through the DM, according to the situation as known by him or her and the reactions of the spied-upon. In the case of a non-player character undertaking a spying mission, a success table is used.

ASSASSIN SPYING TABLE

Level Of The Assassin/Spy	Chance of Success According To Category		
	Simple	Difficult	Extraordinary
1st	50%	30%	10%
2nd	55%	35%	15%
3rd	60%	35%	15%
4th	65%	40%	20%
5th	70%	45%	25%
6th	75%	50%	25%
7th	80%	55%	30%
8th	85%	60%	35%
9th	85%	60%	40%
10th	90%	65%	45%
11th	90%	65%	50%
12th	95%	65%	50%
13th	95%	70%	50%
14th	95%	70%	50%
15th	95%	75%	50%
16th	95%	75%	55%
17th	95%	75%	60%

Time Required To Accomplish Mission:

The length of time necessary to travel to the region in which the spying activity is to take place must be determined by the referee according to circumstances. Once in the necessary locale, the spy will then take a variable period of time to accomplish the mission (or fail), according to the degree of difficulty of the task:

SIMPLE: 1 to 8 days
DIFFICULT: 5 to 40 days
EXTRAORDINARY: As required

Extraordinary missions must be determined by the circumstances of the case. For example, a spy sent to become a member of a secret society might take a month to discover the recruiting requirements of the society, and then spend one or more months making himself or herself eligible for recruitment, and then become insinuated in the group. Thereafter, he or she would gain simple or difficult information according to the time requirements shown, and special information could be gained only as the individual gained more and more status within the organization through continued membership and seemingly outstanding contribution.

Chance Of Discovery:

There always exists a chance of discovery, no matter how simple the mission. The base chance to be discovered is a cumulative 1% per day of time spent spying, subject to a maximum of 10%, minus the level of the spy. Even if the latter brings chance of discovery to a negative percentage, there is always a 1% chance. Modifiers are dependent upon the precautions against spying taken by the spied upon.

18

No Precautions = 1% chance per week
Minimal Precautions = modified % (1% to 10%) chance per week
Moderate Precautions = modified % chance twice per week
Strong Precautions = double modified % chance twice per week

Minimal precautions represent occasional checks on individuals and their activities and some watch on important information. *Moderate precautions* are simply more frequently carried out minimal precautions and more careful questioning of anyone behaving in a suspicious manner. *Strong precautions* include many security checks on individuals and information, as well as counterspies operating to discover any such activity.

If a spy actually becomes a leader in a group, the chance for being detected then drops to that of the category of NO PRECAUTIONS, as the individual is regarded as being "above suspicion", i.e. only certain jealous or ferret-like operatives will still check on the individual.

Chance of discovery will increase tenfold if a spy is caught and another spy is still attempting to operate during a period of 20 to 50 days thereafter.

To find if a spy is discovered, roll percentile dice according to the time period stated. If the mission takes only a fraction of the time stated, roll a third percentile die for tenths of percent. Thus 1% per week equals .14% chance per day, so a roll of 99.9% indicates discovery on a 1 day mission. If a spy is discovered, go to the **SPY FAILURE TABLE** below.

Spy Failure:

If, after spending the requisite time, the spy rolls and is not successful, various possibilities exist. The results are determined on the table below. Note that this table is also used for spy discovery, with appropriate modifiers.

SPY FAILURE TABLE

Dice Score	Result
01-35	Further attempts to gain success are possible, but time to accomplish the mission must again be determined
36-60	Any further spying attempts will be 90% likely to result in failure, discovery, and imprisonment
61-80	Spy caught is in suspicious act, imprisoned, and nothing further is heard*
81-95	Spy is caught with positive proof of spying activity, and is tortured (1-2 dead, 3-4 revealed everything, 5-6 turncoat)*
96-00	Spy is killed or turns coat if counterspies are present

* If counter spies are employed they will give the spy false information and follow him or her to find where he or she came from and who sent him or her to spy in the first place.

Modifiers:

Difficult Mission = +10% on FAILURE dice score
Extraordinary Mission = −5% on FAILURE dice score
Discovered = +25% on FAILURE dice score

Fanatical Spies:

Spies who are absolutely dedicated to their master or a cause cannot be assassins normally hired to spy, but such can exist. These spies will never become double agents. On any dice total over 60 they simply kill themselves.

(Cf. **EXPERT HIRELINGS** for the cost of non-player character spies.)

THIEF ABILITIES

The following additional explanations of thief abilities will help you to prevent abuse of these activities by thieves, and other characters able to use these abilities in whole or in part, in your campaign.

Roll of the dice for any thief function must be kept absolutely secret, so the thief (or similar character) does not know the results!

Back Stabbing: Opponents aware of the thief will be able to negate the attack form. Certain creatures (otyughs, slimes, molds, etc.) either negate surprise or have no definable "back", thus negating this ability.

Picking Pockets: Failure allows additional attempts. The victim might notice and allow the thief to operate anyway in order to track him or her back to the place he or she uses as a headquarters. Up to two attempts at picking a pocket can be made during a round.

Opening Locks: The act of picking the lock to be opened can take from 1-10 rounds, depending on the complexity of the lock. As a rule, most locks will take but 1-4 rounds of time to pick.

Finding And Removing Traps: Use the time requirements for opening locks. Time counts for each function. Small or large traps can be found, but not magical or magically hidden traps.

Moving Silently: Silent movement is the same as normal exploratory movement, i.e. 12' per round as the thief creeps up (croodles) upon the area or victim or whatever. Do NOT inform the thief that his or her dice score indicated a lack of success at this attempted stealth, if that is the case. He or she *thinks* the movement is silent, and the monster or other victim will inform the character of his or her misapprehension soon enough.

Hide In Shadows: As is plainly stated in **PLAYERS HANDBOOK**, this is NEVER possible under direct (or even indirect) observation. If the thief insists on trying, allow the attempt and throw dice, but don't bother to read them, as the fool is as obvious as a coal pile in a ballroom. Likewise, if a hidden thief attempts movement while under observation, the proverbial jig is up for him or her. Naturally, a creature closely pressed in melee is not likely to bother with looking for some thief not directly in the line of sight, but if vision would normally extend to the thief's area of activity, then observation rules apply. Unobserved attempts to hide in shadows must likewise stand the hazard of the dice roll. A score greater than the required number shows that the character's ability is not on a par with his or her intent, and although he or she THINKS hiding has been successful, the creature looking in that direction will note a suspicious outline, form, or whatever. Note also that a thief hiding in shadows is still subject to detection just as if he or she was invisible (see **INVISIBILITY, DETECTION OF INVISIBILITY table**).

Hearing Noise: This is pretty straightforward. The thief, just as any other character, must take off helmet or other obstructing headgear in order to press his or her ear to the door surface in order to hear beyond.

Climbing Walls: This is probably the most abused thief function, although hiding in shadows vies for the distinction. The ability to climb walls is something which is acquired through training and practice, just as are most of the other functions of the thief. The rate at which vertical or horizontal movement is possible depends upon the texture and other conditions of the surface.

WALL CLIMBING TABLE, FEET PER ROUND OF CLIMBING

Wall Surface Is Best Described As:	Condition Of Surface*		
	Non-Slippery	Slightly Slippery	Slippery
very smooth — few cracks	6'	3'	0'
smooth but cracked — somewhat rough	12'	6'	3'
fairly rough and some cracks — very rough	18'	9'	6'
rough and with ledges or many projections	24'	12'	9'

* SLIGHTLY SLIPPERY surfaces *DOUBLE* chances of slipping and falling. SLIPPERY surfaces make chances of slipping and falling TEN TIMES more likely. Thus, a slippery surface cannot be attempted successfully by any thief under 6th level, and even a 10th level thief has a 10% chance per round of slipping and falling.

Be certain to check each round of vertical or horizontal movement for chance of slipping and falling. Surfaces which are inclined inwards move towards greater degrees of difficulty — a non-slippery one being treated as slightly slippery, and a slippery one being virtually unclimbable. Surfaces inclined away from the perpendicular on an outward angle may be treated as either a better surface condition or rougher texture, if the degree of incline is sufficient to make climbing easier.

Most dungeon walls will fall into the fairly rough to rough category. Some will be non-slippery, but most will be slightly slippery due to dampness and slime growth.

Read Languages: This ability assumes that the language is, in fact, one which the thief has encountered sometime in the past. Ancient and strange languages (those you, as DM, have previously designated as such) are always totally unreadable. Even if able to read a language, the thief should be allowed only to get about that percentage of the meaning of what is written as his or her percentage ability to read the tongue in the first place. The rest they will have to guess at. Languages which are relatively close to those known by the thief will not incur such a penalty.

THIEVES AND ASSASSINS SETTING TRAPS

Simple mechanical traps can be set by thieves or assassins. The chance to do so successfully is equal to that of the chance shown for *detecting such traps*, but in this case the assassin operates at an ability level equal to two levels above his or her own and exactly as if he or she were a thief, e.g. a 5th level assassin has the same chance of setting a trap as a 7th level thief does.

Simple traps are those which involve mechanical components which the character setting them has normal access to, such as arrow traps, trip wires, and spring-propelled missiles. Special devices such as poisoned needles, scything blades, and any similar traps with special mechanical components will also require the efforts of one or more specialists — those required to manufacture the component parts.

Whenever a thief or assassin character desires to set a trap, require him or her to furnish you a simple drawing to illustrate how the trap will function. If the chance to successfully set the trap results in failure, there is a chance of causing injury to the trap setter, just as if he or she had set such a trap off. This chance is rolled for separately and is the obverse of the chance for successful setting of a trap. The drawing of the trap will modify the chances for injury in cases where failure results. Modification can be upwards or downwards according to the complexity and danger of the trap. Note that even with a prepared mechanism for a poison needle, for example, the trap must be set, and failure can result. Gloves or protective handwear cannot be worn when setting such traps.

Finally, failure on the first attempt to set a trap does not mean that the thief or assassin can never set the trap. Unlike other similar thief functions, repeated attempts are permissible.

ASSASSINATION EXPERIENCE POINTS

An assassin receives 100 x.p./level of the character assassinated minus or plus 50 x.p. for every level the assassin is greater or lesser than his or her victim. This is modified by multipliers for the degree of difficulty of the mission — simple (X ½), difficult (X 1), or extraordinary (X 1½). The explanations for difficulty given under **SPYING** should be used as guidelines here. The experience given above is added to the regular experience earned for killing the victim, as if he or she were a monster. Experience is also given for the fee the assassin is paid.

Therefore, if an 8th level assassin snuck up on and surprised a 10th level magic-user in the dungeon and successfully assassinated him, the assassin would receive 1,000 x.p. plus another 100 x.p. since the magic-user was 2 levels higher than he. However, since it was a simple mission, the total 1100 x.p. would be multiplied by ½, giving 550 points. This is added to the 2400 x.p. normally received for killing this magic-user, making a final total of 2950 x.p. earned, exclusive of fees.

ASSASSINS' USE OF POISON

Assassins use poison just as any other character does, according to the dictates of the DM. That is, they use the normal tables for poison types (q.v.). When an assassin reaches 9th level (*assassin*), he or she may opt to make a study of poisons. This decision should come from the player in the case of a player character, i.e. do not suggest it or even intimate that such a study can be undertaken. The study will require many weeks and cost from 2,000 to 8,000 g.p. per week. The assassin must find a mentor — an assassin who has already made such a study and actually has put the techniques into practice. In most cases this will be a non-player character assassin of 12th or higher level, who will charge the variable amount. The cost reflects both time and the poisons used in the training. If a player character is involved, he or she must actually have a wide variety of animal, vegetable, and mineral poisons on hand for the training; but he or she can also set the fee as he or she sees fit.

It is not the place of this work to actually serve as a manual for poisons and poisoning. Not only is such a subject distasteful, but it would not properly mesh with the standard poison system used herein. Therefore, the assassin must spend 5-8 weeks to learn each of the following poison skills:

— proper use of all poisons effective in the blood stream only
— proper use of poisons effective through ingestion only
— proper use of contact poisons and poisons effective when in the blood stream or ingested
— the manufacture of poisons and their antidotes

Thus, after 20-32 weeks of study, the assassin will have complete knowledge of 90% of all poisons known. He or she can then use poisons at full normal effect and have the following options as well:

— choose to assassinate by an instantaneous poison
— elect to use a slow acting poison which will not begin to affect the victim for 1-4 hours after ingestion
— elect to use a poison which gradually builds up after repeated doses and kills 1-10 days after the final dose

The assassin must compound the poison, of course. The DM will have to adjudicate this manufacture as he or she deems best. To simulate such manufacture, it is suggested that a week of time and a relatively small outlay (200-1,200 g.p. for materials, bribes, etc.) suffice for any poison. Instantaneous and very slow, undetectable poisons should be more time-consuming and costly, but not greatly so.

This does not guarantee the assassin success, naturally, for he or she must still manage the poisoning and then escape. However, it will give a far better chance and also provide leverage with regard to a slow poison by knowing the antidote. Note that the assassin can stop his or her study at any point, knowing only the knowledge gained in the completed course of study. Also during any course of study, the assassin may not engage in any other activity, or he or she must begin studying again from the beginning of the course. This means that during from 5-8 game weeks the assassin character will be out of play.

One type of poison which assassins can learn to compound is blade venom. Blade venom (always an *insinuative* poison; see **Poison Types**) evaporates quickly. For the first day after its application it does full damage, the second day half, and by the third day none. It is likewise removed by use: on the first hit it will do full damage, on the second hit half damage, and by the third it will be gone. Partially evaporated or used *death* poisons allow the victim a +4 on his or her saving throw.

Poison Types:

The poison of monsters, regardless of its pluses or minuses to the victim's saving throw, is an all-or-nothing affair. That is, either they do no damage, or they kill the victim within a minute or so. Poison potions generally do the same, although you may optionally elect to have any given one be slow-acting, so that the victim will notice nothing for 1-10 hours after quaffing it. Monster poisons are all effective by either ingestion or insinuation into the body and blood stream of the victim. Poison potions must be ingested. If you allow poison use by characters in your campaign, users can purchase ingestive or insinuative poisons only, having to obtain dual-use poisons from monsters.

Purchased poisons are classified and priced as follows:

Poison	Cost/Dose	Onset Time	Damage If Save	Damage If No Save
Ingestive				
A*	5 g.p.	2-8 rounds	10 h.p.	20 h.p.
B**	30 g.p.	2-5 rounds	15 h.p.	30 h.p.
C***	200 g.p.	1-2 rounds	20 h.p.	40 h.p.
D****	500 g.p.	1 segment	25 h.p.	death
E	1,000 g.p.	1-4 turns	30 h.p.	death
Insinuative				
A*	10 g.p.	2-5 rounds	0 h.p.	15 h.p.
B**	75 g.p.	1-3 rounds	0 h.p.	25 h.p.
C***	600 g.p.	1 round	0 h.p.	35 h.p.
D****	1,500 g.p.	1 segment	0 h.p.	death

* Saving throw at +4, chance of tasting/smelling/seeing poison 80%.

** Saving throw at +3, chance of tasting/smelling/seeing poison 65%.

*** Saving throw at +2, chance of tasting/smelling/seeing poison 40%.

**** Saving throw at +1, chance of tasting/smelling/seeing poison 15%.

Assassins use all forms of poison, other than those listed above, at an efficiency which gives the victim +1 on the saving throw; all other character types use them at an efficiency level which allows the victim +2 on saves (in *all* cases). Assassins who have studied poisoning have no penalty. (See **ASSASSINS' USE OF POISONS.**)

THE MONSTER AS A PLAYER CHARACTER

On occasion one player or another will evidence a strong desire to operate as a monster, conceiving a playable character as a strong demon, a devil, a dragon, or one of the most powerful sort of undead creatures. This is done principally because the player sees the desired monster character as superior to his or her peers and likely to provide a dominant role for him or her in the campaign. A moment of reflection will bring them to the un-alterable conclusion that the game is heavily weighted towards mankind.

ADVANCED D&D is unquestionably "humanocentric", with demi-humans, semi-humans, and humanoids in various orbits around the sun of humanity. Men are the worst monsters, particularly high level characters such as clerics, fighters, and magic-users — whether singly, in small groups, or in large companies. The ultra-powerful beings of other planes are more fearsome — the 3 D's of demi-gods, demons, and devils are enough to strike fear into most characters, let alone when the very gods themselves are brought into consideration. Yet, there is a point where the well-equipped, high-level party of adventurers can challenge a demon prince, an arch-devil, or a demi-god. While there might well be some near or part humans with the group so doing, it is certain that the leaders will be human. In co-operation men bring ruin upon monsterdom, for they have no upper limits as to level or acquired power from spells or items.

The game features humankind for a reason. It is the most logical basis in an illogical game. From a design aspect it provides the sound groundwork. From a standpoint of creating the campaign milieu it provides the most readily usable assumptions. From a participation approach it is the only method, for all players are, after all is said and done, human, and it allows them the role with which most are most desirous and capable of identify-ing with. From all views then it is enough fantasy to assume a swords & sorcery cosmos, with impossible professions and make-believe magic. To adventure amongst the weird is fantasy enough without becoming that too! Consider also that each and every Dungeon Master worthy of that title is continually at work expanding his or her campaign milieu. The game is not merely a meaningless dungeon and an urban base around which is plopped the dreaded wilderness. Each of you must design a *world,* piece by piece, as if a jigsaw puzzle were being hand crafted, and each new section must fit perfectly the pattern of the other pieces. Faced with such a task all of us need all of the aid and assistance we can get. Without such help the sheer magnitude of the task would force most of us to throw up our hands in despair.

By having a basis to work from, and a well-developed body of work to draw upon, at least part of this task is handled for us. When history, folk-lore, myth, fable and fiction can be incorporated or used as reference for the campaign, the magnitude of the effort required is reduced by several degrees. Even actual sciences can be used — geography, chemistry, physics, and so forth. Alien viewpoints can be found, of course, but not in quantity (and often not in much quality either). Those works which do not feature mankind in a central role are uncommon. Those which do not deal with men at all are scarce indeed. To attempt to utilize any such bases as the central, let alone sole, theme for a campaign milieu is destined to be shallow, incomplete, and totally unsatisfying for all parties concerned unless the creator is a Renaissance Man and all-around universal genius with a decade or two to prepare the game and milieu. Even then, how can such an effort rival one which borrows from the talents of genius and imaginative thinking which come to us from literature?

Having established the why of the humanocentric basis of the game, you will certainly see the impossibility of any lasting success for a monster player character. The environment for adventuring will be built around humans and demi-humans for the most part. Similarly, the majority of participants in the campaign will be human. So unless the player desires a character which will lurk alone somewhere and be hunted by adventurers, there are only a few options open to him or her. A gold dragon can assume human shape, so that is a common choice for monster characters. If align-ment is stressed, this might discourage the would-be gold dragon. If it is also pointed out that he or she must begin at the lowest possible value, and only time and the accumulation and retention of great masses of wealth will allow any increase in level (age), the idea should be properly squelched. If even that fails, point out that the natural bent of dragons is certainly for their own kind — if not absolute solitude — so what part could a solitary dragon play in a group participation game made up of non-dragons? Dragon non-player characters, yes! As player characters, not likely at all.

As to other sorts of monsters as player characters, you as DM must decide in light of your aims and the style of your campaign. The considered opinion of this writer is that such characters are not beneficial to the game and should be excluded. Note that exclusion is best handled by restriction and not by refusal. Enumeration of the limits and drawbacks which are attendant upon the monster character will always be sufficient to steer the intelligent player away from the monster approach, for in most cases it was only thought of as a likely manner of game domination. The truly ex-perimental-type player might be allowed to play such a monster character for a time so as to satisfy curiosity, and it can then be moved to non-player status and still be an interesting part of the campaign — and the player is most likely to desire to drop the monster character once he or she has examined its potential and played that role for a time. The less intelligent players who demand to play monster characters regardless of obvious con-sequences will soon remove themselves from play in any event, for their own ineptness will serve to have players or monsters or traps finish them off.

So you are virtually on your own with regard to monsters as player characters. You have advice as to why they are not featured, why no details of monster character classes are given herein. The rest is up to you, for when all is said and done, it is your world, and your players must live in it with their characters. Be good to yourself as well as them, and everyone concerned will benefit from a well-conceived, well-ordered, fairly-judged campaign built upon the best of imaginative and creative thinking.

LYCANTHROPY

There have been many different approaches to the disease of lycanthropy. Many are too complicated to understand or are structured so poorly that the werecreature dominates the game. Lycanthropy as a form of player character should be discouraged in AD&D. . This can be done by promoting the human attributes instead of the beast's, thus making lycanthropy undesirable (as it should be).

Some players may not realize that any damage of over 50% of hit points sustained by bites in a fight with a lycanthrope may cause them to be afflicted by the disease. When this happens it may be months after the first night of the change before the character begins to suspect that lycanthropy has taken hold of his or her being. After that first night all that will be remembered is that the character was very ill and extremely tired. In the morning the townspeople quite possibly be combing the countryside looking for a rampaging lycanthrope. The player character may join in the search for the werebeast, not realizing that he or she is the lycanthrope. After a few months of changing, the adventurer will (or should) begin to suspect that something is wrong. On the nights before the full moon the lycanthrope will become withdrawn and a bit edgy, preferring his or her own company to that of others — including family. It may be the torn and shredded clothes he or she wakes up in or the mud and scratches on the character's arms and legs that trigger the realization that he or she may be the werebeast the townspeople are searching for. If at all possible, the DM should try to moderate the campaign so that the players don't know for several months of game time that the character is now a lycanthrope.

Any human player character (humans are the only beings able to contract lycanthropy) bitten for 50% or more of his or her natural hit points has a 100% chance of becoming a lycanthrope of the same type that attacked him or her. If the player eats any belladonna within an hour after being bitten, there is a 25% chance the disease will not manifest itself, and thus the character will not be afflicted by it. If not, then a 12th or higher level patriarch must be found to administer a *cure disease* within three days after being bitten. If the adventurer is only able to find a patriarch of a high enough level after the initial three days, he or she may elect instead to have the priest attempt a *remove curse*. This spell must be performed on the player character when he or she is in wereform. The beast will need to make a monster's saving throw against magic, and while in wereform the creature will fight violently to put as much distance as it can between it and the patriarch performing the spell. If all this fails, there is still hope . . .

At this point, if the player wishes to remain a lycanthrope the two charts given later should be consulted in handling the lycanthrope as a player character. If the adventurer decides to be cured and the methods mentioned thus far have been unsuccessful, he or she may take refuge in a holy/unholy place such as a monastery or an abbey. There the clerics can administer to the afflicted one holy/unholy water laced with a goodly amount of wolfsbane and belladonna prepared by the spiritual methods of that particular religion. This potion is to be consumed by the victim at least twice a day from a silver chalice. No adventuring may be done by the character while he or she is being treated by the clerics. After a month or more (depending upon how advanced the disease is) the player character should be cured and somewhat poorer in the purse, as this procedure is very costly. The clerics will charge for the cost of the herbs and the holy/unholy water as well as for the services rendered. The DM may also wish to include the level of the priest as well as the adventurer into the cost of this treatment.

If the character has died in a fight with a lycanthrope and is resurrected, the disease will be 100% certain if the cleric raising the adventurer is unaware of the disease or fails to follow the proper procedure to eradicate it. The aforementioned cure will work on the werestricken adventurer who has been resurrected. The cleric can use a *cure disease* (if there is still time) or a *remove curse* (if there isn't) on the dead adventurer before employing the *resurrection* spell. If the cleric doesn't take the above safety measures, then it will be necessary to wait until the adventurer becomes a lycanthrope to try to *remove curse* or use the cure with the herbs and holy/unholy water.

If the character opts to remain a lycanthrope, many things will need to be taken into consideration, such as the mental anguish caused by the act of changing. Other things, like conflicting alignments between the character and his or her lycanthrope nature, and what his or her family and friends will do once they discover that their friend and loved one is the werebeast that might have been terrorizing the countryside on the nights of the full

moon, will have to be determined. The more extreme the difference in the alignments of the adventurer and the beast, the more mental anguish the character will be prone to suffer. For example, a lawful good paladin is bitten by a werewolf, which is a chaotic evil creature. He doesn't discover that he has the disease until it is too late. His mental torment is great, especially when the moon is waxing full, up to the time it is full and then for several days afterwards. (The DM may wish to select a mental disorder from the section on INSANITY for the character to suffer from to reflect the effects of the anguish caused by the disease). The paladin, even after being cured, is no longer a paladin because he is no longer pure enough for that honored state. The DM can elect to have the gods send the paladin on a quest in order to restore him to his paladinhood, but it is *not* recommended.

No experience points may be gained by a player character while in lycanthrope form. If the character is a fighter/lycanthrope, the fighter will be able to gain levels only as a fighter, never as a lycanthrope. This applies to all classes. The only way a lycanthrope will ever be able to control the change from man to beast is with time measured by full moons. There will be no control of the change into a werebeast for two years of game time and it will be another year before any control will be gained for the change back into a human. On the nights of a full moon all lycanthropes with less than three years experience as a werebeast will change into their wereform and remain that way from the rise of the moon till dawn.

There are other factors besides the full moon that can cause the release of the werecreature in a person afflicted with lycanthropy. One common cause is stress during a melee. If the character has lost more than one-third of his or her natural hit points during the fight, there is a 50% chance that the werenature will emerge, causing the player character to be disoriented for 1 to 2 rounds (characters with more than two years of experience as a lycanthrope will not suffer this disorientation). During this time, the lycanthrope will be unable to engage in combat. He or she will also sustain damage from the change as shown on the appropriate table given below. Spells used in the vicinity of a lycanthrope such as *monster summoning III-VII*, *conjure animals*, and *animal summoning III* might cause the werenature to be released. It will be up to the DM to decide what spells or magic items could trigger the beast inside the afflicted adventurer. Arguments with other player characters as well as fear could cause the change from man to beast.

All lycanthropes will fight and do damage as described in the MONSTER MANUAL regardless of how long the character has been a lycanthrope. The diseased adventurer will eventually acquire the alignment of the lycanthrope form (if it isn't the same already) within 2 to 12 months.

While in wereform the character will not be interested in any of his or her belongings and will leave them where the change took place. This includes armor and weapons (except for wererats, who will carry swords).

Werebears are the most powerful form of lycanthrope. As with most lycanthropes, they will eventually flee to the woods. Once a werebear engages in combat with a creature of an evil alignment it will fight until it or its opponent is dead. Seventy-five percent of the time, if a monster with an evil alignment is encountered, the werebear will attack immediately.

Wereboars are the most foul-tempered of the lycanthropes. Their temperament is such that they will not join a party unless they can be the leader. If they do join one and are not its leader, they will argue bitterly with anyone who disagrees with them. This action may cause them to change into their wereform from the stress involved in the argument.

Wererats will want to live in the city near humans (humans being one of their favorite foods). If a human is captured and not eaten immediately, it will probably be held for ransom. A wererat will do all it can to keep the party it is with from discovering that it is a lycanthrope. Wererats are the only lycanthropes that will carry a sword or use any kind of a weapon while in animal form. When the marching order of a party is being decided, a wererat will almost always volunteer to be in the rear.

Weretigers are usually interested only in what benefits them. They will tolerate other cats to a certain extent and perhaps even have one for a companion. In human form weretigers can be mistaken for magic-users if they have a domestic cat for an apparent familiar. For this reason many in AD&D will disguise themselves as a magic-user, possibly taking up the trade just enough to give the facade an appearance of realism. Weretigers might have no qualms about turning on their party if the party begins to behave in a manner that the weretiger finds incompatible with its desires.

Werewolves are chaotic evil and therefore very unpredictable, especially in a melee. Werewolves tend to run in packs or family units. Seldom will they join a normal party of adventurers, and if they do, once discovered as a lycanthrope they will turn and attack the party, usually choosing to do so when the adventurers are in combat with another monster.

Change Table For Lycanthropes:

This table will aid the DM in determining the percentage chances of a player character lycanthrope changing into and out of wereform. After six years of experience, lycanthropes will be able to control their change at will.

WANING MOON	1-2 years	3	4	5
Full	100%*	75%	50%	25%
Half	75%**	25%	15%	5%
Quarter	50%	5%	—	—
New Moon	25%**	—	—	—
WAXING MOON				
Quarter	50%	—	—	—
Half	75%**	30%	20%	10%
Full	100%*	80%	55%	30%

* There is no chance for voluntarily changing out of wereform.

** There is only a 25% chance for voluntarily changing out of wereform.

Damage Table:

This table shows how much damage a character takes from armor constriction (before the straps burst and it falls off) during sudden change to lycanthrope form.

Armor Type	Were-bear	Were-boar	Were-rat	Were-tiger	Were-wolf
No Armor	0	0	0	0	0
Leather/Padded	1	1	0	1-2	1
Studded Leather/ Ring Mail	1-2	1-2	1	1-3	1-2
Scale Mail	1-3	1-3	1-2	1-4	1-3
Chain Mail	1-4	1-4	1-2	2-4	1-4
Splint Mail/ Banded Mail	2-4	2-4	1-2	2-5	2-4
Plate Mail	2-5	2-5	1-3	2-5	2-5

ALIGNMENT

Alignment describes the broad ethos of thinking, reasoning creatures — those unintelligent sorts being placed within the *neutral* area because they are totally uncaring. Note that alignment does not necessarily dictate religious persuasion, although many religious beliefs will dictate alignment. As explained under **ALIGNMENT LANGUAGES** (q.v.) this aspect of alignment is not the major consideration. The overall behavior of the character (or creature) is delineated by alignment, or, in the case of player characters, behavior determines actual alignment. Therefore, besides defining the general tendencies of creatures, it also groups creatures into mutually acceptable or at least non-hostile divisions. This is not to say that groups of similarly aligned creatures cannot be opposed or even mortal enemies. Two nations, for example, with rulers of lawful good alignment can be at war. Bands of orcs can hate each other. But the former would possibly cease their war to oppose a massive invasion of orcs, just as the latter would make common cause against the lawful good men. Thus, alignment describes the world view of creatures and helps to define what their actions, reactions, and purposes will be. It likewise causes a player character to choose an ethos which is appropriate to his or her profession, and alignment also aids players in the definition and role approach of their respective game personae. With the usefulness of alignment determined, definition of the divisions is necessary.

Major Divisions:

There are two major divisions of four opposite points of view. All four are not mutually exclusive, although each pair is mutually opposed.

Law And Chaos: The opposition here is between organized groups and individuals. That is, law dictates that order and organization is necessary and desirable, while chaos holds to the opposite view. Law generally supports the group as more important than the individual, while chaos promotes the individual over the group.

Good And Evil: Basically stated, the tenets of good are human rights, or in the case of **AD&D**, creature rights. Each creature is entitled to life, relative freedom, and the prospect of happiness. Cruelty and suffering are undesirable. Evil, on the other hand, does not concern itself with rights or happiness; purpose is the determinant.

There can never exist a lawful chaos or an evil good. These, and their reverses, are dichotomous, This is not to say that they cannot exist in the same character or creature if it is insane or controlled by another entity, but as general divisions they are mutually exclusive pairs. Consider also the alignment graph. If law is opposed to chaos, and good to evil, then the radically opposed alignments are lawful neutral — chaotic neutral, neutral good — neutral evil, lawful good — chaotic evil, and lawful evil — chaotic good. Lawful groups might, for example, combine to put down some chaotic threat, for example, just as readily as good groups would combine to suppress some powerful evil. Basic understanding and agreement, however, is within the general specific alignment, i.e. one of the nine categories. These are defined as follows:

NEUTRALITY: Absolute, or true, neutral creatures view everything which exists as an integral, necessary part or function of the entire cosmos. Each thing exists as a part of the whole, one as a check or balance to the other, with life necessary for death, happiness for suffering, good for evil, order for chaos, and vice versa. Nothing must ever become predominant or out of balance. Within this naturalistic ethos, humankind serves a role also, just as all other creatures do. They may be more or less important, but the neutral does not concern himself or herself with these considerations except where it is positively determined that the balance is threatened. Absolute neutrality is in the central or fulcrum position quite logically, as the neutral sees all other alignments as parts of a necessary whole. This alignment is the narrowest in scope.

NEUTRAL GOOD: Creatures of this alignment see the cosmos as a place where law and chaos are merely tools to use in bringing life, happiness, and prosperity to all deserving creatures. Order is not good unless it brings this to all; neither is randomness and total freedom desirable if it does not bring such good.

NEUTRAL EVIL: Similar to the neutral good alignment, that of neutral evil holds that neither groups nor individuals have great meaning. This ethos holds that seeking to promote weal for all actually brings woe to the truly deserving. Natural forces which are meant to cull out the weak and stupid are artificially suppressed by so-called good, and the fittest are wrongfully held back, so whatever means are expedient can be used by the powerful to gain and maintain their dominance, without concern for anything.

LAWFUL GOOD: Creatures of lawful good alignment view the cosmos with varying degrees of lawfulness or desire for good. They are convinced that order and law are absolutely necessary to assure good, and that good is best defined as whatever brings the most benefit to the greater number of decent, thinking creatures and the least woe to the rest.

LAWFUL NEUTRAL: It is the view of this alignment that law and order give purpose and meaning to everything. Without regimentation and strict definition, there would be no purpose in the cosmos. Therefore, whether a law is good or evil is of no import as long as it brings order and meaning.

LAWFUL EVIL: Obviously, all order is not good, nor are all laws beneficial. Lawful evil creatures consider order as the means by which each group is properly placed in the cosmos, from lowest to highest, strongest first, weakest last. Good is seen as an excuse to promote the mediocrity of the whole and suppress the better and more capable, while lawful evilness allows each group to structure itself and fix its place as compared to others, serving the stronger but being served by the weaker.

CHAOTIC GOOD: To the chaotic good individual, freedom and independence are as important to life and happiness. The ethos views this freedom as the only means by which each creature can achieve true satisfaction and happiness. Law, order, social forms, and anything else which tends to restrict or abridge individual freedom is wrong, and each individual is capable of achieving self-realization and prosperity through himself, herself, or itself.

CHAOTIC NEUTRAL: This view of the cosmos holds that absolute freedom is necessary. Whether the individual exercising such freedom chooses to do good or evil is of no concern. After all, life itself is law and order, so death is a desirable end. Therefore, life can only be justified as a tool by which order is combatted, and in the end it too will pass into entropy.

CHAOTIC EVIL: The chaotic evil creature holds that individual freedom and choice is important, and that other individuals and their freedoms are unimportant if they cannot be held by the individuals through their own strength and merit. Thus, law and order tends to promote not individuals but groups, and groups suppress individual volition and success.

There is no honor among Thieves....

Each of these cases for alignment is, of course, stated rather simplistically and ideally, for philosophical and moral reasonings are completely subjective according to the acculturation of the individual. You, as Dungeon Master, must establish the meanings and boundaries of law and order as opposed to chaos and anarchy, as well as the divisions between right and good as opposed to hurtful and evil. Lawful societies will tend to be highly structured, rigid, well-policed and bureaucratic hierarchical. Class, rank, position, and precedence will be important, so they will be strictly defined and adhered to. On the other hand, chaotic areas will have little government and few social distinctions. The governed will give their consent to government, acknowledging leaders as equals serving those who allowed them to assume leadership. Obedience and service in a chaotic society is given only by those desiring to do so, or by dint of some persuasion, never by requirement.

Alignment With Respect To The Planes:

Obviously, the material planes have no set alignment, nor do the other "inner planes" or the ethereal or astral ones either. However, the "outer planes" show various alignments. This is because they are home to creatures who are of like general alignment. If the curves of the alignment table are carried outwards to the planes, only those planes at the corners will correspond to non-neutral alignments, i.e., lawful good, chaotic good, chaotic evil, and lawful evil. Similarly, those on the horizontal and vertical axes correspond to the neutral-based alignments which support an ethos, i.e. neutral good, chaotic neutral, neutral evil, and lawful neutral. The remainder of the outer plane areas are "gray" areas where alignments shade into each other. Inhabitants of these planes will generally have the same world-view as their fellows on the Prime Material Plane.

Graphing Alignment:

It is of importance to keep track of player character behavior with respect to their professed alignment. Actions do speak far more eloquently than professions, and each activity of a player character should reflect his or her alignment. If a professed lawful evil character is consistently seeking to be helpful and is respecting the lesser creatures, he or she is certainly tending towards good, while if he or she ignores regulations and consistent behavior the trend is towards chaotic alignment (see **PLAYERS HANDBOOK, APPENDIX III, CHARACTER ALIGNMENT GRAPH**). Such drift should be noted by you, and when it takes the individual into a new alignment area, you should then inform the player that his or her character has changed alignment (see **CHANGING ALIGNMENT**). It is quite possible for a character to drift around in an alignment area, making only small shifts

due to behavior. However, any major action which is out of alignment character will cause a major shift to the alignment which is directly in line with the action, i.e., if a lawful evil character defies the law in order to aid the cause (express or implied) of chaotic good, he or she will be either lawful neutral or chaotic neutral, depending on the factors involved in the action.

It is of utmost importance to keep rigid control of alignment behavior with respect to such characters as serve deities who will accept only certain alignments, those who are paladins, those with evil familiars, and so on. Part of the role they have accepted requires a set behavior mode, and its benefits are balanced by this. Therefore, failure to demand strict adherence to alignment behavior is to allow a game abuse.

Lawful good characters should not be allowed to ignore unlawful or shady actions by "looking the other way". If, for example, a party that includes a paladin decides to use poison on a monster that they know is ahead, the DM shouldn't let the paladin be distracted or "led away for a few rounds" when it is patently obvious that the paladin heard the plan. If the player does not take appropriate measures to prevent the action, the DM should warn the paladin that his lack of action will constitute a voluntary alignment change and then let the chips fall where they may!

ALIGNMENT LANGUAGE

Alignment language is a handy game tool which is not unjustifiable in real terms. Thieves *did* employ a special cant. Secret organizations and societies did and do have certain recognition signs, signals, and recognition phrases — possibly special languages (of limited extent) as well. Consider also the medieval Catholic Church which used Latin as a common recognition and communication base to cut across national boundaries. In **AD&D**, alignment languages are the special set of signs, signals, gestures, and words which intelligent creatures use to inform other intelligent creatures of the same alignment of their fellowship and common ethos. Alignment languages are NEVER flaunted in public. They are *not* used as salutations or interrogatives if the speaker is uncertain of the alignment of those addressed. Furthermore, alignment languages are of limited vocabulary and deal with the ethos of the alignment in general, so lengthy discussion of varying subjects cannot be conducted in such tongues.

Each alignment language is constructed to allow recognition of like-aligned creatures and to discuss the precepts of the alignment in detail. Otherwise, the tongue will permit only the most rudimentary communication with a vocabulary limited to a few score words. The speaker could inquire of the listener's state of health, ask about hunger, thirst, or degree of tiredness. A few other basic conditions and opinions could be expressed, but no more. The *specialty tongues* of *Druidic* and the *Thieves' Cant* are designed to handle conversations pertaining to things druidical on the one hand and thievery, robbery and the disposal of stolen goods on the other. Druids could discuss at length and in detail the state of the crops, weather, animal husbandry and foresting; but warfare, politics, adventuring, and like matter would be impossible to detail with the language.

Any character foolish enough to announce his or her alignment by publicly crying out in that alignment tongue will incur considerable social sanctions. At best he or she will be thought unmannerly, rude, boorish, and stupid. Those of the same alignment will be inclined to totally ignore the character, not wishing to embarass themselves by admitting any familiarity with the offender. Those of other alignment will likewise regard the speaker with distaste when overhearing such an outburst. At worst, the character will be marked by those hostile to the alignment in which he or she spoke.

Alignment language is used to establish credentials only after initial communications have been established by other means. Only in the most desperate of situations would any creature utter something in the alignment tongue otherwise. It must also be noted that alignment does NOT necessarily empower a creature to actually speak or understand the alignment language which is general in the ethos. Thus, blink dogs are intelligent, lawful good creatures who have a language of their own. A lawful good human, dwarf, or brownie will be absolutely at a loss to communicate with blink dogs, however, except in the most limited of ways (non-aggression, non-fear, etc.) without knowledge of the creatures' language or some magical means. This is because blink dogs do not intellectually embrace the ethos of lawful good but are of that alignment instinctually; therefore, they do not speak the tongue used by lawful good. This is not true of gold dragons, let us say, or red dragons with respect to their alignment, who do speak their respective alignment languages.

CHANGING ALIGNMENT

Whether or not the character actively professes some deity, he or she will have an alignment and serve one or more deities of this general alignment indirectly and unbeknownst to the character. Changing of alignment is a serious matter, although some players would have their characters change alignment as often as they change socks. Not so!

First, change of alignment for clerics can be very serious, as it might cause a change of deity. (See **DAY-TO-DAY ACQUISITION OF CLERIC SPELLS.**) If a druid changes his or her alignment — that is, becomes other than neutral — then he or she is no longer a druid at all! Change of alignment will have an adverse effect on any class of character if he or she is above the 2nd level.

Immediately upon alignment change actually occurring, the character concerned will lose one level of experience, dropping experience points to take him or her to the very beginning of the next lower level, losing the hit die and/or hit points, and all abilities which accrued to him or her with the lost level. If the alignment change is involuntary (such as that caused by a powerful magic, a curse, etc.), then the character can regain all of the losses (level, hit die, etc.) upon returning to his or her former alignment as soon as is possible and after making atonement through a cleric of the same alignment — and sacrificing treasure which has a value of not less than 10,000 g.p. per level of experience of the character. The sacrificial amount is variable, so use your best judgment as to the total and what and where it should go — magic items to build up the NPC cleric, money out of the campaign, magic items out of the campaign, etc. Similarly, such atonement and sacrifice can be accomplished by a quest. Note that, in all likelihood, the character will desire to retain the new alignment, and it is incumbent upon you as DM to ensure that the player acts accordingly. Some equally powerful means (divine intervention, remove curse, etc.) must be used to restore the original alignment before atonement can begin.

Characters who knowingly or unknowingly change alignment through forethought or actions permanently lose the experience points and level due to disfavor. They must also accept a severe disability in alignment language during a one level transitional period. Until the character has again achieved his or her former level of experience held prior to change of alignment, he or she will not be able to converse in the former alignment's tongue nor will anything but the rudest signaling be possible in the new alignment language. (See **ALIGNMENT LANGUAGE.**) Although it is possible for a character to allow himself or herself to be blown by the winds as far as alignment is concerned, he or she will pay a penalty which will effectively damn the character to oblivion.

A glance at the alignment chart will show that radical alignment change is impossible without magical means. If one is *chaotic good,* it is possible to change to *neutral good* or *chaotic neutral* only, depending upon desire and/or actions. From the absolute *neutral* alignment one can only move to some neutral-based alignment. This represents the fact that the character must divorce himself or herself from certain precepts and views and wholeheartedly embrace another set of values, and human nature is such that without radical personality alteration (such as caused by insanity or magic in the case of this game) such transition must be gradual.

It is assumed that the character's initial alignment has been his or hers for a considerable period prior to the character's emergence as an adventurer. This ethos will not be lightly changed by a stable, rational individual. It is recommended that you do not inform players of the penalty which will occur with alignment change, so that those who seek to use alignment as a means of furthering their own interests by conveniently swapping one for another when they deem the time is ripe will find that they have, instead, paid a stern price for fickleness.

MONEY

PLAYER CHARACTER STARTING MONEY

The amount of funds which each player begins with is kept low to prevent the game from becoming too easy. Players learn from the beginning that they are never able to obtain all of the goods they would like in order to feel safe and satisfied. Explain to players that sums they begin with (see **PLAYERS HANDBOOK, MONEY**) represent inherited monies and savings. A magic-user, for example, has had to expend most ready cash he or she possessed on training; monks are ascetics who don't care about material possessions in any event, so they do not accumulate much money prior to becoming adventurers and treasure seekers.

If you have a difficult campaign, and you opt to bestow a limited number of special items to player characters at the beginning of the game (a potion, a magic goodie such as a +1 dagger, or even something as mundane as a family suit of plate mail) you should adjust starting money accordingly. The game is always supposed to be a challenge, to cause players to want for something, and to wish to adventure with their characters in order to obtain the desired things. Remembering that good players will be able to gain from nearly any successful encounter — there will always be some armor and weapons or equipment to be gained from an adventure — you should not hesitate to be stingy and tight right from the beginning of a campaign!

PLAYER CHARACTER EXPENSES

Each player character will automatically expend not less than 100 gold pieces per level of experience per month. This is simply support, upkeep, equipment, and entertainment expense. These costs are to be deducted by the Dungeon Master automatically, and any further spending by the PC is to be added to these costs. Such expense is justified by the "fact" that adventurers are a free-wheeling and high-living lot (except, of course, for monks). Other miscellaneous expenditures by player characters encompass such things as additional equipment expense for henchmen or hirelings, costs of hirelings, bribes, costs of locating prospective henchmen, and so on. To such costs are to be added:

MAINTENANCE OF HENCHMEN	100 g.p. per level per month*
MAINTENANCE OF STRONGHOLD	1% of total cost of stronghold per month

*This is in **addition** to all treasure shares

Finally, any taxation or other levies must be taken into consideration, along with contributions to the player character's religious organization. All of these costs will help assure the PCs have a keen interest in going out and adventuring in order to support themselves and their many associates and holdings.

You may reduce costs according to prevailing circumstances if you feel it is warranted, but even so doing should not give rise to excess funds on hand in the campaign.

VALUE AND REPUTED PROPERTIES OF GEMS AND JEWELRY

Gems:

The base value of gems found in a treasure can be determined in whole or by lots of 5 or 10 stones by rolling percentile dice:

Dice Score	Base Value	Description	(or Size)
01-25	10 g.p. each	Ornamental Stones	very small
26-50	50 g.p. each	Semi-precious Stones	small
51-70	100 g.p. each	Fancy Stones	average
71-90	500 g.p. each	Fancy Stones (Precious)	large
91-99	1,000 g.p. each	Gem Stones	very large
00	5,000 g.p. each	Gem Stones (Jewels)	huge

Value of a gem depends upon its type, quality and weight. A huge semi-precious stone — carnelian, for example — is worth as much as an average gem stone, quality being equal. Size may vary from stone to stone, a 50 g.p. ornamental stone being of above average size, while a 50 g.p. gem stone would most likely be very small.

Increase Or Decrease Of Worth Beyond Base Value: If you do not place specific value on each gem in a treasure, showing rather the base value of each gem instead, then variation in the worth of each stone should be allowed. This variation will generally result in some increase, although there is a chance for decreasing value as well (see below). To find if a gem increases in value, roll a d10 for each stone, and consult the table below:

Die	Result
1	Stone increases to next higher base value; roll again ignoring results above 8. Stones above 5,000 gold piece value progress as follows: 10,000 GP, 25,000 GP, 50,000 GP, 100,000 GP, 250,000 GP, 500,000 GP, and 1,000,000 GP — the absolute maximum. No stone may increase beyond 7 places from its initial base value.
2	Stone is double base value. Do not roll again.
3	Stone is 10% to 60% above base value. Roll d6 to find new value. Do not roll again on this table.
4-8	Base value shown is unchanged.
9	Stone is 10% to 40% below base value. Roll d4 to find new value. Do not roll again on this table.
0	Stone decreases to next lower base value; roll again on this table, ignoring any result below 2. Stones below 10 gold piece value are: 5 GP, 1 GP, 10 SP, 5 SP, and 1 SP. No stone may decrease beyond 5 places from its initial base value.

When base value only is known, use the table above, and roll for each stone. Stones for which a 1 or a 0 is rolled must be diced for again on the table, but all others are excluded from such rolls. If large numbers of stones are in question, it is suggested that they be diced for in groups in order to make the process less time-consuming.

KEY TO GEM PROPERTIES

transparent (no notation)
translucent *(italics)*
opaque (*)

ORNAMENTAL STONES, Base Value 10 g.p.:

1. Azurite*: mottled deep blue
2. *Banded Agate:* striped brown and blue and white and reddish
3. Blue Quartz: pale blue
4. *Eye Agate:* circles of gray, white, brown, blue and/or green
5. Hematite*: gray-black
6. Lapis Lazuli*: light and dark blue with yellow flecks
7. Malachite*: striated light and dark green
8. *Moss Agate:* pink or yellow-white with grayish or greenish "moss markings"
9. Obsidian*: black
10. Rhodochrosite*: light pink
11. *Tiger Eye:* rich brown with golden center under-hue
12. Turquoise*: light blue-green

SEMI-PRECIOUS STONES, Base Value 50 g.p.:

1. Bloodstone*: dark gray with red flecks
2. Carnelian*: orange to reddish brown (also called Sard)
3. Chalcedony*: white
4. *Chrysoprase:* apple green to emerald green
5. Citrine: pale yellow brown
6. Jasper*: blue, black to brown
7. *Moonstone:* white with pale blue glow
8. Onyx*: bands of black and white or pure black or white
9. Rock Crystal: clear
10. Sardonyx*: bands of sard (red) and onyx (white) or sard*
11. Smoky Quartz: gray, yellow, or blue (Cairngorm), all light
12. Star Rose Quartz: translucent rosy stone with white "star" center
13. Zircon: clear pale blue-green

FANCY STONES, Base Value 100 to 500 g.p.:

1. Amber: watery gold to rich gold (100)
2. Alexandrite: dark green (100)
3. Amethyst: deep purple (100)
4. Aquamarine: pale blue green (500)
5. Chrysoberyl: yellow green to green (100)
6. Coral*: crimson (100)

7. Garnet: red, brown-green, or violet (the most prized) (100) (500)
8. *Jade:* light green, deep green, green and white, white (100)
9. Jet*: deep black (100)
10. Pearl*: lustrous white, yellowish, pinkish, etc. to pure black (the most prized) (100) (500)
11. Peridot: rich olive green (Chrysolite) (500)
12. Spinel: red, red-brown, deep green, or very deep blue (the most prized) (100) (500)
13. Topaz: golden yellow (500)
14. Tourmaline: green pale, blue pale, brown pale, or reddish pale (100)

GEM STONES, 1,000 or more g.p. Base Value:

1. *Black Opal:* dark green with black mottling and golden flecks
2. *Black Sapphire:* lustrous black with glowing highlights (5,000)
3. Diamond: clear blue-white with lesser stones clear white or pale tints (5,000)
4. Emerald: deep bright green
5. *Fire Opal:* fiery red
6. Jacinth: fiery orange (Corundum) (5,000)
7. *Opal:* pale blue with green and golden mottling
8. Oriental Amethyst: rich purple (Corundum)
9. Oriental Emerald: clear bright green (Corundum) (5,000)
10. Oriental Topaz: fiery yellow (Corundum)
11. Ruby: clear red to deep crimson (Corundum) (5,000)
12. Sapphire: clear to medium blue (Corundum)
13. *Star Ruby:* translucent ruby with white "star" center
14. *Star Sapphire:* translucent sapphire with white "star" center

Jewelry:

The base value of jewelry is determined by percentile dice roll, just as with gems:

Dice Roll	Base Value	Description
01-10	100-1,000 g.p.	Ivory or wrought silver
11-20	200-1,200 g.p.	Wrought silver and gold
21-40	300-1,800 g.p.	Wrought gold
41-50	500-3,000 g.p.	Jade, coral or wrought platinum
51-70	1,000-6,000 g.p.	Silver with gems
71-90	2,000-8,000 g.p.	Gold with gems
91-00	2,000-12,000 g.p.	Platinum with gems

Once jewelry's base value is determined, each piece should be checked for workmanship and design by rolling a 10-sided die. Each 1 rolled indicates the piece of jewelry in question is of exceptional value and thus either goes to the highest possible value in its class or to the next higher class (where its base value is re-determined and its workmanship and design are again checked). Any piece of jewelry set with gems must also be checked for the possibility of an exceptional stone in the setting. Any score of 1 on an 8-sided die indicates that the value of the piece of jewelry increases by 5,000 gold pieces, and these exceptional pieces are further checked by rolling a 6-sided die, each successive 1 doubling the increase, i.e., 10,000 g.p., 20,000 g.p., 40,000 g.p., 80,000 g.p., to a maximum of 640,000 gold pieces.

The Dungeon Master can, of course, name what each piece of jewelry is (bracelet, brooch, crown, earrings, necklace, pendant, ring, tiara, etc.), giving its substance and the number and value of its stones.

REPUTED MAGICAL PROPERTIES OF GEMS

Gem Type or Color	Effects or Uses
Agate	Restful and safe sleep
Alexandrite	Good omens
Amber	Wards off diseases
Amethyst	Prevents drunkenness or drugging
Beryl	Wards off foes
Bloodstone	Weather control
Carbuncle	Powers of dragon's sight
Carnelian	Protection from evil
Cats' eye agate	Protection from spirits
Chalcedony	Wards off undead
Chrysoberyl	Protection from possession
Chrysolite	Wards off spells
Chrysoprase	Invisibility
Coral	Calms weather, safety in river crossing, cures madness, stanches bleeding

Diamond	Invulnerability vs. undead
Hematite	Aids fighters, heals wounds
Jacinth	Luck travelling, wards off plague, protection from fire
Jade	Skill at music and musical instruments
Jasper	Protection from venom
Jet	Soul object material
Lapis Lazuli	Raises morale, courage
Malachite	Protection from falling
Malachite & Sunstone	Wards off spells, evil spirits, and poisons
Moonstone	Causes lycanthropy
Olivine	Protection from spells
Onyx	Causes discord amongst enemies
Peridot	Wards off enchantments
Ruby	Gives good luck
Sapphire	Aids understanding of problems, kills spiders, boosts magical abilities
Sapphire, Star	Protection from magic
Sard	Benefits wisdom
Serpentine	Adds to wile and cunning
Topaz	Wards off evil spells
Turquoise	Aids horses in all ways (but stone shatters when it operates)

Black	The Earth - darkness - negation
Blue	The Heavens - truth - spirituality
Clear	The Sun - luck
Green	Venus - reproduction - sight - resurrection
Red	Hemorrhaging control - heat
White	The Moon - enigmatic
Yellow	Secrecy - homeopathy - jaundice

NOTE REGARDING THE MAGICAL PROPERTIES OF GEMS, HERBS, et al.

Regardless of what qualities gems, herbs, and other substances are purported to possess, the mere possession of a score of a type of gem or a bale of some herb will convey absolutely no benefit of magical nature to the character concerned. These special qualities are given herein merely as information for Dungeon Master use in devising special formulae for potions, inks, etc. The information might also prove useful in other ways, particularly with regard to description of magic items, laboratories, and so on. Under no circumstances should you allow some player to convince you to the contrary!

VALUES OF OTHER RARE COMMODITIES

Furs:

Type	Pelt	Trimming*	Cape or Jacket	Coat
beaver	2 g.p.	20 g.p.	200 g.p.	400 g.p.
ermine	4 g.p.	120 g.p.	3,600 g.p.	7,200 g.p.
fox	3 g.p.	30 g.p.	300 g.p.	600 g.p.
marten	4 g.p.	40 g.p.	400 g.p.	800 g.p.
mink	3 g.p.	90 g.p.	2,700 g.p.	5,400 g.p.
muskrat	1 g.p.	10 g.p.	100 g.p.	200 g.p.
sable	5 g.p.	150 g.p.	4,500 g.p.	9,000 g.p.
seal	5 g.p.	25 g.p.	125 g.p.	250 g.p.

*on collar, cuffs, and edges of typical garment

Roll d10 and adjust value as follows:

1 =	−10%	5-8 =	as shown
2 =	−20%	9 =	+10%
3 =	−30%	0 =	+20%
4 =	−40%		

Brocade* / Tapestry	1-20 g.p./square yard
Incense, rare	5-30 g.p./stick
Ivory	3-6 g.p./pound
Pepper	1 g.p./ounce
Perfume, rare	1-6 g.p./dram
Silk	1-3 g.p./square yard
Spice, rare	1-4 s.p./scruple
Unguent, rare	10-60 g.p./gill

*Includes fine carpet and rugs as well

ARMOR, ARMOR CLASS & WEAPONS

TYPES OF ARMOR & ENCUMBRANCE

The encumbrance factor for armor does not consider weight alone; it also takes into account the distribution of the weight of the armor and the relative mobility of the individual wearing the protective material. Therefore, weights for armor shown below are adjusted weights, and base movement speed is likewise shown.

Armor Type	Bulk	Weight*	Base Movement
BANDED	bulky	35#+	9″
CHAIN	fairly	30#+	9″
CHAIN, ELFIN	non-	15#	12″
LEATHER	non-	15#	12″
PADDED	fairly	10#	9″
PLATE (MAIL)	bulky	45#	6″
RING	fairly	25#	9″
SCALE	fairly	40#	6″
SHIELD, LARGE	bulky	10#	—
SHIELD, SMALL	non-	5#	—
SHIELD, SMALL, WOOD	non-	3#	—
SPLINT	bulky	40#	6″
STUDDED (LEATHER)	fairly	20#	9″

*Assumes human-size.

Armor Types:

Banded Mail is a layered armor with padding, light chain, and series of overlapping bands of armor in vulnerable areas. Weight is somewhat distributed.

Chain Mail is padding plus interlocking mesh armor covering the upper and lower body. Vulnerable areas have multiple thicknesses. Weight falls upon the shoulders and waist of the wearer.

Chain, Elfin, is a finely wrought suit of chain which is of thinner links but stronger metal. It is obtainable only from elvenkind who do not sell it.

Leather Armor is shaped *cuir bouli* (leather hardened by immersion in boiling oil) cuirass and shoulder pieces and softer shirt and leggings.

Padded Armor is heavily padded, quilted coat and an additional soft leather jerkin and leggings.

Plate Mail is light chain with pieces of plate — cuirass, shoulder pieces, elbow and knee guards, and greaves. Weight is well distributed. (Plate armor is a full suit of plate which is no more weighty and a bit less bulky, considering what is known as "field plate". If you allow such armor in your campaign, use the same weight, with a 9″ movement base and a base armor class of 2 sans shield. Such armor would be very expensive, c. 2000 g.p.).

Ring Mail is relatively soft leather armor over padding. To the long coat of leather are sewn metal rings. This makes the coat rather heavy and bulky.

Scale Mail is armor similar to ring mail, but overlapping scales of metal are sewn to both coat and leggings—or a skirted coat is worn. As with chain, weight falls mainly on the wearer's shoulders and waist.

Shield, Large, includes such shields as the large Viking round shields or the Norman kite shields. They are made of wood, covered with leather, and bordered with a soft iron banding at the edges.

Shield, Small, is the typical kite and heater shields or small round shields constructed as a large shield, or else made of metal (more rare by far).

Shield, Small, Wooden, is the same as other shields, but it lacks the metal binding and reinforcement, so it will be more easily split.

Splint Mail consists of light chain, greaves, and a leather coat into which are laminated vertical pieces of plate with shoulder guards.

Studded Leather is leather armor to which have been fastened metal studding as additional protection, usually including an outer coat of fairly close-set studs (small plates).

Helmets:

It is assumed that an appropriate type of head armoring will be added to the suit of armor in order to allow uniform protection of the wearer. Wearing of a "great helm" adds the appropriate weight and restricts vision to the front 60° only, but it gives the head AC 1. If a helmet is not worn, 1 blow in 6 will strike at the AC 10 head, unless the opponent is intelligent, in which case 1 blow in 2 will be aimed at the AC 10 head (d6, 1-3 = head blow).

Magic Armor:

When magic armor is worn, assume that its properties allow movement at the next higher base rate and that weight is cut by 50%. *There is no magical elfin chain mail.*

Magic Shields:

Magic shields are no less weighty than their non-magical counterparts, but they are non-bulky with respect to encumbrance.

Shield Use:

A shield is basically a barrier between its wielder and his or her opponent. It is used to catch blows or missiles. It can also be used offensively to strike or push an opponent. The shield can be used fully only to the left or front of the right handed individual. Attacks from the right flank or rear negate the benefits of a shield.

Small Shields: Bucklers and other small shields which are basically held with one hand are moved rapidly by the wielder, but they cover only a small area, so they are less effective by and large. Such shields are less cumbersome and fatiguing in employment, however, so no distinction is made between a small and a normal-sized shield in **AD&D**.

Large Shields: Although a large shield such as a Norman kite shield or a large Viking round shield covers much more of the body, employing one of these shields is far more difficult, as they are cumbersome and fatiguing. Therefore, large shields are treated as but +1 to armor class rating without a shield. Optionally, you may allow them to add +2 to this armor class rating with respect to small (non-war engine or giant hurled) missiles; if you do so, however, be certain that you also keep careful track of encumbrance.

DEXTERITY ARMOR CLASS BONUS

This bonus is in addition to that given by any other forms of protection. The type of armor worn by the character with a dexterity armor class bonus does not adversely affect this bonus, for it is assumed that his or her physical conditioning and training compensate otherwise. (This is particularly applicable with regard to magic armor which is assumed to possess an enchantment which makes it both light and flexible.) The penalty for wearing armor is already subsumed in the defensive bonuses given for it, and if it were further to penalize the character by denying dexterity armor class adjustments, it would be totally invalid.

Modifiers To Dexterity Armor Class Adjustment: Neither penalty nor bonus due to dexterity (the Defensive Adjustment) is considered when the character is subjected to the following attack forms:

Attacks from the rear flank, rear, or strikes from behind (where the character is virtually unable to see the attack coming).

Large missiles such as those hurled by a giant or some form of engine (where the trajectory and speed and size of the missile negate dexterity considerations).

Magical attacks by spell, device, breath weapon, gaze, etc. (note that Defensive Adjustments do apply to saving throws for these attack forms).

WEAPON TYPES, "TO HIT" ADJUSTMENT NOTE

If you allow weapon type adjustments in your campaign please be certain to remember that these adjustments are for weapons versus specific *types* of armor, not necessarily against actual armor class. In most cases,

monsters not wearing armor will not have any weapon type adjustment allowed, as monster armor class in such cases pertains to the size, shape, agility, speed, and/or magical nature of the creature. Not excluded from this, for example, would be an iron golem. However, monsters with horny or bony armor might be classed as plate mail if you so decide, but do so on a case-by-case basis. Naturally, monsters wearing armor will be subject to weapon type "to hit" adjustment.

HIRELINGS

STANDARD HIRELINGS

Most hirelings are dealt with under the section entitled **EXPERT HIRELINGS** — those which are typically employed at such time as the character in question has an established stronghold. Common, standard hirelings are basically the usual craftsmen or laborers taken on by lower level player characters. Men-at-arms (soldiers of mercenary calling) are dealt with under **EXPERT HIRELINGS** (q.v.). Typical standard hirelings are:

STANDARD HIRELINGS TABLE OF DAILY AND MONTHLY COSTS

Occupation	Daily Cost	Monthly Cost*
bearer/porter	1 s.p.	1 g.p.
carpenter	3 s.p.	2 g.p.**
leather worker	2 s.p.	30 s.p.**
limner	10 s.p.	10 g.p.
linkboy	1 s.p.	1 g.p.
mason	4 s.p.	3 g.p.
pack handler	2 s.p.	30 s.p.
tailor	2 s.p.	30 s.p.**
teamster	5 s.p.	5 g.p.
valet/lackey	3 s.p.	50 s.p.

*Monthly rate assumes that quarters are provided for the hireling, and that these quarters contain a bed and like necessities.

**Additional cost is 10% of the normal price of items fashioned by the hireling.

Bearer/Porter: These individuals are laborers who will carry whatever is directed. Each is able to carry up to 50 pounds individually, or double that with a carrying pole or litter or the like.

Carpenter: This occupation assumes most woodworking jobs. A carpenter might be hired to secure a portal, fashion a chest, etc.

Leather Worker: This occupation is principally concerned with the fabrication of leather goods such as back packs, belts, straps, horse tack, etc.

Limner: These individuals do all sign painting, drawing of heraldic devices, etc.

Linkboy: A linkboy is a torch or lantern bearer. They are often youngsters, but mature men also will so serve.

Mason: Any stonework must be done by a mason, and this occupation subsumes plasterers as well.

Pack Handler: These individuals are trained at loading, handling, and unloading beasts of burden such as donkeys, mules, horses, etc.

Tailor: This occupation makes and repairs clothing, bags, shield covers, etc. It also subsumes hatters.

Teamster: Teamsters are basically drivers of carts and wagons. They will also load and unload their vehicles. They are expert animal handlers with respect to their particular specialty of draft animal only, i.e. horses, mules, oxen, or whatever.

Valet/Lackey: This occupation subsumes the various forms of body servants and messengers.

Location Of Standard Hirelings: In general the various occupations represented here are common to most settlements of village-size and above, although each and every village will not be likely to furnish each and every sort of common hireling. Towns and cities will have many available, and each sort will be found in the appropriate section or quarter of the city (or town).

Employment Of Standard Hirelings: This requires the location of the desired individual and the offer of work. If the employment is for only a few days, there will be no real difficulty in locating individuals to take on the job. If the offer is for long term employment, only 1 in 6 will be willing to accept unless a small bonus is offered — a day's wage is too small, but double or treble that is sufficient to make 3 in 6 willing to take service.

Duties: It is not practical to try to determine the time and expenses necessary to accomplish everything possible for the scores of standard hirelings possible to employ, so each DM will have to decide. For example, assume that a player character hires a tailor to make plain blue cloaks for all of his or her henchmen. This will take only about 1 day per garment and cost the stated amount of money plus 5 c.p. (10% of the cost of a cloak) per cloak for materials. However, if the same cloaks were to be fashioned of a material of unusual color and have some device also sewed upon them, time and materials costs would be at least double standard, and probably more.

EXPERT HIRELINGS

If henchmen are defined as the associates, companions, and loyal (to some degree) *followers* of a player character, hirelings are the servitors, mercenaries, and *employees* of such player characters, and they too can have some degree of loyalty based on their accomodations, rate of remuneration, and treatment. Various hirelings of menial nature are assumed to come with the cost of maintaining a stronghold; thus, cooks, lackeys, stableboys, sweepers, and various servants are no concern of the player character. Guards and special hirelings are, however, and such persons must be located and enlisted by the PC or his or her NPC henchmen.

Location of Expert Hirelings: Most expert hirelings can be found only in towns or cities, although some might be located in smaller communities — providing they are willing to pick up and relocate, of course. Employment is a matter of offer and acceptance, and each player character must do his or her own bargaining. The various types of hirelings (listed below) will generally be found in the appropriate section of the community — the Street of Smiths, Weapon Way, Armorers Alley, etc. — or at cheap inns in the case of mercenary soldiers.

Monthly Costs: The cost of each type of expert hireling is shown on the list. This amount is based on all the associated expenditures which go with the position — salary or wage, uniform or clothing, housing, food, and sundry equipment used routinely by the hireling. *Exception:* The cost does not include arms and armor of soldiers, and these items must be furnished to mercenaries over and above other costs. Certain other hirelings incur costs over and above the normal also, when they engage in their occupations. These are indicated on the table by an asterisk (*).

EXPERT HIRELINGS TABLE OF MONTHLY COSTS IN GOLD PIECES

Occupation or Profession	Cost
alchemist	300
armorer	100*
blacksmith	30
engineer-architect	100*
engineer-artillerist	150
engineer-sapper/miner	150
jeweler-gemcutter	100*
mercenary soldier —	
archer (longbow)	4
archer (shortbow)	2
artillerist	5
captain	special
crossbowman	2
footman, heavy	2
footman, light	1
footman, pikeman	3
hobilar, heavy	3
hobilar, light	2
horseman, archer	6
horseman, crossbowman	4
horseman, heavy	6
horseman, light	3
horseman, medium	4
lieutenant	special
sapper/miner	4

serjeant	special
slinger	3
sage	special
scribe	15
ship crew	special
ship master	special
spy	special
steward/castellan	special
weapon maker	100*

  *Cost does not include all remuneration or special fees. Add 10% of the usual cost of items handled or made by these hirelings on a per job basis, i.e. an *armorer* makes a suit of plate mail which has a normal cost of 400 gold pieces, so 10% of that sum (40 g.p.) is added to the costs of maintaining the blacksmith.

Description Of Occupations and Professions:

Alchemist: This profession handles the compounding of magical substances, and the advantages of employing an alchemist are detailed under the section **FABRICATION OF MAGIC ITEMS, Potions.** Alchemists will only be found in cities unless you specifically locate one elsewhere. It will require an offer of 10 to 100 gold pieces bonus money, plus a well-stocked laboratory, plus the assurance of not less than a full year of employment, to attract one to service.

Armorer: This occupation cares for and manufactures armor and shields. One armorer is always required for every 40 soldiers, or fraction thereof, in the employ of the player character, and only spare time can be spent on the manufacture of items, i.e. that fraction of the normal month not spent caring for equipment of troops can be used to make armor, helmets, and/or shields, prorating time according to the number of men — 0 = 100%, 1-5 = 85%, 6-10 = 70%, etc. This includes the armorer and the apprentices which are assumed to be present and cared for by the cost shown. A workroom and forge costing 310-400 g.p. must be available for an armorer, and the skill of the armorer must be determined if armor is to be fashioned:

    01-50 skill level equal to ring, scale, or studded
    51-75 skill level equal to above plus splint
    76-90 skill level equal to all of the above plus chain
    91-00 skill level equal to any sort of armor

If items are to be made, the following times are suggested for an armorer and apprentices working exclusively, assuming a 1 week period in order to set the operation in motion before actual work begins. Armorers occupied for part of the month with caring for the equipment of troops must increase time proportionately.

banded mail	30 days
chain mail	45 days
helmet, great	10 days
helmet, small	2 days
leather armor*	10 days
padded armor**	—
plate mail	90 days
ring mail***	20 days
scale mail***	30 days
shield, large****	2 days
shield, small****	1 day
splinted mail*****	20 days
studded leather armor***	15 days

  * Requires the services of a leather worker and facilities to boil leather in oil.

  ** Requires only the services of a tailor (who will be occupied 30 days with the task).

  *** As with leather armor, and a tailor must be employed as well.

  **** Requires the services of a woodworker.

  ***** Requires the services of a leather worker and a blacksmith.

N.B. For leatherworker, tailor and woodworker, see **STANDARD HIRELINGS.**

Dwarven armorers are twice as efficient but cost three times as much, and they will not generally labor for anyone beyond 1 year of service. **Gnomish armorers** are one and one-half times more efficient than humans and cost twice as much. Dwarves add 25% to skill level roll, gnomes 10%. **Elvish armorers** cost five times the normal rate, and they will fashion only normal chain mail for sale, but it is of the highest quality, and they make it in half the time a human would.

Blacksmith: There must be a blacksmith in any stronghold, and he and his assistants can care for the needs of up to 40 men or horses. Another smith is required for each additional 160 men or horses or fraction thereof. Besides the usual duties (horseshoes, nails, hinges, and miscellaneous bits and pieces) a hired smith can turn out some weaponry each month (each must have a workroom with bellows and forge):

30 arrow heads or quarrel tips, or
10 spear heads, or
5 morning stars, or
2 flails or pole arm heads

Dwarven smiths are three times more efficient and cost ten times as much.

Gnomish smiths are twice as efficient and cost four times as much.

Engineer-Architect: This profession deals with above-ground construction and fortification. In order to build any structure more complex than a simple hut or barn, it is necessary to hire one. An engineer-architect is paid for whole months of employment, even if the work is completed in less than a whole month. He or she also collects an additional fee equal to 10% of the total expenditure on the construction. The building site must be selected or approved by an architect-engineer, or else there is a 75% chance the structure will collapse in 1 to 100 months.

Engineer-Artillerist: This profession deals with the construction and use of siege artillery — catapults, trebuchets, etc. No such engines can be made or properly used without the services of such an individual. If employment is for short term only, say a few months or less, then rates of pay and costs will be increased from 10% to 60%.

Engineer-Sapper/Miner: All underground construction or tunneling, as well as siege operations which require mining, counter-mining, siege equipment (picks, rams, sows, towers, etc.), or trenches, ditches, parapets, and so forth, require the professional services of an engineer-sapper/miner. Dwarves are useful in the capacity of engineer-miner only. They are twice as costly and add 20% to the efficiency of human miners (and dwarven miners will work only for a dwarven engineer-miner, of course).

Jeweler-Gemcutter: This profession allows the character to have rapid and accurate appraisal of any precious metal, gem material, or piece of jewelry (except those which you, as DM, specifically designate as "heretofore unknown"). In addition, the jeweler-gemcutter can set stones in various things (sword hilts, flagons, or whatever) or fashion jewelry from gem material and precious metals. A simple ring will take a week; a bracelet with sculpting two weeks (with stones set, three); while a crown might require a full year of work. Basically, the work merely adds either splendor to the player character's personage by the display, or the value of the materials can be increased by from 10% to 40%, depending on the skill of the individual doing the work. Likewise, as a gemcutter, the individual might well increase the value of a rough or poorly cut stone (those under 5,000 gold piece base value), or the stone might be ruined in the process. Note that jeweler-gemcutters cannot be held responsible for damage. Both functions are shown below:

Jeweler Skill Level

01-20	fair — 10% increase 90% likely
21-50	good — 20% increase 50% likely, +10% otherwise
51-75	superior — 30% increase 60% likely, +10% otherwise
76-90	excellent — 40% increase 70% likely, +10% otherwise
91-00	masterful — 40% increase 60% likely, +20% otherwise

Gemcutter Skill Level*

01-30	shaky — d12, one roll, 1 improves, 10-12 ruins stone
31-60	fair — d12, one roll, 1-2 improves, 12 ruins
61-90	good — d12, one roll, 1-3 improves, 12 ruins
91-00	superb — d20, 1-5 improves, 20 ruins stone

* Roll for this separately after determination of jeweler skill level.

Important: *Players should never know the skill levels of jeweler-gemcutters!*

Dwarven jeweler-gemcutters add 20% to skill level determination rolls. They cost twice as much to employ as far as gold piece outlay is concerned. **Gnome jeweler-gemcutters** add nothing to jeweler's skill but add 30% to gemcutter skill. They likewise cost double with regard to monthly wage.

Mercenary Soldier: The likelihood of encountering any given type of mercenary is strictly up to you as DM. A table below shows suggested probabilities, as well as typical numbers. Types will seldom be mixed. If more than 5 are encountered, 1 will be a serjeant (a leader-type, or equivalent of a non-commissioned officer). It is urged that 1 serjeant for every 10 troops be used as a minimum figure with regard to regular soldiers and leader types. (Captains will have to be hired for each sort of troop type.) Note that regular soldiers are 0 level men-at-arms with 4-7 hit points each.

Dice Score	Troop Type	Number Encountered (d10)			
		1-4	5-7	8-9*	0**
01-04	archer (longbow)	1-4	2-5	3-12	5-20
05-10	archer (shortbow)	1-6	2-8	4-16	5-30
11-12	artillerist	1	2	3	4
13	captain	1	1	1	1
14-20	crossbowman	1-6	2-8	5-20	8-48
21-30	footman, heavy	1-6	2-12	5-30	10-60
31-37	footman, light	1-4	2-8	3-12	5-20
38-40	footman, pikeman	2-5	3-12	5-20	10-40
41	lieutenant	1	1	1	1
42-44	hobilar, heavy	1-3	2-5	3-12	4-16
45-48	hobilar, light	1-4	2-8	3-12	5-20
49	horseman, archer	1-2	1-6	2-8	3-12
50-53	horseman, crossbowman	1-4	2-8	3-12	5-20
54-58	horseman, heavy	1-3	2-5	3-12	4-16
59-70	horseman, light	1-4	2-8	4-16	5-30
71-78	horseman, medium	1-3	2-5	3-12	4-16
79-80	sapper/miner	1-2	1-4	2-5	2-8
81-85	serjeant	1	1	1-2	1-3
86-88	slinger	1-3	1-6	2-8	3-12
89-90	SELECT ANY TYPE OF MISSILE TROOP				
91-96	SELECT ANY TYPE OF FOOTMAN				
97-99	SELECT ANY TYPE OF HORSEMAN				
00	SELECT ANY TYPE OF SPECIALIST OR LEADER				

* With lieutenant if more than 10 soldiers.

** With lieutenant if more than 10 soldiers, with captain if more than 20 soldiers.

Archer (longbow): These troops will be able to operate as light infantry when not employing bows. They can use any typical weapon, for they must be strong and in good health.

Archer (shortbow): These troops will not fight as infantry when not using their bows, unless it is a desperate situation. *In extremis* they will fight as light infantry using short swords, hand axes, and similar weapons. (You may desire to allow certain types — such as the historical Viking warrior types — to be exceptional. If so, these individuals will certainly demand longbowman's wages.)

Artillerist: These troops are required to operate any missile engines larger than a heavy crossbow. They will fight as light infantry only *in extremis*.

Captain: A captain is nothing more than a capable leader, a fighter of 5th, 6th, 7th, or 8th level (according to the d10 score, 1-4 = 5th, 5-7 = 6th, 8-9 = 7th, 0 = 8th) but NOT capable of working upwards. A captain can command as many scores of troops as he or she has levels, i.e., 4th level enables command of 80 men, 5th level enables command of 100 men, etc. In addition, the level of the captain dictates the number of lieutenants which can be controlled. This is exclusive of serjeants and any auxiliary types such as servants, cooks, etc. The monthly cost of a captain is 100 gold pieces per level.

Crossbowman: These soldiers are able to use any sort of crossbow furnished. Each heavy crossbowman will typically desire a light infantryman to accompany him to act as a shield bearer. Crossbowmen will bear hand-held weapons and fight as light foot if meleed by enemy troops.

Footman, heavy: These troops are trained to fight in close formation. They do so regardless of the type of armor thay are equipped with. Weaponry can be sword and shield, axe and shield, pole arms, etc.

Footman, light: These soldiers do not fight in close formation. They are useful in rough terrain, woods, etc.

Footman, pikeman: These soldiers are heavy foot who are especially trained to fight with pikes and also maneuver with them. Mercenary pikemen will be high quality (not militia or levy quality). Heavy footmen can be placed in the center of a pike formation of 100 or more troops, if these troops have trained for not less than two months with the pikemen.

Hobilar, heavy or light: These troops are simply mounted infantry, able to use horses to move but not capable of mounted combat. Thus, hobilars ride to battle but dismount to fight. Some provision must be made to care for the horses, or the hobilars will leave 25% of their number behind to do so.

Horseman, archer: These light troops are generally nomadic types, undisciplined and prone to looting. They will fight hand-to-hand only if circumstances force this action upon them. They can wear leather, ring, or chain mail, and they can carry small shields for use when not plying their bows.

Horseman, crossbowman: All such troops are armed with light crossbows, as heavy weapons are not usable on horseback. They are light troops, but they can wear any sort of armor. They will wield handheld weapons in combat if necessary.

Horseman, heavy: These soldiers are trained to operate in close formation (stirrup-to-stirrup). They are able to use most weapons common to horsemen.

Horseman, light: These soldiers are not trained to operate in close order or formation. They are useful skirmish-raider types only.

Horseman, medium: Similar to heavy cavalry, medium horsemen are trained to operate in formation, but they are generally smaller individuals on lighter horses and do not ride as close to their fellows.

Lieutenant: A lieutenant is an assistant to a captain, or a leader in his or her own right. Fighter level is 2nd (d10 score 1-7) or 3rd (d10 score 8-0), and the lieutenant can command as many decades of troops as he or she has levels. This is exclusive of serjeants, of course. A lieutenant serving under a captain extends the number of troops the captain can effectively command and control. The level of a lieutenant determines how many serjeants he or she is able to direct, these in addition to those normally serving with the troops, i.e., 2 or 3 additional serjeants who can do special duty. The monthly cost of a lieutenant is 100 gold pieces per level. They cannot progress in level.

Sapper/Miner: These troops are required for any military operations which involve use of siege machinery, towers, trenches, mines, etc. Although they will fight only to preserve their lives, they do fight as heavy footmen. They normally wear only light armor because of their duties — leather or studded leather if they are active.

Serjeant: A serjeant is the leader of a small body of troops, a non-commissioned officer equivalent. All serjeants are 1st level fighters but incapable of progressing further. A serjeant can command up to 10 soldiers as an independent unit or assure orders from lieutenants or a captain are carried out. There must be 1 serjeant minimum for every 10 regular soldiers, and there can be 1 per 5. The monthly cost for a serjeant is 10 times the rate of the troops he or she commands, so a serjeant of heavy horsemen costs 60 gold pieces, one of light footmen only 10.

Slinger: Slingers are trained from youth up (as are longbowmen), and are thus rarely encountered. They can wear leather (including studded leather), padded, or ring mail only, but they are also able to employ small shields at the same time as they ply their slings. They are always light infantry, and they are able to use only lesser handheld weapons such as hand axes, clubs, short swords, and daggers.

Non-Human Soldiers:

There can be various units of non-human troops available for mercenary duty, but this depends upon your milieu. It is suggested that as a general

rule such troops be enlisted only where they actually dwell, and only if the player character champions their cause or is a minion of their alignment, religion, or the like, or is a racial hero. The types of soldiers available depends entirely on the race (see **MONSTER MANUAL** for such information). The less intelligent non-humans will serve for from 10% to 60% less cost, but these evil creatures will certainly expect to loot, pillage, and rape freely at every chance, and kill (and probably eat) captives. Dwarves will serve at double rates, or at normal rates if they are basically aiding a champion of their cause and people. Gnomes and halflings will only serve in the latter case. Elves are a difficult case to handle, for they might serve against hated foes, or for a cause, but in either event probably for greater cost or special considerations only. Half humans such as half-elves and half-orcs might be found amongst either human contingents or with those of their non-human parent race. Possible non-human soldiers are:

bugbears	halflings
dwarves	hobgoblins
elves	kobolds
gnolls	lizard men
gnomes	orcs
goblins	

Sage: Sages are a very special case indeed, for they are the encyclopedias, computers, expert opinions, and sort of demi-oracles of the milieu all rolled into one. Even in a quasi-medieval fantasy world, the sum of human knowledge will be so great and so diverse as to make it totally impossible for any one sage to know more than a smattering about many things, a fair understanding of their overall field, and a thorough knowledge of their particular specialty or specialties. The general fields of study for sages are shown hereafter, with special areas of expertise listed under each general category.

Sage Ability:

While any sage is capable of carrying on a discussion in any field of knowledge, what he or she actually has expertise in is an entirely different matter. Thus, any given sage will know the general field of his or her chosen study well, with expertise in two or more special areas, and in addition he or she will be able to give reasonable advice in one or two other fields, but have absolutely no expertise in any of the special categories of the other fields. Note that expertise in a limited number of special categories does not imply that the sage is limited in talent, only that he or she has devoted major effort into limited areas, and his or her knowledge of these special categories will be exceptionally good. When taking the persona of a sage, it is therefore very important for the DM to assume not only the role but also the overview and personal dedication of the character. The number of fields of study (major and minor) and the specialization categories are determined by use of the two tables given hereafter. Find the number of fields of study first:

Dice Score	Minor Fields	Special Categories In Major Field
01 - 10	1	2
11 - 30	1	3
31 - 50	1	4
51 - 70	2	2
71 - 90	2	3
91 - 00	2	4

To use the above information on the following table, first roll for (or choose) one field of study to be the sage's major field, then choose the proper number of special categories within that field. Finally, roll (or choose) the indicated number of minor fields.

Sage Fields Of Study And Special Knowledge Categories:

Humankind 01-30
Art & Music
Biology
Demography
History
Languages
Legends & Folklore
Law & Customs
Philosophy & Ethics
Politics & Genealogy
Psychology
Sociology
Theology & Myth

Demi-Humankind 31-50
Art & Music
Biology
Demography
History
Languages
Legends & Folklore
Law & Customs
Philosophy & Ethics
Politics & Genealogy
Psychology
Sociology
Theology & Myth

Humanoids & Giantkind 51-60
Biology
Demography
History
Languages
Legends & Folklore
Law & Customs
Sociology
Theology & Myth

Physical Universe(s) 61-70
Architecture & Engineering
Astronomy
Chemistry
Geography
Geology & Mineralogy
Mathematics
Meteorology & Climatology
Oceanography
Physics
Topography & Cartography

Fauna 71-80
Amphibians
Arachnids
Avians
Cephalopods & Echinoderms
Crustaceans & Mollusks
Ichthyoids
Insects
Mammals
Marsupials
Reptiles

Flora 81-90
Bushes & Shrubs
Flowers
Fungi
Grasses & Grains
Herbs
Mosses & Ferns
Trees
Weeds

Supernatural & Unusual 91-00
Astrology & Numerology
Cryptography
Divination
Dweomercraeft
Heraldry, Signs & Sigils
Medicine
Metaphysics
Planes (Astral, Elemental & Ethereal)
Planes (Outer)

Chance Of Knowing Answer To A Question:

Question Is	General	Specific	Exacting
Out Of Fields	31%-50%	11%-20%	
In Minor Field	46%-65%	31%-40%	11%-20%
In Major Field	61%-80%	57%-60%	26%-35%
In Special Category	81%-100%	76%-96%	61%-80%

To use the above table each time a particular question is asked, first roll (d10 or d20, as applicable) to determine the sage's *base percentage chance* (within the range shown) to know the answer. When that is determined, roll to see if the sage *does* know the answer. Rolling the indicated base percentage or below indicates that the sage has the knowledge for that particular question.

You must determine if any given question is of general, specific, or exacting nature according to the subject. For example, ''Do giants live on that island?'' is a general sort of a question; ''Do fire giants inhabit the volcanic region of that island?'' is a specific question; and ''Do the fire giants inhabiting the volcanic region of that island possess the Artifact of Alamanzaliz?'' is exacting. Any question asked must be within the scope of knowledge of the player character, or his or her associates at the time, and such inquiries must always be consistent with the learning of the milieu which you have designed. Thus, if you have no gunpowder in the milieu, *no* questions regarding the substance, no matter how phrased,

would be possible, as none of the inquiring parties could possibly have any inkling that such a thing exists anywhere in the multiverse. Be certain to adhere to this rule strictly!

Knowledge of any sage character is not entirely contained within his or her brain. As with any scholar, sages will tend to collect materials which pertain to the fields of study he or she pursues. Thus, the sage must have both living quarters as well as study and library and workroom — a minimum of four rooms of at least 200 square feet each, and if the sage is kept busy answering many questions, then he or she will need more space for the additional materials (books, equipment, life forms, etc.) needed to fulfill the demands of the position. (As DM, make a point of asking for far more than is actually needed, as any dedicated scholar-scientist will desire acquisition of absolutely everything needed or imagined to possess a virtual university and museum. A sage who specializes in flora, for example, might request a root cellar, greenhouse, fungi beds, several acres for growing various plants — all in addition to a bed chamber, study, library, and workroom.)

Sage Characteristics: As with any hireling of importance, abilities, alignment, and even special skills will have to be determined. STRENGTH: d8 +7; INTELLIGENCE: d4 +14; WISDOM: d6 +12; DEXTERITY: standard 3d6; CONSTITUTION: 2d6 +3; CHARISMA: 2d6 +2; ALIGNMENT: (see below)

01-05	CHAOTIC EVIL	41-60	LAWFUL NEUTRAL
06-10	CHAOTIC GOOD	61-80	NEUTRAL
11-20	CHAOTIC NEUTRAL	81-90	NEUTRAL EVIL
21-30	LAWFUL EVIL	91-00	NEUTRAL GOOD
31-40	LAWFUL GOOD		

HIT POINTS: 8d4 + constitution bonuses as applicable.

SPECIAL SKILLS: All sages will have some abilities with respect to spells, for their studies will have empowered them thus. Determine whether spell abilities will be *magic-user, illusionist, cleric,* or *druid* by studies. *Flora* and *fauna* indicate druidical talents, *supernatural* or *unusual* indicates either magic-user or illusionist ability (if magic-user talent is not obviously indicated, assume illusionist ability), studies of the *physical universe* indicate clerical talents (as do such studies as most categories of human, demi-human, and humanoid nature), and art & music and legends & folklore being either clerical or magic-user. When some natural bent is discovered, find the maximum level of the spells known to the sage by rolling a d4 +2 to find a level between 3 and 6, inclusive. This only indicates the *ability* to use spells of up to the level shown — it does not mean that the sage is able to use any spell in particular. Each sage will *possess* 1-4 spells of each level, but at any given time he or she will have no more than 1 of each level available for actual use, the rest being contained in various source books. Find specific spells by random generation. Spells such as *bless, chant, prayer, commune, raise dead, commune with nature,* and *contact other plane* — or their reverse, if applicable, are not within the capabilities of a sage. Naturally, the sage will tend to keep his or her spell knowledge as highly secret, and he or she will likewise have those spells which seem applicable for activities likely to be pursued during the course of the period the sage envisions.

Abilities will change due to aging or special circumstances only. Sages will not increase in hit points, and their special abilities will not increase, either — although if they aquire magic items which are usable by characters of the same profession as that of their special spell ability, they will likely be able to use such items. Spell use is at a level equal to the minimum level at which such a spell could be employed if the sage were of that class, i.e. a sage with third level spell use in magic casts spells at 5th level of ability (the minimum level for a magic-user to cast a third level spell). All sages are middle-aged to venerable in age.

Hiring A Sage: Only fighters, paladins, rangers, thieves, and assassins are able to hire a sage. (Other classes of characters can consult them, however, as explained hereafter.) Any character hiring a sage on a permanent basis must have a stronghold with ample space for the sage, as noted above. A sage will accept service only on a permanent, lifetime basis.

Location Of A Sage: Sages will be found only in large towns and cities. They are typically in or near colleges, schools, universities, libraries, museums, forums, and public speaking places. Sages belong to a Brotherhood, but as a general rule, this association is informal and not likely to have a headquarters at which a sage could be located. (However, the employment of a sage will become common knowledge to all sages within the area.)

Short-Term Employment Of A Sage: Upon locating a sage, any class of character can ask him or her to answer one or more questions. Such short-term employment cannot last beyond one week's time, and the sage will thereafter not be available for at least one game month — as there are more important and constructive things to be done than answering foolish questions, anyway! Remembering the restriction regarding time, use the information found under the *Information Discovery* section hereafter. Costs for short-term employment are 100 gold pieces per day plus the variable amount shown under *Information Discovery* for question difficulty (reflecting costs of obtaining research materials or the information proper through fees, bribes, donations, etc.).

Long Term Employment Of A Sage: If initial reaction of the sage is favorable to the player character attempting to hire him or her, the sage will then entertain any offers of employment on a permanent basis which the character chooses to proffer. As a sage will bring nothing save thinking ability and knowledge, an offer of employment must consider the following:

SUPPORT & SALARY PER MONTH	200 to 1,200 g.p.
RESEARCH GRANTS PER MONTH	200 to 1,200 g.p.
INITIAL MATERIAL EXPENDITURE	20,000 g.p. minimum

Determine salary and grant expectations by random dice rolling of 2d6 for each. Initial material expenditure is a far more important matter, for even if the sage is otherwise satisfied, if this is not met and exceeded then the ability to answer *specific* and *exacting* questions will be sharply curtailed due to lack of reference works, experimental equipment, and so on. A 20,000 g.p. expenditure will allow the sage to operate at 50% of normal efficiency, and for each additional 1,000 g.p. thereafter, the sage will add 1% to efficiency until 90% is reached (upon expenditure of 60,000 g.p.). After 90%, to achieve 100% efficiency the cost per 1% is 4,000 g.p. (for the obviously erudite and rare tomes, special supplies and equipment, etc. — assuming such are available, of course). All told, expenditures must be 100,000 g.p. for 100% sage efficiency in specific and exacting question areas. *Note:* Additional expenditure on materials will increase sage question answering ability in the *general* and *specific* areas as follows: For each 5,000 g.p. and 1 month of uninterrupted study time, the sage can increase his or her knowledge outside his or her fields of study by 1% to a maximum of 5%. At 10,000 g.p. cost and 1 month's time, sage ability in minor fields of study can be brought up by 1% subject likewise to a 5% maximum gain. Addition of another minor field, three maximum, requires 100,000 g.p. expenditure and two years of time. Addition of a major field of study requires 200,000 g.p. and two years' time. Payment *must* be made in advance. No questions can be asked of the sage during the stated period of time, or all is lost.

Information Discovery: It will take only a relatively short period of time, and no costs to speak of, to discover information of a general nature, but as questions become more difficult, the time and cost to give an answer becomes a factor. This is shown on the following table:

Information Discovery Time And Cost Table:

	Nature Of Question Is			
Question Is	General	Specific	Exacting	G.P. Costs
Out Of Fields	1-6 r.	2-24 d.	—	100/d.
In Minor Field	1-4 r.	2-20 d.	5-40 d.	1,000/d.
In Major Field	1-3 r.	1-12 d.	3-30 d.	500/d.
In Special Category	1-2 r.	1-10 h.	2-12 d.	200/d.

r. = rounds
h. = hours
d. = days

Note: All times assume that the sage will be in a position to conduct research and obtain necessary equipment within a day or two of the discovery of the need, and the costs shown assume these activities. If a town or city is not nearby, double times and costs (or compute the sojourn expenditure necessary to arrive at a ocale where the needed materials are to be had, and determine other expenses also). However, if the percentile dice score rolled for knowing the answer to the question is in the lower 20% of the spread, then there will be no costs incurred, as the material is on hand. Thus, if a sage has a 31% to 40% chance of knowing a question, and the dice indicate a 32% chance of knowing it, a following roll of 32% or less indicates knowledge, but a roll of 06% or less indicates that the sage has the information about the question available, and there will be no additional expense. Furthermore, in the *special category* of study, any spread within the lower 80% has no cost,

as this area is where the sage will have accumulated most of his or her materials. As DM you must also use judgment as to related questions, so that if a closely related query is made following one for which an expenditure was necessary, you must determine whether or not the further question or questions would be answerable from the same materials source which was formerly obtained. Naturally, all costs are NOT for materials, some accruing as payments, fees, and bribes.

You may likewise extend the time necessary to answer specific or exacting questions which you believe that the sage would have great difficulty answering due to lack of information available or the particular nature of the question. For example, a query as to how the henchman of the player character could construct an artifact would never be able to be answered positively, but the sage might feel obligated to continue a fruitless search for the knowledge.

Unknown information will always require from 51% to 100% of the maximum time shown to determine that the knowledge is beyond the ability of the sage. All costs will accrue at only half of the stated amount, however. Thus, suppose a sage is asked a question out of any of his or her fields of knowledge. If the question is of general nature, the sage will hedge and talk around the point, or just possibly sit and look wise for 4-6 rounds before answering that the question is beyond his or her learning, and there is no cost involved, as a day was not spent researching. Were the question specific, he or she would require 13-24 days to discover that it was unanswerable and relate this to his or her employer/master. The cost would be 50 g.p. per day, or from 650 g.p. to 1,200 g.p. (in this case probably paid out to others as fees, stipends, and the like trying to find someone with the answer).

Rest And Recuperation: After spending more than 1 day of time answering a question, a sage will need at least 1 day to rest and relax for every 3 he or she spent in research. During this time, he or she will not be able to answer any further queries of anything other than *general* nature, and if the player-character bothers the sage often during this "time off", the sage will demand from 1-2 additional days of time for "special research", and until such time is granted, the sage will expend the maximum amounts of time and expense in answering questions.

Non-Human Or Part Human Sages: Most sages will be human, but if your campaign milieu seems right for sages of dwarven, elven, or any other such race, feel free to use them. However, old and venerable category non-human sages will not be likely to be interested in employment with humans, just as human sages will tend to favor employment with humans, unless their specialization dictates differently.

Scribe: A scribe is principally a secretary or copyist. He or she will be able to record normal things, but never anything of magical nature. Specialists such as scribes able to make maps (or copy them) — cartographers — will be scarce indeed, and generally they will command ten times the cost of a normal scribe. Other specialists would be those able to use codes or ciphers and those able to read and write a language other than the common tongue. These scribes are likewise rare and ten times as costly as the normal sort.

Ship Crew: As with a captain, crewmen must be of the sort needed for the vessel and the waters it is to sojourn in. That is, the crew must be *sailors*, *oarsmen*, or *mates* of either fresh water vessels or salt water vessels. Furthermore, they must be either galley-trained or sailing-vessel-trained. Sailors cost the same as heavy infantry soldiers (2 g.p. per month) and fight as light infantry. They never wear armor but will use almost any sort of weapon furnished. Oarsmen are considered to be non-slave types and primarily sailor-soldiers; they cost 5 g.p. per month, wear any sort of armor furnished, use shields and all sorts of weapons. *Marines* are simply soldiers aboard ship; they cost 3 g.p. per month and otherwise have armor and weapons of heavy foot as furnished. *Mates* are sailor *serjeants* who have special duties aboard the vessel. They conform to specifications of serjeants and cost 30 g.p. per month.

Ship Master: This profession covers a broad category of individuals able to operate a vessel. The likelihood of encountering any given type depends on the surroundings and must be determined by the referee. Types are:

River Vessel Master
Lake Vessel Master
Sea-Coastal Vessel Captain
Galley Captain
Ocean-going Vessel Captain

The latter sort should be very rare in a medieval-based technology milieu. Note that each master or captain will have at least one lieutenant and several mates. These sailors correspond to mercenary soldier lieutenants and serjeants in all respects. For every 20 crewmen (sailors or oarsmen) there must be 1 lieutenant and 2 mates. Sailing any vessel will be progressively more hazardous without master or captain, lieutenants, and mates. (See **WATERBORNE ADVENTURES**). The proper type of master or captain must be obtained to operate whatever sort of vessel is applicable in the waters indicated. Cost for masters, captains and lieutenants is 100 g.p. per month per level of experience. They also are entitled to a share of any prize or treasure taken at sea or on land in their presence. The master captain gets 25%, each lieutenant gets 5%, each mate 1%, and the crewmen share between them 5%. The remainder goes to the player character, of course.

Spy: Spying is a profession which is typically reserved for assassin characters. Other types of characters can be paid to spy, but such activity must be at the discretion of the Dungeon Master. The player character must locate a likely prospect and then employ him or her in some capacity which is in accord with the prospective spy's station and occupation or profession. Then, by means of discussion and offers of payment, the player character must convince the character that he or she should become a spy. The sums offered can range from as little as 100 g.p. to as great as 10,000 or more depending on the situation and the person being approached. If the area where the spy must go is distant, the person or persons to be spied upon dangerous, or the prospective spy of high station, the likelihood of acceptance is low unless the pay is exceptional — in money and possibly magic or land or position or some other valuable consideration. Payment must always be made by installment, part on taking the assignment, the balance on completion of the assignment. Use the **ASSASSIN SPYING TABLE** to determine the success of any mission, treating the spy as a 1st level assassin on his or her first mission, 2nd on the second, etc. Such spies can never become more proficient at spying than 8th level in any event.

"This had better work!"

Steward/Castellan: This occupation pertains to the overseeing of a castle, particularly if the player character owner of the stronghold is not a fighter or cleric or if he or she intends to be away for a time and desires to make certain that the castle is well-run and safe. A steward/castellan is the same as a mercenary soldier captain with respect to level but cost of employment is double (200 g.p./level). However, as he or she is dealing with troops within a stronghold, command ability is double, i.e. 40 troops per level. Generally, a trusted captain will be appointed castellan or steward. Once so appointed, the character will feel affront if asked to take the field as if he or she were nothing more than a common mercenary captain! A castle with a steward/castellan will always be sufficiently garrisoned, have ample food, water reserves, oil, siege equipment and engines, missiles, etc., and will be kept in good repair. Of course, the player character must initially establish the stronghold and its attendant needs for men and supplies of all sorts. Once this has been accomplished, bought, and stocked, the castellan or steward will see that levels are maintained according to the dictates of his or her master. The costs of such work come from standard support costs of the stronghold, but a steward/castellan will see that such funds are actually spent on what they were meant for. **Note:** Loyalty of such a character must be kept high or else disaster might result the first time an enemy approaches the place when the player character is away.

Weapon Maker: A weapon maker is a sort of smith-armorer specializing in the manufacture of high-quality arms. As DM you might desire to divide weapon makers into the three following classes:

BOWYER-ARROWSMITH-FLETCHER
SWORDSMITH-DAGGERSMITH
WEAPONER GENERAL

The bowyer would fashion any sort of bow, including crossbows, and missiles for same. Swordsmith work would be strictly with all forms of swords and daggers. The weaponer would fashion all weapons not made by the other two classes of weapon makers. As with other hirelings of this sort, the weapon maker must have a forge and a workroom. He or she will have various apprentices which are subsumed in the monthly cost. A weapon maker is necessary to support troops, 1 being required to support each 80 men or fraction thereof. If the weapon maker has free time, he or she can turn out weapons at the rate of 1 weapon per day after an initial start-up period of 1 month. Exceptions to this rate are composite and long bows which require a start-up time of 1 year and are turned out at the rate of 2-5 per month thereafter, heavy crossbows which are turned out at a rate of 15 per month, and swords which are made as follows:

scimitar	10/month
sword, bastard	8/month
sword, broad	15/month
sword, long	12/month
sword, short	20/month
sword, two-handed	5/month

Scabbards for all swords will have to be manufactured by a leather worker of some sort. Location of a weapon maker willing to take service with any player character should be difficult.

Daily Employment: Expert hirelings are generally not available for periods of less than one or more months. Soldiers can be hired, but not captains, lieutenants, or serjeants. They recognize hazardous duty, and the cost per day is the same as per month. The supply of such men-at-arms willing to work day-to-day is strictly limited, so if the PCs lose them adventuring, more will not be likely to be found.

HENCHMEN

Henchmen, whether male or female, are greatly desired by the discerning players, for they usually spell the difference between failure and success in the long term view. They are useful in individual adventures as a safety measure against the machinations of rival player characters, provide strength to the character and his or her stronghold, and lastly serve as a means of adventuring when the player character is unable to. Because they are so useful, and because they are typically so devoted, there are charisma limitations as to how many henchmen a PC is able to attract. Knowing this, the real question for the Dungeon Master is who will be attracted? where will they be found? when will they come? and what will the cost be? These questions are answered in detail hereafter.

Level Of Prospective New Henchmen:

As a general rule, only characters of 1st level of experience will be attracted to service with a player character. (If the NPC has already gained a level or more of experience on his or her own, why would the aegis of a PC be sought?!) If the player character attempting to find an NPC henchman is over 6th level, there is a 10% chance that the character found will be 2nd level, and seeking service because of the renown of the PC; if the player character is over 11th level, there is a 25% chance that NPC will be 3rd level, 25% chance for 2nd level, and 50% for 1st level.

Race Of Prospective Henchmen:

The locale in which the non-player character henchman is being sought, the racial distribution in that locale, the race of the prospective liege, and the manner of seeking henchmen, will all bear upon the race of any possible henchmen.

Locale and Racial Distribution: The amount of territory within which the henchman is being sought is of importance, for it determines what character races are available for acquisition. Determine racial percentages that exist within the area, and group them into increments of 5%. For example, a large city of 25,000 might be 80% human, 10% half-orc, and 10% "all others" (dwarf, elf, gnome, half-elf, and halfling).

Racial Specifications: Unless special note is made that only certain races of adventurers are desired, or the notices and broadsides specifically exclude races, the whole of the population base will be eligible, so random samplings will be attracted.

Number of Prospective Henchmen: Human and half-orc characters suitable for level advancement are found at a ratio of 1 in 100. Other races have an incidence of 1 in 50. However, as most of these characters will be other than low level adventurers and already in a situation they are satisfied with — and humans more so than other races, unless the development of the area is primarily other than human — about 1 in 1,000 population will be interested in offers of employment as a henchman. NOTE: This figure must be adjusted by the DM according to the locale, for if it is an active adventuring area, the incidence of prospective henchmen might be as great as 1 in 200, while if it is a settled and staid area, incidence might be as low as 1 in 5,000.

Effective Location of Henchmen: While there might be as many as 25 or more prospective henchmen in the city of 25,000 cited above, the player character desirous of locating one or more for service must be able to reach the NPCs in order to let them know there is a henchman position available. In order to get this sort of information around, there are several methods which can be used singularly or in combination:

Method	Cost	Effectiveness
POSTING NOTICES IN PUBLIC	50 g.p.	10% - 40%
HIRING A CRIER	10 g.p.	1% - 10%
HIRING AGENTS TO SEEK PROSPECTS	300 g.p.	20% - 50%
FREQUENTING INNS AND TAVERNS	special	special

Each method can be tried but once a month with any hope of success. Reduce the percentage chance of effectiveness of each method by 5% when used in combination; this reflects the duplication of effort. The special costs for frequenting inns and taverns is a combination of the price of a round of drinks for the house and a fee to the barkeep to mention the prospective employer to adventurers. For each 10 g.p. (50 g.p. maximum) of fee, there is a 1% - 4% chance of reaching a henchman.

"Dave, get the barbarian in the corner another drink, quick!"

Up to ten establishments can be so worked, but for each visited, the effectiveness of the others is reduced by 1%. Therefore, the PC had better spend in excess of 20 gold pieces in payments to innkeepers and barkeeps if he or she is planning to try this method in more than a few establishments. **Example:** The PC decides to try a media blitz to find a henchman. He posts notices and gets a 30% effectiveness, hires a crier who is 3% effective, hires agents who are 30% effective, and spends 500 g.p. in fees in inns and taverns to get an average 15% effectiveness after overlap. The total coverage is 30% + 3% + 30% + 15% = 78% –15% (use of 3 methods beyond the first at –5% per method) = 63% final total effectiveness. Assume 65% of the total eligible NPC henchmen characters will seek service. Whatever final percentage figure is arrived at, this is multiplied by the total available non-player characters available as henchmen. Use proportions for racial types, unless the methods of informing prospective NPCs neglected some area where a specific race is concentrated.

Length Of Time Required For Responses:

It will take from 2 to 8 days for all prospective henchmen who are going to apply to locate the player character and seek him or her out to apply for the job. During this period of time, the PC must remain in the place he

or she made known as the spot to go for employment. Failure to do so will result in a loss of any applicants coming that day and each day thereafter he or she is not available. When the total number of applicants coming are known by you, divide this number by the number of days during which notice is getting around (2-8), and this will give the number of applicants per day. Always have any odd numbers remaining come during the first or second day.

Treatment Of Prospective Henchmen:

When a character arrives for employment, it is considered poor manners to enspell him or her in any way (except possibly in the case of *know alignment* or *detect good/evil*), to say nothing of physically searching him or her. Direct questions about alignment and religion are usually taken poorly.

Classes Of Prospective Henchmen:

Of the total number of prospective characters who are capable of working upwards in level, the distribution of class will be as follows:

CLERICS	20% (d6, 1 = druid)
FIGHTERS	44% (d10, 1 = ranger, 2 = paladin)
MAGIC-USERS	20% (d6, 1 = illusionist)
THIEVES	15% (d6, 1 = assassin)
MONKS	1%

Non-human characters located will have two classes if they have scores of 14 or greater in two major ability areas, three classes if they have ability scores of 14 or greater in three major areas which match up with those of classes which they are able to work in simultaneously. **Exception:** Those races which can work only in two professions at once will not be exceptional, and regardless of their ability scores they can work in only as many classes as stated in the **PLAYERS HANDBOOK.**

Cost Of Successful Employment:

In addition to the costs of getting prospective henchmen to seek employment, the player character desiring to hire one or more of them must be prepared to make a substantial offer which is comprised of the following considerations:

Initial Payment: Not less than 100 gold pieces per level of the applicant must be offered. This will give a base 25% interest in accepting the position. For each additional 100 gold pieces, interest increases 10% to a maximum of 55%.

Equipment: The prospective henchman must be provided with complete equipment according to his or her class or classes. Any magic items included will make the character more interested in accepting the position, assuming he or she can use such items, of course. For each magic item (exclude arrows except in groups of 5), increase interest by 15%.

Quarters and Support: The PC must offer reasonable housing and promise free food and clothing as needed to the prospective henchman. This simply adds 5% to interest level when offered, but failure to promise such quarters and support will lower interest by 25%.

Activity and Shares: The player character must state what amount of activity the prospective henchman will be given, and what duties and position is envisioned for him or her. Furthermore, the prospective henchman must be told what share of treasure he or she can expect from adventuring, and what division of magic items can be expected.

Characteristics of Henchmen: The characteristics, including alignment, of NPC applicants are discussed under the section, **PERSONAE OF NON-PLAYER CHARACTERS.** You, as DM, can decide how best to reveal all of this information to the PC, some by relating what is "seen", some by actually playing the role of the applicant. If the character asks specific questions, remember that the applicant might take this amiss.

Acceptance Of Employment:

When the basic level of interest is found, and characteristics discovered, roll percentile dice if the PC states a desire to accept the applicant as a henchman. Adding the player character's charisma reaction adjustment to the interest level, and if the dice score does not exceed interest and charisma reaction adjustment, the NPC accepts employment.

Equipment Of Henchmen:

All henchmen will come with nothing except the (normal) clothes they wear. Although they will have a few copper and silver coins, they will have nothing of value — no armor or weapons, nothing! Their wretched state is, in fact, one of the prime motivations for their seeking employment with a successful adventurer.

Exceptional Henchmen:

From time to time player characters will manage to capture or otherwise have in their power characters of higher than 2nd level. This in itself is of no consequence, but what if the player character then makes an offer of henchman status to the other character!

1. If the non-player character is more than two levels greater than the player character, only associate status, possibly for but 1 adventure or undertaking, perhaps for two, will be accepted, regardless of the amount of inducement offered.

2. If the non-player character is from two levels lower to two levels greater than the player character, the NPC will consider only offers of becoming a temporary hireling or an associate for 1-4 weeks or adventures/undertakings.

3. If the non-player character is three or more levels under the level of the player character, he or she will consider the offer, but all of the normal requirements of offer and acceptance must be handled as usual. If the offer is forced (do it or else you die, etc.), the loyalty of the henchman will be that of a *slave*. It will be that of *captured and enlisted* unless a considerable sum of additional money or considerations of magic are given.

Such exceptional henchmen are the sole exception to the rule that henchmen come unequipped, as they might well have considerable goods.

LOYALTY OF HENCHMEN & HIRELINGS, OBEDIENCE AND MORALE

The loyalty of all non-player characters associated with a given player character depends upon many factors. First and foremost is the charisma of the PC, of course. This initial loyalty is modified by subsequent factors and the continuing relations between liege and his or her henchmen and hirelings. Loyalty is important when trouble arises — whether it is some insidious plot from within, a challenge from a rival, or in adventures or warfare. Typical situations which require a check for loyalty, obedience or morale are shown hereafter. Checks are made by adjustment of the base loyalty score (due to the PC's charisma rating). The final total is compared to the result of the percentile dice roll, and if the total is less than the number shown on the dice, the figure or figures in question are disloyal, disobedient, or have poor morale.

TYPICAL LOYALTY, OBEDIENCE, AND MORALE CHECK SITUATIONS

Situation	Failure Result
offered bribe	co-operates
ordered to testify against liege	agrees
has a chance to steal goods	steals
left alone in possible danger	deserts
abandoned	deserts
ordered into possible danger	refuses
ordered to perform heroic act	refuses
ordered to perform heroic and dangerous act	refuses
ordered to rescue party member(s)	refuses
ordered to rescue liege	refuses
in combat with possibly dangerous foe	runs away
liege incapacitated or slain	runs away
offered surrender terms	surrenders
surrounded by superior foe	surrenders
ordered to use up or diminish own magic item	refuses

NORMAL LOYALTY BASE: 50%, +/− charisma adjustment

LOYALTY OF HENCHMEN AND ALLIED CREATURES

Adjusted Loyalty Score	Loyalty
Less than 01	None — will attempt to kill, capture, harm, or desert at first possible opportunity
01-25	Disloyal — will always seek own advantage regardless of circumstances
26-50	Little — will seek own advantage at first sign of weakness
51-75	Fair — will support cause if no great risk is involved
76-00	Loyal — will always attempt to further the ends of the liege, even at great risk
Greater than 00	Fanatical — will serve unquestioningly and lay down own life if necessary without hesitation

LOYALTY BASE MODIFIERS:

Enlistment Or Association	Modifier
associated non-player character	−10%
captured and enlisted	−15%
henchman	+5%
hired mercenary	0%
hired mercenary, short term	− 5%
slave	−30%

Length Of Enlistment or Association*	Modifer
less than 1 month	− 5%
less than 1 year	0%
1 to 5 years	+10%
more than 5 years	+25%

*This includes time between service or length of time that the player character has been generally known and familiar to the figure(s) in question.

Training Or Status Level	Modifier
untrained or peasant	−25%
little training, levied troops	−15%
newly recruited regulars	− 5%
trained regulars	+10%
elite, sub-officers, minor officials/expert hireling	+20%
guards, officers, or major officials/henchmen	+30%

Pay Or Treasure Shared	Modifier
none	−20%
partial, late, or unfair	−10%
average	0%
above average, choice shares	+5%
exceptional, bonuses, gift items*	+10%

*Typically magic items if a henchman is concerned

Discipline/Activity	Modifier
none/one	−10%
lax/little	− 5%
firm and harsh/occasional	0%
firm and fair/often	+10%

General Treatment By Liege	Modifier
inhuman and heartless	−25%
cruel and domineering	−10%*
indifferent and uncaring or variable	− 5%
just and invariable	+10%
just, kind, and invariable	+15%

*Applies only when the liege is not present, is incapacitated or dead; if the liege is near and in power, minuses are treated as pluses — otherwise treat as 0% adjustment (fear).

Racial Preference For -	Liege	Associated Group
antipathy	−5%	−10%
good will	+10%	+5%
hatred	−20%	−15%
neutral	0%	0%
preferred	+20%	+15%
tolerance	0%	− 5%

NOTE: Preference adjustments are cumulative, but only with regard to liege and associates, and with respect to the latter group only the most disliked or most liked are counted.

Alignment Factors

Alignment Is	Liege	Associated Group
1 place removed	0%	0%
2 places removed	−15%	− 5%
3 places removed	−35%	−20%

Examples: lawful evil - lawful neutral = 1 place removed
lawful evil - lawful good = 2 places removed
lawful evil - chaotic good = 3 places removed

Alignment of Liege	Modifier
lawful good	+15%
lawful neutral	+10%
lawful evil	+5%
neutral good	0%
neutral	0%
chaotic good	− 5%
chaotic neutral	−10%
neutral evil	−15%
chaotic evil	−20%

Special Considerations	Modifier
killed faithful henchman or hireling in front of a witness(es)	−40%
tortured faithful henchman or hireling in front of a witness(es)	−30%
reputed to have slain faithful henchmen or hirelings or actually left them to die	−20%
foresworn or oath breaker or deserter	−15%
rumored to have tortured faithful henchmen or hirelings	−10%
discharged faithful henchmen or hirelings without cause	− 5%
given a choice gift or bonus within last two months (hireling) or three months (henchman)	+5%
risked life for within last six months (hireling) or one year (henchman)	+10%
ransomed or rescued within one year	+15%
saved life directly or personally	+25%
uses and diminishes his or her own magic to benefit the NPC (including use of spells, especially cures).	+25%
returned henchman or hireling to normal state from death-like state, had *raised* or *resurrected*	+50%

NOTE: Apply only one penalty and one bonus maximum, whichever of either category is the higher.

Situation Modifiers	Modifier
liege dead or surrounded and outnumbered	−25%
liege hors de combat	−15%
each henchman dead or hors de combat	− 5%
each hit die or level dead, friendly	− 3%
each hit die or level alive, enemy	− 1%
each hit die or level dead, enemy	+1%
each hit die or level alive, friendly	+2%
each henchman present, in sight, alive	+5%
liege present, in sight, alive	+15%

When all modifying factors have been checked, adjust the base loyalty and roll percentile dice as noted above. (If you are certain of your DM ability, most of these factors should be apparent without actually checking them out, simply by empathizing with the character or group in question, and having them act accordingly. Until you are absolutely certain, however, it is urged that you use these tables.)

These rules should be used in conjunction with those given under **Morale** in **COMBAT**.

TIME

TIME IN THE CAMPAIGN

Game time is of utmost importance. Failure to keep careful track of time expenditure by player characters will result in many anomalies in the game. The stricture of time is what makes recovery of hit points meaningful. Likewise, the time spent adventuring in wilderness areas removes concerned characters from their bases of operation — be they rented chambers or battlemented strongholds. Certainly the most important time stricture pertains to the manufacture of magic items, for during the period of such activity no adventuring can be done. Time is also considered in gaining levels and learning new languages and more. All of these demands upon game time force choices upon player characters, and likewise number their days of game life.

One of the things stressed in the original game of **D&D** was the importance of recording game time with respect to each and every player character in a campaign. In **AD&D** it is emphasized even more: YOU CAN NOT HAVE A MEANINGFUL CAMPAIGN IF STRICT TIME RECORDS ARE NOT KEPT.

Use whatever grouping of days you find desirable for your milieu. There is nothing wrong with 7 day weeks and 31, 30 and 28/29 day months which exactly correspond to our real system. On the other hand, there is nothing to prevent you from using some other system if it pleases you and you can keep it straight. What is important to the campaign is that you do, in fact, maintain a time record which logs the activities and whereabouts of player characters and their henchmen.

For the sake of example, let us assume that you begin your campaign on Day 1 of the Year 1000. There are four player characters who begin initially, and they have adventures which last a total of 50 days — 6 days of actual adventuring and 44 days of resting and other activity. At this point in time two new players join the game, one of the original group decides to go to seek the advice of an oracle after hiring an elven henchman, and the remaining three "old boys" decide they will not go with the newcomers. So on Day 51 player A's character is off on a journey, those of B, C, and D are resting on their laurels, and E and F enter the dungeon. The latter pair spend the better part of the day surviving, but do well enough to rest a couple of game days and return for another try on Day 54 — where they stumble upon the worst monster on the first level, surprise it, and manage to slay it and come out with a handsome treasure. You pack it in for the night. Four actual days later (and it is best to use 1 actual day = 1 game day when no play is happening), on Day 55, player characters B, C, and D enter the dungeon and find that the area they selected has already been cleaned out by player characters E and F. Had they come the day after the previous game session, game Day 52, and done the same thing, they would have found the monster and possibly gotten the goodies! What to do about that? and what about old A and his pointy-eared chum off to see the oracle?

Some penalty must accrue to the non-active, but on the other hand, the over-active can not be given the world on a silver platter. Despite time differences, the activities of the newcomers to the campaign should be allowed to stand, as Destiny has decreed that the monster in question could not fall to the characters B, C, and D. Therefore, the creature was obviously elsewhere (not dead) when they visited its lair on Day 52, but it had returned on Day 56. Being aware of time differences between groups of player characters will enable you to prevent the BIG problems. You will know when the adventuring of one such group has gone far enough ahead in game time to call a halt. This is particularly true with regard to town/dungeon adventures.

Returning to player character A and his trek to visit a far-off source of supernatural lore, he and his elven companion set off on Day 51, journey across the land for 11 days, visit the oracle and remain 3 days, then come back in another 11 days (wonder of wonders!). This comes to a total of 25 days all told, counting Day 51, so they come "home" on Day 75 and are set to adventure on Day 77, let us suppose, as a brief rest is in order. Allowing that activity to be not unusual for a single session of play, then player character A and his henchman are ready to play about the same actual time as the other players — only A is at Day 77, B, C, and D are at Day 54, and E and F are at Day 58. The middle group must go first, and alone, or it can opt to "sit around" waiting for A or for E and F or for both parties, or they can operate alone for another short adventure in terms of game time, thus taking advantage of their temporal position. Other options include any of the players singly or in time-related groups going off on outdoor adventures. In the case of players so segregating their characters, it then becomes necessary for you, as DM, to inform prospective participants in a game session that there is a hiatus which will necessitate only certain members of their number playing together, as their respective characters cannot locate the others of the separated groups. At this juncture they should be informed of their options, and if players B, C, and D do not choose to take advantage of their favored position, then game time will pass more swiftly for them, as the other participants must be allowed to adventure — in the dungeon if they so desire. Thus, players E and F would have the choice of awaiting the return of A or of going on adventures which involved only the two characters. In effect, player character A is out of it until game time in the central playing area reaches Day 75, when communications can be made — or until other player characters contact him on his return from the oracle, let us say, assuming nothing important transpired during the return trip.

In effect, the key is the relative import of the player characters' actions in the time frame. Generally, time passes day-for-day, or turn for X number of real minutes during active play. Players who choose to remove their characters from the center of dungeon activity will find that "a lot has happened while they were away", as adventures in the wilderness certainly use up game days with rapidity, while the shorter time scale of dungeon adventuring allows many game sessions during a month or two of game time. Of course, this might mean that the players involved in the outdoors someplace will either have to come home to "sit around" or continue adventuring in wildernesses and perhaps in some distant dungeon as well (if you are kind); otherwise, they will perforce be excluded from game sessions which are taking place during a period of game time in which they were wandering about in the countryside doing other things. This latter sanction most certainly applies to characters learning a new language, studying and training for promotion in level, or off someplace manufacturing magic items.

At some point, even the stay-at-homes will be forced to venture forth into the wilderness due to need, geas, quest, or possibly to escape the wrath of something better avoided. The time lines of various player characters will diverge, meet, and diverge again over the course of game years. This makes for interesting campaigns and helps form the history of the milieu. Groups of players tend to segregate themselves for a time, some never returning to the ken of the rest, most eventually coming back to reform into different bands. As characters acquire henchmen, the better players will express a desire to operate some of theirs independently while they, or their liege lord, are away. This is a perfectly acceptable device, for it tends to even out characters and the game. Henchmen tend to become associates — or rivals — this way, although a few will remain as colorless servitors.

You may ask why time is so important if it causes such difficulties with record-keeping, dictates who can or can not go adventuring during a game session, and disperses player characters to the four winds by its strictures. Well, as initially pointed out, it is a necessary penalty imposed upon characters for certain activities. Beyond that, it also gives players yet another interesting set of choices and consequences. The latter tends to bring more true-to-life quality to the game, as some characters will use precious time to the utmost advantage, some will treat it lightly, and some will be constantly wasting it to their complete detriment. Time is yet another facet which helps to separate the superior players from the lesser ones. If time-keeping is a must from a penalty standpoint, it is also an interesting addition from the standpoint of running a campaign.

TIME IN THE DUNGEON

Keeping track of time in the dungeon (or on any other type of adventure) is sometimes difficult, but it is at least as important as the accurate recording of time in the campaign. As has been mentioned elsewhere, the standard time breakdown is ten one-minute rounds to the turn, and six turns to the hour. All referees should keep a side record of time on a separate sheet of paper, marking off the turns as they pass (melees or other actions which result in fractional turns should be rounded up to make complete turns). It is essential that an accurate time record be kept so that the DM can determine when to check for wandering monsters, and in order to keep a strict check on the duration of some spells (such as *bless, haste, strength,* etc.). The DM must also know how long it has been since the last time the party took a rest. A party should be required to rest at least one turn in six (remember, the average party packs a lot of equipment), and in addition, they should rest a turn after every time they engage in combat or any other strenuous activities.

On occasion, a party may wish to cease movement and "hole up" for a long period, perhaps overnight, resting and recuperating or recovering spells. This does not exempt them from occasional checks for wandering monsters, though the frequency may be moderated somewhat, depending on conditions. Too-frequent interruptions may make spell recovery impossible. Keeping correct records of duration of these periods is absolutely essential.

CHARACTER SPELLS

DAY-TO-DAY ACQUISITION OF CLERIC SPELLS

It is well known to all experienced players that clerics, unlike magic-users, have their spells bestowed upon them by their respective deities. By meditation and prayer the clerics receive the specially empowered words which form the various spells possible for them — although as with the spells of magic-users, the utterance of any given set of key sounds not only causes the desired spell to take effect, but it likewise wipes the memory of the sounds from the mind of the utterer, as each set of sounds is an energy trigger (see **SPELL CASTING**). Of utmost importance, then, is the relationship between cleric and deity.

Each cleric must have his or her own deity, so when a new player opts to become a cleric (including a druid), you must inform them as to which deities exist in your campaign milieu and allow the individual to select which one of them he or she will serve. This will not necessarily establish the alignment of the cleric, so at the same time the cleric player character should also state his or her ethos (not necessarily to the other players). It is then assumed that prior to becoming a first level cleric, the player character received a course of instruction, served a novitiate, and has thoroughly read and committed to memory the teachings of and prayers to his or her chosen deity, so that the character is dedicated to this deity and is able to perform as a cleric thereof. *It is this background which enables the cleric character to use first level spells.*

Furthermore, continued service and activity on behalf of the player character's deity empower him or her to use second level spells as well, but thereafter another agency must be called upon.

Cleric spells of third, fourth, and fifth level are obtained through the aid of supernatural servants of the cleric's deity. That is, through meditation and prayer, the cleric's needs are understood and the proper spells are given to him or her by the minions of the deity.

Cleric spells of sixth and seventh level are granted by direct communication from the deity itself. There is no intermediary in this case, and the cleric has a direct channel to the deity, from whom he or she receives the special power to cast the given spells of these levels.

Lesser clerics, then, draw only upon their education, training, and experience to gain spells, just as higher clerics do when they renew their first and second level spells. In order to gain third, fourth, and fifth level spells, however, higher clerics must reach intermediaries of their respective deities in order to have these powers bestowed upon them from the plane of their deity. When clerics become very great, they must petition their deity personally in order to receive the powerful words which enable the casting of sixth and seventh level cleric spells. It is obvious, therefore, that clerics wishing to use third or higher level spells must be in good standing.

If they have not been faithful to their teachings, followed the aims of their deity, contributed freely to the cause, and otherwise acted according to the tenets of their faith, it becomes unlikely that they will receive intermediary aid unless they make proper atonement and sacrifice. There can be no question that such clerics must be absolutely exemplary in their activities, expressions, and attitudes if they dare to contact their deity directly!

In the former case, where the unfaithful cleric desires third through fifth level spells, the minions (angels, demi-gods, or whatever) will be likely to require the cleric to spend 2-8 days in prayer, fasting, and contemplation of his or her transgressions, making whatever sacrifices and atonement are necessary thereafter, before freely granting those powers once again. Sacrifice and atonement will probably be left to the discretion of the cleric, and it is possible that the minions of the deity will empower him or her with spells to complete these steps, but the cleric had better do the correct thing, or face the consequences.

In the latter case, where the unfaithful cleric desires spells above the fifth level, the deity is certainly going to be highly displeased and absolute. The deity (you, the DM) will point out all of the transgressions, state a course of action which must be followed to regain good graces, grant the spells which the deity deems are necessary to complete the course (but never in excess of those which the cleric could normally use!), and pronounce anathema upon the cleric until satisfactory redemption has been made — i.e., the cleric can not again call upon any help from his or her deity, or its minions, until he or she has regained favor through a course prescribed by the deity.

A cleric who, at this or any juncture, changes deities is going to have a difficult time. His or her former deity will mark the cleric. The new deity (and associated minions) will be suspicious. Once a cleric changes deities, he or she must thereafter be absolutely true to the new calling, or he or she will be snuffed out by some godlike means. It is 90% unlikely that the cleric's first deity will accept him or her back into the fold after falling away, unless some special redemptive agency is involved. There is no salvation for a thrice-changed cleric; he or she is instantly killed. Any change of alignment which causes such a deity change is applicable, unless the change is involuntary. (See **CHANGING ALIGNMENT.**)

Note that the above applies to paladins with respect to their clerical spell powers and to rangers with respect to their druidic clerical spell powers.

ACQUISITION OF MAGIC-USER SPELLS

Inform those players who have opted for the magic-user profession that they have just completed a course of apprenticeship with a master who was of unthinkably high level (at least 6th!). Having been a relatively apt pupil, worked diligently, and made every effort to please, master (or mistress, as the case may be) was kind enough to prepare a special present for the character before he or she goes out into the world to seek his or her fortune. At this juncture request the player to ready a piece of paper which will go into his or her records as a permanent fixture. Instruct the player to entitle the page "FIRST LEVEL SPELLS KNOWN".

While the intelligence of the player character will dictate how many and which spells can be and are known, this knowledge is not automatic. Each and every spell, except those which "master" was generous enough to bestow upon the character, must be found somewhere and recorded in the character's spell books. Thus, if Redouleent the Prestidigitator, intelligence 15, has a repertoire of 7 spells and finds a scroll with yet another, there is a 65% chance that the spell can be understood by that worthy. If, in fact, it can be comprehended, Redouleent must then record the spell in his book (thus destroying that portion of the scroll, of course), and he is now the proud possessor of 8 first level spells — just 3 short of the maximum he'll be able to know.

Returning to the recently-completed apprenticeship, let us now consider the spells given to Redouleent by his wise old master. Obviously, an apprentice must know how to *read magic* to be of use to his master. It is also an absolute must to anyone following the profession of magic-user, so that spell is AUTOMATICALLY on each magic-user character's list of known spells. Then select by random means one spell each from the *offensive, defensive,* and *miscellaneous* categories listed below. Redouleent, or any other player character magic-user will then have a total of 4 — count them — 4 spells with which to seek his (or her) fortune!

Offensive Spells	Defensive Spells	Misc. Spells
1. Burning Hands	Affect Normal Fires	Comprehend Languages
2. Charm Person	Dancing lights	Detect Magic
3. Enlarge	Feather Fall	Erase
4. Friends	Hold Portal	Find Familiar
5. Light	Jump	Identify
6. Magic Missile	Protection From Evil	Mending
7. Push	Shield	Message
8. Shocking Grasp	Spider Climb	Unseen Servant
9. Sleep	Ventriloquism	Write
0. (choose)	(choose)	(choose)

Choice should be left to the player. Note that both *Nystul's Magic Aura* and *Tenser's Floating Disc* must be located by the character; they can never be known at the start. If your campaign is particularly difficult, you may wish to allow choice automatically. You can furthermore allow an extra *defensive* or *miscellaneous* spell, so that the character begins with 5 spells.

Acquisition of Illusionists' Spells

Illusionists do not need the spell *read magic* or anything like it in pursuit of their profession. All illusionist spell books and scrolls are written in a secret tongue which every apprentice learns from his or her mentor. This arcane and difficult language is common to all phantasmal magics, and is necessary for illusionistic conjuring. When an illusionist gains *read magic* at the 14th level (along with several other 1st level magic-user spells), this merely allows him or her to utilize magic-user scrolls that contain spells different from those on the illusionists' list.

When a 1st level illusionist receives his first level spell book from his master, it contains only three spells (*read magic* being unnecessary). The DM should require the player's character to roll a d12 on the table of 1st level illusionist spells, rolling three times and ignoring any rolls that result in duplication. If a DM feels his or her campaign is unusually difficult, he or she may allow the player to choose one or even two of these initial spells.

Spells Beyond Those At Start:

Naturally, magic-user player characters will do their utmost to acquire books of spells and scrolls in order to complete their own spell books. To those acquired, the magic-user will add 1 (and ONLY 1) spell when he or she actually gains an experience level (q.v.). Therefore, most will be frantically attempting to purchase or cozen spells from non-player character magic-users, or even from other player character magic-users.

How you handle NPC magic-users is of utmost importance. There is a special section of the rules regarding non-player characters, and you should follow the suggestions therein carefully. By doing so, players will find that their magic-user characters are unable to acquire new spells — at worst — or must pay so dearly for them in money, magic items, and quests that the game is hardly worth the candle. Of course they will pay the price nonetheless, and that will help you to maintain the campaign as fresh and challenging, as it will rid it of excess treasure and give player characters reason to adventure at the same time.

Superior players will certainly co-operate; thus, spells will in all probability be exchanged between PC magic-users to some extent. No special sanctions need be taken to prevent such exchange — although this co-operation should never be suggested or otherwise encouraged, either. The DM should leave this interaction strictly alone. This is NOT the case when PCs deal with NPC henchmen or hirelings. Non-player character hirelings or henchmen will ABSOLUTELY REFUSE to co-operate freely with player characters, even their own masters or mistresses. Again, this matter is dealt with separately under the section pertaining to the DM's role in operating henchmen and hirelings. As a general rule, they will require value plus a bonus when dealing with their liege. If they will deal with other PCs (or NPCs) at all, they will require double value plus a considerable bonus. For example, Thigru Thorkisen, Magician in the hire of Olaf Blue Cheeks, a 10th level Lord, knows the spell, *suggestion*; and Olaf's associate, Halfdan the Necromancer, requests that he be allowed to copy this spell into his book of third level spells. If Olaf is willing, Halfdan can approach Thigru. If Halfdan has been at least civil to the magician, Thigru will ask nothing more than a third level spell in return, plus another spell, plus some minor magic item such as a set of three potions, a scroll of 3 spells, or perhaps a *ring of invisibility*. If Halfdan had formerly insulted the magician, then the price would be more dear; but supposing the necromancer had actually saved Thigru's life at one time, the cost would be reduced to but a spell exchange and a single potion or scroll of 1 spell.

Naturally, the personality of the henchman or hireling would modify the bargain to some extent. A very avaricious or greedy NPC would ask for more magic items and/or gold too! As a good DM you will have developed the character of each henchman and hireling to the extent that such determinations will be relatively easy.

Finally, the ramifications of spell scarcity are bound to aid your campaign, and not only with regard to excess treasure and magic items. A scroll of but a single spell becomes highly meaningful to the magic-users in the game, especially when it is of a spell heretofore unknown. The acquisition of a book of spells from someplace in the dungeons or wildernesses of the campaign is a benison beyond price! PC and NPC alike will take great pains to guard scrolls and spell books. Magic-users will haunt dusty libraries and peruse musty tomes in the hopes of gleaning but a single incantation to add to their store of magic.

RECOVERY OF SPELLS

Spell recovery, whether cleric/druid or magic-user/illusionist, requires about the same period of time. In order to pray and meditate for a new spell to replace one used, or in order to study and memorize such a spell, it is necessary that the spell-user rest and revitalize his or her mental faculties. Whether one or more spells are to be regained, the minimum time required for complete rest (usually sleep) is that required for the highest spell to be recovered. Minimum rest periods are shown below:

SPELL LEVEL	1 - 2	3 - 4	5 - 6	7 - 8	9
Rest Time	4 hours	6 hours	8 hours	10 hours	12 hours

Thus, if a cleric or magic-user needs only memorize first or second level spells, he or she need only sleep for 4 hours and will then be able to memorize or regain as many such spells as he or she is normally entitled to. On the other hand, if the character in question also wished to include a seventh level spell, rest time would be 10 full hours, even though but a single seventh level spell were to be thus regained, while half a dozen second level spells were also to be regained.

Once rested, an additional one-quarter hour per level of spell must be spent in study/prayer and meditation in order to memorize/acquire the ability to cast each spell.

SPELL CASTING

All magic and cleric spells are similar in that the word sounds, when combined into whatever patterns are applicable, are charged with energy from the Positive or Negative Material Plane. When uttered, these sounds cause the release of this energy, which in turn triggers a set reaction. The release of the energy contained in these words is what causes the spell to be forgotten or the writing to disappear from the surface upon which it is written.

The triggering action draws power from some plane of the multiverse. Whether the spell is an abjuration, conjuration, alteration, enchantment, or whatever, there is a flow of energy — first from the spell caster, then from some plane to the area magicked or enspelled by the caster. The energy flow is not from the caster *per se*, it is from the utterance of the sounds, each of which is charged with energy which is loosed when the proper formula and/or ritual is completed with their utterance. This power then taps the desired plane (whether or not the spell user has any idea of what or where it is) to cause the spell to function. It is much like plugging in a heater; the electrical outlet does not hold all of the electrical energy to cause the heater to function, but the wires leading from it, ultimately to the power station, bring the electricity to the desired location.

Many spells also require somatic motions in conjunction with words. The spoken words trigger the release of the magical energy, and the hand movements are usually required in order to control and specify the direction, target, area, etc., of the spell effects. When spell energy is released, it usually flows to the Prime Material from the Positive or Negative Material Plane. To replace it, something must flow back in reverse. The dissolution and destruction of material components provides the energy that balances out this flow, through the principle of similarity. Sometimes this destruction is very slow, as is the case with druids' mistletoe. Those spells without apparent material components are actually utilizing the air exhaled by the magic-user in the utterance of the spell.

Release of word/sound-stored energy is not particularly debilitating to the spell caster, as he or she has gathered this energy over a course of time prior to the loosing of the power. It comes from outside the spell caster, not from his or her own vital essence. The power to activate even a first level spell would leave a spell caster weak and shaking if it were drawn from his or her personal energy, and a third level spell would most certainly totally drain the caster's body of life!

Because spells tap power from other planes, any improper casting is likely to cause the spell not to function (the heater is turned on, but you haven't plugged it in, or you've plugged it in but not turned it on) or to malfunction (you held onto the prongs of the plug when you tapped the current, or you accidently dropped the heater as you were plugging it in, or perhaps you plugged in some other appliance or device by mistake). Such happenings are covered in the various chances for spell malfunction. If your players inquire as to how spells work, or fail to do so, you can explain, without difficulty, the precepts of the **AD&D** magic spell systems. (For background reading you can direct campaign participants to Vance's **THE EYES OF THE OVERWORLD** and **THE DYING EARTH** as well as to Bellair's **THE FACE IN THE FROST**.)

TRIBAL SPELL CASTERS

Tribal spell casters are found amongst the following races of creatures: BUGBEARS, CAVEMEN, ETTINS, GIANTS, GNOLLS, GOBLINS, HOBGOBLINS, KOBOLDS, LIZARD MEN, OGRES, ORCS, TROGLODYTES, and TROLLS. These spell casters are divided into two types, **shamans** and **witch doctors**.

Shamans are tribal clerics of 7th level or under. **Shamans** have only the following spells (and the reverse, if applicable) which they are able to cast:

First Level	Third Level
cure light wounds	*cure blindness*
detect evil	*cure disease*
detect magic	*dispel magic*
light	*locate object*
protection from evil	*prayer*
resist fear	*remove curse*

Second Level	Fourth Level
augury	*divination*
chant	*exorcise*
detect charm	*neutralize poison*
resist fire	*tongues*
snake charm	
speak with animals	

Note that wisdom does not affect the number of spells of tribal clerics, and the number of spells any such tribal cleric possesses is determined as if the shaman were a character of the appropriate level. There is a limit according to the race of the shaman as to how many levels of experience he or she can possess:

3rd level maximum	5th level maximum	7th level maximum
ettin	bugbear	giant (hill, stone, fire, frost only)
ogre	gnoll	goblin
troglodyte	kobold	hobgoblin
troll	orc	lizard man

Witch doctors are tribal cleric/magic-users. In addition to the maximum level of clerical ability noted above, witch doctors of various races are able to use the following spells (and the reverse, if applicable):

First Level	Second Level
affect normal fires	*audible glamer*
dancing lights	*detect invisibility*
identify	*invisibility*
push	*levitate*
shield	*magic mouth*
ventriloquism	*scare*

The maximum level of magic-user is dependent upon the race of the witch doctor:

2nd level maximum	4th level maximum
bugbear	caveman*
gnoll	goblin
kobold	hobgoblin
lizard man	orc

* Cavemen tribes have normal clerical members.

A tribe will have either shamans or witch doctors, but not both (except cavemen). It is suggested that you include these figures into those tribes you personally determine, not random groups.

SPELL EXPLANATIONS

SPELLS: SPECIAL COMMENTARY FOR REFEREEING

Some considerations, as well as practicality, make it impossible to give a concise list of each spell herein, with name, level, range, duration, area of effect, and so forth tabulated and then special notes appended. A playing aid of this sort will likely be done in the not-too-distant future, and that will serve your needs far better than a spread herein. There are, however, quite a number of special notes which you must be apprised of, as spells are often abused by players.

The type of magic is given in the **PLAYERS HANDBOOK** in order that you may creatively develop material regarding spells — new spells, spell components, spell formulae, or even limitations due to magical repression or other reasons on certain types of spells in some areas. Likewise, specialists can be developed as non-player characters, basing their abilities around the type of magic involved. In short, the type of magic involved in the casting of each spell is there to give you flexibility and a foundation for creativity.

Spell components for a spell are generally lost/used when the spell is cast. **Exceptions:** holy/unholy symbols, druids' mistletoe, *et al.*

Commentary regarding certain spells follows. Be certain to read all of the material and have it at hand whenever a spell user casts a spell for which special considerations are noted.

CLERIC SPELLS

First Level Spells:

Detect Evil: Basically the *degree* of evil (faint, moderate, strong, overwhelming) and its general nature (expectant, malignant, gloating, etc.) can be noted. If the evil is overwhelming, the general bent (lawful, neutral, chaotic) has a 10% chance per level of the cleric of being detectable.

Detect Magic: Only the fact that a dim or strong magic exists can be found by clerics (cf. magic-user spell of the same name).

Light: It should be noted that if this spell is cast upon the visage or before the visual organs of a creature, it will tend to blind it (rather as if a strong light were placed before its eyes), and its attacks and defenses will be a –4 on "to hit", saving throws, and even armor class. Note also that the spell is not mobile, although it can be cast upon a movable or mobile object or creature.

Protection From Evil: Note that this excludes (keeps out) monsters using natural (body) weapon attacks which require touching the protected character.

Second Level Spells:

Augury: This is a general future determinant with only a half hour maximum, so you need not be too exacting with regard to your vagueness. When the *augury* is cast, simply compare the knowledge you have and give the character general impressions of the question asked. "Will we do well if we venture onto the third level?" Answer: "Those who survive will be rich!" Basis: You have a terrible troll near where the character will enter the level (if he does), but the probable party is strong enough to beat it after a hard fight, and the monster guards 10,000 silver pieces and a +1 shield.

Detect Charm: *Charm* spells cast by creatures entitle the charmee to a saving throw versus magic, and if the save is successful, the *detect charm* spell does NOT pick up the fact that the *charm* exists.

Find Traps: This spell will be 10% likely per level of the cleric casting it to be able to note the type of magic involved, i.e. alteration, divination, etc., if it is a magical or magically-concealed trap.

Silence, 15′ Radius: If this spell is cast at a magic resistant creature, and resistance works, silence does NOT encompass the creature. Turning of the spell, in whole or in part, will negate its effects, save for muting sound, if it is turned beyond its radius.

Snake Charm: This spell will be effective against any ophidian or ophidianoid monster such as naga and couatl. Of course, hit point restrictions, resistance to magic, and saving throws apply at all times.

Speak With Animals: This spell will not necessarily make the animal type being conversed with the good and true friend of the cleric, so terseness and evasiveness are likely in basically hostile and reasonably intelligent creatures. The more stupid ones will make inane comments too! Remember to assume the role of an animal, with the appropriate mentality and viewpoint.

Third Level Spells:

Animate Dead: It is, of course, possible to animate the skeletons or corpses of demi-human and humanoid, as well as human, sort. If creatures with more than a basic 1 hit die (or 1 + hit die) are so animated, the number of such skeletons or zombies will be determined in hit dice rather than total numbers. Thus, a cleric of 6th level could animate 6 skeletons of human or humanoid sort which in life had less than 2 hit dice, 3 such undead which in life had less than 3, but 2 or more hit dice, or a single undead creature which had 6, but less than 7, hit dice. For each such additional hit die, the skeleton or zombie will gain another die. Thus, the animated skeleton of a fire giant, an 11 hit die monster, is 10 over the norm for a skeleton normally animated, so it would have 1 + 10 hit dice (11d8). Likewise, a fire giant zombie would have 10 dice over and above the sort of creature typically made into a zombie, so it would have 2 + 10 hit dice (12d8). **N.B.:** This does not enable a cleric to make skeletons or zombies of characters of 2nd or higher level have more hit dice; such undead are simply human skeletons or zombies with 1 or 2 hit dice, nothing more.

Continual Light: As does a *light* spell, this will tend to blind a creature if it is placed on its visual sensory area. The spell can also be placed upon a smallish object, and a lightproof case subsequently used to encase the object so as to make it dark until the covering is removed, i.e. a *continual light* source which expends no fuel and will not blow out. (*Darkness* spells are the bane of this device . . .)

Cure Blindness: This spell will not restore lost visual organs, whether such cause is due to injury or disease. Thus, at your option, the spell can simply remove magical blindness and cure disease or disease-like conditions such as cataracts and glaucoma and various forms of nearsightedness, farsightedness, or astigmatisms common to human eyes; or it can be effective against other eye disorders as well, save those noted above.

Dispel Magic: If this spell is cast upon a magic item it most certainly will have the effect of causing it to be non-operational for 1 round thereafter if the item does not make a saving throw — if the item is not in the possession of any creature, then the item gets no saving throw, and it is non-operational for 1 round. Note that artifacts and relics are NOT subject to this effect. Any *dispel magic* spell must be cast directly at the object, not anything or anyone else, to be so effective.

Glyph Of Warding: If a cleric is on hand to determine that a *glyph of warding* is certainly in existence, an associated magic-user can thereafter use an *erase* spell and possibly (50% + 2%/level of the m-u) remove the *glyph*. As to the design and the names of *glyphs of warding*, design your own or use an encyclopedia to find interesting alphabets to use. You may refer also to **THE WORLD OF GREYHAWK** for other runes and glyphs. For example, here is one such series of glyphs, named.

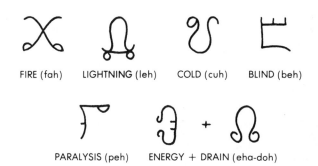

FIRE (fah) LIGHTNING (leh) COLD (cuh) BLIND (beh)

PARALYSIS (peh) ENERGY + DRAIN (eha-doh)

As a *detect traps* spell will see the form of the *glyph*, a cleric might believe he or she knows the name of the *glyph* from past experience, and try to bypass it — possibly with success.

Locate Object: This spell will not enable the caster to find a general class of objects unless the form is nearly the same as that of the majority of others in its class. Thus, stairs have risers and are generally similar, so by means of the spell the caster would be able to locate a flight which closely resembled those he or she pictured in casting the *locate object* spell. However, attempting to find jewelry or a crown or the like requires a certain mental image, and if the image is not generally similar to the desired object(s) within range, the spell will not work, for the image is not familiar/similar to that of the real. In short, desired but unique objects cannot be located by this spell unless they are similar to objects known by the caster.

Prayer: If a *prayer* spell is uttered while another cleric of the same deity is *chanting*, the effect of the two spells are cumulative, i.e. +2 for friendly creatures, −2 for foes. Note that the two spells must be cast by clerics of the same religious persuasion, not merely the same general alignment, and that the *chant* must be in progress while the *prayer* is said.

Speak With Dead: This spell is often subject to abuse due to too liberal DMing. When the cleric asks questions, follow these rules: 1) give answers which are brief, 2) take all questions absolutely literally, and 3) be as evasive as possible if the questioned creature was not friendly to the characters or class or alignment of the spell caster when it lived. Remember, speaking with the dead assumes that the creature has an essence which still exists somewhere, and if it can remember answers to questions, it can remember other things as well . . .

Fourth Level Spells:

Detect Lie: This dweomer does not reveal the truth, nor will it necessarily reveal evasions of the truth; it empowers the caster to detect a lie.

Fifth Level Spells:

Atonement: As the all-in-all of the campaign milieu, you must assume the role of the supernatural powers judging the character making *atonement*. If the action appears to be very sincere, then the deity will be prone to allow *atonement* by means of the spell, with little or no sacrifice in addition, according to the deity's overall nature; so that could mean a few coins in the poor box or a major quest for a relic. The less sincere the character, the greater will be the actions required to complete the spell, i.e. a hollow voice rings forth and commands: "GO FORTH FROM HERE AND RETURN NOT UNTIL YOU BRING CAPTIVE THE HIGH PRIEST OF OSIRIS AND ALL OF THE ALTAR SERVICE OF HIS TEMPLE AS SACRIFICES TO ME IN TOKEN OF THE SINCERITY OF YOUR TRUE REPENTANCE!" And that will be the *final* word from that deity until the deed is accomplished.

Commune: The questions permitted must be asked consecutively in as brief a period as possible, as there is too much bother and disturbance for the supernatural powers otherwise. If the spell caster lags or goes off to do anything else, the spell is broken, over and done with. Note that it is possible for a deity to answer "I don't know", as most deities are not omniscient.

Plane Shift: The material component is similar to a tuning fork, of course, and striking it at the proper time allows the energy vibrations of the person or persons or creature or creatures involved to match those of the desired plane. All you need to do is determine which plane, if you will, attune to which planes, and then when the caster has a metal rod, inform him or her of the note it sounds — an A sharp, for instance, might take one to the Astral Plane, while an A flat will move one to the Elemental Plane of Air, and an A to the Ethereal Plane. Naturally, you can include the octave and even have chords to move a creature to some sub plane, i.e., F sharp minor might move the caster or the subject to the 9th Plane of Hell.

Quest: If the person *quested* agrees to a task, even though this agreement might have been gained by force or trickery, then any chance of avoiding the *quest* (the saving throw) is negated! Those of the same religion as the cleric are not able to avoid a just and deserved *quest* either, and even those of the same alignment having to undertake a just and proper *quest* must have a −4 if they wish to avoid it. A *quest* can be negated by a cleric of greater level than the one which placed the spell, if the cleric so doing is of the same religion as the *quested* creature. Some artifacts or relics can probably negate the spell, and any deity can do so, but only directly.

Sixth Level Spells:

Aerial Servant: The spell caster should be required to show you what form of protective inscription he or she has used when the spell is cast. The three forms mentioned are:

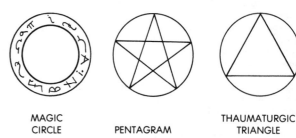

| MAGIC CIRCLE | PENTAGRAM | THAUMATURGIC TRIANGLE |

Blade Barrier: This spell is absolutely stationary. It does not move in any way except with respect to the circling of the blades around the fixed point of the spell center. The plane of rotation of the blades can be horizontal, vertical, or anything in between, however. Note that creatures within the area of the barrier when it is invoked are entitled to a saving throw, and if this save is made, the blades are avoided and no damage is taken.

Conjure Animals: For the list of these creatures see **APPENDIX L: CONJURED ANIMALS.**

Find The Path: This spell is subject to the same sort of abuse as a *locate object* spell is. A locale is not an object. The spell will enable the caster to find a way into or out of some area, but this area must be known or identified in itself, not for what it might house. Thus, one could use it to find a great forest of ash trees but not to find a forest where a green dragon lived. In the latter case the desire is to find an object, not an area or locale. Similarly, use of a *find the path* spell to locate the way to a hoard of platinum pieces is absolutely useless, as it must not be allowed, but the spell could be used to find a level known to have such a hoard of coins, or a cavern with a pool in it might be pointed to, etc. The spell finds a way to a locale or an area, and whatever objects are therein are not meaningful to the spell.

Heal: This spell will not cure serious forms of mental disorders not related to spells or inflicted by injury to the brain.

Word Of Recall: For each plane that the cleric is removed from the plane of his or her designated Sanctuary, there is a 10% cumulative chance that the cleric will be irrevocably lost in the intervening astral or ethereal spaces.

Seventh Level Spells:

Astral Spell: Any magic items can go into the Astral Plane, but most will become non-magical thereon, or on any planes removed from the Prime Material Plane. Those which contain spells which you determine will function on any given plane will function on that plane. Armor and weapons which are +3 or better might also function on other planes, but this is at your option. All artifacts and relics should be allowed to function anywhere. Items which draw their power from a particular plane will be likely to be far more powerful on the plane from whence their power comes, e.g., a *ring of fire resistance* on the Elemental Plane of Fire or a *sword of life stealing* on the Negative Material Plane. For creatures encountered see **APPENDIX C: RANDOM MONSTER ENCOUNTERS, ASTRAL & ETHEREAL ENCOUNTER TABLES.**

Control Weather: To find the prevailing conditions at the time the spell is cast, you must know the clime and the season, of course. Sky conditions (cloudy, foggy, partly cloudy, clear), precipitation, wind speed and direction, and temperature must be determined according to the area. Knowing this, you should have no great problem informing the would-be spell caster as to what sort of weather exists.

Earthquake: Structures very solidly built, with foundations reaching to bedrock, will sustain half damage. Castles so built will take only one-quarter damage if they score above 50% on a saving throw roll. An earth elemental in the spell area has the effect of negating 10% to 100% of the spell effects (d10, 0 = 100%) if the elemental is of forces opposed to the cleric casting the *earthquake* spell.

Gate: Unless you have some facts regarding the minions serving the being called forth by the casting of the *gate* spell, it is necessary to have the being called come. Then, if it is a trifle, it can leave or attack; if it is of middling importance, it can take some positive action to set matters aright, and then demand appropriate repayment; and if the matter is urgent, it can act accordingly and ask whatever is its wont thereafter, if appropriate. However, Asmodeus might send a pit fiend to see what the problem was, and some deity of lawful good might send a ki-rin on the same mission. As to the likelihood of the *gated* being returning without doing something, use a factor of 20% for a trifling matter, 15% of return if the affair is of medial importance, and from 1% to 50% if the matter is very important — 1% indicating that the being finds itself well able to handle the situation and everything pleases or displeases it greatly, 50% if the situation would be risky and it is displeased. Thus, Asmodeus summoned by a party of chaotic good characters to save them from a type VI demon could be a trifle to an important act, depending on what was involved — such as a relic of lawful evil. Asmodeus would certainly do away with the summoners as well as the demon if at all possible. On the other hand, Asmodeus summoned to pit himself against Bahamut would be very likely to turn and do a speedy exit unless the matter was of critical importance to Hell.

Holy/Unholy Word: The speaker must be from the plane upon which it speaks in order to have the utterance send other creatures to their own plane, i.e. a devil on the Prime Material Plane could not use the spell to send away anything, although it could so do if it were in Hell. Creatures sent to their original plane cannot return for 1 day. Creatures slowed by such a spell lose their first round of attack and each odd-numbered round of attack thereafter until the duration of the effect wears off.

Restoration: This spell will cure any and all forms of insanity.

DRUID SPELLS

First Level Spells:

Detect Magic: Only the fact that a dim or a strong magic exists in the area will be noted. (Cf. magic-user spell of the same name.)

Locate Animals: This spell is another which requires a bit of effort on the part of the DM. As it is quite unlikely that each and every species of animal in the area of the spell caster will be recorded, you will have to use the probabilities of your milieu. Obviously, there is 0% chance of locating a polar bear in the jungle, or a jungle cat in a cavern thousands of feet below ground, etc. So the locale is second after the region as to whether or not some animal will be within spell range. Then consider the terrain — mountain lions do not typically roam the prairies, for instance. Lastly, consider the frequency of the animal desired in relation to all of the above. If the animal is within the area of probability, allow a straight percentile roll for frequency: COMMON = 50% chance, UNCOMMON = 25% chance, RARE = 10% chance, VERY RARE = 5% chance. Circumstances will always prevail, so modify as necessary to allow for the surroundings.

Speak With Animals: As noted for the cleric spell of the same name (q.v.), this magic will not make the animal altogether friendly and co-operative.

Second Level Spells:

Animal Friendship: This spell will only function if the druid actually wishes to be the animals' friend. If the druid has ulterior motives, the animals will always sense it.

Charm Person Or Mammal: If at the same time this spell is cast the subject is struck by any spell, missile or weapon which inflicts damage, the creature will make its saving throw at +1 per point of damage sustained. Naturally, this assumes damage is inflicted by members of the spell caster's party.

Remember that a charmed creature's or person's priorities are changed as regards the spell-caster, but the charmed one's basic personality and alignment are not. The spell is not *enslave* person or mammal. A request that a charmee make itself defenseless or that he/she/it be required to give up a valued item or cast a valuable spell or use a charge on a valued item (especially against the charmee's former associates or allies) could allow an immediate saving throw to see if the charm is thrown off. In like manner, a charmed figure will not necessarily tell everything he/she/it knows or draw maps of entire areas. A charmed figure *can* refuse a request, if such refusal is in character and will not directly cause harm to the charmer. Also, a *charm* spell does not substantially alter the charmee's feelings toward the charmer's friends and allies. The charmed person or creature will not react well to the charmer's allies making suggestions like "Ask him this question . . ." The charmee is oriented toward friendship and acceptance of the charmer, but this does not mean that he/she/it will put up with verbal or physical abuse from the charmer's associates.

Create Water: It is not possible to *create water* within living material, i.e. it is not possible to cast the spell upon a creature and create liquid in any part of its body.

Feign Death: The recipient of this dweomer consumes air at 1/100th of the normal rate. Any poison within the system of the spell recipient is effectively slowed so as to cause no harm whatsoever for the duration of the spell.

Fire Trap: The spell can be removed/negated by a *dispel magic* as is normal.

Heat Metal: Elfin chain mail is not subject to this spell. All ferrous-based magic armor is entitled to a saving throw versus *Magical fire*. If the save is successful, the *heat metal* spell does NOT affect it.

Locate Plants: For the likelihood of any given plant type to be within the area of the spell, consult the foregoing discussion regarding the spell *locate animals*. It will generally be more difficult to adjudicate matters botanical, however, as the distribution of plant species is not as widely known as that of animals. As a rule, most herbs will grow only in temperate regions, most spices in tropical regions. If you have never heard of the plant, assume it is rare or very rare, and give appropriate percentages.

Obscurement: A *gust of wind* spell will cause the vapor to swirl and dissipate in 25% of the normal time, so that instead of the *obscurement* lasting for 4 rounds per level it will last for but 1 round per level, once the *gust of wind* has been cast, of course.

Produce Flame: If the druid chooses to hurl the flame, treat it as a missile, but any target is considered to be at *short range*. If a miss occurs, use the grenade-like missile principle to determine where the flame strikes.

Warp Wood: Attempting to affect the wood of a magically held or *wizard locked* door is another matter. The level of the druid is compared to the level of the magic-user, and only if the latter is of lower level than the former will the spell have any chance of working. For each level of experience greater than the magic-user, the druid has a 20% chance of warping dweomered wood.

Third Level Spells:

Call Lightning: If a djinn or an air elemental is on hand to form a whirlwind, the druid is able to summon half-strength lightning strokes therefrom.

Snare: The material of the noose can be cut with any magic blade, or a non-magical sharp instrument with a "to hit" bonus of +2 or better.

Summon Insects: If thick smoke or hot flames are near the target creatures, the insects called forth will NOT go near the intended victim — those who might be considered dazed or burned to a crisp. The spell thus fails. Likewise, if the victim steps into such an area, all insects are gone that instant, so that next round it may act normally.

Tree: Note that the druid can appear as a conifer, bush, etc. The armor class of such a plant is that of the druid, and its hit points are likewise those of the druid.

Fourth Level Spells:

Animal Summoning I: For probable animals in the area see the foregoing commentary on *Locate Animals*. The animals typically summonable are:

APES	BABOONS	BADGERS
BADGERS, GIANT	BEARS, BLACK	BEAVERS, GIANT

BOARS, WILD	BOARS, WARTHOGS	BULLS
CAMELS, WILD	CATTLE, WILD	CROCODILES, NORMAL
DOGS, WILD	EAGLES, GIANT	GOATS, GIANT
HERD ANIMALS*	HORSES, WILD	HYENAS
JACKALS	JAGUARS	LEOPARDS
LIZARDS, GIANT	LYNX, GIANT	OWLS, GIANT
RAMS, GIANT	RATS, GIANT	SNAKE, POISONOUS
SNAKE, SPITTING	WEASEL, GIANT	WOLVES
WOLVES, DIRE	WOLVERINES	

*Summonable only by specific type of animal.

You will note that animals with 4 + n hit dice are included. If the druid names such an animal type, allow summoning if otherwise indicated, but limit the number appearing to 1-3.

Call Woodland Being: These sorts of creatures are the type which should generally be indicated on area maps as to location and numbers. However, if by chance you are faced with the problem of a druid casting this spell where such information is not at hand, use the following random percentage possibilities:

Creature Type Called	Light	Type of Woodlands Moderate/Sylvan	Dense/Virgin
2-8 brownies	30%	20%	10%
1-4 centaurs	5%	30%	5%
1-4 dryads	1%	25%	15%
1-8 pixies	10%	20%	10%
1-4 satyrs	1%	30%	10%
1-6 sprites	15%	10%	5%
1 treant	0%	5%	25%
1 unicorn	0%	15%	20%

Add 1% per level of the druid casting the spell except where 0%. Check in order for each type by rolling percentile dice, and if at the end of the list nothing is indicated, there are no woodland beings within spell range. For example, a 10th level druid begins the spell in a sylvan wood. There is a 30% chance for brownies, but the dice roll shows 35, so none come, then a 40% chance for centaurs gets a dice score of 72, but finally a 35% chance for dryads gets a dice roll of 10, so from 1-4 dryads will come. Since the *call* was successful, no further checks are made.

Dispel Magic: See the comments on the cleric spell of the same name for the effects of the spell upon an item.

Hallucinatory Forest: Touching the illusory growth will neither inform the individual as to its nature nor will it affect the magic.

Fifth Level Spells:

Transmute Rock To Mud: Rate of sinking is 1' per segment, i.e. 1' per 6 seconds or 10' per minute (round). Brush thrown upon the surface will stop sinking of creatures able to climb atop it (use discretion as to the amount of brush and the weight of creatures). Ropes can be used to pull creatures out of the mire, assuming that sufficient power is available — 1 man/man, 10 men/horse (or vice versa).

Wall Of Fire: It is not possible for the spell caster to move at all and maintain concentration on the *wall of fire*.

Sixth Level Spells:

Anti-Animal Shell: This shell is non-mobile. Humans, even though able to use magic, are non-magical, as are dwarves, elves, etc.

Conjure Fire Elemental: A *holy/unholy* word will send any elemental back to its plane.

Fire Seeds: As with missiles of the type produced by a *produce flame* spell, all *fire seed* missiles are considered to be short range, and misses are handled as described in the **GRENADE-LIKE MISSILES** subsection of **COMBAT.**

Turn Wood: Even magical weapons with wooden sections will be turned. An *anti-magic shell* will protect from this spell, and a *dispel magic* will have normal chances of wiping out its effects.

Wall Of Thorns: Dexterity bonus to armor class is NOT considered in this

case. If a *wall of fire* results from the burning of the thorns, the side towards the druid will be the non-harmful one.

Seventh Level Spells:

Chariot Of Sustarre: This vehicle and its steeds are from the Elemental Plane Of Fire; therefore, they are subject to forced return to this plane (such as by *dispel magic, holy/unholy word,* etc.).

Conjure Earth Elemental: As noted regarding fire elementals, a *holy/unholy word* will send the creature back to its own plane.

Fire Storm: The reverse, *fire quench,* will cause a *flame tongue* (flaming) sword to be extinguished unless it makes a successful saving throw versus a CRUSHING BLOW. Once extinguished thus, the weapon becomes non-magical.

Reincarnation: Regardless of the form of the creature in which the character is reincarnated, allow the new form to progress as far as possible in characteristics and abilities. For example, a badger character could grow to giant size, have maximum hit points, plus bonus points for a high constitution, and the intelligence level of its former character. A centaur reincarnation might eventually gain hit dice up to 5, 6, 7, or even 8, and it would be eligible to wear armor, use magic items, etc.

MAGIC-USER SPELLS

First Level Spells:

Charm Person: Attacks causing damage upon the subject person will cause a saving throw bonus of +1 per hit point of damage sustained in the round that the *charm* is cast.

Comprehend Languages: The reverse, *confuse languages,* can be cast upon a scroll to make it unreadable, but a second *comprehend languages* spell will then succeed.

Detect Magic: This spell detects the intensity of the magic (dim, faint, moderate, strong, very strong, intense) and there is a 10% chance per level of the caster that the type (abjuration, alteration, etc.) can be found as well, although if a dual type, the detection percentage applies to both and must be rolled for separately.

Enlarge: All garments and equipment worn by a subject of this spell should be considered to automatically drop off if held by straps or fasteners, otherwise to split away during growth, so it is not possible to "squeeze someone to death in their armor" by means of an *enlarge.* Material components possessed will not change size. Coats of mail, however, will be ruined if growth occurs while worn. Note that you can opt to make a target wearing objects an impossible task for an *enlarge* spell unless the character is actually touched so as to distinguish the creature from the objects.

Erase: This spell might be useful against a *glyph of warding* (q.v.).

Find Familiar: If the magic-user opts to send away a familiar, he or she may never again find another until the former is killed or dies. Purposely killing or causing to be killed a familiar (or former familiar) is most likely to find great disfavor with the gods, assuming, of course, that this pertains to the magic-user and his or her associated familiar. Note that spell duration concerns the finding of the familiar. Once it is found, the familiar will serve until killed. To determine animal availability, see the fourth level druid spell, *Animal Summoning I.*

"One false move, wizard, and your familiar gets it!"

Light: This spell can effectively blind an opponent as noted under the commentary on the cleric spell of the same name.

Message: This is not a *tongues* spell, and speech will be as normal for the spell caster.

Protection From Evil: This spell prevents attacks which employ parts of the body of affected creatures. (Cf. cleric spell of the same name.)

Sleep: Unless a single creature is designated as the target of a *sleep* spell in a mixed group, the *sleep* spell will first affect the lowest level/hit dice targets.

Tenser's Floating Disc: The caster cannot ride on the *Disc*. The *Disc* always follows the magic-user.

Unseen Servant: The created force has no shape, so it cannot be clothed.

Write: Ink for use with this spell is only 10% likely to be located at any given apothecary/alchemist in a town, or double that for a city. Ink will come in a flask which will be sufficient to inscribe 2-4 spells. The cost will be 200 to 500 gold pieces. You should devise whatever formula for manufacture of this substance you desire. Ichor of slithering tracker, octopus ink, and powdered gems are a fair place to start from.

Second Level Spells:

Detect Evil: The magic detects only the intensity of the evil. (Cf. cleric spell of the same name.)

Invisibility: See the **INVISIBILITY** section under **THE ADVENTURE.**

Locate Object: See the cleric spell of the same name for complete commentary.

Rope Trick: Those climbing the rope and gaining the safety of the extra-dimensional space are able to see *out* of it clearly, as if they were observing through a window of about 3' width by 5' height. Those outside can not see in.

Stinking Cloud: A *gust of wind* spell will blow this away in 1 round after contact. If it is cast in a place where there is considerable air movement, the *stinking cloud* will move in the direction of the air current at from 1" to 6" per round, depending on air speed. For each 1" of such movement, shorten its duration by 1 round.

Web: If this spell is cast without two firm anchoring places, the webs collapse and entangle themselves, effectively negating the spell.

Wizard Lock: The caster can always pass through his or her own *wizard locked* portal freely.

Third Level Spells:

Dispel Magic: For the effects of this spell on a magic item, see the cleric spell of the same name.

Feign Death: For the rate of air consumption and effects on poisoning, see the cleric spell of the same name.

Gust Of Wind: This spell is particularly useful against such spells as *obscurement*, *stinking cloud*, and *cloudkill* (qq.v.).

Lightning Bolt: Note that physical damage is not exceptional, so that if a solid wall is struck, the bolt effectively rebounds its full remaining distance. If it strikes a barrier which is shattered/broken through by the force of the stroke, then the bolt continues beyond.

Monster Summoning I: For a list of monsters summoned see **APPENDIX M: SUMMONED MONSTERS.**

Phantasmal Force: The magic-user must know of and understand the force/creature he/she is making an illusion of. Thus, if the caster has never cast a fireball or has never seen a dragon turtle, his illusion of such will be very poor.

Protection From Evil, 10' Radius: As heretofore noted, this spell prevents use of body weaponry by affected creatures.

Fourth Level Spells:

Charm Monster: It is needful to point out that this spell does not suddenly empower the caster, or his or her associated characters, with any special means of communications. If the caster is unable to convey to the charmed creature his or her instructions, then the monster will simply refrain from harming the spell caster, and the others in the area, if any, will still be subject to its attentions, hostile or otherwise. Similar to a *charm person* spell, if damage is inflicted on the charmee at the same time (round) as the spell is cast, then the saving throw is made at +1 for each 1 point of damage so inflicted.

Dig: This spell will inflict 5-20 hit points of damage if cast upon a clay golem.

Extension I: This spell must be cast after the spell to be extended, whether by another spell-user during the same round, or the initial spell caster or another immediately preceding the casting of the *extension*. If a round elapses, the *extension* goes for naught.

Fire Trap: A *dispel magic* has the possibility stated to remove the *fire trap*. If it fails to do so, the trap is not affected and is not triggered.

Minor Globe Of Invulnerability: The *globe* gives off a faint shimmering when it forms. Third level spells from devices — fireballs or lightning, for example — will not penetrate its sphere.

Monster Summoning II: For a list of monsters summoned see **APPENDIX M: SUMMONED MONSTERS.**

Polymorph Others: As is continually pointed out, henchmen and hirelings will NOT desire to be subjected to the effects of this spell! Furthermore, level of experience is not a part of a character's form, so it is quite foolish and totally impossible to attempt to *polymorph* a creature into an nth level character. Likewise, profession is not form, so attempting to *polymorph* a fighter, thief, etc. results in human form and nothing more. Shape changers (lycanthropes, deities, druids, vampires, certain dragons, jackalweres, dopplegangers, mimics, et al.) will be affected for but one round, then will return to their former form.

Rary's Mnemonic Enhancer: When this is used to gain additional lower level spells, the magic-user must then memorize the spells and equip himself or herself with the requisite components.

Wizard Eye: The ocular device magically formed has substance and it has form which might be detected (cf. **INVISIBILITY**). Solid objects prevent the passage of a *wizard eye*, although it can pass through a space no larger than a small mouse hole (about one-half inch diameter).

Fifth Level Spells:

Animate Dead: See the cleric spell of the same name for a detailed commentary.

Cloudkill: The caster is able to cast this spell so that it forms around him or her, if this is desired. However, any creatures staying within the cloud for more than 1 round, even though they have 7 or more hit dice/levels, will take 1-10 hit points of damage on the second and each succeeding round.

Conjure Elemental: See the cleric spell, *aerial servant*, for details of protective inscriptions.

Contact Other Plane: See the section on **INSANITY.**

Extension II: See *extension I*, above.

Leomund's Secret Chest: For a list of random creatures which might come from the Ethereal Plane, see **APPENDIX C: RANDOM MONSTER ENCOUNTERS.**

Monster Summoning III: For a list of monsters summoned see **APPENDIX M: SUMMONED MONSTERS.**

Transmute Rock To Mud: For commentary see the druid spell of the same name.

Wall Of Force: A *rod of cancellation* or a *sphere of annihilation* will bring down the *wall of force*, the former being used fully in the process, and the latter drawing any and all small objects into its vortex in the process. (Small objects are those weighing less than 100 g.p. and within 1" radius of the *sphere*.) The diamond dust for the spell must be the equivalent of stone(s) of not less than 10,000 g.p. value.

Wall Of Iron: If the *wall of iron* is created vertically, there is a 50% chance either way for its falling left or right, ahead or backwards, depending on its placement. It would take not less than 30 strength points with at least 400 pounds mass to affect this probability, and then only 1% for each pound over 300 or strength point over 30. If the caster concentrates specially, it is possible to double the area by halving the thickness.

Wall Of Stone: Any use of the wall as a bridge must be arched and buttressed. This will require 50% of the total volume of the wall, so a 20th level magic-user normally may create 400 square feet in surface area 5 feet thick. To use it as bridge, only 200 square feet can be considered, so a span 5 feet wide and 40 feet long could be made (assuming the chasm to be bridged was about 38' wide). Unsupported spans will automatically collapse of their own weight if over 20' across.

Sixth Level Spells:

Anti-Magic Shell: It must be pointed out that creatures on their own plane are normal creatures, so this spell cast upon the Elemental Plane of Fire, for example, would hedge out none of the creatures of the plane.

Control Weather: For commentary on this spell, see the cleric spell of the same name.

Death Spell: Creatures with less than 1 hit die count as only ½ a creature which otherwise has less than 2 hit dice. If such creatures are subjected to the spell, count them off thusly, although the maximum number affected cannot exceed 80 in any event.

Enchant An Item: When casting the *permanency* spell on an item, the magic-user need only roll 2 or better with d20 to avoid loss of a constitution point. Formulae for magic items are suggested under **FABRICATION OF MAGIC ITEMS** (q.v.).

Extension III: See *extension I.*

Geas: The casting time is also the total time the magic-user has to word the *geas* spell. It is otherwise similar to a *quest* (q.v.).

Glassee: The strength of the glassy area is the same as that of the original material.

Monster Summoning IV: For a list of monsters summoned see **APPENDIX M: SUMMONED MONSTERS.**

Move Earth: The practical limitation on the area of effect of this spell is a 24" square area, with four hours of casting time, exclusive of elemental conjuration.

Otiluke's Freezing Sphere: The sling stone-sized application of this spell has a 4" range if hurled by hand, otherwise as a sling bullet. All ranges by hand are short; otherwise treat it as a slung missile. Use the **GRENADE-LIKE MISSILES TABLE** to find where misses strike.

Reincarnation: See the cleric spell of the same name for commentary on this spell.

Spiritwrack: Only one specially illuminated vellum sheet may be prepared by the magic-user and be in his or her possession and/or control at the same time. This will be realized by any magic-user as soon as a second is begun. It is not possible to have two such sheets naming the same being either, as the magic of the naming will be held within the first, but as soon as the second is made, it will go therein. Finally, no creature can make such a sheet naming itself.

Stone To Flesh: In casting this spell upon a stone block, the magic-user can cause the area of effect to be cylindrical if so desired, so a passage can be thus made. Maximum diameter is 3', minimum 1'.

Seventh Level Spells:

Drawmij's Instant Summons: The special jewel used will have a magic-

ally-created inscription naming the object it will summon. The inscription is invisible and readable only by means of a *read magic* spell to all but the caster of the spell. Items contained within a *Leomund's Secret Chest* are not subject to this spell.

Duo-Dimension: See **APPENDIX C: RANDOM MONSTER ENCOUNTERS, ASTRAL & ETHEREAL ENCOUNTER TABLES.**

Monster Summoning V: For a list of monsters summoned see **APPENDIX M: SUMMONED MONSTERS.**

Phase Door: This spell provides an escape route for high level magic-users, although phase spiders can see and use it with ease. A *gem of seeing*, *true seeing*, and *true sight* will reveal the presence of a *phase door*.

Eighth Level Spells:

Clone: Only humans, demi-humans and humanoids may be cloned.

Glassteel: The armor class of this substance is 1.

Monster Summoning VI: For a list of monsters summoned see **APPENDIX M: SUMMONED MONSTERS.**

Permanency: There is only a 5% chance of the spell caster actually losing a point of constitution if the spell is cast upon a non-living thing.

Serten's Spell Immunity: Although it should be rather obvious, the spell works against nearly any form of *enchantment/charm*. Thus:

Forget, Hypnotism, Ray of Enfeeblement	+9
Antipathy/Sympathy, Confusion, Mass Suggestion	+7
Chaos, Feeblemind, Otto's Irresistible Dance	+5

Any other such spells can be adjudicated from the list in the **PLAYERS HANDBOOK** and herein.

Ninth Level Spells:

Astral Spell: See the cleric spell of the same name for commentary.

Gate: See the cleric spell of the same name for commentary.

Imprisonment: To find what number of creatures are freed, roll percentile dice to find the density of imprisoned creatures before rolling for the number. Multiply the first roll by the second, rounding any remainders to the nearest whole. For each such creature freed there is only a 10% chance that it will be in the area of the spell caster. Use the **RANDOM MONSTER TABLES** of **APPENDIX C** for these, using d20 for level, any number of 9 or higher indicating a 9th level monster.

Monster Summoning VII: For a list of monsters summoned, see **APPENDIX M: SUMMONED MONSTERS.**

Prismatic Sphere: At the commencement of this spell, each color is shimmering, but each represents a successive layer, rather like an onion. The first MUST be brought down before the second can be affected, etc. Any creature passing through gets the effect of each and every color layer still existing.

Time Stop: Use a stop watch or silent count to time this. The caster must be able to complete his or her acts before spell duration expires, or else he or she will likely be found in an embarrassing act. The use of a *teleport* spell just before the spell duration of the *time stop* expires is permissible.

ILLUSIONIST SPELLS

First Level Spells:

Gaze Reflection: The creature that has its gaze reflected by this spell is entitled to a saving throw.

Light: This spell can effectively blind an opponent as noted in the commentary of the cleric spell of the same name.

Second Level Spells:

Detect Magic: For commentary on this spell see the cleric spell of the same name, NOT the magic-user spell.

Fog Cloud: A *gust of wind* spell will dissipate the cloud in a single round.

Invisibility: See the section on **INVISIBILITY** for commentary.

Third Level Spells:

Illusionary Script: The cost of the lead-based ink is 100 to 400 gold pieces, plus the alchemist's profit of 100 g.p.

Invisibility, 10' Radius: See the **INVISIBILITY** section.

Rope Trick: See the magic-user spell of the same name for commentary.

Fourth Level Spells:

Improved Invisibility: *Improved invisibility* has the effect of moving considerations for detection of such invisibility downwards by two places compared to other forms of *invisibility*. See **INVISIBILITY** for commentary.

Phantasmal Killer: If the affected individual is somehow brought to an unconscious state, the spell can not do harm.

Fifth Level Spells:

Shadow Door: The invisibly fleeing illusionist can be detected (cf. **INVISIBILITY**), but there must be active and concentrated attempts to do so. This will not simply be noticed in passing, as attention will be on the *shadow door*.

Shadow Magic: The caster is actually tapping a power source, even though the majority of the spell is illusion, thus the 1 hit point of damage per level of the caster.

Sixth Level Spells:

Conjure Animals: For a list of animals see **APPENDIX L: CONJURED ANIMALS.**

Demi-Shadow Magic: This spell also allows the caster to tap a source of power as noted under *shadow magic*.

Seventh Level Spells:

Astral Spell: See **APPENDIX C.: RANDOM MONSTER ENCOUNTERS, ASTRAL & ETHEREAL ENCOUNTER TABLES** for a list of creatures which can be met.

Vision: Consider this spell similar to a *contact other planes* for handling purposes. Unrelated *visions* should contain some cryptic clue as to what the caster is seeking. Even on a 10 or better, be certain to make the *vision* as unclear and indirect as possible.

Final Note:

Remember that the reverse of any spell must be separately memorized, and that each requires special components.

THE ADVENTURE

ADVENTURES IN THE OUTDOORS

It is necessary to have a reasonably well-detailed, large scale map for conducting adventures outdoors. Naturally, the initial adventuring in the campaign will be those in the small community and nearby underground maze. For whatever reason — player desire, *quest* or *geas*, or because of your own direction — adventuring will sooner or later move to the outdoors. What you must do to handle this is not difficult following the general procedures given below.

First, decide how you wish to proceed regarding the world at large. If you have plenty of time and ideas, you should design a continent (or a large portion thereof) which perfectly meshes with your initial setting. If this is not possible, obtain one of the commercially available milieux, and place

the starting point of your campaign somewhere within this already created world. At the risk of being accused of being self-serving, I will mention parenthetically that my own **WORLD OF GREYHAWK**, (published by TSR), was specifically designed to allow for insertion of such beginning milieux, variety being great and history and organization left purposely sketchy to make interfacing a simple matter. Whatever course you opt for, the scale of such world maps should be in the neighborhood of 20 to 40 miles per hexagon. Such areas allow mapping of considerable territories and are optimal for movement and smaller scale maps as well, dividing each large hex into blocks of smaller hexes, 5 across the middle or 5 across each face, as desired.

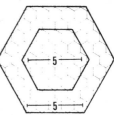

Adventuring outdoors actually covers several sorts of adventuring, for it is a catch-all term for all activities not in underground or urban settings. Thus, under this general heading will be 4 major subheadings: **LAND ADVENTURES, ADVENTURES IN THE AIR, WATERBORNE ADVENTURES,** and **UNDERWATER ADVENTURES.**

Movement rates for land and water adventures are shown under movement. Underwater movement is the same as dungeon and similar indoors movement rates, as the locale of such adventures is always limited in area.

LAND ADVENTURES

Starting from the point of origin, your players will move over not only varying types of terrain but through areas of varying human/demi-human population as well. Just as terrain will affect the frequency and type of monsters encountered, so will population dictate likelihood and type of encounter. You must, therefore, show population density on your large scale map — or at least have some idea of it in mind as adventurers move across the land. The chance of encounter is set with the following bases:

Chance Of Encounter:

Population Density	Base Chance Of Encounter
relatively dense	1 in 20
moderate to sparse/patrolled	1 in 12
uninhabited/wilderness	1 in 10

FREQUENCY OF ENCOUNTER CHANCE TIME CHECKS:

Type Of Terrain	Check For Encounter At					
	Morning	Noon	Evening	Night	Midnight	Pre-Dawn
Plain	x	-	x	-	x	-
Scrub	x	-	x	x	-	x
Forest	x	x	x	x	x	x
Desert	x	-	-	x	-	x
Hills	-	x	-	x	-	x
Mountains	x	-	-	x	-	-
Marsh	x	x	x	x	x	x

x = check for encounter

- = do not check unless party numbers over 100 creatures

Procedure: Daylight hours consist of morning, noon, and evening; night consists of night, midnight, and pre-dawn. These times equate to periods of about an hour after the party sets forth for the day, the mid-point of the journey, and near the end when camp is being made with respect to daylight hours. During hours of darkness, equate the periods to first, middle, and end sleep periods. Where only 1 or 2 chances for encounter exist, you may vary the time as you see fit in order to avoid player reliance on information which they should not be privy to. When an encounter check is indicated, roll the appropriate die, and if a 1 results, an encounter takes place. In this event, go to the appropriate table for the terrain, and determine randomly what sort of monster is being encountered. **Note:** In areas where you have detailed the monster population, a random determination should not be necessary, as this information should be recorded by you.

When an actual meeting does occur, consult the explanations accompanying the table for any special procedures to follow. Attempts by the encountering party to *evade* are dealt with under **COMBAT, PURSUIT AND EVASION OF PURSUIT** (q.v.).

Encounter Distance: If either party is surprised, the encounter distance is determined by subtracting the value of surprise (as determined by the die which indicated that the condition existed) from normal encounter distance. Normal encounter distance is 6″ to 24″ (6d4). Thus, on a surprise roll of 1, for example, encounter distance is 5″ to 23″ (6d4 −1), on a 2 the distance is 4″ to 22″, etc. In addition to shortening encounter distance, surprise also allows the surprising party to have that number of segments as shown on the die as the surprise factor as free and unanswered activity to move, attack, flee, etc. (See **SURPRISE.**) In addition to modification for surprise, terrain will also modify encounter distance as follows:

Scrub — −1 per die on all 3's and 4's
Forest— −1 per die on all numbers (00's are possible)
Marsh— −1 per die on all 2's, 3's, and 4's

Plain, desert, hills, and mountains do not alter encounter distance variables unless one of the three modifying types of terrain also exists. If final encounter distance is 1″ or less, than a *confrontation* will usually take place.

Confrontation: Confrontation indicates that the adventurers and some monster have met at close proximity, and some interaction is likely to take place. There are, however, modifying circumstances:

1) If the monsters are intelligent and would normally deem themselves to be weaker than the party of adventurers, then they will always seek to avoid such confrontation.

2) If the party of adventurers surprises the monsters and elects to flee the encounter, they may attempt to avoid confrontation by using free segments of action to move out of confrontation distance and evade the monsters.

Confrontation interaction can consist of any number of actions, singly or in combination — parley and reaction, spell casting, missile fire, melee combat, etc.

Movement:

As mentioned previously, movement rates have been given elsewhere. There rates assume that a party of from 1 to 100 creatures are concerned. If more than 100 are in the party, reduce movement rate by 1 mile per day for each additional 100 or fraction thereof, but in no event should such adjustment slow the rate of movement of the party to below 50% of normal speed.

Becoming Lost: Any party not guided by a creature knowledgeable of the countryside through which the party is moving, or which is not following a well defined course (river, road, or the like), or which is not using a well-drawn and correct map, might become lost. This is determined prior to the commencement of a day's movement. Determination is based on the terrain:

Terrain Type	Chance Of Becoming Lost	Direction
Plain	1 in 10	60° left or right
Scrub	3 in 10	60° left or right
Forest	7 in 10	any
Rough	3 in 10	60° left or right
Desert	4 in 10	60° left or right
Hills	2 in 10	60° left or right
Mountains	5 in 10	120° left or right
Marsh	6 in 10	any

To find the direction of movement if a party is lost, roll d6, 1-3 indicating left, 4-6 indicating right. Each hex face is 60°. If a loss of direction of 120° is possible, roll a second d6, 1-3 indicating a 60° direction loss, 4-6 indicating 120°. In any direction, loss is possible, roll a single d6, with results being read off clockwise considering the intended direction of travel as 12 o'clock, and giving 2 chances for complete loss and movement in the exact opposite direction, thus: 1 = right ahead, 2 = right behind, 3-4 = directly behind, 5 = left behind, and 6 = left ahead, i.e. there is NO chance of the party ever accidentally moving in the desired direction when the die indicates the condition of being lost exists. Direction of lost movement is illustrated below:

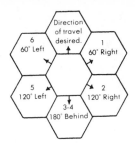

Procedure For Lost Parties:

As soon as the die roll indicates the party is lost, determine the direction. If it is onto a space which has previously been travelled over and mapped by the party, then they will recognize that they became lost. Tell them that they moved in **X** direction, rather than that which was desired, but they have seen landmarks and realize their error. If movement is into an area where the party has not already been and mapped, then immediately roll again to determine if the party will be lost the next day also. If no such lost direction is indicated, then the party will realize it has made an error the next day; but meanwhile describe terrain as if they had actually moved in the desired direction, i.e. as if they had not been lost with regards to direction. This will, of course, result in the erroneous mapping of a space until corrected. If the party will also be lost the following day, the procedure above is followed until they are no longer lost. At that point, they will realize that they have *not* been moving in the desired direction, or series of directions, but they will NOT know just where they became lost. They will have to back-track and attempt to locate the last space which they mapped correctly and go on again from that place.

It must be understood that parties following a correct map will never become lost. Procedures are only for exploration of unmapped terrain.

Rest: Movement rates are postulated on sufficient daily rest periods so as to obviate the necessity for any protracted rest periods of a day or more during the course of any journey. If normal movement rate is exceeded, however, then special rest periods in addition to any subsumed brief breaks in travel are required. This is detailed below:

Forced Movement: It is possible to make forced marches up to twice the distance shown for daily movement rate. Such forced movement increases the daily rate in 10% increments, from 10% to 100% at the option of the party, to a maximum of double normal movement rate; but as soon as a total of 100% of additional normal movement rate is reached, or as soon as the party determines to assume non-forced movement, whichever first occurs, a mandatory rest period must be enforced. Rest period depends upon the total percentage of forced movement:

10% - 30% = 1 hour per 10%
40% - 60% = 2 hours per 10%
70% - 100% = 3 hours per 10%

To find the time required for enforced rest, simply find the total percentage of rest time and deduct this from normal daily movement rate. Thus, 30% means that 30% of movement the next day is deducted, as the party rested during that period. At 3 hours per 10% increment of forced movement, 70% equals 210%, so 2 full days, plus 10% of a third day must be spent in rest from the forced march.

Failure to rest after normal movement is equal to 100% means that beasts of burden have a cumulative chance of dropping dead of 10% per 10% increment of additional movement of any sort. Other creatures lose 1 level of ability or hit die in the same manner, until 0 is reached and exhaustion kills them. Such loss of vitality, whether by beast of burden, creature, or character requires a full 8 hours of additional rest for each such 10% increment, hit die, or level of ability lost. For example, a 12th level fighter who moves an additional 90% of movement after exceeding normal movement by 100% must rest 72 hours, consecutively, in order to regain 12th level of ability. Prior to that period of rest, the character is effectively 3rd level!

ADVENTURES IN THE AIR

To be able to fly is one of mankind's oldest and strongest fantasies. In the world of **AD&D**, this wish can often be fulfilled. However, travel and combat in the air is often much different from that which takes place in the two-dimensional realm of the earthbound, so much so that it must needs have a special section devoted to it.

AERIAL TRAVEL

Long-distance aerial travel can be accomplished by use of either magical device or flying mount. Certain magic items (such as a *broom* or *carpet of flying*) do not have limited duration of use, and thus are the most efficient forms of such travel (though a *broom of flying* may not be very comfortable to use for hours on end).

Your players may want to know how far they can go in a day on a *flying carpet* (or other similar device). For the purposes of long-distance aerial travel, assume every 3″ of speed equals one mile per hour. Thus, a *broom of flying*, with a speed of 30″, can fly long distances at an average speed of 10 m.p.h., and can cover about 100 miles in a day (assuming ten hours of semi-continuous travel during daylight). The above formula does *not* necessarily apply to short-distance travel.

If your players are unimpressed by these kinds of distances, remind them that in a pre-technological civilization they are little short of miraculous. Some of your players may have walked as far as twenty miles in one day. Ask them to remember how far it was.

Flying Mounts:

Most flying mounts will be either griffons, hippogriffs or pegasi. All of these should be very difficult to acquire, and even harder to train. None of these types will mix with the others (griffons will eat pegasi or hippogriffs if given a chance, and hippogriffs confined with pegasi will bully-rag them whenever possible).

Griffons are often nasty and bad-tempered. If captured when very young and trained, however, they can become fiercely loyal mounts. Their loyalty is non-transferable once fixed, so they must be disciplined and trained solely by the intended rider. The griffon must be trained and exercised by its owner on a fairly regular basis while it is a fledgling (up to age six months) in order to accustom it to his or her presence and the bridle, blanket, saddle, etc. When the griffon is half-grown a period of intensive training must begin, which will last at least four months. The daily routine must never be broken for more than two days, or the griffon's wild nature will assert itself and all progress will be lost. After two months of this intensive training, it will be possible to begin to fly the griffon. This will be a period of training for mount and owner alike, as the rider must learn how to deal with a new dimension, and he will probably have no teacher but himself. Imagine the confusing tumult of giant wings, the rush of air, the sudden changes in altitude, and you will realize why an inexperienced rider absolutely *cannot* handle a flying mount.

Griffons, like all large flying creatures, eat enormous amounts of food, especially after prolonged aviation. Moreover, they are carnivores, and thus very expensive to feed. Care and keeping of a griffon will be a constant strain on the largest treasure hoard. Costs will probably run in the area of 300-600 g.p. per month. It will require special quarters, at least three grooms and keepers, and occasionally an entire horse for dinner (diet will differ, but similar arrangements must be made for all flying mounts).

Hippogriffs are not so difficult to train as griffons, but neither are they as dependable in a pinch. A training process basically similar to that previously described will be necessary, though occasionally an animal trainer can substitute for the master for short periods if he or she is tied up elsewhere. Once broken, hippogriffs may possibly serve more than one master. They are omnivores, and thus somewhat less expensive to feed than griffons.

Pegasi are greatly valued for their speed, which makes them virtually the fastest things in the air. Their training is a long process similar in many respects to that of griffons. They will serve only *good* characters — all others will find them totally intractable. Like griffons, their loyalty is given to only one master in a lifetime.

All flying mounts must rest one hour for every three they fly, and they can never fly more than nine hours a day. During their rest periods they will eat as if famished: this means meat for griffons or hippogriffs, and green living plants, preferably of a succulent nature, or fine hay and oats, for pegasi.

Use of more exotic types of flying mounts will generally require some form of spell control (such as *charm monster*), though the more intelli-

gent ones may possibly give their permission and cooperation in certain circumstances. This does not ensure ease of handling and stability on the part of the rider, however. Likewise, griffons, hippogriffs and pegasi can be charmed and ridden.

To be able to fight while flying any aerial mount requires considerable practice. To become adept at aerial archery entails at least two months of continual practice (cf. **AERIAL COMBAT, Aerial Missile Fire**).

AERIAL COMBAT

Most creatures which can fly do so by means of wings, either natural or magically augmented (as in such inherently magical beings as demons and devils, dragons, griffons, etc.). Most winged creatures must be constantly flapping their wings to provide enough thrust to keep their weight in the air. Some creatures are light enough and powerful enough to allow them to actually hover in one place, but most must be constantly moving forward. This means that aerial combat is nearly always going to be a swoop and slash, hit-and-run affair. Grappling of opponents in the air will generally result in both of them plummeting to the ground, unless they are at a high altitude and disengage almost immediately. Even then, it is a risky business. Only beings with the ability to hover (gained either through quick and powerful wings or some form of magical flight) will be able to engage in combat that resembles the round-after-round melee system employed in ground battle.

It will therefore be seen that maneuverability is of prime importance in conducting aerial combat. Flying combatants — whether they are eagles or dragons, men mounted on broomsticks, or hippogriffs — must make attack passes at their opponents, wheel about in the air, and attack again. Those which are more maneuverable will be able to change direction and speed in a shorter time than those which are less maneuverable, and thus have some advantage in pursuit and avoidance.

To conduct an aerial battle, a DM must know the speed, maneuverability and attack modes of each creature involved.

Speed:

Speed of flight of each creature is listed with the other information in the **AD&D MONSTER MANUAL**, and it will be noted again in the list of aerial creatures at the end of this section. When conducting aerial combat that takes place entirely in the air, it will be convenient to convert *inches per turn* to *inches* (or *hexes*) *per round*.

For the sake of standardization, all flying creatures can climb at one-half, and dive at twice the stated movement rate. They will be able to climb one foot for every three feet they move forward, but they may dive up to one foot downward for each foot travelled forward (i.e., at a 45-degree angle. None of the above applies to creatures with class A maneuverability, which can move in any direction they choose.). When diving, all creatures' physical attacks will do double damage to all targets which are not themselves diving. This includes diving attacks at earthbound creatures which come from a height of 30 feet or more. There is no damage penalty for attack while climbing. No creature will be able to climb above 5000 feet (due to lack of breathable air) as a general rule, but you may alter the ceiling if you wish.

Maneuverability:

Naturally, every type of flying creature maneuvers differently from every other type, but in order to make the game playable and aerial combat possible, maneuverability has been broken down into five classes. These vary from A to E, most maneuverable to least maneuverable. Note that the stated amount the creature can turn per round assumes that the creature is moving at full speed. Creatures moving at half speed turn as one class better. Winged creatures cannot move at less than one-half speed and remain airborne (except for class B).

Class A: Creature can turn 180° per round, and requires 1 segment to reach full airspeed. Creature requires 1 segment to come to a full stop in the air, and can hover in place. Class A creatures have total and almost instantaneous control of their movements in the air. Examples: djinn, air elementals, aerial servants, couatl.

Class B: Creature can turn 120° per round, and requires 6 segments to reach full airspeed. Creature requires 5 segments to come to a full stop in the air, and can hover in place. Examples: *fly* spell, sprites, sylphs, giant wasps, ki-rin.

Class C: Creature can turn 90° per round, and requires 1 round to reach full airspeed. Examples: *carpet* or *wings of flying,* gargoyles, harpies, pegasi, lammasu, shedu.

Class D: Creature can turn 60° per round, and requires 2 rounds to reach full airspeed. Examples: pteranodons, sphinxes, *mounted* pegasi.

Class E: Creature can turn 30° per round, and requires 4 rounds to reach full airspeed. Examples: dragons, rocs, wyverns.

Attack Modes:

As mentioned previously, grappling in the air is usually out of the question. This means that many different creatures will use considerably different combat tactics in the air, and their "natural" methods of attack will often be substantially altered. The following list should help the DM determine how certain creatures will fight in the air. Speed and maneuverability class are also listed. For reasons of space or redundancy, not all flying creatures have been included. Once familiar with the system, the DM should be able to apply it to any aerial monster.

Aerial servant: 24″, class A. If forced to fight, an aerial servant usually resorts to battering.

Chimera: 18″, class E. The chimera is a clumsy flyer, and prefers to use its breath weapon in aerial battles. It can use its claws or attack with *one* of its heads.

Cockatrice: 18″, class C. The cockatrice is not a strong, steady flyer, and will not go above 300′ unless provoked into one of its screaming fits of rage. In any case, it will never fly for more than 2-5 turns before landing to rest. The cockatrice's power to turn *flesh to stone* is an awful one, as it often need only hit to destroy its enemies, and those petrified in the air usually fall and shatter!

Couatl: 18″, class A. The couatl's favorite tactic is to throw loops around other flying creatures and constrict them so that neither couatl nor prey can fly. Both plummet to the earth, but the couatl turns ethereal just before impact and thus escapes being crushed.

DAEMONS:

Nycadaemon: 36″, class D. Though heavy, nycadaemons are powerful flyers, and can build up great speed and momentum. They act much like flying battering rams, striking for 2-12 points of damage when they hit (or as much as 3-18 if they hit another flyer head-on, though this will also damage the nycadaemon 1-4 points). A nycadaemon will try to run its prey close to the ground and then close for a grapple. The wings will be used to batter and confuse and slow their fall, as it attempts to bring its opponent down to the ground where leverage and its full physical strength can be brought to bear.

DEMONS:

Succubus: 18″, class C. Succubi prefer not to melee in the air or on the ground, and will use guile, treachery and *etherealness* whenever possible.

Type I: 18″, class C. These vulture-demons generally slash with their rear talons.

Type IV: 12″, class E. **Type VI:** 15″, class D. These two huge demon types will try to bring their foes to the ground, much like nycadaemons.

DEVILS: All devils' power of *illusion* makes them difficult and dangerous aerial opponents.

Erinyes: 21″, class C. Erinyes will slash with their envenomed dagger or use their *rope of entanglement* to foul opponents' wings and make them fall.

Horned devil: 18″, class D. Horned devils will attempt to impale with their fork and rip with their tails as they pass.

Pit Fiend: 15″, class D. These mightiest of devils will usually attempt to force their prey to the ground, where they can leisurely tear them

limb from limb. Their clubs and tails are dangerous weapons in the air.

DINOSAURS:

Pteranodon: 15″, class C. These creatures' light bone structure makes them unwilling to collide with other creatures in the air, but if necessary they will attempt to spear with their long, pointed beaks. Their preferred method of attack is to drop upon earthbound creatures from above, lift them up to several hundred feet and then allow them to plummet to their deaths.

Djinni: 24″, class A. Djinn, like all creatures from the aerial plane, are nearly impossible to catch in the air. When a swooping creature approaches them, they simply move aside. In addition, their ability to *create illusions* and *become invisible* ensures that all aerial combat will take place only when and where the djinni desires. They are openly contemptuous of those who need wings to fly, or magical aviators such as magic-users and efreet.

Dragon: 24″ or 30″, class E. Lack of maneuverability due to large size may seem to put dragons at a disadvantage in the air, but their powerful breath weapons somewhat make up for this. On an attack pass, a dragon can either bite or use its claws — never both. A dragon may choose to breathe on an approach and then pass and slash with fang or claw.

Eagle, giant: 48″, class D. Giant eagles commonly attack with their talons. They share with their smaller cousins the ability to plummet almost to the ground and then suddenly break their fall and pull out or land safely.

Efreeti: 24″, class B. As with djinn, efreet use their *invisibility* and *illusion* abilities to good effect in aerial combat.

Elemental, air: 36″, class A. Air elementals gain +1 to hit and +2 on each die of damage they inflict when fighting in the air. They move in the same manner as djinn.

Gargoyle: 15″, class C. Gargoyles will attempt to spear with their horn or slash with their claws (never both).

Griffon: 30″, class C (class D when mounted). A griffon will either slash with its forward talons or bite with its powerful beak.

Harpy: 15″, class C. Harpies will use either their leg talons or a weapon in aerial battle. Like eagles, they can plummet straight down and then pull out.

Hippogriff: 36″, class C (class D when mounted). Hippogriffs fight in much the same manner as griffons.

Ki-rin: 48″, class B. Ki-rin will generally attack with their horn to impale.

Lammasu: 24″, class C. Lammasu will use their claws if forced to fight. They are hard to hit in the air, as they can *dimension door* away from an attack path.

Manticore: 18″, class E. Manticores are clumsy flyers, but they will not hesitate to fling their tail spikes at opponents who come too close (cf. **AERIAL COMBAT, Aerial Missile Fire**). They can also employ their front claws.

MEN: Men, like monsters, must behave differently in the air than on the ground. Most flying combat involving humans consists of magical or magically-equipped flyers rising above a melee to gain a positional advantage for the purpose of spell- or missile-casting. This actually isn't as easy as most players would like to think it is, as the different forms of magical flight often have requirements which interfere with such actions.

Levitation: Once effected, this spell takes no concentration on the part of the caster except during changes of height, so it is quite useful when a magic-user desires to rise above a melee to acquire an open field of fire for his or her spells. The major drawback is that figures rising out of a battle are automatically assumed to be magic-users and will immediately attract most if not all of their opponents' missile fire. Recipients of the *levitation* spell who wish to use bows from their elevated position will find that they are not totally stable, and thus shooting is slightly more difficult. Such archers will shoot at −1 "to hit". This is cumulative, subtracting another point from the archer's chance to hit for each successive round of fire until −3 is reached, as the archer becomes increasingly unstable. Continued firing will not lower the archer's chances beyond –3, and any round spent not firing (or fighting) will allow him or her to stabilize and start again at –1. Slinging, casting javelins or spears, or actually swinging a weapon (such as a sword) will be at double the minuses "to hit" for archery, i.e., –2, –4, –6. Due to the lack of leverage and something to "push" against, it is impossible to cock a heavy or medium crossbow while levitating (let your players find this out for themselves!). *Levitating* persons are marvelous targets for flying creatures. They can generally be treated as earthbound targets which are easier to get at, and fight at a disadvantage.

The DM should remember that though the recipient of a *fly* spell has full control of his or her movement, the height of a recipient of *levitation* is always under the control of the caster, and if that person is otherwise occupied, no vertical movement is possible (of course, this does not apply to magical devices such as *boots of levitation*, though everything else in the foregoing section is applicable).

Fly spell: Utilizing a *fly* spell takes as much concentration as walking, so most spells could be cast while *flying*, either while hovering or moving slowly (3″ or less). There is no penalty for archery while *flying* (assuming the archers are hovering — if they are moving, see **AERIAL COMBAT, Aerial Missile Fire**), but there are minuses for slinging or swinging weapons, and these are the same as the penalties for archery while *levitating*, i.e., –1 to hit, cumulative per successive rounds until –3 is reached. Persons using a *fly* spell (or a magical device which confers that power upon the bearer, such as a *ring of flying*) will move at maneuverability class B. *Flying* persons involved in ground melees attract missile fire much as *levitators* do. *Flying* persons involved in combat with other aerial creatures do so in the same manner as any other creature of their maneuverability class.

Broom of flying: These devices must be moving at least half speed to function. With practice, they can be controlled by the rider's knees, so an experienced broomsman can melee in the air. However, all spell use is impossible while riding a broom, though some magical devices (such as wands) could be used. Brooms are maneuverability class C.

Carpet of flying: Carpets are the most stable of flying devices, and thus the most valuable. Though they are class C as pertains to maneuverability, they can hover or move at any speed the controller desires (up to the stated maximum). While hovering or moving slowly they are ideal platforms for spell- or missile-casting (quick motion tends to disrupt magical concentration, even if the spell-user is not the one controlling the carpet). They are not so easily adapted to aerial melee, as passengers will tend to get knocked off the carpet and fall to the ground. Attempts to weave straps or seat belts into a *flying carpet* will generally destroy its dweomer.

Wings of flying: These devices are maneuverability class C and the wearer must be moving at least half speed to maintain flight. Though the *wings* leave the aviator's hands free for fighting, it is impossible to concentrate enough to cast spells due to the continual bodily motion involved. This does not prohibit the use of some magical devices that duplicate spell effects (rings, wands, etc.). Like an eagle, the wearer of *wings of flying* can plummet a great distance and still pull out safely if the wings have not been previously damaged.

Flying mounts: All flying mounts will move at one maneuverability class worse than normal when mounted. This applies even if the rider is as small as a halfling or gnome. The only exceptions to this are E class creatures such as dragons, which are large enough to carry human-sized riders at no penalty. Normal spell use while riding a flying mount is of course impossible (though certain magic devices may be used).

Pegasus: 48″, class C (class D when mounted). In flight, pegasi fight with their front hooves.

Peryton: 21″, class C. A peryton will attempt to impale with its sharp horns.

Pseudo-dragon: 24″, class B. Pseudo-dragons rely on their poisonous stingers in aerial combat.

Roc: 30″, class E. Rocs generally attack using their huge and powerful talons. Amazingly enough, considering their great size, they can plummet straight down like eagles and then arrest their fall by a sudden unfurling of their wings.

Shedu: 24″, class C. Shedu will strike with their powerful hooves if they become involved in aerial combat, though their power to become *ethereal* allows them to avoid this if they so desire.

Sphinx: 24″, 30″ or 36″, class D. The various sphinxes nearly always employ their fore claws in an aerial battle, though the roar of the androsphinx is also a potent weapon, as it weakens opponents and could make them unable to fly.

Wyvern: 24″, class E. On an attack pass, a wyvern will attempt to either bite or sting.

Conducting Combat:

Conducting aerial combat will be much simplified if the DM will remember that most flying monsters simply cannot execute complicated maneuvers like barrel rolls or loop-the-loops. Most can do nothing more than climb, dive and/or turn, and all of these actions are easily simulated and quantified using speed and maneuverability classes.

There are two methods you can use to conduct aerial combat. The first way is simple but less accurate. The second method is more accurate but requires the use of hex paper or a hex map. Though both can be done on paper, the best way to visualize the relative positions of the combatants is to employ miniature figures or paper counters. A running record of absolute (or relative) altitude should be kept, either on a separate sheet or on a small piece of paper under each figure or counter.

The simple method is to move each flyer in the direction they are facing at the beginning of the move, and execute the turn at the end by simply refacing the flyer in its new direction. Speed would be in actual inches of movement, or some ratio thereof.

A more accurate method entails the use of hex paper so that actual arc turns can be indicated, and so that these turns may take place at any time during a move.

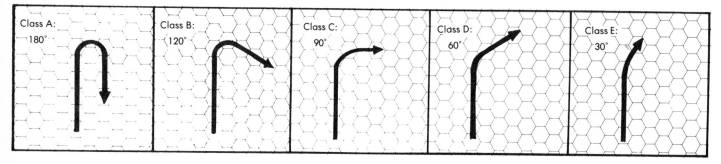

Turns will actually take place through several hexes (the only exceptions to this are creatures from the elemental plane of air, which can turn on a dime in any direction they wish). A turn need not be executed through consecutive hexes. To illustrate, here are possible variant turns for a class B flyer, which can turn up to 120° in one round:

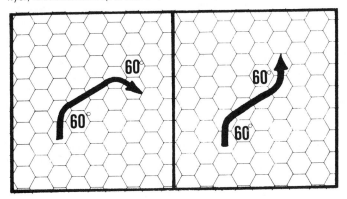

The orders for the first example would read: Straight 1, right 60°, straight 3, right 60°, straight 1.

Each flyer can move 1 hex per 3″ of speed; thus, a gargoyle with a speed of 15″, could move 5 hexes, while a griffon, with a speed of 30″, could move 10. Keep in mind climbing and diving speed alterations.

In both the simple and complex methods, movement should be simultaneous. If there are several players involved, you may wish to have them write out their moves ahead of time (the DM, of course, is not obligated to do this). If two opponents are clearly making for each other, and it is within their ability to intercept but their written orders would cause them to miss, some slight adjustment should be made.

Aerial Missile Fire: For all missiles fired in the air, treat short range as medium (−2 to hit) and medium range as long (−5 to hit) as pertains to chance of hitting. Fire at objects at long range will always miss. The above applies to missile firers on flying mounts or using a *broom or wings of flying* only if they have spent several months in practice. Otherwise, they will not be able to hit at all. The range penalties also apply to missile-firing creatures such as manticores (treat as composite long bow as pertains to range). Note that the above applies only to those who are moving. Those hovering with a *fly* spell or on a *carpet of flying* will suffer no penalties. Those levitating will be penalized as delineated in earlier subsection **Attack Modes, Men: Levitation.**

Dragons and similar creatures with breath weapons (such as chimerae) will have a slightly harder time hitting other flying creatures. For this reason, moving aerial targets of flying dragons add +2 to their saving throws.

Damage: Any winged creature which sustains damage greater than 50% of its hit points will be unable to maintain flight and must land. Any winged creature which sustains more than 75% damage will not even be able to control its fall, and will plummet to the ground. This simulates damage to the wings, as in aerial combat, the wings will be a prime point of vulnerability. Feathered wings are not as easy to damage as membranous wings, and in flight should be given an extra hit point value equal to one-half the normal hit points of the creature they support, for the purpose of figuring how much damage need be taken before the creature can no longer fly. Thus, a griffon with 30 hit points would add an additional illusory 15 points in aerial combat, for a flight-damage total of 45, and thus would be able to take 23 points of damage before it would be forced to land. In contrast, a membrane-winged creature like a succubus with 30 hit points would only be able to sustain 15 points of damage before it could no longer fly. *Under no conditions are the extra flight-damage points to be added to the monster's actual hit points for the purpose of absorbing damage.* A flying monster will only be able to sustain the normal amount of damage it usually takes in order to incapacitate or kill it, i.e., if the exemplary griffon above takes 31 points of damage from dragon breath, it is dead.

As a final note, remember that heroic aviators who leap into the saddle of their hippogriff and rise to battle without taking a couple of rounds to strap in will tend to fall out in the first round of melee, and it is 1-6 hit points of damage for every ten feet they fall (up to a maximum 20-120 points).

WATERBORNE ADVENTURES

In due course your players will evince a desire to travel by water. Rivers, lakes and the seas have always provided mankind with a means of transportation and livelihood as well. From the first raft and reed boat, ambatche and catamaran, the waters have beckoned men to come and explore. This form of adventure certainly awaits the participants of an **AD&D** campaign — with a vengeance! Encounters are dealt with in **APPENDIX C: RANDOM MONSTER ENCOUNTERS, WATERBORNE ENCOUNTERS,** this being subdivided into fresh and salt water encounters. Information regarding ships, their armament and crews, is detailed here. The rules are general in nature to allow playing at any scale or upon any playing surface desired (hex or square grid, floor, etc.).

General Classes of Vessels:

Rowboat: Small boats, with or without a sail, which are rowed by oars or paddled, fall into this category. A ship's longboats, dugout canoes, skiffs and punts are likewise considered rowboats. A normal crew for a rowboat can be from one to ten or more men depending on its size. Rowboats do not come equipped with armament and don't function well in breezes above 19 miles per hour.

Barges/Rafts: These are long, somewhat rectangular craft designed primarily for river transportation. A few larger and sturdier types are used for lake and coastal duties. Barges generally have a shallow draft, as do rafts — the former having a bow and side freeboard, with the latter having neither. The Egyptian Queen Hatshepsut's obelisk barge is a prime example of a working barge. Crafts constructed of fagots bound together, or made of stretched hides, such as the umiak, are considered barges in most cases. The same is true of sampans and jangadas. Normal crew for a barge varies between 20 and 100 or more men, depending on the size of the ship and its purpose. If the barge is a working vessel, such as Queen Hatshepsut's, it is conceivable that it could require as many as 100 men, if not more, to man such a mammoth barge. Sampans and jangadas, on the other hand, do not require a great crew to man them. Sampans need only three to ten men while jangadas require as few as one. Barges and rafts don't usually come with armament, but can be so equipped if desired. These types of vessels do not function well in winds above moderate breezes.

Galleys: These are long, slim oared ships. Some of the earlier types of galleys are the Greek and Roman biremes, triremes, and quadriremes. These galleys have 2, 3, and 4 banks of oars. The type most commonly used in **AD&D** is the drakkar, the Viking Dragon Ship. This is a square-sailed, oared ship having a single mast that can be unstepped. She is the easiest to maneuver in choppy waters because the planks are overlapped and riveted together (clinker built). This gives her the ability to move with the waves instead of forcing her hull through them. Crew for galleys depend on their size. Some can have as few as 30 men manning the oars while others have been known to have 200 or more. Most galleys, because of the need of space for the men at the oars, do not venture far from land. The general construction is such that even though she is seaworthy it is more comfortable to be near land or sail the rivers and make camp on the shore. Armament on galleys ranges from a ram to ballistae. Some of the larger ones may even sport a catapult.

Merchant Ships: This type of ship is most commonly a small wide-hulled vessel having a single mast and a lateen sail. She is not only favored by merchants, but pirates as well. She can be moved by sweeps at rowboat speed. Cogs, carracks and caravels of the 13th and 14th centuries are considered to be excellent merchant ships because of their sturdiness and the few sailors required to man them. Most ships of this type can feasibly carry a hundred or more men, but because of on-board conditions and money, ships are manned by a minimal crew of at least 10 men, including the officers. Pirates are the exception when manning ships. They will fill the ship with men, sailing up and down the coast for about a week, plunder if they can, and then put into port. Typical armament for this kind of ship includes ballistae and perhaps a catapult.

Warships: These vessels tend to be fast, but at most times not very seaworthy, particularly the earlier ones. The ultimate warship for the purpose of **AD&D** is the nao. She is squaresailed like the cog, but features two or more masts and is of caravel construction. She also has a distinctive overhanging forecastle and a rounded stern. The crew of a warship generally consists of 2 or 3 men to work each ballista, 3 or 4 men to handle the catapult and the rest to man the sails. It is possible to have 100 or more men on board, but because of the shortage of space for food and fresh water, the number is usually considerably less.

Hull Values:

The hull value or the defensive point value is how much damage the ship can sustain before sinking (any time that damage reaches one-third or more of this value, repairs must be made). For damage done to a ship by various attack forms, see **Siege Attack** under **CONSTRUCTION AND SIEGES**. To determine the number of points each ship can have, see the table below and roll accordingly.

Type of Vessel	Hull Value Range
Rowboat	1-4
Barge, small	1-6
Barge, large	2-8
Galley, small	2-12
Galley, large	4-16
Merchant, small	6-36
Merchant, large	12-48
Warship	7-42

Repairing Damage:

Any time damage reaches one third to one half of a ship's hull value, repairs can be made at sea. If the damage is more than one half, the ship must put into port for repairs. The amount of time and repairs needed as well as the cost involved will be at the DM's option.

Length and Width:

The average length and width of most ships is given below. It will be up to the DM or the players buying or constructing them to determine exactly how long and wide any ship will be.

Ship	Length	Width
Rowboat	8'-20'	2'-4'
Barge, small	15'-20'	8'-12'
Barge, large	25'-45'	12'-20'
Galley, small	30'-60'	8'-15'
Galley, large	120'-160'	20'-30'
Merchant, small	25'-40'	10'-15'
Merchant, large	50'-80'	15'-25'
Warship	70'-100'	15'-25'

Crew:

See **Ship Master** and **Ship Crew** under **EXPERT HIRELINGS**.

Wind Direction and Force:

Wind direction and its force are important in determining if sails, oars, both, or neither can best be used in propelling the ship. Currents of course will aid or hinder the ship, but it will be up to the DM to decide what currents, if any, will be in the oceans. Wind force will need to be determined for movement abilities and damage if the force is above Strong Gale.

Direction (d8)

1	North	5	Northwest
2	South	6	Northeast
3	East	7	Southwest
4	West	8	Southeast

Force (3d6)

		Miles Per Hour
3	Calm	0-1
4-8	Light Breeze	2-7
9-12	Moderate Breeze	8-18
13-15	Strong Breeze	19-31
16	Strong Gale	32-54
17	Storm	55-72
18	Hurricane	73-136

Any wind of strong gale force or better will have a percentage chance to do damage to the ship. There is also a chance for men to be blown overboard. The amount of damage and how many men may be blown overboard will be determined by the DM. Checks are made every 6 hours, or until winds subside.

	Strong Gale	Storm	Hurricane
Capsizing	1%	20%	40%
Broken mast	5%	25%	45%
Broken beams	10%	35%	50%
Torn sail and/or fouled rigging	20%	45%	65%
Man overboard	10%	50%	70%

Exhaustion:

Exhaustion will occur after the crew has rowed at their normal speed for 8-10 hours or at maximum speed for 30 minutes. This applies only to galleys or any other oared vessel.

Movement:

Any oared ship can move forward from a complete standstill in one round. Galleys are able to do a pivot only if they are dead still in the water. This action requires a certain amount of skill or else the oars may be damaged. Any ship wanting to turn must let her momentum carry her twice her length before such a procedure may begin.

Movement From a Standstill Position to Normal Speed:

Barge, small	2 rounds
Barge, large	5 rounds
Galley, small	3 rounds
Galley, large	6 rounds
Merchant, small	5 rounds
Merchant, large	1 turn
Warship	1 turn

Speed:

The table below indicates how fast ships can sail or be oared at normal and maximum speed.

Ship Type	Normal Sail	Maximum Sail*	Normal Oar	Maximum Oar**
Rowboat	2 mph	3 mph	1 mph	2 mph
Barge, small	2 mph	3 mph	1 mph	1 mph
Barge, large	1 mph	2 mph	½ mph	1 mph
Galley, small	6 mph	9 mph	5 mph	8 mph
Galley, large	4 mph	7 mph	4 mph	8 mph
Merchant, small	5 mph	7 mph	½ mph	1 mph
Merchant, large	3 mph	5 mph	¼ mph	½ mph
Warship	4 mph	6 mph	½ mph	1 mph

* Based on the wind force of Strong Breeze.

** For short periods of 10-20 minutes.

Burn Damage of Controlled Fires:

For every 10 flaming arrows, every flaming catapult missile, and every 5-dice *fireball* and up (i.e., a 10-dice *fireball* requires a double check) that hits, burn damage will have to be determined. *Lightning bolts* will have to be checked for burn damage at increments of 8-dice. Anything below that only does structural damage (see **CONSTRUCTION AND SIEGES, SIEGE ATTACK VALUES**). When a *lightning bolt* does burn damage, subtract 3 from the roll for the kind of damage that is done (for example, a 15 is rolled, 15 − 3 = 12; twelve is the number on the table to determine damage).

Fire Damage (3d6)

		Hull Damage Equivalent
3-7	Light damage	1 point of hull damage
8-10	Light to moderate damage	2-4 points of hull damage
11-13	Moderate damage	3-6 points of hull damage
14-15	Moderate to heavy damage	4-8 points of hull damage
16-18	Heavy damage	5-10 points of hull damage

Light damage: Almost no damage. Requires no immediate attention. When a ship has sustained more than 3 light damages, consider it to be light to moderate damage.

Light to moderate damage: Minor damage done. No immediate repairs needed. When a ship has sustained 2 light damages and 1 light to moderate damage or 2 light to moderate damages, consider it to be moderate damage.

Moderate damage: A few minor repairs needed before the ship can get underway. When a ship has sustained 2 moderate damages, consider it to be moderate to heavy damage.

Moderate to heavy damage: Many minor repairs needed or several major ones needed before the ship may sail. When a ship has sustained 2 moderate to heavy damages, consider it to be heavy damage.

Heavy damage: Extensive repairs needed to ship's sails and mast. Rigging burned badly.

The DM will have to decide what part of the ship took damage. The amount will be determined by what did the damage to the ship. This will have to be subtracted from the ship's hull value.

Ships' Burning Time of Uncontrolled Fires:

Damage done to a ship by fire that equals or surpasses the hull value is considered a fire that is no longer under control by the men aboard. Also, any fires magically fed and not countered have a 75% chance of spreading out of control due to the time, lack of men or capable magic-user, or other circumstances.

Ship Type	Burning Time
Rowboat	1 turn
Barge, small	1-2 turns
Barge, large	1-4 turns
Galley, small	1-3 turns
Galley, large	1-6 turns
Merchant, small	2-8 turns
Merchant, large	3-12 turns
Warship	3-12 turns

Ramming:

Before any battle in which ramming is intended, the mast must be unstepped and secured on deck. Ramming (which can only be done by galleys) must be done head-on at full speed, with the galley striking the target ship at a 60-90° angle. After striking, the ramming ship must backwater immediately or risk sinking with the ship it rammed or being boarded by her crew if the hole is above the water line.

Grappling and Boarding:

Grappling is done when the men of one ship, by means of a grapnel and rope, attempt to secure their craft to another ship (or something else, should it be desired). There is a 25% chance that the men aboard the grappled ship will be able to successfully sever the line or remove the grapnel. If the attempt to remove the grapnel fails, the ship may find herself boarded by the men of the other ship. If both ships are of the same type, i.e., two galleys, then there are no bonuses for melee. However, if it is the crew of a galley trying to board a merchant ship or warship, the latter will attack with a +1 while the former with a –1. The reason is that the men aboard the merchant or warship have the advantage of height, and are fighting down at the men on the galley. When this happens, the men in the galley usually outnumber the men on the higher ship, by as much as three to one in some cases. This applies to all ships that are built with two or more decks.

Melee:

Human-like vs. human-like: On-board combat will be as normal melee combat in a dungeon. Sahuagin, lacedon (ghouls), kopoacinth (gargoyles), koalinth (hobgoblins) and men (buccaneers and pirates) will attempt to board the ship. Other human-like creatures such as nixies, aquatic elves, tritons, sea hags and mermen cannot or will not try to board.

Human-like vs. non-human: The men on a ship will be at a disadvantage fighting monsters in the water. A squid will try to encircle the ship with its tentacles and sink it. Other sea monsters may be just as dangerous.

See the **MONSTER MANUAL** for specifics of each monster.

Sinking a Ship:

There are several ways to sink a ship. One is to ram her, damaging her hull

and thus forcing her to take on water (see **Ramming**). Depending on the size of the ship and the location and size of the hole, it may take from 1-12 turns before she sinks below the surface of the water (rowboats and small rafts are the only vessels that will sink in less than 1 turn). Burning is another way to sink a ship. She will burn to her waterline and everything beneath that will sink (see **Burn Damage of Controlled Fires**). A rowboat hit directly with a boulder will sink immediately. It will take several direct hits with a boulder before enough damage is done to cause a merchant ship or warship to sink (see **Hull Values** and **Siege Engines**). The weather is also a factor that can cause a ship to capsize and eventually sink (see **Wind Direction and Force**). Some monsters, such as a Sea Snake or a Dragon Turtle, will also attempt to capsize a ship if they should choose to attack it.

Ship's Capture:

The capturing of a ship occurs when all the crew aboard one ship have died, surrendered, or are rendered helpless and unable to fight (trapped in the hold, for example). To determine if surrender will take place, compare the crews of both sides. If one side is greater by 3 to 1, surrender is inevitable by the side that is outnumbered. The captain of the losing side may refuse to surrender and order his men to continue fighting (a roll of 1 on a d6 indicates that his men will obey). Surrender does not apply to player characters. They decide whether or not they want to surrender.

Swimming:

Swimming will be impossible in any type of metal armor with the exception of magic armor. Any character wearing magic armor will be encumbered and the only stroke possible will be the dog paddle. It is possible to swim in leather and padded armor, but it is awkward and there is a 5% chance of drowning per hour. All heavy possessions must be discarded or the chance of drowning increases by 2% for every 5 pounds on the character's person other than his or her leather or padded armor. This includes weapons, purses filled with gold and/or gems, backpacks and hard boots. One unsheathed dagger may be carried by the adventurer between his or her teeth. Swimming during winds above 35 miles per hour will be almost impossible, and there is a 75% chance of drowning.

General Naval Terminology:

Aft — the rear part of a ship.
Corvice — a bridge with a long spike in its end used by the Romans for grappling and boarding.
Devil — the longest seam on the bottom of a wooden ship.
Devil to pay — chalking the seam of the same name. When this job is assigned, it is given to the ship's goof-off and thus comes the expression "You will have the devil to pay".
Fore — the forward part of a ship.
Fore Castle — a fortified wooden enclosure resembling a castle in the fore of a ship.
Hoist Sails — to raise the sails.
Lower the sails — to let the sails down.
Port — the left side of a ship; also a city or town where ships may take refuge or load and unload cargo.
Shearing off oars — accidentally or intentionally breaking oars of one or more ships when attempting to board or cripple the ship if it did not retract its oars.
Starboard — the right side of a ship.
Step — to put the mast up.
Stern — a section of the aft of a ship.
Stern Castle — the same as a fore castle except that it is in the stern of the ship.
Stroke — the drummer and the beat he sets for the oarsmen on a galley.
Top Castle — a fortified structure on the mast.
Unstep — to take down the mast.
Weigh Anchor — means the anchor is clear of the bottom.

UNDERWATER ADVENTURES

As all readers of fantasy know, the ocean floor is home to numerous ancient submarine civilizations and dark, green realms of creatures half-man and half-fish. Your players may have heard tales of the mountains of sunken loot that have been collected there over the centuries, of such things as pearls the size of a man's head, of beautiful mermaids with green eyes and blue skin . . . If they should find some way to investigate these stories, how will you handle it? This section deals with methods for conducting underwater scenarios.

Breathing:

The first major concern in underwater adventures is breathable air. Magic-users have the advantage in this area, as they have access to several spells that can solve the problem of submarine respiration. These include *water breathing* (which is also a druidical spell), *airy water*, *shape change*, or even *wish*, which might be made to work for the whole party (illusionists would use *alter reality*). They can also *polymorph others* into forms that can breathe water. However, most non-magic-users will probably find the use of magic items or potions safer and more reliable. These include *potions of water breathing* or items like the *helm of underwater action* or the *cloak of the manta ray* (which help in movement as well as respiration). The DM may also find it expedient to create such things as "air pills" or seaweed herbs that confer the temporary power to breathe water when ingested. Most methods of underwater breathing are of limited duration, so most submarine adventures will be similar to dungeon adventures as regards time actually spent underwater. Players will have to get to their destination, accomplish their mission and return in a matter of turns, rather than days or weeks as in other outdoor adventures. If extended campaigns are desired, the DM will have to ensure that the players can acquire some sort of equipment or comestible that will allow them to stay underwater for an unlimited time.

Movement:

There are two possible modes of movement underwater: swimming and walking. Swimming is not possible in any type of armor heavier than leather (except magic armor), or when encumbered with more than 20 pounds of equipment of any type (add or subtract 1 pound for each 100 g.p. worth of strength bonus or penalty). Though submersion in water makes everything "weigh less" due to buoyancy, actual mass of equipment is unchanged, and the same density that causes the illusion of less weight also causes a resistance to movement that slows it down considerably. Therefore, movement (either swimming or walking) is the same as the speeds used in dungeons, even though underwater movement is "outdoors". Average movement is a function of encumbrance in exactly the same ratios as in dungeon movement.

Persons able to swim (due to lack of encumbrance, not innate natatorial ability) will be able to move vertically as well as horizontally, and at the same rate of speed. Remember that swimming persons are vulnerable to attack from every direction.

Characters encumbered with more than about 20 pounds of gear will be forced to walk on the floor of the ocean, lake, river, or whatever. They will have to negotiate underwater hills, coral outcroppings, shipwrecks, seaweed forests, etc., in the normal manner, i.e., they will have to go around or through them. Characters equipped with a *ring of free action* or other magic item that confers the same power will be able to move normally and cover distance as if in the wilderness — that is, three times dungeon rate.

Vision:

Distance of vision will vary according to depth (available light) and obscuring objects. Basically, characters will be able to see objects and movement up to 50' away in fresh water and 100' away in salt water. The depth limit of vision is the same as the distance limit: characters can see until they go below 50' in fresh or 100' in salt water. Below this depth vision will be obscured. You may wish to vary the distance as function of depth to make this slightly more accurate, so that characters in fresh water could see 50' at a depth of 10', 40' at a depth of 20', and so on in segments of 10' until vision is 0' at 60' of depth. The same formula would apply to salt water, starting with 100' of distance at 10' of depth. Use of a *light* spell would allow vision up to 30' distance regardless of depth, or add 10' of vision to any distance shorter than 60' (whichever is greater). The visual capability of a *helm of underwater action* will quintuple normal vision as pertains to both distance and depth.

Infravision and ultravision are useful underwater, and their distance limits are the same as in dungeon settings. There are some problems, however: infravision users may become confused due to shifting currents and layers of different-temperatured water, as water exchanges heat more slowly than air and therefore is of a less even temperature. Distance of ultravision is halved at 100' depth and reduced to zero below 200', as ultraviolet "light" does not penetrate beyond that depth in sufficient quantities for sight.

Other objects will also obscure vision. Seaweed or sea grass will reduce vision to 10' or perhaps nil for those within it, depending on its density. Sea grass can be anywhere from 3' to 30' in height, while seaweed can take practically any size or shape the DM desires. In any case, shoals of either will totally obstruct vision, and anything may be hiding within! Schools of fish can also blind and confuse with their masses and quick movements. Mud can also be a big problem, especially as pertains to combat on the bottom, where violent movement may kick it up in great clouds, totally blocking vision as long as the movement lasts and for 7-12 (d6 + 6) rounds afterwards, unless there is a current to carry it away. Even light sources cannot penetrate the muddiest water.

Combat:

Underwater combat is difficult for normal land-born characters. Due to water resistance, effective use of crushing or cleaving weapons will not be possible — only thrusting weapons will be of any use (this means spears, tridents, daggers, stabbing swords, etc.). Human-types will also be somewhat slowed underwater, so aquatic creatures will always get the first chance to hit, unless the human is armed with a significantly longer weapon than the opponent. Only those characters with *free action* ability (from a ring, helm or otherwise) will be able to move as if above water: they can use any type of weapon they could normally use, and they receive no reaction penalty.

Nets will prove useful as an adjunct to thrusting weapons underwater, especially if both of the combatants are swimming. There are several ways nets could be used.

Two or more characters could stretch a large net between them and foul up attackers or combatants by maneuvering it so that their opponents become entangled therein. This is most effective vs. charging or unsuspecting opponents, who will have less chance of avoiding it.

Nets wielded single-handedly in combat must be weighted. As the net is thrown, it is given a slight horizontal spin. The spin causes centrifugal force to move the weighted ends out, which keeps the net open and untangled. If thrown correctly, it will slow and stop spinning as it arrives at its target, the weights then pulling the net down over the victim. Nets can be thrown one foot for every point of the thrower's strength. Underwater races can throw nets an average of 15', sahuagin 20'. Weighted nets can also be dropped upon non-swimmers on the ocean floor to drag them down or incapacitate them. Some battle nets have little hooks or barbs attached at every intersection to ensure that targets will be unable to escape easily.

All of the undersea races use nets, particularly aquatic elves, locathah, and mermen; the most adept of all are the sahuagin. They will often set ambushes involving many small nets or one huge net several hundred feet in diameter. These may be concealed in seaweed or left floating near the surface, disguised as something else. The sahuagin are masters of combat network as well, and will often fight with a net in one hand (to entangle and confuse) and a short, jabbing trident in the other.

The underwater combat net is a difficult weapon to use, and player characters who attempt it will do so at -4 to hit (unless they undergo extensive training and choose the underwater net as a weapon of proficiency. Such training must take place underwater).

Except for certain specially-made crossbows, use of missile weapons is generally impossible underwater. Special crossbows which will function underwater can be made by knowledgeable bowyers for ten times the normal price. Effective underwater range of these will be one-half normal (dungeon distances).

If characters intend to go somewhere where normal missile weapons could be of use (like the great air-filled domes of Atlantis), bows and missiles must be kept dry. This is doubly true of such things as scrolls and books, of course.

Spell use underwater will be limited to the same ranges and distances as in dungeons. In addition, there are problems with spell preparation, as many material components will be altered by or will not work correctly underwater. Some spells will be altered in effects as well. Fire-based spells (such as *fireball*) will not function at all underwater (except within the radius of an *airy water* spell). Electrical spells will be conducted to the entire surrounding area — a *lightning bolt* will behave as a *fireball*, etc. As Dungeon Master, you can alter whatever spell preparations or effects you deem necessary and reasonable.

Underwater spell use:

The following spells cannot be cast or will not function underwater:

Cleric:

3rd level — *speak with dead**
4th level — *lower water*
        *speak with plants**
5th level — *atonement**
        flame strike
        insect plague
6th level — *aerial servant*
7th level — *control weather*
        wind walk

Druid:

1st level — *predict weather*
2nd level — *fire trap*
        heat metal (though its reverse, *chill metal*, will work)
        *produce flame**
3rd level — *call lightning*
        *pyrotechnics**
        summon insects
4th level — *animal summoning I*
        call woodland beings
        *produce fire**
5th level — *animal summoning II*
        control winds
        insect plague
        pass plant
        wall of fire
6th level — *animal summoning III*
        conjure fire elemental
        fire seeds
        weather summoning
7th level — *Chariot of Sustarre*
        control weather
        creeping doom
        fire storm

Magic-user:

1st level — *affect normal fires**
        *burning hands**
        find familiar
2nd level — *pyrotechnics**
3rd level — *fireball*
        *flame arrow**
        gust of wind
4th level — *fire charm*
        fire shield — *hot flame** (the cold flame version of this spell
          will still function)
        fire trap
        wall of fire
        distance distortion
6th level — *control weather*
        *guards and wards**
        lower water
7th level — *cacodemon**
        delayed blast fireball
8th level — *incendiary cloud*
        *polymorph any object**
9th level — *meteor swarm*

Illusionist:

1st level — *wall of fog**
3rd level — *illusionary script**
7th level — *first level magic-user spells:*
        *affect normal fires**
        *burning hands**

* = spells that can be cast and will function within the bounds of an *airy water* spell.

The effects of the following spells will be substantially altered when cast underwater:

Cleric:

6th level — *part water:* this spell can be used to form a "tunnel" through deep water, no wider than 10' in diameter.
7th level — *earthquake:* effects are as follows:
    TERRAIN
        Underwater — causes shock waves stunning all within range who fail to save vs. death magic for 5-20 rounds.

Druid:

7th level — *conjure earth elemental:* an earth elemental conjured underwater will have to stay in the sea, lake, or river floor from which it was conjured, and cannot venture into the water. However, it may still assault creatures or constructions resting on or in the ground.

Magic-user:

3rd level — *fly:* this spell will enable the recipient to swim easily at any depth desired, even if encumbered or normally too heavy to float. Maximum speed is 9''.
        lightning bolt: underwater, this spell resembles a fireball as pertains to area of effect. Instead of a stroke, the electrical discharge takes the form of a 2'' radius sphere, centering on the point where a stroke would originate were the spell cast above water. All those within the sphere will suffer the full effect (saving throw indicates one-half damage).
4th level — *ice storm:* the icy hail formed by this spell will be very large but weak in downward force, inflicting only 1-10 hit points of damage before floating to the surface. Sleet will melt instantly and have no effect.
        wall of ice: a wall of ice can be formed underwater, but it will immediately float to the surface and bob about like an ice floe.
5th level — *conjure elemental:* air and fire elementals cannot be conjured under water at all. Earth elementals can be conjured only as described above under *conjure earth elemental.* There is no problem about conjuring water elementals, of course.
6th level — *Otiluke's freezing sphere:* this spell is extremely dangerous to the caster if invoked in its first manifestation while submerged. The globe of absolute zero matter, when formed underwater, will instantly freeze the water around the caster into a block of ice of a volume equal to 50 cubic feet per level of the caster. This will last a number of rounds equal to the level of the caster. Unless immediate aid is forthcoming, the magic-user will suffocate (the ice-entombed magic-user will immediately float to the surface, of course).
        part water: see 6th level clerical spell *part water* (above) for comments on this spell.

TRAVEL IN THE KNOWN PLANES OF EXISTENCE

The Known Planes of Existence, as depicted in **APPENDIX IV** of the **PLAYERS HANDBOOK**, offer nearly endless possibilities for **AD&D** play, although some of these new realms will no longer be fantasy as found in swords & sorcery or myth but verge on that of science fiction, horror, or just about anything else desired. How so? The known planes are a part of the "multiverse". In the Prime Material Plane are countless suns, planets, galaxies, universes. So too there are endless parallel worlds. What then of the Outer Planes? Certainly, they can be differently populated if not substantially different in form.

Spells, magic devices, artifacts, and relics are known ways to travel to the planes. You can add machines or creatures which will also allow such travel. As far as the universe around your campaign world goes, who is to say that it is not possible to mount a roc and fly to the moon(s)? or perhaps to another planet? Again, are the stars actually suns at a distance? or are they the tiny lights of some vast dome? The hows and wherefores are yours to handle, but more important is what is on the other end of the route.

For those of you who haven't really thought about it, the so-called planes are your ticket to creativity, and I mean that with a capital C! *Everything* can be absolutely different, save for those common denominators necessary to the existence of the player characters coming to the plane. Movement and scale can be different; so can combat and morale. Creatures can have more or different attributes. As long as the player characters can somehow relate to it all, then it will work. This is not to say that you are expected to actually make each and every plane a totally new experience — an impossibly tall order. It does mean that you can put your imagination to work on devising a single extraordinary plane. For the rest, simply use **AD&D** with minor quirks, petty differences, and so forth. If your players wish to spend most of their time visiting other planes (and this could come to pass after a year or more of play) then you will be hard pressed unless you rely upon other game systems to fill the gaps. Herein I have recommended that **BOOT HILL** and **GAMMA WORLD** be used in campaigns. There is also **METAMORPHOSIS ALPHA, TRACTICS,** and all sorts of other offerings which can be converted to man-for-man role-playing scenarios. While as of this particular writing there are no commercially available ''other planes'' modules, I am certain that there will be soon — it is simply too big an opportunity to pass up, and the need is great.

Astral and ethereal travel are not difficult, as the systems for encounters and the chances for the hazards of the *psychic wind* and *ether cyclone* are but brief sections of **APPENDIX C: RANDOM MONSTER ENCOUNTERS,** easily and quickly handled. Other forms of travel, the risks and hazards thereof, you must handle as you see fit. For instance, suppose that you decide that there is a breathable atmosphere which extends from the earth to the moon, and that any winged steed capable of flying fast and far can carry its rider to that orb. Furthermore, once beyond the normal limits of earth's atmosphere, gravity and resistance are such that speed increases dramatically, and the whole journey will take but a few days. You must then decide what will be encountered during the course of the trip — perhaps a few new creatures in addition to the standard ones which you deem likely to be between earth and moon.

Then comes what conditions will be like upon Luna, and what will be found there, why, and so on. Perhaps here is where you place the gateways to yet other worlds. In short, you devise the whole schema just as you did the campaign, beginning from the dungeon and environs outward into the broad world — in this case the universe, and then the multiverse. You need do no more than your participants desire, however. If your players are quite satisfied with the normal campaign setting, with occasional side trips to the Layers of the Abyss or whatever, then there is no need to do more than make sketchy plans for the eventuality that their interests will expand. In short, the planes are there to offer whatever is needed in the campaign. Use them as you will.

OUTDOOR MOVEMENT

As the scale of maps will differ from campaign to campaign, general movement rates are given, and you can adapt them to the scale of your campaign maps accordingly. Some variation in movement rate is justifiable, but the distances shown should neither be increased or decreased substantially.

MOVEMENT AFOOT IN MILES/DAY

Burden	Normal	Terrain Is Rugged	Very Rugged
light	30	20	10
average	20	10	5
heavy	10	5	2

MOVEMENT MOUNTED IN MILES/DAY

Mount	Normal	Terrain Is Rugged	Very Rugged
light	60	25	5
medium	40	20	5
heavy	30	15	5
draft	30	15	5
cart*	25	15	—
wagon*	25	10	—

* Road, track or open terrain only.

Light burden assumes an average man travelling with no more than 25 pounds of additional weight in food, weapons, and other equipment.

Average burden assumes an average man travelling with from 26 to 60 pounds of gear of all sorts.

Heavy burden assumes an average man with more than 60 pounds of gear but less than 90 pounds.

Adjust all weight assumptions by strength and race factors.

Normal terrain assumes basically open ground, scrub, typical desert, light forest, low hills, small watercourses, etc. With respect to vehicular movement it assumes roadways through such terrain or smooth fields (steppes, plains, etc.).

Rugged terrain assumes rough ground, snow, forests, steep hills, large water courses, etc. With respect to vehicular movement it assumes either roadways through such terrain or tracks/paths through normal terrain.

Very rugged terrain assumes broken ground, deep snow and ice, heavy forests, marshy ground, bogs, bluffs, mountains, and broad watercourses.

Note: You must determine for yourself which terrain areas are impassable to mounted movement or any normal travel. Generally large swamps and high mountains fall into this category.

MOVEMENT AFLOAT, OARED OR SCULLED IN MILES/DAY

Vessel Type	Lake	Marsh	River*	Sea	Stream
raft	15	5	15	—	10
boat, small	30	15	35	—	25
barge	20	5	20	—	—
galley, small	40	5	40	30	—
galley, large	30	—	30	30	—
merchant, small	10	—	15	20	—
merchant, large	10	—	10	15	—
warship	10	—	10	20	—

MOVEMENT AFLOAT, SAILED IN MILES/DAY

Vessel Type	Lake	Marsh	River*	Sea	Stream
raft	30	10	30	—	15
boat, small	80	20	60	—	40
barge	50	10	40	—	—
galley, small	70-80	—	60	50	—
galley, large	50-60	—	50	50	—
merchant, small	50-60	—	50	50	—
merchant, large	25-35	—	35	35	—
warship	40-50	—	40	50	—

* See below for effects of current on movement.

Lake assumes a large body of water, at least two to three miles broad and several times as long, minimum.

Marsh assumes a shallow body of water overgrown with aquatic vegetation but with considerable open channels; this does not include a bog but does include swamps.

River assumes a body of water at least three times as wide as the vessel afloat upon it is long (that is, the smallest river is at least 40' wide) and navigable to the vessel considered, usually because of familiarity and/or piloting. For current effect, subtract its speed times eight (C × 8) from movement when moving upriver, adding this same factor to movement for downriver traffic unless navigational hazards disallow — in which case adjust to a multiplier of two or four times current accordingly.

Sea (and ocean) movement assumes generally favorable conditions. It is not possible to herein chart ocean currents, prevailing winds, calms, or storms, for these factors are peculiar to each milieu. Currents will move vessels along their route at their speed. Prevailing winds will add or subtract from movement somewhat (10% to 30%) depending on direction of travel as compared to winds. Calms will slow sailed movement to virtually nil. Storms will have a likelihood of destroying vessels according to the strength of the storm and the type and size of the vessel. To simulate these effects during long voyages, reduce the movement rates shown by a variable of 5% to 20% (d4, 1 = 5%, 2 = 10%, etc.).

Stream assumes a body of water under 40' width. The effects of currents are the same as for river movement.

For description of vessel types, see **WATERBORNE ADVENTURES.**

INFRAVISION & ULTRAVISION

Infravision:

As explained in **PLAYERS HANDBOOK,** infravision is the ability to see light waves in the infrared spectrum. Characters and various creatures with infravisual capability out to 60′ (standard) are basically picking up radiation from their surroundings. Therefore they note *differences* in thermal radiation, hot or cold. They do not "see" things which are the same temperature as their surroundings. Thus, a room in a dungeon might look completely blank, as walls, floor, ceiling, and possibly even some wooden furniture within are all of the same temperature. Openings in the walls should show up rather plainly, as space anywhere else will, and if you are generous, you can allow different substances to radiate differently even if at the same temperature, i.e. the wood in the example above would be discernible if care was used in scanning the room infravisually. Note that air currents might show as cold or warm layers. Except where very warm or very cold objects are concerned, vision of this sort is roughly equal to human norm on a dark and cloudy night at best. Note also that monsters of a very cold or very warm sort (such as a human) can be tracked infravisually by their footprints. Such tracking must occur within 2 rounds of their passing, or the temperature difference where they had trodden will dissipate.

Light sources which give off heat also absolutely prevent normal infravision from functioning within their sphere of illumination. (Explain this as the effect of trying to see into the dark when the observer is in a brightly lit area.) It requires not less than two segments to accustom the eyes to infravision after use of normal vision.

Creatures with infravisual capability of unusual nature, such as those which see infravisually to 90′, are actually emitting infrared radiation from their eyes and seeing what is within this visual range by receiving the reflected radiation. Such creatures can easily distinguish floor, ceiling, wall, and other areas, as well as furnishings within an area. The eyes of all such creatures will appear as very brightly glowing red when observed by any other creature with standard infravision. Most monsters inhabiting underground areas will have this form of infravision.

Infravision outdoors enables the individual to see figures which are warm or cold at 100′ to 300′, depending on temperature extremes. Vision is otherwise equal to a bright, starry night, with full moonlight.

Ultravision:

Ultravision is the ability to see radiation above violet in the normal visible spectrum. Unless this ability is of highly unusual nature, so as to be able to see far into this spectrum, ultravision will not be useful underground (where radiation is screened out) without some source of ultravisual emanation. Magic weapons which shed illumination spoil ultravisual capability, just as heat does infravision. As noted in **PLAYERS HANDBOOK,** ultravision enables the viewer to see outdoors at night as if he or she were in twilight, so vision extends clearly for about 100 yards, dimly to about 300. On particularly cloudy nights, ultravisual capability is reduced to about half normal, i.e. clear sight to 50 yards, dim to 150 yards.

INVISIBILITY

"Now I'll sneak up on the monster invisibly!" How often has this cry rung forth from eager players in your campaign? How often have you cursed because of it? Never fear, there are many answers to the problem of invisibility, and most difficulties will be resolved after you read the following rules and suggestions regarding the subject.

Invisibility is not what most players desire it to be. It is neither a sound-proofing nor an odor preventative. Normal sound issues from the invisible creature, just as normal odors do. Monsters might well be able to hear, smell, or see the invisible character. Furthermore, the associates of the invisible party are not able to see him or her any better than foes are, so this can cause problems, too. Now consider a *silence* spell and large area *invisibility* cast upon a party. Imagine the chaos within the area as characters stub their toes on the heels of the person before them, with the inability to hear *anything* so that falls, suggestions as to what should be done, or orders cannot be heard. Consider also that dust on the floor will betray most invisibility, as will dust or powder in the air. Think of a door opening without any visible cause; will this cause suspicion in the mind of the viewer (particularly when the surroundings are taken into account!)? You bet it will!

Invisibility spells are broken when attack occurs, but what about devices? Becoming invisible takes but a twinkling, but if the party is observed doing so, there is no reason why an opponent cannot attack with the standard penalty (−4) for inability to see the target. Likewise, becoming visible takes only a second, but thereafter the foe is able to clearly observe the attacker for a return of the compliment, as it must be assumed that it requires a full round to again activate the magic which enables the character to be non-visible.

Invisibility to animals, the first level druid spell, does not allow attack, but it is pretty well proof against stupid animals. *Invisibility* devices generally duplicate the spell or else make the user likely to be undetected that turn or round, indetectability being stated as a percentage chance. CHECK EACH PERIOD AS APPLICABLE UNDER THE SITUATION. *Dust of disappearance* does not negate sound or odor either, so it is basically the same as an *invisibility* spell which allows invisible attack. *Psionic invisibility* is a mind control ability ("The Shadow Knows!") which is more similar to the druidic *invisibility to animals*, for the affected creature(s) does not notice sounds or odors from the psionic. Note, however, that this form of invisibility is sharply limited in that it works only on a set maximum number of creatures according to their combined levels/hit dice. In no event is the thief ability to *hide in shadows* to be treated the same as invisibility as regards disappearance (see **CHARACTER CLASSES, THIEF ABILITIES** for further details).

Finally, we have the consideration of the ability to detect invisible creatures even though they are not actually seen. This is explainable as the observer's ability to note a minor disturbance in the air — a shimmering or haze — or by keen hearing, and/or keen sense of smell. The table below gives the probability of detection of *invisibility* according to level/hit dice.

DETECTION OF INVISIBILITY TABLE

Level or Hit Dice of Creature	Intelligence Ability Rating							
	0-1	2-4	5-7	8-10	11-12	13-14	15-16	17+
7/7 & 7 +	—	—	—	—	—	—	—	5%
8/8 & 8 +	—	—	—	—	—	—	5%	10%
9/9 & 9 +	—	—	—	—	—	5%	10%	15%
10/10	—	—	—	—	5%	15%	20%	25%
11/10+ − 11	—	—	—	5%	15%	25%	30%	35%
12/11+ − 12	—	—	5%	15%	25%	35%	40%	45%
13/12+ − 13	—	5%	10%	25%	35%	45%	50%	55%
14/13+ − 14+	5%	10%	15%	35%	45%	55%	65%	75%
15 & +	10%	15%	20%	45%	55%	65%	80%	95%

Note: You may give unintelligent creatures with keen hearing or sense of smell the equivalent of intelligence to reflect detection of invisible creatures.

Check each round the creature is exposed to invisibility. Once detected, the invisible creature will be kept track of thereafter, as the detector will be able to note the cause. Any attacks incur the −4 penalty of attacking an invisible opponent, of course, and the invisible creature likewise is entitled to +4 on saving throws.

MIRRORS

It is important for DMs to remember that in order to be reflective, a mirror must have a light source.

DETECTION OF EVIL AND/OR GOOD

It is important to make a distinction between character alignment and some powerful force of evil or good when this detection function is considered. In general, only a *know alignment* spell will determine the evil or good a character holds within. It must be a great evil or a strong good to be detected. Characters who are very strongly aligned, do not stray from their faith, and who are of relatively high level (at least 8th or higher) might radiate evil or good if they are intent upon appropriate actions. Powerful monsters such as demons, devils, ki-rin and the like will send forth emanations of their evil or good. Aligned undead must radiate evil, for it is this power and negative force which enables them to continue existing. Note that none of these emanations are noticeable without magical detection.

In like fashion, powerful magic items which have some purpose as

respects alignment will radiate evil or good — unless they are aligned with neutrality, which is neither, of course. Most other magic items will most certainly not, even though their effect might be for evil or good. Likewise, items which are not magical but which have powerful effects will probably not give any evil or good aura. Poison is a prime example. It is perfectly neutral and has no aura whatsoever. Unholy water will emanate evil, just as holy water will radiate good. Places sanctified to some deity of evil or good will certainly give off an appropriate aura.

Thus, a trap, for example, is neutral and gives no evil or good reading. If the same trap leads victims to the lair of Juiblex, for instance, there will be an aura of evil about it; while if it brings victims into the realm of Bahamut, it will send out an aura of good. Using these guidelines, you should have little difficulty in adjudicating the attempts of characters empowered to detect evil or good to do so. As a side note, be sure to remember that all such detection requires not less than one round of stillness and concentration whether the power is from some inner source (paladins, for example), or by some external means (spells, swords, etc.). Therefore, the character must stop, have quiet, and intently seek to detect the aura.

LISTENING AT DOORS

In addition to the simple exercise of observation, many times characters will desire to *listen*, ear pressed to a portal, prior to opening and entering. This requires a special check, in secret, by you to determine if any sound is heard. Because of this, continual listening becomes a great bother to the DM. While ear seekers will tend to discourage some, most players will insist on having their characters listen at doors at every pretense. First, make certain that you explain to players that *all* headgear must be removed in order to listen. Those wearing helmets will probably have to remove a mail coif and padded cap as well, don't forget. The party must also be absolutely silent, and listening will take at least one round.

Silent creatures — undead, bugbears, etc. — will never be heard. Sleeping or resting or alerted creatures will not be heard either. If there is something for the listener to hear behind the door, the following probabilities will determine if any sound is heard:

Race Of Listener	Chance Of Hearing Noise
Dwarf	2 in 20 (10%)
Elf	3 in 20 (15%)
Gnome	4 in 20 (20%)
Half-Elf	2 in 20 (10%)
Halfling	3 in 20 (15%)
Half-Orc	3 in 20 (15%)
Human	2 in 20 (10%)

Keen-eared individuals will gain a bonus of 1 or 2 in 20 (5% or 10%). Use chance of hearing a noise to determine if a character is keen-eared the first time he or she listens at a door, and if it is indicated, tell the player to note the fact for his or her character. Player characters will not initially have hearing problems (as they wouldn't have survived if they had them). During the course of adventuring, great noise might cause hearing loss. Handle this as you see fit. A loss of hearing might negate the chance to hear something behind a door without any other noticeable effects.

Hearing Noise: When a die roll indicates a noise has been heard, tell the player whose character was listening that he or she heard a clink, footstep, murmuring voices, slithering, laughter, or whatever is appropriate. (Of course, some of these noises will be magical, e.g., *audible glamer* spells, not anything which will be encountered at all!) Be imprecise and give only vague hints; never say, "You hear ogres," but "You hear rumbling, voice-like sounds." Failure to hear any noise can be due to the fact that nothing which will make noise is beyond the portal, or it might be due to a bad (for the listener) die roll. Always roll the die, even if you know nothing can be heard. Always appear disinterested regardless of the situation.

Maximum Number Of Listeners: Each listener will take up about 2½' of space, so up to three can listen at a typical dungeon door.

Maximum Length Of Time For Listening: Only three attempts can be made before the strain becomes too great. After the third attempt, the listeners must cease such activity for at least five rounds before returning to listening again.

COMBAT

ENCOUNTERS, COMBAT, AND INITIATIVE

Combat is divided into 1 minute period *melee rounds*, or simply *rounds*, in order to have reasonably manageable combat. "Manageable" applies both to the actions of the combatants and to the actual refereeing of such melees. It would be no great task to devise an elaborate set of rules for highly complex individual combats with rounds of but a few seconds length. It is not in the best interests of an adventure game, however, to delve too deeply into cut and thrust, parry and riposte. The location of a hit or wound, the sort of damage done, sprains, breaks, and dislocations are not the stuff of heroic fantasy. The reasons for this are manifold.

As has been detailed, hit points are not actually a measure of physical damage, by and large, as far as characters (and some other creatures as well) are concerned. Therefore, the location of hits and the type of damage caused are not germane to them. While this is not true with respect to most monsters, it is neither necessary nor particularly useful. Lest some purist immediately object, consider the many charts and tables necessary to handle this sort of detail, and then think about how area effect spells would work. In like manner, consider all of the nasty things which face adventurers as the rules stand. Are crippling disabilities and yet more ways to meet instant death desirable in an open-ended, episodic game where participants seek to identify with lovingly detailed and developed player-character personae? Not likely! Certain death is as undesirable as a give-away campaign. Combat is a common pursuit in the vast majority of adventures, and the participants in the campaign deserve a chance to exercise intelligent choice during such confrontations. As hit points dwindle they can opt to break off the encounter and attempt to flee. With complex combat systems which stress so-called realism and feature hit location, special damage, and so on, either this option is severely limited or the rules are highly slanted towards favoring the player characters at the expense of their opponents. (Such rules as double damage and critical hits must cut both ways — in which case the life expectancy of player characters will be shortened considerably — or the monsters are being grossly misrepresented and unfairly treated by the system. I am certain you can think of many other such rules.)

One-minute rounds are devised to offer the maximum of choice with a minimum of complication. This allows the DM and the players the best of both worlds. The system assumes much activity during the course of each round. Envision, if you will, a fencing, boxing, or karate match. During the course of one minute of such competition there are numerous attacks which are unsuccessful, feints, maneuvering, and so forth. During a one-minute melee round many attacks are made, but some are mere feints, while some are blocked or parried. One, or possibly several, have the chance to actually score damage. For such chances, the dice are rolled, and if the "to hit" number is equalled or exceeded, the attack was successful, but otherwise it too was avoided, blocked, parried, or whatever. Damage scored to characters or certain monsters is actually not substantially physical — a mere nick or scratch until the last handful of hit points are considered — it is a matter of wearing away the endurance, the luck, the magical protections. With respect to most monsters such damage is, in fact, more physically substantial, although as with adjustments in armor class rating for speed and agility, there are also similar additions in hit points. So while a round of combat is not a continuous series of attacks, it is neither just a single blow and counter-blow affair. The opponents spar and move, seeking the opportunity to engage when an opening in the enemy's guard presents itself.

Because of the relatively long period of time represented by the round, dexterity (dexterity, agility, speed, quickness) is represented by a more favorable armor class rating rather than as a factor in which opponent strikes the first blow. Likewise, weapon length and relative speed factors are not usually a consideration. (See **Initiative** and **Charging** below, however.) The system of **AD&D** combat maximizes the sense of hand-to-hand combat and the life-and-death character of melee without undue complication. Because of this, you, the DM, are enabled to conduct such portions of a game without endless resort to charts, tables, procedure clarifications, and over-lengthy time requirements. Players, on the other hand, will not become bored with endless dice rolling and rules consulting, but at the same time will have a reasonable chance to seek escape for their characters should the affair go badly. The steps for encounter and combat are as follows:

1. Determine if either or both parties are SURPRISED.

2. Determine *distance*, if unknown, between the parties.

3. If both parties are unsurprised, or equally surprised, determine INITIATIVE for that round.

4. Determine the results of whatever actions are decided upon by the party with initiative:

   A. *Avoid* engagement (flee, slam door, use magic to escape, etc.) if possible.
   B. Attempt to *parley*.
   C. *Await* action by other party.
   D. Discharge missiles or magical device attacks or cast spells or turn undead.
   E. Close to striking range, or charge.
   F. Set weapons against possible opponent *charge*.
   G. Strike blows with weapons, to kill or subdue.
   H. Grapple or hold

5. Determine the results of whatever actions are decided upon by the party which lost the initiative (as per A. through H. above).

6. Continue each melee round by determination of distance, initiative, and action until melee ends due to fleeing, inability to continue, or death of one or both parties.

Surprise:

The term *surprise* is basically self-explanatory. A surprised party is caught unawares or unprepared. In such circumstances the non-surprised (or less-surprised) party has an immediate advantage which is reflected in the granting of 1 or more *segments* of initiative, during which the active (non- or less surprised) party can take actions 4. A. through H., wholly or partially depending on several modifying factors. The surprise segment is 6 seconds. Avoiding, parleying, awaiting the action of the surprised, missile discharge, and setting of weapons (typically spears or spearing types of pole arms) are possible. Most spells cannot be cast in a single segment, although first level magic-user/illusionist spells are usually but 1 segment long, as are some other spells, and these spells are possible to use in a surprise segment. Other, longer casting time spells can only be begun in the first segment of surprise. Similarly, the distance separating the parties may be too great to close during a single segment, even by charging, and melee striking or grappling might not be possible. However, during the surprise segment or segments, the surprised party is unable to react in any way, so the latter actions might be possible.

Surprise is determined by rolling a six-sided die for each party concerned, modifying the result by using the most favorable member of the party concerned, i.e. a ranger, surprised only on a roll of 1, will represent the whole of a group of other character types. Note, however, the effect of dexterity as detailed below. The same holds for mixed types of monsters. If surprise is indicated for both parties concerned, the party which has lesser surprise subtracts its result from the result of the greater to find the number of segments the latter are inactive. Nonetheless, it is possible for both parties to be surprised equally — with surprise thus having no effect.

Surprise is usually expressed as a 2 in 6 chance for all parties concerned, i.e. a six-sided die is rolled with a 1 or 2 indicating surprise. Some monsters are more capable of surprising foes than the normal 2 in 6 probability, and some cannot be surprised as easily, so they have a reduced probability — 1 in 6, 1 in 8, etc. Each 1 of surprise equals 1 segment (six seconds) of time lost to the surprised party, and during the lost time the surprising party can freely act to escape or attack or whatever. If both parties are surprised, then the effect is negated or reduced:

Surprise Dice Difference	Lost Segments
0	0
1 (2-1, 3-2, etc.)	1
2 (3-1, 4-2, etc.)	2
3 (4-1, 5-2, etc.)	3

Assume the party of characters comes upon a monster. They have 2 of 6 chances to surprise, and the monster also has 2 in 6. A six-sided die is rolled for the party, another for the monster. Both sides could be surprised, or either could be surprised. This is shown on the table below:

Party's Die	Monster's Die	Surprise Effect
3 to 6	3 to 6	none
1	1	both surprised
2	2	both surprised
1 or 2	3 to 6	party surprised
3 to 6	1 or 2	monster surprised
1	2	party surprised
2	1	monster surprised

Example: Party A is surprised on a roll of 1 or 2, while party B is surprised only on a roll of 1. A rolls 2 and B rolls 1, so A is inactive due to surprise for 1 segment. Had B rolled a 2, it would not have been surprised at all, and A would have been inactive for 2 segments.

Example: Party A is surprised only on a roll of 1, but party B surprises on 5 in 6 (d6, 1-5) due to its nature or the particular set of circumstances which the DM has noted are applicable to this encounter. The favorable factor normally accruing to party A is 1, i.e., parties of this sort are normally surprised on 1 or 2, but this party is surprised only on a 1 — therefore they have an additional 1 in 6 to their favor (and *not* a 50% better chance). Party B will surprise them on 5 in 6 less 1 in 6, or 4 in 6. Assume A rolls a 4, so it is surprised for 4 segments unless B rolls a 1, in which case A party's inactive period will be only 3 segments, or if B rolls a 2, in which case surprise will last for only 2 segments (4 − 1 = 3, 4 − 2 = 2).

Because the party surprised is (relatively) inactive, the surprising party will be able to attempt telling blows during each segment of surprise as if the segment were an entire round! That is, a fighter able to attack twice during a normal round of combat will be able to do so twice during each surprise segment, so dice are rolled for hit determination accordingly. Even if distance prevents striking with weapons, the discharge of arrows, bolts or hand-hurled weapons is permissible at three times the normal rate providing the weapon/missiles are ready, otherwise at normal rates for rounds. Once surprise segments are over, melee proceeds normally on a round-by-round basis.

Prior detection negates the possibility of surprise. Thus, magical devices can possibly negate surprise by detection of thoughts or intentions. Noise can negate surprise considerations, whether the sound is the normal progress of the party or the effect of a fruitless attempt to open a door. Light can spoil the chance of surprise. The particular condition of a monster can likewise negate any chance of it being surprised. In any event, it is of utmost importance to realize that surprise can be and often is unilateral. That is, one party can be surprised while the other, somehow aware of the other's presence, can NOT be so taken. In all such cases, merely roll for the party which is subject to the condition and do not roll for the other.

Dexterity Reaction In Surprise: This factor (**Dexterity Table I, PLAYERS HANDBOOK**) affects both *surprise* and *mutual surprise* situations. In the former case the penalty (−3 to −1) or bonus (+1 to +3) allows the surprised party *on an individual basis only* the opportunity to mitigate the condition. That is, if there is a dexterity penalty, the individual will suffer that many additional segments of time in a surprised state. On the other hand, if the dexterity bonus applies the individual negates that many segments of surprise as far as the individual only is concerned. Dexterity reaction bonus for surprise *never* creates surprise in an opponent party or in an individual with regard to its penalty factor; it adds to existing surprise or detracts from it, and only as far as the particular individual is concerned, not for any other individuals concerned. As DM you will undoubtedly decide that there are situations where penalty and/or bonus do not apply, such as when an individual is otherwise prepared or when the individual is in the act of pulling chain mail over his or her head. Such adjudication is properly within the scope of refereeing the game, and you should feel free to deny either case as you see fit.

Factors Contributing To Surprise:

When one side or another is surprised, this general term can represent a number of possible circumstances. In the first place it simply represents actual surprise — that is, the opponent was unprepared for the appearance/attack. The reason for this could be eating, sleeping, waste elimination, attention elsewhere, no weapon ready, etc. While each possible cause of surprise could be detailed, with a matrix and factors of time for recovery from the condition calculated to a nicety, the overall result would not materially add to the game — in fact, the undue complication would detract from the smooth flow of play.

The second factor represented in surprise is morale. What is the effect of being taken unaware and/or unprepared upon the surprised party? Reactions are not only hampered by circumstances of a physical nature. Panic or fear reactions to the situation take their toll. Again, this is all subsumed in the single surprise roll determination for each side, and in the simple set of rules governing what transpires when one or the other is surprised.

Finally, the surprising group must be able to assess the situation and act upon it, so surprise doesn't mean that the party with the advantage has automatically achieved victory and triumph. What is gained is the opportunity to act as is seen best in the circumstances — be it to flee the encounter, get the "drop" on the surprised, or to attack with spells, missiles, or blows. Of course, the other side is then forced to react to whatever the surprising side has chosen to do.

Distance:

When encounters occur, the distance between concerned parties will be 5″ to 10″ (d6 + 4) subject to the following modifying factors:

1. **Line of Sight:** If this is unobstructed and light is involved, the distance possible for determination of another party present is virtually infinite. It could likewise be sharply restricted due to obstructions.

2. **Noise:** If one party is making considerable noise which is discernible by the other party, the latter will have the options of fleeing or concealment; the former negating the encounter, the latter allowing distance to be 1″ to 4″ before discovery by the noisy party.

3. **Actual Area:** If the encountered party is in a small area, distance between the two can be no greater than the maximum distance possible for discovery of the one by the other, i.e. opening a door into a 20′ X 20′ room will mean the distance between the two parties can be under 10′, 10′ or thereabouts, or 20′ (d6, 1-2 = striking distance, 3-4 = 10′ distance, 5-6 = 20′ distance).

4. **Planned or Unplanned Appearance:** The sudden precipitation of one party upon the other due to any of a number of factors (*teleportation*, *dimension door* spell, other magical means, a chute, etc.) will cause distance similar to that found when actual area is a factor.

5. **Surprise:** Surprise can only be a factor in close encounter situations. If either or both parties are surprised, the distance must be either 1″ to 3″ or it must be less as determined under the actual area modifier. Thus if the actual area were a 40′ X 60′ room, if surprise exists the distance between the parties will be 1″ to 3″.

6. **Light:** The illumination factor or visual capability of the concerned parties will affect encounter distance as follows:

   A. A light source reliance limits the encounter distance to twice the normal vision radius of the source (2 X radius of the light source).
   B. Infravision and/or ultravision operate only to the stated limit of their range and limit encounter distance accordingly.

Initiative:

Surprise gives initiative to the non- or less-surprised party. It is otherwise determined when an encounter occurs and at the start of each combat round. It indicates which of the two parties will act/react. Again, a d6 is rolled, and the scores for the two parties are compared. (It is recommended that such initiative rolls be made openly unless there is some reason to hide that of the encountered monster party — such as special bonuses which would be unknown to the player characters involved.) The higher of the two rolls is said to *possess the initiative* for that melee round. (While it is not accurate to roll one die for all individuals comprising each party, it is a convenient and necessary expedient. Separate rolls could be made for each member of two small groups, for instance, but what happens to this simple, brief determination if one party consists of 9 characters and 6 henchmen and the other of 7 giants and 19 dire wolves, let us say?) Possession of initiative allows the individuals to take action or reaction as desired according to the foregoing list of alternatives, and as detailed hereafter. The dexterity or speed of individuals or weapons is not considered in the 1 minute round except as hereafter noted.

Initiative For Creatures With Multiple Attack Routines: When one or more creatures involved in combat are permitted to use their attack routines twice or more often during the round, then the following initiative determinants are employed. When the attack routine may be used twice, then allow the side with this advantage to attack FIRST and LAST with those members of its group who have this advantage. If it is possessed by both parties, the initiative roll determines which group strikes FIRST and THIRD, which group strikes SECOND and LAST. If one or both groups have members allowed only one attack routine, it will always fall in the middle of the other attacks, the order determined by dicing for initiative, when necessary. If one party has the ability to employ its attack routines thrice, then the other party dices for initiative to see if it, or the multi-routine group, strikes first in the mid-point of the round. Extrapolate for routines which occur four or more times in a round by following the method above. Note that a *routine* is the attack or attacks usual to the creature concerned, i.e. a weapon (or weapons) for a character, a claw/claw/bite routine for a bear (with incidental damage assessed as it occurs — the hug, for example). A 12th level fighter is allowed attack routines twice in every odd numbered melee round, for example, and this moves up to three per round if a *haste* spell is cast upon the fighter. Damage from successful attacks is assessed when the ''to hit'' score is made and damage determined, the creature so taking damage having to survive it in order to follow its attack routine.

Ties: It will often occur that initiative determination results in a tie. This merely indicates that each party has equal chances for acting and that attacks occur simultaneously. In cases of equal initiative score, damage accrues to both groups regardless of what is inflicted.

Inflicting Damage: Except as noted under **Ties**, above, damage (or the general results of some attack routine such as a *turning* of undead or casting of a *slow* spell) is inflicted upon the reacting party prior to allowing these creatures their portion of action in the melee round. Thus, some of the members of the party which does not have the initiative might be caught in a *web* spell, others might be *turned* by a cleric, and some damaged or killed/destroyed by other spells, missile discharge, and blows from hand-held weapons before they ever have a chance to themselves act. The reacting party's action could be an attempt to flee, cast spells, hurl missiles, or melee — it does not matter. If the reacting party does use attack routines, for example, the damage so inflicted will be assessed immediately. This could well mean that if they win the initiative roll next round they can attack a second time, doing damage accordingly, before the opponent party can act.

ENCOUNTER REACTIONS

Any intelligent creature which can be conversed with will react in some way to the character that is speaking. Reaction is determined by rolling percentile dice, adjusting the score for charisma and applicable loyalty adjustment as if the creature were a henchman of the character speaking, and the modified score of the percentile dice is compared to the table below:

Adjusted Die Score	Reaction
01 (or less)-05	Violently hostile, immediate attack*
06-25	Hostile, immediate action*
26-45	Uncertain but 55% prone toward negative
46-55	Neutral — uninterested — uncertain
56-75	Uncertain but 55% prone toward positive
76-95	Friendly, immediate action
96-00 (or greater)	Enthusiastically friendly, immediate acceptance

* Or morale check if appropriate.

Avoiding:

It is always possible to flee from an undesired confrontation if the other party is surprised. It is never possible to flee from an encounter where the opponent party is in striking range. (See **Breaking Off From Melee,** below.) A party can always flee an encounter if it gains the *first* initiative. Whether or not the opponent party will follow in pursuit of the fleeing party depends on the following factors:

1. What you, the Dungeon Master, have stated in your key concerning the party, if applicable. This is first and foremost in ALL cases.

2. What the stated characteristics of the creature(s) involved are. That is,

if player characters, do they say they will pursue, or if monsters, does their description say that they will always seek to pursue?

3. Obvious deterrents to pursuit, such as a pool of flaming oil, a secured portal, etc. will modify monster behavior accordingly.

4. Fleeing party behavior and/or possessions noted by the opponent party will modify pursuit desire.

5. Relative speed will cause the pursuing party to cease fruitless chase if they are obviously being outdistanced (except if the pursuers are player characters who must state they are halting such chase).

6. Otherwise 50% of the time (d6, 1-3 = pursuit, 4-6 = break off pursuit).

Parleying:

Upon encountering another party, the party with initiative can always elect to attempt some form of communication. This can be a friendly gesture, a throwing down of arms, offering of treasure, or some spoken word or phrase. Just what this effect will be is determinable only by the DM considering the prevailing circumstances. It is safe to say that a group of elves attempting to parley with a red dragon will find their efforts generally unsuccessful unless they also have some obvious advantage which the dragon is aware of. It is common for player characters to attack first, parley afterwards. It is recommended that you devise encounters which penalize such action so as to encourage parleying attempts — which will usually be fruitless, of course!

Awaiting Action:

This is self-explanatory, not an attempt to parley but neither an attack. It is seldom utilized by experienced adventurers.

MISSILE DISCHARGE

This is the usual loosing of arrows and bolts, hurling of axes, hammers, javelins, darts, etc. It also includes the hurling of rocks by giants, manticore tail spike throwing, and so on. It can occur simultaneously with magical device attacks, spell casting, or turning of undead. Magical device and spell attacks can negate the effects of or damage some missiles, i.e., arrows fired off simultaneously with the discharge of a *fireball* spell, or a javelin hurled into an *ice storm*, or a dwarven hammer tossed at an opponent struck by a *fireball* or *lightning bolt*. As referee you will have to determine the final results according to circumstances. This is not difficult using the **ITEM SAVING THROW** table.

Likewise, discharge of missiles into an existing melee is easily handled. It is permissible, of course, and the results might not be too incompatible with the desires of the discharging party. Assign probabilities to each participant in the melee or target group according to sheer numbers. In the case of participants of varying size use half value for size ''S'', normal value for size ''M'', and one and one-half value for size ''L'' creatures which are not too much larger than man-size. Total the values for each group and ratio one over the other. If side A has 4 man-sized participants, and side B has 3 smaller than man-sized participants and 1 size ''L'' bugbear, the ratio is 4:3. Then, according to the direction of the missile discharge, determine hits by using the same ratio. If 7 missiles were loosed, 4 would have a chance to hit side A, 3 side B. In cases where the ratio does not match the number of missiles, convert it to a percentage chance: 1/7 = 14% or 15%, depending on whether the missiles are coming from ahead of side A (14%) or from behind (15%). Thus 4/7 = 56% or 60% chance per missile that it will hit side A. The minor difference represents the fact that there will be considerable shifting and maneuvering during combat which will tend to expose both opponents to fire on a near equal basis. Such missiles must then be assigned (by situation or by random determination) to target creatures, a ''to hit'' determination made, and damage assessed for those which do hit.

Large missiles will be treated in the same fashion.

If one opponent group is significantly larger than the other, accurate missiles which have a small area of effect can be directed at the larger opponent group with great hope of success. You may assign a minor chance of the missile striking a friend if you wish, but this writer, for instance, always allows archery hits to hit a giant or a similar creature engaged against a human or smaller opponent.

Missiles from giants are approximately 1' in diameter, as are those from small catapults. Those from large catapults (and trebuchets) are approximately 2' in diameter.

See also **GRENADE-LIKE MISSILES** and **Special "To Hit" Bonuses.**

Strength Bonus Considerations: The strength bonus for hitting and damage does not apply to missiles unless the character so entitled specifically takes steps to equip himself or herself with special weapons to take advantage of the additional strength. This will result in the weapon having an additional chance to hit and do the additional damage as well. In no event will it add to the effective range of the character's weapon. Thus, the character will employ a heavier missile or a more powerful bow and heavier arrows or larger sling missiles to gain the advantage of strength. To do so, he or she must obtain the special weapon or weapons, and this is within the realm of your adjudication as DM as to where and how it will be obtained, and how much cost will be involved.

Dexterity Penalty And Bonus Considerations: The *Dexterity Attacking Adjustment* is for missile firing considerations when initiative is considered. It adjusts the initiative die roll for the concerned individual only. Thus, it may well allow the concerned individual to discharge a missile prior to the opponent's attack even though the opponent has gained the initiative otherwise or vice versa. More important, this factor also gives the individual a "to hit" penalty or bonus when discharging a missile at an opponent.

Special Note Regarding Giant And Machine Missiles:

When giants hurl boulders or any of the various siege machines (ballistae, catapults, etc.) fire missiles, target characters do not gain dexterity bonus considerations to armor class when "to hit" computations are made. Consider this as follows: Character A has an armor class rating of −2, but as dexterity accounts for 2 of these factors, AC rating drops to 0 if a giant is hurling rocks at the character or if some machine is discharging missiles at him or her.

Missile Fire Cover And Concealment Adjustments:

Adjust the *armor class of the target creature* as follows if cover (hard substances which protect) or concealment (soft substances which screen) exists:

TARGET HAS ABOUT	ARMOR CLASS BONUS
25% cover	+2
50% cover	+4
75% cover	+7
90% cover	+10
25% concealment	+1
50% concealment	+2
75% concealment	+3
90% concealment	+4

25% is cover or concealment to the knees, or part of the left or right side of the body screened; it might also be a target which is seen for only three-quarters of a round. Men on a walled parapet would typically be 25% covered. 50% cover or concealment equals protection or screening to the waist, half of one side of the body, or being seen for only half the round. Figures in thick brush would be at least 50% concealed; men on a castle wall with embrasures and merlons would be at least 50% covered. Shuttered embrasures and narrow windows would provide 75% cover, while arrow slits offer 90% cover.

For the effect of cover on magic, see **SPELL CASTING DURING MELEE, Effect of Cover on Spells and Spell-like Powers.**

GRENADE-LIKE MISSILES: BOULDERS AND CONTAINERS OF ACID, HOLY/UNHOLY WATER, OIL, POISON

Hurling various containers of liquid is a common tactic in dungeon adventures in particular. For game purposes it is necessary to make certain assumptions regarding all such missiles.

Size:		
	Acid —	½ pint (8 oz.)
	Holy/Unholy Water —	¼ pint (4 oz.)
	Oil —	1 pint (16 oz.)
	Poison —	¼ pint (4 oz.)

Effect:

Liquid Contents	Area of Effect	Splash	Damage From a Direct Hit
—acid	1' diameter	1 h.p.	2-8 h.p.
—holy/unholy water	1' diameter	2 h.p.	2-7 h.p.
—oil, alight	3' diameter	1-3 h.p.*	2-12 h.p. + 1-6 h.p.**
—poison	1' diameter	special	special

* Flaming oil splashed on a creature will burn for 1-3 segments, causing 1 hit point of damage per segment.

** Direct hit with flaming oil causes 2-12 hit points of damage the first round, and 1-6 additional hit points of damage the second round, but then burns out.

Range: The range of all such container missiles is 3". Beyond 1" is medium, and beyond 2" is long (−2 and −5 "to hit" respectively).

Hits: When the die roll indicates the missile has hit, then it is necessary to roll again to see if the container shatters or not — use the BLOW, CRUSHING column on the **ITEM SAVING THROW MATRIX** —unless special procedures were taken to weaken the container, i.e. the container was specially scored, it is particularly fragile, etc. Damage occurs only if the container breaks, except with regard to oil which must be alight (flaming) to cause damage. If oil has been specially prepared by insertion of a rag into the opening of the container (or wrapped around the neck of the container) and set afire prior to hurling, it will burst into flame when the container breaks upon target impact; otherwise, a torch or other means of causing combustion must be brought into contact with the oil.

Poison special is dependent upon whether or not the poison is a contact poison or if the container was hurled into the ingestive or respiratory orifice on the target creature. In the latter case, breakage is not necessary if the container was unstoppered; if stoppered check saving throw for breakage using the BLOW, NORMAL column of the **ITEM SAVING THROW MATRIX.**

Splash Hits: All creatures within three feet of the impact and breaking point of the container missile must save versus poison or be splashed with the contents of the shattered container.

Boulders: Boulders, for game purposes, are considered to be 1' in diameter for giants, 2' in diameter for siege engines. Range and damage specifications for siege machines are given in the appropriate section. (See **MONSTER MANUAL** for giants' abilities.)

A dropped boulder (or any heavy weight) will do damage as follows: each 14 lbs. of weight will inflict one point of damage per foot of distance dropped between 10' and 60' (distances above 60' are treated as 60'). Alternately, each 14 lbs. of weight will inflict a flat 1-6 hit points of damage.

Misses: If the "to hit" die roll indicates a miss, roll 1d6 and 1d8. The d6 indicates the **distance in feet** the missile was off target. (If the target was large, simply compute the distance from the appropriate portion of the target, i.e. the character aims at a section of the floor which is 1' square, and miss distance is measured from the appropriate edge as explained below.) The d8 indicates the **direction** in which the distance in feet of the miss is measured:

1 = long right	5 = short left
2 = right	6 = left
3 = short right	7 = long left
4 = short (before)	8 = long (over)

At short range you may optionally use d4 to determine distance off target, but then use d8 for long range distance determination. If the missile is hurled at a plane such as a wall, read long as high, short as low, measuring up the wall and then along the ceiling or down and then along the floor.

Lighting Oil: If a torch is used to attempt to light spilled oil, use above procedures for misses, as it still could land in the puddle of oil or oil covered area. A lantern should be handled similarly, but also allow it a 2' diameter flaming oil area.

Crossing Flaming Oil: Leaping over a puddle of flaming oil will cause no damage, unless the creature so doing is highly inflammable. Creatures with garments of cloth must save versus FIRE, NORMAL on the ITEM SAVING THROW MATRIX or have their garments catch fire. Walking through or standing in flaming oil will cause the creature to take 1-6 hit points of damage per melee round.

Holy/Unholy Water: All forms of **undead**, as well as creatures from the lower planes (demons, devils, night hags, night mares, nycadaemons, etc.) are affected by HOLY WATER. Paladins, lammasu, shedu, ki-rin, and similar creatures of good alignment (or from the upper planes) are affected by UNHOLY WATER. The liquid causes the affected creature to suffer a burning as if struck by acid. Undead in non-material form cannot be harmed by holy water, i.e. until a ghost takes on material form, it is unaffected, and a vampire in gaseous form cannot be harmed by holy water.

SPELL CASTING DURING MELEE

These functions are fully detailed in **PLAYERS HANDBOOK.** Their commencement is dictated by initiative determination as with other attack forms, but their culmination is subject to the stated casting time. Both commencement and/or completion can occur simultaneously with missile discharge, magical device attacks, and/or turning undead. Being struck by something during casting will spoil the spell.

Spell-casters will always insist that they are able to use their powers during combat melee. The DM must adjudicate the *success* of such use. Consider this: The somatic (movement) portions of a spell must be begun and completed without interruption in a clean, smooth motion. The spell as a whole must be continuous and uninterrupted from beginning to end. Once interrupted, for any reason whatsoever, the spell is spoiled and lost (just as if used). Spells cannot be cast while violently moving — such as running, dodging a blow, or even walking normally. They are interrupted by a successful hit — be it blow, missile, or appropriate spell (not saved against or saveable against).

Thus, casting a spell requires that a figure be relatively motionless and concentrating on the effort during the entire course of uninterrupted casting. For example, a magic-user casting a *fireball* must be in sight of the intended area of effect during the course of the spell (although an associate *could* be there to open a door intervening between caster and target area at an appropriate time — provided the timing was correct, of course). The caster cannot begin a spell, interrupt it just prior to completion, run to a different area, and then complete the spell; interruption instantly cancels it. Unless a spell has no somatic components, the caster cannot be crouching, let alone prone, during casting.

It can thus be understood that spell casting during a melee can be a tricky business, for a mere shove at any time can spoil the dweomer! Any spell can be attempted, but success is likely to be uncertain. Use the following procedure for spells cast during melee:

1. Spell casters must note what spell they intend to cast at the beginning of each round prior to any knowledge of which side has initiative.

2. Attacks directed at spell casters will come on that segment of the round shown on the opponent's or on their own side's initiative die, whichever is applicable. (If the spell caster's side won the initiative with a roll of 5, the attack must come then, not on the opponent's losing roll of 4 or less.) Thus, all such attacks will occur on the 1st-6th segments of the round.

3. Intelligent monsters able to recognize the danger of spells will direct attacks against spell casters if not engaged by other opponents so as to be prevented from so doing.

4. The spell caster cannot use his or her dexterity bonus to avoid being hit during spell casting; doing so interrupts the spell.

5. Any successful attack, or non-saved-against attack upon the spell caster interrupts the spell.

Because spell casting will be so difficult, most magic-users and clerics will opt to use magical devices whenever possible in melee, if they are wise.

Magical Device Attacks:

These attacks are the spell-like discharge functions of rods, staves, wands and any similar items. These attacks can occur simultaneously with the discharge of missiles, spell casting, and/or turning undead. The time of such discharge by any magical device is subject to initiative determination. (See also **Combat Procedure**, below.)

Effect Of Cover On Spells and Spell-like Powers:

Hard cover will increase chances for saving throws as noted. Cover equal to 90% (or better) will also give the target creatures the benefit of no damage whatsoever if the appropriate saving throw is successful.

Monster Charm Power:

The magical charming power of creatures such as nixies and vampires is much more powerful than that of the simple *charm person* spell. While it will eventually wear off, until it does, the charmee is subject to mental commands by the charmer, unlike either the *charm person* or *charm monster* spell. This means that a monster-charmed character does not need to speak the creature's language to understand commands from the monster which charmed it, although only basic emotions or simple commands can be mentally communicated to the charmee unless some mutual language is common to both the charmer and the charmee. While the *charmed* character is not an automaton, he or she will certainly hasten to carry out whatever instructions or commands are received from the charmer, except those which are obviously self-destructive. This relatively complete control of the charmee's mind enables the charmer to make the victim almost totally subject to its will, including giving up personal possessions, betraying associates, and so forth. Mental communication between charmer and charmee extends only to sight range or up to a 60' radius if not in sight range. Magic circles of protection (spells or specially drawn) will break the communication link and seemingly cause the *charm* to be broken, but unless magically dispelled, or until the power of the magic wears off, the effect is again evident when the charmee is outside such protection.

TURNING UNDEAD

As stated on the **CLERICS AFFECTING UNDEAD TABLE,** this function may be attempted only once by each cleric. Of course, if there are two, both may attempt the function, each trying once, etc. There is also an exceptional case where turning may be practiced more than once by each and every cleric concerned. This occurs in cases where multiple forms of creatures subject to turning are involved. If the cleric attempting the turning is successful against any or all types within the group of multiple forms of undead, that type or multiple types, to the maximum number indicated by the dice roll or otherwise indicated by the rules, are turned, and on the next round the cleric so successful may attempt to turn other undead of the group. This process may continue as long as each successive attempt is successful and the cleric lives. Undead so turned (from the group of multiple types) are lowest hit dice types to highest hit dice types, i.e. first listed to last listed on the table. Any failure to turn undead disallows a further attempt by the same cleric. Turning can occur at the same time as missile discharge, magical device attacks, and/or spell casting. It also is subject to initiative determination.

If the undead are in a mixed group — for example, 1 vampire, 3 ghasts, and 8 ghouls — you may opt to disallow any turning or other effect if the most powerful member — in the example above, the vampire — is not affected by the cleric. Naturally, this rule applies only to groups of mixed undead where the lesser are following or serving the greater. Mindless undead, skeletons and zombies, cannot be considered. Otherwise, the cleric will affect undead according to the die score, with the possibility of the lesser monsters being turned or otherwise affected, while greater ones are unaffected.

Evil Clerics: Anything below a result of *T* indicates that the undead are *compelled* to do some service. Treat this in the same way as an invisible stalker serving a magic-user. The length of service so compelled is equal to 24 hours minus the minimum score the cleric needed to compel such service. **Example:** A 9th level evil cleric meets a lich, and scores 20 on the die roll, so the lich will be neutral and not attack for 8 hours (24-16); later the same cleric encounters a vampire, and scores a 12, so the vampire will join the evil cleric and serve as a member of the cleric's group for up to 14 hours (24-10). A successful result of "T" indicates that the undead will remain neutral or serve for a full 24 hour period. A "D" result indicates co-operative service by the undead as long as the evil cleric renews his or her control every 6 days. In any of the above cases, hostile acts against the undead or associated creatures will certainly cause the cleric's effects to be totally broken and negated entirely. Hostile acts include entry into an area which the affected creatures have been commanded to guard, attempts to remove guarded items or treasure belonging to the affected creatures, attempts to prevent the affected creatures from carrying out commands, or actual attack by spell, weapon, or other forms which cause the affected creatures harm.

N.B.: Any commanded creature will immediately be freed from clerical compulsion upon the unconsciousness (excepting normal sleep) or death of the cleric who successfully compelled them to service. This will result in the affected undead or other affected creature or creatures either leaving or attacking the cleric and his or her group according to the existing circumstances. Consider treatment and risk when arriving at the action the affected creature takes. Mindless undead will simply do nothing, losing all animation and direction.

Counter-Affecting: A cleric of opposite alignment may attempt to negate the effects of a cleric who has affected undead or other creatures. The table is consulted, and if the countering cleric is successful, the affected undead are freed of the effects of the first cleric's efforts. Of course, this counter will *not* restore any undead destroyed/damned by a good cleric. This counter may in turn be countered, etc. This may continue indefinitely until one or the other cleric fails and is no longer eligible to affect undead *et al.* When affected creatures have clerical effects countered, they are powerless to take any action on the following round.

Evil Areas: You may wish to establish areas where evil has made special power bases, i.e., an evil shrine, temple, or whatever. Such areas must be limited, of course — the shrine to perhaps a 10" by 10" area, the temple to twice that area. Such areas will automatically reduce the chance of any cleric affecting undead or other creatures within their precincts by a previously stipulated factor — perhaps 1 or 2 in the shrine area, 3 or 4 in the temple area. This power can be destroyed only by desecration of the evil, i.e. breaking of the evil altar service, pouring of holy water upon the altar, *blessing and prayers,* and whatever other actions you, as DM, deem sufficient. Thus, in an area specially consecrated to evil, undead and associated creatures from the lower planes are far more difficult to handle. The corollary to this is that on the lower planes themselves, good clerics are totally unable to affect the evil creatures who dwell upon them, while on the upper planes, an evil cleric would have no effect upon a paladin. *Good areas* are similar bases of power for such creatures, and evil clerics will have lesser chances of affecting paladins or similar good aligned creatures.

FURTHER ACTIONS

Close To Striking Range:

This merely indicates that the party concerned is moving at base speed to engage the opponent. The base speed is inches, indicating tens of feet in the dungeon or similar setting indoors, tens of yards outdoors. All normal activity and bonuses are permitted when so doing. This action is typically taken when the opponent is over 1" distant but not a long distance away. Play goes to the next round after this, as melee is not possible, although other activity can, of course, take place such as that detailed above.

Charge:

This action brings the charging party into combat on the charge round, but there are a number of considerations when it is taken.

Movement Rate Outdoors: Movement *bonus* for charging in normal outdoor settings is 33⅓% of base speed for bipedal creatures, 50% for quadrupeds. (Cf. TSR's **SWORDS & SPELLS.**)

Movement Rate Indoors: The indoor/dungeon rate is greatly reduced due to the conditions. Therefore, *all movement at the charge is double base speed,* remembering that encumbered creatures are not allowed the charge. **Note:** The opponent must be within 10' distance at the termination of the charge in order for any blows to be struck during that round.

Armor Class of Charging Creatures: There is no dexterity bonus allowed for charging creatures. Creatures with no dexterity bonus become 1 armor

class lower, i.e. easier to hit. Thus an AC 3 creature becomes AC 4. There is no penalty to AC 10 creatures for charging, however.

Melee At End of Charge: Initiative is NOT checked at the end of charge movement. The opponent with the longer weapon/reach attacks first. Charging creatures gain +2 on their "to hit" dice if they survive any non-charging or charging opponent attacks which occur first. Weapon length and first strike are detailed under **Strike Blows.**

Only one charge move can be made each turn; thus an interval of 9 rounds must take place before a second charge movement can be made.

Set Weapons Against Possible Opponent Charge:

Setting weapons is simply a matter of bracing such piercing weapons as spears, spiked pole arms, forks, glaives, etc. so as to have the butt of the shaft braced against an unyielding surface. The effect of such a weapon upon a charging (or leaping, pouncing, falling, or otherwise onrushing) opponent is to cause such opponent to impale itself and take double normal damage if a hit is so scored. **Example:** Character A sets her spear with its butt firmly braced upon the floor just as a giant toad hops at her (attacking); if the spear impales the creature, it will score double indicated damage (d8 × 2). Note that in this case initiative is automatically given to the set spear as it will obviously take effect prior to any attack routine of the toad, and that two dice are not rolled, but the result of the d8 roll is multiplied by 2.

Strike Blows:

As previously stated, initiative is the key factor as to which side strikes blows first each melee round. This is modified by creatures with multiple attack routines, whether by natural or magical ability (such as *haste*). It is also modified by weapon length when one opponent is charging (or otherwise closing precipitously) into melee contact.

Simultaneous Initiative: When opponents in melee have tied for initiative, blows (attack routines included) occur simultaneously, except when both opponents are using weapons. Each weapon has a *speed factor,* and in the case of otherwise simultaneous blows, the opponent with the weapon which has the lower speed factor will strike first. Thus, a blow from a fist occurs before a blow with a dagger (1 to 2), a dagger before a short sword (2 to 3), a short sword prior to a hammer (3 to 4), and so on.

Weapon Speed Factor: This number is indicative of the wieldiness of any particular weapon, how long it takes to ready the weapon against an opponent, or how long it takes to recover and move it in its attack mode. A pike, for example, is a 13, as it must be lowered, grasped, and then held/thrust firmly. Such a weapon is not usable in dungeon settings, or anywhere else without masses of other pikes to support it. In the latter case, an opponent surviving the first attack from the bearer of the pike will likely be able to strike several times before recovery of the pike for a second thrust. This is further detailed below. A two-handed sword, with a 10 speed factor, likewise requires a lengthy readying time and recovery period after its attack due to its size and weight.

When weapon speed factor is the determinant of which opponent strikes first in a melee round, there is a chance that one opponent will be entitled to multiple attacks. Compare the score of the lower-factored weapon with that of the higher. If the difference is at least twice the factor of the lower, or 5 or more factors in any case, the opponent with the lower factored weapon is entitled to 2 attacks *before* the opponent with the higher weapon factor is entitled to any attack whatsoever. If the difference is 10 or greater, the opponent with the lower-factored weapon is entitled to 2 attacks *before* the opponent is allowed to attack, and 1 further attack at the same time the opponent with the higher-speed-factored weapon finally is allowed to attack. Note that such speed factor considerations are not applicable when either closing or charging to melee, but after an initial round of combat, or in cases where closing/charging was not necessary, the speed factor considerations are applicable.

Other Weapon Factor Determinants: The speed factor of a weapon also determines when the weapon strikes during the course of the round with respect to opponents who are engaged in activity other than striking blows. Thus, suppose side A, which has achieved initiative (action) for the round, has a magic-user engaged in casting a spell. Compare the speed factor of the weapon with the number of segments which the spell will require to cast to determine if the spell or the weapon will be cast/strike first, subtracting the losing die roll on the initiative die roll from the weapon factor and treating negative results as positive. **Example:** A sword with a factor of 5 (broad or long) is being used by an opponent of a magic-user attempting to cast a *fireball* spell (3 segment casting time). If the sword-wielding attacker was represented by a losing initiative die roll of 1, the spell will be cast *prior* to the sword's blow. A 2 will indicate that the spell and the blow are completed simultaneously. A 3-5 will indicate that the blow has a *chance* of striking (if a successful "to hit" roll is made) before the spell is cast, arriving either as the spell is begun or during the first segment of its casting. Suppose instead that a dagger were being employed. It has a speed factor of only 2, so it will strike prior to spell completion if the initiative roll which lost was 1-4 (the adjusted segment indicator being 1, 0, 1, 2 respectively) and simultaneously if the die score was a 5. If the weapon being employed was a two-handed sword (or any other weapon with a speed factor of 10, or 9 for that matter) there would be no chance for the reacting side to strike the spell caster prior to completion of the *fireball*. Note that even though a spell takes but 1 segment to complete, this is 6 seconds, and during that period a reacting attacker might be able to attack the magic-user or other spell caster prior to actual completion of the spell! If combat is simultaneous, there is no modification of the weapon speed factor.

Striking To Subdue: This is effective against some monsters (and other creatures of humanoid size and type) as indicated in the **MONSTER MANUAL** (under **DRAGONS**) or herein. Such attacks use the flat, butt, haft, pommel, or otherwise non-lethal parts of the weapons concerned but are otherwise the same as other attacks. Note that unless expressly stated otherwise, all subduing damage is 75% temporary, but 25% of such damage is actually damaging to the creature being subdued. This means that if 40 hit points of subduing damage has been inflicted upon an opponent, the creature has actually suffered 10 hit points of real damage. The above, of course, does not apply to player characters.

Grapple And Hold: See **NON-LETHAL AND WEAPONLESS COMBAT PROCEDURES.**

Special "To Hit" Bonuses:

The following general rules will be of assistance when you must adjudicate melee combat or missile fire:

Opponent encumbered, held by one leg, off balance, etc.	+2
Opponent stunned, held by both legs, *slowed*, partially bound, etc.	+4
Opponent magically asleep, *held*, paralyzed, or totally immobile	Automatic

(Cf. **MELEE, Magically Sleeping or Held Opponents**.)

Apply bonuses to the chance of the opponent being struck. The opponent will gain no dexterity bonus, of course. In totally immobilized and powerless situations, the opponent can be fully trussed, slain, or whatever in 1 round, so no bonus need be given.

See also **MELEE, Flank And Rear Attacks.**

MORALE

Morale checks are used to determine the amount of will to fight in non-leader NPCs, and can be applied both to henchmen and hirelings of character types and groups of intelligent opponent monsters (see also **Loyalty of Henchmen & Hirelings, Obedience and Morale**). Base unmodified morale score is 50%.

Morale Checks Made When
Faced by obviously superior force*	check each round
25% of party** eliminated or slain	check at +5%
Leader unconscious	check at +10%
50%+ of party** eliminated or slain	check at +15%
Leader slain or deserts	check at +30%

* Such as in melee when one force is hitting twice as often as the other.

** Or individual taking this much personal wound damage.

Other Morale Check Modifiers
Each enemy deserting	−5%
Each enemy slain	−10%
Inflicting casualties without receiving any	−20%
Each friend killed	+10%
Taking casualties without receiving any	+10%
Each friend deserting	+15%
Outnumbered & outclassed by 3 or more to 1	+20%

MORALE SCORES

Henchmen or Associated Creatures:

For each creature take the base morale (loyalty) score and cast percentile dice. Adjust the score for penalties and bonuses, and if the adjusted score is equal to or less than the loyalty score, morale is good. If the number exceeds the loyalty score, the creature will react according to the morale failure table below.

Monsters, Intelligent:

Each monster has a base morale of 50%, +5%/hit die above 1, +1%/hit point above any hit dice. If a morale check is required, scoring and reaction are as stated above for henchmen *et al*.

MORALE FAILURE

1% to 15%	fall back, fighting
16% to 30%	disengage-retreat
31% to 50%	flee in panic
51% or greater	surrender

The difference between the maximum score needed to retain morale and the number actually rolled, as adjusted, is the % of morale failure.

PURSUIT AND EVASION OF PURSUIT

There are two cases of pursuit and evasion of pursuit. The first is in underground situations, and the second is in outdoor settings. There are various special circumstances which pertain to each case, so each will be dealt with separately.

Pursuit And Evasion In Underground Settings:

When player characters, with attendant hirelings and/or henchmen, if any, elect to retreat or flee from an encounter with a monster or monsters, a possible pursuit situation arises. Whether or not pursuit will actually take place is dependent upon the following:

1. If the matrix or key states that the monster(s) in question will pursue, or if the **MONSTER MANUAL** so states, then pursuit will certainly occur.

2. If the monster or monsters encountered are semi-intelligent or under, hungry, angry, aggressive, and/or trained to do so, then pursuit will be 80% likely to occur (d10, 1 through 8).

3. If the monster or monsters encountered are of low intelligence but otherwise suit the qualifications of 2., above, then pursuit will occur with the following probabilities:

    A. If the party outnumbers the potential pursuers, then pursuit is 20% likely.

    B. If the party is about as numerous as the potential pursuers, then pursuit is 40% likely.

    C. If the party is outnumbered by the potential pursuers, then pursuit is 80% likely.

    D. If condition C. exists, and furthermore, the potential pursuers conceive of themselves as greatly superior to the party, then pursuit is 100% certain.

Pursuit will have 3 separate cases:

1. **The pursued are faster than the pursuers:** Unless there are extenuating circumstances, such as a ranger NPC or an invisible stalker or a slithering tracker pursuing, then pursuit will end as soon as any one of the following conditions is met:

A. The pursued are in sight but over 100' distant; or

B. The pursued are out of sight and were over 50' distant when they so left the perception of the pursuer(s); or

C. Pursuit has continued over 5 rounds, and the pursuer has not gained perceptibly upon the pursued.

2. **The pursued are of equal speed to the pursuers:** As in case 1. above, pursuit will end as soon as any 1 of the following conditions are met:

A. The pursued are in sight but over 150' distant; or

B. The pursued are out of sight and were over 80' distant when they left the perception of the pursuer(s); or

C. Pursuit has continued over 1 turn, and the pursuer has not gained perceptibly upon the pursued.

3. **The pursuer is faster than the pursued:** The pursuit will be broken off only if one of the following occurs:

A. The pursued are out of sight and were over 200' distant when they left the perception of the pursuer(s); or

B. The pursuer is unable to continue due to reasons of physical endurance.

Modifiers To Pursuit: There are several circumstances which will affect the pursuer. These are:

1. **Barriers:** Physical or magic barriers will slow or halt pursuit, i.e. a locked portal, a broken bridge, a *wall of fire*, etc.

2. **Distractions:** Actual or magic distractions will be from 10% to 100% likely to cause pursuit to falter or cease altogether. For example, a *dancing lights* spell moving away from a fleeing party which has extinguished its light sources might distract pursuers, just as a *phantasmal force* of a strong helper joining the pursued might cause the pursuers to cease pursuit. Similarly, if the pursued passed through or near some other creatures which would be hostile to the pursuing force, or at least not friendly to the pursuers, then it is quite possible that the creatures passed through and the pursuers would become embroiled. **N.B.:** The likelihood of any distraction being successful is a matter for individual adjudication by the DM, using **AD&D** principles and common sense as they apply to the particular circumstances prevailing. There are also 2 sub-cases here:

A. **Food:** Food, including rations and/or wine, will be from 10% to 100% likely to distract pursuers of low intelligence or below, providing the food/wine is what they find palatable. Roll a d10 to find the probability, unless you have a note as to how hungry or food-oriented the creatures are. Add 10% to the result for every point of intelligence below 5, and give a 100% probability for non-intelligent creatures pursuing. If probability is under 100%, roll the d10 a second time, and if the result is equal to or less than the probability determined, then the pursuers break off pursuit for 1 round while the food/wine is consumed.

B. **Treasure:** Treasure, including precious metals, gems, jewelry, rare stuffs such as ivory or spices, valuable items, and/or magic will be 10% to 100% likely to cause pursuers of low or greater intelligence to be distracted. Pursuers of low intelligence will have an additional 10% per 10 items (regardless of actual value) dropped, i.e. 20 copper pieces have a 20% additional probability of causing a distraction. The value of items dropped, known or presumed or potential, will likewise cause pursuers of average or greater intelligence to be more likely to be distracted. For each 100 g.p. value or potential value, add 10% to base probability. Roll the d10 a second time to see if potential and actual interest are the same, just as is done when food is used as a possible distraction. (Note, however, that very small items of value — notably, gems and the like — would have a chance of going completely unnoticed in the heat of pursuit.) If success occurs, the pursuer will be distracted for 1 round, or the length of time necessary to gather up the treasure, whichever is the greater.

3. **Multiple Choice:** It will most often come to pass that the pursued take a

route which enables them to cause the pursuer(s) to have to make decisions as to which direction the pursued took in their flight. Thus, at a branching passage where there are 3 possible ways which could have been taken, there is a basic 2 in 3 chance that the pursuer(s) will take the wrong passage. Likewise, if there are a door and a passage, there is a 1 in 2 chance of wrong choice. This base chance assumes that the pursuer cannot see the pursued when choice is made, that sound does not reveal the direction of flight, that smell does not reveal direction of flight, nor do any other visual, audial, or olfactory clues point to the escape path. As DM, you will have to adjudicate such situations as they arise. The following guidelines might prove helpful:

LIGHT: Straight line of sight is near infinite, any corner cuts distance to 60'.

NOISE: Characters in metal armor can be heard for 90', hard boots can be heard at 60', relatively quiet movement can be heard at 30'.

ODORS: Normal scent can be detected by creatures hunting or tracking by scent for several hours — even in a dungeon setting. Scent can be masked with various things — mustard powder, oil of citronella, crushed stinging nettle, etc.

Building Interiors: Treat these settings the same as one underground, as applicable.

Procedure For Determination Of Evasion Underground: If it is discovered that a pursuit situation exists, and the player-party elects to evade rather than confront pursuers, then record the relative speeds of pursued and pursuer. Move the pursued party as many 10's of feet as their *slowest* member is able to travel, and likewise move the pursuing party as many 10's of feet as its *fastest* member can travel, noting positions of slower members, if any, as well. This movement is accomplished on the map, of course. Three such movement phases are (for game purposes) equal to 1 round. At the end of any movement portion where any number of the pursued party is within 10' or less of any number of the pursuing party, confrontation must take place between the concerned members of the parties. (At this point the remainder, if any, of the pursued party may elect to stop flight or continue evasion attempts as they wish.) Also, at the end of each movement portion it is necessary to check the 3 SEPARATE PURSUIT CASES and any PURSUIT MODIFIERS to see if the pursued party has succeeded in evading the pursuers. Keep track not only of the route of flight, but also of the amount of game time so spent, as some pursuit will automatically cease after a set period without confrontation.

Mapping During Flight: No mapping is ever possible. Give no distance measures in moving the pursued. Give no compass directions either!

Pursuit And Evasion In Outdoor Settings:

Pursuit in the outdoors is generally similar to that in settings underground or indoors. The 3 general rules of likelihood of pursuit apply. However, pursuit will certainly continue until evasion is successfully accomplished. In outdoor settings, evasion is accomplished in a different manner, the variables being the relative speed of movement and size of the parties concerned and the type of terrain over which pursuit takes place. Available light is also a factor.

BASE CHANCE OF EVADING PURSUIT OUTDOORS:	80%

MOVEMENT SPEED ADJUSTMENT	
— Pursued is faster	+10%
— Both parties are of equal speed	0%
— Pursuer is faster	−20%

TERRAIN ADJUSTMENT	
— Plain, desert, open water	−50%
— Scrub, rough, hills, marsh	+10%
— Forest, mountains	+30%

SIZE OF PARTIES INVOLVED ADJUSTMENT	
— Pursued party totals fewer than 6 creatures	+10%
— Pursued party totals 6-11 creatures	0%
— Pursued party totals 12-50 creatures	−20%
— Pursued party totals over 50 creatures	−50%
— Pursuing party totals fewer than 12 creatures	−20%
— Pursuing party totals 12-24 creatures	0%
— Pursuing party totals over 24 creatures	+10%

AVAILABLE LIGHT ADJUSTMENT	
— Light equal to full daylight	−30%
— Light equal to twilight	−10%
— Light equal to bright moonlight	0%
— Light equal to starlight	+20%
— Light equal to dark night	+50%

Procedure For Determination Of Evasion Outdoors: Upon encountering creatures from which the player-party flees in order to evade, determine if a condition of surprise exists. If the player-party has surprised the creature encountered, evasion is automatic. If no surprise exists, then follow the procedure below. If the party encountering the creatures is surprised, then no evasion is possible, and confrontation is unavoidable.

Find the chance for evasion by adjusting the base chance according to variables. The pursued party rolls percentile dice, and if the number generated is less than or equal to the adjusted base chance of evasion, then they have had immediate success at eluding the pursuers. Otherwise, pursuit continues unless the pursuers are faster than the pursued and can close within 1 hour, in which case confrontation must take place. Continuing pursuit requires an evasion check every game hour. After the initial check each game hour another must be made just as is initially done, with the added stipulation that any result of 0% or less indicates immediate confrontation and no further chance of evasion.

Special Note Regarding Fatigue: No rules for exhaustion and fatigue are given here because of the tremendous number of variables, including the stamina of the characters and creatures involved. Thus, characters mounted on horses have gradually slowing movement, but this is not a factor unless pursuing creatures tire more or less rapidly than do the mounts. You must judge these factors in a case of continuing pursuit. Fatigue merely slows movement and reduces combat effectiveness. Exhaustion will generally require a day of complete rest to restore the exhausted creatures. Always bear in mind that humans inured to continuous running, for example, can do so for hours without noticeable fatigue, i.e., those such as Apache Indians, Zulu warriors, etc. Do not base your judgment on the typical modern specimen.

MELEE

The term melee includes striking with bodily weapons such as teeth, fangs, tusks, tushes, claws, nails, talons, paws, etc. It also includes striking with various objects and weapons. The **COMBAT TABLES** are used for determination of hits, and the amount of damage scored is given in either the **MONSTER MANUAL** or the **PLAYERS HANDBOOK** (for weapons). It also includes **NON-LETHAL AND WEAPONLESS COMBAT PROCEDURES** (q.v.). While combat includes melee, melee does not include such facets of combat as missile fire, spell casting, etc. In general, the procedure followed in melee is explained under **ENCOUNTERS, COMBAT, AND INITIATIVE** or **NON-LETHAL AND WEAPONLESS COMBAT PROCEDURES.** Special considerations are given here.

Number Of Opponents Per Figure:

Physical size and space will dictate limitation upon the number of opponents able to engage a single figure in melee. If **Official ADVANCED DUNGEONS & DRAGONS** miniature figures are used to represent the creatures involved in a melee, then these miniatures will dictate the number of opponents which can be involved. Beware of using other fantasy miniature figures, as most of them are not designed to the specific scale and do not conform to the standards of the **MONSTER MANUAL** (or even necessarily conform to 25mm scale!). In other cases use the following rule of thumb:

1. If the single figure is size S, 4 size M or 2 size L figures are all that can attack it under optimum conditions during any single round. 6 size S figures can attack it, however, space permitting.

2. If the single figure is size M, it can be attacked by a maximum of 8 size S opponents, 6 size M, or 4 size L.

3. If the single figure is size L, a maximum of 12 size S, 8 size M, or 6 size L figures can engage it at one time.

Modifiers are impossible to detail fully, as they include the physical circumstances prevailing at the time. It is obvious that a figure in a narrow passage or in a corner can be attacked only from a limited front. Similarly, the shape of the single figure and the attackers will be a factor, as a giant snake has more body space subject to attack than does a giant, unless the attackers are able to fly or otherwise attack the entire vertical surface of the giant. Any long-bodied creature has more area open to attack, and wide-bodied creatures, or those which employ some natural body weaponry which requires contact with the opponent, will be more restricted with respect to the number of attackers possible, viz. how many constrictor snakes can effectively attack an opponent? Two basic grid systems are shown below, one with hexagons, one with squares. These grids demonstrate how multiple opponents engage a single figure. (See also **Flank And Rear Attacks**, hereafter.)

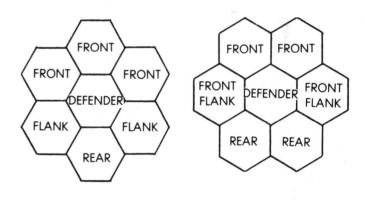

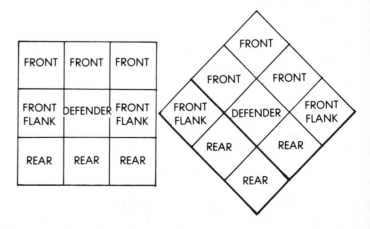

To determine the number of opponents which can attack the single defender, use squares or hexes of one inch per face for 25mm scale, or you may simply view the illustrations used above and mentally visualize the situation. For example, in the case of a human being attacked by giant rats, 2 of the attackers would certainly be able to fit into each hexagon (if normal rats were attacking, 4 per hex) so 6 would attack frontally, 4 from flank positions, and 2 from the rear. If these same giant rats were attacking a centaur, for instance, the number of flank attacks would certainly be increased to allow 2 more hexes (4 more attackers gaining flank attack advantage).

Special Types Of Attacks:

Flank Attacks: All flank attacks negate any defender armor class addition for shield. Attacks against a rear flank, where the opponent is virtually unable to view the attackers, negate dexterity armor class bonus.

Rear Attacks: Opponents attacking from the rear gain a +2 to hit, negate any consideration for shield, and also negate any consideration for dexterity.

Stunned, Prone or Motionless Opponents: Treat all such opponents as if being attacked from the rear, but in this case the "to hit" bonus is +4 rather than +2.

Magically Sleeping or Held Opponents: If a general melee is in progress, and the attacker is subject to enemy actions, then these opponents are automatically struck by any attack to which they would normally be subject, and the maximum damage possible according to the weapon type is inflicted each time such an opponent is so attacked. The number of attacks or attack routines possible against such an opponent is twice the number normally allowed in a round. Otherwise, such opponents may be automatically slain, or bound as appropriate to materials at hand and size, at a rate of one per round. Note that this does not include normally sleeping opponents (see **ASSASSINS' TABLE FOR ASSASSINATIONS**).

Invisible Opponents: Invisible opponents are always at an advantage. They can only be attacked if they are attacking or otherwise detected somehow. These opponents always cause the attacker to attack at a –4 on "to hit" rolls because of the invisibility. They can never be attacked from flank or rear positions unless the attacker can see them (thus they are, in fact, visible!).

Important Note Regarding "To Hit" Adjustments:

Certain spells such as *curse*, *prayer*, and *protection from evil* adjust the chance "to hit" of either the attacker or the defender or both. Such changes MUST be made to the armor class of the figure concerned, not to the dice score rolled in attacking. An inspection of the combat tables will show that the dice roll progression will make some opponents *hit proof* if the dice rolls are adjusted downwards rather than the armor class being moved upwards. (At some point, the upwards armor class adjustment could also make such opponents virtually invulnerable, but this is less likely and not necessarily undesirable.) *Example:* A reverse *bless*, a *curse*, is cast upon opponents. Therefore, the effective armor class of the side which cast the spell will be raised by one category, so that a figure normally of armor class 4 will be treated as 3, 3 as 2, etc. By so doing it is still possible for opponents to roll natural 20s and thus score hits.

Who Attacks Whom:

As with missile fire, it is generally not possible to select a specific opponent in a mass melee. If this is the case, simply use some random number generation to find out which attacks are upon which opponents, remembering that only a certain number of attacks can usually be made upon one opponent. If characters or similar intelligent creatures are able to single out an opponent or opponents, then the concerned figures will remain locked in melee until one side is dead or opts to attempt to break off the combat. If there are unengaged opponents, they will move to melee the unengaged enemy. If the now-unengaged figures desire to assist others of their party, they will have to proceed to the area in which their fellows are engaged, using the movement rates already expressed.

Meleeing An Opponent Spell Caster:

If an opponent spell caster attempting a spell is in melee, and is attacked by weapon or punched, grappled, or overborne, there is a likelihood of the opponent not being able to cast the spell. In the case of hits with weapons or successful striking with a punch, the spell caster will absolutely be prevented from completion of the spell (and furthermore the entire spell is LOST). In the case of grappling or overbearing, the spell caster will absolutely be prevented from spell completion if the attack form is successful, and the spell is wasted in this case also. Both cases assume the attack occurring prior to completion of the spell, of course.

Attacks With Two Weapons:

Characters normally using a single weapon may choose to use one in each hand (possibly discarding the option of using a shield). The second weapon must be either a dagger or hand axe. Employment of a second weapon is always at a penalty. The use of a second weapon causes the character to attack with his or her primary weapon at –2 and the secondary weapon at –4. If the user's dexterity is below 6, the *Reaction/Attacking Adjustment* penalties shown in the **PLAYERS HANDBOOK** are added to EACH weapon attack. If the user's dexterity is above 15, there is a downward adjustment in the weapon penalties as shown, although this never gives a positive (bonus) rating to such attacks, so that at 16 dexterity the secondary/primary penalty is –3/–1, at 17 –2/0, and at 18 –1/0.

The secondary weapon does not act as a shield or parrying device in any event.

Breaking Off From Melee:

At such time as any creature decides, it can break off the engagement and flee the melee. To do so, however, allows the opponent a free attack or attack routine. This attack is calculated as if it were a rear attack upon a stunned opponent. When this attack is completed, the retiring/fleeing party may move away at full movement rate, and unless the opponent pursues and is able to move at a higher rate of speed, the melee is ended and the situation becomes one of encounter avoidance.

Monks' Open Hand Melee:

Despite their training and capabilities, monks are not supermen or superwomen. The **PLAYERS HANDBOOK** states that they are able to stun or kill opponents with open hand attacks, and this is so; but such opponents are limited in general to man-size or smaller. This is indicated below:

A MONK AT 1ST LEVEL IS CAPABLE OF STUNNING OR KILLING ONLY AN OPPONENT OF MAN-SIZE (M) OR SMALLER. FOR PURPOSES OF THIS DETERMINATION, MAN-SIZE SHALL BE:

Maximum Height: 6' 6"
Maximum Weight: 300#

For each level above the 1st, the monk will gain additional stunning/killing ability at the rate of 2 inches of height and 50 pounds of opponent weight per level of experience gained. Thus:

Monk's Level	Opponent Maximum Height	Opponent Maximum Weight
2nd	6' 8"	350#
3rd	6' 10"	400#
4th	7'	450#
5th	7' 2"	500#
6th	7' 4"	550#
7th	7' 6"	600#
8th	7' 8"	650#
9th	7' 10"	700#
10th	8'	750#
11th	8' 2"	800#
12th	8' 4"	850#
13th	8' 6"	900#
14th	8' 8"	950#
15th	8' 10"	1,000#
16th	9'	1,050#
17th	9' 2"	1,100#

At the upper levels (13th and above) you may wish to allow a variation upwards of some considerable height and weight — perhaps an additional 1" to 2" and 50# per level so as to allow some chance versus the larger and heavier creatures such as hill giants.

Important: Monks' stunning/killing ability can only apply to living things. Undead cannot be affected (and an open hand hit on an undead creature could be very undesirable from the monk's standpoint in any event — especially if the creature causes damage by touch, for the monk touching the undead creature then is the same as the reverse). Golems and dopplegangers cannot be affected. Damage from open hand attacks still accrues if the monster can be so hit otherwise.

Actions During Combat And Similar Time-Important Situations:

The activity of player characters and player character-directed creatures must be stated precisely and without delay at the start of each melee round or before the appropriate divisions of other situations where exact activity must be known. If you are a stickler, you may require all participants to write their actions on paper. Conversation regarding such activities is the same as if player characters were talking aloud, of course.

Delay in deciding what is to be done should be noted, as such hesitation will basically mean that the individual is not doing anything whatsoever during the period, but he or she is simply standing by and dithering, trying to arrive at a decision as to what should be done. Considering the melee round as 1 full minute, actually time a participant, and you will see what is meant . . . . In a similar vein, some players will state that they are going to do several actions, which, if allowed, would be likely to occupy their time for many rounds. For example: "I'll hurl oil at the monster, ignite it, drink my *potion of invisibility,* sneak up behind it, and then stab it in the back!" How ambitious indeed. Where is the oil? In a pouch, of course, so that will take at least 1, possibly 2 segments to locate and hurl. If the potion is in the character's back pack, 3 or 4 segments will be taken up just finding it, and another 1 segment will be required to consume its contents. (See **DRINKING POTIONS.**) Now comes the tricky part, sneaking up. Assuming that the potion has taken effect, and that our dauntless character has managed to transfer his or her weapon back to his or her hand (for certainly all the other activity required the character to at least put the weapon in the off hand), he or she is now ready to creep around the fringe of the combat and steal up behind the foe to smite it in the back. If the space is not too crowded (remember, his or her friends can't see the invisible character either) and the monster not too far away, the time should only amount to about a round or so. Therefore, the character's actions will fill something over two complete rounds.

As DM, simply note these actions, and begin them accordingly. Then, when the player starts to give instructions about additional activity, simply remind him or her that he or she is already engaged in the former course, and that you will tell him or her when that is finished and new instructions are in order. If the player then changes plans, take the character from its current state and location accordingly.

Example of Melee:

Party A (player characters) is composed of Aggro the Axe, a 4th level fighter; Abner, a 5th level magic-user; Arkayn, a 4th level cleric; and Arlanni, a 2nd level thief. They are hastening down a dungeon corridor in order to avoid an encounter with a large group of goblins, whose territory they are now leaving. It is a ten-foot wide corridor and they are moving with the cleric, fighter, and thief in a line in front, followed closely by the magic-user. Suddenly they round a bend and confront party B, who are earnestly engaged in squabbling over some treasure. Party B is composed of Gutboy Barrelhouse, a 6th level dwarf fighter; Balto, a 1st level monk; Blastum, a 4th level magic-user; and Barjin, a 4th/5th level half-elf fighter/magic-user.

The first thing the DM must do is determine if either party is *surprised.* He rolls a d6 for party B (where the players can see it, since there are no secret modifiers) and a 2 comes up. The leader for the players rolls and gets a 4 for party A. Party B is surprised (since they rolled a 2), and will be inactive for 2 segments.

Next the DM checks distance, and finds that the parties are only 10' apart — sufficiently near to close and strike.

Party A immediately recognizes party B as a group of "evil marauders" they were warned against and moves to attack. First, Arlanni the thief, who had her sling ready (as the player had stated previous to the encounter), fires a shot at Blastum, who is obviously a magic-user. A sling bullet gains +3 "to hit" vs. no armor. Arlanni would usually need an 11 to hit, but now needs only an 8. She rolls a 5, and misses.

Aggro the fighter rushes forward to attack the nearest opponent, who happens to be Balto, the monk. Balto is wearing no armor, so Aggro needs a base 8 to hit Balto. However, Aggro is using a +1 hand axe, and furthermore an axe is +1 to hit vs. no armor, so Aggro's adjusted amount needed to hit is only 6 (or, alternately, the cumulative +2 could be added to whatever he rolls to improve his chances of rolling an 8 or better). Aggro rolls a 14 and hits Balto, but only 1 point of damage is rolled, plus a 1 point bonus from the magic axe (2 points total), and Balto can take 4.

Meanwhile, Abner and Arkayn have been preparing short (first level) spells. The cleric shouts a *command* of "surrender!" at Gutboy Barrelhouse, but Gutboy is 6th level and thus gets a saving throw. Furthermore, he is a dwarf with a constitution of 16, and thus saves at +4. He therefore needs a 10 or better to save (instead of a 14). He rolls a 17 and saves easily. Unfortunately, he is almost simultaneously hit by two *magic missiles* from Abner, the magic-user. Against these there is no save, and Gutboy suffers 6 points of damage (from a possible 4-10).

As party B is surprised for 2 segments, party A has a chance to hit in each segment as if they were full rounds (this does not apply to spell use, of course). In the second segment, Arlanni chooses to set down her crossbow and unsheathe her sword. Aggro would normally get another chance to hit Balto, who would be inactive for another segment, but Balto's dexterity allows him a +1 reaction adjustment, which means that he personally will be surprised for one less segment than the rest of his party. So this segment he is up and on his guard, and Aggro does not get another hit attempt this round. Arkayn the cleric readies his mace as Abner steps back and begins to unroll a scroll for use next round.

Now initiative dice are rolled, and party A's score is lower, so party B gets to react to the assault. Balto attacks Aggro (who is in AC 2) with his staff. He needs a base 18 to hit, and the −7 armor class adjustment for sword vs. plate mail and shield makes this a 20. He (the DM) rolls a 19 — almost, but not quite! Gutboy Barrelhouse and Barjin the fighter/magic-user both attack Arkayn. That cleric's AC is only 5. Gutboy has +1 to hit due to strength, and his hammer's armor class adjustment vs. scale mail and shield is +1, so he needs a 9 or better to hit (11 before bonuses). He rolls a 12 and hits for 5 points of damage (including 1 point of bonus damage from strength). Barjin, with a sword, needs a 13 or better to hit Arkayn. He rolls a 13 exactly, and hits for 6 more points of damage. Arkayn is starting to have second thoughts about this whole affair.

Meanwhile, Blastum has been preparing a *shocking grasp* spell, and now he steps forward and touches (rolls a successful "to hit" die score) Arlanni the thief, delivering 10 points of damage (1-8 + 4). There is no saving throw: Arlanni has only 8 hit points, and dies.

On the left, Aggro again attacks Balto with his axe. He rolls a 12 and hits him for 5 points. Balto only had two points left, so he is dead.

Arkayn chooses to attempt to hit Gutboy Barrelhouse. The dwarf is clad in splint mail, but he is carrying a +2 shield, so his effective armor class is 1 (though his AC *type* is 3). Arkayn needs a base 17 to hit AC 1, but using a mace vs. AC *type* 3 gives him a +1 armor class adjustment, so he really only needs a 16 or better. He rolls a 7 and misses.

During this time Abner has been reading a *web* spell from the scroll, and now it takes effect. The *web* stretches from wall to wall and entangles Gutboy, Barjin, Blastum (who was beginning spell preparations, though now they're ruined and the spell is lost), and the unfortunate Arkayn, who was too near not to get caught. All attempt saving throws, but only Gutboy Barrelhouse makes his, and thus is only partially entangled. However, even his 17 strength will not enable him to escape the *web* in time to avoid being subsequently subdued or killed by Aggro or *slept* by Abner. The melee is effectively over: Arkayn can be helped out of the *web* by his friends, while Barjin and Blastum are basically helpless to avoid whatever the player characters have in mind concerning them.

As you can see, a large number of things can happen in each round of melee, yet this whole fight took only two minutes of game time. Some melees will last far longer. It may seem at first as if there is a tremendous number of confusing variables that modify the action, but you'll be surprised at how quickly you'll be able to conduct a complicated melee and routinely cover every point. An experienced DM can do it with only an occasional reference to the tables (though it is not recommended that you try this — wait until it comes naturally). The main thing to remember is to do everything in an orderly, step-by-step fashion. Deal with your players' actions and reactions one by one instead of all at once, or you will never be able to keep track of what round it is, and who's doing what when.

NON-LETHAL AND WEAPONLESS COMBAT PROCEDURES

It is not uncommon for players to be weaponless at some stage of a game — or for better players to wish to attack an opponent bare-handed in order to most effectively neutralize that opponent's potential; whether to subdue or slay when neutralized is another matter. *Three basic attack modes are recommended:* PUMMEL, GRAPPLE, OVERBEAR. Each method of attack is explained separately, and each has its own table and modifiers.

Variable Applicable To All Pummeling, Grappling, and Overbearing Attacks: The attacker takes the number of the column he or she normally uses for weapon attacks, 1 being that for the lowest levels, 2 being that for the next group of levels, and so on. To this number he or she adds the score of a secretly rolled d6, i.e. 1-6. The defender does the same, but the die score is that of a d4. The attacker may use this variable for:

1) a bonus to his or her base chance to pummel, grapple, or overbear, OR

2) a bonus to the score rolled for a successful pummeling, grappling, or overbearing attack.

The defender may use the variable for:

1) a penalty (subtraction) to the attacker's base chance to pummel, grapple, or overbear, OR

2) a penalty (subtraction) to the attacker's pummeling, grappling, or overbearing attack which has succeeded.

The decision as to how to use the variable must be made prior to each attack.

Unconscious parties gain no such variable.

Pummel: This attack form is aimed at battering an opponent into unconsciousness. It can be used with fists or dagger pommel (as in *pummel*) as weapons. 25% of damage sustained is actual; the remaining 75% is restored at the rate of 1 hit point per round. Whenever an opponent reaches 0 hit points, unconsciousness occurs. It lasts for 1 round, plus 1 round for every point of damage beyond 0 hit points which has been sustained, i.e. 4 hit points equals 5 rounds of unconsciousness. An unconscious opponent can be trussed or slain in 1 round.

Determination of First Attack Initiative: First attack initiative is determined by surprise, charging to attack, higher dexterity, or higher die roll — in that order. Whichever first occurs determines the first attack for the round, so in most cases the pummeling attacker will go first in the first round.

Base Score to Hit: The base score on percentile dice is opponent AC value times 10 to arrive at a percentage chance to hit, i.e. AC 10 = 100%, AC 9 = 90%, all the way to AC ratings of 0 and minus numbers which indicate no chance or a negative chance to score a hit. The base chance to hit is modified as follows:

Attacker's dexterity, per point	+1%
Attacker's strength, per point over 15	+1%
Attacker's AC, per point, with negative AC being treated as positive by type*	+1%
Opponent slowed	+10%
Opponent stunned	+20%
Opponent prone without shield or ready weapon and/or helpless	AUTOMATIC HIT
Opponent base movement over 12″**	−5%
Opponent *hasted* (includes *speed* potion)	−10%

* Magical protections such as rings, bracers, cloaks, etc. do not count as AC, so ignore them; encumbrance = AC 10.

** Do not count if unable to move freely — down, cornered, encumbered, etc.

In each round of weaponless melee, there will be two pummeling attacks, and possibly several blows per attack. The attacker determines if a strike is

successful, and then whether or not it does any damage and how much, if any. Percentile dice are rolled, and the score is modified as shown below. The **PUMMELING TABLE** is then consulted.

Attacker's strength —	
per point over 12	+1%
per 10% over 18	+2%
Using wooden butt or mailed fist	+5%
Using metal pommel	+10%
Opponent slowed	+10%
Opponent stunned	+20%
Opponent helpless	+30%
Active defender —	
per point of dexterity over 14	−2%
employing shield	−10%
Leather or padded armor	−10%
Chain, ring, scale, or studded mail	−20%
Magical cloak or ring	−30%
Banded, plate, or splint mail	−40%
Helmet, open-faced	−5%
Helmet, nasaled but otherwise open	−10%
Helmet, visored or slitted	−20%

PUMMELING TABLE

Adjusted Dice Score	Result	Hit Points of Damage Scored
under 01	blow misses, opponent may counter	none
01-20	ineffective blow, strike again	none
21-40	glancing blow, off balance*	2 + strength bonus
41-60	glancing blow, strike again	4 + strength bonus
61-80	solid punch, off balance*	6 + strength bonus
81-00	solid punch, strike again	8 + strength bonus
over 00	crushing blow, opponent is stunned**	10 + strength bonus

* Series ends, determination of next strike must be made.

** Opponent unable to attack for 1 full round.

Grapple: This attack form is aimed at holding the opponent and rendering him or her helpless. Damage sustained is 25% actual and 75% incidental which is restored at 1 hit point per round. As in pummeling attacks, a score of 0 equals unconsciousness, 1 round plus 1 round for each point of minus damage sustained.

Determination of First Attack Initiative: Surprise, charging to attack, higher dexterity, higher die roll — in that order.

Base Score to Grapple: Multiply attacker's armor class by 10, ignoring magical devices (bracers, cloaks, rings, etc.), but adding 1 for each +1 of magical armor, to find a percentage chance from 100% to 0%. **Note:** The attacker cannot grapple if either or both hands are holding anything. The base chance to grapple is modified as follows:

Attacker's dexterity, per point	+1%
Defender's armor protection is —	
leather or padded	+10%
chain, ring, scale	+20%
banded, plate, splint	+30%
Opponent slowed or stunned	+20%
Opponent base movement 3″ faster	−10% per 3″
Opponent *hasted* (includes *speed* potion)	−20%

In each round of grappling combat there will be an attack and a counter. Any existing hold automatically goes first until broken. Once it is determined that a grappling attack succeeds, the percentile dice must be rolled again to find what hold is gained. The dice roll is modified as follows:

Attacker's dexterity, per point	+1%
Attacker's strength —	
per point	+1%
per 10% over 18	+1%
Opponent slowed	+10%
Opponent stunned	+20%
Opponent helpless	+30%
Per 10% weight difference (attacker)	±5%
Per 10% height difference* (attacker)	±5%

Opponent dexterity, per point over 14	−2%
Opponent strength —	
per point over 12	−1%
per 10% over 18	−1%
Opponent wearing banded or plate mail	−10%
Opponent wearing gorget and helmet	−10%
Opponent using shield	−10%

* Halved if prone.

Bonuses and penalties are totalled and the result added to the result of the percentile dice roll. The **GRAPPLING TABLE** is then consulted for the result.

GRAPPLING TABLE

Adjusted Dice Score	Result	H.P. or Special Damage Scored
under 21	waist clinch, opponent may counter	none
21-40	arm lock//forearm/elbow smash	1 + strength bonus
41-55	hand/finger lock//bite	2 + strength bonus
56-70	bear hug/trip	3 + strength bonus
71-85	headlock//flip or throw	5 + strength bonus
86-95	strangle hold//head butt	6 + strength bonus
Over 95	kick/knee/gouge	8 + strength bonus, opponent stunned

Any hold shown remains in effect from round to round unless the opponent scores a higher percentage hold, i.e. arm lock breaks a waist clinch, a hand/finger lock breaks an arm lock, and so forth. Damage accrues until a hold is broken or until the holder elects to try for a different hold. The opponent may still inflict damage by lesser hold results shown after the double slashes (//). These might result in both opponents falling to the ground and continuing their grappling there. **Note:** If the opponent is stunned, a second attack may immediately be made, and the stunned opponent cannot counter for 1 round.

Overbear: This attack form aims at quickly taking the opponent to a prone position, incidentally inflicting damage, and allowing either a pummel or grappling follow-up attack. The attacker can have either or both hands otherwise employed — carrying a shield, weapon, etc. 50% of damage inflicted is actual, the balance is restored at the rate of 1 point per round. Once an opponent is overborne, some other form of combat MUST take place.

Determination of First Attack Initiative: Surprise, charging to attack, higher dexterity, higher die roll — in that order. Attacker attempting to overbear need not go first to so attack.

Base Score to Hit: Same as grappling attack. If overbearing attack succeeds, roll percentile dice again, and modify the resulting total by the following:

Attacker's strength —	
per point	+1%
per 10% over 18	+2%
Opponent slowed or 1 foot held	+10%
Rushing or leaping to attack	+15%
Opponent stunned or both feet held	+20%
Per 10% weight difference	±10%
Per 10% height difference	±5%
Opponent's strength —	
per point over 14	−1%
per 10% over 18	−2%
Opponent's dexterity, per point over 14*	−2%
Opponent braced	−10%

OVERBEARING TABLE

Adjusted Dice Score	Result	Hit Points of Damage Scored
under 21	bounce off or avoided, opp. may ctr.	none
21-40	slip down and grab leg	none
41-60	opponent staggered, attack again	1 + strength bonus
61-80	opponent knocked to knees	2 + strength bonus
81-00	opponent knocked to hands and knees	3 + strength bonus
over 00	opponent knocked flat, stunned for 1 round	4 + strength bonus

General Notes:

Multiple Opponent Attacks: It is possible for as many opponents as will physically be able to attack a single adversary to engage in pummeling, grappling, or overbearing attack modes. Attack order must first be determined. Attack from behind negates the shield and dexterity components of the defending creature. Hits are determined, then results, in order of attack.

Monsters using these attack modes will choose the most effective if they are human or humanoid and have above average intelligence, otherwise they will use the modes in random fashion. Creatures will always attack to overbear if they do not use weapons, except bears and similar monsters who seek to crush opponents by hugging attacks (these are grappling).

Opponents With Weapons Used Normally: If the opponent of a grappling, pummeling or overbearing attack has a weapon, the opponent will always strike first unless the attacker has surprise. Any weapon hit does NO damage, but it does indicate that the attacker trying to grapple, pummel or overbear has been fended or driven off, and the attack is unsuccessful. The weapon-wielder then has the opportunity to strike at the weaponless one "for real", if he or she so chooses. Surprised opponents with weapons have no chance for a fending-off strike, unless the attacker must use all surprise segments to close to grapple, pummel, or overbear.

Monks: Even if grappled, pummeled, or overborne, monks are able to conduct open hand combat normally until stunned or unconscious.

COMBAT TABLES

Using The Combat Tables:

Find the level of the attacker on the appropriate chart and matrix that with the armor class of the defender. The resulting number or greater must be rolled on a d20 for a successful hit. Penalties and bonuses may modify either the die roll or the number needed to hit, as long as one method is used consistently.

ATTACK MATRICES FOR MISSILE AND MELEE COMBAT, CLERICS AFFECTING UNDEAD, PSIONIC COMBAT

I. Attack Matrices for Dwarves, Elves, Gnomes, Half-Elves, Halflings, Half-Orcs, and Humans
 A. Clerics, Druids, and Monks
 B. Fighters, Paladins, Rangers, and 0 Level Halflings and Humans
 C. Magic-Users and Illusionists
 D. 1. Thieves and Assassins
   2. Assassins' Table for Assassinations

II. Attack Matrix for Monsters

III. Matrix for Clerics Affecting Undead

IV. Matrices for Psionic Combat
 A. Psionic vs. Psionic in Mental Combat
 B. Psionic Attack upon Defenseless Psionic
 C. Psionic Blast Attack upon Non-Psionic Creature
 D. Psionic Attack Ranges and Damage Adjustment

Opponent Armor Class Description (If Armor is Worn):

Armor Class	Type of Armor
2	Plate mail + shield
3	Splint or banded mail + shield/plate mail
4	Chain mail + shield/splint or banded mail
5	Scale mail + shield/chain mail
6	Studded leather or ring mail + shield/scale mail
7	Leather or padded armor + shield/studded leather or ring mail
8	Leather or padded armor
9	Shield only
10	None

Armor class below 10 is not possible except through cursed items. Armor class above 2 is easily possible due to magical bonuses and dexterity bonuses. To determine a "to hit" number not on the charts, project upwards by 1's (5% increments), repeating 20 six times before continuing with 21 (cf. **MATRIX I.A.**).

I.A. ATTACK MATRIX FOR CLERICS, DRUIDS AND MONKS

Opponent Armor Class	20-sided Die Score to Hit by Level of Attacker						
	1-3	4-6	7-9	10-12	13-15	16-18	19+
-10	25	23	21	20	20	20	19
-9	24	22	20	20	20	19	18
-8	23	21	20	20	20	18	17
-7	22	20	20	20	19	17	16
-6	21	20	20	20	18	16	15
-5	20	20	20	19	17	15	14
-4	20	20	20	18	16	14	13
-3	20	20	19	17	15	13	12
-2	20	20	18	16	14	12	11
-1	20	19	17	15	13	11	10
0	20	18	16	14	12	10	9
1	19	17	15	13	11	9	8
2	18	16	14	12	10	8	7
3	17	15	13	11	9	7	6
4	16	14	12	10	8	6	5
5	15	13	11	9	7	5	4
6	14	12	10	8	6	4	3
7	13	11	9	7	5	3	2
8	12	10	8	6	4	2	1
9	11	9	7	5	3	1	0
10	10	8	6	4	2	0	-1

Missiles: -5 at **long** range, -2 at **medium** range.

I.C. ATTACK MATRIX FOR MAGIC-USERS AND ILLUSIONISTS

Opponent Armor Class	20-sided Die Score to Hit by Level of Attacker				
	1-5	6-10	11-15	16-20	21+
-10	26	24	21	20	20
-9	25	23	20	20	20
-8	24	22	20	20	19
-7	23	21	20	20	18
-6	22	20	20	19	17
-5	21	20	20	18	16
-4	20	20	20	17	15
-3	20	20	19	16	14
-2	20	20	18	15	13
-1	20	20	17	14	12
0	20	19	16	13	11
1	20	18	15	12	10
2	19	17	14	11	9
3	18	16	13	10	8
4	17	15	12	9	7
5	16	14	11	8	6
6	15	13	10	7	5
7	14	12	9	6	4
8	13	11	8	5	3
9	12	10	7	4	2
10	11	9	6	3	1

Missiles:* -5 at **long** range, -2 at **medium** range.

*Normal, **not** magical.

I.B. ATTACK MATRIX FOR FIGHTERS, PALADINS, RANGERS, BARDS, AND 0 LEVEL HALFLINGS AND HUMANS*

Opponent Armor Class	20-sided Die Score to Hit by Level of Attacker									
	0	1-2	3-4	5-6	7-8	9-10	11-12	13-14	15-16	17+
-10	26	25	23	21	20	20	20	18	16	14
-9	25	24	22	20	20	20	19	17	15	13
-8	24	23	21	20	20	20	18	16	14	12
-7	23	22	20	20	20	19	17	15	13	11
-6	22	21	20	20	20	18	16	14	12	10
-5	21	20	20	20	19	17	15	13	11	9
-4	20	20	20	20	18	16	14	12	10	8
-3	20	20	20	19	17	15	13	11	9	7
-2	20	20	20	18	16	14	12	10	8	6
-1	20	20	19	17	15	13	11	9	7	5
0	20	20	18	16	14	12	10	8	6	4
1	20	19	17	15	13	11	9	7	5	3
2	19	18	16	14	12	10	8	6	4	2
3	18	17	15	13	11	9	7	5	3	1
4	17	16	14	12	10	8	6	4	2	0
5	16	15	13	11	9	7	5	3	1	-1
6	15	14	12	10	8	6	4	2	0	-2
7	14	13	11	9	7	5	3	1	-1	-3
8	13	12	10	8	6	4	2	0	-2	-4
9	12	11	9	7	5	3	1	-1	-3	-5
10	11	10	8	6	4	2	0	-2	-4	-6

Missiles: −5 at **long** range, −2 at **medium** range.

*Note: Half-elves use the attack matrix as elves do, while non-player character half-orcs use the attack matrix for monsters. Dwarves, elves and gnomes are never lower than 1st level (unlike halflings and humans, which may be of 0 level). Bards fight at their highest level of *fighter* experience.

Special Note Regarding Fighters' Progression: This table is designed to allow fighters to advance by 5% per level of experience attained, rather than 10% every 2 levels, if you believe that such will be helpful in your particular campaign. If you opt for a per level advancement in combat ability, simply use the table but give a +1 "to hit" bonus to fighters who attain the second level of experience shown in each group of 2 levels, i.e. 1-2, 3-4, etc. You may, of course, elect not to allow per level combat advancement.

I.D.1. ATTACK MATRIX FOR THIEVES AND ASSASSINS

Opponent Armor Class	20-sided Die Score to Hit by Level of Attacker					
	1-4ᵃ	5-8ᵇ	9-12ᶜ	13-16ᵈ	17-20ᵈ	21+ᵈ
-10	26	24	21	20	20	20
-9	25	23	20	20	20	19
-8	24	22	20	20	20	18
-7	23	21	20	20	19	17
-6	22	20	20	20	18	16
-5	21	20	20	19	17	15
-4	20	20	20	18	16	14
-3	20	20	19	17	15	13
-2	20	20	18	16	14	12
-1	20	20	17	15	13	11
0	20	19	16	14	12	10
1	20	18	15	13	11	9
2	19	17	14	12	10	8
3	18	16	13	11	9	7
4	17	15	12	10	8	6
5	16	14	11	9	7	5
6	15	13	10	8	6	4
7	14	12	9	7	5	3
8	13	11	8	6	4	2
9	12	10	7	5	3	1
10	11	9	6	4	2	0

Missiles: -5 at **long** range, -2 at **medium** range.

ᵃ Thieves and assassins double damage from a surprise **back stab**.

ᵇ Thieves and assassins triple damage from a surprise **back stab**.

ᶜ Thieves and assassins quadruple damage from a surprise **back stab**.

ᵈ Thieves and assassins quintuple damage from a surprise **back stab**.

I.D.2. ASSASSINS' TABLE FOR ASSASSINATIONS*

Level of the Assassin	Level of the Intended Victim									
	0-1	2-3	4-5	6-7	8-9	10-11	12-13	14-15	16-17	18+
1	50%	45%	35%	25%	10%	1%	---	---	---	---
2	55%	50%	40%	30%	15%	2%	---	---	---	---
3	60%	55%	45%	35%	20%	5%	---	---	---	---
4	65%	60%	50%	40%	25%	10%	1%	---	---	---
5	70%	65%	55%	45%	30%	15%	5%	---	---	---
6	75%	70%	60%	50%	35%	20%	10%	1%	---	---
7	80%	75%	65%	55%	40%	25%	15%	5%	---	---
8	85%	80%	70%	60%	45%	30%	20%	10%	2%	---
9	95%	90%	80%	70%	55%	40%	30%	20%	5%	---
10	99%	95%	85%	75%	60%	45%	35%	25%	10%	1%
11	100%	99%	90%	80%	65%	50%	40%	30%	15%	5%
12	100%	100%	95%	85%	70%	55%	45%	35%	20%	10%
13	100%	100%	99%	95%	80%	65%	50%	40%	25%	15%
14	100%	100%	100%	99%	90%	75%	60%	50%	35%	25%
15	100%	100%	100%	100%	99%	85%	70%	60%	40%	30%

*Or attacks on helpless opponents by any character class (see **COMBAT** section).

The percentage shown is that for success (instant death) under near optimum conditions. You may adjust slightly upwards for perfect conditions (absolute trust, asleep and unguarded, very drunk and unguarded, etc.). Similarly, you must deduct points if the intended victim is wary, takes precautions, and/or is guarded. If the assassination is being attempted by or in behalf of a player character a complete plan of how the deed is to be done should be prepared by the player involved, and the precautions, if any, of the target character should be compared against the plan. Weapon damage always occurs and may kill the victim even though "assassination" failed.

II. ATTACK MATRIX FOR MONSTERS (Including Goblins, Hobgoblins, Kobolds, and Orcs)

Opponent Armor Class	20-sided Die Score to Hit by Monster's Hit Dice Number											
	up to 1-1	1-1	1	1+	2-3+	4-5+	6-7+	8-9+	10-11+	12-13+	14-15+	16+
-10	26	25	24	23	21	20	20	20	20	19	18	17
-9	25	24	23	22	20	20	20	20	19	18	17	16
-8	24	23	22	21	20	20	20	20	18	17	16	15
-7	23	22	21	20	20	20	20	19	17	16	15	14
-6	22	21	20	20	20	20	19	18	16	15	14	13
-5	21	20	20	20	20	20	18	17	15	14	13	12
-4	20	20	20	20	20	19	17	16	14	13	12	11
-3	20	20	20	20	19	18	16	15	13	12	11	10
-2	20	20	20	20	18	17	15	14	12	11	10	9
-1	20	20	20	19	17	16	14	13	11	10	9	8
0	20	20	19	18	16	15	13	12	10	9	8	7
1	20	19	18	17	15	14	12	11	9	8	7	6
2	19	18	17	16	14	13	11	10	8	7	6	5
3	18	17	16	15	13	12	10	9	7	6	5	4
4	17	16	15	14	12	11	9	8	6	5	4	3
5	16	15	14	13	11	10	8	7	5	4	3	2
6	15	14	13	12	10	9	7	6	4	3	2	1
7	14	13	12	11	9	8	6	5	3	2	1	0
8	13	12	11	10	8	7	5	4	2	1	0	-1
9	12	11	10	9	7	6	4	3	1	0	-1	-2
10	11	10	9	8	6	5	3	2	0	-1	-2	-3

Note: Any plus above +3 equals another hit die, i.e. 6+6 equals 7 hit dice.

Missiles: -5 at **long** range, -2 at **medium** range.

CREATURES STRUCK ONLY BY MAGIC WEAPONS

Despite special defenses which protect certain creatures from attacks by non-magical weapons, these monsters can be effectively hit by attackers as follows:

Defender Is Hit By Weapon	Attacker Must Have The Following		
	Hit Only By	OR	Hit Dice Of*
+1 or better	+1 or better		4 + 1 or more
+2 or better	+2 or better		6 + 2 or more
+3 or better	+3 or better		8 + 3 or more
+4 or better	+4 or better		10 + 4 or more

* This does not apply to characters of any sort.

This provides for magical properties and sizes of the attacking monster. Thus, massive hill giants can effectively attack most creatures, and all other types of giants can affect everything save a few gods.

III. MATRIX FOR CLERICS AFFECTING UNDEAD, et al.

Type of Undead	Level of Cleric Attempting to Turn†									
	1	2	3	4	5	6	7	8	9-13	14+
Skeleton	10	7	4	T	T	D	D	D*	D*	D*
Zombie	13	10	7	T	T	D	D	D	D*	D*
Ghoul	16	13	10	4	T	T	D	D	D	D*
Shadow	19	16	13	7	4	T	T	D	D	D*
Wight	20	19	16	10	7	4	T	T	D	D
Ghast	--	20	19	13	10	7	4	T	T	D
Wraith	--	--	20	16	13	10	7	4	Tⁱ	D
Mummyᵃ	--	--	--	20	16	13	10	7	4	T
Spectreᵇ	--	--	--	--	20	16	13	10	7	T
Vampireᶜ	--	--	--	--	--	20	16	13	10	4
Ghostᵈ	--	--	--	--	--	--	20	16	13	7
Licheᵉ	--	--	--	--	--	--	--	19	16	10
Special**ᶠ	--	--	--	--	--	--	--	20	19	13

† Paladins turn undead et al. as a cleric two levels below their level.

* Number affected is 7-12 rather than 1-12.

** Evil creatures from lower planes such as minor demons, lesser devils, mezzodaemons, night hags, from 1-2 in number. (As a rule of thumb, any creature with armor class of −5 or better, 11 or more hit dice, or 66% or greater magic resistance will be unaffected.)

[a] A paladin of 1st or 2nd level can be turned by an **evil** cleric.

[b] A paladin of 3rd or 4th level can be turned by an **evil** cleric.

[c] A paladin of 5th or 6th level can be turned by an **evil** cleric.

[d] A paladin of 7th or 8th level can be turned by an **evil** cleric.

[e] A paladin of 9th or 10th level can be turned by an **evil** cleric.

[f] A paladin of 11th or higher level can be turned by an **evil** cleric.

Procedure: A d20 is rolled, and if the *number* shown is matched or exceeded by the die roll the undead are turned. From 1-12 (or 7-12 or 1-2) undead (or evil creatures from lower planes) are affected:

1. **Evil clerics** cause the creatures to take neutral or friendly attitude according to a reaction dice score. Neutral undead will ignore the cleric and his or her party; friendly ones will follow the cleric and join the adventure.

2. **Good clerics** cause the creature to move directly away from his or her person, and stay as far away as possible for not less than 3 nor more than 12 rounds, moving at full speed for the duration if at all possible. The turned undead will be able to come back again, but they are subject to further turning by the cleric.

Failure to score the number shown, or greater, means the turning was unsuccessful. No further attempt by the cleric can be made with respect to the particular undead, and they may proceed to attack or otherwise operate unconstrained.

T: This symbol indicates automatic turning — whether to influence by an evil cleric or actual driving away by a good cleric.

D: This symbol indicates the cleric has automatically brought the undead into friendly status (evil cleric) or destroyed or damned them (good cleric).

-: No effect upon the undead is possible where a dash is shown.

The progression on the table is not even. A variable increment of 5% appears — 19, 20. It is included to reflect two things. First, it appears to allow lower level clerics a chance to turn some of the tougher monsters. It disappears (at 4th level) and reappears again only when the clerics have reached a high level (8th and up). This reflects the relative difficulty of these clerics when faced with turning away the worst of evil creatures, but also allows the table to have them completely destroy the weaker undead. If for some reason you must have an exact progression, follow the columns for levels 1, 2, and 3, correcting to the right from there — and thus rather severely penalizing the clerics of upper levels, but by no means harming play balance. Column 4 will then read, top to bottom: T, 4, 7, 10, 13, 16, 19, 20. Do not otherwise alter the table as it could prove to be a serious factor in balance — weakening or strengthening clerics too greatly.

IV.A. PSIONIC VS. PSIONIC IN MENTAL COMBAT

Total Psionic Strength	Attack Mode	Defense Mode				
		Mind Blank$_1$	Thought Shield$_2$	Mental Barrier$_3$	Intellect Fortress$_8$	Tower of Iron Will$_{10}$
	Psionic Blast$_{20}$	3	7	4	1	0
01	Mind Thrust$_4$	12	4	0	0	1
to	Ego Whip$_7$	8	3	0	0	0
25	Id Insinuation$_{10}$	1	6	8	1	1
	Psychic Crush$_{14}$	2%	---	---	---	---
	Psionic Blast$_{20}$	6	9	6	2	0
26	Mind Thrust$_4$	15	6	1	0	2
to	Ego Whip$_7$	12	4	0	0	0
50	Id Insinuation$_{10}$	2	8	10	3	3
	Psychic Crush$_{14}$	5%	2%	1%	---	---
	Psionic Blast$_{20}$	10	12	9	4	1
51	Mind Thrust$_4$	18	9	2	2	3
to	Ego Whip$_7$	17	6	1	1	1
75	Id Insinuation$_{10}$	4	11	13	7	6
	Psychic Crush$_{14}$	9%	4%	2%	1%	---
	Psionic Blast$_{20}$	15	16	13	7	2
76	Mind Thrust$_4$	22	13	5	4	5
to	Ego Whip$_7$	23	9	3	2	3
100	Id Insinuation$_{10}$	7	15	17	12	10
	Psychic Crush$_{14}$	14%	7%	5%	3%	2%
	Psionic Blast$_{20}$	21	21	18	11	4
101	Mind Thrust$_4$	26	18	9	7	8
to	Ego Whip$_7$	30	13	6	4	6
125	Id Insinuation$_{10}$	11	20	22	18	15
	Psychic Crush$_{14}$	20%	11%	9%	6%	4%
	Psionic Blast$_{20}$	28	27	24	16	7
126	Mind Thrust$_4$	30	24	16	11	12
&	Ego Whip$_7$	38	18	10	7	10
up	Id Insinuation$_{10}$	16	26	28	25	21
	Psychic Crush$_{14}$	27%	16%	14%	10%	7%

Total Psionic Strength is the *attacker's* attack and defense point strength total *prior* to the subtraction of attack points for the current attack segment and defense points for the current defense mode for that same segment. (These points, along with losses, if any, are taken only at the end of the segment.) ALL ATTACKS AND DEFENSES ARE SIMULTANEOUS.

The **Attack Mode** is compared to the **Defense Mode**, reading across, and a result is obtained.

Numbers indicate the number of *points of defense strength* lost.

Psychic Crush shows the percentage chance of instantly killing the opponent. Any score above that shown for the defensive mode used indicates *no effect.* A dash indicates no possible chance of causing instant death.

When both sides have attacked once and defended once the psionic combat segment is over. All points of strength expended in attacking and defending are totaled separately, points lost due to attack are added, and a new **Total Psionic Strength** is determined for each side. EXCEPTION: If a *psychic crush* succeeds, the defender is dead, and adjustments are made only for the victor's strength.

Note: The subscripted numbers following the names of the attack and defense modes (as in *Psionic Blast$_{20}$*) are the costs, in attack or defense points respectively, of using the modes.

IV.B. PSIONIC ATTACK UPON DEFENSELESS PSIONIC

Current Attack Strength & Attack Mode	Defender's Psionic Strength Total						
	10-59	60-109	110-159	160-209	210-259	260-309	310+
01-25							
Psionic Blast	D	C	C	15	10	5	5
Mind Thrust	W	W	40	35	30	25	20
Ego Whip	30	25	20	15	10	5	5
Id Insinuation	40	35	30	25	20	15	10
Psychic Crush	72%	60%	50%	40%	30%	20%	10%
26-50							
Psionic Blast	S	D	C	C	15	10	5
Mind Thrust	W	W	W	40	35	30	25
Ego Whip	35	30	25	20	15	10	5
Id Insinuation	R	40	35	30	25	20	15
Psychic Crush	75%	62%	52%	42%	32%	22%	12%
51-75							
Psionic Blast	W	S	D	C	C	15	10
Mind Thrust	P	W	W	W	40	35	30
Ego Whip	40	35	30	25	20	15	10
Id Insinuation	R	R	40	35	30	25	20
Psychic Crush	79%	65%	55%	45%	35%	25%	15%
76-100							
Psionic Blast	P	W	S	D	C	C	15
Mind Thrust	P	P	W	W	W	40	35
Ego Whip	P	40	35	30	25	20	15
Id Insinuation	R	R	R	40	35	30	25
Psychic Crush	84%	69%	59%	49%	39%	29%	19%
101-125							
Psionic Blast	K	P	W	S	D	C	C
Mind Thrust	P	P	P	W	W	W	40
Ego Whip	I	P	40	35	30	25	20
Id Insinuation	R	R	R	R	40	35	30
Psychic Crush	90%	74%	64%	54%	44%	34%	24%
126 & up							
Psionic Blast	K	K	P	W	S	D	C
Mind Thrust	P	P	P	P	W	W	W
Ego Whip	I	I	P	40	35	30	25
Id Insinuation	R	R	R	R	R	40	35
Psychic Crush	97%	80%	70%	60%	50%	40%	30%

Defender's Psionic Strength Total is the score prior to any reductions, even though the current total for the individual could be as low as 0.

The attacker's **Current Attack Strength & Attack Mode** are compared with the **Defender's Psionic Strength Total**, reading across, and a result is obtained.

Numbers indicate the number of the defender's **psionic attack points** lost.

Letters:

C = *Confused* for 2-8 rounds, no psionic activity possible

D = *Dazed* for 1-4 turns, no psionic or other activity

I = *Idiocy*, psionic ability lost forever, though idiocy is curable by a *heal* spell

K = *Killed*, raising/resurrection is possible, but psionic ability is lost

P = *Permanent* loss of one attack or defense mode or psionic discipline, and *dazed* as above

S = *Sleeping* is a coma for 1-4 weeks (catatonic state 99% likely to be mistaken for death)

R = *Robot*, meaning mind is under control of the victor until released or 2-8 weeks have elapsed and a saving throw versus magic is made

W = *Wounded* psionically, one attack or defense mode or psionic discipline unusable for 2-8 weeks

Note: Psionic creatures with *mind bar* ability will take damage only after *all* psionic strength is lost, so treat *letter* results as −40 points until 0 is reached.

Damage accruing beyond the point where 0 psionic attack points was reached results in physical damage (hit points) being taken by the defender on a point for point basis.

IV.C. PSIONIC BLAST ATTACK UPON NON-PSIONIC CREATURE

The psionically attacking creature must have a *current* psionic attack strength of 100 or more; if current strength is 99 or fewer attack points, the creature cannot use a psionic blast attack upon a *non-psionic*.

Attacked Creature's Total Intelligence & Wisdom**	Saving Throw at Attack Range		
	Short	Medium	Long
0-5	20	19	18
6-9	18	17	16
10-13	16	15	14
14-17	14	13	12
18-21	12	11	10
22-25	10	9	8
26-29	8	7	6
30-33	6	5	4
34-35	4	3	2
36-37	2	1	0
38 & up	0	-1	-2

Attacked Creature's Total Intelligence & Wisdom	Death	Coma	Sleep	Stun	Confuse	Enrage	Panic	Feeblemind	Permanent Insanity	Temporary Insanity	Mild Insanity
0-5	01-85	86-99	00	—	—	—	—	—	—	—	—
6-9	01-10	11-90	91-99	00	—	—	—	—	—	—	—
10-13	01	02-15	16-90	91-99	00	—	—	—	—	—	—
14-17	—	01	02-10	11-90	91-99	00	—	—	—	—	—
18-21	—	—	01	02-15	16-90	91-99	00	—	—	—	—
22-25	—	—	—	01	02-15	16-90	91-99	00	—	—	—
26-29	—	—	—	—	01	02-15	16-90	91-99	00	—	—
30-33	—	—	—	—	—	01	02-15	16-90	91-99	00	—
34-35	—	—	—	—	—	—	01	02-20	21-85	86-99	00
36-37	—	—	—	—	—	—	—	01	02-15	16-90	91-00
38 & up	—	—	—	—	—	—	—	—	01	02-15	16-00

Saving Throw Dice Adjustments

Additions		Subtractions	
magic-user	+1	panicked	-1
cleric	+2	enraged	-1
elf	+2	confused	-2
Intellect Fortress in 10'	+2	hopeless	-3
mind blank spell	+2	stunned	-3
dwarf	+4	using psionic related power*	-4
halfling	+4	using *ESP* device	-5
helm of telepathy †	+4	feebleminded	**
Tower of Iron Will in 3'	+6	insane	***
mind bar	+6		

† The *helm of telepathy* will cause the attacker to be *stunned* for 1-4 rounds if the defender's saving throw is successful.

* These powers or spells are: *astral projection/spell, augury, charm monster, charm person, clairaudience, clairvoyance, confusion, detect evil/good, detect magic, dimension door, divination, empathy, enlarge, ESP, etherealness, feeblemind, feign death, geas, invisibility* (any sort), *know alignment, levitation, locate object, magic jar, plane shift, polymorph self, quest, shape change, suggestion, symbol, telekinesis, telepathy, teleportation, true seeing.*

** A feebleminded person has a combined intelligence and wisdom score of 0-5.

*** Insane creatures cannot be psionically attacked. (See **INSANITY.**)

DEATH: Creature can be brought back to life as is usual.

COMA: 2-12 days where creature cannot be awakened.

SLEEP: 5-20 turns where creature cannot be awakened.

STUN: 2-8 turns where character is at usual stunned condition (see **COMBAT**).

CONFUSE: 1-4 turns as per the spell of the same name.

ENRAGE: 2-8 rounds and creature affected must immediately launch a spell or physical attack upon any opponent or other creature. During enraged period, creature will not think of defense or any action save attacking.

PANIC: 2-8 rounds with reaction as a *fear* spell from a 4th level magic-user.

FEEBLEMIND: This lasts until a *heal, restoration,* or *wish* is used. The creature's combined intelligence & wisdom is in the 0-5 range when so affected. All memory of spells is gone, and the affected creature cannot attack or defend.

PERMANENT INSANITY: This lasts until a *heal, restoration,* or *wish* is used. Select TWO forms of insanity from the table herein, and have affected creature behave accordingly as long as the condition lasts.

TEMPORARY INSANITY: 2-12 weeks duration, otherwise as above.

MILD INSANITY: 1-4 weeks duration, ONE form of insanity only, otherwise as above.

Note Regarding Insanity: In most cases the fact that the creature has been inflicted will NOT be immediately evident to associates. Behavior will make the condition suspect as appropriate to the form of affliction.

IV.D. PSIONIC ATTACK RANGES AND DAMAGE ADJUSTMENT

Attack Mode	Attack Range		
	Short	Medium	Long
A. Psionic Blast	2″	4″	6″
B. Mind Thrust	3″	6″	9″
C. Ego Whip	4″	8″	12″
D. Id Insinuation	6″	12″	18″
E. Psychic Crush	5″	---	---

Attacks in series add 50% to range for **each** psionic linked, i.e. 2=200% of range, 3=250% of range, etc. Expenditure of double or treble points by an individual will double or treble range of attack modes B, C, or D.

Attack Mode	Area of Effect
A. Psionic Blast	½″ base, 6″ length, 2″ terminus cone
B. Mind Thrust	1 creature
C. Ego Whip	1 creature
D. Id Insinuation	2″ x 2″ area within range
E. Psychic Crush*	1 creature

* User may use only defense mode G, Thought Shield.

Medium range attacks reduce damage by 20%, fractions rounded up.

Long range attacks reduce the attacker's effective total psionic strength by one category (25 points) and reduce damage by 20%, fractions rounded up. If the attacker is already in the 01-25 strength range, damage is reduced 50%, fractions being dropped.

PSIONIC COMBAT NOTES

a.) Creatures involved in psionic combat cannot engage in any other activity. However, psionic combat takes place very quickly — in segments rather than rounds — and is usually over in a very short time. For this reason, when psionic combat is begun, a good DM will usually just stop everything else until it is taken care of.

b.) Psionically-attacked creatures will automatically throw up a defense if they can do so, and will use the best type (most applicable) they can.

c.) It is possible to engage in only one psionic activity *in addition to defense modes* at a time, i.e., a psionic, while defending, could either attack or use a psionic discipline. It is never possible to attack and use a psionic discipline or to use two psionic disciplines simultaneously.

d.) In psionic combat table IV.C. **(Psionic Blast Attack Upon Non-Psionic Creature)**, the attacked creature's total intelligence and wisdom is used to figure saving throws. However, wisdom is not a standard given attribute of monsters. To compute the wisdom of non-psionic monsters, use the following table:

Intelligence of Creature	Wisdom Range
Low	2-8
Average	3-12
Very/Highly	4-16
Exceptional/Genius	8-18 (2d6 + 6)
Supra-Genius	8-20 (4d4 + 4)
Godlike	9-24 (3d6 + 6)

Creatures below *low* intelligence have negligible wisdom.

SAVING THROW MATRICES

I. SAVING THROW MATRIX FOR CHARACTERS AND HUMAN TYPES

Character Class and Experience Level		Paralyzation, Poison or Death Magic	Petrification or Polymorph*	Rod, Staff or Wand	Breath Weapon**	Spell***
			Attack to be Saved Against			
Clerics[a]	1-3	10	13	14	16	15
	4-6	9	12	13	15	14
	7-9	7	10	11	13	12
	10-12	6	9	10	12	11
	13-15	5	8	9	11	10
	16-18	4	7	8	10	9
	19+	2	5	6	8	7
Fighters[b]	0	16	17	18	20	19
	1-2	14	15	16	17	17
	3-4	13	14	15	16	16
	5-6	11	12	13	13	14
	7-8	10	11	12	12	13
	9-10	8	9	10	9	11
	11-12	7	8	9	8	10
	13-14	5	6	7	5	8
	15-16	4	5	6	4	7
	17+	3	4	5	4	6
Magic-Users[c]	1-5	14	13	11	15	12
	6-10	13	11	9	13	10
	11-15	11	9	7	11	8
	16-20	10	7	5	9	6
	21+	8	5	3	7	4
Thieves[d]	1-4	13	12	14	16	15
	5-8	12	11	12	15	13
	9-12	11	10	10	14	11
	13-16	10	9	8	13	9
	17-20	9	8	6	12	7
	21+	8	7	4	11	5

   * Excluding *polymorph wand* attacks.

  ** Excluding those which cause petrification or polymorph.

*** Excluding those for which another saving throw type is specified, such as death, petrification, polymorph, etc.

[a]   Includes Druids.

[b]   Includes Paladins, Rangers, and 0 level types.

[c]   Includes Illusionists.

[d]   Includes Assassins and Monks.

N.B.: A roll of 1 is **always** failure, regardless of magical protections, spells, or any other reasons which indicate to the contrary.

Multi-class characters, characters with two classes, and bards check the matrix for each class possessed, and use the **most favorable** result for the type of attack being defended against.

II. SAVING THROW MATRIX FOR MONSTERS

A.   **All monsters use the matrix for characters.**

B.   Hit dice equate to Experience Level, with additional pluses in hit points moving the creature upwards by one hit die. Further die levels are added for each increment of four additional points. Therefore, for the purpose of determining saving throw levels, 1 + 1 through 1 + 4 hit dice becomes 2, 1 + 5 through 1 + 8 becomes 3, 2 + 1 through 2 + 4 also becomes 3, 2 + 5 through 2 + 8 becomes 4, etc.

C.   Most monsters save as fighters, except:

    1.   Those with abilities of other character classes gain the benefit of the most favorable saving throw score, i.e. be it cleric or magic-user or thief.

    2.   Those with no real offensive fighting capabilities save according to their area of ability — cleric, magic-user, thief, etc.

D.   Non-intelligent creatures save at an Experience Level equal to one-half their hit dice, rounded upwards, except with regard to **poison or death magic.**

III. SAVING THROW MATRIX FOR MAGICAL AND NON-MAGICAL ITEMS

Attack Form & Number

Item Description	acid	crushing blow	normal blow	disintegrate	fall	fireball	magical fire	normal fire	frost	lightning	electricity
	1	2	3	4	5	6	7	8	9	10	11
Bone or Ivory	11	16	10	20	6	17	9	3	2	8	1
Ceramic	4	18	12	19	11	5	3	2	4	2	1
Cloth	12	6	3	20	2	20	16	13	1	18	1
Crystal or Vial	6	19	14	20	13	10	6	3	7	15	5
Glass	5	20	15	20	14	11	7	4	6	17	1
Leather or Book	10	4	2	20	1	13	6	4	3	13	1
Liquid*	15	0	0	20	0	15	14	13	12	18	15
Metal, hard	7	6	2	17	2	6	2	1	1ᵃ	11	1
Metal, soft or Jewelry**	13	14	9	19	4	18	13	5	1	16	1
Mirror***	12	20	15	20	13	14	9	5	6	18	1
Parchment or Paper	16	11	6	20	0	25	21	18	2	20	1
Stone, small or Gem	3	17	7	18	4	7	3	2	1	14	2
Wood or Rope, thin	9	13	6	20	2	15	11	9	1	10	1
Wood or Rope, thick	8	10	3	19	1	11	7	5	1	12	1

* Potions, magical oils, poisons, acids while container remains intact.

** Includes pearls of any sort.

*** Silvered glass. Treat silver mirror as "Metal, soft," steel as "Metal, hard."

ᵃ If exposed to extreme cold then struck against a very hard surface with force, saving throw is -10 on die!

Magical Items: Magical items gain +2 on all rolls plus +1 for each plus they have above +1, i.e. +1 = +2 on saving throw, +2 = +3 on saving throw. Furthermore, the magic item gains +5 on saving throws against attack forms in its own mode, i.e. blow vs. shield, *fireball* vs. *ring of fire resistance* or *fireball wand*.

Non-Magical Items: Those items which do not exactly conform to item descriptions above can be interpolated. It is assumed that the item in question is actually exposed to the form of attack, i.e. the blow falls on the item, the fall is such as to not cushion the item, the fire actually contacts the item, etc. As with magical items, non-magical items gain +5 versus attacks in their own mode.

Attack Forms

1. Acid
2. Blow, Crushing
3. Blow, Normal
4. Disintegration
5. Fall
6. Fireball (or breath)
7. Fire, Magical
8. Fire, Normal (oil)
9. Frost, Magical
10. Lightning Bolt
11. Electrical Discharge/Current

1. **Acid:** This assumes a considerable volume of strong acid (black dragon or giant slug spittle) or immersion for a period which would affect the item.

2. **Blow, Crushing:** This assumes that the item is struck by a weighty falling object or a blow from an ogre's or giant's weapon, for example. Another example would be a (ceramic) flask of oil or a (crystal or glass) vial of holy water hurled against a hard surface or dropped from a height. A piece of cloth can be ripped or torn by a crushing blow.

3. **Blow, Normal:** This assumes an attack by a normal-strength opponent or only fairly heavy object which strikes the object. This also applies to a (ceramic) flask of oil or a (crystal or glass) vial of holy water hurled against a tough, but slightly yielding, surface.

4. **Disintegration:** This is the magical effect.

5. **Fall:** This assumes the item falls about 5' and comes into contact with a hard (stone-like) surface. A softer surface (wood-like) gives a +1 on the saving throw, and a fleshy-soft surface gives +5. For each 5' over the first 5' the item falls, subtract -1 from the die roll to save.

6. **Fireball:** This is the magical *fireball*, *meteor swarm*, (red) dragon breath, etc.

7. **Fire, Magical:** This is the magical *wall of fire, fire storm, flame strike*, etc.

8. **Fire, Normal:** This assumes a hot fire such as produced by a blazing wood fire, flaming oil, and the like. The item in question would have to be exposed to the fire for an amount of time sufficient to have an effect, i.e. paper or parchment for but 1 melee round, cloth for 2, bone or ivory for 3, etc.

9. **Frost, Magical:** This is the magical frost or cold such as a white dragon breathes or spells such as *cone of cold* or *ice storm*.

10. **Lightning Bolt:** This is magical attack from lightning called from the sky, blue dragon breath, etc.

11. **Electrical Discharge/Current:** The "shock" of an electric eel, magical items, traps, etc.

SAVING THROWS

The term *saving throw* is common enough, coming to us from miniature wargames and **D&D.** It represents the chance for the figure concerned to avoid (or at least partially avoid) the cruel results of fate. In **AD&D** it is the same. By means of skill, luck, magical protections, quirks of fate and the aid of supernatural powers, the character making his or her saving throw takes none or only part of the indicated results — *fireball* damage, poisoning, being turned to stone, or whatever. The various saving throws are shown on the appropriate tables — for characters, monsters, and items as well. When someone or something fails to roll the number shown, or better, whatever is coming comes in full. To better understand the concept of the saving throw, the following is offered:

As has been often pointed out, **AD&D** is a game wherein participants create personae and operate them in the milieu created and designed, in whole or in part, by the Dungeon Master and shared by all, including the DM, in imagination and enthusiasm. The central theme of this game is the interaction of these personae, whether those of the players or those of the DM, with the milieu, including that part represented by the characters and creatures personified by the DM. This interaction results in adventures and deeds of daring. The heroic fantasy which results is a blend of the dramatic and the comic, the foolish and the brave, stirring excitement and grinding boredom. It is a game in which the continuing epic is the most meaningful portion. It becomes an entity in which at least some of the characters seem to be able to survive for an indefinite time, and characters who have shorter spans of existence are linked one to the other by blood or purpose. These personae put up with the frustrations, the setbacks, and the tragedies because they aim for and can reasonably expect to achieve adventure, challenge, wealth, glory and more. If player characters are not of the same stamp as Conan, they also appreciate that they are in effect writing their own adventures and creating their own legends, not merely reliving those of someone else's creation.

Yet because the player character is all-important, he or she must always — or nearly always — have a chance, no matter how small, a chance of somehow escaping what otherwise would be inevitable destruction. Many will not be able to do so, but the escapes of those who do are what the fabric of the game is created upon. These adventures become the twice-told tales and legends of the campaign. The fame (or infamy) of certain characters gives lustre to the campaign and enjoyment to player and DM alike as the parts grow and are entwined to become a fantastic history of a never-was world where all of us would wish to live if we could.

Someone once sharply criticized the concept of the saving throw as ridiculous. Could a man chained to a rock, they asked, save himself from the blast of a red dragon's breath? Why not?, I replied. If you accept fire-breathing dragons, why doubt the chance to reduce the damage sustained from such a creature's attack? Imagine that the figure, at the last moment, of course, manages to drop beneath the licking flames, or finds a crevice in which to shield his or her body, or succeeds in finding a way to be free of the fetters. Why not? The mechanics of combat or the details of the injury caused by some horrible weapon are *not* the key to heroic fantasy and adventure games. It is the character, how he or she becomes involved in the combat, how he or she somehow escapes — or fails to escape — the mortal threat which is important to the enjoyment and longevity of the game.

If some further rationale is needed to explain saving throws versus magic, here is one way of looking at it. Magical power is energy from another plane channeled through this one by the use of certain prescribed formulae. The magic obeys (or disobeys) the magic-user because he or she controls and constrains it by a combination of the formulae and willpower. As magic-users advance in level, their willpower increases through practice, and so does their control. Inherently magical creatures exercise such control instinctively.

A character under magical attack is in a stress situation, and his or her own will force reacts instinctively to protect the character by slightly altering the effects of the magical assault. This protection takes a slightly different form for each class of character. Magic-users understand spells, even on an unconscious level, and are able to slightly tamper with one so as to render it ineffective. Fighters withstand them through sheer defiance, while clerics create a small island of faith. Thieves find they are able to avoid a spell's full effects by quickness . . .

So a character manages to avoid the full blast of the *fireball*, or averts his or her gaze from the basilisk or medusa, or the poisonous stinger of the giant scorpion misses or fails somehow to inject its venom. Whatever the rationale, the character is saved to go on. Of course, some saves result in the death of the character anyway, as partial damage causes him or her to meet death. But at least the character had some hope, and he or she fought until the very end. Stories will be told of it at the inn, and songs sung of the battle when warriors gather around the campfire. Almost, almost he managed to reach the bend in the passage where the fell breath of the blue dragon Razisiz could not reach, but at the last moment his toe struck a protrusion, and as he stumbled the dragon slew him!

Saving Throw Modifiers:

DM Stipulations: You may assign modifiers to any saving throws as you see fit, always keeping in mind game balance.

Rule Stipulations: Some attack forms will always give an adjustment to saving throws because of the creature considered, e.g., a large spider's poison attack is always at a plus on the saving throw dice. Some attack forms always receive adjustments against certain creatures also. Check facts regarding the characters and/or monsters concerned.

Magical Devices and Protections: Various magic items (rings, armor, shields, etc.) allow saving throw dice modifications. In general, these modifiers are cumulative, unless otherwise stated. Some spells will also cause such modifications. It is necessary to familiarize yourself with all such information by having a working knowledge of both **MONSTER MANUAL** and **PLAYERS HANDBOOK**, as well as this volume.

Circumstantial Adjustments: Such adjustments are quite similar to DM stipulations. That is, if a character is standing in a pool of water holding a sword in his steel-gauntleted hand when the blue dragon breathes at him, you just might wish to slightly alter his chances of saving. In like manner, you might wish to give this same character one-half or NO damage from a red dragon's breath in the same circumstances. (In this same fashion you may feel no constraint with respect to allotting pluses to damage so meted out to players, adjusting the score of each die upwards or downwards as you see fit because of prevailing circumstances.)

Certain Failure: As shown on the table, a 1 is ALWAYS a failure, regardless of magical modifiers to the contrary. However, as DM you may adjust such failures according to prevailing circumstances, although any adjudication which negates failure on a roll of 1 is not recommended at all. Another rule you may wish to consider is allowing a save (where applicable) on a natural 20, regardless of penalties.

Item Saving Throws:

These saving throws are self-explanatory in general. It is a case of either saving or failing. Potions and liquids which do not make their saving throws should be noted secretly by you — unless the player concerned has

his or her character check to determine if the fluid was harmed. Such failure will not otherwise be notable without examination and testing.

Artifacts & Relics: Because of the very nature of these items, you may desire to disallow any destruction or harm to these items by common normal or magical means. This rule may apply to some, all, or none as you deem best in the circumstances of your campaign. You might, for example, decide that all such items have an additional +3 on their saving throw dice, and that certain obviously potent items are subject to harm only from other artifacts and relics or attacks by gods or similarly powerful beings.

Poison Saving Throws For Characters:

For those who wonder why poison does either killing damage (usually) or no harm whatsoever, recall the justification for character hit points. That is, damage is not actually sustained — at least in proportion to the number of hit points marked off in most cases. The so called damage is the expenditure of favor from deities, luck, skill, and perhaps a scratch, and thus the saving throw. If that mere scratch managed to be venomous, then DEATH. If no such wound was delivered, then NO DAMAGE FROM THE POISON. In cases where some partial damage is indicated, this reflects poisons either placed so that they are ingested or used so as to ensure that some small portion does get in the wound or skin of the opponent.

Poison Saving Throws For Monsters:

There are exceptions to the death (or damage) rule for poison. Any creature with a thick layer of fat (where blood vessels and nerves are virtually non-existent) will be totally immune to poison from creatures which are not able to penetrate this fat layer when injecting their poison. All swine, wereboars included, will be in this protected class. Similarly, very large creatures poisoned by very small ones are not likely to be affected. Even the poison of the deadly coral snake would not be likely to harm an apatosaurus. Giants would simply smash giant centipedes without fear of their poison — which would cause a swelling and rash, perhaps, at worst. Whenever a situation arises where poison is involved, consider both of these cases in reaching a decision.

MAGIC ARMOR AND SAVING THROWS

The magical properties of the various sorts of magic armor will sometimes, but not always, add bonuses to saving throw dice rolls made by wearers. All cases cannot be dealt with, for there will undoubtedly be many special circumstances which occur. There are guidelines, however, which will generally serve. Saving throws will NOT be aided by magic armor against:

    GAS
    POISON
    SPELLS WHICH DO NOT CAUSE PHYSICAL DAMAGE*

* *petrification, polymorph, magic jar, charm.*

Saving throw rolls WILL receive an armor bonus against:

    ACID, EXCEPT WHEN IMMERSION OCCURS
    DISINTEGRATION
    FALLING DAMAGE
    FIRE, MAGICAL AND OTHERWISE
    SPELLS WHICH CAUSE PHYSICAL DAMAGE*

* Exception: Metallic armor will NOT add to saving throws versus electrical attacks, although nonmetallic armor will do so.

Of course, where no saving throw is permitted, magic armor does not then give such an option unless otherwise stated.

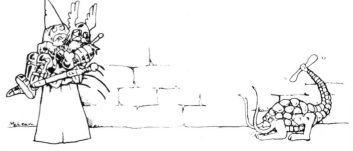

PROGRESSION ON THE COMBAT TABLES

A quick glance at the progression of numbers on the **COMBAT TABLES** will reveal that 20 is repeated. This reflects the fact that a 20 indicates a "perfect" hit. It also incidentally helps to assure that opponents with high armor class value are not "hit proof" in most cases. Should any DM find that this system offends his or her sensibilities, the following modification is suggested: Consider the repeated 20 as a perfectly-aimed attack which does not gain any benefit from strength or magical properties of any sort — spell, missile, or weapon. That is, the 20 must be attained by a roll of *natural 20*. All bonuses accrue only up to and including a total of 20, so that even if a character attacked with a bonus for strength of +3 and a +3 magic sword he or she would have to roll a *natural* 20 in order to score a hit on any creature normally hit by the second or successive repetitions of 20, i.e. the bonus (+3 in the example) could not exceed a total score of 20 unless an *actual* 20 is rolled. Thus, the **COMBAT TABLES** could be amended to read like this:

21 (natural 20 plus at least +1 bonus)
20 (natural)
20 (natural)
20 (natural)
20 (natural)
20 (natural)
20 (die result + bonuses to total)
19 (die result + bonuses to total)

This then gives the advantage of allowing creatures to hit and be hit, yet it denies any undue advantages, as the second and all successive 20s, as well as all "to hit" scores above 20 require a natural die roll of 20.

HIT POINTS

It is quite unreasonable to assume that as a character gains levels of ability in his or her class that a corresponding gain in actual ability to sustain physical damage takes place. It is preposterous to state such an assumption, for if we are to assume that a man is killed by a sword thrust which does 4 hit points of damage, we must similarly assume that a hero could, on the average, withstand five such thrusts before being slain! Why then the increase in hit points? Because these reflect both the actual physical ability of the character to withstand damage — as indicated by constitution bonuses — and a commensurate increase in such areas as skill in combat and similar life-or-death situations, the "sixth sense" which warns the individual of some otherwise unforeseen events, sheer luck, and the fantastic provisions of magical protections and/or divine protection. Therefore, constitution affects both actual ability to withstand physical punishment hit points (physique) and the immeasurable areas which involve the sixth sense and luck (fitness).

Harkening back to the example of Rasputin, it would be safe to assume that he could withstand physical damage sufficient to have killed any four normal men, i.e. more than 14 hit points. Therefore, let us assume that a character with an 18 constitution will eventually be able to withstand no less than 15 hit points of actual physical damage before being slain, and that perhaps as many as 23 hit points could constitute the physical makeup of a character. The balance of accrued hit points are those which fall into the non-physical areas already detailed. Furthermore, these actual physical hit points would be spread across a large number of levels, starting from a base score of from an average of 3 to 4, going up to 6 to 8 at 2nd level, 9 to 11 at 3rd, 12 to 14 at 4th, 15 to 17 at 5th, 18 to 20 at 6th, and 21 to 23 at 7th level. Note that the above assumes the character is a fighter with an average of 3 hit points per die going to physical ability to withstand punishment and only 1 point of constitution bonus being likewise assigned. Beyond the basic physical damage sustained, hits scored upon a character do not actually do such an amount of physical damage.

Consider a character who is a 10th level fighter with an 18 constitution. This character would have an average of 5½ hit points per die, plus a constitution bonus of 4 hit points, per level, or 95 hit points! Each hit scored upon the character does only a small amount of actual physical harm — the sword thrust that would have run a 1st level fighter through the heart merely grazes the character due to the fighter's exceptional skill, luck, and sixth sense ability which caused movement to avoid the attack at just the right moment. However, having sustained 40 or 50 hit points of damage, our lordly fighter will be covered with a number of nicks, scratches, cuts and bruises. It will require a long period of rest and recuperation to regain the physical and metaphysical peak of 95 hit points.

Recovery of Hit Points:

When a character loses hit points in combat or to some other attack form (other than being drained of life energy levels), there are a number of different means by which such points can be restored. Clerics and paladins are able to restore such losses by means of spells or innate abilities. Magical devices such as potions operate much the same way, and a *ring of regeneration* will cause automatic healing and revitalization in general of its wearer. Commonly it is necessary to resort to the passage of time, however, to restore many characters to full hit point strength.

For game purposes it is absolutely necessary that the character rest in order to recuperate, i.e. any combat, spell using, or similar activity does not constitute rest, so no hit points can be regained. For each day of rest a character will regain 1 hit point, up to and including 7 days. However a character with a penalty for poor constitution must deduct weekly the penalty score from his or her days of healing, i.e., a −2 for a person means that 5 hit points healing per week is maximum, and the first two days of rest will restore no hit points. After the first week of continuous rest, characters with a bonus for high constitution add the bonus score to the number of hit points they recover due to resting, i.e., the second week of rest will restore 11 (7 + 4) hit points to a fighter character with an 18 constitution. *Regardless of the number of hit points a character has, 4 weeks of continuous rest will restore any character to full strength.*

Zero Hit Points:

When any creature is brought to 0 hit points (optionally as low as −3 hit points if from the same blow which brought the total to 0), it is *unconscious*. In each of the next succeeding rounds 1 additional (negative) point will be lost until −10 is reached and the creature dies. Such loss and death are caused from bleeding, shock, convulsions, non-respiration, and similar causes. It ceases immediately on any round a friendly creature administers aid to the unconscious one. Aid consists of binding wounds, starting respiration, administering a draught (spirits, *healing* potion, etc.), or otherwise doing whatever is necessary to restore life.

Any character brought to 0 (or fewer) hit points and then revived will remain in a coma for 1-6 turns. Thereafter, he or she must rest for a full week, minimum. He or she will be incapable of any activity other than that necessary to move slowly to a place of rest and eat and sleep when there. The character cannot attack, defend, cast spells, use magic devices, carry burdens, run, study, research, or do anything else. This is true even if *cure* spells and/or *healing* potions are given to him or her, although if a *heal* spell is bestowed the prohibition no longer applies.

If any creature reaches a state of −6 or greater negative points before being revived, this could indicate scarring or the loss of some member, if you so choose. For example, a character struck by a *fireball* and then treated when at −9 might have horrible scar tissue on exposed areas of flesh — hands, arms, neck, face.

EFFECTS OF ALCOHOL AND DRUGS

Characters under the influence of alcohol, narcotics, or other similar drugs will be affected as follows:

INTOXICATION TABLE

Effect on	State of Intoxication		
	Slight	Moderate	Great*
Bravery	+1	+2	+4
Morale	+5%	+10%	+15%
Intelligence	−1	−3	−6
Wisdom	−1	−4	−7
Dexterity	0	−2	−5
Charisma	0	−1	−4
Attack dice	0	−1	−5
Hit points	0	+1	+3

* beyond great intoxication persons become comatose and will sleep for 7 to 10 hours.

Notes on Intoxication Table:

Bravery is covered in the **NON-PLAYER CHARACTER CHARACTERISTICS** section of this book. Increases in bravery simply move the character upwards until "foolhardy" is attained.

Morale pertains only to non-player characters.

Intelligence, Wisdom, Dexterity and **Charisma** indicate the number of points the various characteristics are lowered temporarily due to intoxication.

Attack dice for missile or melee combat are lowered according to the penalty shown. Note that opponent saving throws vs. magical attacks made by an intoxicated character are raised by the same number (1 or 5 - - 5% or 25%).

Hit points are increased due to the effects of the drug on the intoxicated character. He or she can physically withstand more punishment.

RECOVERY FROM INTOXICATION

Time is the only cure for intoxication, although certain stimulants will shorten the recovery time.

INTOXICATION RECOVERY TABLE

Intoxication Level*	Recovery Time	Stimulant Effect	
		Mild	Strong
Slight	1-2 hours	x .80	x .50
Moderate	2-4 hours	x .85	x .55
Great	4-6 hours	x .90	x .55
Comatose	7-10 hours	x .95	x .60

* as time passes the affected person moves upwards in intoxication level.

Mild stimulants will have no harmful effects.

Strong stimulants have a 5% chance per application of lowering the character's constitution by 1 point. This is permanent.

INSANITY

When a character is struck by insanity due to mental attack, curse, or whatever, you may assign the type of madness according to the seriousness of the affliction or determine the affliction randomly using the table below. Each type of insanity listed thereon is described in game terms. As DM you will have to assume the role of the insane character whenever the madness strikes, for most players will not be willing to go so far. Note that this list is not so comprehensive as to preclude any addition you desire — just be sure that you follow the spirit of the rules here.

TYPES OF INSANITY

1. dipsomania*	11. mania
2. kleptomania*	12. lunacy
3. schizoid*	13. paranoia
4. pathological liar*	14. manic-depressive
5. monomania	15. hallucinatory insanity
6. dementia praecox	16. sado-masochism
7. melancholia	17. homicidal mania
8. megalomania	18. hebephrenia
9. delusional insanity	19. suicidal mania
10. schizophrenia	20. catatonia

* These mild insanities **are** subject to psionic attack (see **PSIONIC COMBAT TABLES**).

1. **Dipsomania:** This mild insanity form manifests itself periodically. About once per week, or whenever near large quantities of alcoholic beverages, the afflicted will begin drinking excessive quantities of ale, beer, wine, or like spiritous liquors. Such drinking will continue until the character passes out. It is 50% likely that the **dipsomania** will continue when he or she awakens if anywhere near alcohol, 10% likely otherwise (in which case the individual will seek to find drink and become violent if denied).

2. **Kleptomania:** This is another mild insanity form which manifests itself in an ardent desire, in this case an uncontrollable urge to steal any small object available. The afflicted will furtively pocket small items, regardless of their worth, whenever the opportunity presents itself, and he or she will usually seek out such opportunities. There is a 90% probability of being seen stealing if the character is being observed. This desire to take things is absolutely uncontrollable, and the

individual will lie to avoid being prevented the opportunity, or when caught.

* Kleptomaniac thieves or assassins have a –10% on their stealing ability due to the overpowering urge to immediately steal an item.

3. **Schizoid:** This rather mild insanity form manifests its effects in a personality loss. The afflicted has no personality of his or her own, so he or she will select a role model and make every attempt possible to become like that character. Selection will be based upon as different a person as is possible with regard to the insane character. Thus an insane magic-user will begin to follow the habits of a fighter, for example, dressing and speaking like that character and seeking to be like him or her in all ways.

4. **Pathological Liar:** This form of insanity is evident after conversing with the individual for a short period of time. The afflicted character will begin making outrageous statements regarding his or her abilities, possessions, experiences, or events. Whenever anything important or meaningful is discussed or in question, the afflicted can not tell the truth, and not only will he or she lie, but do so with the utmost conviction, absolutely convinced that the prevarication is truth.

5. **Monomania:** This character will seem absolutely normal until presented with an idea, goal, or similar project which seems promising or purposeful to him or her. As of then, the character will become obsessed with the accomplishment of the purpose. He or she will think of nothing else, talk of nothing else, plan and act to accomplish nothing save the fixed end. The monomaniac will brook no swerving from any friend or associate, and he or she will insist that such individuals serve the "cause" with the same devotion that the afflicted character shows. (Hostility and violence could result, and certainly not a little suspicion and mistrust if co-operation is not heartfelt . . .) Once the desired end has been accomplished, the insane character will manifest symptoms of **dementia praecox** (6., below) until a new purpose is found.

6. **Dementia Praecox:** The afflicted character will be quite uninterested in any undertaking when suffering from this form of madness. Nothing will seem worthwhile, and the individual will be continually filled with lassitude and a tremendous feeling of ennui. No matter how important the situation, it is 25% probable that the afflicted will choose to ignore it as meaningless to him or her.

7. **Melancholia:** Similar to **dementia praecox**, this malady makes the afflicted given to black moods, fits of brooding, and feelings of hopelessness. The afflicted will be 50% likely to ignore any given situation due to a fit of **melancholia** coming upon him or her.

8. **Megalomania:** With this condition, the insane character will be absolutely convinced that he or she is the best at everything the smartest, wisest, strongest, fastest, handsomest, and most powerful character of his or her profession. The afflicted will take immediate umbrage at any suggestion to the contrary, and he or she will demand the right to lead, perform any important act, make all decisions, etc. (This one is VERY dangerous.)

9. **Delusional Insanity:** Similar to **megalomania**, in this state the deluded will be convinced that he or she is a famous figure a monarch, demi-god, or similar personage. Those who "fail" to recognize the afflicted as such will incur great hostility. In normal affairs, this individual will seem quite sane, but the afflicted will act appropriate to a station which he or she does not actually have and tend to order around actual and imaginary creatures, draw upon monies and items which do not exist, and so on.

10. **Schizophrenia:** This form of insanity has the well-known "split personality" trait. From 1 to 4 separate and distinct personalities can exist in the afflicted — base the number upon the severity of the insanity. Likewise, the difference from one personality to the next should reflect the severity of the affliction. Each "new" personality will be different in alignment, goals, and preferences. (A very severe case might have a different class also, but without coincidental possession, the new personality emerging will not have the actual abilities he or she may think that she possesses.) The onset of **schizophrenia** is random, 1 in 6 per day, with a like chance of a new (or return to the old) personality emerging. However, whenever a stress situation — decision, attack, etc. — arises, the 1 in 6 chance of **schizophrenia** striking must be checked every round in which the stress continues.

11. **Mania:** Somewhat like **schizophrenia,** this form of insanity strikes suddenly (1 in 6 chance per turn, lasts 2-12 turns, then 1 in 6 chance per turn of return to normalcy) and violently. The afflicted will become hysterical, enraged, or completely maniacal (d6 for determination, equal chances). The insane character will shriek, rave, and behave in a violent manner, possessing an 18/50, 18/75, or 18/00 strength according to the state he or she is in. (Note that a female can possess 18/00 strength when afflicted, as can non-human races otherwise limited to lesser strengths.) The maniac is unreasoning when spoken to, but he or she will possess great cunning. The afflicted will desire to avoid or to do something according, but not necessarily appropriate, to the situation at hand. When the maniacal state passes, the afflicted will not remember his or her insane actions and will not believe that he or she is insane.

12. **Lunacy:** This violent and often homicidal state occurs whenever the moon is full, or nearly full. The afflicted character will generally behave as one in a maniacal state, with paranoid (q.v.), hallucinatory (q.v.), or homicidal (q.v.) tendencies. When the moon is absent or in its first or last quarters, the afflicted will be melancholiac. At other times, he or she will be relatively normal — perhaps a bit suspicious and irascible.

13. **Paranoia:** At the onset of this derangement, the afflicted becomes convinced that "they" are plotting against him or her, spying, listening, and always nearby. As the affliction develops over several days, the insane character will become convinced that everyone around is part of this plot. Conversations are about him or her, laughter is directed at him or her, and every action of former friends is aimed at deluding him or her so as to fulfill the "plot". The paranoid will be principally concerned about position or goods first, but as the insanity advances, he or she will "realize" that the plotters are actually after his or her life. The paranoid will evidence signs of increasing suspicion, take elaborate precautions with locks, guards, devices, and food and drink. In the later stages of the affliction, he or she will evidence highly irrational behavior, hire assassins to do away with "plotters", and even become homicidal in order to "protect" his or her life. Paranoids will trust absolutely no one when the affliction has advanced, regarding their former close associates and friends as their worst enemies.

14. **Manic-Depressive:** This alternating insanity form causes the afflicted to swing from one state to the other in 1 to 4 day intervals. When excited, the afflicted is 90% likely to become maniacal (11., above), and when disappointed or frustrated is 90% likely to become highly melancholic. Thus, in addition to the usual 1 to 4 day cycle of mania-depression, he or she can jump from one state to the other depending on outside stimuli.

15. **Hallucinatory Insanity:** This form of malady causes the afflicted to see, hear, and otherwise sense things which do not exist. The more exciting or stressful the situation, the more likely the individual is to hallucinate. Common delusions are: ordinary objects which do not exist, people nearby or passing when there are none, voices giving the afflicted information or instructions, abilities or form which the character does not really have (strength, sex, wings, etc.), threatening creatures appearing from nowhere, etc. It is 50% likely that the insane individual will behave normally until stimulated or under stress. Hallucinations will then commence and continue for 1 to 20 turns after the excitement/stress passes.

16. **Sado-Masochism:** This form of insanity is coupled with maniacal urges and behavior. The afflicted individual is equally likely to be in a sadistic or masochistic phase. In the former, he or she will have an obsessive desire to inflict pain (and probably death) upon any living thing encountered. However, after so doing, the insane character will return to a relatively normal state for 1 to 3 days. Likewise, when in a masochistic state the afflicted individual will have an overwhelming urge to be hurt and will act accordingly. After so doing, normalcy returns for 1 to 3 days. Note that friends and associates do not matter to the afflicted individual, nor do enemies.

17. **Homicidal Mania:** The individual afflicted with this form of insanity appears absolutely normal. He or she will behave with what seems to be complete rationality, and nothing unusual will be noted regarding the individual — except that he or she will occasionally manifest an unique interest in weapons, poisons, and other lethal devices. The insanity form causes the afflicted to be obsessed with the desire to kill. This desire must be fulfilled periodically — 1 to 4 day intervals. The victim must be human (or of the same race as the character if non-human). If prevented from killing, the frustrated individual will become uncontrollably maniacal and attack the first person he or she encounters, wildly seeking to slay. After such an occurrence, however, the afflicted will fall into a fit of **melancholia** for 1-6 days before returning to a homicidal state once again.

18. **Hebephrenia:** When afflicted by this form of insanity, the character will evidence a withdrawal from the real world. He or she will wander aimlessly, talk to himself or herself, giggle and mutter, and act childishly — sometimes even reverting to such a state as to desire to play childish games with others. This insanity is constant, but if sufficiently irritated by someone nearby, the afflicted is 75% likely to become enraged and maniacal, attacking the offender fiercely. If the insane individual does not become so enraged, he or she will become catatonic for 1-6 hours and then revert to hebephrenic behavior once again.

19. **Suicidal Mania:** This form of insanity causes the afflicted character to have overwhelming urges to destroy himself or herself whenever means is presented — a perilous situation, a weapon, or anything else. The more dangerous the situation or item, the more likely the individual is to react self-destructively. Use a scale of 10% to 80% probability, and if the afflicted does not react suicidally, then he or she will become melancholic for 1 to 6 days. If he or she is frustrated in suicidal attempts, then the character will become maniacal for 2 to 8 turns, and then fall into melancholy for 2 to 12 days.

20. **Catatonia:** When struck with this form of insanity, the character completely withdraws from reality. He or she will sit staring and unmoving, will not react to any outside stimuli, and will eventually die of dehydration if left alone. The catatonic individual can be moved, led around, fed, and so forth; but he or she will do nothing personally. If continually provoked and irritated in order to get a response, there is a 1% cumulative chance per round that the insane individual will react with **homicidal mania.** Once provocation ceases, **catatonia** returns.

Naturally, these forms of insanity are not clinically correct. They are designed to conform to game terms and situations. Their inclusion is to fill in an area of the game where a condition exists and no adequate explanation is otherwise given (cf. **DISEASE**).

EXPERIENCE

ADJUSTMENT AND DIVISION OF EXPERIENCE POINTS

The judgment factor is inescapable with respect to weighting experience for the points gained from slaying monsters and/or gaining treasure. You must weigh the level of challenge — be it thinking or fighting — versus the level of experience of the player character(s) who gained it. With respect to monsters, each hit die balances 1 experience level, counting each *special ability* and each *exceptional ability* as an additional hit die, and also counting any hit point plus as an additional hit die. Dividing the total adjusted hit dice equivalent of the monsters slain by the total of all levels of experience of all characters who had a part (even if only 1 missile, blow, spell, etc.) in the slaying yields a fraction which is the measure of challenge. If the numerator is greater than the denominator, then full experience should be awarded. If the denominator is greater, use the fraction to adjust the amount of experience by simple multiplication. (Note: It may be necessary to adjust character level in the same manner as is done with monster hit dice in order to gain a true evaluation; as, for example, 12 orcs are not equal to a wizard!) Therefore, the following rule applies:

If the average hit dice or level is 10 times greater than the average level or hit dice, there must be an adjustment of *at least* halving or doubling the experience point (x.p.) award as the circumstances dictate, except if the lesser group is approximately 20 times more numerous than the greater value group.

(20 orcs might prove troublesome to a wizard, but even that is subject to the circumstances of the encounter.)

Tricking or outwitting monsters or overcoming tricks and/or traps placed to guard treasure must be determined subjectively, with level of experience balanced against the degree of difficulty you assign to the gaining of the treasure.

Division of Experience Points:

How treasure is divided is actually in the realm of player decision. Experience points (x.p.) for slain monsters, however, is *strictly* your prerogative. It is suggested that you decide division of x.p. as follows:

1. X.p. for the slain monsters are totalled.

2. All surviving characters who took part (no matter how insignificantly) in slaying the monsters are totalled.

3. X.p. total is divided by the number of characters, each getting an equal share.

4. **Exception:** Monsters slain single-handedly — and a magic-user protected by fighters keeping off the enemy so he or she can cast spells which slay monsters is NOT fighting single-handed — accrue x.p. only to the slayer and are not included in steps 1. through 3. above.

Example: A party of 12 characters encounters monsters; in the ensuing battle all characters fight, 2 are slain, and the x.p. for monsters killed total 4,300, so each survivor gains 430 — adjusted for difficulty and for being actual player characters or halved for henchman characters.

EXPERIENCE VALUE OF TREASURE TAKEN

Gold Pieces: Convert all metal and gems and jewelry to a total value in gold pieces. If the relative value of the monster(s) or guardian device fought equals or exceeds that of the party which took the treasure, experience is awarded on a 1 for 1 basis. If the guardian(s) was relatively weaker, award experience on a 5 g.p. to 4 x.p., 3 to 2, 2 to 1, 3 to 1, or even 4 or more to 1 basis according to the relative strengths. For example, if a 10th level magic-user takes 1,000 g.p. from 10 kobolds, the relative strengths are about 20 to 1 in favor of the magic-user. (Such strength comparisons are subjective and must be based upon the degree of challenge the Dungeon Master had the monster(s) pose the treasure taker.)

Treasure must be physically taken out of the dungeon or lair and turned into a transportable medium or stored in the player's stronghold to be counted for experience points.

All items (including magic) or creatures sold for gold pieces prior to the awarding of experience points for an adventure must be considered as treasure taken, and the gold pieces received for the sale add to the total treasure taken. (Those magic items not sold gain only a relatively small amount of experience points, for their value is in their usage.)

Note: Players who balk at equating gold pieces to experience points should be gently but firmly reminded that in a game certain compromises must be made. While it is more "realistic" for clerics to study holy writings, pray, chant, practice self-discipline, etc. to gain experience, it would not make a playable game roll along. Similarly, fighters should be exercising, riding, smiting pelts, tilting at the lists, and engaging in weapons practice of various sorts to gain real expertise (experience); magic-users should be deciphering old scrolls, searching ancient tomes, experimenting alchemically, and so forth; while thieves should spend their off-hours honing their skills, "casing" various buildings, watching potential victims, and carefully planning their next "job". All very realistic but conducive to non-game boredom!

EXPERIENCE POINTS VALUE OF MONSTERS

The following table is for determination of x.p. to be awarded for slain opponent creatures. If the monster is particularly powerful, double the Exceptional Ability Addition may be awarded.

Experience Level or Monster's Hit Dice*	Basic X.P. Value (BXPV)	X.P. Per Hit Point (XP/HP)	Special Ability X.P. Bonus (SAXPB)**	Exceptional Ability X.P. Addition (EAXPA)***
up to 1 − 1	5	1	2	25
1 − 1 to 1	10	1	4	35
1 + 1 to 2	20	2	8	45
2 + 1 to 3	35	3	15	55
3 + 1 to 4	60	4	25	65
4 + 1 to 5	90	5	40	75
5 + 1 to 6	150	6	75	125
6 + 1 to 7	225	8	125	175
7 + 1 to 8	375	10	175	275
8 + 1 to 9	600	12	300	400
9 + 1 to 10+	900	14	450	600
11 to 12+	1300	16	700	850
13 to 14+	1800	18	950	1200
15 to 16+	2400	20	1250	1600
17 to 18+	3000	25	1550	2000
19 to 20+	4000	30	2100	2500
21 and up	5000	35	2600	3000

* Treat peasants/levies as up to 1 − 1, men-at-arms as 1 − 1 to 1, and all levels as the n + 1 hit dice category.

** Typical *special abilities:* 4 or more attacks per round, missile discharge, armor class 0 or lower, special attacks (blood drain, hug, crush, etc.), special defenses (regeneration, hit only by special and/or magic weapons), high intelligence which actually affects combat, use of minor (basically defensive) spells.

*** Typical *exceptional abilities:* energy level drain, paralysis, poison, major breath weapon, magic resistance, spell use, swallowing whole, weakness, attacks causing maximum damage greater than 24 singly, 30 doubly, 36 trebly, or 42 in all combinations possible in 1 round.

Judicious application of these guidelines will assume that an equitable total number of experience points are given for slaying any given monster. Special ability bonus awards should be cumulative, i.e., a gargoyle attacks 4 times per round and can be hit only by magic weapons, so a double *Special Ability X.P. Bonus* should be awarded. Likewise, if there are multiple *exceptional abilities*, the awards should reflect this. If an otherwise weak creature has an extraordinary power, multiply the award by 2, 4, 8, or even 10 or more.

Examples:

1. A giant centipede with 2 hit points has BXPV of 5, XP/HP total of 2 and a EAXPA (for poison) of 25 — totalling 32 x.p.

2. An owl bear with 30 hit points has BXPV of 150, XP/HP total of 180 and a SAXPB of 75 — totalling 405 x.p.

3. A 10-headed hydra with 80 hit points has BXPV of 900, XP/HP total of 880 and a SAXPB (for multiple attacks) of 450 — totalling 2230 x.p.

4. An ancient spell-using red dragon of huge size with 88 hit points has a BXPV of 1300, XP/HP total of 1408, SAXPB of 2800 (armor class + special defense + high intelligence + saving throw bonus due to h.p./die), and an EAXPA of 2550 (major breath weapon + spell use + attack damage of 3-30/bite) — totalling 7758 x.p.

The **ALPHABETICAL RECAPITULATION OF MONSTERS (APPENDIX E)** contains standard experience point values for monsters slain. These are suggested values, and you may alter them to suit your campaign.

SPECIAL BONUS AWARD TO EXPERIENCE POINTS

If your campaign is particularly dangerous, with a low life expectancy for starting player characters, or if it is a well-established one where most players are of medium or above level, and new participants have difficulty surviving because of this, the following *Special Bonus Award* is suggested:

Any character killed and subsequently restored to life by means of a spell or device, other than a *ring of regeneration*, will earn an experience point bonus award of 1,000 points. This will materially aid characters of lower levels of experience, while it will not unduly affect earned experience for those of higher level. As only you can bestow this award, you may also feel free to decline to give it to player characters who were particularly foolish or stupid in their actions which immediately preceded death, particularly if such characters are not "sadder but wiser" for the happening.

GAINING EXPERIENCE LEVELS

Experience points are merely an indicator of the character's progress towards greater proficiency in his or her chosen profession. UPWARD PROGRESS IS NEVER AUTOMATIC. Just because Nell Nimblefingers, Rogue of the Thieves' Guild has managed to acquire 1,251 experience points does NOT mean that she suddenly becomes Nell Nimblefingers the Footpad. The gaining of sufficient experience points is necessary to indicate that a character is *eligible* to gain a level of experience, but the actual award is a matter for you, the DM, to decide.

Consider the natural functions of each class of character. Consider also the professed alignment of each character. Briefly assess the performance of each character after an adventure. Did he or she perform basically in the character of his or her class? Were his or her actions in keeping with his or her professed alignment? Mentally classify the overall performance as:

E — Excellent, few deviations from norm = 1
S — Superior, deviations minimal but noted = 2
F — Fair performance, more norm than deviations = 3
P — Poor showing with aberrant behavior = 4

Clerics who refuse to help and heal or do not remain faithful to their deity, fighters who hang back from combat or attempt to steal, or fail to boldly lead, magic-users who seek to engage in melee or ignore magic items they could employ in crucial situations, thieves who boldly engage in frontal attacks or refrain from acquisition of an extra bit of treasure when the opportunity presents itself, "cautious" characters who do not pull their own weight — these are all clear examples of a POOR rating.

Award experience points normally. When each character is given his or her total, also give them an alphabetic rating — E, S, F, or P. When a character's total experience points indicate eligibility for an advancement in level, use the alphabetic assessment to assign *equal* weight to the behavior of the character during each separate adventure — regardless of how many or how few experience points were gained in each. The resulting total is then divided by the number of entries (adventures) to come up with some number from 1 to 4. *This number indicates the number of WEEKS the character must spend in study and/or training before he or she actually gains the benefits of the new level.* Be certain that all decimals are retained, as each .145 equals a game day.

Not only must game time be spent by the character desiring advancement, but treasure will have to be spent as well. The amount of gold pieces, or the equivalent in value in gems, jewelry, magic items, etc., is found by using the following simple formula:

LEVEL OF THE TRAINEE CHARACTER × 1,500 = WEEKLY COST DURING
STUDY/TRAINING.

The level of the aspiring character should be computed at current (not to be gained) level.

Initial study and/or training must be conducted under the tutelage of a character of the same class and profession as the trainee, i.e., a fighter must train under a fighter, a paladin under a paladin, a druid under a druid, etc. Note that the tutor might possibly accept some combination of gold and service in return for his tutelage, at the DM's option. **Exception:** *A character with a performance score under 2 need not be tutored, but the study and/or training time will be twice the indicated period, i.e. 1 week becomes 2, 1.2 weeks becomes 2.4 weeks, etc.* If a character has a performance score of 2 or greater, and he or she is unable to locate a mentor to train under, the character must remain at his or her current level until such time as a tutor can be located and the necessary training and/or study course paid for and completed before any gain of experience level is granted. Note that self-training costs more, as expenses are per week, and the potential option of service is excluded.

Training under a higher level character applies only to characters who are below the "name", or nominal upper level, of their class and profession. These upper levels for each class are shown below:

CLERIC	High Priest
DRUID	Druid
FIGHTER	Lord
PALADIN	Paladin
RANGER	Ranger Lord
MAGIC-USER	Wizard
ILLUSIONIST	Illusionist
THIEF	Master Thief
ASSASSIN	Assassin
MONK	Superior Master
BARD	*special*

Characters who have achieved "name" level must merely spend game time equal to the number of weeks indicated by performance in self-conducted training and/or study. Costs (in g.p. or equivalent) of the exercise then become a function of class:

CLERIC = 2,000/level/week (vestments & largess)
FIGHTER = 1,000/level/week (tithes & largess)
MAGIC-USER = 4,000/level/week (equipment, books, experiments, etc.)
THIEF = 2,000/level/week (tools, equipment, etc.)

Bards are a special profession, as they have already earned levels as fighter and thief. Once they begin gaining experience as bards, each must pay tuition to his respective college. These payments and donations must be at least 50% of all monetary gains plus an additional 1,000 g.p. per level upon gaining a higher one. (Contributions and payments must be made to a druid whose level of experience is such that he or she is able to use more of their highest level spells than the bard is.) In any event, the funds so received do NOT accrue to the druid but pass to the amorphous organization of druidical colleges.) Failure to make the required contributions prevents the bard from level advancement. Otherwise, bards do not need to spend extra time in training and study other than a single week — alone or in company with a druid to whom contributions and payments may be made — upon attaining experience points sufficient to advance one level of experience.

All training/study is recorded in game time. The period must be uninterrupted and continuous. He or she cannot engage in adventuring, travel, magic research of any nature other than that concerned with level advancement, atonement, etc. If there is a serious hiatus in the course of training/study, the character loses all of the benefits of the time spent prior to the interruption, as well as the total funds advanced for the training/study, and he or she must begin anew if a level of experience is to be gained. Under no circumstances can a character gain additional experience points by any means until he or she actually acquires the higher level through the required training/study course. Thus, a character who successfully adventures and gains experience points which not only equal a new level but are almost sufficient to gain yet a second such level, cannot opt to forego the period of training and study necessary to go up a level in favor of gaining a few more points and training and studying for two levels at once. ONCE A CHARACTER HAS POINTS WHICH ARE EQUAL TO OR GREATER THAN THE MINIMUM NUMBER NECESSARY TO MOVE UPWARDS IN EXPERIENCE LEVEL, NO FURTHER EXPERIENCE POINTS CAN BE GAINED UNTIL THE CHARACTER ACTUALLY GAINS THE NEW LEVEL. This rule applies to bards, as noted (for failure to make the necessary contributions and payments).

THE CAMPAIGN

Unlike most games, **AD&D** is an ongoing collection of episode adventures, each of which constitutes a session of play. You, as the Dungeon Master, are about to embark on a new career, that of universe maker. You will order the universe and direct the activities in each game, becoming one of the elite group of campaign referees referred to as DMs in the vernacular of **AD&D**. What lies ahead will require the use of all of your skill, put a strain on your imagination, bring your creativity to the fore, test your patience, and exhaust your free time. Being a DM is no matter to be taken lightly!

Your campaign requires the above from you, and participation by your players. To belabor an old saw, Rome wasn't built in a day. You are probably just learning, so take small steps at first. The milieu for initial adventures should be kept to a size commensurate with the needs of campaign participants — your available time as compared with the demands of the players. This will typically result in your giving them a brief background, placing them in a settlement, and stating that they should prepare themselves to find and explore the dungeon/ruin they know is nearby. As background you inform them that they are from some nearby place where they were apprentices learning their respective professions, that they met by chance in an inn or tavern and resolved to journey together to seek their fortunes in the dangerous environment, and that, beyond the knowledge common to the area (speech, alignments, races, and the like), they know nothing of the world. Placing these new participants in a small settlement means that you need do only minimal work describing the place and its inhabitants. Likewise, as player characters are inexperienced, a single dungeon or ruins map will suffice to begin play.

After a few episodes of play, you and your campaign participants will be ready for expansion of the milieu. The territory around the settlement — likely the "home" city or town of the adventurers, other nearby habitations, wilderness areas, and whatever else you determine is right for the area — should be sketch-mapped, and places likely to become settings for play actually done in detail. At this time it is probable that you will have to have a large scale map of the whole continent or sub-continent involved, some rough outlines of the political divisions of the place, notes on predominant terrain features, indications of the distribution of creature types, and some plans as to what conflicts are likely to occur. In short, you will have to create the social and ecological parameters of a good part of a make-believe world. The more painstakingly this is done, the more "real" this creation will become.

Eventually, as player characters develop and grow powerful, they will explore and adventure over all of the area of the continent. When such activity begins, you must then broaden your general map still farther so as to encompass the whole globe. More still! You must begin to consider seriously the makeup of your entire multiverse — space, planets and their satellites, parallel worlds, the dimensions and planes. What is there? why? can participants in the campaign get there? how? will they? Never fear! By the time your campaign has grown to such a state of sophistication, you will be ready to handle the new demands.

Setting Things In Motion:

There is nothing wrong with using a prepared setting to start a campaign, just as long as you are totally familiar with its precepts and they mesh with what you envision as the ultimate direction of your own milieu. Whatever doesn't match, remove from the material and substitute your own in its place. On the other hand, there is nothing to say you are not capable of creating your own starting place; just use whichever method is best suited to your available time and more likely to please your players. Until you are sure of yourself, lean upon the book. Improvisation might be fine later, but until you are completely relaxed as the DM, don't run the risk of trying to "wing it" unless absolutely necessary. Set up the hamlet or village where the action will commence with the player characters entering and interacting with the local population. Place regular people, some "different" and unusual types, and a few non-player characters (NPCs) in the various dwellings and places of business. Note vital information particular to each. Stock the goods available to the players. When they arrive, you will be ready to take on the persona of the settlement as a whole, as well as that of each individual therein. Be dramatic, witty, stupid, dull, clever, dishonest, tricky, hostile, etc. as the situation demands. The players will quickly learn who is who and what is going on — perhaps at the loss of a few coins. Having handled this, their characters will be equipped as well as circumstances will allow and will be ready for their bold journey into the dangerous place where treasure abounds and monsters lurk.

The testing grounds for novice adventurers must be kept to a difficulty factor which encourages rather than discourages players. If things are too easy, then there is no challenge, and boredom sets in after one or two games. Conversely, impossible difficulty and character deaths cause instant loss of interest. Entrance to and movement through the dungeon level should be relatively easy, with a few tricks, traps, and puzzles to make it interesting in itself. Features such as rooms and chambers must be described with verve and sufficiently detailed in content to make each seem as if it were strange and mysterious. Creatures inhabiting the place must be of strength and in numbers not excessive compared to the adventurers' wherewithal to deal with them. (You may, at this point, refer to the sample dungeon level and partial encounter key.)

The general idea is to develop a dungeon of multiple levels, and the deeper adventurers go, the more difficult the challenges become — fiercer monsters, more deadly traps, more confusing mazes, and so forth. This same concept applies to areas outdoors as well, with more and terrible monsters occurring more frequently the further one goes away from civilization. Many variations on dungeon and wilderness areas are possible. One can build an underground complex where distance away from the entry point approximates depth, or it can be in a mountain where adventurers work upwards. Outdoor adventures can be in a ruined city or a town which seems normal but is under a curse, or virtually anything which you can imagine and then develop into a playable situation for your campaign participants.

Whatever you settle upon as a starting point, be it your own design or one of the many modular settings which are commercially available, remember to have some overall plan of your milieu in mind. The campaign might grow slowly, or it might mushroom. Be prepared for either event with more adventure areas, and the reasons for everything which exists and happens. This is not to say that total and absolutely perfect information will be needed, but a general schema is required. From this you can give vague hints and ambiguous answers. It is no exaggeration to state that the fantasy world builds itself, almost as if the milieu actually takes on a life and reality of its own. This is not to say that an occult power takes over. It is simply that the interaction of judge and players shapes the bare bones of the initial creation into something far larger. It becomes fleshed out, and adventuring breathes life into a make-believe world. Similarly, the geography and history you assign to the world will suddenly begin to shape the character of states and peoples. Details of former events will become obvious from mere outlines of the past course of things. Surprisingly, as the personalities of player characters and non-player characters in the milieu are bound to develop and become almost real, the nations and states and events of a well-conceived **AD&D** world will take on even more of their own direction and life. What this all boils down to is that once the campaign is set in motion, you will become more of a recorder of events, while the milieu seemingly charts its own course!

CLIMATE & ECOLOGY

It is of utmost importance to some Dungeon Masters to create and design worlds which are absolutely correct according to the laws of the scientific realities of our own universe. These individuals will have to look elsewhere for direction as to how this is to be accomplished, for this is a rule book, not a text on any subject remotely connected to climatology, ecology, or any science soft or hard. However, for those who desire only an interesting and exciting game, some useful information in the way of advice can be passed along.

Climate: Temperature, wind, and rainfall are understood reasonably well by most people. The distance from the sun dictates temperature, with the directness of the sun's rays affecting this also. Cloud cover also is a factor, heavy clouds trapping heat to cause a "greenhouse effect". Elevation is a factor, as the higher mountains have less of an atmosphere "blanket". Bodies of water affect temperature, as do warm or cold currents within them. Likewise air currents affect temperature. Winds are determined by rotational direction and thermals. Rainfall depends upon winds and available moisture from bodies of water, and temperatures as well. All of the foregoing are relevant to our world, and should be in a fantasy world, but the various determinants need not follow the physical laws of the earth. A milieu which offers differing climates is quite desirable because of the variety it affords DM and player alike.

The variety of climes allows you to offer the whole gamut of human and monster types to adventurous characters. It also allows you more creativity with civilizations, societies and cultures.

Ecology: So many of the monsters are large predators that it is difficult to justify their existence in proximity to one another. Of course in dungeon settings it is possible to have some in stasis or magically kept alive without hunger, but what of the wilderness? Then too, how do the human and humanoid populations support themselves? The bottom of the food chain is vegetation, cultivated grain with respect to people and their ilk. Large populations in relatively small land areas must be supported by lavish vegetation. Herd animals prospering upon this growth will support a fair number of predators. Consider also the tales of many of the most fantastic and fearsome beasts: what do dragons eat? Humans, of course; maidens in particular! Dragons slay a lot, but they do not seem to eat all that much. Ogres and giants enjoy livestock and people too, but at least the more intelligent sort raise their own cattle so as to guarantee a full kettle.

When you develop your world, leave plenty of area for cultivation, even more for wildlife. Indicate the general sorts of creatures inhabiting an area, using logic with regard to natural balance. This is *not* to say that you must be textbook perfect, it is merely a cautionary word to remind you not to put in too many large carnivores without any visible means of support. Some participants in your campaign might question the ecology — particularly if it does not favor their favorite player characters. You must be prepared to justify it. Here are some suggestions.

Certain vegetation grows very rapidly in the world — roots or tubers, a grass-like plant, or grain. One or more of such crops support many rabbits or herd animals or wild pigs or people or whatever you like! The vegetation springs up due to a nutrient in the soil (possibly some element unknown in the mundane world) and possibly due to the radiation of the sun as well (see the slight tinge of color which is noticeably different when compared to Sol? . . .). A species or two of herbivores which grow rapidly, breed prolifically, and need but scant nutriment is also suggested. With these artifices and a bit of care in placing monsters around in the wilderness, you will probably satisfy all but the most exacting of players — and that one probably should not be playing fantasy games anyway!

Dungeons likewise must be balanced and justified, or else wildly improbable and caused by some supernatural entity which keeps the whole thing running — or at least has set it up to run until another stops it. In any event, do not allow either the demands of "realism" or impossible make-believe to spoil your milieu. Climate and ecology are simply reminders to use a bit of care!

TYPICAL INHABITANTS

The bulk of the people met on an adventure in an inhabited area — whether city, town, village, or along the roads through the countryside, will be average folk, with no profession as adventurers know it, and no special abilities for clericism, fighting, magic, or thievery. They are simply typical, normal people (as you define typical and normal for the milieu, of course). When dealing with these types, it is suggested that the following factors be used:

General Classification	Hit Points	Combat Ability
sedentary females	1 - 3	−3
sedentary males	1 - 4	−2
active females	1 - 4	−1
active males	2 - 5	0 level
laboring females	2 - 5	0 level
laboring males	2 - 7	0 level

Sedentary occupations are those where the individual does nothing, or is a clerk, scribe, etc.

Active occupations are those involving considerable movement and activity such as a serving maid, carpenter, etc.

Laboring occupations are strenuous and include farming, mining, and most menial labor tasks.

SOCIAL CLASS AND RANK IN ADVANCED DUNGEONS & DRAGONS

There is no random table for determination of a character's social status to be found here. That is because the inclusion of such a factor will either tell you little or nothing of useful nature, or it will abridge your freedom with respect to development of your campaign milieu. That is, if such a table tells you only a little so as not to force a social structure upon your campaign, the table can contain nothing of use. If it states rank, it presupposes you will, in fact, have such classes in your campaign when you might not desire them at all. There are dozens of possible government forms, each of which will have varying social classes, ranks, or castes. Which sort you choose for your milieu is strictly your own prerogative. While this game is loosely based on Feudal European technology, history and myth, it also contains elements from the Ancient Period, parts of more modern myth, and the mythos of many authors as well. Within its boundaries all sorts of societies and cultures can exist, and there is nothing to dictate that their needs be Feudal European. In **THE DRAGON** magazine (#25; Vol. 3, No. 11, May 1979) there appeared an article written by me which outlines this very precept and lists a number of government forms which could be employed by the DM in his or her milieu. Actually, some, all, or none of them could appear in the "world" of any given campaign. To aid the harassed referee, I have listed these forms again. Additionally, a list of nobility (or authorities) in various medieval cultures is given. I

have included the latter as many DMs prefer to base their campaign upon a society of this sort, for they can then draw upon its historical data for game purposes.

Once a set of social structures and cultures has been devised for the campaign, you may or may not find it useful to assign rank, class, or caste to player characters. Will your society have hereditary rank? Will it go only to males? females? both equally? Will only the first-born inherit? Will any inheritance of property be required to be the entire estate to one individual? Deciding government form and culture might well delineate much of the social structure of the nation, state, or city in question. Let us assume a social structure of an aristocracy which is non-hereditary. Members of this ruling class are those who have served in the military, own property of 100 or more acres extent, and pay an annual tax of not less than 10 gold pieces on their income. Land ownership may be waived in the case of merchants and tradesmen whose business is such that they pay not less than 20 gold pieces in taxes each year. In any event, the aristocrats are the only persons eligible for any government office, command of the military, and from their number are elected senators who pass laws and legislate in general. Former senators are eligible to election to various tribunals and judgeships. Former military officers are appointed by senatorial vote to keep the peace and police the land.

The majority of citizens of this state are small land holders, tradesmen, and various workers. They provide the food and goods and labor which make the economy stable. These people are likewise obligated to serve in the military, and if they serve with distinction, they will be awarded land or stipends which will elevate them to the aristocracy. Of course, industry, marriage or other means can move any of these citizens to a higher status. Only a few persons are actually enslaved — criminals and captives of war. A large number of the workers are bound to labor for a fixed period, and some must likewise serve apprenticeships. These individuals have the hope of eventually earning sufficient funds to become landowners or rich merchants or tradesmen themselves.

In such a society, adventurers would come from the younger children of aristocrats — those who will inherit little and wish to remain in the favored class. Some would come from the middle group — adventurous persons who aim at becoming members of the aristocracy through successes in such adventures. Few, if any, would come from the lowest class, i.e. the bondsmen and common laborers. Assigning a social class to player characters in such a society would not have any particular value unless you also devised various rivalries within the classes.

With this brief example in mind, it is easy to see how pointless it is to blindly plug in a set of "birth tables" based on some form of hereditary, quasi-European nobility which may have absolutely no meaning within any of the states of your campaign milieu. Furthermore, any use of such material must be carefully considered even if your campaign does have such a society and titles of rank, viz. do you really believe that one of your player characters should be the first born son of a major noble or a ruler? If so, why is he adventuring? Where are his guards and retainers? Does his father know his whereabouts? If so, why is he allowing the heir to his title and estates to risk his life in such a foolish manner? Similarly, do such tables have a logical precedence and order? Are there offices which do not logically belong within a feudal society? Are there classes which are contradictory, anachronistic, or meaningless? Unless you specifically tailor your milieu to fit such tables, it is likely that there will be far too many "yes" answers to the above questions. The intelligent verdict must be that each DM has to accept the responsibility of deciding for himself or herself if assigning class distinctions is a vital part of his or her campaign. If such is necessary, then the DM must further accept the work of devising his or her own logical birth tables, drawn from a society, culture, and government form developed to fit the overall milieu. This is unquestionably a tall order. Those referees who lack time will find that it is perhaps better for them to utilize one of the several campaign scenarios commercially available, adding personal touches, of course, but basically relying on the cultural and societal developments of the unit.

Even with such ready-made campaign settings, you may or may not wish to include social classes immediately for player characters. My own **GREY-HAWK** campaign, for example, assumes all player characters (unless I personally place one who is otherwise) are freemen or gentlemen, or at worst they can safely represent themselves to be so. (Note that the masculine/human usage is generic; I do not like the terms *freecreatures* or *gentlebeings*!) Outstanding activity can (and has) brought knighthood or social status to certain characters. This was carefully planned as a reward if the characters succeeded, and it now allows them much latitude of action and assurance of reliable aid in certain realms — but it likewise has earned them the enmity of others. With all of that out of the way, consider the list of a few of the possible governmental forms and then the lists of noble/official titles.

Government Forms:

AUTOCRACY — Government which rests in self-derived, absolute power, typified by a hereditary emperor, for example.

BUREAUCRACY — Government by department, rule being through the heads of the various departments and conducted by their chief administrators.

CONFEDERACY — Government by a league of (possibly diverse) social entities so designed as to promote the common good of each.

DEMOCRACY — Government by the people, i.e. the established body of *citizens*, whether through direct role or through elected representatives.

DICTATORSHIP — Government whose final authority rests in the hands of one supreme head.

FEODALITY — Government of a feudal nature where each successive layer of authority derives power and authority from the one above and pledges fealty likewise.

GERIATOCRACY — Government reserved to the elderly or very old.

GYNARCHY — Government reserved to females only.

HIERARCHY — Government which is typically religious in nature and generally similar to a feodality.

MAGOCRACY — Government by professional magic-users only.

MATRIARCHY — Government by the eldest females of whatever social units exist.

MILITOCRACY — Government headed by the military leaders and the armed forces in general.

MONARCHY — Government by a single sovereign, usually hereditary, whether an absolute ruler or with power limited in some form (such as the English monarchs, limited in rule by the Magna Carta).

OLIGARCHY — Government by a few (usually absolute) rulers who are co-equal.

PEDOCRACY — Government by the learned, savants, and scholars.

PLUTOCRACY — Government by the wealthy.

REPUBLIC — Government by representatives of an established electorate who rule in behalf of the electors.

THEOCRACY — Government by god-rule, that is, rule by the direct representative of the god.

SYNDICRACY — Government by a body of syndics, each representing some business interest.

This listing is by no means exhaustive, and you should feel free to use other forms, or invent your own, as the needs of your particular campaign direct.

Royal And Noble Titles: (Northern European):

Emperor/Empress			
King/Queen			
	Archbishop		
Duke/Duchess		Pfalzgraf	
Prince/Princess		Herzog	
Marquis/Marquise		Margrave	
Count (Earl)/Countess		Graf	
	Bishop		
Viscount/Viscountess		Waldgraf	
Baron (Thane)/Baroness			
	Abbot		
Baronet		Freiherr	Seigneur
Knight		Ritter	Chevalier
	Prior		

Knights are non-hereditary peers. Their precedence (or importance) falls variously depending upon the order of knighthood they hold. Various officials of the court will rank amongst the nobility; an excellent discussion of this will be found in a good encyclopedia under *Precedence,* or in the appropriate section of TSR's **WORLD OF GREYHAWK.**

Royal And Noble Titles: (Asian Forms):

	Padishah	Maharaja	Kha-Khan	
				Tarkhan
Sultan	Shah	Rajah	Ilkhan	
Dey	Caliph			
Bey			Orkhon	
Bashaw				
Pasha				
Emir	Amir		Khan	
	Sheikh	Nawab		
	Malik			

You may find it interesting to mix titles, invent them, and place the whole in the campaign setting you devise accordingly. Research in various histories will be helpful, as will be a copy of a good thesaurus.

THE TOWN AND CITY SOCIAL STRUCTURE

Cities and towns have typically attracted the independent and free-thinking sorts, as they offer more opportunity for such lifestyles, even considering the medieval (rather intolerant) community. In towns and cities there are few nobles and gentlefolk of knightly status. The social structure can be shown as follows:

Upper Class: Nobles, gentlemen, the wealthiest of merchants and most important guildmasters, from which are drawn the most important law makers and executives.

Middle Class: Merchants and guildmasters, with master artisans and the like making up the balance. They provide lesser officials.

Lower Class: Tradesmen, journeymen, laborers, and all others form the lower class. From their number is drawn the common council.

This gives a typical medieval city or town government a structure which is formed of:

MAYOR, MAGISTRATE, or BURGOMASTER — probably a lifetime office drawn only from the upper class.

ALDERMEN, BURGHERS, or BURGESSES who are chosen by the upper class to serve as the major officers under the mayor *et al.* The judiciary and military commanders of the municipality are likely to fall within this stratum.

ALDERMEN are elected by the middle class. Law enforcement officials, customs officials, and tax officials all come from the middle class, too.

COUNCILORS of the common council are likely to be selected by the upper and middle classes as well as the free lower class. From this class are drawn the petty officials, so roles are advisory or administrative only.

The constabulary of a town or city will be drawn in part from citizen soldiers, the city watch or police force and militia called up in times of great need. Most other soldiery, by far the bulk in most cases, will be hired mercenaries. When any army is fielded, the leading men of the city are likely to be in overall command, with assistance from mercenary captains, the force being a composite of the municipal levies and the hired soldiers. (**Note:** Such forces could be of considerable magnitude in battle, as noted by the history of London, for example, or the military history of the Hanseatic League.)

ECONOMICS

There is no question that the prices and costs of the game are based on inflationary economy, one where a sudden influx of silver and gold has driven everything well beyond its normal value. The reasoning behind this is simple. An active campaign will most certainly bring a steady flow of wealth into the base area, as adventurers come from successful trips into dungeon and wilderness. If the economy of the area is one which more accurately reflects that of medieval England, let us say, where coppers and silver coins are usual and a gold piece remarkable, such an influx of new money, even in copper and silver, would cause an inflationary spiral. This would necessitate you adjusting costs accordingly and then upping dungeon treasures somewhat to keep pace. If a near-maximum is assumed, then the economics of the area can remain relatively constant, and the DM will have to adjust costs only for things in demand or short supply — weapons, oil, holy water, men-at-arms, whatever.

The economic systems of areas beyond the more active campaign areas can be viably based on lesser wealth only until the stream of loot begins to pour outwards into them. While it is possible to reduce treasure in these areas to some extent so as to prolong the period of lower costs, what kind of a dragon hoard, for example, doesn't have gold and gems? It is simply more heroic for players to have their characters swaggering around with pouches full of gems and tossing out gold pieces than it is for them to have coppers. Heroic fantasy is made of fortunes and king's ransoms in loot gained most cleverly and bravely and lost in a twinkling by various means — thievery, gambling, debauchery, gift-giving, bribes, and so forth. The "reality" **AD&D** seeks to create through role playing is that of the mythical heroes such as Conan, Fafhrd and the Gray Mouser, Kothar, Elric, and their ilk. When treasure is spoken of, it is more stirring when participants know it to be TREASURE!

You may, of course, adjust any prices and costs as you see fit for your own milieu. Be careful to observe the effects of such changes on both play balance and player involvement. If any adverse effects are noted, it is better to return to the tried and true. It is fantastic and of heroic proportions so as to match its game vehicle.

DUTIES, EXCISES, FEES, TARIFFS, TAXES, TITHES, AND TOLLS

What society can exist without revenues? What better means of assuring revenues than taxation, and all of the names used in the title of this section are synonymous with *taxes* — but if it is called something different perhaps the populace won't take too much umbrage at having to pay and pay and pay . . .

It is important in most campaigns to take excess monies away from player characters, and taxation is one of the better means of accomplishing this end. The form and frequency of taxation depends upon the locale and the social structure. *Duties* are typically paid on goods brought into a country or subdivision thereof, so any furs, tapestries, etc. brought into a town for sale will probably be subject to duty. *Excises* are typically sums paid to belong to a particular profession or practice a certain calling; in addition, an excise can be levied against foreign currency, for example, in order to change it into the less remarkable coin of the realm. *Fees* can be levied for just about any reason — entering a city gate is a good one for non-citizens. *Tariffs* are much the same as duties, but let us suppose that this is levied against only certain items when purchased — rather a surtax, or it can be used against goods not covered by the duty list. *Taxes* are typically paid only by residents and citizens of the municipality and include those sums for upkeep of roads and streets, walls, gates, and municipal expenses for administration and services. Taxation is not necessarily an annual affair,

for special taxes can be levied whenever needful, particularly upon sales, services, and foreigners in general. *Tithes* are principally religious taxation, although there is no prohibition against the combination of the secular with the sacred in the municipality. Thus, a tithe can be extracted from all sums brought into the community by any resident, the monies going to the religious organization sponsored by the community or to that of the character's choosing, at your option. (Of course, any religious organizations within a municipality will have to pay heavy taxes unless they are officially recognized by the authorities.) *Tolls*, finally, are sums paid for the use of a road, bridge, ferry, etc. They are paid according to the numbers of persons, animals, carts, wagons, and possibly even materials transported.

If the Gentle Reader thinks that the taxation he or she currently undergoes is a trifle strenuous for his or her income, pity the typical European populace of the Middle Ages. They paid all of the above, tolls being *very* frequent, with those trying to escape them by use of a byway being subject to confiscation of all goods with a fine and imprisonment possible also. Every petty noble made an extraction, municipalities taxed, and the sovereign was the worst of all. (Eventually merchants banded together to form associations to protect themselves from such robbery, but peasants and other commoners could only revolt and dream of better times.) Barter was common because hard money was so rare. However, in the typical fantasy milieu, we deal with great sums of precious metals, so use levies against player character gains accordingly. Here is an example of a system which might be helpful to you in developing your own.

The town charges a 1% duty on all normal goods brought into the place for sale — foodstuffs, cloth and hides, livestock, raw materials and manufactured goods. Foreigners must also pay this duty, but at double rate (2%). Luxury items and precious goods — wine, spirits, furs, metals such as copper, gold, etc., jewelry and the like — pay a tariff in addition to the duty, a 5% of value charge if such are to be sold, and special forms for sale are then given to the person so declaring his wares (otherwise no legal sale is possible). Entry fee into the town is 1 copper piece per head (man or animal) or wheel for citizens, 5 coppers for non-citizens, unless they have official passports to allow free entry. (Diplomatic types have immunity from duties and tariffs as regards their personal goods and belongings.) Taxes are paid per head, annually at 1 copper for a peasant, 1 silver for a freeman, and 1 gold piece for a gentleman or noble; most foreign residents are stopped frequently and asked for proof of payment, and if this is not at hand, they must pay again. In addition, a 10% sales tax is charged to all foreigners, although no service tax is levied upon them. Religion is not regulated by the municipality, but any person seeking to gain services from such an organization must typically pledge to tithe. Finally, several tolls are extended in order to gain access to the main route from and to the municipality — including the route to the dungeon, of course.

Citizens of the town must pay a 5% tax on their property in order to defray the costs of the place. This sum is levied annually. Citizenship can be obtained by foreigners after residence for one month and the payment of 10 gold pieces (plus many bribes).

The town does not encourage the use of foreign currency. Merchants and other business people must pay a fine of 5% of the value of any foreign coins within their possession plus face certain confiscation of the coins, so they will typically not accept them. Upon entering the town non-residents are instructed to go to the Street of the Money Changers in order to trade their foreign money for the copper "cons", silver "nobs", gold "orbs", and platinum "royals". Exchange rate is a mere 90%, so for 10 foreign copper pieces 9 domestic copper "commons" are handed out. Any non-resident with more than 100 silver nobles value in foreign coins in his or her possession is automatically fined 50% of their total value, unless he or she can prove that entry into the town was within 24 hours, and he or she was on his or her way to the money changers when stopped. Transactions involving gems are not uncommon, but a surtax of 10% is also levied against sales or exchange of precious stones and similar goods.

MONSTER POPULATIONS AND PLACEMENT

As the creator of a milieu, you will have to spend a considerable amount of time developing the population and distribution of monsters — in dungeon and wilderness and in urban areas as well. It is highly recommended that you develop an overall scheme for both population and habitation. This is not to say that a random mixture of monsters cannot be used, simply selecting whatever creatures are at hand from the tables of monsters shown by level of their relative challenge. The latter method does provide a rather fun type of campaign with a "Disneyland" atmosphere, but long range play becomes difficult, for the whole lacks rhyme and reason, so it becomes difficult for the DM to extrapolate new scenarios from it, let alone build upon it. Therefore, it is better to use the random population technique only in certain areas, *and even then to do so with reason*. This will be discussed shortly.

In general the monster population will be in its habitat for a logical reason. The environment suits the creatures, and the whole is in balance. Certain areas will be filled with nasty things due to the efforts of some character to protect his or her stronghold, due to the influence of some powerful evil or good force, and so on. Except in the latter case, when adventurers (your player characters, their henchmen characters, and hirelings) move into an area and begin to slaughter the creatures therein, it will become devoid of monsters.

Natural movement of monsters will be slow, so there will be no immediate migration to any depopulated area — unless some power is restocking it or there is an excess population nearby which is able to take advantage of the newly available habitat. Actually clearing an area (dungeon or outdoors territory) might involve many expeditions and much effort, perhaps even a minor battle or two involving hundreds per side, but when it is all over the monsters will not magically reappear, nor will it be likely that some other creatures will move into the newly available quarters the next day.

When player characters begin adventuring they will at first assume that they are the most aggressive types in the area — with respect to characters, of course. This is probably true. You have other characters in the area, of course, and certainly many will be of higher level and more capable of combatting monsters than are the new player characters. Nonetheless, the game assumes that these characters have other things to do with their time, that they do not generally care to take the risks connected with adventuring, and they will happily allow the player characters to stand the hazards. If the characters who do the dirty work are successful, the area will be free of monsters, and the non-player characters will benefit. Meanwhile, the player characters, as adventurers, automatically remove themselves to an area where there are monsters, effectively getting rid of the potential threat their presence poses to the established order. There is an analogy to the gunfighter-lawman of the "Wild West" which is not inappropriate. In some cases the player characters will establish strongholds nearby which will help to maintain the stability of the area — thus becoming part of the establishment. Your milieu might actually encourage such settlement and interaction if you favor politics in your campaign. The depopulation and removal to fresh challenge areas has an advantage in most cases.

As DM you will probably have a number of different and exciting dungeons and wilderness and urban settings which are tied into the whole of the milieu. Depopulation of one simply means that the player characters must move on to a fresh area — interesting to them because it is *different* from the last, fun for you as there are new ideas and challenges which you desire your players to deal with. Variety is, after all, the spice of **AD&D** life too! It becomes particularly interesting for all parties concerned when it is a meaningful part of the whole. As the players examine first one facet, then another, of the milieu gem, they will become more and more taken with its complexity and beauty and wish to see the whole in true perspective. Certainly each will wish to possess it, but none ever will.

Variety of setting is easily done by sketching the outlines of your world's "history". Establishing power bases, setting up conflicts, distributing the creatures, bordering the states, and so forth, gives the basis for a reasoned — if not totally logical in terms of our real world — approach. The multitude of planes and alignments are given for such a purpose, although they also serve to provide fresh places to adventure and establish conflicts between player characters as well.

Certain pre-done modules might serve in your milieu, and you should consider their inclusion in light of your overall schema. If they fit smoothly into the diagram of your milieu, by all means use them, but always alter them to include the personality of your campaign so the mesh is perfect. Likewise, fit monsters and magic so as to be reasonable within the scope of your milieu and the particular facet of it concerned. Alter creatures freely, remembering balance. Hit dice, armor class, attacks and damage, magical and psionic powers are all mutable; and after players become used to the standard types a few ringers will make them a bit less sure of things. Devising a few creatures unique to your world is also recommended. As a DM you are capable of doing a proper job of it provided you have had some hours of hard experience with rapacious players. Then you will know

not to design pushovers and can resist the temptation to develop the perfect player character killer!

In order to offer a bit more guidance, this single example of population and placement will suffice: In a border area of hills and wild forests, where but few human settlements exist, there is a band of very rich, but hard-pressed dwarves. They, and the humans, are hard pressed because of the existence of a large tribe of orcs. The latter have invited numbers of ogres to join them, for the resistance of the men and dwarves to the orcs' looting and pillaging has cost them not a few warriors. The orcs are gaining, more areas nearby are becoming wilderness, and into abandoned countryside and deserted mines the ferocious and dark-dwelling monsters of wilderness and dungeon daily creep. The brave party of adventurers comes into a small village to see what is going on, for they have heard that all is not well hereabouts. With but little help they must then overcome the nasties by piecemeal tactics, being careful not to arouse the whole to general warfare by appearing too strong. This example allows you to develop a logical and ordered placement of the major forces of monsters, to develop habitat complexes and modules of various sorts — abandoned towns, temples, etc. It also allows some free-wheeling mixture of random critters to be stuck in here and there to add uncertainty and spice to the standard challenge of masses of orcs and ogres. You, of course, can make it as complex and varied as you wish, to suit your campaign and players, and perhaps a demon or devil and some powerful evil clerics are in order . . . .

Just as you have matrices for each of your dungeon levels, prepare like data sheets for all areas of your outdoors and urban areas. When monsters are properly placed, note on a key sheet who, what, and when with regard to any replacement. It is certainly more interesting and challenging for players when they find that monsters do not spring up like weeds overnight — in dungeons or elsewhere. Once all dragons in an area are slain, they have run out of dragons! The likelihood of one flying by becomes virtually nil. The "frontier" moves, and bold adventurers must move with it. The movement can, of course, be towards them, as inimical forces roll over civilization. Make it all fit together in your plan, and your campaign will be assured of long life.

PLACEMENT OF MONETARY TREASURE

Wealth abounds; it is simply awaiting the hand bold and strong enough to take it! This precept is basic to fantasy adventure gaming. Can you imagine Fafhrd and the Gray Mouser without a rich prize to aim for? Conan without a pouchful of rare jewels to squander? And are not there dragons with great hoards? Tombs with fantastic wealth and fell guardians? Rapacious giants with spoils? Dwarven mines brimming with gems? Leprechauns with pots of gold? Why, the list goes on and on!

The foregoing is, of course, true; but the matter is not as simple as it might seem on the surface. First, we must consider the logic of the game. By adventuring, slaying monsters or outwitting opponents, and by gaining treasure the characters operating within the milieu advance in ability and gain levels of experience. While **AD&D** is not quite so simplistic as other such games are regarding such advancement, it nonetheless relies upon the principle of *adventuring* and success thereat to bestow such rewards upon player characters and henchmen alike. It is therefore incumbent upon the creator of the milieu and the arbiter of the campaign, the Dungeon Master, to follow certain guidelines and charges placed upon him or her by these rules and to apply them with intelligence in the spirit of the whole as befits the campaign milieu to which they are being applied.

A brief perusal of the character experience point totals necessary to advance in levels makes it abundantly clear that an underlying precept of the game is that the amount of treasure obtainable by characters is graduated from small to large as experience level increases. This most certainly does not intimate or suggest that the greater treasures should be in the hundreds of thousands of gold pieces in value — at least not in readily transportable form in any event — but that subject will be discussed a bit later. First and foremost we must consider the placement of the modest treasures which are appropriate to the initial stages of a campaign.

All monsters would not and should not possess treasure! The TREASURE TYPES given in the **MONSTER MANUAL** are the optimums and are meant to consider the maximum number of creatures guarding them. Many of the monsters shown as possessing some form of wealth are quite unlikely to have any at all. This is not a contradiction in the rules, but an admonition to the DM not to give away too much! Any treasure possessed by weak, low-level monsters will be trifling compared to what numbers of stronger monsters might guard. So in distributing wealth amongst the creatures which inhabit the upper levels of dungeons/dungeon-like areas, as well as for petty monsters dwelling in small numbers in the wilderness, assign it accordingly. The bulk of such treasure will be copper pieces and silver. Perhaps there will be a bit of ivory or a cunningly-crafted item worth a few gold pieces.

Electrum will be most unusual, gold rare, and scarcer still will be a platinum piece or a small gem! Rarest of all, treasure of treasures — the magic item — is detailed hereafter (**PLACEMENT OF MAGIC ITEMS**). If some group of creatures actually has a treasure of 11 gold pieces, another will have 2,000 coppers and yet a third nothing save a few rusty weapons. Of course, all treasure is not in precious metals or rare or finely made substances. Is not a suit of armor of great value? What of a supply of oil? a vial of holy water? weapons? provisions? animals? The upper levels of a dungeon need not be stuffed like a piggy bank to provide meaningful treasures to the clever player character.

Assign each monster treasure, or lack thereof, with reason. The group of brigands has been successful of late, and each has a few coppers left from roistering, while their leader actually has a small sum of silver hid away — coupled with salvaged armor, weapons, and any odd supplies or animals they might have around. This will be a rich find indeed! The giant rats have nothing at all, save a nasty, filthy bite; but the centipedes living beneath a pile of rotting furniture did for an incautious adventurer some years ago, and his skeletal remains are visible still, one hand thrust beneath the debris of the nest. Hidden from view is a silver bracelet with an agate, the whole thing being valued at 20 gold pieces. Thus, intelligent monsters, or those which have an affinity for bright, shiny objects, will consciously gather and hoard treasures. Others will possibly have some as an incidental remainder of their natural hunting or self-defense or aggressive behavior or whatever. Naturally, some monsters will be so unfortunate as to have nothing of value at all, despite their desire to the contrary — but these creatures *might* know of other monsters (whom they hate and envy) who do have wealth!

In more inaccessible regions there will be stronger monsters — whether due to numbers or individual prowess is immaterial. These creatures will have more treasure, at least those with any at all. Copper will give way to silver, silver to electrum, electrum to gold. Everyday objects which can be sold off for a profit — the armor and weapons and suchlike — will be replaced by silks, brocades, tapestries, and similar items. Ivory and spices, furs and bronze statues, platinum and gems and jewelry will trickle upwards from the depths of the dungeon or in from the fastness of wilderlands. But hold! This is not a signal to begin throwing heaps of treasure at players as if you were some mad Midas hating what he created by his touch. Always bear in mind the effect that the successful gaining of any treasure, or set of treasures, will have upon the player characters and the campaign as a whole. Consider this example:

A pair of exceedingly large, powerful and ferocious ogres has taken up abode in a chamber at the base of a shaft which gives to the land above. From here they raid both the upper lands and the dungeons roundabout. These creatures have accumulated over 2,000 g.p. in wealth, but it is obviously not in a pair of 1,000 g.p. gems. Rather, they have gathered an assortment of goods whose combined value is well in excess of two thousand gold nobles (the coin of the realm). Rather than stocking a treasure which the victorious player characters can easily gather and carry to the surface, you maximize the challenge by making it one which ogres would naturally accrue in the process of their raiding. There are many copper and silver coins in a large, locked iron chest. There are pewter vessels worth a fair number of silver pieces. An inlaid wooden coffer, worth 100 gold pieces alone, holds a finely wrought silver necklace worth an incredible 350 gold pieces! Food and other provisions scattered about amount to another hundred or so gold nobles value, and one of the ogres wears a badly tanned fur cape which will fetch 50 gold pieces nonetheless. Finally, there are several good helmets (used as drinking cups), a bardiche, and a two-handed sword (with silver wire wrapped about its hilt and a lapis lazuli pommel to make it worth three times its normal value) which complete the treasure. If the adventurers overcome the ogres, they must still recognize all of the items of value and transport them to the surface. What is left behind will be taken by other residents of the netherworld in no time at all, so the bold victors have quite a task before them. It did not end with a mere slaying of ogres . . . .

In like manner the hoard of a dragon could destroy a campaign if the treasure of Smaug, in **THE HOBBIT**, were to be used as an example of what such a trove should contain. Not so for the wise DM! He or she will place a few choice and portable items, some not-so-choice because they are difficult to carry off, and finally top (or rather bottom and top) the whole with mounds, piles, and layers of copper pieces, silver, etc. There will be much there, but even the cleverest of players will be more than hard put to figure out a way to garner the bulk of it after driving off, subduing, or slaying the treasure's guardian. Many other avaricious monsters are eagerly awaiting the opportunity to help themselves to an unguarded dragon hoard, and news travels fast. Who will stay behind to mind the coins while the rest of a party goes off to dispose of the better part of the loot? Not their henchmen! What a problem . . .

In the event that generosity should overcome you, and you find that in a moment of weakness you actually allowed too much treasure to fall into the players' hands, there are steps which must be taken to rectify matters. The player characters themselves could become attractive to others seeking such gains. The local rulers will desire a share, prices will rise for services in demand from these now wealthy personages, etc. All this is not to actually penalize success. It is a logical abstraction of their actions, it stimulates them to adventure anew, and it also maintains the campaign in balance. These rules will see to it that experience levels are not gained too quickly as long as you do your part as DM!

PLACEMENT OF MAGIC ITEMS

Just as it is important to use forethought and consideration in placing valuable metals and other substances with monsters or otherwise hiding them in dungeon or wilderness, the placement of magic items is a serious matter. Thoughtless placement of powerful magic items has been the ruination of many a campaign. Not only does this cheapen what should be rare and precious, it gives player characters undeserved advancement and empowers them to become virtual rulers of all they survey. This is in part the fault of this writer, who deeply regrets not taking the time and space in **D&D** to stress repeatedly the importance of *moderation*. Powerful magic items were shown, after all, on the tables, and a chance for random discovery of these items was given, so the uninitiated DM cannot be severely faulted for merely following what was set before him or her in the rules. Had the whole been prefaced with an admonition to use care and logic in placement or random discovery of magic items, had the intent, meaning, and spirit of the game been more fully explained, much of the give-away aspect of such campaigns would have willingly been squelched by the DMs. The sad fact is, however, that this was not done, so many campaigns are little more than a joke, something that better DMs jape at and ridicule — rightly so on the surface — because of the foolishness of player characters with astronomically high levels of experience and no real playing skill. These god-like characters boast and strut about with retinues of ultra-powerful servants and scores of mighty magic items, artifacts, relics adorning them as if they were Christmas trees decked out with tinsel and ornaments. Not only are such "Monty Haul" games a crashing bore for most participants, they are a headache for their DMs as well, for the rules of the game do not provide anything for such play — no reasonable opponents, no rewards, nothing! The creative DM can, of course, develop a game which extrapolates from the original to allow such play, but this is a monumental task to accomplish with even passable results, and those attempts I have seen have been uniformly dismal.

Another nadir of Dungeon Mastering is the "killer-dungeon" concept. These campaigns are a travesty of the role-playing adventure game, for there is no development and identification with carefully nurtured player personae. In such campaigns, the sadistic referee takes unholy delight in slaughtering endless hordes of hapless player characters with unavoidable death traps and horrific monsters set to ambush participants as soon as they set foot outside the door of their safe house. Only a few of these "killer dungeons" survive to become infamous, however, as their participants usually tire of the idiocy after a few attempts at enjoyable gaming. Some lucky ones manage to find another, more reasonable, campaign; but others, not realizing the perversion of their DM's campaign, give up adventure gaming and go back to whatever pursuits they followed in their leisure time before they tried **D&D**.

AD&D means to set right both extremes. Neither the giveaway game nor the certain death campaign will be lauded here. In point of fact, DMs who attempt to run such affairs will be drumming themselves out of the ranks of **AD&D** entirely. **ADVANCED DUNGEONS & DRAGONS** aims at providing not only the best possible adventure game but also the best possible refereeing of such campaigns.

Initial placement of magic items in dungeon and wilderness is a crucial beginning for the campaign. In all such places you must NEVER allow random determination to dictate the inclusion of ANY meaningful magic items. Where beginning/low-level player characters are concerned, this stricture also applies to the placement of any item of magic. Furthermore, you need never feel constrained to place or even allow any item in your campaign just because it is listed in the tables. Certainly, you should never allow a multiplicity, or possibly even duplication, of the more powerful items. To fully clarify this, consider the development of a campaign as follows:

In stocking the setting for initial play in the campaign, you must use great care. Consider the circumstances of the milieu and the number of player characters who will be active in it. Then, from the lists of possible items, choose a selection which is commensurate with the setting and the characters involved. For example, you might opt for several potions, a scroll of 1 spell, a wand, a pair of *boots of elvenkind*, several +1 magic arrows, and a +1 magic dagger. As these items will be guarded by relatively weak creatures, you will allow only weak items. The potions will be *healing, heroism, levitation* or the like. The spell on the scroll will be low level — first or second. If you do decide placement of the wand is appropriate, you will make certain that its guardian will use it in defense, and the instrument will have few charges left in any event, with a power which is not out of line with the level of the characters likely to acquire it. The magical *boots* might be worn by a denizen of the area. While the magic arrows might not be used against adventurers, the +1 dagger will be. With all this in mind, you place the items in the countryside and first/upper level of the dungeon/dungeon-like setting. You never allow more than a single item or grouping (such as 3 magic arrows) to a treasure, nor more treasures with magic items than 1 in 5 to 1 in 10, as this is an initial adventuring setting.

As the campaign grows and deeper dungeons are developed, you exercise the same care in placement of selected and balanced magic items. Of course, at lower levels of the dungeon you have more powerful single items or groupings of disparate items, but they are commensurate with the challenge and ability of participants. Guardians tend to employ the items routinely, and others are hidden ingeniously to escape detection. Likewise in the expanding world around the starting habitation you place monsters and treasures, some with magic. You, the DM, know what is there, however, as you have decided what it will be and have put it there for a purpose — whether for the overall direction of the campaign, some specific task, or the general betterment of player characters to enable them to expand their adventuring capabilities because they are skillful enough to face greater challenges if they manage to furnish themselves with the wherewithal to do so.

In those instances where a randomly discovered monster has a nearby lair, and somehow this lair contains treasure, do not allow the dice to dictate a disaster for your campaign. If their result calls for some item of magic which is too powerful, one which you are not certain of, or one which you do not wish to include in the game at this time, you will be completely justified in ignoring it and rolling until a result you like comes up, or you can simply pick a suitable item and inform the players that this is what they found. It is only human nature for people to desire betterment of their position. In this game it results in player characters seeking ever more wealth, magic, power, influence, and control. As with most things in life, the striving after is usually better than the getting. To maintain interest and excitement, there should always be some new goal, some meaningful purpose. It must also be kept in mind that what is unearned is usually unappreciated. What is gotten cheaply is often held in contempt. It is a great responsibility to Dungeon Master a campaign. If you do so with intelligence, imagination, ingenuity, and innovation, however, you will be well rewarded. Always remember this when you select magic items for placement as treasure!

TERRITORY DEVELOPMENT BY PLAYER CHARACTERS

When player characters reach upper levels and decide to establish a stronghold and rule a territory, you must have fairly detailed information on hand to enable this to take place. You must have a large scale map which shows areas where this is possible, a detailed cultural and social treatment of this area and those which bound it, and you must have some extensive information available as to who and what lives in the area to be claimed and held by the player character. Most of these things are provided for you, however, in one form or another, in this work or in the various playing aid packages which are commercially available. The exact culture and society of the area is up to you, but there are many guides to

help you even here.

Assume that the player in question decides that he will set up a stronghold about 100 miles from a border town, choosing an area of wooded hills as the general site. He then asks you if there is a place where he can build a small concentric castle on a high bluff overlooking a river. Unless this is totally foreign to the area, you inform him that he can do so. You give him a map of the hex where the location is, and of the six surrounding hexes. The player character and his henchmen and various retainers must now go to the construction site, explore and map it, and have construction commence.

If you have not already prepared a small scale map of the terrain in the area, use the random generation method when the party is exploring. Disregard any results which do not fit in with your ideas for the place. Both you and the player concerned will be making maps of the territory — on a scale of about 200 yards per hex, so that nine across the widest part will allow the superimposition of a large hex outline of about one mile across. Use actual time to keep track of game time spent exploring and mapping (somewhat tedious but necessary). Check but once for random monsters in each hex, but any monster encountered and not driven off or slain will be there from then on, excepting, of course, those encountered flying over or passing through. After mapping the central hex and the six which surround it, workers can be brought in to commence construction of the castle. As this will require a lengthy period of game time, the player character will have to retain a garrison on the site in order to assure the safety of the crew and the progress of the work (each day there will be a 1 in 20 chance that a monster will wander into one of the seven hexes explored by the character, unless active patrolling in the territory beyond the area is carried on).

While the construction is underway, the character should be exploring and mapping the terrain beyond the core area. Here the larger scale of about one mile per hex should be used, so that in all the character can explore and map an entire campaign hex. There are MANY one mile hexes in a 30 mile across campaign hex, so conduct movement and random monster checks as is normal for outdoor adventuring. Again, any monsters encountered will be noted as living in a hex, as appropriate, until driven out or killed. However, once a hex is cleared, no further random monster checks will be necessary except as follows:

1) Once per day a check must be made to see if a monster has wandered into one of the border hexes which are adjacent to unexplored/uncleared lands.

2) Once per week a check must be made to see if a monster has wandered into the central part of the cleared territory.

Monsters which are indicated will generally remain until driven out or slain. Modifiers to this are:

1) Posting and placement of skulls, carcasses, etc. to discourage intelligent creatures and monsters of the type able to recognize that the remains are indicative of the fate of creatures in the area.

2) Regular strong patrols who leave evidence of their passing and aggressively destroy intruders.

3) Organized communities whose presence and militia will discourage all but organized groups who prey on them or certain monsters who do likewise.

Assuming that the proper activity is kept up and the castle is finished, then the player character and entourage can take up residence in the stronghold. By patrolling the territory regularly — about once per week on a sweep basis, or daily forays to various parts of the area, the character will need only check once each week for incursions of wandering monsters (see **APPENDIX C: RANDOM MONSTER ENCOUNTERS**) on the **Uninhabited/Wilderness** table. Checks must also be made on the **Inhabited** table. If no road goes through the territory, then but one such check per week is necessary. If a road goes through, then three checks per week must be made on the **Inhabited** table. (This can be profitable if the encounters are with merchants and pilgrims, less so with certain other types . . . .)

At such time as a territory has more than 30 miles of inhabited/patrolled land from center to border, then only the second type of monster checks are made, and all unfavorable ones, save one per month, are ignored. This reflects the development of civilization in the area and the shunning by monsters of the usual sort — things such as ankheg might love it, however, and bandits may decide to make it a regular place of call. As usual, any monsters not driven off or slain *will* settle down to enjoy the place. If regular border patrols are not kept up, then the territory will revert to wilderness status — unless the lands around it are all inhabited and patrolled. In the latter case all of the unsavory monsters from the surrounding territory will come to make it a haven for themselves.

Because this is a fantasy adventure game, it is not desirable to have any player character's territory become tame and staid. There must always be a chance for some monster to enter the area and threaten the well-being of its inhabitants. What is the answer if the territory is located in the heart of some powerful state? Intrigue and petty wars, of course! If the territory of a player character is part of a nation, then there will be jealous neighbors, assassins, and the like to threaten him or her. In this case you will have to devote more personal effort to seeing to it that there is still adventure and excitement involved in maintaining the fief.

In territories hacked from the wilderness, the "fame" of the owner will eventually spread so as to attract inhabitants to the safety (?) of the area. They will begin to appear after the player character's stronghold is finished and patrols have generally cleared the area. The populace will match the area and the alignment of the character. When a random monster check reveals some form of creature who properly matches the potential inhabitant type for the territory, then have them move in and settle down, making proper subservience calls upon the master of the territory, naturally. Hamlets, thorps, and various other settlement forms will eventually be established here and there in the area, starting near the castle and working towards the fringe of the territory. Once these territories become settled and population abounds (relatively speaking) they can be used as centers for activity — good or evil or whatever. That is, they can attract more of the ilk which inhabit them, draw opponents sworn to exterminate them, trigger raids or reprisals, etc. Much of this depends upon some action being taken — hopefully by the player character forming active groups from the population base and doing something, but as a last resort action which you initiate by setting up a series of circumstances which will bear upon the territory.

Fighters and clerics will be the principal territorial developers. Magic-users will typically become involved to a lesser extent, for they have many more demands upon their time. The real benefit of having player characters develop territory is the addition to your milieu. These areas become focal points for action in the campaign if properly encouraged and handled, and if things grow a bit slow, a DM-invented threat to some territory is bound to get things moving with elan.

Going back to the construction of the stronghold, when the player elects to build he or she must be required to furnish you with a duplicate set of plans of the castle grounds, its dungeons, and interiors as well. At the same time you can give the player a free hand in drawing a small scale map of the area immediately around his or her stronghold — say, on a 1 hex to 30 yards basis, so about a one-half mile area hex can be depicted on a normal sheet of small hex paper, and a bit beyond shown as needed. With your copy of this map you can plan sieges or other attacks as they occur.

If for any reason a player who has developed territory gives up the campaign, or simply drops the character in favor of another, you can then take over these areas and run them as you like to benefit your campaign. In all respects, then, development of territory by player characters is a highly desirable aspect of the campaign. It gives added purpose to play, and provides long periods where the player can be actively involved in the actual direction of the campaign milieu, which will eventually benefit things regardless of what transpires at a later date.

PEASANTS, SERFS, AND SLAVES

In feudalistic societies, no person not of gentle or noble birth would be allowed weapons of offense, other than those for hunting. Therefore, swords, lances, maces, etc. would be totally banned. In societies which heavily oppress the commoners, serfs and/or slaves will be even more restricted than common peasants. They can have no weapon of any sort whatsoever. They cannot leave their area, be it a farm, estate, village, or whatever. They are chattel.

Peasants, serfs, and slaves generally resent this treatment. Revolts of these sorts of peoples are common in history. Any character who forces peasantry, serfdom, or slavery upon any inhabitants of an area he or she

controls will have to be very careful to guard against uprisings. The oppressed folk will most certainly attempt an uprising once every five years, minimum. If there is weakness noted, there will be an uprising immediately. Peasants will demand more freedom, rights, and lesser taxes; serfs will be attempting to gain peasant status; slaves will simply desire to slay their former masters and escape to somewhere where they can be free. Exact details of such uprisings are not possible here, but you should be able to determine them without undue difficulty. The oppressed populace will give rise to about 1 fighter for every 5 total, as men, women, and just about anybody able to carry a club or a knife will join in. Arms and armor (if any) will be scant and crude. Troops will be 0 level, peasant class. Tactical ability will usually tend to be nil. The exception is if some mercenary group aids peasants, or if some slaves have had military experience.

If a rising does occur, the player character must suppress it as soon as possible. If it lasts more than one month, the revolting folk will gain experience, organization, recruits, and better weapons and armor. Therefore, for each full month of successful revolt, add 10% to the number of people in revolt, assume 10% of the total force becomes equal to regular men-at-arms in training and armor and weapons, and allow them greater tactical ability. After six months of successful revolt, the rebellion can be assumed to have taken on the status of a civil war, and the revolutionaries will be able to field something approximating a regular military force.

A SAMPLE DUNGEON

LEVEL KEY   1 square = 10'

STAIRS UP =
TRAP DOOR =

STAIRS DOWN =
SECRET TRAP DOOR = ⓢ

DOOR =
STREAM =

SECRET DOOR = S
CONCEALED DOOR = C

WANDERING MONSTERS

Non-Crypt Areas (Generally Northern Portion of Map):

Die	Result
1	3-12 goblins (patrolling from area 7.-8.)
2	2-5 bandits (from area 4.-5.)
3	7-12 giant rats
4	1-2 fire beetles (from area 12.-13.)

Crypt Areas:

Die	Result
1	1-2 ghouls (from area 24.)
2	1 3rd level evil cleric & 2 hobgoblins (from area 35.-37.)
3	7-12 giant rats
4	2-5 skeletons (patrolling from area 27.)

MONASTERY CELLARS & SECRET CRYPTS

1. ENTRY CHAMBER: A damp and vaulted chamber 30' square and arched to a 20' high center roof. Arches begin at 8' and meet at a domed peak. Walls are cut stone block, floor is rough. Thick webs hide ceiling. See A & B below.

    A. LARGE SPIDER: AC 8; Move 6"*15"; HD: 1 + 1 (HP 6). There are also nine 1 HP young spiders hiding in the upper part of the webs. This monster lurks directly over a central litter of husks, skin, bones, and its own castings, awaiting new victims to drop upon. It will always attack by surprise unless the webs it is in are burned (which will do 3 HP damage to the spider and kill the young). There are 19 silver pieces in the litter on the ground, while a goblin skull there has a 50 gold piece garnet inside which will only be noticed if the skull is picked up and examined.

    B. ROTTING SACKS: There are 10 moldy sacks of flour and grain stacked here. The cloth is easily torn to reveal the contents. If all of them are opened and searched, there is a 25% probability that the last will have YELLOW MOLD in it, and handling will automatically

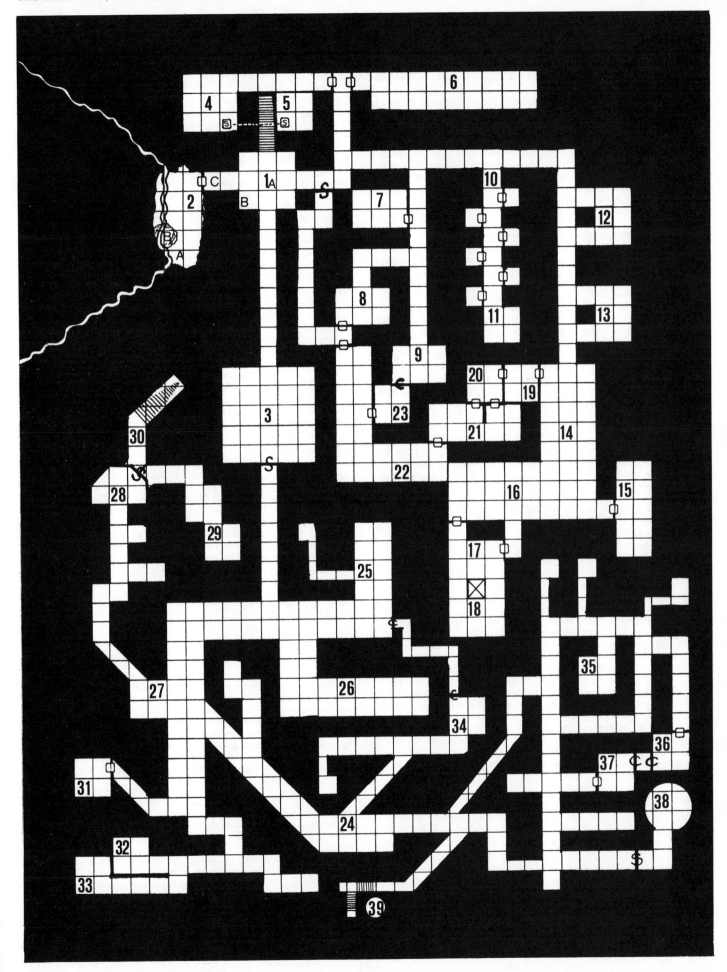

cause it to burst and all within 10' must save versus poison or die in 1 turn.

    C.   Heavy oak door with bronze hardware is remarkable only in that if any character listens at it, he or she will detect a moaning which will rise and then fade away. Unbeknownst to listeners, it is the strong breeze which goes through area 2. AS SOON AS THIS DOOR IS OPENED, A WIND GUST WILL EXTINGUISH TORCHES AND BE 50% LIKELY TO BLOW OUT LANTERNS AS WELL. The wind continues to make the corridor impossible for torches until the door is shut.

2.   WATER ROOM: This natural cavern was roughly worked to enlarge it. Torches cannot be lit. When the monastery was functioning, the place was filled with casks and barrels and buckets, but now only 8 rotting barrels remain (location A.) and there are 3 buckets scattered about. Several of the barrels hold water — they were new and being soaked to make them tight.

    B.   THE LIMED-OVER SKELETON OF THE ABBOT is in this pool of water, but it appears to be merely a somewhat unusual mineral formation. Clutched in the bony fingers is the special key which will allow the secret door at location 28. to open to the treasury room (29.) rather than to the steps which lead down to the caverns (steps down at 30.). If the remains are disturbed in any way, a cylindrical object will be noticed, the thing being dislodged from where it lay by the skeleton, and the current of the stream carrying it south (downstream) at 6" speed. To retrieve it a character must be in the stream and score "to hit" as if it were AC 4 in order to catch it. It is a watertight ivory tube with a vellum map of the whole level inside. However, slow seepage has made all but a small portion blur and run into ruin. The map shows only areas 1., 2., the passage to 3., a smudge where 3. is and the passage to 24. about 20' south of the secret door leading from 3. to 24. — the latter being shown with miniature sarcophagi drawn in the 80' or so not water soaked and ruined.

    STREAM: This is cold and fast flowing. It is from 5' to 7' wide and 3' to 5' deep. It enters on the north from a passage which it fills entirely, and it exits to the south in the same manner.

    POOL: The pool is about 10' long and 15' wide. It is about 4' deep at its edge and 7' in the center. There are a score or so of small, white blind fish in it, and under the rocks are some cave crayfish, similarly blind and white.

3.   EMPTY CEREMONIAL CHAMBER: This large place appears to be a dead end. It has roof supports similar to chamber 1, but the vaulted ceiling dome here is fully 25' high. When the monastery was functioning, the faithful were brought here after death, consecrated, and then carried to their final resting place by silent monks after the mourners left. A wooden platform, supposedly merely a dais for ceremony and religious rites, was placed against the south wall. This platform being 9' off the ground enabled the use of the secret door in the south wall — this portal being 8½' wide, 10' high, and 10' above the floor of the chamber. Amongst the 7 small protruding knobs of stone about 9½' above the floor, the 7th pushes in to trigger the door mechanism, and the portal will swing inward (swings east) with a grinding noise. The only clue which still remains are socket holes in the south wall. There are 2 at the 20' and 2 at the 30' line (that is, on either side of the centermost 10' south wall space). Each pair has 1 socket at about 4' height, 1 at about 8'. Each socket is ½' × ½' square and a little deeper. The first socket hole examined by the party will have several splinters of wood (from the platform, of course) which might prove to be another clue to thinking players.

4.   (Etc.)

THE FIRST DUNGEON ADVENTURE

Assume that you have assembled a group of players. Each has created a character, determined his or her race and profession, and spent some time carefully equipping these neophyte adventurers with everything that the limited funds available could purchase. Your participants are now eagerly awaiting instructions from you as to how to find the place they are to seek their fortunes in. You inform them that there is a rumor in the village that something strange and terrible lurks in the abandoned monastery not far from the place. In fact, one of the braver villagers will serve as guide if

they wish to explore the ruins! (This seemingly innocent guide might be nothing more than he seems, or possibly an agent of some good or evil power, or a thief in disguise, or just about anything else. In this case, however, let it be a thief, for reasons you will discover soon.) The party readily agrees, and so the adventure begins.

You inform them that after about a two mile trek along a seldom-used road, they come to the edge of a fen. A narrow causeway leads out to a low mound upon which stand the walls and buildings of the deserted monastery. One of the players inquires if the mound appears to be travelled, and you inform the party that only a very faint path is discernible — as if any traffic is light and infrequent. Somewhat reassured, another player asks if anything else is apparent. You describe the general bleakness of the bog, with little to relieve the view save a few clumps of brush and tamarack sprouting here and there (probably on bits of higher ground) and a fairly dense cluster of the same type of growth approximately a half mile beyond the abandoned place. Thus, the party has only one place to go — along the causeway — if they wish to adventure. The leading member of the group (whether appointed or self-elected, it makes no difference) orders that the party should proceed along the raised pathway to the monastery, and the real adventure begins.

The so-called guide, the thief, is a 3rd level non-player character. You placed him in the village and gave the reason for his being there as a desire for a huge fire opal which the abbot of the place is said to have hidden when the monastery was under siege. The fellow died, according to legend, without revealing it to anyone, so somewhere within the ruins lies a fortune. But this particular thief lacks courage, so he has been living frugally in the village while seeking some means of obtaining the gem without undue risk to himself. Now, he has the party to serve as his means. If they invite him along, then he will go — with seeming reluctance, of course. If they do not, he will lurk near the entrance hoping to obtain any loot they will have gleaned from the adventure when they return, doing so either by stealth or by force if the party is sufficiently weakened from the perils they have faced.

Before you are three maps: a large-scale map which shows the village and the surrounding territory, including the fen and monastery, the secret entrance/exit from the place, and lairs of any monsters who happen to dwell in the area; at hand also is a small-scale (1 square to 10' might be in order) map of the ruined monastery which shows building interiors, insets for upper levels, and a numbered key for descriptions and encounters; lastly, you have the small scale map of the storage chambers and crypts beneath the upper works of the place (refer to the section, **THE CAMPAIGN**), likewise keyed by numbers for descriptions and encounters. So no matter what action the party decides upon, you have the wherewithal to handle the situation. When they come to the area shown on the second map, the one depicting the monastery complex, you set aside map one, and begin a more detailed narrative of what they "see", possibly referring to the number key from time to time as they explore the place.

Movement within buildings is actually the same as in an underground setting. Each square represents an area of 10' per side, and movement is very slow as observation and map making and searching takes considerable time. Base movement rate translates to 1 square per 1 factor in a turn (10 minute period). In like manner, examination and mapping of a room or chamber will require about a 10 minute period. Thorough searching of contents and examination of walls, floor, and possibly the ceiling as well is also a lengthy process. How are doors and secret doors opened? and what about locks and fastenings? It is vital that the DM know such details thoroughly, so that the mundane processes of dungeon adventuring can be carried out rapidly, clearly, and in a fashion which will be interesting and exciting.

Movement And Searching: You must make some arbitrary decisions regarding the time expended in activities which are not strictly movement. Travelling along a corridor and mapping its length takes 1 turn per 90', assuming a base move of 9". How long does it take to move along but a short section of passage, open a door, enter the room beyond, and search it? Such variables as passage length, condition of the portal (locked, stuck, or normal), size of the room beyond, and thoroughness of the search make an absolute determination of time nearly impossible. There are many variations of player character activity — looking for signs of use of the corridor, listening for noise, looking for traps, inspection of walls for secret doors, etc. — all of which compound the need for an arbitrary handling of time. If a few fixed references are used, the task becomes a good deal easier, however. Therefore, the following suggestions are offered:

DOOR — search for traps:	1 round
DOOR — listening for noise:	1 round
ROOM — mapping, and casually examining a 20′ × 20′ area:	1 turn
ROOM — thoroughly searching after initial examination*:	1 turn
SECRET DOOR — checking for by simple tapping of floor or wall, by 10′ × 10′ area:	1 round
SECRET DOOR — thorough examination for means to open, by 10′ × 10′ area:	1 turn

* This assumes that, in fact, the area has items which can be checked for traps, examined, contents searched, hidden compartments looked for, and so on. If there are many containers and much furniture in the area, the time might actually be double that shown. If the place has nothing but some odds and ends, then a casual examination will discover all there is to know about the place (short of a check for secret doors) and a thorough search is contra-indicated.

Detection Of Unusual Circumstances, Traps, And Hearing Noise: Regardless of the means, it takes effort and concentration to perform any of these activities. A gnome, for instance, must remain relatively quiet and concentrate for a turn to detect facts about an underground setting. Likewise, a dwarf must work at it. An elf doesn't detect secret doors 16⅔% of the time by merely passing them unless he or she is actually concentrating on the act. A character with a sword must have it out and be thinking about its power in order for the weapon to communicate anything to him or her. To sum it all up, DON'T GIVE PLAYERS A FREE LUNCH! Tell them what they "see", allow them to draw their own conclusions and initiate whatever activity they desire. You are the source of their input, a time keeper, and the motivator of all not connected with them. That is sufficient to keep you busy, rest assured.

Assume that your players are continually wasting time (thus making the so-called adventure drag out into a boring session of dice rolling and delay) if they are checking endlessly for traps and listening at every door. If this persists, despite the obvious displeasure you express, the requirement that helmets be doffed and mail coifs removed to listen at a door, and then be carefully replaced, the warnings about ear seekers, and frequent checking for wandering monsters (q.v.), then you will have to take more direct part in things. Mocking their over-cautious behavior as near cowardice, rolling huge handfuls of dice and then telling them the results are negative, and statements to the effect that: "You detect nothing, and nothing has detected YOU so far — ", might suffice. If the problem should continue, then rooms full with silent monsters will turn the tide, but that is the stuff of later adventures.

Doors: As a rule of thumb, all doors are hard to open and hard to keep closed or open for player characters, while inhabitants of the dungeon find little difficulty in these regards. Regardless of how a door opens, it is usual that its weight and condition require that force be used to swiftly operate it. This is represented by the roll of d6 for each person involved in pushing, pulling, lifting, sliding, or whatever. A roll of 1 or 2 typically indicates success, anything above indicates the door still remains unopened. (Cf. **PLAYERS HANDBOOK, Character Abilities,** *Strength.*) Very heavy doors might reduce chances by half. Locked doors might only open if two or even three simultaneous 1's are rolled. Most doors are about 8′ wide, and this allows up to three characters to attempt opening. A door of 3′ or less width allows but a single character to make an attempt. If wooden doors (always metal bound, naturally) are broken down by axes and the like, it will take some time — a full turn is usual — and require at least 3 checks to see if nearby and/or wandering monsters are attracted by the noise. Doors can also be blasted away by *fireballs* and other spells, for example. This will not be likely to draw monsters to the vicinity immediately. Any such destruction will, however, attract the attention of all passing creatures and possibly cause future problems. Intelligent dungeon inhabitants will certainly make efforts to repair damage if it is in their interest to do so. Finally, metal doors (usually locked) will be very difficult to open, requiring a *knock* spell or similar means most of the time.

Concealed Doors: These are doors which are hidden in some way — behind a curtain, covered with plaster, a trap door under a rug, etc. They differ from a secret door in that once their concealment is uncovered they are obviously doors.

Secret Doors: These are portals which are made to appear to be a normal part of the surface they are in. They can possibly be sensed or detected by characters who are actively concentrating on such activity, or their possible location may be discovered by tapping (though the hollow place could be another passage or room beyond which has no portal in the

hollow-sounding surface). Discovery does not mean that access to the door mechanism has been discovered, however. Checking requires a very thorough examination of the possible secret door area. You may use either of two methods to allow discovery of the mechanism which operates the portal:

1. You may designate probability by a linear curve, typically with a d6. Thus, a secret door is discovered 1 in 6 by any non-elf, 2 in 6 by elven or half-elven characters, each character being allowed to roll each turn in checking a 10′ × 10′ area. This also allows you to have some secret doors more difficult to discover, the linear curve being a d8 or d10.

2. You may have the discovery of the existence of the secret door enable player characters to attempt to operate it by actual manipulation, i.e. the players concerned give instructions as to how they will have their characters attempt to make it function: "Turn the wall sconce.", "Slide it left.", "Press the small protrusion, and see if it pivots.", "Pull the chain."

It is quite acceptable to have a mixture of methods of discovering the operation of secret door.

With these basic points in mind, let us return to the action of the first dungeon adventure. Assuming that the abandoned monastery is merely a burned-out shell, with nothing but rubble and ruin within, the players spend only a few minutes of real time "looking around" before they discover a refuse-strewn flight of steep and worn stone stairs leading downward. "Ahah!", exclaims the leader of the group, "This must be the entrance to the dungeons. We'll find what we are looking for there." The other players voice agreement, and so the real adventure begins. What is said by the Dungeon Master will be prefaced by the letters DM, while the party of player characters will be prefaced by either LC (for leader), or OC (for any of the other player characters speaking).

DM: "What are you going to do now?"

LC: "Light our torches, and go down the steps!"

DM: "Fine, but I'll need the 'marching order' you will be in." (At this point the players either write down the names of characters with each in its respective rank, or place their painted miniature figures in actual formation. As minimum width is about 3⅓′ per character: a 5′ wide corridor requires single file, a 10′ wide passage means up to 3 may be abreast, and up to 6 abreast can move down a 20′ wide passageway.) "Please note what formation you will take in a 5′ wide passage, and what your marching order will be in a 20′ wide area, also."

LC: (After a brief discussion with the other players:) "Here is the information on this sheet of note paper. We'll change it only if one of us is wounded, lost, or killed."

DM: "Why are the gnome and the halfling in the front rank, the magic-user in the middle, and the human fighter and cleric in the rear?"

LC: "That way all 5 of us can act when we encounter an enemy! The magic-user can cast spells over the heads of the short characters in front, and the pair in the back rank can do likewise, or fire missiles, or whatever is needed, including a quick move to the front!"

DM: (Nodding agreement) "You remember that the torches will spoil the infravisual capabilities of the gnome and the halfling, don't you?"

LC: "Certainly, but the humans must be able to see! We will go down the stairs now, with weapons drawn and ready."

DM: "You descend southward, possibly 30′ laterally, and at the end of the stairway you see an open space."

LC: "Enter the area and look around."

DM: "You are in a chamber about 30′ across to the south and 30′ wide east and west. There are 10′ wide passages to left and right and ahead, each in the center of the respective walls. The stairway you descended likewise enters the chamber in the center of the north wall."

LC: "What else do we see?"

DM: "The floor is damp and rough. There are arches supporting the ceiling, starting from a spot about 8' above the floor and meeting about 20' height in the central dome of the place — it is difficult to tell, because the whole ceiling area is covered with webs . . . . Possibly old cobwebs. Oh yes. There are some mouldering sacks in the southwest corner, and some rubbish jumbled in the center of the floor — which appears to be dirt, old leather, rotting cloth, and possibly sticks or bones or something similar."

LC: (A confused babble breaks out at this point, with players suggesting all sorts of different actions. The leader cautions them and tries for a careful, reasoned, methodical approach.) "The gnome and the halfling will hand their torches to the fighter (me) and the cleric. They will then look down the east and west passages, while I check the one straight ahead to the south. The cleric will check the sacks, and the magic-user will examine the pile of refuse in the center of the chamber. Everyone agree?"

OC: "Sure!" says the player with the cleric character, "I'm moving over to the sacks now, sticking close to the lefthand wall."

DM: "What are the rest of you doing? As indicated? Tell me how you are doing it, please." (If miniature figures and a floor plan are being used, each player can simply move his or her figurine to show route of movement and final position. Otherwise, each player must describe actions just as the cleric character player did above.)

LC: "They are now in position, what is seen and what happens?"

DM: "Just as the three are about in position to look down the passages, and while the cleric is heading for the rotting bags, the magic-user cries out, and you see something black and nasty looking upon her shoulder!"

LC: "EVERYBODY, QUICK! SEE WHAT'S ATTACKED HER!" Then turning to the referee: "We rush over to help kill whatever has attacked her! What do we see?"

DM: "A large spider has surprised her. As she went to examine the refuse it dropped from its web. It landed on her back and bit her. Before you can take any action, she must make a saving throw with +2 on her die, of course, and then she and the spider must dice for initiative and fight a round of combat. After that the rest can try to do something."

OC: (The magic-user.) "A 16, did I make it?!" (This said as she rolls the die to make the required saving throw against the spider's poison.)

DM: "Yes. Easily, so you take only 1 hit point of damage. While you mark it down, I'll roll for the spider's initiative — beat a 3."

OC: (Again the magic-user.) "A 5. If that means I can act before the spider does, I'll grab it and throw it on the floor and stamp on it with my boot!"

DM: "Roll a d20, and we'll see if you hit." The die score indicates that the magic-user would hit an opponent of the armor class of the large spider, so the DM states: "You grab the spider, but as you do so, you are now allowing the monster to attack you, even though you had the initiative, and it bites at your hand as you hurl it to the floor!" (Amidst groans of horrified anticipation from the players, the DM rolls a d20, but the low number which results indicates a clean miss by the arachnid.) "Yug! The nasty thing misses you, and it is now scuttling along the floor where you tossed it!"

LC: "Who is nearest to the spider? Whomever it is will smash it with a weapon!"

DM: "It was hurled down to the southwest, and it is now heading for the wall there to climb back into its web overhead. The cleric is nearest to it."

OC: (The cleric, of course.) "I squash the nasty thing with my mace!" and here the player, having already gained savoir faire, rolls a d20 to see if his strike is successful. A 20, and a beaming player shouts: "I got it!"

DM: "You're right, and you do . . . (with these words the DM rolls a d6 to determine the amount of damage) SIX POINTS! That's heavy — heavy enough to kill it, in fact. It is smashed to pieces. What now?"

LC: "Everybody will do what we set out to do in the first place. If nothing valuable or interesting is in the sacks, the cleric will then help the magic-user search the refuse and burn the webs overhead in case there are any more spiders hiding up there."

DM: "The sacks hold rotten grain, so the cleric will go and help the magic-user as ordered. They find the refuse consists of castings, some husks of small victims of the spider, hide, bones, a small humanoid skull, and 19 silver pieces. Do you now fire the webs overhead?"

LC: "Examine the skull first. What kind of humanoid was it? Can we tell?"

DM: "Possibly a goblin. When you are looking at it more closely, you see that there is a small gem inside — a garnet."

LC: That's more like it! Put it safely in your pouch, along with the silver pieces, Good Cleric, and light the spiderweb."

DM: "The strands burn quickly, flame running along each and lighting others touched. You see several young spiders crisped as the mass of webs near the top of the chamber catches fire."

LC: "That's that. What is seen down the three corridors leading out of the place?"

DM: "The east passage appears to turn north after about 30' or so, the south tunnel runs straight as far as can be seen, and the west corridor ends in a door at about 20'."

LC: "Come on, fellow adventurers, let's head west and see what lurks beyond the door!" The other players concur, so marching order is re-established, and the gnome and halfling lead the way.

DM: "Okay, you are marching west: 10', 20', and the passage ends in a door to the west. It is a great, heavy thing, bound in corroded bronze. There is a huge ring in the center."

LC: "Magic-user, step forward and listen at the door. Gnome and halfling, see which way it opens, and get ready to do so."

DM: (Rolling a d6 behind a screen so that the players cannot see the result which would normally indicate if noise were detected or not, if applicable, when a character listens. In this case the DM knows what will be heard, but pretends otherwise.) "There is a faint moaning sound — you can't really tell what it is — which rises and then fades away. The door pulls inwards towards you, the hinges on the left."

LC: "We all get ready, I'll nock an arrow, and the magic-user will ready her magic missile spell. As soon as we are set the cleric and the gnome will pull the door open, the cleric closest to the hinged side. Ready? GO!"

DM: "Each of you who are opening the door roll a d6 for me to see if you succeed. I see from your character sheets that the gnome has a normal strength, so he'll need a 1 or 2, the cleric has 17 strength, so he'll do it on a 1, 2, or 3." (Eager hands roll the dice, and each succeeds in rolling a score low enough to indicate success.) Smiling, the DM continues: "The door groans inward, and a blast of cold, damp air gusts into the passage where you are, blowing out both torches!" (Here, as about 3 turns have elapsed, the DM rolls a d6 to see if a 'wandering monster' appears; the resulting 5 indicates none.)

LC: (Thinking quickly.) "Halfling and gnome, what do you see with your infravision!? Should we slam the door?"

DM: "It takes a few seconds for their eyes to adjust to the darkness, and then they tell you that they can detect no creatures — everything appears to be the same temperature, cold."

LC: "Cleric, it is time to use your light spell, for we'll never get torches lit in this wind. Cast it on your 10' pole." (There is a delay while the cleric complies, and then:) "We are now poking the bright end of the pole into the place and looking; tell us what we see."

DM: The space behind the door is only rough-hewn and irregular. It appears to be a natural cave of some sort which was worked to make it larger in places. It is about 25' across and goes 40' south. A small stream — about 15' wide at one place, but only 6' or 7' wide elsewhere — runs south along the far wall. There are 3 buckets and several barrels in the place, but nothing else."

LC: "Check the ceiling and the floor. No more nasty surprises for us! If we note nothing unusual, we will check out the buckets and barrels quickly." (Aside to the others:) "This was probably the water supply room for the monastery, so I doubt if we'll find anything worthwhile here."

OC: "Where exactly is the wide spot in the stream? I think that I'll check out that pool." (The DM tells the player where it is, so he heads over to the place.) "Now, I'm looking into the water with the bright end of my staff actually thrust into the liquid, what happens?"

DM: "First, the others checking the containers find that they held nothing but water, or are totally empty, and that the wood is rotten to boot. You see a few white, eyeless fish and various stone formations in a pool of water about 4' to 6' deep and about 10' long. That's all. Do you wish to leave the place now?"

LC: "Yes, let's get out of here and go someplace where we can find something interesting."

OC: "Wait! If those fish are just blind cave types, ignore them, but what about the stone formations? Are any of them notable? If so, I think we should check them out."

DM: "Okay. The fish are fish, but there is one group of minerals in the deepest part of the pool which appears to resemble a skeleton, but it simply — "

OC: "If the pole will reach, I'll use the end to prod the formation and see if it is actually a skeleton covered with mineral deposits from the water! I know the Shakespearean bit about a 'sea change'!"

DM: "You manage to reach the place and prodding it breaks off a rib-like piece. You see bone beneath the minerals. As you prod, however, a piece of the formation is caught by the current — a cylindrical piece about a foot long — and it rolls downstream."

LC: "Run as fast as I can to get ahead of it, jump in, and grab it! Quick! Some of you get ready to pull me out if the water is over my head!"

DM: "You manage to get ahead of the piece, jump into water about 4' deep, and grab at it, but you must roll a d20 'to hit' to see if you can manage to grasp the object before it is swept past you and goes downstream into the pipe-like tunnel which the stream flows out through." (The player rolls and scores high enough to have hit armor class 4, the value the DM has decided is appropriate to the chance of grasping, so the DM continues:) "You are in luck this adventure! You have the object, and it seems to be an ivory or bone tube with a waterproof cap."

LC: "As soon as my fellows help me out of the stream, we'll examine it carefully, and if all appears okay, we'll dry it off thoroughly and open it very gently."

DM: "There is nothing difficult involved, so after drying it off on the gnome's cape, you break the seal and pull out the stopper. Inside is a roll of vellum."

LC: "Let's get out of here now, shut the door, get some torches going again, and then read whatever is on the scroll." (The others agree, and in a few moments, the actions have been taken care of.) "Now, carefully remove the scroll and see what is on it."

DM: "The tube must have allowed a bit of water to seep in slowly, for there are parts of the scroll that are smudged and obliterated, but you can see it is a map of the passages under the monastery. You recognize the stairs down and the water supply room. It looks as if the eastern portion is smeared beyond recognition, but you see that the south passage runs to a blurred area, and beyond that you see a large area with coffin-like shapes drawn along the perimeter. That's all you can determine."

LC: "We go back east 20', which takes us back to the entry chamber, and then we'll head south down the long corridor there. We will look carefully at the map we found to see if it shows any traps or monsters along our route."

DM: "You are at the mouth of the passageway south in the center of the south wall of the entry chamber. The map doesn't indicate any traps or monsters, so you go south down the passage — 10', 20', 30', 40', 50', 60', 70', 80', 90'. The passageway is unremarkable, being of stone blocks and natural stone, with an arched ceiling about 15' high. At 90' you come into the northern portion of a 50' × 50' chamber. It is bare and empty. There are no exits apparent. It seems to be a dead end place." (Here the DM makes a check to see if any 'wandering monsters' come, but the result is a 2 on d6, so there are none.) "What are you going to do?"

LC: "We'll look at our map again. Does this look as if it were the room with the coffin-shapes?"

DM: "Certainly not. The place seems to be about where the blotched area is, but there are no passageways out of it."

LC: "Let's tap along that south wall, especially in the center 30' to see if it sounds hollow. The cleric, gnome, and halfling will do the tapping, while the magic-user and I watch back the way we came."

DM: (Rolling a few dice behind the screen several times, knowing that tapping won't show anything, as the secret door is 10' above the floor:) "The entire wall sounds VERY solid. You spend a full 10 minutes thoroughly checking, even to the far east and west, and all 3 are convinced it is not hollow beyond. However, the gnome, who you placed in the middle, noted some strange holes in the wall. These were square places cut into the natural stone, each about half a foot per side and a bit deeper. There were 2 at the 20' and 2 at the 30' line, 1 above the other, the lower at about 3', and the higher at about 6'. He found some small splinters of wood in one."

OC: "Does the smudged area give us any clue as to what the holes could be for? Let's feel around inside them to see if there are levers or catches or something . . ."

LC: "Yes. Look at the map, and carefully check those holes with daggers first — we don't want to lose fingers or hands!" (When all that comes to naught:) "Can anyone think of why there would be wood splinters in the holes? That must be some sort of a clue!"

OC: "The only thing I can think of is that the holes are sockets for some sort of wooden construction —"

LC: "Sure! How about a ramp or stairs? How high is the ceiling in this place?"

DM: "Oh, it must be at least 25' or more."

LC: "Let's form a human pyramid and see if there's a secret door higher up on the wall — right here in the center where the passage seems to go on southwards. I'll form the base, and the rest of you help the gnome and the halfling up, and hold them there (use the pole!), while they tap. What do they discover?"

DM: "The halfling at the top of the stack has a 1 in 6 chance of slipping and bringing you all down." (A roll of 4 follows, so:) "But it doesn't happen, and both the gnome and the halfling manage a few taps, and even that feeble work seems to indicate some sort of space beyond."

LC: "Let's change the plan a bit. The cleric and I will hoist the gnome up and hold his legs firmly while he checks around for some way to open the secret door. Meanwhile, the halfling and the magic-user will guard the entrance so that we won't be attacked by surprise by some monster while thus engaged."

DM: "You accomplish the shuffle, and let's see if anything comes — " (A d6 roll for wandering monsters again gives a negative result.) "The guards see nothing, and what is the gnome doing now?"

OC: (The gnome:) "I'll scan the stone first to see if there are marks or some operating device evident."

DM: "Some stone projections seem rather smooth, as if worn by use. That's all you are able to note."

OC: "Then I'll see if I can move any of the stone knobs and see if they operate a secret door! I'll push, pull, twist, turn, slide, or otherwise attempt to trigger the thing if possible."

DM: "The fist-sized projection moves inwards and there is a grinding sound, and a 10' × 10' section of the wall, 10' above the floor in the center part, swings inwards to the right."

OC: (The gnome:) "I'll pull myself up into the passage revealed, and then I'll see if I can drive in a spike and secure my rope to it, so I can throw the free end down to the others."

DM: "You get up all right, and there is a crack where you can pound in a spike. As you're doing it, you might be in for a nasty surprise, so I'll let you roll a six-sider for me to see your status — make the roll! (Groans as a 1 comes up indicating surprise. The DM then rolls 3 attacks for the ghoul that grabbed at the busy gnome, and one claw attack does 2 hit points of damage and paralyzes the hapless character, whereupon the DM judges that the other 3 would rend him to bits. However, the DM does NOT tell the players what has happened, despite impassioned pleas and urgent demands. He simply relates:) "You see a sickly gray arm strike the gnome as he's working on the spike, the gnome utters a muffled cry, and then a shadowy form drags him out of sight. What are you others going to do?"

LC: "Ready weapons and missiles, the magic-user her *magic-missile* spell, and watch the opening."

DM: "You hear some nasty rending noises and gobbling sounds, but they end quickly. Now you see a group of gray-colored human-like creatures with long, dirt- and blood-encrusted nails, and teeth bloodied and bared, coming to the opening. As they come to the edge you detect a charnel smell coming from them — 4 of them, in fact."

What will the party do? Will the cleric realize that they are ghouls and attempt to turn them? Will he succeed? If not, there may well be no survivors. If so, what treasure lies beyond? Possibly the great gem . . . but the thief still awaits the party's return. Well, that is the stuff from which adventures are spun, and now you know how to spin your own.

NON-PLAYER CHARACTERS

PERSONAE OF NON-PLAYER CHARACTERS

It is often highly desirable, if not absolutely necessary, to have well-developed non-player characters (NPCs). In order to easily develop these personae, the tables below are offered for consideration. Note that the various facts and traits are given in a sequence which allows the character to develop itself — with judicial help from the DM. Thus, *Alignment, Appearance, Possessions,* and then *General Tendencies* are given. The first three will, of necessity, modify the fourth, and the latter will similarly greatly modify the other traits.

The personae of special NPCs should be selected (and embellished, if you wish) from the tables (or see THE ROGUES GALLERY from TSR). Other NPCs can be developed randomly, or by a combination of random and considered selection. No fewer than three *General Tendencies* should be determined, and several more can be added if the DM desires. Of course, some are contradictory, and if a random selection indicates such dichotomy, roll until noncontradictory tendencies are discovered. In like manner, successively generated traits should not conflict with the *General Tendencies* previously developed — unless the NPC is *insane*, in which case such conflict is quite permissible. A brief explanation of each fact and trait is given after the tables.

ADJUSTMENTS TO ABILITY DICE ROLLS FOR NON-PLAYER CHARACTERS

Race

Dwarf	strength +1, constitution +1, charisma −1
Elf	intelligence +1, dexterity +1
Gnome	wisdom +1, constitution +1, charisma −1
Halfling	dexterity +1, constitution +1

Class	Minimum Score or Adjustment to Ability Dice Roll*
Cleric	wisdom +2
Druid	12/14 minimum wisdom/charisma
Fighter	strength +2, constitution +1
Ranger	as fighter, 12 minimum wisdom
Paladin	as fighter, 17 minimum charisma
Magic-User	intelligence +2, dexterity +1
Illusionist	15/15 minimum intelligence/dexterity
Monk	12/15/15 minimum strength/wisdom/dexterity
Thief	dexterity +2, intelligence +1
Assassin	as thief, strength +1

Occupation	
Laborer	strength +1 to +3
Mercenary (level 0)	strength +1, constitution +3 4 minimum hit points
Merchant/Trader	12/12 minimum intelligence/charisma

* Note that these are adjustments **in addition to** those noted in the **AD&D PLAYERS HANDBOOK.** In spite of all additions, normal ability limits cannot be exceeded.

FACTS TABLES

Alignment (d10)
1. lawful good
2. lawful neutral
3. lawful evil
4. neutral evil
5. chaotic evil
6. chaotic neutral
7. chaotic good
8. neutral good
9. neutral
0. neutral

Possessions (or wealth) (d10)
1. none
2. scant
3. scant
4. average
5. average
6. average
7. average
8. above average
9. exceptional
0. superabundant

Appearance (roll separately for each category)

Age (d10)	General (d10)
1. young	1. dirty
2. youthful	2. clean
3. youthful	3. unkempt
4. mature	4. immaculate
5. mature	5. rough
6. mature	6. ragged
7. mature	7. dandyish
8. middle-aged	8. foppish
9. old	9. non-descript
0. ancient	0. imposing

Sanity (d10)
1. very stable
2. normal
3. normal
4. normal
5. normal
6. normal
7. neurotic
8. unstable
9. insane*
0. maniacal*

* Roll again, and if either **insane** or **maniacal** is indicated a second time, the character then conforms to that sanity level; in all other cases the second roll stands in place of the first.

TRAITS TABLES

General Tendencies (d12, d6)
1. optimist
2. pessimist
3. hedonist
4. altruist
5. helpful/kindly
6. careless
7. capricious/mischievous
8. sober
9. curious/inquisitive
10. moody
11. trusting
12. suspicious/cautious
13. precise/exacting
14. perceptive
15. opinionated/contrary
16. violent/warlike
17. studious
18. foul/barbaric
19. cruel/callous
20. practical joker/prankster
21. servile/obsequious
22. fanatical/obsessive
23. malevolent
24. loquacious

Personality (d8, d8)

1-5 Average	6-7 Extroverted	8 Introverted
1. modest	1. forceful	1. retiring
2. egoist/arrogant	2. overbearing	2. taciturn
3. friendly	3. friendly	3. friendly
4. aloof	4. blustering	4. aloof
5. hostile	5. antagonistic	5. hostile
6. well-spoken	6. rude	6. rude
7. diplomatic	7. rash	7. courteous
8. abrasive	8. diplomatic	8. solitary/secretive

Disposition (d10)
1. cheerful
2. morose
3. compassionate/sensitive
4. unfeeling/insensitive
5. humble
6. proud/haughty
7. even tempered
8. hot tempered
9. easy going
0. harsh

Intellect (d10)
1. dull
2. average
3. average
4. active
5. active
6. dreaming
7. ponderous
8. anti-intellectual
9. scheming
0. brilliant

Nature (d6)
1. soft-hearted
2. forgiving
3. hard-hearted
4. unforgiving
5. jealous
6. vengeful

Materialism (d6)
1. aesthetic
2. intellectualist
3. average
4. covetous
5. greedy
6. avaricious

Honesty (d8)
1. scrupulous
2. very honorable
3. truthful
4. average
5. average
6. average
7. liar
8. deceitful

Bravery (d8)
1. normal
2. normal
3. normal
4. foolhardy
5. brave
6. fearless
7. cowardly
8. craven

Energy (d8)
1. slothful
2. lazy
3. normal
4. normal
5. normal
6. energetic
7. energetic
8. driven

Thrift (d8)
1. miserly
2. mean
3. thrifty
4. average
5. average
6. spendthrift
7. spendthrift
8. wastrel

Morals (d12)
1. aesthetic
2. virtuous
3. normal
4. normal
5. lusty
6. lusty
7. lustful
8. immoral
9. amoral
10. perverted*
11. sadistic*
12. depraved*

Piety (d12)
1. saintly
2. martyr/zealot
3. pious
4. reverent
5. average
6. average
7. average
8. average
9. impious
10. irreverent
11. iconoclastic
12. irreligious

* Roll again; if **perverted, sadistic,** or **depraved** is again indicated, the character is that; otherwise, the second roll tells the true morals, and the first roll is ignored in favor of the second.

Interests (d12, d6)
1. religion	13. wines & spirits
2. legends	14. foods & preparation
3. history	15. gambling
4. nature	16. drugs
5. horticulture	17. collector*
6. husbandry	18. collector*
7. exotic animals	19. collector*
8. hunting	20. collector*
9. fishing	21. community service
10. handicrafts	22. altruism
11. athletics	23. none
12. politics	24. none

* See **Collections** table below.

Collections (d12)
1. knives & daggers
2. swords
3. weapons
4. shields & weapons
5. armor
6. books & scrolls
7. minerals & gems
8. ornaments & jewelry
9. coins & tokens
10. trophies & skins
11. porcelain, china & crystal
12. artwork*

* This includes tapestries, paintings, statuary, carvings, etc.

FACTS

Alignment is preferably selected for created NPCs. For encountered NPCs, the DM can select the alignment or generate it randomly, as best suits the particular situation.

Appearance:

Age can be actual or apparent — such as by means of disguise, magic, etc.

General (appearance) can be due to the existing circumstances or a true characteristic. Appearance will be modified by possessions.

Possessions indicate the number of garments, adornment, weapons, goods, property, etc., according to the circumstances particular to the NPC in question. Actual and apparent possessions can differ greatly — the miserly individual, for example, will never display wealth.

Sanity is the measure of the mental balance of the NPC against the norm. The type of insanity or maniacal bent is usually determined by **Traits** rolls.

TRAITS

General Tendencies are given to guide and direct the generation of following traits and the operation of the NPC in actual play. Conflicting **Traits** should be disregarded unless the NPC is *insane*. Some tendencies have two listings separated by a slash. The DM should either immediately select one — in the case of a predetermined NPC — or list both and select the one which better suits the NPC when the balance of the other **Traits** are determined — in cases of encountered NPCs.

Personality:

Average indicates a typical personality type with one or more outstanding tendencies. The average personality will seldom be noticeably outstanding in any of its tendencies until the NPC is well-known through dealings and association.

Extroverted personalities are more readily apparent, as will be their outstanding tendencies. The extroverted NPC will be gregarious and tend toward being in positions which deal with people or power.

Introverted indicates that the NPC is basically inwardlooking and prefers his or her own company to that of others. Monks and hermits are

two good, if not polar, examples. The encountered NPC introvert will seldom be in a people-oriented occupation or with a large party of humans.

Disposition is the indicator of the general inclination of the NPC personality with regard to mood or manner.

Nature describes the disposition tendencies, and as a modifier it must be carefully watched to avoid contradiction, i.e. compassionate and hard-hearted, unfeeling and softhearted.

Bravery indicates the courage of the NPC with regard to threat, risk, hazard, etc.

Intellect describes to the DM the manner in which the NPC's mental processes function, and it will modify the intelligence rating in four out of eight cases (dreaming — brilliant). The "dreaming" and "ponderous" intellects will tend to ratiocinate more slowly. The "scheming" intellect will, at times, perform brilliantly, and the "brilliant" intellect will perform above its stated intelligence rating due to discernment and insight.

Energy is basically self-explanatory. The "driven" individual is certainly neurotic, typically obsessive, and often fanatical.

Thrift, like energy, is self-explanatory. The various degrees of saving and spending must be considered with care.

Materialism denotes the regard the NPC has for goods and property. **Thrift** and **Materialism** complement each other.

Honesty describes the NPC's basic veracity and tendencies in dealing with others.

Piety is the rating of the religious view of the NPC. "Saintly" will be modified to fit the alignment of the NPC, and the **Piety Trait** must fit the character class as well.

Morals refer to the sexual tendencies of the NPC, although this **trait** rating can be used with regard to some ethical questions.

Interests describe the pastimes, avocations and hobbies of NPCs. More than one **Interest** is possible for those characters which are not otherwise obsessive or devoted to some vocation or calling.

Collections simply indicate the field of **Interest** of the "Collector". Other sorts can be added as desired. In game use, the collector of swords, for example, will be a likely contact for player characters wishing to dispose of such weapons gained as loot during an adventure.

NON-PLAYER CHARACTER ENCOUNTER/OFFER REACTION ADJUSTMENTS

Sanity		Disposition	
neurotic	– 1% to 6%	any	+/– 1% to 6%
insane	+/– 1% to 10%		
maniacal	+/– 1% to 20%	**Nature**	
		any	+/– 1% to 4%
General Tendencies			
any	+/– 1% to 8%	**Bravery**	
		any	+/– 1% to 20%
Personality			
any	+/– 1% to 8%	**Materialism**	
		any	+/– 1% to 20%

HEIGHT AND WEIGHT TABLES

MALES

	Height In Inches			Weight In Pounds		
	Average	–	or +	Average	–	or +
Dwarf	48	1-4	1-6	150	2-16	2-24
Elf	60	1-4	1-6	100	1-10	1-20
Gnome	42	1-3	1-3	80	2-8	2-12
Half-elf	66	1-6	1-6	130	1-20	1-20
Halfling	36	1-3	1-6	60	2-8	2-12
Half-orc	66	1-4	1-4	150	2-16	4-40
Human	72	1-12	1-12	175	3-36	5-60

FEMALES

	Height In Inches			Weight In Pounds		
	Average	–	or +	Average	–	or +
Dwarf	46	1-4	1-4	120	2-16	2-20
Elf	54	1-4	1-6	80	1-10	2-12
Gnome	39	1-3	1-3	75	1-8	1-8
Half-elf	62	1-6	1-6	100	1-12	2-16
Halfling	33	1-3	1-3	50	2-8	2-8
Half-orc	62	1-3	1-3	120	3-18	4-32
Human	66	1-6	1-8	130	3-30	4-48

HEIGHT AND WEIGHT DETERMINATION

	Height			Weight		
	Under	Avg.*	Over	Under	Avg.**	Over
Dwarf	01-15	16-80	81-00	01-20	21-65	66-00
Elf	01-10	11-80	81-00	01-15	16-90	91-00
Gnome	01-20	21-85	86-00	01-20	21-75	76-00
Half-elf	01-35	36-90	91-00	01-20	21-85	86-00
Halfling	01-10	11-90	91-00	01-10	11-50	51-00
Half-orc	01-45	46-75	76-00	01-30	31-55	56-00
Human	01-20	21-80	81-00	01-25	26-75	76-00

* For average height roll % dice: 01-30 = shorter by 1-4½'', 71-00 = taller by 1-4½'' (1-3½'' for races under 5' tall).

** Weight as above, adjust by 1-8 # (1-4 if 100# or less).

LANGUAGE DETERMINATION

The following is to be used primarily to determine knowledge of languages in NPCs (and such things as magic swords), as player characters generally should be required to learn foreign languages from others when the opportunity and inclination present themselves. This is subject to alteration, of course, pending conditions in individual campaigns.

RANDOM LANGUAGE DETERMINATION TABLE

Dice Roll	Language	Dice Roll	Language
01	Brownie	45-49	Halfling
02-03	Bugbear	50-51	Hobgoblin
04	Centaur	52-54	Kobold
05	Dragon, Black	55	Lammasu
06	Blue	56-58	Lizard Man
07	Brass	59	Manticore
08	Bronze	60	Medusian
09	Copper	61	Minotaur
10	Gold	62	Naga, Guardian
11	Green	63	Spirit
12	Red	64	Water
13	Silver	65	Nixie
14	White	66	Nymph
15	Dryad	67-70	Ogrish
16-20	Dwarvish	71	Ogre Magian
21-25	Elvish	72-76	Orcish
26	Ettin	77	Pixie
27	Gargoyle	78	Salamander
28	Giant, Cloud	79	Satyr
29	Fire	80	Shedu
30	Frost	81	Sprite
31-33	Hill	82	Sylph
34	Stone	83	Titan
35	Storm	84	Troll
36-39	Goblin	85	Xorn
40	Gnoll	86-00	Human foreign or other*
41-44	Gnome		

* Select a foreign tongue, choose an unlisted creature language, or select at random by ignoring rolls over 85, if the first two options are not desired.

SPECIAL ROLES OF THE DUNGEON MASTER

As the DM you are game moderator, judge, jury, and supreme deity. You are also actively engaged in actual role playing throughout the course of the campaign, from game to game, as you must take the persona of each and every henchman and/or hireling involved. (See also **Monsters**, hereafter.) To play such roles to the hilt, it is certainly helpful to the DM if he or she has player characters of his or her own in some other campaign.

Henchmen: Regardless of their loyalty, henchmen are individuals. Play them for their liege just as if they were your player characters, modified by whatever circumstances and special characteristics are applicable. Begin creating the persona of such a non-player character as soon as he or she appears on the scene, without recourse to the book characteristics. It will thereafter become easier and more natural for you to re-assume the persona as needed. The most important rule to remember is that the henchman is an individual, with likes, dislikes, feelings, and so on. The henchman is likely to aspire to greater things too, and he or she will tend to look out for personal interests. Bullying, duping, cheating, and similar maltreatment will certainly be resented. The henchman will talk about it with others of his class and fellow henchmen and hirelings. Henchmen will never loan out money or valuables without security — particularly if one instance of failure to repay or loss has occurred previously. Loyalty will certainly drop in this case, and if such action is repeated, loyalty will be lost in most cases. If their liege is so bold as to suggest that the henchmen should make loans to other characters, there will be flat refusal in all likelihood. The key here is playing the henchman as if he or she were an actual person — better still if the character is somewhat greedy and avaricious. Interest should be paid on loans. Use of a henchman's valuables, such as a magic item, should be based on the holding of some equal or better object of similar nature, certainly one usable by the henchman, and the promise of some payment in addition — such as a minor item of magic! (See also **ACQUISITION OF MAGIC-USER SPELLS.**)

Some few players will actually play their henchmen as individual characters, not merely as convenient extensions of their main player character. In these rare cases, your involvement with these henchmen will be minimal. It is far more probable that the players will attempt to manipulate their henchmen, and you will counter all such attempts by active assumption of the role or roles. You will keep low-intelligence characters behaving accordingly, clever ones possibly tricking their master, and so on.

Hirelings: As these characters serve strictly as employees, they should be played as such — mercenaries interested in doing their job and collecting their pay. Unusual indeed will be circumstances which see a hireling volunteering for extra work/service. Rather, a hireling seeks to do only as much as is absolutely minimal to fulfill terms of employment. If more is desired, more must be offered. Playing such roles is relatively easy, and if groups are involved, concentrate on the personae of the leaders. Otherwise, hirelings can be treated as henchmen as far as involvement is concerned.

Monsters: Taking the role of some of the monsters — those who happen to be human or humanoid — is not a difficult task for the DM, but sometimes it is hard to get into the personae of particularly nauseating creatures or minions of purity or whatever. Such creatures might well be beyond the realm of experience of the referee, and understandably so. Nonetheless, such monsters must be carefully played by the DM.

Each and every monster must be played as closely to its stated characteristics as is possible. Clever ones should be played with cleverness, stupid ones with stupidity, ferocious ones with ferocity, cowardly ones with cowardice, and so on. In all cases, the DM is absolutely obligated to play the monster in question to the best of his or her ability according to the characteristics of the monster and the circumstances of the encounter. A magic-using creature will intelligently select the best (or what the creature believes will be the best) spell or magic device for attack/defense. Intelligent monsters will make use of magic items in their treasure hoard! Thinking monsters will tend to flee from encounters which are going badly in order to live and fight another day. There is no reason why monsters can not learn from encounters, employ flaming oil, set up ambushes, and so forth according to their capabilities and resources.

Other Non-Player Characters: The host of merchants, shopkeepers, guardsmen, soldiers, clerics, magic-users, fighters, thieves, assassins, etc. are likewise all yours to play. Again, this is simply a matter of assuming the station and vocation of the NPC and creating characteristics — formally or informally according to the importance of the non-player character. These NPCs will have some alignment, but even that won't be likely to prevent a bit of greed or avariciousness. Dealing with all such NPCs should be expensive and irritating. Consider the two following examples:

The fighter, Celowin Silvershield, enters a strange town seeking aid from a

high level magic-user in order to turn an associate back to flesh (after a most unfortunate encounter with a cockatrice). His inquiries at a tavern meet with vague answers until several rounds of drinks have been purchased, and the proprietor generously tipped. Wending his way from tavern to wizard's tower, Celowin is accosted by a beggar, and he is pestered unendingly until he either pays off or calls for the watch. Paying off will attract a swarm of other beggars. Calling for the watch can be nearly as dangerous, as they could resent a foreigner's refusal to deem a native beggar worthy of a copper or two. Despite such possible misadventures, the fighter finally comes to the tower of Llewellyn ap-Owen, a wizard of high repute. However, Celowin's knocking is answered by a lesser person, the warlock Tregillish Mul, the wizard's henchman. Mul informs the eager fighter that: "Lofty Llewellyn is far too busy to see anyone at this time. Good day!" Unless Celowin is quick in offering some inducement, the warlock will slam the tower door and forget about the intrusion.

Now let us assume that Celowin's bribe was sufficient to convince Tregillish Mul to arrange an appointment with his master, and furthermore that such appointment is actually timely. Now old ap-Owen is rather testy, for he was in the middle of an experiment which is now *absolutely ruined*, and must be begun all over again, just because this stupid sword-swinger managed to convince Mul-the-lackwit that something was more important than a wizard's spell research! Well, this fellow Celowin had better have a good reason for interruption, and further, the pay had better be good . . . . Celowin will have to pay through the nose, in cash and in magic items, to get the magic-user to turn stone to flesh once again. But suppose Celowin has no item which Llewellyn could use? The wizard will take something he cannot use personally, for he undoubtedly has all sorts of henchmen and hirelings who can employ these things, not to mention the possibility of trading or selling. In no event will money ever serve to replace magic items! Furthermore, if no magic is available, then a geas can be laid to get some!

These examples show how varying roles are played without great difficulty simply by calling upon observation of basic human nature and combining it with the particular game circumstances applicable. Once established, it is quite easy to recall the personae of frequently consulted or encountered NPCs. If such intercourse becomes very frequent, considerable additional development of the character or characters concerned, and their surroundings, will certainly be in order. Thus, in many ways, the campaign builds and grows of its own volition and within its own parameters.

HIRING NON-PLAYER CHARACTERS TO CAST SPELLS OR USE DEVICES

It is a certainty that your players will seek outside aid many times during the course of your campaign. At times a particular spell — or device able to deliver a magical power — will be necessary or very helpful to a party, and so they will seek out a cleric or magic-user to hire for the service. The most common spells sought are various cures and informational spells. The players should know from the outset that there is no free lunch anywhere, and that the performance of any service is going to cost a "reasonable" sum. A few sample prices for spells are listed below. Note that these charges are based on characters of similar alignment and religion as the cleric requesting the service at the headquarters of the cleric in question.

Cleric Spell Requested	Cost in Gold Pieces (See Below)
astral spell	5,000 per person
atonement	500 per level of experience of the recipient
augury	300
bless	5 per person per level of spell caster
commune	1,000 plus 500 per question
continual light	500
control weather	10,000
cure blindness	1,000
cure disease	1,000
cure light wounds	100
cure serious wounds	350
cure critical wounds	600
detect evil/good	100 (assumes device being checked)
detect magic	150 (assumes device being checked)
dispel evil/good	1,000
dispel magic	100 per level of spell caster
divination	1,000
earthquake	10,000

Cleric Spell Requested	Cost in Gold Pieces (See Below)
exorcise	1,000 per level of spell caster
find the path	500 per level of spell caster
gate	50,000
glyph of warding	100 per level of spell caster
heal	200 per point of healing
neutralize poison	1,000
part water	1,000 per level of spell caster
plane shift	4,000
prayer	50 per level of spell caster
protection from evil	50 per level of spell caster
purify food & drink	100
raise dead	1,000 plus 500 per level of spell caster
regenerate	15,000
remove curse	500 per level of spell caster
resist cold	50 per level of spell caster
resist fire	100 per level of spell caster
restoration	10,000 plus a like amount per level of experience of the recipient
silence	100 per level of spell caster
slow poison	200 per level of spell caster
speak with dead	100 per level of spell caster
tongues	500
true seeing	400 per level of spell caster

Prices can be adjusted for faithful, lower level characters. Likewise, they can be upped a bit for those who are not regular attendees of services. If the caster is expected to travel any distance, but not at risk, factors will be as much as doubled. If at any risk, the cleric is likely to refuse or charge five or more times the rates shown.

Attack spells are not shown in order to discourage hiring of spell casters for such purposes. As a general rule, *no specially hired spell caster will ever accompany a party on an adventure of any sort*, except in circumstances planned and directed by the Dungeon Master.

When non-cleric spell casters are hired, they will likewise consider alignment and personal risk in setting fees. Whether casting spells or using a magical device supplied to them by the party, there will always be a substantial charge. Should any of good, particularly lawful good, alignment complain, note that "the worker is worthy of his hire" and similar Scriptural quotes might be called for in order to silence complaints. If death results due to payment failure, point out that the player has "gone to his (or her) reward" — how can that be bad? In the event that the cleric would actually further the cause of the deity and alignment by doing the service, payment can be deferred until the party has the wherewithal to do so; however, this deferral will certainly adjust the fee upwards, or possibly require a normal fee and special service from the party in addition.

To forestall the *charming* of spell casters in order to get them to perform services of this nature, note that such characters will always be 25% likely to cast a spell as close as possible to the opposite of that he or she is instructed to cast. This is due to the befuddled state of mind and the psychic duress of the *charm* spell operating on the individual's mind.

It is also worth mentioning that NPC spell casters are NOT going to take continual interruptions too kindly, even if the party so doing is of the same faith and alignment and pays well. At some point the spell caster will get fed up with it and begin raising rates. (The players should not rely upon those outside their group to keep their members viable. They must learn self-reliance or else pay the price one way or another.)

MONSTERS AND ORGANIZATION

As has been stressed herein, you will find that it is necessary to assume the various roles and personae of all creatures not represented by players. This can be particularly difficult in combat situations. You must be able to quickly determine what the monsters involved will do in any given situation, and this can be particularly difficult in combat situations.

It is necessary that you make a rule to decide what course of action the monsters will follow BEFORE the party states what they are going to do. This can be noted on the area key or jotted down on paper. Having such notes will save you from later arguments, as it is a simple matter to show disgruntled players these "orders" when they express dissatisfaction with the results of such an encounter. The intelligence and wisdom of concerned monsters are principal determinants of their actions and/or

reactions. Consider also cunning and instinct. It is also important to remember that *lawful* indicates an organized and ordered approach, while *chaotic* means a tendency towards random, individual action and disorganization; but these modifiers must also be judged in light of the monsters concerned, of course.

Examples of the responses of six different types of monsters follow. The situation will be the same in each example: The 'party' (whose composition and levels are unimportant for the example and would obviously vary in each situation anyway) will be attacking the monsters in the examples in two situations. SITUATION 1 (S1) is where encounter occurs for the first time, and while the party inflicts casualties upon the monsters, victory is denied; the party then leaves with its wounded, regroups, and returns one full week later to finish the job. SITUATION 2 (S2) is where the party, rested, healed, and ready for action, has now re-encountered the monsters in question. In both situations the response of the monsters concerned will be detailed so you can use the examples in handling actual play.

EXAMPLE I: The party has entered a crypt under an old temple and attacked skeletons and zombies encountered there.

S1: The monsters will respond only as the crypts are entered in turn. Being effectively mindless, they have no co-ordination in their attacks, and no pursuit will occur when the party breaks off.

S2: There will be no change in response on the part of the skeletons and zombies. Those destroyed will not have been replaced (assuming, of course, that some evil cleric is not nearby) by reinforcements. Doors and furniture previously damaged or destroyed will not have been repaired.

EXAMPLE II: The party has located and attacked a colony of giant ants.

S1. Although giant ants have only "animal intelligence", the colony is an organized society wherein individuals are part of a greater whole; thus, response will be ordered. Warrior ants will meet the attackers, and workers will remove bodies, items dropped, and any rubble caused by the combat. If the queen is threatened, the workers will attack also. When the party breaks off the action, there is but slight chance of pursuit.

S2. In the interim, pupae reaching maturity (perhaps 1-6 warriors and 3-12 workers) will have replaced casualties incurred during the first encounter. Destroyed tunnels will have been repaired, new tunnels possibly dug, and general activity of the colony carried on normally. Warriors will again meet the party (although they might be reduced in number). When the queen is killed, all organized activity will cease.

EXAMPLE III: The party has found a cave complex which is the lair of an orc band.

S1. The orcs might have a warning device (a drum, horn, gong, bell, etc.) available for use by the guards posted at the entrance to their lair. The larger the number of orcs, the greater the chance that such a device will be on hand. As soon as the attack occurs, one or two orcs will rush to inform the group that they are under attack, assuming that opportunity allows. Response to the attack will be disorganized, wave attacks being likely, with the nearest orcs coming first, and the leaders (most likely to be at the rear of the complex) coming up near the last. Some traps might be set along the complex entry. Resistance will stiffen as the leaders (and ogres, if any) come up. When the party retires, there is a fair chance for pursuit — a general harassment by the boldest fighters amongst the orcs.

S2. There is not much chance that the chaotic orcs will have sent for reinforcements, although some few losses might have been replaced by returning group members. Any damage or destruction in the cave complex will have been repaired. There is a great likelihood that more guards will be on duty and some warning device ready to alert the group, as discipline will be attempted because of the attack. Response to the attack will be more immediate, and leaders and spell casters will be ready to fight. (If the party camped too near the orcs during the intervening week, there is a chance that the orcs might have located and raided the place!)

EXAMPLE IV: The party comes upon a small town and openly assaults the place.

S1. Town guards will give warning immediately, and while there will not be an alarm device at each post, there will be a central bell, gong, or whatever to alert the entire citizenry of attack. When this sounds, trained militia bands will arm, muster, and move to designated locations to repel the attack. The citizens, regardless of alignment (and this includes characters with adventurer classes), will be likely to join to fight attackers, for the general welfare of the community will come first. When the party breaks off their attack, pursuit is highly possible if the town has sufficient forces available to do so on the spot.

S2. The town will have sought whatever reinforcements they could by means of employment of mercenaries, requests to nearby fortresses and towns for men-at-arms, and *all* able-bodied persons will be formed into militia bodies. Any destruction wrought by the initial assault will have been repaired as time and ability allowed. Guards will be doubled or trebled, and local spell casters will have their most effective and powerful offensive and defensive magicks ready. Scouting parties will have been sent out and the approach of the attacking party will be likely to be known. Pursuit will be very likely if the second attack fails so as to allow it.

EXAMPLE V: The party encounters a bandit camp and engages in combat.

S1. The entire camp will be organized and ready for action on the spur of the moment. As soon as the guard pickets sound the alarm, reaction will be swift. Defensive traps, snares, and pits will make up a part of the defensive ring of the camp. Bandits will move to take up assigned posts. Counterattacks will be thrown against the party at appropriate times. When the action is broken off, thieves, assassins, or even monks who might be members of the bandit group will move to track and follow the party to discover what its subsequent actions are and if another attack will ensue.

S2. There is a great likelihood that the entire encampment will be GONE (without a trace of where it went) if the attacking party was obviously of sufficient power to cause serious trouble if it attacked again. If still there, the traps, pits, and snares will have been more carefully hidden and will be more numerous also. Ambushes might be set along the most probable route of approach to the camp for the party's second attack. A few more bandits might have been enlisted or called in from groups out raiding. All guards will have been doubled or trebled, all men more alert than ever, and all possible preparations made. During the interim an assassination attempt upon one or more of the members of the party might have been made (assuming that the bandits have an assassin character amongst their number), an attempt to insinuate a spy into the party might have been made, and/or a raid upon the party's camp may have been carried out by the bandits. If the party retires, pursuit will certainly take place if bandit strength still allows.

EXAMPLE VI: The party discovers a fortress and attacks.

S1. Guards will instantly sound a warning to alert the place. Alarms will be sounded from several places within the fortress. Leaders will move to hold the place, or expel invaders, with great vigor. Spell casters will be likely to have specific stations and assigned duties — such as casting *fireballs, lighting bolts, flame strikes, cloudkills, dispel magics,* and like spells. Defenders are out to KILL, not deal stupidly or gently with, attackers, and they will typically ask no quarter, nor give any. In like fashion, traps within the fortress will be *lethal.* As action continues, commanders will assess the party's strengths, weaknesses, defense, and attack modes and counter appropriately. If the party is within the fortress, possible entry points and escape routes will be sealed off. When the attackers pull back, it is very likely that they will be counterattacked, or at least harassed. Additionally, members of the force of the stronghold will track the party continually as long as they are within striking distance of the fortress.

S2. The fortress will most likely have replaced all losses and have reinforcements in addition. An ambush might be laid for the attackers when they approach. A sally force will be ready to fall upon the attackers (preferably when engaged in front so as to strike the flank or rear). Siege machinery, oil, missiles, etc. will be ready and in good supply. Repairs to defenses will be made as thoroughly as time and materials permitted. Weak areas will have been blocked off, isolated, and trapped as well as possible under the circumstances. Leaders will be nearby to take immediate charge. Spell casters might be disguised as guards, or hidden near guard posts, in order to surprise attackers. Any retreat by the attackers will be followed up by a hot pursuit.

As DM you must base actions and responses upon what the *logical* activities possible to the monsters encountered would be when attacked first and then later. You assume the part of the creatures involved and act accordingly. If the attacking party does not have the savoir-faire to assess and properly handle the encounter — and this could well mean leaving as quickly as possible and not returning to get a second bloody nose — then they deserve whatever befalls them. It is absolutely necessary that the Dungeon Master remember that a seriously threatened person will reply with the *strongest* possible attack/defense measure in order to assure his or her well-being. (This could, of course, indicate a feigned surrender, pretended friendliness, fighting to the death or dozens of other reactions according to the circumstances and intelligence/wisdom of the individual involved.) The best course might actually be running away — something which intelligent creatures and many not-so-intelligent animals will be prone to do when there is no other choice save useless death. So, then, does a threatened cleric cast a *know alignment* spell upon an aggressor? Or a *hold person*? Obviously, the latter choice is far more logical in 99% of the cases, and so you should have monsters behave. Skeletons and zombies will mindlessly be slaughtered. Giant ants will march to destruction in behalf of their colony, but more intelligent creatures will react with a greater variety of defenses, counterattacks, and so on in order to assure their safety.

USE OF NON-HUMAN TROOPS

Demi-human troops are unlikely to serve a human master who is not otherwise supporting a cause of the particular race. Some small number might serve with a henchman of their own race, but not large bodies except for short periods of time, most probably when danger threatens their area. You might allow exceptions to this as they become compatible with your campaign. Similarly, half-elves might enlist bodies of elves, halflings might enlist dwarves or elves, etc.

Lizard men will serve a human master only because of fear or religious awe. Either case requires continual maintenance in order to keep the lizard men serving. Communications will probably be a problem. Lizard men troops will also tend to fall upon dead and wounded of either side and devour them if not strictly officered at *all* times.

Non-human troops, bugbears and humanoids, will be very difficult to handle. They will tend to fight amongst each other (cf. **Compatibility Of Non-Human Troops** below), fight with humans nearby — whether friendly or not (25% chance if friendly), run from battle if they see troops on their own side retiring or retreating, and fall to looting at the first opportunity. Communications are also a great problem. If the master is strong and powerful and gives them cause to fear disobedience, it will be of some help in disciplining such troops. Likewise, if there are strong leaders within each body of such troops, threatening and driving them on, they will be more likely to obey. Weakness in leadership, or lack of officering, will certainly cause these troops to become unruly and impossible to control. Probability of control for each type of troops is shown below:

Race of Troops	No Officers & Weak Leader	No Officers & Strong Leader	Officers & Strong Leader
Bugbear	30%	50%	80%
Gnoll	30%	40%	80%
Goblin	40%	50%	90%
Hobgoblin	20%	40%	90%
Kobold	25%	50%	95%
Lizard man	10%	60%	100%
Orc	20%	50%	90%

Whenever orders are given or combat takes place, find the appropriate column and roll thereon. If the dice score exceeds the percentage shown, the troops disobey in some manner — refuse to move, attack any disliked creatures nearby, loot, run away, etc. Note that it is not possible to have a weak leader and effective officers. Strong leaders will be tested often. Granting the troops a high rate of pay is generally viewed as weakness in a leader.

Compatibility Of Non-Human Troops: The general compatibility of demi-human troop types can be determined by consulting the **PLAYERS HANDBOOK, RACIAL PREFERENCES TABLE.** Lizard men are hated by all demi-humans and humanoids save kobolds, and even the latter are suspicious of them (just as human troops are). Of the various races of humanoids, many will bully or attack one another as indicated on the table below.

HUMANOID RACIAL PREFERENCES TABLE

	Basic Acceptability Of Racial Type					
Race	Bugbear	Gnoll	Goblin	Hobgoblin	Kobold	Orc
Bugbear	P	T*	G	A*	A*	A*
Gnoll	T	P	A*	N	A*	T*
Goblin	G	A	P	T	G	N
Hobgoblin	T	N	N*	H**	A*	T*
Kobold	A	H	G	A	P	A
Orc	A	N	T*	N	A*	H**

* Indicates that the race will bully and harass such humanoids.

** Assumes that the others of this race are of a rival tribe.

Notes On The Table:

P: P indicates some preference and compatibility or even possible friendliness between them with appropriate co-operation.

G: G indicates that some *goodwill* exists, and so no hostility and some co-operation is possible.

T: T indicated the races can *tolerate* each other, and open hostilities are not likely to be evident.

N: N indicates *neutral negative* feelings on the part of these races, and that there will be no move to aid them if anything ill befalls.

A: A indicates *antipathy* and an active dislike which will break into open hostility if the opportunity presents itself. If *leaders or overseers are weak, these creatures will desert.*

H: H indicates *hatred*, possibly kept in check by fear, which will certainly break into open hostilities at the first opportunity, or else the hating humanoids will *desert at the first chance* if near a strong body of such hated creatures.

Use the table whenever humanoid troops are fighting or even serving side by side (within 12″ of each other without any intervening troops or screen so that the other humanoids are visible). Have the troops behave according to the letter key.

CONSTRUCTION & SIEGE

UNDERGROUND CONSTRUCTION

As Dungeon Master you will be interested in the subject of dungeon building for two reasons. Most important is the work which will take place in various underground settings you devise for your players. Work will probably be in progress prior to their venturing into the labyrinth, during the course of their adventures therein, and even after they have moved on to some other project or task. Later, high level player characters will build their own strongholds, and they will desire some dungeon mazes thereunder. Although the volume of material given herein is by no means that of a text on mining, it should be more than adequate for quick and easy handling of the task in your campaign.

MINING: CUBIC VOLUME OF ROCK PER 8 HOURS LABOR PER MINER

	Type of Rock Being Mined		
Race Of Miner Working	Very Soft	Soft	Hard
gnoll, halfling, human	75′	50′	25′
gnome, kobold	80′	60′	30′
goblin, orc	85′	65′	30′
dwarf, hobgoblin	90′	70′	35′
ogre	150′	100′	50′
hill giant	250′	150′	75′
fire giant, frost giant	300′	200′	100′
stone giant	500′	350′	175′

Multiple Workers: For game purposes, assume that each extra miner will cause an appropriate additional volume of rock to be mined, providing that there is room in the shaft. Assuming that a typical shaft will be 10′ wide, and arched to a 16′ (or so) peak, including scaffolding, where appropriate, the maximum number of miners, by race, per 10′ wide shaft is shown below; increase the number for wider or narrower shafts accordingly, although any miner larger than man-sized needs a 10′

minimum width in which to work.

Race	Maximum Number Per 10′ Wide Shaft
dwarf, gnome, goblin, halfling, kobold	16
hobgoblin, human, orc	12
gnoll	8
ogre	6
giant, any type	4

Multiple Shifts: There is no reason to limit work to one-third of the day. If there is need, construction can be carried on 24 hours per day, as long as there are enough fresh workers every 8 hours to do so. No worker may toil more than 8 hours per day.

Natural Area: Where natural passages and cave/cavern space exists, there can be no work, or minor work only to straighten, enlarge, or whatever. Computing the amount of rock necessary to be mined for such passages or spaces is no great matter. The existence of such natural areas is another matter altogether. You can always assume that the basically subterranean races of creatures discover such natural cave areas and select them purposely. For player characters, you might wish to allow the following chances for finding a natural cave area:

Type Of Rock Being Mined	Chance for Natural Space
limestone (very soft)	1 in 10
other sedimentary rocks (soft)	1 in 50
lava (hard)	1 in 20
other igneous rocks (hard)	1 in 100

The size of such natural areas will typically be small to very large and with many passages in the case of limestone only. Igneous rock areas will be short passages or small caves only. Lava area spaces will tend to be tubes, often fairly large and long. Other sedimentary areas will be smallish and not extensive.

General Note: As a rule, player characters will not be able to get races of creatures such as kobolds, hobgoblins, orcs, gnolls, ogres, and giants to perform mining labor. These creatures would far rather steal, rob, and kill for their income. Fear of enslavement will sometimes prove successful for a time, but guarding the unwilling miners, and the hard task of getting them to work at their optimum rate will be difficult problems for the taskmaster. Miners have tools, which make quite efficient weapons, so 1 comparable guard per 4 workers is about the minimum. Slave or unwilling labor is from 50% to 80% as efficient, depending on how many foremen are on hand to watch and drive the laborers. If 1:16, efficiency is 50%, if 1:12 it is 60%, 1:8 means 70%, and 1:4 brings efficiency to 80% normal. Thus, for every 4 unwilling miners there must be a guard and a supervisor. Of course, if ogres were doing the work, the guard and the task master would have to be equal to ogres in hit dice/power — 4th level fighters or ogres, or comparable, for example.

CONSTRUCTION TIME

Earth Excavation: The cost of the ditch 100′ in length, 10′ deep, and 20′ wide assumes that a crew of 3-4 men work for six weeks. If soil is heavy clay, time will be doubled.

Stone Constructions: Fortress-like stone constructions take about one week per 10′ cubic section. Adding 50% to the expenditure will double the rate of construction, but to triple the rate of construction, expenditure must be increased to 250% of the base cost — the maximum increase in construction rate. Normal stone buildings as shown on the cost list, require four months to construct, including interior work. All times assume building materials are on hand. Quarry work and transportation, if any, are additional cost and time factors. Architect costs are also additional.

Wood Constructions: Wooden buildings take approximately one-half the time it takes to construct similar buildings with stone. Wooden hoardings, for example, can be built at the rate of a 10′ section per day.

There are so many variable factors involved that the times given for completion of any given construction must be vague. If you do not wish to spend undue amounts of time calculating, it is suggested that you use the following rough estimates for construction time:

Moat house, shell keep, small castle	1 year + 2-8 months
Small castle with outer and inner walls, medium castle	2 years + 1-6 months

Medium castle with outer and inner walls,
large castle   3 years + 2-8 months
Large concentric castle, walling average town   5 years + 1-12 months

Times assume that an architect has prepared plans in advance, and that normal costs are expended in construction. If additional monies are spent, time is reduced as noted for stone constructions. With respect to walling urban areas, citizens who willingly labor to speed construction will reduce time by 50%.

CONSTRUCTIONS

Construction	Cost in G.P.
Arrow slit	3
Arrow slit, crossletted	5
Barbican	4,000
Bartizan, 10' d., 20' h.	300
Batter, plinth or splay	50
Battlement, 14' l.	20
Building, stone	500
Building, wood	200
Buttress, stone, 3' w., 5' d., 10' h.	15
Catwalk, wooden, 10' l.	10
Ditch, 100' l., 10' d., 20' w.	100
Door, iron, 4' w., 7' h.	100
Door, secret, 2' w., 4' h.	50
Door, trap, 2' w., 3' l.	2
Door, wooden, 4' w., 7' h.	10
Door, wooden, reinforced, 4' w., 7' h.	25
Drawbridge, 10' w., 15' l.	400
Embrasure shutters	3
Gatehouse, stone	2,000
Hoardings, wooden, 10' l.	10
Machicolation, stone, 10' l.	100
Merlon, 4' w., 3' d., 5' h.	6
Merlon, pierced with arrow slit, 4' w., 3' d., 5' h.	10
Moat, 100' l., 10' d., 20' w.	250
Murder hole	10
Palisade, wooden, 100' l., 10' h.	100
Parapet, stone, 10' l.	10
Pilaster, 5' w., 3' d., 10' h.	25
Pit, 5' cube	4
Portcullis, 10' w., 15' h.	500
Rampart, earth, 100' l., 10' h.	100
Stairs, stone, 10' rise, 3' w.	50
Stairs, wooden, 10' rise, 3' w.	10
Tower, round, 20' d., 30' h.	850
Tower, round, 30' d., 30' h.	1,350
Tower, round, 40' d., 30' h.	1,600
Tower, square, 10' sq., 30' h.	600
Tower, square, 20' sq., 30' h.	900
Tower, square, 30' sq., 30' h.	1,200
Tunnel, underground, 5' w., 8' h., 10' l.	100
Wall, bastion, 5' w., 20' h., 40' l.	500
Wall, curtain, 10' w., 20' h., 100' l.	1,000
Window, shuttered, 2' w., 4' h.	7
Window, shuttered & barred, 2' w., 4' h.	10

Arrow slit: Each arrow slit assumes a space behind it in which the bowman stands, ½' w., 4' l.

Arrow slit, crossletted: As the name implies, this is a straight slit with a cross slit for crossbows.

Barbican: The barbican is a solid stone outwork with two 30' diameter by 30' high round towers and a connecting building 20' wide by 30' long by 20' high. It must be properly pierced and battlemented. The barbican can include a gate or can be a simple outwork.

Bartizan: This is a small tower built to provide flanking fire on curtain walls or as an additional firing platform.

Batter, plinth or splay: These terms describe a sloping support which strengthens wall or tower bases, hindering attack by machine or humans.

Battlement: These are the parapet (or sill), embrasures, and merlons set atop a wall to provide cover for bowmen. If the surface is not broad, a catwalk (q.v.) must also be constructed. A 14' section of battlement will

typically have two 4' wide merlons and two embrasures 3' wide.

Building, stone: This is a single course (1' thick) of dressed or field stone with 120' of outside walls 20' high, with two wooden floors (second and attic), two flights of stairs, a peaked roof, and one wooden door. Cellar excavation, ground flooring, windows, interior walls, and additional doors are extra. The cost to increase wall thickness is 10% of initial cost per course of stone (1' thickness). Thus, the building upgraded to 10' thick walls (and appropriate outer dimensions) would cost 500 G.P. plus 90%, or a total of 950 gold pieces. The cost of a stone building can be used for computing interior dungeon walls.

Building, wood: This is the same as stone building above, but walls are framed with planks, total thickness ½'.

Buttress, stone: This is a wall support generally used for reinforcing the outside surface of a curtain wall, tower, etc. To buttress a wall up to 20' height, the equivalent of three buttress sections is needed.

Catwalk: This is a sturdy platform about 3' wide which is built upon a wall or palisade to enable defenders to shoot or fight over the top of the construction.

Ditch: This is a trench excavated as an obstacle, with sloped, compacted, and sodded sides. If a rampart of earth is built immediately above one side of a ditch the cost of the rampart is only 20% of the amount shown. The cost of ditching can be used for computing the cost of excavating for cellars, basements, dungeons, etc.

Door, iron: An iron door is typically set into stone with three long hinges/supports. It consists of plates about one inch thick bolted to a frame about one-half that thickness. The cost of larger or smaller or thicker doors is 2 g.p./sq. ft. of one-half inch iron added to or subtracted from the basic door cost. It has an iron bar on one side.

Door, secret: This is a stone portal which operates by counter-poise or pivot, with a hidden mechanism to trigger operation. There is no reduction for smaller portals, and the cost for larger ones is 5 g.p. per square foot of increased size.

Door, trap: This is a stout wooden door about two inches thick set into a floor. It is raised by an iron ring which is constructed as part of the trap door. Each additional square foot of trap door costs 1 s.p.

Door, wooden: This is a sturdy door of hardwood (maple, ash, etc.) about three inches thick. A square foot of additional wood (or for less wood) in the door is 2 s.p. The door is barred on one side by a two-by-four.

Door, wooden, reinforced: This is a stout oaken door, four inches thick, bound with iron bands and secured by a 3x6 oaken bar. Each square foot of alteration is valued at 5 s.p.

Drawbridge: This is a bridge of six-inch thick hardwood planks bound with iron and attacked to great chains which pass through the wall of the stronghold. These chains are used to raise the drawbridge by means of a winch and capstan bars and held fast by pawl and ratchet. Each 1 square foot alteration is valued at 2 g.p.

Embrasure shutters: These wooden pieces mask an embrasure. They are constructed in two sections, independent of each other, which rest firmly against the merlons on either side but swing out from the bottom to allow archery.

Gatehouse, stone: A gatehouse is a building of stone with walls 5' thick, two reinforced doors guarding a portal 10' wide by 12' high, a portcullis, and machicolated battlements atop the structure. It is 30' high to the battlement; the battlement is 7' high. The gatehouse has 140' of outer walls. Two barbettes cover its gate side.

Hoardings, wooden: This is a very stout wooden catwalk projecting in front of a wall. It has embrasures, a peaked roof connecting it to the battlement, and holes in the flooring to enable defenders to hurl and discharge missiles at attackers at the wall foot.

Machicolation, stone: This is a stone projection which moves the battlement out over the outer face of the wall. It has spaces in the stone flooring which allow missiles to be discharged to the space at the wall foot.

Merlon: A stone section rising above the parapet to provide cover for defenders atop a wall or tower is a merlon. The merlon can be pierced with a slit for additional missile power.

Moat: A water-filled ditch (properly packed and graveled in most cases) comprises a moat.

Murder hole: This is a slit, crossletted slit, or similar opening in a floor to command a passageway below. In combination with inner portcullis, inner wall slits, and pits, they make an entrance passage in a gatehouse or similar structure very unhealthy for attackers.

Palisade: A wooden fence of logs about six inches thick sunk into the ground from 4' to 6' forms a palisade. A palisade is usually built atop a rampart and equipped with a catwalk in order to turn the upper portion into a parapet.

Parapet, stone: This is a low stone wall 3' high and 3' thick (or deep) to provide cover for defenders. It is crenelated by placement of merlons.

Pilaster: This is a pillar-like reinforcement about as thick at its base as at its top.

Pit: A pit is a hole covered by a wooden or metal lid. The lid is removed when attackers threaten the work in which it is in. A pit is typically walled and floored with finished stone.

Portcullis: This is a grille of reinforced wooden or iron bars which is raised and lowered by counter-weights and winch. For each square foot of alteration adjust the cost by 2 gold pieces.

Rampart, earth: A rampart is a layered, packed, and sodden earthen wall, usually topped by a palisade. (See also **ditch.**)

Stairs, stone: Solid stone for the first 10' rise, the stone staircase must be buttressed if it rises beyond 10'.

Staircase, wooden: Typical stairs are built of sturdy hardwood.

Tower, round: A stone cylinder, without doors, arrow slits, or battlements, a round tower has one stone floor, a flat stone roof, and spiral stone stairs to the roof. The walls of 20' diameter towers are 5' thick, those of a 30' diameter tower are 6' thick, and those of a 40' diameter tower are 7' thick.

Tower, square: See **tower, round** above. A 10' square tower has walls 3' thick.

Tunnel, underground: A straight shaft generally used as an escape route, the underground tunnel is assumed to be dug through soft earth and floored, walled and roofed in rough stone. If it is dug through hard earth the cost will increase by 100%. If the tunnel is mined through solid rock the cost will be 500% of the figure shown.

Wall, bastion: This is a curved wall section, typically hemispherical, built into a curtain wall to provide flanking fire. It has no battlement.

Wall, curtain: This is a straight wall section without battlements. If it is built above 20' height it must be thickened or supported by buttresses, pilasters, etc.

Window, shuttered: A typical opening in a wall, it is covered by wooden shutters of one inch thickness.

Window, shuttered & barred: This is a typical window protected by a single bar with spurs to either side to prevent entrance through its aperture. Bars on wider windows can be multiples of the type above or crossbar grilled.

SIEGE ENGINES AND DEVICES OF WAR

Occasionally the need to handle various siege equipment and artillery will arise. While the conduct of largescale battles is not a subject for this work, the 1:1 use of such machines can be dealt with easily herein.

Engine or Device	Cost in G.P.
Ballista (or mangonel or scorpion)	75
Catapult, heavy	200

Catapult, light	150
Cauldron, suspended	50
Gallery, covered (or tortoise)	350
Hoist	150
Mantlet, movable	15
Ram	500
Ram catcher	20
Siege tower	800
Sow	500
Trebuchet	500

Ballista: A war engine which fires a heavy, spear-like missile. The cost of missiles for a ballista is comparable to javelin cost.

Catapult: An engine operating by tension or torsion which hurls heavy missiles. Combustibles, rocks, dead animals, barrels of sewage, etc. can be used as ammunition.

Cauldron, suspended: A huge iron pot for boiling or flaming liquid. It is suspended in such a manner so as to allow it to be tipped easily in order to spill its contents on attackers.

Gallery, covered: A sometimes movable construction, typically a heavy timber frame, with green hides protecting the wood. It has a double roof, one peaked to shed missiles and liquids. It is used to provide cover for attackers operating against a wall. Width is 12', height 12', length 20'.

Hoist: A frame with fulcrum and lever, the lever equipped at one end with a basket which can hoist up to 4 attackers to a height of 30' to assault a construction.

Mantlet, movable: A wooden wall, with wheels for movability, and a slit for archery. It is typically 6' wide, 8' long, and several inches thick. The mantlet is slanted backward at a slight angle.

Ram: A movable gallery equipped with a heavy log suspended from two roof beams by chains. The log is shod in iron and used to batter through defenses.

Ram catcher: A fork or hook of iron on a long pole. It is lowered by defenders to catch and hold a ram (or sow) at work on a wall. The defenders then raise the catcher to disable or break the ram.

Siege tower: A mobile wooden tower, typically a beam frame with slats and green hides to protect it from fire. It is 16' square at the base, 40' high, with a 10' square parapet at the top. At 30' height there is a drawbridge 10' square. The lower portion is for locomotion. A ladder leads up the back or interior to drawbridge deck and the upper parapet, with two intermediate floors.

Sow: A pick/screw device, otherwise conforming to the ram, for use against stonework.

Trebuchet: A large siege engine which fires very heavy missile loads a great distance by means of lever and counterpoise.

WAR MACHINE FIRE TABLES

Use the tables below to determine "to hit" probabilities whenever siege engines/war machines fire:

Device	Range Min.	Range Max.	Damage S-M	Damage L	Rate of Fire	Crew Min.	Crew Max.
Ballista (scorpion)	¼''	32''	2-12	3-18	¼-½	2	4
Catapult, heavy	18''	36''	2-24	4-16	¼	6	10
Catapult, light (onager)	15''	30''	2-20	3-12	¼	4	6
Ram*	0''	¼''	9-16	7-12	½	10	20
Sow*	0''	¼''	9-16	13-24	½	10	20
Trebuchet	24''	48''	3-30	5-20	¼	8	12

* Damage possible only if victim is directly in front of the boom device (ram, pick, or screw).

Range is the distance from engine to target creature. The trajectory of ballista missiles is basically a flat one, while those from catapults and trebuchets have a high arch. Minimum range basically reflects arching trajectory. The range for rams and sows is only the maximum swing of the boom and indicates the proximity of the engine housing to target (normally a construction).

Damage variable is self-explanatory.

Rate of fire can be achieved only with at least a minimum crew. If less than the minimum number of crewmen are available, then rate of fire drops to at best 50% of normal. The maximum number of crew enables a ballista to double its normal rate of fire. All other engines gain nothing (except less chance of dropping below minimum requirements for normal rate of fire) by having crew above minimum numbers shown.

Hit Determination:

Artillerists must operate all missile engines in order to allow them a chance to hit. (You may, at your option, allow fighters to opt to learn various artillery engines in lieu of normal hand weapons.) The level of the crew chief determines the chance "to hit", i.e. if a 0 level fighter, then the first column, if a 1st or 2nd level then the second column, etc. ALL TARGETS, REGARDLESS OF ACTUAL ARMOR CLASS, ARE CONSIDERED AS AC 0 FOR PURPOSES OF "TO HIT" DETERMINATION, EXCEPT BALLISTA TARGETS WHICH ARE ALWAYS CONSIDERED TO BE AC 10 IF EXPOSED TO SIGHT. If a direct hit is scored, determine damage according to target size.

I. **Direct Fire Machines:**

    ballistae
    mangonels
    scorpions

II. **Indirect Fire Machines:**

    catapults
    onagers
    trebuchet

Adjust the base number "to hit" by using the following tables of modifiers. Roll d20, and if the number equals or exceeds the adjusted base number, a hit has been scored.

Target Movement:	Bonuses and Penalties
Stationary	+3
Movement rate less than 3"	0
Movement rate 3"-12"	−3

Target Size:	Bonuses and Penalties
Man size or smaller	−2
Horse and rider size or small ship size	0
Giant size, small building or medium ship size	+2
Medium building or large ship size	+4
Large building, castle wall, etc.	+6
Subsequent shots after initial rating shot (only if target is stationary)	+4

Weather Conditions (Ships Only)	Bonuses and Penalties
Calm	+1
Light to moderate breeze	0
Strong breeze to strong gale	−2
Storm	−4

Type of Fire	Bonus
Direct Fire	+4

If a catapult or trebuchet miss occurs, go to the **GRENADE-LIKE MISSILES** section to find where the missile struck. Misses will always pass over, to the left, to the right, or fall short of the closest appropriate part of the target, even if this causes the missile to fall short or exceed the minimum or maximum range restrictions.

As noted in the **GRENADE-LIKE MISSILES** section, missiles from small catapults are considered to be of 1' diameter, those from trebuchets 2'. Ballista missiles are akin to spears.

Field Of Fire: The arc of fire of missile engines is as follows:

Ballista	45° left or right
Catapult, heavy	15° left or right
Catapult, light	30° left or right
Trebuchet	10° left or right

Intervening objects will not be likely to interfere with the flight of arched missiles from catapults or trebuchets, unless they impose themselves near the engine or the target. Thus, a trebuchet could arch its missile over a 40' high wall which was more than 6" distant from it and less than 6" from the target. As ballista missiles are on a flat trajectory, objects between the engine and the target will interrupt the flight path of these missiles.

Cover: Target creatures which can be seen only partially or which are totally unseen cannot be hit by catapult or trebuchet missiles in the normal manner. A target area must be named and the **GRENADE-LIKE MISSILES** determination is then used to find where the missile actually hits. Ballista fire is not possible when target is unseen. If they are partially visible, use the **MISSILE FIRE COVER AND CONCEALMENT ADJUSTMENTS.**

Siege Damage: The damage caused to constructions by the various engines, as well as that caused by various monsters and spells, is detailed under **SIEGE ATTACK VALUES** (q.v.).

SIEGE ATTACK VALUES

	Points Of Damage Against			
Means Of Attack	Wood	Earth	Soft Stone	Hard Rock
Bigby's Clenched Fist	1*	—	½*	¼*
Catapult missile, heavy	6	—	4	2
Catapult missile, light	4	—	2	1
Dig	—	10	—	—
Disintegrate	2	2	2	2
Earth elemental	2*	10*	2*	1*
Earthquake	5-60	5-30	5-60	5-30
Fireball	½**	—	—	—
Giant, cloud, stone, storm	3*	—	1*	½*
Giant, fire or frost	2*	—	1*	½*
Giant, hill	1*	—	½*	¼*
Giant-hurled boulder —				
cloud, fire, or frost	4	—	2	1
stone or storm	6	—	4	2
Golem, iron	3*	1*	2*	1*
Golem, stone	3*	1*	1*	½*
Horn of blasting	18	6	8	4
Lightning bolt	½**	—	—	—
Move earth	—	20	—	—
Ram	1*	—	¼*	—
Sow (pick or screw)	½*	½***	½*	¼*
Treant	8*	2*	2*	1*
Trebuchet missile	8	—	5	3

  * Damage shown is per round of attack by this mode.

  ** Damage shown is per level of the spell caster employing the spell, and assumes fire damage following; if the wooden target is protected by green hides, is wet, etc., reduce damage by 50%.

  *** Damage inflicted only if sow is equipped with a screw device.

Soft stone includes fired brick, limestone, sandstone. **Hard rock** is granite and similar material.

Additional Attack Forms:

Mining assumes that a tunnel will be driven under a construction, shored up, filled with combustibles, and then fired so as to burn out supports. If successful, this will breach a 10' wide section of curtain wall or cause 10 points of damage to other sorts of constructions.

Sapping assumes that workers, under protection of a gallery, for example, are able to dig away at earth or stone. This mode of attack is slow. To represent it, give it the damage done by a sow, but on a per turn, rather than per round, basis.

It is important that the reader understand that all values are representative only. The entire process of siege warfare would prove interminable in a campaign, so it has been speeded up here to force sallies and counter attacking or the fall of the fortress.

CONSTRUCTION DEFENSIVE VALUES

Construction	Defensive Point Value
Barbican	150*
Bartizan	25
Batter, plinth, or splay	20**
Battlement	12
Building, stone (per course)	10
Building, wood	8-16
Buttress	20**
Door, iron	10
Door, wooden	1
Door, wooden, reinforced	3
Drawbridge	10-15
Gate (double reinforced doors)	8-12
Gatehouse, stone	120
Hoarding, wooden	2
Merlon	10
Palisade, wooden	6-12
Parapet, stone	20
Pilaster	15**
Portcullis	12
Rampart	20***
Tower, round	40-80
Tower, square	30-50
Wall, bastion	40
Wall, curtain	20****
Window, shuttered	4
Window, shuttered & barred	12

* Excludes any values for gates or portcullis.

** All these defensive points must be destroyed before the construction supports can be affected, i.e., a tower with a batter is valued at 20 additional points.

*** Unaffected by missiles from catapults or from battering or picking.

**** This indicates the strength of a curtain wall 10' thick in an area 10' wide by 10' high; if a breach, rather than a hole, is desired, the wall must be destroyed from top to bottom.

SIEGE ENGINES AND DEVICES OF WAR DEFENSIVE VALUES

Device	Defensive Point Value
Ballista	2
Catapult, heavy	6
Catapult, light	4
Cauldron, suspended	2
Gallery, covered	10
Hoist	4
Mantlet, movable	3
Ram	12
Siege Tower	16
Sow	12
Trebuchet	8

CONDUCTING THE GAME

ROLLING THE DICE AND CONTROL OF THE GAME

In many situations it is correct and fun to have the players dice such things as melee hits or saving throws. However, it is your right to control the dice at any time and to roll dice for the players. You might wish to do this to keep them from knowing some specific fact. You also might wish to give them an edge in finding a particular clue, e.g. a secret door that leads to a complex of monsters and treasures that will be especially entertaining. You do have every right to overrule the dice at any time if there is a particular course of events that you would like to have occur. In making such a decision you should *never* seriously harm the party or a non-player character with your actions. "ALWAYS GIVE A MONSTER AN EVEN BREAK!"

Examples of dice rolls which should always be made secretly are: listening, hiding in shadows, detecting traps, moving silently, finding secret doors, monster saving throws, and attacks made upon the party without their possible knowledge.

There will be times in which the rules do not cover a specific action that a player will attempt. In such situations, instead of being forced to make a decision, take the option to allow the dice to control the situation. This can be done by assigning a reasonable probability to an event and then letting the player dice to see if he or she can make that percentage. You can weigh the dice in any way so as to give the advantage to either the player or the non-player character, whichever seems more correct and logical to you while being fair to both sides.

Now and then a player will die through no fault of his own. He or she will have done everything correctly, taken every reasonable precaution, but still the freakish roll of the dice will kill the character. In the long run you should let such things pass as the players will kill more than one opponent with their own freakish rolls at some later time. Yet you do have the right to arbitrate the situation. You can rule that the player, instead of dying, is knocked unconscious, loses a limb, is blinded in one eye or invoke any reasonably severe penalty that still takes into account what the monster has done. It is very demoralizing to the players to lose a cared-for-player character when they have played well. When they have done something stupid or have not taken precautions, then let the dice fall where they may! Again, if you have available ample means of raising characters from the dead, even death is not too severe; remember, however, the constitution-based limit to resurrections. Yet one die roll that you should NEVER tamper with is the SYSTEM SHOCK ROLL to be raised from the dead. If a character fails that roll, which he or she should make him or herself, he or she is FOREVER DEAD. There MUST be some final death or immortality will take over and again the game will become boring because the player characters will have 9+ lives each!

HANDLING TROUBLESOME PLAYERS

Some players will find more enjoyment in spoiling a game than in playing it, and this ruins the fun for the rest of the participants, so it must be prevented. Those who enjoy being loud and argumentative, those who pout or act in a childish manner when things go against them, those who use the books as a defense when you rule them out of line should be excluded from the campaign. Simply put, ask them to leave, or do not invite them to participate again.

Peer pressure is another means which can be used to control players who are not totally obnoxious and who you deem worth saving. These types typically attempt to give orders and instructions even when their characters are not present, tell other characters what to do even though the character role they have has nothing to do with that of the one being instructed, or continually attempt actions or activities their characters would have no knowledge of. When any such proposals or suggestions or orders are made, simply inform the group that that is no longer possible under any circumstances because of the player in question. The group will then act to silence him or her and control undesirable outbursts. The other players will most certainly let such individuals know about undesirable activity when it begins to affect their characters and their enjoyment of the game.

Strong steps short of expulsion can be an extra random monster die, obviously rolled, the attack of an *ethereal mummy* (which always strikes by surprise, naturally), points of damage from "blue bolts from the heavens" striking the offender's head, or the *permanent* loss of a point of charisma (appropriately) from the character belonging to the offender. If these have to be enacted regularly, then they are not effective and stronger measures must be taken. Again, the ultimate answer to such a problem is simply to exclude the disruptive person from further gatherings.

INTEGRATION OF EXPERIENCED OR NEW PLAYERS INTO AN EXISTING CAMPAIGN

A viable campaign is likely to suffer some attrition as it progresses, with players dropping out for one reason or another, and new participants coming into the campaign milieu. Some of these newcomers will be experienced players from other campaigns and have special characters which they wish to continue with. Other experienced players will have no characters, but they will have useful knowledge of the game which puts them apart from true novices. Finally, there will be the totally uninitiated participants — those who have only a vague idea of the game or who have absolutely no information as to what it is all about. These three types of new players will have to be integrated into a campaign which could be in nearly any state of maturity, with the majority of players being low, middle, or high level. To accomplish a smooth transition, I suggest that the most applicable form of those given below be followed.

Transferring player characters from other campaigns to yours is appreciated by the participants coming into the milieu, as they have probably spent a good deal of time and effort with their characters, and a certain identification and fondness will have been generated. You can allow such integration if the existing player character is not too strong (or too weak) for your campaign and otherwise fits your milieu with respect to race and class. The arsenal of magic items the character has will have to be examined carefully, and it is most likely that some will have to be rejected.

If several of such player characters are coming into your game at the same time, they can actually be of lower level than the balance of participants as long as they co-operate and adventure together rather than with the others until they have approached parity with the group. If the character or characters of the new participant or participants are too powerful for the campaign, the players will have to accept the fact and develop some new characters; however, it is not wrong to let them know that some future time might see a state of maturity which will allow the joining of the new characters with their old as co-operating equals or as leader and henchmen.

Experienced players without existing characters should generally be brought into the campaign at a level roughly equal to the average of that of the other player characters. If the average is 4th level, for example, an "average" die or d4 + 1 can be rolled to find a level between 2 and 5. This actually works well even if the average experience level of the campaign is 5th, 6th, 7th, or even 8th, especially when the "averaging" die is used. If the experience level is above 8th, you will wish to start such newcomers out at 4th or higher level. After all, they are not missing out on anything, as they already played beginning character roles elsewhere, and they will not have to be virtually helpless and impotent characters in your campaign, as you give them a substantial level to begin with — 4th, 5th, or 6th for instance. You might be in a position to take a different approach if there are several experienced newcomers in your campaign by adapting the method given below for the complete neophyte.

The inexperienced player should be allowed the joy of going on a dungeon adventure as a neophyte. You will recall how much fun it was when you didn't really know what was going on or which monster was which or how to do anything but loved every second of it! Throwing a green player into a group of veteran **AD&Ders** destroys all hope of that, for the inexperienced player will be suppressed or repressed or both. If there is only one neophyte in your campaign, set up a special area for 1st level of experience play, and likewise set aside some time for the individual to play alone — a couple of the experienced players can act the part of some mercenary men-at-arms, as well as the roles of various tradesmen and others the new player meets in the course of play, and have a lot of fun in the bargain; but all actions, reactions, and decision making will be left strictly up to the neophyte (with no hints or other help from the others). If several green participants are being integrated at the same time, the experienced players will not be needed to help out, but otherwise the

"It's a great new fantasy role-playing game. We pretend we're workers and students in an industrialized and technological society."

procedure is the same. After a few adventures the newcomers will be seasoned a bit to be allowed to join in with major expeditions on occasion. When 3rd or 4th level has been reached it is generally acceptable to allow full co-operation between the less experienced and veteran players, for at that point the former should be able to contribute something to play and greatly benefit from adventuring with the "old hands".

Be careful not to allow magic items from other campaigns to come into yours with integrated player characters, as this could upset your milieu or at least give the player character something he or she never was meant to have. See **NON-STANDARD MAGIC ITEMS** for details. Considered use of inherited or bestowed magic items is certainly urged with respect to integration of experienced players with new characters into a group of middle or high level characters. Similarly, if a neophyte is to be worked into the campaign as quickly as possible, yet allowing the enjoyment of first adventuring to be unique to him or her, extra funds and a minor item or two should be included when the character is developed. The object of this is to keep the campaign viable, for it is almost certain that attrition will occur, and you will need to bring in new players as smoothly as possible in order to maintain your milieu, but you will also need to make the integration as enjoyable as possible for them and for your veteran players as well.

MULTIPLE CHARACTERS FOR A SINGLE PLAYER

There is no absolute prohibition regarding multiple characters belonging to a single player. Where it is deemed beneficial, the Dungeon Master may allow multiple characters as he or she sees fit. For instance, when the major character of a player is off on some special trip, he or she may be allowed to use a new character, rather than playing the part of one of his or her character's henchmen. In fact, one player can have several characters providing he or she is a good, co-operative campaign participant capable of properly handling such multiple roles.

In general the multiple characters belonging to a single player should not be associates. One should not "know" information, or be able to communicate knowledge which is peculiar to him or her to the other. One such character should not automatically regard another controlled by the same player as a friend. Money and/or valuable items cannot be freely interchanged. In short, each such character must be played as an individual. As DM, you must be prepared to step in and take the part of one such character if the player is abusing the privilege of having multiple characters. Do so quickly and firmly, and the player will be likely to understand that you will brook no foolishness — particularly if the character you take the persona of becomes hostile and aggressive to demands from the other.

In campaigns where there are only a few players, or where only a few of the many players are really good players, it is likely that each (good) player will have several characters. Over the course of many games, some will be on reasonable, if not friendly, terms with others, some will avoid others, and some will actually be enemies. Explain to your players that you don't object to them having multiple characters if they are willing to play each as a separate and distinct individual, and that should be sufficient advice to any player capable of handling two or more characters.

INTERVENTION BY DEITIES

If the supernatural powers of the various Outer Planes could and would continually and constantly involve themselves in the affairs of the millions upon the Prime Material Plane, they would not only be so busy as to get neither rest nor relaxation, but these deities would be virtually handling their own affairs and confronting each other regularly and often. If an entreaty for aid is heard one time in 100, surely each and every deity in the multiverse would be as busy as a switchboard operator during some sort of natural disaster. Even giving each deity a nominal number of servants able to supply aid to desperate adventurers, the situation would be frenzied at best. Add to this the effects of various spells — *commune, contact other plane, gate.* It is obvious that intervention by a deity is no trifling matter, and it is not to be allowed on a whim, even if characters are *in extremis!*

This is not to dictate that deities will never come to characters. Serving some deity is an integral part of **AD&D**. The mighty evil gods, demons, and devils are prone to appear when their name is spoken — provided they stand the possibility of gaining converts to their cause. The forces of good might send some powerful creature of like alignment to aid characters on a mission in their behalf. Certainly in the case of some contest between opposing deities all sorts of intervention will take place — but always so as not to cause the deities themselves to be forced into direct confrontation! Otherwise, the accumulation of hit points and the ever-greater abilities and better saving throws of characters represents the aid supplied by supernatural forces.

In most cases, therefore, you will have to determine the involvement of deities as you develop the scenario or series of scenarios of your campaign. (In my own **Greyhawk Campaign** there have been 9 demi-gods, 3 demon lords, and a handful of Norse and other gods involved in the course of many years of play. Once or twice there has been divine intervention — and twice the powers of the infernal region have come at the mention of a certain name . . . .) Spur of the moment intervention can be handled as follows: If the character beseeching help has been exemplary in faithfulness, then allow a straight 10% chance that some creature will be sent to his or her aid if this is the first time the character has asked for help. If 00 is rolled, there is a percentage chance equal to the character's level of experience that the deity itself will come, and this chance is modified as follows:

Each previous intervention in behalf of the character	–5%
Alignment behavior only medial	–5%
Alignment behavior borderline	–10%
Direct confrontation with another deity required by the situation	–10%
Character opposing forces of diametrically opposed alignment	+1%
Character serving deity proximately (through direct instructions or by means of some intermediary)	+25%

Note: Deities will not intervene on the planes which are the habitation of other deities, i.e., the Outer Planes. They will neither venture to involve themselves in the Positive and Negative Material Planes. Intervention in the Elemental Planes is subject to DM option, based upon the population he or she has placed there. (If there are elemental gods, the deities from the Outer Planes will NOT go there.) Intervention occurs only on the Prime Material, Astral, or Ethereal Planes in most cases.

Demi-Gods And Gods:

If a demi-god or god is deprived of its material body by any means whatsoever, (including being "killed" on the Prime Material Plane), then it is sent back to its own particular plane. This process is similar to that of slaying the material form of some demon or devil.

THE ONGOING CAMPAIGN

While it might seem highly unlikely to those who have not been involved in fantasy adventure gaming for an extended period of time, after the flush of excitement wears off — perhaps a few months or a year, depending on the intensity of play — some participants will become bored and move to other gaming forms, returning to your campaign only occasionally. Shortly thereafter even your most dedicated players will occasionally find that dungeon levels and wilderness castles grow stale, regardless of subtle differences and unusual challenges. It is possible, however, for you to devise a campaign which will have a very minimal amount of participant attrition and enthusiast ennui, and it is not particularly difficult to do so.

As has been mentioned already, the game must be neither too difficult to survive nor so easy as to offer little excitement or challenge. There must always be something desirable to gain, something important to lose, and the chance of having either happen. Furthermore, there must be some purpose to it all. There must be some backdrop against which adventures are carried out, and no matter how tenuous the strands, some web which connects the evil and good, the opposing powers, the rival states and various peoples. This need not be evident at first, but as play continues, hints should be given to players, and their characters should become involved in the interaction and struggle between these vaster entities. Thus, characters begin as less than pawns, but as they progress in expertise, each eventually realizes that he or she is a meaningful, if lowly, piece in the cosmic game being conducted. When this occurs, players then have a dual purpose to their play, for not only will their player characters and henchmen gain levels of experience, but their actions have meaning above and beyond that of personal aggrandizement.

But if serious purpose is integral to a successfully ongoing campaign, there must be moments of relief as well. Such counterplots can be lesser and different themes within the whole, whether some side dungeon or quest, a minor altercation between petty nobles, or whatever. Occasional "pure fun" scenarios can be conducted also. That is, moments of silliness and humor help to contrast with the grinding seriousness of a titanic struggle and relieve participants at the same time. After all, **ADVANCED DUNGEONS & DRAGONS** is first and foremost a game, a pastime for fun and enjoyment. At times the fun aspect must be stressed. Thus, in my "Greyhawk Campaign" I included an "Alice In Wonderland" level, and while it is a deadly place, those who have adventured through it have uniformly proclaimed it as great fun because it is the antithesis of the campaign as a whole. Similarly, there are places where adventurers can journey to a land of pure Greek mythology, into the future where the island of King Kong awaits their pleasure, or through the multiverse to different planets, including Jack Vance's "Planet of Adventure", where they hunt sequins in the *Carabas* while Dirdir and Dirdirmen hunt them.

Of course, such areas represent a considerable investment in time and effort. Many of you will not have hours to spend creating these diversions, so it might seem that your campaign is doomed to eventual stagnation. Not so. The various prepared modules available commercially are ideal for use as sidelights to the whole of your game. In addition, there are many games which can be "plugged into" your **AD&D** campaign to serve as relief. After all is said and done, role playing is role playing and the setting is not of paramount importance. The trick is to adapt one system to the other so as to enable continuity of the characters from **AD&D** into the other setting. This allows not only a refreshing change, but it also poses new problems to participants and adds new factors to your campaign — new abilities, new weapons, etc. TSR has many games and rules systems which can be used with this game to expand and invigorate your campaign. Space does not permit detailed explanations of how to do this with each and every possible system, but two readily lend themselves to both the spirit of **AD&D** and its systems: **BOOT HILL** and **GAMMA WORLD**.

Sixguns & Sorcery:

Whether or not you opt to have a time/space warp throw **BOOT HILL** gunfighters into your **AD&D** world, or the adventurers from your fantasy milieu enter a Wild West setting, the conversions are the same. Converting and discovering character statistics is handled as follows:

CHARACTER ABILITIES

BOOT HILL CHARACTER CONVERSION TO AD&D	AD&D CHARACTER ABILITIES TO BOOT HILL STATISTICS
Strength as shown; 19 = 18/50, 20 = 18/75	**Speed** dexterity score = % score
Intelligence use 3d6 to determine	**Gun Accuracy** all have 01 initially, each 6 rounds fired add +1 until a maximum of 25
Wisdom use 3d4 to determine	**Throwing Accuracy** use normal attack tables for **AD&D**
Dexterity 6 base +1 per 10% of **BOOT HILL** speed rating to a maximum of 16	**Strength** as shown, 18/up to 51 = 19, 18/51 and greater = 20
Constitution use 3d6 to determine	**Bravery** 100 modified as follows: cleric = –2 × wisdom fighter* = –1 × wisdom magic-user = –3 × wisdom thief = –4 × wisdom * or monk
Charisma use d8 + 4 to determine	**Experience** initially NO experience, subject to later results

Hit Dice: Each **BOOT HILL** character is equal to a 2nd level fighter (2d10 + constitution bonus, if any). In addition, for each category of gunfighting experience a **BOOT HILL** character has, add one additional level of fighter ability, i.e. add 1d10 + applicable bonus.

Armor Class: As in **AD&D**, so most **BOOT HILL** characters will have AC 10 (no armor) at least initially.

Saving Throws: BOOT HILL characters save at their fighter level as noted above under **hit dice.**

Fighting Ability: BOOT HILL characters have fighter level as noted above under hit dice.

Movement: Base unarmored movement for **BOOT HILL** characters is 12″. Horses are all light.

Turn Sequence: Use the normal **AD&D** turn sequence unless both sides are using firearms, in which case use the **BOOT HILL** turn sequence and first shot determination. When the **AD&D** turn sequence is used, then for *initiative* give +1 to **BOOT HILL** characters who are unarmored and using firearms.

Weapon Range: BOOT HILL inches convert to **AD&D** inches (″).

Rate Of Firearms: Use the rate of fire shown in **BOOT HILL** as the number of shots allowed per round, with NO penalty for firing more than 1 shot. As the round is a full minute, you may optionally allow DOUBLE rate of fire, with a -10% penalty for all shots fired above the standard rate of fire, the penalty being cumulative, i.e. 3 extra shots = 30% penalty on each extra shot. *Reloading* rate equals segments per round, so that any firearm can be completely reloaded in 1 round.

First Shot Determination Base Number Adjustments:

Weapon Speed Factor	=	AD&D Missile Weapon Rate Of Fire	=	Weapon Class
8-13		½		VS
6-7		1		S
5		2		BA
4		3		A
2-3		-		F
1		-		VF

Adjustment For Actual Armor:

Armor Class Due To Armor Worn	First Shot Determination Modifier (Penalty)
10	0
9	-1
8	-2
7*	-3
6	-4
5	-5
4	-6
3	-7
2	-8

* All magic armor is classed as AC 7 for purposes of this determination. Note that magic rings, bracers, and similar protections which are not armor equate to AC 10 for this purpose.

Hit Determination Modifier:

Armor Class	Modifier
10	0
9	-1
8	-1
7	-2
6	-2
5	-3
4	-3
3	-4
2	-4
1	-5
0	-5
-1	-6
-2	-6
etc.	etc.

Special Note: Do not include dexterity bonus to armor class for purposes of modifying hit determination.

Wounds: Each hit causes damage as follows, several hits from the same weapon being computed separately:

Weapon	Damage	Range Modifier S	M	L
Arrow, tomahawk (hand axe), etc.		ALL AS IN AD&D		
Derringer	1-4	+2	+1	0
Other Hand Gun	1-8	+3	+1	0
Shotgun	1-10	+2	0	-1
Scatter gun	1-8	+1	0	-1
Other Shoulder Arms	2-8	+2	+1	0
Gatling Gun	1-8	+2	+1	0
Cannon (canister)	3-12	+4	+2	0
Dynamite (per stick)*	4-24	-	-	-

* No saving throw allowed. You may optionally allow a save, treating the explosion as if it were a *fireball*, but damage base must then be increased to 6-36 hit points.

Any circumstances not covered here can be extrapolated from this work and/or **BOOT HILL**. Referees might well find that some **AD&D** monsters and characters will prove interesting inhabitants for old mines or hidden valleys . . .

Transferral Of Fire Arms To The AD&D Campaign: Unless you desire to have gunpowder muddying the waters in your fantasy world, it is strongly urged that **BOOT HILL** firearms be confined to specific areas, and when gunpowder is brought into the fantasy world it becomes inert junk — ergo, no clever alchemist can duplicate it. Likewise, dynamite and similar explosives become inert.

Mutants & Magic:

Readers of **THE DRAGON** might already be familiar with the concept of mixing science fantasy and heroic fantasy from reading my previous article about the adventures of a group of **AD&D** characters transported via a *curse scroll* to another continuum and ending up amidst the androids and mutants aboard the *Starship Warden* of **METAMORPHOSIS ALPHA**. Rather than go back over that ground again, it seems more profitable to discuss instead the many possibilities for the DM if he or she includes a gateway to a post-atomic war earth a la **GAMMA WORLD**. The two game systems are not alien, and interfacing them is not difficult. The challenges are very interesting for **AD&D** characters, and it might get one of the participants interested enough to get a separate **GAMMA WORLD** campaign going, thus giving all of you a new field for gaming, and most important give you a break from DMing continually.

CHARACTER ABILITIES

GAMMA WORLD CHARACTERS CONVERTED TO AD&D	AD&D CHARACTER ABILITIES TO GAMMA WORLD STATISTICS
Strength as shown, 18 receives no percentile roll	**Strength (Physical)** as in **AD&D**, with percentile bonus included
Intelligence as shown	**Intelligence** as shown
Wisdom use mental strength	**Strength (Mental)** use wisdom
Dexterity as shown	**Dexterity** as shown
Constitution as shown	**Constitution** as shown
Charisma as shown	**Charisma** as shown
Magic Resistance NONE	**Radiation Resistance** NONE

Hit Dice: GAMMA WORLD characters should be allowed to retain their total (based on their constitution), while **AD&D** characters should retain their hit dice and bonus points gained by level.

Armor Class: Depending on whether the action is on a **GW** or an **AD&D** world, convert the armor classes by using the following tables:

GAMMA WORLD ARMOR TO AD&D ARMOR CLASS #		AD&D ARMOR TO GAMMA WORLD ARMOR CLASS #	
NO PROTECTION	10	NONE	10
Shield only	9	Shield only	9
Furs or skins	8	Leather or padded	8
Furs or skins & shield/ cured hide armor/ plant fiber armor/ partial carapace	7	Leather or padded & shield/studded leather/ring mail	7
Cured hide or plant fiber armor & shield or total carapace	6	Studded leather or ring & shield/ scale mail (& shield) /chain mail	6
Sheath armor/piece metal armor/total carapace	5	Chain mail & shield/ banded or splint mail	5
Sheath armor or piece metal armor or total carapace & shield	4	Banded or splint mail & shield/plate mail (& shield)	4
Powered plate/plastic armor	0	Magic armors from AC 1 to –2	3
Powered alloy/energized /inertia/powered scout /battle armor	–4	Magic armors from AC –3 to –6	2
Powered attack/ assault armor	–8	Magic armors from AC –7 to –10	1

Saving Throws: As noted, **GW** characters get no save against magic (spells), although some mental mutations will modify this rule (see below). Likewise, **AD&D** characters are not allowed any radiation resistance. *Poison* saves should use the **GW** matrix in a **GAMMA WORLD** area, otherwise the **AD&D** system is used. All other saving throws are as per **AD&D**, with **GW** characters being considered as fighters (those with mental mutations approximating spell abilities should gain the benefit of saving as a 1st-5th level magic-user if the saving throw category therefore is superior to that of fighters). Level of ability is based on the number of experience points the **GW** character has earned, each step equalling 1 level, i.e. 0 - 2,999 = 1st level, 3,000 - 5,999 = 2nd level, 6,000 - 11,999 = 3rd level, 12,000 - 24,999 = 4th level, etc.

Fighting Ability: **GW** characters in an **AD&D** world fight at the level indicated by their accumulated experience points. **AD&D** characters in a **GW** campaign use the latter system of resolution to hit, regardless of level.

Movement: Use the **AD&D** movement rates for characters, as the scales are roughly equal.

Turn Sequence: Use **AD&D**, considering a search move as a round, and a combat melee round as a segment.

Weapon Range: Outdoors convert **GAMMA WORLD** meters to **AD&D** inches (''), the latter being yards. In an underground setting do NOT lower ''artifact'' weapons from **GW** to **AD&D** inches (''), triple their ranges to make up for the ground scale being reduced to one-third outdoor.

Rate of Fire: Use **AD&D**, converting **GW** combat melee turns to **AD&D** round segments when applicable.

Initiative: Use the **AD&D** system.

''To Hit'' Bonuses: Allow all bonuses normal to characters in each game, except that *strength* of **GW** will give bonuses rather than dexterity (which will improve armor class of **GW** characters not wearing ''artifact'' protection).

Damage: As shown in **AD&D** for all weapons except those found only in **GW**. In the latter case, damage is as shown in **GAMMA WORLD**.

Fatigue: Ignore fatigue, or you may opt to use it only for **GW** characters.

Mental Combat: Unless **AD&D** psionic abilities are present use the **GW** system (otherwise the **AD&D** psionic combat system). Wisdom indicates mental strength. See also below.

Spells: Magic-users without their books will not be able to regain spells. Clerics in a **GW** world setting will be totally out of touch with their deity or deities, and so they will be unable to regain spells above second level. Certain mental mutation powers resemble spells, and vice versa. *Mental defenselessness*, for instance, will allow any illusion/phantasm or enchantment/charm spell to function automatically against him, her, or it. A *mental defense shield* will give a bonus of +4 on saving throw dice rolls against the very same form of attacks, and detect both mental powers and magic. Furthermore, characters with this ability would certainly have all five forms of psionic defense modes to use. *Mental control over physical state* would enable override of *hold* spells and paralysis effects also. *Mental control* used against any **AD&D** creature would be regarded as a *magic jar* attempt. Likewise, certain **AD&D** spells would be very helpful against **GW** characters, creatures, and weapons: *minor globe of invulnerability*, for example, would prevent mental attack forms which approximate spells of up to 3rd level (inclusive). *Invulnerability to normal missiles* would be effective against slug throwers, needlers, and fragmentation devices as well as medieval technology missiles. A *wall of force* would stop many beams and rays as well, but blasters and torc grenades, basically disintegration weapons, would bring it down instantly. Whenever any case arises, use the examples and principles above to help you adjudicate the result.

Artifacts: The **GW** ''artifacts'' (except those with chemical bases which could be reproduced) will operate in the **AD&D** world, just as most magic items will function in a **GW** setting. **AD&D** characters are limited in ability with regard to **GW** ''artifacts'' to those operable under **Chart A.** Furthermore, they receive a +1 on their die rolls. Clerics and magic-users with an intelligence of 15 or better may negate this restriction, and the penalty to dice rolls as well, through practice or research. Each successful operation of an ''artifact'' allows a 10% cumulative chance of negating the penalty. Research on the object will allow a 1% cumulative chance of operating **Charts B** and **C** items as follows: Each day of research on type **B** objects, with a 100 g.p. per day expenditure, each week of research on **C** objects with a 1,000 gold piece per week cost. (Naturally, such study and research must be uninterrupted and undisturbed.)

Any ''artifact'' or magic items which are demonstrated for characters with usage instructions given will allow operation without the charts. **AD&D** characters will, however, use ''artifact'' weapons which differ greatly from weapons or magic items to which they are accustomed at 4 levels of experience lower than they normally would. Each successful use allows a 25% chance for such characters to increase in expertise, (i.e., lose a penalty level) until they eventually reach normal ability. (Such characters might also receive special consideration when handling firearms in a **BOOT HILL** situation, being familiar with hand and shoulder arms, and gaining a base 25 accuracy, for example, with a 50 maximum after practice.)

MAGICAL RESEARCH

CREATION OF HOLY/UNHOLY WATER

Only clerics, excluding druids, are able to prepare holy water — or unholy water in the case of evil clerics. As a third level spell is involved, it requires a cleric of not less than 5th level of experience to manage to create such fluid. The process is as follows:

A specially *blessed/cursed* basin of fine workmanship and precious metal (copper, silver, electrum, gold, or platinum) must be fashioned for the cleric. This vessel must be engraved with the holy/unholy symbols of the cleric's deity or deities, and it must be within a special repository of finely crafted and carefully worked rare wood, with a base, pedestal, chest-like holder and lid — the whole being known as a font. The basin is placed within the font, and the cleric then casts the following spells in succession, while robed in formal vestments appropriate to his or her religious persuasion:

create water
purify food & drink (the water) or its reverse
bless or its reverse
chant (1 full turn)
prayer

The amount of water created depends upon the metal of the receptacle, and this is shown hereafter, along with suggested costs for the various parts of the font. Once created, the holy/unholy water cannot leave the font for more than a turn without losing its efficacy unless it is placed within specially *blessed/cursed* vials of crystal — either rock or special leaded glass. Each empty vial is worth 2-5 gold pieces.

Holy/Unholy Water Receptacles:

Metal	Capacity For Creation	Minimum-Maximum Basin Cost	Font Cost
copper	6 vials	130 - 180 g.p.	200 g.p.
silver	10 vials	1900 - 2400 g.p.	500 g.p.
electrum	18 vials	8000 - 12000 g.p.	1000 g.p.
gold	32 vials	19000 - 22000 g.p.	1500 g.p.
platinum	50 vials	110000 - 200000 g.p.	2000 g.p.

You may allow combination metal vessels with capacity according to the composition, found by interpolation of the above capacity figures, i.e., a copper basin chased with silver and set with silver rim and handles would hold 8 vials and cost 50% of the copper vessel plus 50% of the silver vessel price. Fonts and basins must be designed and constructed on special order, the process taking 4-10 (2d4 + 2) weeks.

Capacities are designed for game purposes so as to limit supplies of holy/unholy water. They can be justified by the rationale that the deities find more precious metals more pleasing than those of less worth, so they are prone to grant more favor upon such offering vessels.

Limit Of Creation: Holy water or unholy water may be made but once per week. The ritual takes a full day of prayers and meditation, followed by the actual ritual, followed by a need for not less than 8 hours of rest and repose. Only one holy/unholy water font per religious edifice is possible, as deities look upon anything other as unworthy and excessive.

Defilement Of Fonts: If any non-believer *blesses/curses* an *unholy/holy* font, or uses less refined means such as excreting wastes into a font or basin, the whole is absolutely desecrated, defiled, and unfit. It must be smelted down and remade *in toto*. The cost will be 20% to 50% of the normal figures shown above, and the process will take from 4 to 6 weeks. Note that either method of defilement requires actual contact with the font and its vessel. Any *blessing* or *cursing* from a distance will be absolutely ineffectual and wasted. Relics might either defile by touch or prevent defilement by being encased within the font or receptacle, at your option.

Note Regarding The Drinking Of Holy Water:

Ingesting or bathing with holy water will have the beneficial effect of slowing the onset of lycanthropy or of becoming undead. For each vial so used, the process is slowed by from 1-4 turns. This time delay is to be secretly determined and noted.

SPELL RESEARCH

Whether from the desire to create a new spell or from dissatisfaction with a lack of power, it is certain that the magic-users in your campaign will eventually get around to inquiring about the procedures necessary to research and create a spell. Whether the spell is new or a listed spell which the character has been unable to locate during the course of his or her adventuring, the process is nearly the same. First, you must determine two salient facts: Is the character of sufficient intelligence to "know" another spell of that level? Is the desired spell of a level which the character's ability allows? Success demands positive replies to both questions. However, regardless of any negative responses, information will not be passed to the inquirer, for he or she should be able to discover such obstacles without recourse to the DM, and failure to do so indicates a lack of good

judgment on the character's part which will be evidenced by lack of success only after fruitless research.

Determination Of Spell Level: New spells might pose a small problem, as it will require some study on your part, but most of the burden can be shifted to the player. When desire to research a new spell is stated, inform the player that his or her character must carefully draft the details of the spell, i.e., you must have a typed copy of the spell in the same format as used in the **PLAYERS HANDBOOK.** Only when this is in your hands should you consider the power of the spell. Meanwhile do not discuss the matter with the player — at least as DM to player; it might be necessary to take the part of a sage and discuss the spell with the player character, for example, but that is entirely different. Once you have the details of the spell, compare and contrast it with and to existing spells in order to determine its level and any modifications and additions you find necessary in order to have it conform to "known" magic principles. Any super-powerful, absolute killer, or like spell must be thrown out immediately. Be certain to consider all of the ramifications of a spell and all of the descriptive wording, to weed out spells which give the user some extraordinary, undeserved, and/or unwarranted power. Anything better than the 9th level spells (7th level with respect to clerics) is in the category of *impossible*. Allow research, but it will always be useless.

Check the range, duration, area of effect, and saving throw in particular to see that the spell has limits and restrictions. You might well wish to place more rigid restrictions than are shown. Similarly you might add components and/or lengthen casting time. After analysis of the spell and adjustment of its parameters, you will be in a position to assign it a level. If the spell is a variation of an existing spell, with only minor differences, improvements, or extended effects, it will probably be only one level higher. If it is superior in two categories, place it two levels higher, and so forth. If it is a spell which is markedly different from all others, find the spell or spells which most closely resemble it, and then set its level according to the relative power of those covered in the book compared to the new spell. Spells with combination functions are at *least* equal in level to the sum of the spell functions *plus a level*, i.e., a spell which combined *audible glamer* with *phantasmal force* would be 6th level (a 2nd level plus a 3rd level plus 1 level for combining spells).

Cost Of Research: The basic cost for spell research is only 200 gold pieces per spell level per week. Note, however, that this assumes that the researcher has a laboratory (or shrine in the case of a cleric) and library at hand (built up in gaining levels of experience and whatever other reasons are applicable). To the base cost must be added a weekly variable of 100 to 400 gold pieces per level of the spell, the variable accounting for additional materials needed. If no library of materials is owned by the researcher, the base cost increases by a factor of 10 (2,000 gold pieces per spell level per week), the researcher being assumed to be acquiring arcane texts and scrolls, thus creating a library. The *player* must establish the amount to be spent, based on his or her appraisal of the level, *without assistance from the DM!*

Length Of Research: Initial preparations and research will consume a number of weeks equal to the level of the spell being researched. After this initial period, there exists a chance to achieve success, the chance being given weekly. Research therefore will always extend to a number of weeks equal to the level of the spell being researched plus 1, i.e., a 1st level spell will take a minimum of 2 weeks research. Research expense accrues each and every week. There is no limit to the extension of research, although practically, even minimal expenditure will result in successful research after the basic period plus 6 or so weeks on the average.

Conditions Under Which Spell Research Is Possible: It is absolutely mandatory for the researcher to be of sound mind and body and to have privacy and seclusion free from interruption during the course of his or her spell study. This necessity precludes any adventuring or general interaction during the period of research. It requires about 8 hours per day of work, and only an hour or two per day can be spent doing other things — instructing underlings, disbursing funds, etc. Any interruption of research will be a setback. Each day of such hiatus will cause 1 full week of lost time. Also, as noted above, a library must be at hand, and this means that either the researcher must have his or her own stronghold or highly private quarters, or obtain them prior to beginning the project. If a personal library is not possessed, the research must be carried on in or within one day's journey of a town or city in which the research materials can be obtained.

Research Materials: Acquisition of materials includes not only texts and scrolls, but also various components for the material needs of the spell.

Written works cover the whole spectrum of knowledge, as the researcher must be aware of any and all aspects of the magic he or she wishes to use. Thus, works on history, geography, astrology, alchemy, etc. must be obtained.

Chance Of Success: The base chance of success is 10%, plus the intelligence score of the researcher (wisdom with respect to clerics), plus the level of the character researching the spell, minus twice the level of the spell being researched: $10\% + I + L - 2 \times$ spell level = base chance for success. This base chance is modified upwards in 10% increments by doubling of maximum base cost per level of the spell (2,000 gold pieces). Thus, an expenditure of base cost + variable + 2,000 g.p. on a per spell level basis increases base chance from 10% to 20%, and 4,000 g.p. additional per spell level increases base chance from 10% to 30%, and so on, to a maximum base chance of 50% (expenditure of 8,000 gold pieces additional per spell level). Insufficient expenditure means a 0% success chance.

Determination Of Success: After the initial research period (equal to the level of the spell in weeks), find the base chance, adjust by intelligence, character level, and spell level, and secretly roll percentile dice. Any score greater than the percentage of success chance indicates a negative result. Continue to check for success each successive game week as long as research is uninterrupted and proper funding for the work continues. Remember, if a spell that is impossible for the character is being researched, this procedure remains constant, but there will NEVER be success, and the dice roll is simply frosting. (Eventually, even the most determined and least wise will begin to understand their aim is fruitless.)

Confidentiality Of New Spells: Once a player succeeds in researching a new spell, it is his or her character's alone. Only that character has the proper formula, and no mention of the spell should be made by you.

Additional Notes: There is no way that costs in money or time can be reduced. Likewise, conditions must be as set forth. Research materials must be obtained. It is possible to use another's facilities, but this will most certainly not reduce costs. Gathering a library assumes that the character is in a metropolitan area with libraries, booksellers, etc. from which copies can be obtained. If such is necessary, this must be done prior to the beginning of actual research, as it will take about one week per spell level to gather sufficient materials — the greater the level of the spell, the more esoteric and rare the tomes needed.

FABRICATION OF MAGIC ITEMS, INCLUDING POTIONS AND SCROLLS

It is an obvious premise of the game that magic items are made somewhere by someone or something. A properly run campaign will be relatively stringent with respect to the number of available magic items, so your players will sooner or later express a desire to manufacture their own. *Do not tell them how this is to be accomplished!* In order to find out, they must consult with a sage (q.v.) or a high level character of the proper profession, the latter being detailed a bit hereafter.

Magic items are made by high level magic-users, except those items which are restricted to clerics and special racial items and books, artifacts and relics. Books (including tomes, librams and manuals), artifacts, and relics are of ancient manufacture, possibly from superior human or demi-human technology, perhaps of divine origin, thus books, artifacts, and relics cannot be made by players and come only from the Dungeon Master. Dwarven and elven manufactured items — the +3 *dwarven war hammer*, certain other magic axes and hammers, *cloaks* and *boots of elvenkind*, magic arrows, magic bows in some cases, and even some magic daggers and swords — are likewise beyond the ken of player characters of these races. Only very old, very intelligent and wise dwarves and elves who have attained maximum level advancement are able to properly forge, fashion, and/or make these items and have the appropriate magicks and spells to change them into special items — i.e., these items are likewise the precinct of the DM exclusively.

This still leaves an incredible range of magic items which player characters can aspire to manufacture. It is a sad fact, however, that these aspirations must be unsatisfied until the player character achieves a level of ability which is one greater than nominal highest level — high priest, druid, wizard, illusionist. That is, a player character must be at least an 11th level high priest, an archdruid, a 12th level wizard or an 11th level illusionist in order to manufacture magic items (except with respect to potions and scrolls, as will be discussed hereafter). Furthermore, a player character

may manufacture only those items particular to his or her profession or items which are usable by professions not able to so make magic items only. Thus, a cleric is unable to fashion a wand usable by magic-users or illusionists, a magic-user cannot manufacture a clerical magic item, etc. There is a further prohibition upon clerics regarding the making of items which are prohibited to their profession or which are of opposite alignments; this restraint does not extend into the sphere of magic-users as a class. Thus, clerics cannot manufacture magic swords, though magic-users can.

Manufacture Of Potions:

Potions may be made by any magic-user of 7th level or above, if he or she enlists the aid of an alchemist (q.v.). At levels above the 11th, such assistance is no longer mandatory, although it will reduce the amount of money and time the player character must spend making the potion by 50% of the compounding/infusing time normally required, as the alchemist will be so employed instead.

In order to begin manufacture of a potion (and they may be made only one at a time), the magic-user must have a proper laboratory with fireplace, workbench, brazier, and several dozen alembics, flasks, dishes, mortar and pestle, basins, jugs, retorts, measuring devices, scales, and so forth! Such implements are not easily obtained, being found only at alchemical shops or produced upon special orders by stone masons, potters, glass blowers, etc. Initial outlay for the creation of a workshop, assuming that the place already has a fireplace, would cost between 200 and 1,000 g.p. This cost is based on the relative availability of the tradesmen and goods necessary to complete the work room and stock it properly. The DM may certainly require a greater expenditure if the campaign has inflation and/or shortages. In addition, upkeep of the laboratory requires a further monthly outlay of 10% of the total cost of the place, exclusive of any special provisions or protections, in order to stock basic fuel and supplies, replace broken equipment, and so on when the laboratory is in use. (**Note:** The place is *always* in use if the player character has an alchemist in his or her employ, for the alchemist will continually putter and experiment, always to no particular end, when not engaged in specific work for the magic-user.)

In order to avoid the length and complication of separate formulae for each type of potion, the following simple system is given. Both the cost in gold pieces and the days of compounding and infusing are determined by use of the experience points award (as shown on the list of magic items) amounts. If no experience points are shown, then the potion has a 200 g.p. base for cost and time determination. The point award for a given potion is also the amount of gold pieces the magic-user must pay in order to concoct the basic formula — with rare herbs and spices and even more exotic ingredients. The number of days required to brew the potion is the same figure, each hundred or fraction thereof indicating one full day of compounding time to manufacture the liquid, i.e., 250 x.p. = 250 g.p. basic costs and 3 full days of time.

Most important to the manufacture of a potion is the substance of its power, the special ingredient. The list of potions and special ingredients possible is given for your convenience only. You may opt for any reasonable special ingredient you deem suitable for a potion, keeping in mind difficulty of obtaining the material (hopefully high or greater) and its sympathetic equivalency or relationship to the end result of quaffing the potion.

Poison: Only assassins of 9th or higher level may concoct "potions" of poison — or any other sort of poison, for that matter. Refer to the section on assassins for details of special forms of poison. No laboratory or alchemist is needed, but cost and time are found as if a normal potion was being prepared.

Suggested Special Ingredients For Potions:

Type of Potion	Suggested Special Ingredient(s)
animal control	organ or gland from representative type or types to be controlled
clairaudience	human or simian thalamus gland or ear from an animal with keen hearing
clairvoyance	human or simian thalamus gland or eye from an animal with keen sight
climbing	insect legs (giant)
delusion*	doppleganger flesh or rakshasa ichor
diminution	powdered kobold horn and wererat blood

dragon control	brain of the appropriate dragon type	
ESP	mind flayer brain	
extra-healing	troll blood or hair of a saint**	
fire resistance	fire elemental phlogiston or salamander scales	
flying	hippogriff feathers and wyvern blood	
gaseous form	vampire dust or ogre magi teeth	
giant control	brain of appropriate giant type	
giant strength	drops of sweat from appropriate giant type	
growth	ogre magi gland	
healing	ogre magi blood of thread of saint's garment**	
heroism	heart of lion or similar giant cat	
human control	vampire eye or nixie blood	
invisibility	invisible stalker ichor	
invulnerability	gargoyle horn or lycanthrope skin	
levitation	beholder eye (from stalk) or will-o-wisp essence	
longevity	dragon blood and treant sap or elf blood	
oil of etherealness	shedu fat or demon brain	
oil of slipperiness	purple worm gland or liver of giant pike	
philter of love	dryad hair	
philter of persuasiveness	harpies' tongues or devil tongue	
plant control	shrieker spores and umber hulk eye	
polymorph (self)	mimic skin or succubus hair	
poison	special	
speed	pegasus heart and giant weasel blood	
super-heroism	giant wolverine blood and minotaur heart	
sweet water	water elemental eye or triton blood	
treasure finding	gold dragon scale and six different powdered gem stones	
undead control	dust of freshly destroyed spectres or vampire brain or ghost ectoplasm or lich tongue	
water breathing	water naga blood or nixie organs	

* Alternatively, a 5% to 20% failure percentage can be assigned to all potion manufacture, and those which are failures become *delusion* potions of the sort which was being attempted, i.e., *animal control*, *flying*, etc.

** Possible only if a cleric compounds the potion.

Manufacture of Scrolls:

Scrolls are exceptional in that they are simply storage space for spells of one sort or another. Clerics, druids, magic-users, and illusionists inscribe scrolls with spells applicable to their particular professions. *Protection* spells are scribed by either magic-users or clerics, the determination being as follows:

Clerical Protection Spells	Magic-User Protection Spells
DEVILS	DEMONS
POSSESSION	ELEMENTALS
UNDEAD	LYCANTHROPES
	MAGIC
	PETRIFICATION

Curse scrolls can be made by any sort of spell user noted above.

Scrolls may be inscribed only by characters of 7th or higher level, and the spells placed upon the scroll must be of a level which the inscribing character is able to employ, i.e. a 9th level magic-user could not place a 7th level spell on a scroll. (Note that the *write* spell enables the magic-user to inscribe his or her own *reference* works so as to be able to read and remember higher level spells than he or she is currently able to use; it does not enable casting or scroll inscription.)

A scroll of spells may be inscribed only upon pure and unblemished papyrus, parchment, or vellum — the latter being the most desirable. Any mistake will doom the effort to failure. A fresh, virgin quill must be used for each spell transcribed. The quill must be from a creature of strange or magical nature, i.e. a griffon, harpy, hippogriff, pegasus, roc, sphinx of any sort, and similar monsters you elect to include (demons, devils, lammasu, etc.).

The material upon which the scroll of spells is to be written can be purchased at the following cost guidelines:

papyrus, per sheet	2 g.p. and up	+5% chance of failure
parchment, per sheet	4 g.p. and up	±0% chance of failure
vellum, per sheet	8 g.p. and up	−5% chance of failure

The type of material used will affect the likelihood of successful transcription, as listed above. Special quills cannot normally be purchased, for only common goose or similar feather instruments are available in shops. The would-be inscriber must arrange for the special writing tools as he or she can.

Ink is a very special requirement. Scroll spell ink, just as the ink for detailing spells in spell books, is compounded only by the inscriber from secret and strange ingredients. The basic medium should be sepia from a giant squid or ink from a giant octopus. To this liquid must be added blood, powdered gems, herbal and spice infusions, draughts concocted from parts of monsters, and so on. An example of a formula for the ink required to scribe a *protection from petrification* spell is shown below:

1 oz. giant squid sepia
1 basilisk eye
3 cockatrice feathers
1 scruple of venom from a medusa's snakes
1 large peridot, powdered
1 medium topaz, powdered
2 drams holy water
6 pumpkin seeds

Harvest the pumpkin in the dark of the moon and dry the seeds over a slow fire of sandalwood and horse dung. Select three perfect ones and grind them into a coarse meal, husks and all. Boil the basilisk eye and cockatrice feathers for exactly 5 minutes in a saline solution, drain, and place in a jar. Add the medusa's snake venom and gem powders. Allow to stand for 24 hours, stirring occasionally. Pour off liquid into bottle, add sepia and holy water, mixing contents with a silver rod, stirring widdershins. Makes ink sufficient for one scroll.

Other ink formulas will be devised similarly according to the dictates of the DM. Ingredients should suit the overall purpose of the ink. It is recommended that each different spell to be transcribed require a different ink compound — clerical spells requiring more venerated and holy materials, druid spells being basically rare roots and herbs in infusions, and so on. Garments, wrappings, dust, sweat, tears, teeth, fangs, organs, blood, and so forth are all ideal components.

Once material, quill, and ink are ready, the spell scriber must actually write the magical runes, glyphs, symbols, characters, pictograms, and words upon the surface of the scroll. Transcription must be from his or her scroll books or upon an altar (for clerics and druids). Special candles and incense must be burning while the inscription is in progress. Clerics must have prayed and specially sacrificed to their deity, while magic-users must have drawn a magic circle and remain uninterrupted. PREPARATION REQUIRES ONE FULL DAY FOR EACH LEVEL OF THE SPELL BEING SCRIBED ON THE SCROLL. A 1st level spell takes one day, a 2nd level spell two, etc. Time so spent must be continuous with interruptions only for rest, food, sleep, and the like. If the inscriber leaves the scroll to do anything else, the magic is broken, and the whole effort is for naught.

Failure: There is a basic 20% chance that a mistake, smudge, or flaw in the scroll will make the spell useless. To this base chance is added 1% per level of the spell being inscribed, so that total failure chance is from 21% to 29%, minus the level of the character attempting to write the spell. Thus, if a 14th level cleric is attempting to write a 7th level spell on a *parchment* scroll, the failure chance is 20% + 7% − 14% = a 13% chance. After the requisite materials and preparations have been taken care of, the player character must then spend the full time necessary to inscribe the scroll spell. Thereafter, a percentile dice roll greater than the percentage chance of failure equals success.

If multiple spells are being scribed, a failure of one means that no further spells may be placed upon the scroll. In any event, a maximum of seven spells may be written on a single scroll. As a spell is read from the scroll, its letters and figures writhe and glow, the magic is effected, and then the lines fade and are gone forever. (In order for a magic-user or illusionist to transcribe a heretofore unknown spell from a scroll to his or her books, a *read magic* and then a period of time equal to that necessary to place the spell on the scroll are required; this likewise causes the spell to disappear from the scroll.)

The scriber of the spell does not need a *read magic* spell to use his or her own scroll spells, just as clerics and druids never need the aid of magic to read appropriate scroll spells.

Fabrication Of Other Magic Items:

All of the various other magic items will require the use of the magic spell, *enchant an item*, save clerical items.

With respect to the former, you must determine which spells and ingredients are necessary to the manufacture of each specific magic item. For example, a player character wizard of 15th level desires to make a *ring of spell storing*. He or she commissions a platinumsmith to fashion a ring of the finest quality, and pays 5,000 g.p. for materials and labor. He or she then casts the *enchant an item* spell according to the **PLAYERS HAND-BOOK** instructions. As DM, you now inform him or her that in order to contain and accept the spells he or she desires to store in the device, a scroll bearing the desired spells must be scribed, then a *permanency* spell cast upon the scroll, then the scroll must be merged with the ring by some means (typically a *wish* spell). As all of that could not be done in time, the ring would have to be prepared with the *enchant an item* spell again. Of course, you could tell the player before, if you are soft-hearted or he or she is intelligent enough to ask before starting the ball rolling.

The above-mentioned *ring of spell storing* could be made without the benefit of a *permanency* spell, and spells could be stored within, but they could only be called forth once, and then the ring would be useless. Wands and other chargeable items do not require *permanency*, and of course they are used up when all the charges are gone. Items with a permanent dweomer (such as weapons, armor, most rings and miscellaneous magic items) do require a *permanency* spell to be made continuously operational.

Clerics and druids making an item which is applicable to their profession must spend a fortnight in retreat, meditating in complete isolation. Thereafter, he or she must spend a sennight fasting. Finally, he or she must pray over and purify the item to become magical (this process takes but a day). Of course, the item must be of the finest quality just as detailed in the *enchant an item* spell description. Thereafter the cleric or druid must place the item upon his or her altar and invoke the direct favor of his or her deity to instill a special power into the item. There is a 1% per day cumulative chance that the item will then be empowered as desired, providing the cleric or druid has been absolutely exemplary in his or her faith and alignment requirements. Furthermore, if the item is one with charges, the cleric or druid must then take it into seclusion and cast the requisite spells upon it, doing so within 24 hours of its being favored by the deity. In other cases, the item need only be sanctified to the appropriate deity in order to complete its manufacture.

In all cases, the manufacture of any magic item other than a potion or scroll will be so debilitating as to necessitate the maker to rest for one day for each 100 g.p. of the item's experience point value, i.e. one with a 2,000 experience point value means 20 days of complete rest. During this period, the character can do *nothing* except eat, rest, undertake *mild* exercise, and sleep — all in relative isolation. No adventuring or spell use is possible during this period!

Fabrication Of Magic Items By Illusionists:

Though different spells are employed, the process of fabrication of magic items which illusionists use is not really very different from that used by magic-users. It is almost exactly similar as regards costs in both time and money. Some processes are also nearly identical, such as the making of scrolls, which may be done at the 7th level and up.

At the 11th level illusionists may be able to create one-shot or charged magic items, things without a permanent dweomer, such as potions or a *wand of illusion*, for example. Such items are really merely storehouses of magical energy which can be released in various ways. Like any other

spell-caster, the illusionist must fashion the item out of rare and expensive materials, but instead of using *enchant an item* to prepare the item to receive its enchantment, the illusionist uses *major creation* to subtly alter its structure in a magical direction so that it can receive and retain the necessary spells. During the next 16 hours after casting the *major creation*, the illusionist instills the primary initial dweomers into the item, and if his concentration is interrupted even once during this period, the item instantly fades and forever disappears, like an illusion that has been dispelled.

Beginning at 14th level an illusionist may attempt to make items with a truly permanent dweomer, such as a +1 dagger or a *ring of protection*, for example. This entails a similar process to the one described above. The crucial difference is that after a *major creation* spell has been used to adjust the material object, an *alter reality* must be cast to fix it permanently in place and make it able to contain a permanent magic. Thus, with a great expense in time, money and preparation, *major creation*, *alter reality* and *true sight* spells, and an unflawed gem worth not less than 10,000 g.p., an illusionist might be able to create a *gem of seeing*.

The basic thing to remember if details are in question is that illusionists are a sub-class of magic-users, and except for what has been outlined above, what applies to magic-users applies to illusionists as well.

Fabrication Of Magic Items By Charmed Or Enslaved Magic-Users:

It is absolutely necessary that you take note that any sort of charmed, magically persuaded, or otherwise enslaved magic-user will be totally unable to function in such a manner as to allow the fabrication of any sort of magic item — scroll, potion, or otherwise. The discipline and concentration demanded by such activity absolutely precludes individuals of this sort from manufacturing magic items. If a player character should attempt to have such a character fabricate items, allow the usual amounts of time and money to be expended, and then inform him or her that the results are negative. If the player character opts to have the enslaved individual continue, say nothing, but the attempts will continue to be fruitless.

NON-STANDARD MAGIC ITEMS

There are two considerations respecting non-standard magic items. The first is your invention and inclusion of them in your campaign, and this is expected and encouraged. You should put your imagination and inventiveness to work this way. Standard items can be varied so as to make it more interesting when your players are familiar with the usual forms. New devices can be created to add freshness and new dimensions to the game. Special magic items can be devised to complement some special situation or to serve as a special reward for overcoming some special monster or difficult area. All such creations, however, must be made with care. The items must be such as to not unbalance the game. They must not make one player character too strong, either with respect to opponents or his or her fellows or to the campaign or to the game system as a whole. Items which are expended after a single use, those with limited usages, and those with variable effects are most desirable. As it is very likely that every campaign will have its special items, the second consideration comes up.

Other referees will not generally know what special powers or restrictions such items have. Thus, they will not be usable in campaigns other than that from which they came in most cases. You, as a referee, should simply cause any such items brought into your campaign to disappear. Never take a player's word for any item. Do not allow its use in your campaign unless you know his or her DM and get a full explanation *in writing* from that person which details the properties of the item. Do not allow a player to bulldoze you in any manner regarding this. Simply inform the person that he or she must have left the item in his or her former area, as it is not around in yours! This solves the problem of having a possible imbalance brought into your carefully designed campaign. This ties directly to the section dealing with **INTEGRATION OF EXPERIENCED OR NEW PLAYERS INTO AN EXISTING CAMPAIGN** (q.v.).

Note: Altered *form* of a standard **AD&D** item is not a new or non-standard item, i.e., a cap which causes its wearer to be *invisible* is the same as a *ring of invisibility*.

USE OF MAGIC ITEMS

COMMAND WORDS

In order to use a rod, staff or wand, it is usually necessary to know the proper command word. There are several possible ways to acquire this knowledge. If the item is/was in the possession of an opponent, it may be possible to learn the appropriate word or phrase directly, either by noting what he or she says when using the item, or by causing the possessor to divulge the information through force or trickery. It is common for spell-users to keep such information recorded among their hidden scrolls and spell books, in case their memories should somehow become impaired (or simply prove insufficient) and the words be forgotten.

If none of these sources should fit the situation, and the item was not found with an accompanying scroll explaining its use and history, it may be necessary to resort to informational spells such as *contact other plane, legend lore* or *speak with dead.*

CRYSTAL BALLS & SCRYING

Various devices for seeing at a distance (such as *crystal balls,* various scrying devices such as dishes or pans of water or mirrors, and spells such as *clairaudience*) are detectable. If the creature being observed in this manner is a spell user, then consult the table given for **DETECTION OF INVISIBILITY** in the section entitled **INVISIBILITY.** Find the creature's level/hit dice and intelligence, and then use the table as if an invisible creature were to be detected, checking each round.

If crystal balling or scrying in any other form is detected by the observed, then it can be stopped by the use of *darkness* or *dispel magic,* the observed simply noting the small disturbance in the air caused by the magical viewing and casting the spell upon that spot, thus causing the scrying to cease for the length of the *darkness* spell or for a full day in the case of *dispel magic.*

DRINKING POTIONS

It takes but a segment (6 seconds) to open and consume the typical potion. Thereafter, however, a certain delay will occur while the contents are ingested and the magical properties of the potion take effect. The delay will be from 2-5 segments as a rule. When a potion is imbibed, simply roll d4, add +1 to the result, and in that number of segments the effects of the dose will take full effect. You may establish specific times for various potions if you so desire, but this is a complication which is not generally recommended.

APPLYING OILS

Magic oils, not being consumed, are treated differently. The contents are poured over hands and body and smeared appropriately. This will require normal opening time and decanting, i.e., 1 segment. Spreading the oil will require 2-5 segments also, just as detailed for potions to take effect.

POTION MISCIBILITY

The magical mixtures and compounds which comprise potions are not always compatible. You must test the miscibility of potions whenever:

1) two potions are actually intermingled, or

2) a potion is consumed by a creature while another such liquid already consumed is still in effect

While it is possible to prepare a matrix which lists each potion type and cross references each to show a certain result when one is intermingled with the other, such a graph has two drawbacks. First, it does not allow for differences in formulae from alchemist and/or magic-user. Second, it will require continual addition as new potion types are added to the campaign. Therefore, it is suggested that the following table be used — with, perhaps, the decision that a *delusion* potion will mix with anything, that *oil of slipperiness* taken with *oil of etherealness* will always increase the chance for the imbiber to be lost in the Ethereal Plane for 5-30 days to 50%, and *treasure finding* mixed with any other type of potion will always yield a lethal poison. Whatever certain results you settle upon for your campaign, the random results from the table apply to all other cases.

POTION MISCIBILITY TABLE

Dice Score	Result
01	EXPLOSION! Internal damage is 6-60 h.p., those within a 5″ radius take 1-10 h.p. if mixed externally, all in a 10′ radius take 4-24 hit points, no save.
02-03	Lethal poison results, and imbiber is dead; if externally mixed, a poison gas cloud of 10′ diameter results, and all within it must save versus poison or die.
04-08	Mild poison which causes nausea and loss of 1 point each of strength and dexterity for 5-20 rounds, no saving throw possible; one potion is cancelled, the other is at half strength and duration. (Use random determination for which is cancelled and which is at half efficacy.)
09-15	Immiscible. Both potions totally destroyed, as one cancelled the other.
16-25	Immiscible. One potion cancelled, but the other remains normal (random selection).
26-35	Immiscible result which causes both potions to be at half normal efficacy when consumed.
36-90	Miscible. Potions work normally unless their effects are contradictory, e.g. *diminution* and *growth,* which will simply cancel each other.
91-99	Compatible result which causes one potion (randomly determined) to have 150% normal efficacy. (You must determine if both effect **and** duration are permissible, or if **only** the duration should be extended.)
00	DISCOVERY! The admixture of the two potions has caused a special formula which will cause one of the two potions only to function, but its effects will be permanent upon the imbiber. (Note that some harmful side effects could well result from this . . .)

Roll for miscibility secretly whenever it occurs. Give no uncalled-for clues until necessary.

ENERGY DRAINING BY UNDEAD OR DEVICE

When a character loses a level of energy, he or she loses an experience level. That is, he or she loses hit points equal to those gained with the acquisition of the former experience level (including bonus points for constitution), all abilities gained with the experience level now lost, and experience points sufficient to bring the total possessed to the mid-point of the next lower level. If this brings the character below 1st level of experience, then the individual is a 0 level person never capable of gaining experience again. If a 0 level individual is drained an energy level, he or she is dead (possibly to become an undead monster). In order to allow for the possibility of the loss of hit dice due to energy level draining, you might require that players record the score of each hit die rolled for their characters, so that when a level is lost the appropriate number of hit points also lost can be known immediately.

A multi-classed character (or character with two classes) who is drained of an experience level always loses the highest level he or she has gained (e.g., a halfling 2nd level fighter/3rd level thief would lose one level of thieving ability). If all levels are equal, the highest level of the class which requires the greatest amount of experience points is lost. If a multi-classed character (e.g., a fighter/magic-user) is struck by a creature which drains two levels, a level is drained from each class.

When a character is drained of all energy levels, he or she might become an undead monster of the same sort which killed him or her. (See the appropriate paragraphs pertaining to the undead monsters concerned in the **MONSTER MANUAL.**) These lesser undead are controlled by their slayer/drainer. Each has but half the hit dice of a normal undead monster of this same type. Lesser vampires have but half their former level of experience with respect to their profession (cleric, fighter, etc.) at the time they initially encountered and were subsequently slain/drained by their now-master vampire, i.e., an 8th level thief killed by a vampire, even though drained to below 0 level in the process, returns as a 4th level thief vampire, as appropriate. However, upon the destruction of their slayer/drainer, such lesser undead *gain* energy levels from characters they subsequently slay/drain until they reach the maximum number of hit dice (and their former level of class experience as well, if applicable) appropriate to their type of undead monster. Upon reaching full hit dice status, they are able to slay/drain and control lesser undead as they once were.

TREASURE

RANDOM TREASURE DETERMINATION

I. MAP OR MAGIC DETERMINATION

01-10 = Map Table (II.)
11-00 = Magic Items Table (III.)

If the treasure in a monster's lair indicates that maps or magic are there, you will often have to determine which are present by random number generation with percentile dice. This is simple and the table shows which tables to use to determine the result. This system can be used for monsters you place on the outdoor map as well as for monsters randomly encountered by a party exploring in the wilderness. In any event, you will have to make a number of additional dice rolls to find exactly what is within the treasure trove.

II. MAP TABLE

Dice	Result
01-05	False map
06-70	Map to monetary treasure
71-90	Map to magic treasure
91-00	Map to a combined hoard

If a map is indicated, you must generate a number between 01 and 00 to discover what the map leads to. However, the contents of the map itself are a problem, for how can it be possible to direct each DM properly considering the infinite number of possibilities under which the map will be located? The answer is that this writer can only suggest. A map should **never** list its treasure, only show its location.

When a map is purposely placed by the DM it is obviously incumbent upon him or her to satisfy both its requirements — to what it leads and where it leads. Randomly discovered maps are not an overwhelming problem. In the dungeon they can show a route down, up or (if the lair is at an edge of the level map) off into an area you have not yet drawn. Use the **RANDOM DUNGEON GENERATION** tables to set out a course which their map will "show". There is no reason why the treasure cannot be guarded, or why monsters cannot be encountered along the way, as long as the whole fits reasonably together, i.e. the map owner placed the guards or was unable to get the treasure because of these monsters. Generally, the whole route can be quite long or only a few hundred feet. If the treasure is particularly rich you might wish to have it hidden leagues away in another lost dungeon, along the course of a long underground river, or something similar. The direction of your campaign is strictly your own province.

Maps found outdoors in a monster's lair can lead into an underground labyrinth, a few miles in the wilderness to some hidey-hole, lair, ruins, or even in a town. Direction is easily determined by a quick roll of d8, basing the compass on 1 being north (or whatever) and simply counting round (2 is northeast, 3 is east, etc.). The table below may be used as a guide if you wish:

01-20	labyrinth of caves found in the lair
21-60*	outdoors, 5-8 miles distant
61-90*	outdoors, 10-40 miles distant
91-00*	outdoors, 50-500 miles distant

* Treasure shown on the map is:

01-10	buried and unguarded
11-20	hidden in water
21-70	guarded in a lair
71-80	somewhere in a ruins
81-90	in a burial crypt
91-00	secreted in a town

Elaborate as you see fit. For containment, concealment and trapping, refer to the tables given with the **RANDOM DUNGEON GENERATION.**

Note that relatively low-value treasures will not be as well guarded as those of great value.

II.A. MONETARY TREASURE

Dice	Result
1-2	20,000-80,000 copper pieces (2d4), 20,000-50,000 silver pieces (d4 + 1)
3-5	5,000-30,000 electrum pieces (5d6)
6-10	3,000-18,000 gold pieces (3d6)
11-12	500-2,000 platinum pieces (5d4)
13-15	10-100 gems (d10 × 10)
16-17	5-50 pieces of jewelry (5d10)*
18	Roll twice, discounting rolls above 17
19	Roll thrice, discounting rolls above 17
20	Each monetary item above

* Specific types of jewelry can be determined on the **Jewelry and Items Typically Bejewelled Table** (part of **Appendix I, DUNGEON DRESSING**) if desired.

This table shows the parameters for each sort of goods to be found in a treasure of this sort. Random number generation with d20 discovers which sorts of goods are in the trove. You will observe that the table is weighted towards large quantities of coins which will require a train to remove — or must be left entirely if foreplanning is not observed.

(As with any treasure not taken immediately, you must set a percentage chance for it to be stolen away if it is abandoned by the discoverers. Their actions and precautions will serve as guidelines. If a monster guarded the treasure, the likelihood of it being taken elsewhere could increase greatly.)

Base value of gems and jewelry can be determined when the treasure is actually divided and disposed of.

II.B. MAGIC TREASURE

Dice	Result
1-5	Any item rolled on Magic Item Table, plus 4 Potions
6-8	Any 2 items rolled on Magic Item Table
9-12	1 Sword, 1 Armor or Shield, 1 Miscellaneous Weapon
13-14	Any 3 items, no Sword or Potions
15-18	Any 6 Potions and any 6 Scrolls
19	Any 4 items, 1 is a Ring, 1 is a Rod
20	Any 5 items, 1 is a Rod, 1 is Miscellaneous Magic

This random determination table needs no explanation. Because of its weighting, and the weighting of the MAGIC ITEMS table, most treasures will have magic potions, scrolls, armor and weapons. This is carefully planned so as to prevent imbalance in the game. Keep potent magic items rare. (Increase scarcity by destroying or stealing what is found!)

II.C. COMBINED HOARD

Dice	Result*
01-20	1-2 Monetary Treasure and 1-5 Magic Treasure
21-40	6-10 Monetary Treasure and 1-5 Magic Treasure
41-55	3-5 & 6-10 Monetary Treasure and 1-5 & 15-18 Magic Treasure
56-65	1-2, 3-5 & 6-10 Monetary Treasure and 9-12 & 13-14 Magic Treasure
66-75	6-10 & 11-12 Monetary Treasure and 6-8 & 15-18 Magic Treasure
76-80	3-5, 6-10, 11-12 & 16-17 Monetary Treasure and 1-5 & 9-12 Magic Treasure
81-85	20 Monetary Treasure and map to 1-5 Magic Treasure
86-90	20 Monetary Treasure and map to 19 Magic Treasure
91-96	Map to 1-2 & 3-5 Monetary Treasure, 20 Magic Treasure on hand
97-00	Map to 11-12 & 13-15 Monetary Treasure plus 15-18 Magic Treasure, 20 Magic Treasure on hand

* Key the results to the proper listings from the prior two tables.

These are the real finds, which can satisfy even the most avaricious dwarf's greed. Note that when it says "1-2 Monetary Treasure", for instance, it means the treasure indicated by a die result of 1 or 2 on the MONETARY TREASURE sub-table. Combined hoards should be hidden, trapped and guarded! They should be located in distant places too!

III. MAGIC ITEMS

Dice	Results
01-20	Potions (A.)
21-35	Scrolls (B.)
36-40	Rings (C.)
41-45	Rods, Staves & Wands (D.)
46-48	Miscellaneous Magic (E.1.)
49-51	Miscellaneous Magic (E.2.)
52-54	Miscellaneous Magic (E.3.)
55-57	Miscellaneous Magic (E.4.)
58-60	Miscellaneous Magic (E.5.)
61-75	Armor & Shields (F.)
76-86	Swords (G.)
87-00	Miscellaneous Weapons (H.)

As mentioned previously, the MAGIC ITEMS table is weighted towards results which balance the game. Potions, scrolls, armor and arms are plentiful. Rings, rods and miscellaneous items of magic represent only a 25% occurrence on the table. This is so done in order to keep magic-users from totally dominating play. They are sufficiently powerful characters without adding piles of supplementary goodies. What they gain from the table will typically be used up and discarded.

When determination of a magic item is needed simply roll percentile dice and consult table III. Complete explanations of each category follow, but as many items duplicate or closely resemble the effects of various magic spells, you will need a copy of **ADVANCED DUNGEONS & DRAGONS, PLAYER'S HANDBOOK** for reference.

The suggested experience point (x.p.) values are for characters who keep the items. Gold piece sale values are the usual sums which characters will be paid for magic items, and if so sold, the x.p. award should be based on the selling price of the items, not the x.p. value. Also remember that a character is assumed to retain an item, thus getting the low x.p. value for it, if he or she sells it to another player character. (See **EXPERIENCE.**)

Note: Many magical items are of an expendable nature, where their power is depleted with each use and eventually used up. The Dungeon Master can use his discretion in setting such limitations on other particular items, if he wishes.

III.A. POTIONS

Dice	Result	Experience Point Value	G.P. Sale Value
01-03	Animal Control*	250	400
04-06	Clairaudience	250	400
07-09	Clairvoyance	300	500
10-12	Climbing	300	500
13-15	Delusion**	---	150
16-18	Diminution	300	500
19-20	Dragon Control*	500-1,000	5,000-9,000
21-23	ESP	500	850
24-26	Extra-Healing	400	800
27-29	Fire Resistance	250	400
30-32	Flying	500	750
33-34	Gaseous Form	300	400
35-36	Giant Control*	400-900	1,000-6,000
37-39	Giant Strength* (F)	500-750	900-1,400
40-41	Growth	250	300
42-47	Healing	200	400
48-49	Heroism (F)	300	500
50-51	Human Control*	500	900
52-54	Invisibility	250	500
55-57	Invulnerability (F)	350	500
58-60	Levitation	250	400
61-63	Longevity	500	1,000
64-66	Oil of Etherealness	600	1,500
67-69	Oil of Slipperiness	400	750
70-72	Philter of Love	200	300
73-75	Philter of Persuasiveness	400	850
76-78	Plant Control	250	300
79-81	Polymorph (self)	200	350
82-84	Poison**	---	---
85-87	Speed	200	450
88-90	Super-Heroism (F)	450	750

91-93	Sweet Water	200	250
94-96	Treasure Finding	600	2,000
97	Undead Control*	700	2,500
98-00	Water Breathing	400	900

* Effectiveness on type of creature controlled must be determined by die roll; consult item explanation.

** The Dungeon Master must mislead the possessor of the potion so as to convince him that it is not harmful. (See the appropriate item description for particulars.)

(F) = Fighters only may use

III.B. SCROLLS*

Dice	Result	Spell Level Range
01-10	1 spell	1-4
11-16	1 spell	1-6
17-19	1 spell	2-9 (d8 + 1) or 2-7* (d6 + 1)
20-24	2 spells	1-4
25-27	2 spells	1-8 or 1-6*
28-32	3 spells	1-4
33-35	3 spells	2-9 or 2-7*
36-39	4 spells	1-6
40-42	4 spells	1-8 or 1-6*
43-46	5 spells	1-6
47-49	5 spells	1-8 or 1-6*
50-52	6 spells	1-6
53-54	6 spells	3-8 (d6 + 2) or 3-6* (d4 + 2)
55-57	7 spells	1-8
58-59	7 spells	2-9
60	7 spells	4-9 (d6 + 3) or 4-7* (d4 + 3)
61-62	Protection — Demons	(2,500 x.p.)
63-64	Protection — Devils	(2,500 x.p.)
65-70	Protection — Elementals	(1,500 x.p.)
71-76	Protection — Lycanthropes	(1,000 x.p.)
77-82	Protection — Magic	(1,500 x.p.)
83-87	Protection — Petrification	(2,000 x.p.)
88-92	Protection — Possession	(2,000 x.p.)
93-97	Protection — Undead	(1,500 x.p.)
98-00	Curse**	

* 30% of all scrolls are of clerical nature (dice 71-00), and 25% of all clerical scrolls are druidical. 10% of all magic-user scrolls are illusionist. This applies only to scrolls 01-60 above. Asterisked numbers indicate clerical spell levels.

** It is incumbent upon the Dungeon Master to do his utmost to convince players that a cursed scroll should be read. This is to be accomplished through duplicity, coercion and threat, etc. — i.e., any scroll not read has a chance of fading in normal air, but this can be noted by the archaic wording if read in the still dungeon atmosphere. A curse takes effect immediately; suggested curses are:

01-25 —	Reader *polymorphed* to monster of equal level which attacks any creatures nearby
26-30 —	Reader turned to liquid and drains away
31-40 —	Reader and all within 20' radius transported 200 to 1,200 miles in a random direction
41-50 —	Reader and all in 20' radius transported to another planet, plane or continuum
51-75 —	Disease fatal to reader in 2-8 turns unless cured
76-90 —	Explosive runes
91-99 —	Magic item nearby is ''de-magicked''.
00 —	Randomly rolled spell affects reader at 12th level of magic-use

Experience Points (x.p.) Value:

Awarded only to characters who can use the spell(s); the award should be 100 x.p. per spell level. *Protection* scrolls are noted as to x.p. value on the table itself.

Gold Piece (g.p.) Sale Value:

Any scroll can be sold in the "open market" for three times its x.p. value. *Protection* scrolls sell for five times x.p. value.

III.C. RINGS

Dice	Result	Experience Point Value	G.P. Sale Value
01-06	Contrariness	---	1,000
07-12	Delusion	---	2,000
13-14	Djinni Summoning‡	3,000	20,000
15	Elemental Command	5,000	25,000
16-21	Feather Falling	1,000	5,000
22-27	Fire Resistance	1,000	5,000
28-30	Free Action	1,000	5,000
31-33	Human Influence‡	2,000	10,000
34-40	Invisibility	1,500	7,500
41-43	Mammal Control‡	1,000	5,000
44	Multiple Wishes‡	5,000	25,000
45-60	Protection	2,000-4,000	10,000-20,000
61	Regeneration	5,000	40,000
62-63	Shooting Stars	3,000	15,000
64-65	Spell Storing	2,500	22,500
66-69	Spell Turning	2,000	17,500
70-75	Swimming	1,000	5,000
76-77	Telekinesis‡	2,000	10,000
78-79	Three Wishes‡	3,000	15,000
80-85	Warmth	1,000	5,000
86-90	Water Walking	1,000	5,000
91-98	Weakness	---	1,000
99	Wizardry‡ (M)	4,000	50,000
00	X-Ray Vision	4,000	35,000

(M) = Magic-user use only.

‡ These rings contain the most powerful magical abilities and may possess only a limited number of magical charges before being depleted, at the DM's option.

III.D. RODS, STAVES, & WANDS

Dice	Result	Experience Point Value*	G.P. Sale Value*
01-03	Rod of Absorption (C,M)	7,500	40,000
04	Rod of Beguiling (C,M,T)	5,000	30,000
05-14	Rod of Cancellation (any)	10,000	15,000
15-16	Rod of Lordly Might (F)	6,000	20,000
17	Rod of Resurrection (C)	10,000	35,000
18	Rod of Rulership (any)	8,000	35,000
19	Rod of Smiting (C,F)	4,000	15,000
20	Staff of Command (C,M)	5,000	25,000
21-22	Staff of Curing (C)	6,000	25,000
23	Staff of the Magi (M)	15,000	75,000
24	Staff of Power (M)	12,000	60,000
25-27	Staff of the Serpent (C)	7,000	35,000
28-31	Staff of Striking (C,M)	6,000	15,000
32-33	Staff of Withering (C)	8,000	35,000
34	Wand of Conjuration (M)	7,000	35,000
35-38	Wand of Enemy Detection (any)	2,000	10,000
39-41	Wand of Fear (C,M)	3,000	15,000
42-44	Wand of Fire (M)	4,500	25,000
45-47	Wand of Frost (M)	6,000	50,000
48-52	Wand of Illumination (any)	2,000	10,000
53-56	Wand of Illusion (M)	3,000	20,000
57-59	Wand of Lightning (M)	4,000	30,000
60-68	Wand of Magic Detection (any)	2,500	25,000
69-73	Wand of Metal & Mineral Detection (any)	1,500	7,500
74-78	Wand of Magic Missiles (any)	4,000	35,000
79-86	Wand of Negation (any)	3,500	15,000
87-89	Wand of Paralyzation (M)	3,500	25,000
90-92	Wand of Polymorphing (M)	3,500	25,000
93-94	Wand of Secret Door & Trap Location (any)	5,000	40,000
95-00	Wand of Wonder (any)	6,000	10,000

* Assumes full charges are in item.

(C) = Usable by the cleric class only.

(F) = Usable by the fighter class only.

(M) = Usable by the magic-user class only.

(T) = Usable by the thief class only.

(any) = Usable by any class unless otherwise prohibited.

III.E. MISCELLANEOUS MAGIC

TABLE (III.E.) 1.

Dice	Result	Experience Point Value	G.P. Sale Value
01-02	Alchemy Jug	3,000	12,000
03-04	Amulet of Inescapable Location	---	1,000
05	Amulet of Life Protection	5,000	20,000
06-07	Amulet of the Planes	6,000	30,000
08-11	Amulet of Proof Against Detection and Location	4,000	15,000
12-13	Apparatus of Kwalish	8,000	35,000
14-16	Arrow of Direction	2,500	17,500
17	Artifact or Relic (see **Special** table hereafter)	---	---
18-20	Bag of Beans	1,000	5,000
21	Bag of Devouring	---	1,500
22-26	Bag of Holding	5,000	25,000
27	Bag of Transmuting	---	500
28-29	Bag of Tricks	2,500	15,000
30-31	Beaker of Plentiful Potions	1,500	12,500
32	Boat, Folding	10,000	25,000
33	Book of Exalted Deeds (C)	8,000	40,000
34	Book of Infinite Spells	9,000	50,000
35	Book of Vile Darkness (C)	8,000	40,000
36	Boots of Dancing	---	5,000
37-42	Boots of Elvenkind	1,000	5,000
43-47	Boots of Levitation	2,000	15,000
48-51	Boots of Speed	2,500	20,000
52-55	Boots of Striding and Springing	2,500	20,000
56-58	Bowl Commanding Water Elementals (M)	4,000	25,000
59	Bowl of Watery Death (M)	---	1,000
60-79	Bracers of Defense	500*	3,000*
80-81	Bracers of Defenselessness	---	2,000
82-84	Brazier Commanding Fire Elementals (M)	4,000	25,000
85	Brazier of Sleep Smoke (M)	---	1,000
86-92	Brooch of Shielding	1,000	10,000
93	Broom of Animated Attack	---	3,000
94-98	Broom of Flying	2,000	10,000
99-00	Bucknard's Everfull Purse	1,500/2,500/ 4,000	15,000/25,000/ 40,000

* Per armor class above 10, i.e., AC 6 is worth 2,000 in x.p., 12,000 g.p. if sold.

TABLE (III.E.) 2.

Dice	Result	Experience Point Value	G.P. Sale Value
01-06	Candle of Invocation (C)	1,000	5,000
07-08	Carpet of Flying	7,500	25,000
09-10	Censer Controlling Air Elementals (M)	4,000	25,000
11	Censer of Summoning Hostile Air Elementals (M)	---	1,000
12-13	Chime of Opening	3,500	20,000
14	Chime of Hunger	---	---
15-18	Cloak of Displacement	3,000	17,500
19-27	Cloak of Elvenkind	1,000	6,000
28-30	Cloak of Manta Ray	2,000	12,500
31-32	Cloak of Poisonousness	---	2,500
33-55	Cloak of Protection	1,000*	10,000*
56-60	Crystal Ball (M)	1,000**	5,000**
61	Crystal Hypnosis Ball (M)	---	3,000

Dice		Exp. Pt.	G.P.
62-63	Cube of Force	3,000	20,000
64-65	Cube of Frost Resistance	2,000	14,000
66-67	Cubic Gate	5,000	17,500
68-69	Daern's Instant Fortress	7,000	27,500
70-72	Decanter of Endless Water	1,000	3,000
73-76	Deck of Many Things	---	10,000
77	Drums of Deafening	---	500
78-79	Drums of Panic	6,500	35,000
80-85	Dust of Appearance	1,000	4,000
86-91	Dust of Disappearance	2,000	8,000
92	Dust of Sneezing and Choking	---	1,000
93	Efreeti Bottle	9,000	45,000
94	Eversmoking Bottle	500	2,500
95	Eyes of Charming (M)	4,000	24,000
96-97	Eyes of the Eagle	3,500	18,000
98-99	Eyes of Minute Seeing	2,000	12,500
00	Eyes of Petrification	---***	---***

* Per plus of protection.

** Add 100% for each additional feature.

*** If reverse effect, 12,500 x.p. and 50,000 g.p. sale value.

TABLE (III.E.) 3.

Dice	Result	Experience Point Value	G.P. Sale Value
01-15	Figurine of Wondrous Power	100*	1,000*
16	Flask of Curses	---	1,000
17-18	Gauntlets of Dexterity	1,000	10,000
19-20	Gauntlets of Fumbling	---	1,000
21-22	Gauntlets of Ogre Power (C, F, T)	1,000	15,000
23-25	Gauntlets of Swimming and Climbing (C, F, T)	1,000	10,000
26	Gem of Brightness	2,000	17,500
27	Gem of Seeing	2,000	25,000
28	Girdle of Femininity/Masculinity (C, F, T)	---	1,000
29	Girdle of Giant Strength (C, F, T)	200	2,500
30	Helm of Brilliance	2,500	60,000
31-35	Helm of Comprehending Languages & Reading Magic	1,000	12,500
36-37	Helm of Opposite Alignment	---	1,000
38-39	Helm of Telepathy	3,000	35,000
40	Helm of Teleportation	2,500	30,000
41-45	Helm of Underwater Action	1,000	10,000
46	Horn of Blasting	5,000	55,000
47-48	Horn of Bubbles	---	---
49	Horn of Collapsing	1,500	25,000
50-53	Horn of the Tritons (C, F)	2,000	17,500
54-60	Horn of Valhalla	1,000**	15,000**
61-63	Horseshoes of Speed	2,000	10,000
64-65	Horseshoes of a Zephyr	1,500	7,500
66-70	Incense of Meditation (C)	500	7,500
71	Incense of Obsession (C)	---	500
72	Ioun Stones	300***	5,000***
73-78	Instrument of the Bards	1,000****	5,000****
79-80	Iron Flask	---	---
81-85	Javelin of Lightning (F)	250	3,000
86-90	Javelin of Piercing (F)	250	3,000
91	Jewel of Attacks	---	1,000
92	Jewel of Flawlessness	---	1,000/facet
93-00	Keoghtom's Ointment	500	10,000

* Per hit die of the figurine.

** Double for a bronze horn, triple for an iron horn.

*** Per stone.

**** Per level of instrument for Bards.

TABLE (III.E.) 4.

Dice	Result	Experience Point Value	G.P. Sale Value
01	Libram of Gainful Conjuration (M)	8,000	40,000
02	Libram of Ineffable Damnation (M)	8,000	40,000
03	Libram of Silver Magic (M)	8,000	40,000
04	Lyre of Building	5,000	30,000
05	Manual of Bodily Health	5,000	50,000
06	Manual of Gainful Exercise	5,000	50,000
07	Manual of Golems (C, M)	3,000	30,000
08	Manual of Puissant Skill at Arms (F)	8,000	40,000
09	Manual of Quickness of Action	5,000	50,000
10	Manual of Stealthy Pilfering (T)	8,000	40,000
11	Mattock of the Titans (F)	3,500	7,000
12	Maul of the Titans	4,000	12,000
13-15	Medallion of ESP	1,000/3,000	10,000/30,000
16-17	Medallion of Thought Projection	---	1,000
18	Mirror of Life Trapping (M)	2,500	25,000
19	Mirror of Mental Prowess	5,000	50,000
20	Mirror of Opposition	---	2,000
21-23	Necklace of Adaptation	1,000	10,000
24-27	Necklace of Missiles	50*	200*
28-33	Necklace of Prayer Beads (C)	500**	3,000**
34-35	Necklace of Strangulation	---	1,000
36-38	Net of Entrapment (C, F, T)	1,000	7,500
39-42	Net of Snaring (C, F, T)	1,000	6,000
43-44	Nolzurs' Marvelous Pigments	500***	3,000***
45-46	Pearl of Power (M)	200****	2,000****
47-48	Pearl of Wisdom (C)	500	5,000
49-50	Periapt of Foul Rotting	---	1,000
51-53	Periapt of Health	1,000	10,000
54-60	Periapt of Proof Against Poison	1,500	12,500
61-64	Periapt of Wound Closure	1,000	10,000
65-70	Phylactery of Faithfulness (C)	1,000	7,500
71-74	Phylactery of Long Years (C)	3,000	25,000
75-76	Phylactery of Monstrous Attention (C)	---	2,000
77-84	Pipes of the Sewers	1,750	8,500
85	Portable Hole	5,000	50,000
86-00	Quaal's Feather Token	500/1,000	2,000/7,000

* Per hit die of each missile.

** Per special bead.

*** Per pot of pigments.

**** Per level of spell.

"Well, either it allows a magic-user to throw the various Bigby's hand spells, or it's a +2 backscratcher. So far we're not sure which . . . ."

TABLE (III.E.) 5.

Dice	Result	Experience Point Value	G.P. Sale Value
01	Robe of the Archmagi (M)	6,000	65,000
02-08	Robe of Blending	3,500	35,000
09	Robe of Eyes (M)	4,500	50,000
10	Robe of Powerlessness (M)	---	1,000
11	Robe of Scintillating Colors (C, M)	2,750	25,000
12-19	Robe of Useful Items (M)	1,500	15,000
20-25	Rope of Climbing	1,000	10,000
26-27	Rope of Constriction	---	1,000
28-31	Rope of Entanglement	1,250	12,000
32	Rug of Smothering	---	1,500
33	Rug of Welcome (M)	6,500	45,000
34	Saw of Mighty Cutting (F)	1,750	12,500
35	Scarab of Death	---	2,500
36-38	Scarab of Enraging Enemies	1,000	8,000
39-40	Scarab of Insanity	1,500	11,000
41-46	Scarab of Protection	2,500	25,000
47	Spade of Colossal Excavation (F)	1,000	6,500
48	Sphere of Annihilation (M)	3,750	30,000
49-50	Stone of Controlling Earth Elementals	1,500	12,500
51-52	Stone of Good Luck (Luckstone)	3,000	25,000
53-54	Stone of Weight (Loadstone)	---	1,000
55-57	Talisman of Pure Good (C)	3,500	27,500
58	Talisman of the Sphere (M)	100	10,000
59-60	Talisman of Ultimate Evil (C)	3,500	32,500
61-66	Talisman of Zagy	1,000	10,000
67	Tome of Clear Thought	8,000	48,000
68	Tome of Leadership and Influence	7,500	40,000
69	Tome of Understanding	8,000	43,500
70-76	Trident of Fish Command (C, F, T)	500	4,000
77-78	Trident of Submission (F)	1,250	12,500
79-83	Trident of Warning (C, F, T)	1,000	10,000
84-85	Trident of Yearning	---	1,000
86-87	Vacuous Grimoire	---	1,000
88-90	Well of Many Worlds	6,000	12,000
91-00	Wings of Flying	750	7,500

TABLE (III.E.) Special.

Dice	Result	G.P. Sale Value*
01	Axe of the Dwarvish Lords	55,000
02	Baba Yaga's Hut	90,000
03-04	Codex of the Infinite Planes	62,500
05-20	Crown of Might	50,000
21	Crystal of the Ebon Flame	75,000
22	Cup and Talisman of Al'Akbar	85,000
23-24	Eye of Vecna	35,000
25	Hand of Vecna	60,000
26	Heward's Mystical Organ	25,000
27	Horn of Change	20,000
28-29	Invulnerable Coat of Arnd	47,500
30-31	Iron Flask of Tuerny the Merciless	50,000
32	Jacinth of Inestimable Beauty	100,000
33	Johydee's Mask	40,000
34-35	Kuroth's Quill	27,500
36-37	Mace of Cuthbert	35,000
38	Machine of Lum the Mad	72,500
39-40	Mighty Servant of Leuk-O	185,000
41-47	Orb of the Dragonkind	10-80,000
48-63	Orb of Might	100,000
64	Queen Ehlissa's Marvelous Nightingale	112,500
65-66	Recorder of Ye'Cind	80,000
67-68	Ring of Gaxx	17,500
69-74	Rod of Seven Parts	25,000
75-91	Sceptre of Might	150,000
92	Sword of Kas	97,000
93-98	Teeth of Dahlver-Nar	5,000/tooth
99	Throne of the Gods	---
00	Wand of Orcus	10,000

* These items bring no experience points.

III.F. ARMOR AND SHIELD

Dice	Result	Experience Point Value	G.P. Sale Value
01-05	Chain Mail +1	600	3,500
06-09	Chain Mail +2	1,200	7,500
10-11	Chain Mail +3	2,000	12,500
12-19	Leather Armor +1	300	2,000
20-26	Plate Mail +1	800	5,000
27-32	Plate Mail +2	1,750	10,500
33-35	Plate Mail +3	2,750	15,500
36-37	Plate Mail +4	3,500	20,500
38	Plate Mail +5	4,500	27,500
39	Plate Mail of Etherealness	5,000	30,000
40-44	Plate Mail of Vulnerability	---	1,500
45-50	Ring Mail +1	400	2,500
51-55	Scale Mail +1	500	3,000
56-59	Scale Mail +2	1,100	6,750
60-63	Splint Mail +1	700	4,000
64-66	Splint Mail +2	1,500	8,500
67-68	Splint Mail +3	2,250	14,500
69	Splint Mail +4	3,000	19,000
70-75	Studded Leather +1	400	2,500
76-84	Shield +1	250	2,500
85-89	Shield +2	500	5,000
90-93	Shield +3	800	8,000
94-95	Shield +4	1,200	12,000
96	Shield +5	1,750	17,500
97	Shield, large, +1, +4 vs. missiles	400	4,000
98-00	Shield −1, missile attractor	---	750

65% of all armor is man-sized, 20% is elf-sized, 10% is dwarf-sized, and but 5% gnome or halfling sized.

III.G. SWORDS

Dice	Result	Experience Point Value	G.P. Sale Value
01-25	Sword +1	400	2,000
26-30	Sword +1, +2 vs. magic-using & enchanted creatures	600	3,000
31-35	Sword +1, +3 vs. lycanthropes & shape changers	700	3,500
36-40	Sword +1, +3 vs. regenerating creatures	800	4,000
41-45	Sword +1, +4 vs. reptiles	800	4,000
46-49	Sword +1, Flame Tongue: +2 vs. regenerating creatures +3 vs. cold-using, inflammable, or avian creatures +4 vs. undead	900	4,500
50	Sword +1, Luck Blade	1,000	5,000
51-58	Sword +2	800	4,000
59-62	Sword +2, Giant Slayer	900	4,500
63-66	Sword +2, Dragon Slayer	900	4,500
67	Sword +2, Nine Lives Stealer	1,600	8,000
68-71	Sword +3	1,400	7,000
72-74	Sword +3, Frost Brand: +6 vs. fire using/ dwelling creatures	1,600	8,000
75-76	Sword +4	2,000	10,000
77	Sword +4, Defender	3,000	15,000
78	Sword +5	3,000	15,000
79	Sword +5, Defender	3,600	18,000
80	Sword +5, Holy Avenger	4,000	20,000
81	Sword of Dancing	4,400	22,000
82	Sword of Wounding	4,400	22,000
83	Sword of Life Stealing	5,000	25,000
84	Sword of Sharpness	7,000	35,000
85	Sword, Vorpal Weapon	10,000	50,000
86-90	Sword +1, Cursed	400	---
91-95	Sword −2, Cursed	600	---
96-00	Sword, Cursed Berserking	900	---

Note: 70% of swords are longswords, 20% are broadswords, 5% are short (small) swords, 4% are bastard swords, 1% are two-handed swords.

III.H. MISCELLANEOUS WEAPONS

Dice	Result	Experience Point Value	G.P. Sale Value
01-08	Arrow + 1, 2-24 in number	20	120
09-12	Arrow + 2, 2-16 in number	50	300
13-14	Arrow + 3, 2-12 in number	75	450
15	Arrow of Slaying	250	2,500
16-20	Axe + 1	300	1,750
21-22	Axe + 2	600	3,750
23	Axe + 2, Throwing	750	4,500
24	Axe + 3	1,000	7,000
25-27	Battle Axe + 1	400	2,500
28-32	Bolt + 2, 2-20 in number	50	300
33-35	Bow + 1	500	3,500
36	Crossbow of Accuracy, + 3	2,000	12,000
37	Crossbow of Distance	1,500	7,500
38	Crossbow of Speed	1,500	7,500
39-46	Dagger + 1, + 2 vs. creatures smaller than man-sized	100	750
47-50	Dagger + 2, + 3 vs. creatures larger than man-sized	250	2,000
51	Dagger of Venom	350	3,000
52-56	Flail + 1	450	4,000
57-60	Hammer + 1	300	2,500
61-62	Hammer + 2	650	6,000
63	Hammer + 3, Dwarven Thrower	1,500	15,000
64	Hammer of Thunderbolts	2,500	25,000
65-67	Javelin + 2	750	5,000
68-72	Mace + 1	350	3,000
73-75	Mace + 2	700	4,500
76	Mace of Disruption	1,750	17,500
77	Mace + 4	1,500	15,000
78-80	Military Pick + 1	350	2,500
81-83	Morning Star + 1	400	3,000
84-88	Scimitar + 2	750	6,000
89	Sling of Seeking + 2	700	7,000
90-94	Spear + 1	500	3,000
95-96	Spear + 2	1,000	6,500
97	Spear + 3	1,750	15,000
98-99	Spear, Cursed Backbiter	---	1,000
00	Trident (Military Fork) + 3	1,500	12,500

EXPLANATIONS AND DESCRIPTIONS OF MAGIC ITEMS

POTIONS (III.A.)

Potions are typically found in ceramic, crystal, glass, or metal flasks in enough quantity to provide one person with one complete dose so as to be able to achieve the effects which are given hereafter for each type of potion. Potion containers can be other than as described at your option. As a general rule they should bear no identifying marks, so that the players must sample from each container in order to determine the nature of the liquid. However, even a small taste should suffice to identify a potion in some way — even if just a slight urge. As Dungeon Master you should add a few different sorts of potions, both helpful and harmful, of such nature as to cause difficulties in identification. In addition, the same type of potion, when derived from different sources, might smell, taste, and look differently.

Unless otherwise stated, the effects of a potion will last for 4 complete turns plus 1-4 additional turns (d4). If half of a potion is quaffed, the effects will last one-half as long in some cases. Potions take effect 2-5 segments **after** they are imbibed.

While potions can be compounded by magic-user/alchemist teams at a relatively low cost, they must have an actual potion to obtain the formula for each type. Furthermore, the ingredients are always rare and/or hard to come by. This aspect of potions, as well as the formulation of new ones by players, is detailed in the appropriate subsection of the **MAGICAL RESEARCH** rules.

Animal Control: This potion enables the imbiber to empathize with and control the emotions of animals of 1 type, i.e. cats, dogs, horses, etc. The number of animals so controlled depends upon size: 5-20 animals of the size of giant rats, 3-12 animals of about man-size, or 1-4 animals of about ½ ton or more in weight. The sort of animal which can be controlled depends upon the particular animal as indicated by die roll (d20):

1-4	mammal/marsupial
5-8	avian
9-12	reptile/amphibian
13-15	fish
16-17	mammal/marsupial/avian
18-19	reptile/amphibian/fish
20	all of the above

Animals with intelligence of 5 (low intelligence) or better are entitled to a saving throw versus magic. Control is limited to emotions or drives unless some form of communication is possible. Note that many monsters cannot be controlled by the use of this potion, nor can humans, demi-humans, or humanoids. (Cf. Ring of Mammal Control.)

Clairaudience: This potion empowers the creature drinking it to hear as the third level magic-user spell of the same name (q.v.). It can be used, however, to clairaudit unknown areas within 3''. Its effects last for 2 turns only.

Clairvoyance: This potion empowers the individual to see as the third level magic-user spell, clairvoyance (q.v.). It differs from the spell in that unknown areas up to 3'' distant can be seen. Its effects last for 1 turn only.

Climbing: Imbibing this potion enables the individual to climb as a thief, up or down vertical surfaces, with only a base 1% chance of slipping and falling. (Check at the halfway point, d%, 01 equals a fall.) A climbing potion is effective for 1 turn plus 5 to 20 rounds. For every 1,000 g.p. weight equivalent carried by the character, there is an additional 1% added to chance of slipping. If the climber wears armor, there are the following additions to the slipping/falling chance:

studded leather	1%
ring mail	2%
scale mail	4%
chainmail	7%
banded or splinted armor	8%
plate mail	10%
magic armor, any type	1%

Delusion: This potion affects the mind of the character so that he or she believes the liquid is some other potion (healing, for example, is a good choice — damage is "restored" by drinking it, and only death or rest after an adventure will reveal that the potion only caused the imbiber to believe that he or she was aided). If several individuals taste this potion, it is still 90% probable that they will all agree it is the same potion (or whatever type the DM announces or hints at).

Diminution: When this potion is quaffed, the individual, and all he or she carries and wears, will diminish in size to as small as 5% of normal size. If half of the contents are swallowed, the person shrinks to 50% of normal size. The effects of this potion last for 6 turns plus 2-5 turns (d4 + 1).

Dragon Control: This potion enables the individual drinking it to cast what is in effect a charm monster spell upon any dragon with 6''. The dragon is entitled to a saving throw versus magic, but it is made at –2 on the die. There are various sorts of dragon control potions, as shown below (d20):

1-2	white dragon control
3-4	black dragon control
5-7	green dragon control
8-9	blue dragon control
10	red dragon control
11-12	brass dragon control
13-14	copper dragon control
15	bronze dragon control
16	silver dragon control
17	gold dragon control
18-19	evil dragon control*
20	good dragon control**

* Black, blue, green, red, white.

** Brass, bronze, copper, gold, silver.

Control lasts for from 5-20 (5d4) rounds.

ESP: The ESP potion bestows an ability which is the same as the second level magic-user spell of the same name (q.v.), except that its effects last for 5-40 (5d8) rounds, i.e. 5 to 40 minutes.

Extra-Healing: This potion restores 6-27 (3d8 + 3) hit points of damage when wholly consumed, or 1-8 hit points of damage for each one-third potion.

Fire Resistance: This potion bestows magical invulnerability to all forms of normal fire (such as bonfires, burning oil, or even huge pyres of flaming wood) upon the person drinking it. It furthermore gives resistance to such fires as generated by molten lava, a *wall of fire*, a *fireball*, fiery dragon breath and similar intense flame/heat. All damage from such fires is reduced by −2 from each die of damage, and if a saving throw is applicable, it is made at +4. Note: If but one-half of the potion is consumed it confers invulnerability to normal fires and half the benefits noted above (−1, +2). The potion lasts 1 turn, or 5 rounds for half doses.

Flying: A flying potion enables the individual drinking it to fly in the same manner as the third level magic-user spell, *fly* (q.v.).

Gaseous Form: By imbibing this magical liquid, the individual causes his or her body, as well as what it carries and wears, to become gaseous in form and able to flow accordingly at a base speed of 3″/round. (A *gust of wind* spell, or even normal strong air currents, will blow the gaseous form backwards at air speed.) The gaseous form is transparent and insubstantial. It wavers and shifts. It cannot be harmed except by magical fires or lightnings, in which case damage is normal. A whirlwind will inflict double damage upon any creature in *gaseous form*. When in such condition the individual is able to enter any space which is not airtight, i.e., a small crack or hole which allows air to penetrate also allows entry by a creature in gaseous form. The entire potion must be consumed to achieve this result, and the effects last the entire duration.

Giant Control: A full potion of this draught must be drunk in order to make its effects be felt. It will influence 1 or 2 giants as if a *charm monster* spell were affecting them. If only 1 giant is so influenced, it is entitled to a saving throw versus magic at −4 on the die roll; if 2 are influenced the die rolls are at +2. The type of giant subject to a particular potion is randomly determined as follows:

1-5	hill giant
6-9	stone giant
10-13	frost giant
14-17	fire giant
18-19	cloud giant
20	storm giant

Control lasts for only 5-30 (5d6) rounds.

Giant Strength: When a *giant strength* potion is consumed the individual gains great strength and bonuses to damage when he or she scores a hit with any hand-held or thrown weapon. It is also possible for the person to hurl rocks as shown on the table below. Note that the type of *giant strength* gained by drinking the potion is randomly determined on the same table:

Die Score	Strength Equivalent	Weight Allow.	Damage Bonus	Rock Hurling Range	Rock Hurling Base Damage	Bend Bars/ Lift Gates
1-6	Hill Giant	+ 4,500	+ 7	8″	1-6	50%
7-10	Stone Giant	+ 5,000	+ 8	16″	1-12	60%
11-14	Frost Giant	+ 6,000	+ 9	10″	1-8	70%
15-17	Fire Giant	+ 7,500	+10	12″	1-8	80%
18-19	Cloud Giant	+ 9,000	+11	14″	1-10	90%
20	Storm Giant	+12,000	+12	16″	1-12	100%

Compare these abilities to the character *strength* ability and to the *girdle of giant strength*. The potion can be used only by fighters. Note this does not give the same powers as a *girdle*.

Growth: This potion causes the person consuming it to enlarge in both height and weight, his or her garments and other worn and carried gear likewise growing in size. Strength is increased sufficiently to allow bearing normal armor and weapons, but does not add to combat. Movement increases to that of a giant of approximately equal size. Each quarter of the potion consumed causes 6′ height growth, i.e. a full potion increases height by 24′.

Healing: An entire potion must be consumed in a single drinking (round) in order for this liquor to restore 4-10 (2d4 + 2) hit points of damage. (Cf. *extra-healing*.)

Heroism: This potion gives the imbiber a temporary increase in life energy levels if he or she has fewer than 10 levels of experience. This is shown below:

Level of Consumer	Number of Energy Levels Bestowed	10-sided Dice for Accumulated Damage Bestowed
0	4	4
1st-3rd	3	3 + 1
4th-6th	2	2 + 2
7th-9th	1	1 + 3

When the potion is quaffed, the individual fights as if he or she were at the experience level bestowed by the magic of the elixir. Damage sustained is taken first from magically gained hit dice and bonus points. This potion is restricted to use by men-at-arms and fighters.

Human Control: A potion of *human control* allows the imbiber to control up to 32 levels/hit dice of humans/humanoids/demi-humans as if a *charm person* spell had been cast, and the human types to be controlled are entitled to saving throws versus magic. Any pluses on hit dice are rounded *down* to the lowest whole die, i.e. 1 + 2 = 1, 2 + 6 = 2. The type of human(s) which can be controlled is randomly determined on the table below:

1-2	Dwarves
3-4	Elves/Half-Elves
5-6	Gnomes
7-8	Halflings
9-10	Half-Orcs
11-16	Humans
17-19	Humanoids (gnolls, orcs, goblins, etc.)
20	Elves, Half-Elves, and Humans

This potion lasts for from 5-30 rounds.

Invisibility: When this potion is consumed it confers *invisibility* similar to the spell of the same name (q.v.). As actions involving combat cause termination of the non-visible state, the individual possessing the potion can quaff a single gulp — equal to 1/8 of the contents of the container — to bestow *invisibility* for 3-6 turns.

Invulnerability: This potion confers immunity to non-magical weapons and attacks from creatures with no magical properties (see **CREATURES STRUCK ONLY BY MAGICAL WEAPONS**) or with fewer than 4 hit dice. Thus, an 8th level character without a magical weapon could not harm the imbiber of an *invulnerability* potion. It further improves armor class rating by 2 classes and gives a bonus of +2 to the individual on his or her saving throws versus all forms of attack. Its effects are realized only when the entire potion is consumed, and they last for 5-20 rounds. Only fighters can use this potion.

Levitation: A *levitation* potion enables the consumer to *levitate* in much the same manner as the second level magic-user spell of the same name (q.v.). The potion allows levitation of the individual only, subject to a maximum weight of 6,000 g.p. equivalent, so it is possible that the individual drinking the potion could carry another person.

Longevity: The *longevity* potion reduces the character's game age by from 1-12 years when it is imbibed, but each time one is drunk there is a 1% cumulative chance that it will have the effect of reversing all age removal from previously consumed *longevity* potions. The potion otherwise restores youth and vigor. It is also useful to counter magical or monster-based aging attacks. The entire potion must be consumed to achieve the results.

Oil of Etherealness: This potion is actually a light oil which is applied externally to the dress and exposed flesh. It then confers *etherealness*. In the ethereal state the individual can pass through solid objects — sideways, upwards, downwards — or to different *planes*. Naturally, the individual cannot touch non-ethereal objects. The oil takes effect 3 rounds after application and it lasts for 4 + 1-4 turns unless removed with a weak acidic solution prior to the expiration of its normal effective duration. It can be applied to objects as well as creatures; one potion is sufficient to anoint a normal human and such gear as he or she typically carries (2 or 3 weapons, garments, armor, shield, and the usual miscellaneous gear carried). Ethereal individuals are invisible. (Cf. *phase door* spell, and **TRAVEL IN THE KNOWN PLANES OF EXISTENCE** hereafter.)

Oil of Slipperiness: Similar to the *oil of etherealness* described above, this liquid is to be applied externally. This application makes it impossible for the individual to be grabbed or grasped/hugged by any opponent or constricted by snakes or tentacles. (Note that a roper could still inflict weakness, but that the monster's tentacles could not entwine the opponent coated with *oil of slipperiness*.) In addition, such obstructions as webs, magical or otherwise, will not affect an anointed individual; and bonds such as ropes, manacles, and chains can be slipped free. Magical ropes and the like are not effective against this oil. If poured on a floor or on steps there is a 95% chance/round that creatures standing on the surface will slip and fall. The oil lasts 8 hours to wear off normally, or it can be wiped off with an alcohol solution (such as wine).

Philter of Love: This potion is such as to cause the individual drinking it to become *charmed* (cf. *charm* spells) with the first creature seen after consuming the draught, or actually become enamored and *charmed* if the creature is of similar race and of the opposite sex. Charming effects wear off in 4 + 1-4 turns, but the enamoring effects last until a *dispel magic* spell is cast upon the individual.

Philter of Persuasiveness: When this potion is imbibed the individual becomes more charismatic. Thus, he or she gains a bonus of 25% on reaction dice rolls. The individual is also able to *suggest* (cf. the magic-user *suggestion* spell) once per turn to as many creatures as are within a range of 3″ of him or her.

Plant Control: A *plant control* potion enables the individual who consumed it to influence the behavior of vegetable life forms — including normal plants, fungi, and even molds and shambling mounds — within the parameters of their normal abilities. The imbiber can cause the vegetable forms to remain still/silent, move, entwine, etc. according to their limits. Vegetable monsters with intelligence of 5 or higher are entitled to a saving throw versus magic. Plants within a 2″ × 2″ square can be controlled subject to the limitations set forth above, for from 5-20 rounds. Self-destructive control is not directly possible if the plants are intelligent. (Cf. *charm plants* spell.) Control range is 9″.

Poison: A *poison* potion is simply a highly toxic liquid in a potion flask. Typically, *poison* potions are odorless and of any color. Ingestion, introduction of the poison through a break in the skin, or possibly just skin contact, will cause death. Poison can be weak (+4 to +1 on saving throw), average, or deadly (−1 to −4 or more on the saving throw). Some poison can be such that a *neutralize poison* spell will simply lower the toxicity level by 40% — say from a -4 to a +4 on saving throw potion. You might wish to allow characters to hurl poison flasks (see **COMBAT**).

Polymorph (self): This potion duplicates the effects of the fourth level magic-user spell of the same name (q.v.) in most respects.

Speed: A potion of *speed* increases the movement and combat capabilities of the imbiber by 100%. Thus, a movement rate of 9″ becomes 18″, and a character normally able to attack but once per round would gain double attacks in a round. Note that this does not reduce spell casting time, however (cf. *haste* spell). Use of a *speed* potion ages the individual by 1 year. The other effects last for 5-20 rounds, the aging is permanent.

Super-Heroism: This potion gives the individual a temporary increase in life energy levels (cf. *heroism* potion) if he or she has fewer than 13 levels of experience:

Level of Consumer	Number of Energy Levels Bestowed	10-sided Dice for Accumulated Damage Bestowed
0	6	5
1st-3rd	5	4 + 1
4th-6th	4	3 + 2
7th-9th	3	2 + 3
10th-12th	2	1 + 4

It is otherwise the same as a *heroism* potion, but its effects last from but 5 to 30 melee rounds.

Sweet Water: This liquid is not actually a potion to be drunk (though if it is drunk it will taste good), but it is to be added to other liquids in order to change them to pure, drinkable water. It will neutralize poison and ruin magic potions (no saving throw). The contents of the container will change up to 100,000 cubic feet of polluted or salt or alkaline water to fresh water. It will turn up to 1,000 cubic feet of acid into pure water. The effects

of the potion are permanent, but subject to later contamination or infusion after an initial period of 5-20 rounds.

Treasure Finding: A potion of *treasure finding* empowers the drinker with a location sense, so that he or she can point to the direction of the nearest mass of treasure. The treasure must be within 24″ or less, and its mass must equal metal of at least 10,000 copper pieces or 100 gems or any combination thereof. Note that only valuable metals (copper, silver, electrum, gold, platinum, etc.) and gems (and jewelry, of course) are located; worthless metals or magic without precious metals/gems are not found. The consumer of the potion can "feel" the direction in which the treasure lies, but not its distance. Intervening substances other than special magical wards or lead-lined walls will not withstand the powers which the liquor bestows upon the individual. The effects of the potion last for from 5-20 rounds. (Clever players will attempt triangulation.)

Undead Control: This potion in effect gives the imbiber the ability to *charm* certain undead (ghasts, ghosts, ghouls, shadows, skeletons, spectres, wights, wraiths, vampires, and zombies). The *charming* ability is similar to the magic-user spell, *charm person* (q.v.). It affects a maximum of 16 hit dice of undead, rounding down any hit point additions to hit dice to the lowest die, i.e. 4 + 1 equals 4 hit dice. The undead are entitled to saving throws versus magic only if they have intelligence. Saving throws are made at −2 due to the power of the potion, but the effects wear off in from 5-20 rounds. To determine type of undead affected by a particular potion, roll d10 and consult the following table:

Die Roll	Undead Type
1	Ghasts
2	Ghosts
3	Ghouls
4	Shadows
5	Skeletons
6	Spectres
7	Wights
8	Wraiths
9	Vampires
0	Zombies

Water Breathing: It is 75% likely that a *water breathing* potion will contain two doses, 25% probable that there will be four in the container. The elixir allows the character drinking it to breathe normally in liquids which contain oxygen suspended within them. This ability lasts for one full hour per dose of potion quaffed, with an additional 1-10 rounds (minutes) variable. Thus, a character who has consumed a *water breathing* potion could enter the depths of a river, lake, or even the ocean and not drown while the magical effects of the potion persisted.

SCROLLS (III.B.)

Scrolls will generally be found in cylinders — tubes of ivory, jade, leather, metal, or wood. You may require that players read certain magic runes/writings inscribed on tubes in order to open the container in some cases. This enables you to have *read magic* (or *comprehend languages*) spells taken and used, as well as giving the possibility for traps (*symbols*, *explosive runes*) and curses along with a powerful scroll.

Each scroll is written in its own magical cypher, so to understand what sort of scroll has been found the ability to *read magic* must be available. Once a scroll is read to determine its contents, a *read magic* will not be needed at a subsequent time to invoke the magic. Note that even a *map* will appear magical until the proper spell is used. Reading a scroll to find its contents does not invoke its magic unless it is a specially triggered *curse*. The latter scroll appears to be a scroll of any sort. It radiates no evil or special aura beyond the magical.

Scrolls not read to determine contents immediately are from 5% to 30% likely to fade; it is your option to set the percentage or use a d6 to randomly determine it for each scroll.

When scrolls are examined, the following table can be used to find their nature:

First Roll	Second Roll
01-70 Magic-user	then 01-10 Illusionist
71-00 Cleric	then 01-25 Druid

Only the indicated class of character can use the scroll, except thieves.

Protection scrolls can be read by *any* class or race of character even with-out a magic spell.

Spell Level of Scroll Spells: All scroll spells are assumed to be written so as to make it as easy and quick as possible for the writer. Thus, the level of the spell, its characteristics with respect to range, duration, area of effect, etc., where level is a factor, is typically but 1 level higher than that required to actually use the spell, but *never below 6th level of experience.* Thus, a sixth level magic-user spell is written at 13th level of ability, a seventh at 15th level, etc. A scroll *fireball* or *lightning bolt* spell is of 6 dice (6d6) in most cases, but as DM you may decide to make certain scroll spells more powerful by increasing the level at which they are written; however, this will certainly affect the chance of spell failure as given below:

Magic Spell Failure: If a spell-user acquires a scroll with a spell(s) of a level(s) not yet usable by the character, the spell-user may still attempt to use the spell; the chance of failure, or other bad effect, is 5% per level difference between the character's present level and the level of magic use at which the spell could be used. For example, a 1st level magic-user finds a scroll with a *wish* spell inscribed upon it. The chance of failure is 85%, as *wish* is a spell of 9th level magic attained at 18th level of magic use — 18 − 1 = 17 × 5% = 85%. Dice are rolled, and any score of 85 or less indicates failure of some sort, and the following table is consulted:

Level Difference	Total Failure	Reverse or Harmful Effect
1-3	95%	5%
4-6	85%	15%
7-9	75%	25%
10-12	65%	35%
13-15	50%	50%
16 and up	30%	70%

Use of Scroll Spells: When any given scroll is read for purposes of copying the spell's formula (so as to be able to "know" it) or to release its magic, the writing completely and permanently disappears from the scroll. The magic content of the spell is bound up in the writing, and use releases and erases it. Thus, reading a spell from a scroll of 7 spells makes the thing a scroll of 6 spells. No matter what a player may attempt, a *scroll* spell is usable but once and once only. No exceptions should be made save in the case where you have a special magic item in mind — perhaps a scroll which can be read from once per week or whatever — and always only in rare finds.

Note Regarding Use Of Scroll Spells: Those characters able to read and employ scroll spells may do so regardless of other restrictions, and once the spell is known, it is not necessary to use a special *read magic* in order to effect its powers. Reading of such scrolls is possible even to magic-users who are otherwise unable to employ such a spell for any reason whatsoever, be it inability to learn or above level of use — although in the latter case there is a chance of spell failure (q.v.). Ability to use scroll spells does not permit a cleric to use a druid spell, a magic-user spell, or a magic-user to use a cleric spell. Likewise, it does not extend the ability of spell use to non-spell-using characters except with respect to *protection* scrolls.

Spell Level Range: This gives the parameters for random determination of spell level for those scrolls you do not set beforehand. When spell level is determined it is a simple matter to randomly find which particular spell it is by consulting the appropriate **SPELL TABLES** (cf. **PLAYER'S HANDBOOK**).

Protection Scrolls:

Protection from Demons: This scroll requires 1 full round to read if it is to protect against all sorts of demons, including demon princes, 7 segments to protect against demons of type VI or lower, and only 3 segments to protect against type III or lower. The circle of protection generated springs outwards from the scroll reader in a 10' radius. No demon protected against can penetrate the circle physically or magically or in any way, but the person(s) within can launch attacks, if otherwise possible, upon demons. The protection moves with the reader of the scroll. Its effect lasts for 5-20 (5d4) rounds.

Note that the protection radius is not an actual physical globe, and if the user forces a demon into a place from which further retreat is impossible (e.g., a corner), and then continues forward until the demon would be within the radius of the circle, the demon is *not* harmed, and the protection

is considered voluntarily broken and disappears. There is no way in which this can be used as an offensive weapon.

Protection from Devils: This scroll is nearly identical to the *protection from devils* scroll. It requires 1 round to read if it is to protect against all kinds of devils, including arch-devils, 7 segments to protect against greater devils or lower, and 3 segments to protect against lesser devils or lower.

Protection from Elementals: Reading time: 6 segments. There are 5 varieties of this scroll:

01-15	*Protection from Air Elementals* (including aerial servants, djinn, invisible stalkers, and wind walkers)
16-30	*Protection from Earth Elementals* (including xorn)
31-45	*Protection from Fire Elementals* (including efreet and salamanders)
46-60	*Protection from Water Elementals* (including tritons and water weirds)
61-00	*Protection from All Elementals*

The magic protects the reader and all within 10' of him or her from the kind of elemental noted, as well as elemental creatures of the same, or all, planes. The circle of protection affects a maximum of 24 hit dice of elemental creatures if the scroll is of a *specific* elemental type, 16 hit dice if it is against *all* sorts of elementals. The spell lasts for 5-40 (5d8) rounds. Attack out of the circle is possible, as is attack into it by any elemental creature with more hit dice than are protected against or by several elemental creatures — those in excess of the protected number of hit dice being able to enter and attack.

Protection from Lycanthropes: Reading time: 4 segments. There are 7 types of this scroll:

01-05	*Protection from Werebears*
06-10	*Protection from Wereboars*
11-20	*Protection from Wererats*
21-25	*Protection from Weretigers*
26-40	*Protection from Werewolves*
41-98	*Protection from all Lycanthropes*
99-00	*Protection from Shape-Changers*

The magic circle from the reading of the scroll extends in a 10' radius. It moves with the person who read the scroll. Each scroll protects against 49 hit dice of lycanthrope(s), rounding all hit points pluses downwards unless they exceed +2. The protection is otherwise similar to that against elementals. The *protection from shape-changers* scroll protects against monsters (except gods and god-like creatures) able to change their form to that of man; i.e. dopplegangers, certain dragons, druids, jackalwere, and those under the influence of polymorph spells, as well as all actual lycanthropes. The magic lasts for 5-30 rounds.

Protection from Magic: Reading time: 8 segments. This scroll invokes a very powerful and invisible globe of anti-magic in a 5' radius from the reader. It prevents any form of magic from passing into or out of its confines, but normal things are not restricted by it. As with other protections, the globe of anti-magic moves with its invoker. Any magical item which touches the globe must be saved for with a 50% likelihood of the object being drained of all magic from the power of the globe, i.e. save equals 11 or better with d20. The protection lasts for 5-30 (5d6) rounds.

If multiple magic items encounter the globe simultaneously, the leading item (a magic sword held in advance of its holder, for instance) is the first affected, then the others are checked in order of decreasing power until the first item fails its save, at which time the globe is cancelled and the item is drained of its magic.

Protection from Petrification: Reading time: 5 segments: A 10' radius circle of protection extends from, and moves with, the reader of this scroll. All within its confines are absolutely immune to any attack forms, magical or otherwise, which cause flesh to turn to stone. The protection lasts for 5-20 (5d4) rounds.

Protection from Possession: Reading time: 1 round. This scroll generates a magic circle of 10' radius which extends from, and moves with, the reader. All creatures within its confines are protected from possession by magical spell attacks such as *magic jar*; attack forms aimed at possession or mental control or psychic energy drain which are psionically based or magically based; or demon, devil, night hag, or similar creature possession (obsession). This protects even dead bodies if they are within the magic circle. The protection lasts for 10 to 60 rounds in 90% of these scrolls; 10% have power which lasts 10 to 60 turns, but the protection is *stationary*.

Protection from Undead: Reading time: 4 segments. When this scroll is read a 5' radius circle of protection extends from, and moves with, the reader. It protects all within its circumference from all physical attacks from undead (ghasts, ghosts, ghouls, shadows, skeletons, spectres, wights, wraiths, vampires, zombies) but not magic spells or other attack forms. If a creature leaves the protected area it is then subject to physical attack as well. The protection will restrain up to 35 hit dice/levels of undead; excess hit dice/levels can pass through the circle. It remains in effect for 10-80 (10d8) rounds. Note: some *protection* scrolls of this nature will protect only against certain types of undead (one or more) rather than all undead, at the DM's option. (Cf. POTIONS, *Undead Control* for a die roll table.)

Special Note: All *protection* scrolls are cumulative in effect but not in duration.

RINGS (III.C.)

All magic rings will normally radiate magic, but most are impossible to detect as magic rings without some mystic means. Furthermore, all magic rings look alike, so that determination of a given ring's magical powers is very difficult. The ring must be put on and various things tried in order to find what it does. This requires patience on your part, but the game demands it. No ring radiates good or evil.

No more than 2 magic rings can be worn by a character at the same time. If more are worn, then none will function. No more than 1 magic ring can be worn on the same hand; a 2nd will cause both to be useless. Rings must be worn on the fingers. Rings on toes, in ear lobes, etc. do not function as magic rings.

Rings' spell-like abilities function as 12th level of magic use unless the power requires a higher level of magic use. The latter function at the minimum level of magic use necessary to cast the equivalent spell.

Magic rings can be worn and used by all character classes and humans/-humanoids not specifically prohibited elsewhere. You might allow "monsters" with digits to wear rings, and some can actually benefit from them. For example, a troll ("thin and rubbery") could wear a *ring of regeneration* and gain its benefits in addition to its normal regenerative abilities.

Rings can be used by any race of character, but those worn by gnomes, dwarves, and halflings have a 20% chance per use of malfunctioning. If a malfunction occurs the ring simply does not work. This applies to cursed rings (*contrariness, delusion, weakness*) as well; if they do not work they are recognized and can be removed.

Note: The symbol ‡ appearing on the RINGS table (III.C.) and in the following descriptions denotes rings of the most powerful magical abilities, which will often possess a limited number of magical charges at the option of the DM.

Ring of Contrariness: This magic ring is cursed so as to make its wearer unable to agree with any idea or statement or action. Once put on, the ring can be removed only after a *remove curse* spell is cast upon the individual wearing it. Because of the curse, the wearer will resist any attempts to cast such a spell. Furthermore, the *contrariness* ring will have one of the following additional magical properties:

01-20	*Flying*
21-40	*Invisibility*
41-60	*Levitation*
61-70	*Shocking Grasp* (once per round)
71-80	*Spell Turning*
81-00	*Strength* (18/00)

Note that *contrariness* can *never* be removed from the ring. The wearer will use his or her own powers, plus those of the ring, to retain it on his or her finger. The wearer of the ring will never damage him or herself. If, for example, other characters suggest that the wearer should make certain that attacks upon him or her are well-defended against, or that he or she should not strike his or her own head, the ring wearer will *agree* — possibly attacking or striking at the speaker's head — because obviously the

result must be contrary in this case. If a *ring* of *contrariness* turns spells, the cumulative *remove curse* cast upon the individual wearing it must equal or exceed 00 (100%).

Ring of Delusion: A *delusion ring* will convince the wearer that it is some other sort of ring, a ring of whatever sort the wearer really desires. As the wearer will be completely convinced that the ring is actually one with other magical properties, he or she will unconsciously use his or her abilities of any sort (including those of other magical items available) to actually produce a result commensurate with the supposed properties of the *delusion ring*. As referee, you will have to be most judicious in determining how successful the self-delusion can be, as well as how observers can be affected and what they will observe. The ring can be removed at any time.

Djinni Summoning‡: One of the many fabled rings of fantasy legend, the "genie" ring is most useful indeed, for it is a special "gate" by means of which a certain djinni can be summoned from the Elemental Plane of Air. When the ring is rubbed the summons is served, and the djinni will appear on the next round. The djinni will faithfully obey and serve the wearer of the ring, but if the servant of the ring is ever killed, the ring becomes non-magical and worthless. See **ADVANCED DUNGEONS & DRAGONS, MONSTER MANUAL**, for details of a djinni's abilities and capabilities.

Ring of Elemental Command: The 4 types of *elemental command* rings are very powerful. Each appears to be nothing more than a lesser ring (detailed below), but each has certain other powers as well as the following common properties:

1. Elementals of the plane to which the ring is attuned cannot approach within 5' of or attack the wearer; or, if the wearer desires, he or she may forego this protection and instead attempt to *charm* the elemental (saving throw applicable at –2 on the die). If the latter fails, however, total protection is lost and no further attempt at charming can be made, but the secondary properties given below will then function with respect to the elemental.

2. Creatures, other than normal elementals, from the plane to which the ring is attuned attack at –1 on their "to hit" dice, the ring wearer takes damage at –1 on each hit die, makes applicable saving throws from the creature's attacks at +2, all attacks are made by the wearer of the ring at +4 "to hit" (or –4 on the elemental creature's saving throw), and the wearer does +6 damage (total, not per die) adjusted by any other applicable bonuses and/or penalties. Any weapon used by the ring wearer can hit elementals or elemental creatures even if it is not magical.

3. The wearer of the ring is able to converse with the elementals or elemental creatures of the plane to which the ring is attuned, and they will recognize that he or she wears the ring, so they are at least going to show a healthy respect to the wearer. If alignment is opposed, this respect will be *fear* if the wearer is strong, *hatred* and a *desire to slay* if the wearer is weak.

4. In addition, the possessor of a *ring of elemental command* will suffer a saving throw penalty as follows:

Air	–2 vs. fire
Earth	–2 vs. petrification
Fire	–2 vs. water or cold
Water	–2 vs. lightning/electricity

5. Only one power (whether major or minor) of a *ring of elemental command* can be in use at one time.

—Air: The wearer can at will produce the following magical effects:

> *gust of wind* (once per round)
> *fly*
> *wall of force* (once per day)
> *control winds* (once per week)
> *invisibility*

The ring will appear to be nothing other than an *invisibility ring* until a certain condition is met (such as having the ring *blessed*, slaying an air elemental, or whatever you determine as necessary to activate its full potential).

—Earth: The wearer can at will produce the following magical effects:

stone tell (once per day)
passwall (twice per day)
wall of stone (once per day)
stone to flesh (twice per week)
move earth (once per week)
feather fall

The ring will appear to be nothing other than a *ring of feather falling* until the condition you establish is met.

—Fire: The wearer can at will produce the following magical effects:

burning hands (once per turn)
pyrotechnics (twice per day)
wall of fire (once per day)
flame strike (twice per week)
fire resistance

The ring will appear to be nothing other than a *ring of fire resistance* until the condition you establish is met.

—Water: The wearer can at will produce the following magical effects:

purify water
create water (once per day)
water breathing (5' radius)
wall of ice (once per day)
airy water
lower water (twice per week)
part water (twice per week)
water walking

The ring will appear to be nothing other than a *ring of water walking* until the condition you establish is met.

Rings operate at 12th level of experience, or the minimum level needed to perform the equivalent magic spell, if greater, with respect to range, duration, or area of effect determinations which might apply. The additional powers take only 5 segments to bring forth.

Ring of Feather Falling: This ring protects its wearer by automatic activation of a *feather fall* if the individual falls 5' or more. (Cf. *feather fall* spell.)

Ring of Fire Resistance: The wearer of this ring is totally immune to the effects of normal fires — torches, flaming oil, bonfires, etc. Very large and hot fires, molten lava, demon immolation, hell hound breath, or a *wall of fire* spell will cause 10 hit points of damage per round (1 per segment) if the wearer is directly within such conflagration. Exceptionally hot fires such as red dragon breath, pyrohydra breath, *fireballs*, *flame strike*, *fire storm*, etc. are saved against at +4 on the die roll, and all damage dice are calculated at –2 per die, but each die is never less than 1 in any event. (As a rule of thumb, consider very hot fires as those which have a maximum initial exposure of up to 24 hit points, those of exceptional heat 25 or more hit points.)

Ring of Free Action: This ring enables the wearer to move and attack freely and normally whether attacked by a *web*, *hold*, or *slow* spell, or even while under water. In the former case the spells have no effect, while in the latter the individual moves at normal (surface) speed and does full damage even with such cutting weapons as axes and scimitars and with such smashing weapons as flails, hammers, and maces, insofar as the weapon used is held rather than hurled. This will not, however, enable *water breathing* without the further appropriate magic.

Ring of Human Influence‡: This ring has the effect of raising the wearer's charisma to 18 with respect to encounter reactions with humans/humanoids. The wearer can make a *suggestion* to any human or humanoid conversed with (saving throw applies). The wearer can also *charm* up to 21 levels/hit dice of human/humanoids (saving throws apply) just as if he or she were using the magic-user spell, *charm person*. The two latter uses of the ring are applicable but once per day. *Suggestion* or *charm* requires 3 segments of casting time.

Ring of Invisibility: The wearer of an *invisibility ring* is able to become invisible at will, instantly, This non-visible state is exactly the same as the magic-user *invisibility* spell (q.v.), except that 10% of these rings also have *inaudibility* as well, making the wearer absolutely silent. If the wearer wishes to speak, he or she breaks all silence features in order to do so.

Ring of Mammal Control‡: This ring enables its wearer to exercise complete control over mammals with intelligence of 4 or less (*animal* or *semi*-intelligent mammals). Up to 30 hit dice of mammals can be controlled. Control extends to such limits as to enable the wearer to have the creatures controlled actually kill themselves, but complete concentration is required. (Note: the ring does not affect bird-mammal combinations, humans, semi-humans, and monsters such as lammasu, shedu, manticores, etc.) If you are in doubt about any monster, it is NOT a mammal.

Obviously, rats, weasels, herd animals, dolphins, and even unicorns are mammals, but intelligence will preclude control of the better ones. Control time is 3 segments.

Ring of Multiple Wishes‡: This ring contains from 2-8 (2d4) *wish* spells (q.v.). As with any *wish*, you must be very judicious in how you handle the request. If players are greedy and grasping, be sure to "crock" them. Interpret their wording exactly, twist the wording, or simply rule the request is beyond the power of the magic. In any case, the *wish* is used up, whether or not (or how) the *wish* was granted. Note that no *wish* is able to cancel the decrees of god-like beings, unless it comes from another such creature.

Ring of Protection: A *ring of protection* increases the wearer's armor class value and saving throws versus all forms of attack. A +1 ring raises AC by 1, say from 10 to 9 and gives a bonus of +1 on saving throw die rolls. The magical properties of a *ring of protection* are cumulative with all other magical items of protection except as follows:

1. The ring does not add to armor value if magical armor is worn, although it does add to saving throw die rolls.

2. More than 1 *ring of protection* operating on the same person, or in the same area, do not combine protection; only one — the strongest, if applicable — will function, so a pair of +2 *protection* rings are still only +2.

To determine the value of the protection ring use the table below:

01-70	+1
71-82	+2
83	+2, 5' radius protection
84-90	+3
91	+3, 5' radius protection
92-97	+4 on AC, +2 on saving throws
98-00	+6 on AC, +1 on saving throws

The *radius* bonus of 5' extends to all creatures within its circle, but applies only to their saving throws, i.e. only the ring wearer gains armor class additions.

Ring of Regeneration: There are 2 forms of this ring: The standard *regeneration ring* restores 1 hit point of damage (and will replace lost limbs or organs eventually also) per turn. It will bring its wearer back from death (but if poison is the cause, the saving throw must be made or else the wearer dies again from the poison still in his or her system). Only total destruction of all living tissue by fire or acid or similar means will prevent *regeneration*. Of course the ring must be worn, and its removal stops regeneration processes. The rare form is the *vampiric regeneration ring*. This ring bestows one-half of the value of hit points of damage the wearer inflicts upon opponents in hand-to-hand (melee, non-missile, non-spell) combat immediately upon its wearer (fractions dropped). It does not otherwise cause regeneration or restore life, limb or organ. To determine which type of ring is discovered roll percentile dice: 01-90 = *ring of regeneration*, 91-00 = *vampiric regeneration ring*. In no case can the wearer's hit point total exceed that initially generated.

Ring of Shooting Stars: This ring has 2 modes of operation, both working only in relative darkness. During night hours, under the open sky, the *shooting stars ring* will perform the following functions:

dancing lights (once per hour) — as the spell
light (twice per night), 12" range — as the spell
ball lightning (once per night) — see below
shooting stars (special) — see below

The *ball lightning* function releases 1 to 4 balls of lightning at the wearer's option. These glowing globes exactly resemble *dancing lights*, and the ring wearer controls them as he or she would control *dancing lights*. These spheres have a 12″ range and a 4 round duration. They can be moved at 4″ per round. Each sphere is about 3′ in diameter, and any creature it touches or comes near to dissipates its charge (save versus magic equals one-half damage as the contact was across an air gap). The charge values are:

4 lightning balls	2-8 hit points damage each
3 lightning balls	2-12 hit points damage each
2 lightning balls	5-20 hit points damage each
1 lightning ball	4-48 hit points damage

Release can be simultaneous or singular, during the course of 1 round or as needed throughout the night.

The *shooting stars* are glowing missiles with fiery trails, much like a *meteor swarm*. 3 *shooting stars* can be released from the ring each week, simultaneously or one at a time. They impact for 12 hit points of damage and burst (as a *fireball*) in a 1″ diameter sphere for 24 hit points of damage. Any creature struck will take full damage from impact plus full damage from the *shooting star* burst. Creatures within the burst radius must save versus magic to take only one-half damage, i.e. 12 hit points of damage, otherwise they too take the full 24 hit points of damage. Range is 7″, at the end of which the burst will occur, unless an object or creature is struck before that. The *shooting stars* follow a straight line path. A creature in the path must save versus magic or be impacted upon by the missile, and saving throw rolls are at -3 within 2″ of the ring wearer, -1 within 2″ to 4″, normal beyond 4″.

Indoors at night, or underground, the ring has the following properties:

faerie fire (twice per day) — as the spell
spark shower (once per day) — see below

The *spark shower* is a flying cloud of sizzling purple sparks, which fan out from the ring for 20′ to a breadth of 10′. Creatures within this area take from 2-8 hit points of damage each if no metallic armor is worn or no metallic weapon is held, 4-16 otherwise.

Range, duration, and area of effect of functions are the minimum for the comparable spell unless otherwise stated. Casting time is 5 segments.

Ring of Spell Storing: A *ring of spell storing* will contain 2-5 (d4 + 1) spells which the wearer can employ just as if he or she were a spell user of the level appropriate to use the spell in question. The class of spells contained within the ring is determined in the same fashion as the spells on scrolls. The level of each spell is determined as follows:

cleric: d6, if 6 is rolled roll d4 instead
druid: as cleric
magic-user: d8, if 8 is rolled roll d6 instead
illusionist: as cleric

Which spell type of any given level is contained by the ring is also randomly determined. The ring has the empathic ability to impart to the wearer the names of its spells. Once class, level, and type are determined, the properties of the ring are *fixed* and *unchangeable*. Once a spell is cast from the ring, it can only be restored by a character of appropriate class and level of experience, i.e. a 12th level magic-user is needed to restore a 6th level magic-user spell to the ring. Spells stored require 5 segments each to cast.

Ring of Spell Turning: This ring distorts the three normal dimensions with respect to magic spells directed at its wearer. Any spell cast at an individual will usually rebound, in part or perhaps in whole, upon the spell caster. The distance between, and area occupied by, the victim (the ring wearer) and the spell caster are not as they seem when the magic activates the *spell turning* ring. Three important exceptions must be noted:

1. Spells which affect an area, and which are not cast directly at the ring wearer, are not turned by the ring.

2. Spells which are delivered by touch are not turned.

3. Magic contained in devices (rods, staves, wands, rings, and other items) which are triggered without spell casting are not turned. Note: a scroll spell is *not* considered a device.

When a spell is cast at an individual wearing a *ring of spell turning* percentile dice are rolled and rounded to the nearest decimal, i.e. 1-5 is

dropped, 6-9 adds 10, so 05 equals 0%, but 96 equals 100%. The score of the percentile dice indicates what portion of the spell has been turned back upon its caster.

Damage is determined and awarded proportionately. Saving throws (for both opponents) are adjusted upwards by +1 for each 10% below 100%, i.e. 80% = +2, 70% = +3, . . .10% = +9. Even with such adjustments in saving throw it is possible that both target individual and spell caster will end up polymorphed into bullfrogs!

Note Regarding Ring of Spell Turning: Unless the percentile dice score for the *turning* effect is 09 or less or 91 or more, this ring will allow a saving throw against spells which normally have none. The effect of the save will be to negate or inflict half normal damage as appropriate to the spell in question. For each 10% of the spell *turned*, allow a 5% chance (1 in 20) to save. Thus, if 11-19 is rolled, a roll of 20 saves, 20-29 allows a 19-20 to save, 30-39 allows 18-20, and so on. Example: An illusionist casts a *maze* spell upon a fighter wearing a *ring of spell turning*. The *maze* spell normally allows no saving throw, but the ring turns 34% of the spell effect. The fighter has a 15% chance to save against the spell (34% on the *turning*); otherwise it will take full normal effect. The illusionist must also save (100% – 34% = 66%, or 6 10% increments, which converts to a 30% chance to save) by rolling a 15-20 or be *mazed* also. Saving in this case will negate spell effect. This special saving throw is NOT modified by race, magic items, or any other condition, including existing spells.

Spells which affect a certain number of levels which are aimed at the ring wearer must be able to affect as many levels as the wearer and the spell caster combined. If this condition is fulfilled, then the procedure above applies to ultimate effect determination.

In the case of the ring wearer desiring to receive a spell, he or she must remove the *spell turning* ring to be able to do so.

Psionic attacks are not considered as spell casting.

If the spell caster and spell recipient both wear *spell turning* rings a resonating field is set up, and one of the following results will take place:

01-70	spell drains away without effect
71-80	spell affects both equally at full effect
81-97	both rings are drained permanently
98-00	both individuals go through a rift into the *Positive Material Plane*

Ring of Swimming: The *ring of swimming* bestows the ability to swim at a full 21″ base speed upon the wearer, assuming, of course, he or she is clad only in garments appropriate for such activity. It further enables the wearer to dive up to 50′ into water without injury, providing the depth of the water is at least 1½′ per 10′ of diving elevation; and the wearer can stay underwater for up to 4 rounds without needing a breath of air. Surface swimming can continue for 4 hours before a 1 hour (floating) rest is needed. The ring confers the ability to stay afloat under all but typhoon-like conditions.

Ring of Telekinesis‡: This ring enables the wearer to telekinese objects in the same manner as the fifth level magic-user spell, *telekinesis* (q.v.). The amount of weight which can be so moved, however, is variable. Roll percentile dice to find the strength of the ring:

01-25	250 g.p. maximum
26-50	500 g.p. maximum
51-89	1,000 g.p. maximum
90-99	2,000 g.p. maximum
00	4,000 g.p. maximum

Telekinesis time is only 1 segment to begin the effect.

Ring of Three Wishes: Although the ring contains 3 *wish* spells instead of a variable number, it is otherwise the same as a *multiple wish* ring except that 25% (01-25) contain 3 *limited wish* spells (q.v.).

Ring of Warmth: A *warmth* ring provides its wearer with body heat even in conditions of extreme cold where the wearer has no clothing whatsoever. It also provides restoration of cold-sustained damage at the rate of 1 hit point of damage per turn. It increases saving throws versus cold-based attacks by +2 and reduces damage sustained by -1 per die.

Ring of Water Walking: This ring enables the wearer to walk upon any liquid without sinking into it; this includes mud, quicksand, oil, running water, and even snow. The ring wearer's feet do not actually contact the surface he or she is walking upon when liquid or water is being walked upon (but oval depressions about 1½' long and 1 inch deep per 100 pounds of weight of the walker will be observed in hardening mud or set snow). Rate of movement is standard movement for the individual wearing the ring. Up to 1,200 pounds weight can be supported by a *water walking* ring.

Ring of Weakness: This cursed ring causes the wearer to lose 1 point of strength and 1 point of constitution per turn until the individual reaches 3 in each ability area. This loss is not noticeable until the individual actually observes his or her weakened state due to some exertion (such as combat or heavy lifting), for the ring will also make the wearer *invisible* at will (and also cause the rate of strength and constitution point loss to double). Note that when full *weakness* is attained the wearer will be unable to function in his or her class. The *weakness* ring can be removed only if a *remove curse* spell, followed by a *dispel magic* spell, is cast upon the ring. There is a 5% chance that the ring is reversed, being a *ring of berserk strength*. This form gradually increases strength and constitution to 18 each (roll percentile dice for bonus strength if the wearer is a fighter). Increase is 1 point per ability per turn. However, once 18s in both abilities are reached, the wearer will always melee with any opponent he or she meets, immediately, regardless of circumstances. Points lost from the ring are restored by rest on a 1 day for 1 point basis, with 1 point of each ability lost being restored in 1 day of rest. Berserk strength is lost when the ring is removed, as are constitution points gained.

Ring of Wizardry: Only magic-users can benefit from this type of ring. Other classes, even those with spell ability, can neither use nor understand the working of a *ring of wizardry*. The ring *doubles* spell ability (i.e. the number of spells a magic-user may prepare each day) in one or more spell levels. To determine the properties of a given ring use the table below:

01-50	doubles first level spells
51-75	doubles second level spells
76-82	doubles third level spells
83-88	doubles first and second level spells
89-92	doubles fourth level spells
93-95	doubles fifth level spells
96-99	doubles first through third level spells
00	doubles fourth and fifth level spells

Ring of X-Ray Vision: A *ring of X-ray vision* empowers its possessor with the ability to see into and/or through substances which are impenetrable to normal sight. Vision range is 20', with the viewer seeing as if it were normal light due to expanded vision capability. *X-ray vision* will penetrate 20' of cloth, wood, or similar animal or vegetable material, up to 10' of stone or 10 inches of many metals:

Substance Scanned	Thickness Penetrated per Round of X-Raying	Maximum Thickness
Animal matter	4'	20'
Vegetable matter	2½'	20'
Stone	1'	10'
Iron, Steel, etc.	1 inch	10 inches
Lead, Gold, Platinum	*nil*	*nil*

It is possible to scan 100 square feet of area during 1 round; thus during 1 turn the wearer of the ring could scan a full area of stone 10' wide, 10' high and 10' thick, or 100' wide, 10' high, and 1' thick. Secret compartments, drawers, recesses, and doors are 90% likely to be located by X-ray vision scanning. Even though this ring enables its wearer to scan secret doors, traps, hidden items, and the like, it also limits his or her use of the power, for it drains 1 point of constitution if used more frequently than once every 6 turns. If it is used 3 turns in 1 hour the user loses 2 points from his or her total constitution score, 3 if used 4 turns, etc. Constitution loss is recovered at the rate of 2 points per day of rest. Constitution of 2 means the wearer is exhausted and *must* rest immediately. No activity, not even walking, can be performed until constitution of 3 or better is restored.

RODS, *et al.* (Including Staves and Wands) (III.D.)

Rods are about 3' long and as thick as your thumb. Staves are about 5' or 6' long and as thick as a young sapling, i.e. about an inch and a half at the base, tapering to an inch at the tip, although they can be of nearly equal diameter throughout, knurled, etc. Wands are 1¼' long and slender. Rods

are fashioned from metal, strange wood, ivory or bone. They can be plain or decorated and carved, tipped or not. Staves are typically fashioned of wood, often carved, usually metal bound and shod, and likely to be gnarly and twisted. They can be unusual or appear to be ordinary. Wands are of ivory, bone, or wood and are usually tipped with something — metal, crystal, stone, etc. They are fragile and tend to break easily.

Rods and wands will usually be found in cases or similar storage places. Staves stand sturdily alone. In neither case is concealment precluded, of course.

Unless noted to the contrary, these items will have the following number of *charges*; each time the item is used, there is an expenditure of 1 charge (the user will not necessarily be aware of the number of charges in an item):

rods	50 charges minus 0 to 9 (d10 – 1)
staves	25 charges minus 0 to 5 (d6 – 1)
wands	100 charges minus 0 to 19 (d20 – 1)

Most of these items can be recharged by spell users of sufficiently high level. This is discussed elsewhere under the heading **FABRICATION OF MAGIC ITEMS.** Note that a rod, staff or wand completely drained will become forever useless, crumbling to powder as its last charge is expended.

Use of Rods, Staves, and Wands:

Any device of this nature which discharges some form of magic over a distance (that is, the device does not require touch or contact with the object or creature to be affected) must generally have a command word *spoken* in order to cause the device to function. Thus, a *wand of lightning*, for example, might require the utterance of the key word "blitzen" in order to discharge, or it might have a key phrase to cause it to function, such as "Watt and ampere, volt and ohm" (possibly even extending to: " . . . let this discharge find its home!"). A *wand of polymorphing*, or other similar device performing a like function, would require a key word and the new form to be made by the power: "Xot's the word, be a bird!" or some such. Magical silence will most certainly prevent such devices from functioning.

(See also **USE OF MAGIC ITEMS, COMMAND WORDS.**)

Rods:

Unless specified otherwise, rods radiate a magical effect which influences creatures hostile to the wielder.

Rod of Absorption: This rod acts as a magnet and draws magic spells of any nature (cleric, druid, magic-user, or illusionist) into itself, nullifying their effects but storing their *potential* within until the wielder chooses to release this energy in the form of spells of his or her own casting. The magic absorbed must have been directed *at* the character possessing the rod. (Cf. *ring of spell turning*). The wielder can instantly detect the spell level and decide on whether to react or not when the rod absorbs it. The wielder can use the energy to cast any spell he or she has memorized, in but 1 segment, without loss of spell memory, as long as the spell so cast is of equal or lesser level than the one absorbed. Excess levels are stored as potential, and can be cast in like manner (in 1 segment with no spell memory loss) as any level of spell so long as the wielder knows the spell and has it memorized.

The *rod of absorption* can never be recharged. It absorbs 50 spell levels and can thereafter only discharge any remaining potential it might have within. The wielder will know this upon grasping the item. If it has charges used, this indicates that it has already absorbed that many spell levels and they have been used.

Example: a cleric has a *rod of absorption* and uses it to nullify the effect of a *hold person* spell cast at him by a magic-user. The rod now has absorbed 3 spell levels, can absorb 47 more, and the cleric can, in 1 segment, cast any first, second, or third level spell he or she has memorized, *without* memory loss of that spell, by using the stored potential of the rod. Assume the cleric casts a *hold person* back. This spell is only second level to him or her, so the rod then holds 1 spell level of potential, and can absorb 47 more still, with 2 charges permanently disposed of.

Rod of Beguiling: This rod enables its possessor to radiate an emotional and mental wave of fellow-feeling to all creatures with any intelligence whatsoever (1 or higher intelligence). The effect is to cause all such creatures within a 2" radius of the device to be virtually charmed by the individual and beguiled into regarding him or her as their comrade, friend, and/or mentor (no saving throw). The beguiled creatures will love and respect the rod wielder. They will trustingly listen and obey insofar as communication is possible, and the instruction seems plausible and does not outwardly consign the beguiled to needless injury or destruction or go against their nature or alignment. Each charge of the rod beguiles for 1 turn. It can be recharged.

Rod of Cancellation: This dreaded rod is a bane to all classes, for its touch will drain *any* item of *all* magical properties unless a saving throw versus the cancellation is made. Contact is made by scoring a normal "to hit" score in combat melee.

Saving Throw	Item
20	potion
19	scroll
17	ring
14	rod
13	staff
15	wand
12	miscellaneous magic item
3	artifact or relic
11 (8)	armor or shield (if +5)
9 (7)	sword (holy sword)
10	miscellaneous weapon*

* Several small items, such as magic arrows or bolts, together in one container will be drained simultaneously.

If the score indicated, or higher, is not rolled (d20), the item is drained. Upon the item's draining, the rod itself becomes brittle and is no longer potent. Drained items are not restorable, even by wish.

Rod of Lordly Might: This rod has functions which are spell-like as well as uses as a magic weapon of different sorts. It also has several more mundane workings. The *rod of lordly might* is metal, thicker than other rods, with a flanged ball at one end and various studs along its length. It weighs 10 pounds, thus requiring 16 or greater strength to wield properly (−1 on "to hit" die rolls for *each* point of strength below 16).

The spell-like functions of the rod are:

1. *Paralyzation* upon touch if the wielder so commands

2. *Fear* upon all enemies viewing it if the wielder so desires (6" maximum range)

3. *Drain* 2-8 hit points from the opponent touched and bestow them upon the rod wielder (up to the rod wielder's normal maximum; cf. *ring of regeneration*)

Each such function draws off 1 charge from the rod. The functions entitle victims to saving throws versus magic, with the exception of function 3. above which requires a successful "hit" during melee combat.

The weapon uses of the rod are:

1. +2 mace as is

2. +1 *sword of flame* when button #1 is pushed — a blade springs forth from the ball, which becomes the hilt, while the handle shortens the weapon to an overall length of 3'

3. +4 battle axe when button #2 is pushed — blade springs forth at the ball, and the whole lengthens to a 4' length

4. +3 spear when button #3 is pushed — the sword blade springs forth, and the handle can be lengthened up to 12', for an overall length of from 6' minimum to 15' maximum (the latter length highly suitable for lance employment).

These functions do not use charges.

The mundane uses of the rod are:

1. Climbing pole — when button #4 is pushed a spike which can anchor in granite is extruded from the butt, while the tip sprouts 3 sharp hooks; the rod lengthens 5' per segment until button #4 is pushed

again or until 50' is reached. In either case, horizontal bars of 3 inch length then fold out from the sides, 1' apart, in staggered progression. The rod is firmly held by spike and hooks and will bear up to 4,000 pounds (40,000 g.p. equivalent) weight. It retracts by pushing button #5.

2. The same function will force open doors if the rod's base is planted 30' or less from the portal to be forced and is in line with it. The force exerted is equal to storm giant strength.

3. When button #6 is pushed the rod will indicate magnetic north and give the possessor a knowledge of approximate depth beneath the surface (or height above it) he or she is.

These functions do not use charges either.

The *rod of lordly might* cannot be recharged. When its charges are exhausted, all spell-like functions cease as do weapon functions 2 and 3, but the rod continues to work in all other ways.

Rod of Resurrection: This rod enables the cleric to resurrect the dead — even elven, dwarven, gnome, or halfling — as if he or she were of high enough level to cast the spell, and no rest will be required as the rod bestows the lifegiving effects. The rod can be used once per day. The number of charges used to resurrect a character depends on class and race:

			plus	
cleric	1		dwarf	3
druid	2		elf	4
fighter	2		gnome	3
paladin	1		half-elf	2
ranger	2		halfling	2
magic-user	3		half-orc	4
illusionist	3		human	1
thief	3			
assassin	4			
monk	3			
bard	2			

Multi-classed characters use the least favorable category. The rod cannot be recharged.

Rod of Rulership: The individual who possesses this magic rod is able to exercise rulership (command the obedience and fealty) of creatures within 12" when he or she activates the device. From 200 to 500 hit dice (or levels of experience) can be ruled, but creatures with 15 or greater intelligence and 12 or more hit dice/levels are entitled to a saving throw versus magic. Ruled creatures will obey the wielder of the *rod of rulership* as if he or she were their absolute suzerain, but if some command given is absolutely contrary to the nature of the commanded, the magic will be broken. The rod takes 5 segments to activate. Each charge lasts for 1 turn. The rod cannot be recharged.

Rod of Smiting: This rod is a +3 magic weapon which inflicts 4-11 (d8 + 3) hit points of damage. Against golems the rod does 8-22 (2d8 + 6) hit points of damage, any score of 20 or better completely destroys the monster, but any hit upon a golem drains 1 charge. The rod does normal damage (4-11) versus creatures of the *outer planes* such as demons, devils, and night hags. Any score of 20 or better draws off 1 charge and causes triple damage: (d8 + 3) × 3. The rod cannot be recharged.

Staves:

Unless inapplicable or otherwise specified, staves function at the 8th level of magic-use, i.e. their spell discharge is that of an 8th level of experience magic-user with respect to range, duration, area of effect.

The magic functions of a staff generally require only 2 segments to discharge, but the device must then build up power again, and this requires 8 segments.

Damage is nominally 8d6 with respect to *fireballs*, *lightning bolts*, etc.

Staff of Command: This device has 3 functions, only 2 of which will be effective if the wielder is a magic-user, but all 3 work when the staff is in a cleric's hands. The 3 functions are:

1. *Human influence:* This power duplicates that of the *ring* of the same name. Each *suggestion* or *charm* draws 1 charge from the staff.

2. *Mammal control/animal control:* This power functions only as *mammal control* (as the ring of that name) when the staff is used by a magic-user, but in the hands of a cleric it is *animal control* (as the potion of that name, all types of animals listed). Either use drains 1 charge per turn or fraction thereof.

3. *Plant control:* This function duplicates that of the potion of the same name, but for each 1" square area of plants controlled for 1 turn or less 1 charge is used. A magic-user cannot control plants at all.

The staff can be recharged.

Staff of Curing: This device can *cure disease, cure blindness, cure wounds* (6-21 hit points — 3d6 + 3), or *cure insanity.* Each function drains 1 charge. The device can be used but once per day on any person (dwarf, elf, gnome, half-elf, halfling, half-orc included), and no function may be employed more than twice per day, i.e. the staff can only function 8 times during a 24 hour period. It can be recharged.

Staff of the Magi: This potent staff contains many spell powers and other functions as well so as to be a walking arsenal in one device. The staff has the following powers which do not drain charges:

> detect magic
> enlarge
> hold portal
> light
> protection from evil/good

The following powers drain 1 charge per usage:

> invisibility   fireball
> knock   lightning bolt
> pyrotechnics   ice storm
> web   wall of fire
> dispel magic   passwall

These powers drain 2 charges per usage:

> whirlwind   conjure elemental
> plane travel   telekinesis

The *whirlwind* is identical to that caused by a djinni (q.v.). *Plane travel* is similar to the psionic ability of *probability travel* (q.v.), but travel is possible only to the various planes. The staff can be used to conjure 1 *elemental* (q.v.) of each type per day, each having 8 hit dice. *Telekinesis* is at 8th level also, i.e. 200 pounds maximum weight.

The *staff of the magi* adds +2 to all saving throws versus magic. The staff can be used to *absorb* magic-user spell energy directed at its wielder, but if the staff absorbs energy beyond its charge limit it will explode just as if a "retributive strike" (see below) had been made. The spell levels of energy absorbed count only as recharging the staff, but they cannot be redirected immediately, so if *absorption* is desired, that is the only action possible by the staff wielder that round. Note also that the wielder has no idea of how many spell levels are cast at him, for the staff does not communicate this knowledge as does a *rod of absorption*. Therefore, absorbing spells can be risky. Absorption is the only way this staff can be recharged.

Retributive strike is a breaking of the staff. It must be purposeful and declared by the magic-user wielding it. When this is done all levels of spell energy in the staff are released in a globe of 3" radius. All creatures within 1" of the broken staff take hit points of damage equal to 8 times the number of spell levels of energy (1 to 25), those between 1"-2" take 6 × levels, and those 2"-3" distant take 4 × levels. Successful saving throws versus magic indicate only one-half damage is sustained. The magic-user breaking the staff has a 50% chance of *plane travelling* to another plane of existence, but if he or she does not, the explosive release of spell energy totally destroys him or her. This, and the *staff of power*, are the *only* magic items capable of a retributive strike.

Staff of Power: The *staff of power* is also a very potent magic item, with offensive and defensive abilities. It has these powers:

> continual light   magic missile or lightning bolt
> darkness, 5' radius   ray of enfeeblement
> levitation   cone of cold or fireball

These functions cost 1 charge each. The following powers drain 2 charges each:

> shield, 5' radius
> globe of invulnerability
> paralyzation

Paralyzation is a ray from the end of the staff which extends in a cone 4" long and 2" wide at its base.

The wielder of this staff gains +2 on armor class and saving throws. He or she may use the staff to smite opponents. It strikes as a +2 magic weapon and does 3-8 hit points of damage; if 1 charge is expended, the staff does double damage, but 2 charges do not triple damage.

A *staff of power* can be broken for a *retributive strike* (cf. *staff of the magi*). The staff can be recharged.

You may determine alternate powers shown by random die roll.

Staff of the Serpent: There are 2 varieties of this staff, the "Python" and the "Adder".

The *python* strikes as a +2 magic weapon and does 3-8 hit points of damage when it hits. If the cleric throws the staff to the ground, its 6' lengthens and thickens to become a constrictor snake, 25' long (AC 3, 49 hit points, 9" movement). This happens in 1 round. The snake will *entwine* if it scores a hit, the opponent being constricted for 4-10 hit points of damage per round, and the victim will be so engaged until it or the *python* is destroyed. Note that the *python* will return to its owner upon command. If it is destroyed while in snake form the staff is destroyed.

The *adder* strikes as a +1 magic weapon and does 2-4 hit points of damage when it hits. Upon command the head of the staff becomes that of an actual serpent (AC 5, 20 hit points). This head remains for 1 full turn. When a hit is scored, damage is not increased, but the victim must save versus poison or be slain. Only evil clerics will employ an *adder* staff. If the snake head is killed, the staff is destroyed.

Neither staff has or requires charges. 60% of these staves are *pythons.*

Staff of Striking: This oaken staff is the equivalent of a +3 magic weapon. (If weapon vs. armor type adjustment is made, the *staff of striking* is always treated as the most favorable weapon type vs. any armor.) It causes 4-9 (d6+3) points of damage when a hit is scored. This expends a charge. If 2 charges are expended, bonus damage is doubled (d6+6); if 3 charges are expended, bonus damage is tripled (d6+9). No more than 3 charges can be expended per strike. The staff can be recharged.

Staff of Withering: The *staff of withering* is a +1 magic weapon. A hit from it causes 2-5 points of damage. If 2 charges are expended when a hit is scored, the creature struck will also age 10 years, its abilities and life span adjusted for the resulting age increase. If 3 charges are expended when a hit is made, 1 of the opponent creature's limbs can be made to shrivel and become useless unless it saves versus magic (check by random number generation for which member is struck). Note that ageless creatures (undead, demons, devils, etc.) cannot be aged or withered. Each effect of the staff is cumulative, so that 3 charges will score damage, age, *and* wither. Aging a dwarf is of little effect, while aging a dragon could actually aid the creature.

Wands:

Wands perform at 6th level of experience with respect to the damage they cause, range, duration, area of effect, etc. unless otherwise stated.

At your option 1% of all wands are trapped to backfire.

Wand of Conjuration: Grasping of this device enables a magic-user to immediately recognize any cast or written magic-user conjuration/summoning spell (*unseen servant, monster summoning, conjure elemental, death spell, invisible stalker, limited wish, symbol, maze, gate, prismatic sphere, wish*). The wand has the following powers which require expenditure of 1 charge:

> unseen servant
> monster summoning*

> * A maximum of 6 charges may be expended, 1 per level of the *monster summoning*, or 6 *monster summoning I*, 3 *monster summoning II*, 2 *monster summoning III*, or any combination totalling 6. The magic-user must be of a sufficient experience level to cast the appropriate *summoning* spell. The *monster summoning* takes 5 segments.

The wand can also conjure up a *curtain of blackness* — a veil of total black which absorbs all light. The *curtain of blackness* can cover a maximum area of 600 square feet (60' × 10', 40' × 15', 30' × 20'), but it must stretch from ceiling to floor, wall to wall. The *curtain* costs 2 charges to conjure. The veil of total lightlessness can be penetrated only by physical means or magic. The wand also enables its wielder to construct a *prismatic sphere* (or *wall*), one color at a time, red to violet, at a 1 charge per color cost. Each function of the wand takes 5 segments of time, and only 1 function per round is possible. The wand may be recharged.

Wand of Enemy Detection: This wand gives off a pulse and points in the direction of any hostile creature(s) intent upon the bearer of the device. The creature(s) can be invisible, ethereal, astral, out of phase, hidden, disguised, or in plain sight. Detection range is a 6'' sphere. The function requires 1 charge to operate for 1 turn. The wand can be recharged.

Wand of Fear: When the *fear* wand is activated a pale amber ray springs from the tip of the wand, a cone 6'' long by 2'' in base diameter, which flashes on in 1 segment and instantly disappears. Each creature touched by the ray must save versus a *wand* or react as per the *fear* spell (first level cleric spell, *remove fear* reversal), i.e. turn and move at fastest possible speed away from the wand user for 6 rounds. Each usage costs 1 charge. It can operate but once per round. The wand can be recharged.

Wand of Fire: This wand can be employed in 4 separate functions which duplicate the following magic-user spells:

1. *Burning hands:* The wand emits a plane of fire, a fan-shaped sheet 10' wide at its terminus and 12' long. Each creature touched takes 6 hit points of damage. The plane appears in 1 segment, shoots forth its dark red flames, and snuffs out in less than 1 second. It expends 1 charge.

2. *Pyrotechnics:* This function exactly duplicates the spell of the same name. It requires 2 segments to activate. It expends 1 charge.

3. *Fireball:* The wand coughs forth a pea-sized sphere which streaks out to the desired range (or to a maximum range of 16'') and bursts in a fiery violet-red blast, exactly as a *fireball* cast by a spell of that name would. The function takes 2 segments. It expends 2 charges. The *fireball* does 6 hit dice of damage, but all 1's rolled are counted as 2's, i.e. the burst does 12-36 hit points. A saving throw versus *wand* is applicable.

4. *Wall of fire:* The wand can be used to draw a fiery curtain of purplish-red flames which exactly duplicates the *wall of fire* spell cast by a magic-user, i.e. a sheet of flame 12 square '' (1'' × 12'', 2'' × 6'', 3'' × 4'', etc.) which lasts for 6 rounds, causes 8-18 hit points damage (2d6 + 6) if touched (2-8 hit points if within 1'' of the fire, 1-4 if within 2''), and can also be made as a ring-shape around the wand user (but the circle is only 2¼'' in diameter). This function requires 3 segments. It expends 2 charges.

The *wand of fire* can operate but once per round. It can be recharged.

Wand of Frost: A *frost* wand can perform 3 functions which duplicate magic-user spells:

1. *Ice storm:* A silvery ray springs forth from the wand and in 1 segment an *ice* (or *sleet*) *storm* occurs up to 6'' distant from the wand holder. This function requires 1 charge.

2. *Wall of ice:* The silvery ray will form a *wall of ice*, 6 inches thick, and a square area equal to 6'' (1'' × 6'', 2'' × 3'', etc.) in 2 segments at a cost of 1 charge.

3. *Cone of cold:* Dancing white crystalline motes spray forth from the wand in a cone with a 6'' length and a terminal diameter of 2''. The cold comes forth in 2 segments but lasts but 1 second. The temperature is c. −100° F., and damage is 6 hit dice, treating all 1's rolled as 2's (6d6, 12-36). The cost is 2 charges per use. Saving throw versus a *wand* is applicable.

The wand can function but once per round, and may be recharged.

Wand of Illumination: This wand has 4 separate functions, 3 of which approximate magic-user spells, and 1 of which is singular:

1. *Dancing lights:* In 1 segment the wand will produce this effect at a cost of 1 charge.

2. *Light:* The *illumination* wand sends forth *light* in 2 segments time at an expenditure of 1 charge.

3. *Continual light:* This function requires only 2 segments to perform, but the cost is 2 charges.

4. *Sunburst:* When this effect is called forth the wand delivers a sudden flash of brilliant greenish-white light, with blazing golden rays. The range of this *sunburst* is 12'' maximum, and its duration is but 1/10 of a second. Its area of effect is a globe of 4'' diameter. Any undead within this globe take 6-36 hit points of damage, with no saving throw. Creatures within or facing the burst must save versus a *wand* or be blinded for 2-12 segments and unable to do anything during that period. (Of course, the creatures in question must have ocular organs sensitive to the visible light spectrum). The function requires 3 segments and expends 3 charges.

The wand can be recharged.

Wand of Illusion: The *illusion* wand creates both audible and visual illusions (cf. *audible glamer, phantasmal force*). The wand emits an invisible ray, with a 14'' maximum range. The effect takes 3 segments to commence. The wand wielder must concentrate on the *illusion* in order to maintain it, but he or she may move normally (not melee) and still do so. Each portion — audible and visual — costs 1 charge to effect and 1 per round to continue. The wand may be recharged.

Wand of Lightning: This wand has 2 functions which closely resemble magic-user spells:

1. *Shock:* This function causes the recipient to take 1-10 hit points of damage, with no saving throw, when struck in melee combat. Any ''to hit'' score discounts metallic armor and shield (giving opponents armor class 10) but not plain leather or wood. Magic bonuses on metallic armor do not affect armor class, but such items as a *ring of protection* do. The shock uses 1 charge.

2. *Lightning bolt:* The possessor of the wand can discharge a bolt of *lightning*. The stroke can be either the forked or straight bolt (cf. magic-user spell, *lightning bolt*). Damage is 12-36 (6d6, treating 1's as 2's), but a saving throw is applicable. This function uses 2 charges. It requires 2 segments to discharge.

The wand may be recharged. It can perform but 1 function per round.

Wand of Magic Detection: This wand is similar in operation to the *enemy detection* wand. If any form of magic is in operation, or a magic item exists, within a 3'' radius, the *magic detection* wand will pulse and point to the strongest source. Note that the wand will point to a person upon whom a spell has been cast. Operation requires 1 round, and successive rounds will point out successively less powerful magic radiations. The category of magic (abjuration, alteration, etc.) can be determined if one round is spent concentrating on the subject emanation. 1 charge is expended per turn (or fraction thereof) of use. Starting with the second round of continuous use, there is a 2% cumulative chance per round that the wand will temporarily malfunction and indicate non-magical items as magical, or vice-versa. The wand may be recharged.

Wand of Metal and Mineral Detection: This wand also has a 3″ radius range and pulses and points to the largest mass of metal within its effective area of operation. However, the wielder can concentrate on a specific metal or mineral type (gold, platinum, quartz, beryl, diamond, corundum, etc.); if the specific type is within range the wand will point to any and all places it is located, and the wand possessor will know the approximate quantity as well. Each operation requires 1 round. Each charge powers the wand for 1 full turn. The wand may be recharged.

Wand of Magic Missiles: The *missiles* wand discharges *magic missiles* which are similar to those of the first level magic-user spell, *magic missile*. The device fires a *magic missile* which causes 2-5 hit points of damage. It operates as the spell of the same name, always hitting its target when wielded by a magic-user, otherwise requiring a "to hit" die roll. Each missile takes 3 segments to discharge, and costs 1 charge. A maximum of 2 may be expended in 1 round. The wand may be recharged.

Wand of Negation: This device operates to negate the spell or spell-like function(s) of rods, staves, wands and other magical items. The individual with the *negation* wand points the device, and a pale gray beam shoots forth to touch the target — device or individual. This will totally negate any wand function, and make any other spell or spell-like function from a device 75% likely to be negated, whether it is a low-level spell, or even if it is an ultra-powerful spell. Operation of the wand requires but 1 segment of a round. It can function but once per round, and each negation drains 1 charge. The wand cannot be recharged.

Wand of Paralyzation: This wand shoots forth a thin ray of bluish color to a maximum range of 6″. If the ray touches any creature it must save versus *wands* or be rigidly immobile for from 5-20 rounds. A save indicates the ray missed, and there is no effect. Each operation takes 3 segments and costs 1 charge. The wand may operate once per round. It may be recharged. (Note that as soon as the ray touches 1 creature it *stops*; the wand can attack only 1 target per round.)

Wand of Polymorphing: The *polymorphing* wand emits a green beam, a thin ray which darts forth to a maximum distance of 6″. If this beam touches any creature, it must make its saving throw versus *wands* (success indicating a miss) or be *polymorphed (others)* as the spell of the same name (q.v.). The wand wielder may opt to form the victim into a snail, frog, insect, etc. as long as the result is a small and inoffensive creature. The possessor of the wand may elect to *touch* a creature with the device instead. When this is done (unwilling creatures must be *hit* and they are also entitled to a saving throw) the recipient is surrounded by dancing motes of sparkling emerald light, and then transforms into whatever creature-shape the wand wielder has stated. This is the same magical effect as the *polymorph (self)* spell (q.v.). Either function requires 3 segments. Each draws 1 charge. Only 1 function per round is possible. The wand may be recharged.

Wand of Secret Door and Trap Location: This wand has an effective radius of 1½″ for secret door location, 3″ for trap location. When the wand is energized it will pulse and point to whichever thing it is to locate if a secret door/trap is within location range. Note that it locates either one or the other, not both during one operation. It requires 1 round to function and draws 1 charge. The wand may be recharged.

Wand of Wonder: The *wand of wonder* is a strange and unpredictable device which will generate any number of strange effects, randomly, each time it is used. The usual effects are shown on the table below, but you may alter those for any or all of these wands in your campaign as you see fit, although it is recommended that you follow the *pattern* shown. The functions of the wand are:

01-10	*slow* creature pointed at for 1 turn
11-18	*deludes* wielder for 1 round into believing the wand functions as indicated by a second die roll
19-25	*gust of wind,* double force of spell
26-30	*stinking cloud* at 3″ range
31-33	*heavy rain* falls for 1 round in 6″ radius of wand wielder
34-36	summon rhino (1-25), elephant (26-50) or mouse (51-00)
37-46	*lightning bolt* (7″ × ½″) as wand

47-49	*stream of 600 large butterflies* pour forth and flutter around for 2 rounds, blinding everyone (including wielder)
50-53	*enlarge* target if in 6″ of wand
54-58	*darkness* in a 3″ diameter hemisphere at 3″ center distance from wand
59-62	*grass grows* in area of 16″ square before wand, or grass existing there grows to 10 times normal size
63-65	*vanish* any non-living object of up to 1,000 pounds mass and up to 30 cubic feet in size (object is ethereal)
66-69	*diminish* wand wielder to 1/12′ height
70-79	*fireball* as wand
80-84	*invisibility* covers wand wielder
85-87	*leaves grow* from target if in 6″ of wand
88-90	*10-40 gems* of 1 g.p. base value shoot forth in a 3″ long stream, each causing 1 h.p. of damage to any creature in path — roll 5d4 for number of hits
91-97	*shimmering colors* dance and play over a 4″ × 3″ area in front of wand — creatures therein blinded for 1-6 rounds
98-00	*flesh to stone* (or reverse if target is stone) if target is within 6″

The wand uses 1 charge per function. It may not be recharged. Where applicable, saving throws should be made.

MISCELLANEOUS MAGIC (III.E., 1. through 5. and Special)

As the name implies, this category is a catch-all for many sorts of magical items. Some are powerful, others weak; some are highly desirable, others are deadly to the finder. The number of such items is great in order to make it improbable that there will be duplicates in a campaign — or at least not more than 2 or 3.

Use care in revealing information regarding any item found by players. Describe an item only in the most general of terms, viz. wood, metal, cloth, leather, etc. Allow player questions to simulate visual and tactile examination. A cloak appears as a cloth object — only examination will reveal its form and probable nature. Likewise, do not simply blurt out the properties and powers of an item. It must be held, or worn, or whatever; and experiment and experience are the best determinators of magical qualities if some other means is not available (a bard, sage, *commune* spell, etc.).

Items are listed alphabetically. **Artifacts** and **relics** are listed (1%) on table E.1., directing the reader to E. **Special** for enumeration. These items are detailed after all other *miscellaneous magic*. If you do not desire such an item to occur, substitute a *bag of beans,* or the next item on the table.

Unless noted by class letter in parenthesis after a listing, items are usable by any class not otherwise prohibited. Class letters are (C) clerics, (F) fighters, etc. and each listing includes appropriate sub-classes.

Special Note: All magical *books, librams, manuals, tomes,* etc. appear to be "normal" works of arcane lore. Each is completely indistinguishable from the other by visual examination of the outer parts or by detection for magic aura. Bard characters will have normal chances of finding out the nature of such writings, as will an *identify* spell from a magic-user. Otherwise, *only a wish* will be useful in typing a magical writing, i.e. *alter reality, commune, contact higher planes, limited wish, true seeing, true sight,* and other spells or powers are useless. A *wish* will reveal *general* contents of a book, telling what characteristics or class is most affected (*not* necessarily benefited) by the work. It requires a second *wish* to determine *exact* contents. After being perused by a character, most of these magical works will vanish forever, but those which are non-beneficial to the reader will typically be attached to the character, and he or she will be unable to be rid of it. If the work benefits another alignment of character, the possessor is *geased* to conceal and guard the writing. As Dungeon Master you should use your judgment and imagination as to exactly how these items will be treated, using the rules herein as parameters.

TABLE (III.E.) 1.

Alchemy Jug: This magical device can pour forth varying liquids upon command. The quantity of each liquid is dependent upon the liquid itself. The *jug* can pour only 1 kind of liquid on any given day, 7 pourings maximum. The liquids pourable and quantity per pouring are:

salt water	16 gallons
fresh water	8 gallons
beer	4 gallons
vinegar	2 gallons
wine	1 gallon
ammonia	1 quart
oil	1 pint
aqua regia	2 gills (8 oz.)
alcohol	1 gill (4 oz.)
chlorine	8 drams (1 oz.)
cyanide	4 drams (½ oz.)

The jug will pour forth 2 gallons per round, so it will require 8 rounds to complete 1 pouring of salt water.

Amulet of Inescapable Location: This device is typically worn on a chain or as a brooch which pins on. It appears to be an amulet which prevents location, scrying (crystal ball viewing and the like), or detection/influence by *ESP/telepathy*. Actually, the amulet doubles the likelihood and/or range of these location and detection modes, however. Normal determination attempts, including *detect magic*, will not reveal its true nature.

Amulet of Life Protection: This pendant or brooch device serves as a ward for the psyche (soul). The wearer cannot be *possessed* by *magic jar* spell or any similar mental attack, including demonic or diabolic means. If the wearer is slain, the psyche enters the amulet and is protected for 7 full days. Thereafter it goes to the plane of its alignment, however. If the *amulet* is destroyed during the 7 days, the psyche is utterly and irrevocably annihilated. Note: psionic attack modes *psionic blast* or *psychic crush* will not harm the wearer.

Amulet of the Planes: The *amulet of the planes* is a device which enables the individual possessing it to transport himself or herself instantly to or from any one of the upper levels of the *Outer Planes*. This travel is absolutely safe, but until the individual learns the device, transport will be random. Roll d6, 1-3 = do not add 12, 4-6 = add 12 to d12 for 1-24 random results:

1-2	*Seven Heavens*
3	*Twin Paradises*
4	*Elysium*
5	*Happy Hunting Grounds*
6-7	*Olympus*
8	*Gladsheim*
9	*Limbo*
10	*Pandemonium*
11-12	*Abyss*
13	*Tarterus*
14	*Hades*
15	*Gehenna*
16-17	*Nine Hells*
18	*Acheron*
19	*Nirvana*
20	*Arcadia*
21-24	*Prime Material Plane*

You may alternately have the following results:

22	*Ethereal Plane*
23	*Astral Plane*
24	*Prime, but alternate Earth*

Amulet of Proof Against Detection and Location: This device wards the wearer against all divination and mental or magical location and/or detection. The wearer cannot be detected through *clairaudience*, *clairvoyance*, *ESP*, *telepathy*, *crystal balls*, or any other scrying devices. No aura is discernible on the wearer, and predictions cannot be made regarding him or her, unless some powerful being is consulted.

Apparatus of Kwalish: When initially found this item will certainly appear as a large iron barrel. It has a secret catch which opens a hatch in one end.

Inside are 10 levers:

1	extend legs and tail/retract same
2	uncover forward porthole/cover same
3	uncover side portholes/cover same
4	extend pincers and feelers/retract same
5	snap pincers
6	forward/left or right
7	backwards/left or right
8	open "eyes" with *continual light* inside/close "eyes"
9	raise (levitate)/sink
10	open hatch/close hatch

The *apparatus* moves forward at a 3" speed, backwards at 6". The 2 pincers extend forward 4' and snap for 2-12 hit points damage each if they hit a creature — 25% chance, no reduction for armor, but dexterity reduction applies. The device can operate in waters up to 900' deep. It can hold 2 human-sized persons and enough air to operate for 2-5 hours at maximum capacity. The *apparatus* is AC 0 and will take 100 hit points damage to cause a leak, 200 to stave in a side. When the device is fully operating the whole appears as something like a giant lobster.

Arrow of Direction: An *arrow of direction* typically appears to be a normal (or possibly magic) arrow. Its magical properties make it function much as a *locate object* spell, however, empowering the arrow to show the direction of the desired way. Once per day the device can be tossed into the air; it will fall and point towards the desired way, and this process can be repeated 7 times during the next 7 turns. Note: the arrow will point only towards requested way/location. The request can be only for one of the following: stairway (up or down), sloping passage (up or down), dungeon exit or entrance, cave, cavern. Requests must be phrased by distance (nearest, farthest, highest, lowest) or by direction (north, south, east, west, etc.).

Bag of Beans: This bag is constructed of heavy cloth. It is about 2' wide and 4' long (the size of any other bag or large sack). When it is opened and examined it will reveal several large pebble-like objects. If these objects are dumped out of the bag they will each explode for 5-20 hit points of damage each, all creatures within a 10' radius must save versus magic or take full damage. To be removed safely, the *beans* in the bag must be taken out by hand; telekinesis will not work, nor can they be worked out using tools in any way which will not explode them. Each pebble-like bean must be placed in dirt and watered. From each, in succession, will spring some creature or object. It is suggested that 3-12 beans are optimum, and only 1 or 2 will be beneficial, the others being monsters or useless things. For example:

#1	3 shriekers spring up and begin wailing
#2	an *ice storm* strikes the area
#3	a poisonous raspberry bush with animated runners shoots up, but each of its 5-20 berries is a gem of 100 or 500 g.p. base value (or perhaps just worthless glass)
#4	a hole opens in the ground; a purple worm can be below or a djinni ring . . .
#5	smoke and gases cover an area of 50' radius for 5 turns, and creatures therein cannot see and will be blinded for 1-6 rounds even when they step out of the cloud
#6	a wyvern grows instantly and attacks; its sting is a *javelin of piercing*
#7	poison gas seeps out slowly forming a cloud of 20' radius which persists for 1 turn; while it lasts it might turn some dirt at its center to magic dust (appearance, vanishing, sneezing and choking . . .)

Thought, imagination and judgment are required with this item.

Bag of Devouring: This bag appears as a typical sack — possibly appearing to be empty, possibly as having *beans* in its bottom. The sack is, however, the lure used by an extra-dimensional creature. It is one of its feeding orifices. Any substance of animal or vegetable nature is subject to "swallowing" if it is thrust within the bag. The *bag of devouring* is 90% likely to ignore any initial intrusions, but anytime it senses living human flesh within, it is 60% likely to close and attempt to draw the whole victim within — base 75% chance for success less strength bonus for "damage", each +1 = –5% on base chance. Thus an 18 strength character (with +2 damage) is only 65% likely to be drawn into the bag, while a 5 strength character (with –1 damage) is 80% likely to be drawn in. The bag radiates magic. It can hold up to 30 cubic feet of matter. It will act as a *bag of hold-*

ing (normal capacity), but each turn it has a 5% cumulative chance of "swallowing" the contents and then "spitting the stuff out" in some non-space. Creatures drawn within are consumed in 7 segments of a round, eaten, and forever gone.

Bag of Holding: As with other magic bags, this one appears to be a common cloth sack of about 2' X 4' size. The *bag of holding* opens into a non-dimensional space, and its inside is larger than its outside dimensions. Regardless of what is put into this item, the *bag of holding* always weighs a fixed amount. This weight, the bag's weight limit in contents, and its volume content are dependent upon its quality as shown below:

Dice	Weight	Weight Limit	Volume Limit
01-30	15 pounds	250 pounds	30 cubic feet
31-70	15 pounds	500 pounds	70 cubic feet
71-90	35 pounds	1,000 pounds	150 cubic feet
91-00	60 pounds	1,500 pounds	250 cubic feet

If overloaded, or sharp objects are placed within so as to pierce it, the bag will rupture and be ruined, and the contents will be lost forever in the vortices of nilspace.

Bag of Transmuting: This magical sack appears to be a *bag of holding* of one of the 4 quality types. It will perform properly for 2-5 uses (or more if the usages are made within a few days time). However, at some point the magic field will waver, and precious metals and gems within the bag will be turned into common metals and stones of no worth. When emptied, the bag will burst to pour forth these transmuted metals and minerals. Any magic items (other than artifacts and relics) placed in the bag will become ordinary and dull lead, glass or wood as appropriate (no saving throw) once the transmuting effects have begun.

Bag of Tricks: As is usual, a *bag of tricks* appears to be of typical size for sacks, and visual or other examination will not reveal any contents. However, if an individual reaches inside, he or she will feel a small, fuzzy object. If this is withdrawn and tossed 1' to 20' away, it will balloon into one of the following animals, which will obey and fight for the individual who brought it into being until the current combat terminates. The animals inside a *bag of tricks* are dependent upon which sort of bag is found. Roll d10 to determine which type:

Type 1-5

Die	Animal	AC	Hit Dice	Hit Points	Damage per Attack
1	Weasel	6	½	2	1
2	Skunk	9	½	2	Musk
3	Badger	4	1 + 2	7	1-2/1-2/1-3
4	Wolf	7	2 + 2	12	2-5
5	Lynx, giant	6	2 + 2	12	1-2/1-2/1-4 — 1-3/1-3
6	Wolverine	5	3	15	1-4/1-4/2-5 + musk
7	Boar	7	3 + 3	18	3-12
8	Stag, giant	7	5	25	4-16 or 1-4/1-4

Type 6-8

Die	Animal	AC	Hit Dice	Hit Points	Damage per Attack
1	Rat	7	½	2	1
2	Owl	7	½	3	1-3/1-3
3	Dog	7	1 + 1	6	1-4
4	Goat	7	1 + 1	8	1-6
5	Ram	6	2	10	2-5
6	Bull	7	4	20	1-6/1-6
7	Bear	6	5 + 5	30	1-6/1-6/1-8 — 2-12
8	Lion	5/6	5 + 2	28	1-4/1-4/1-10 — 2-7/2-7

Type 9-0

Die	Animal	AC	Hit Dice	Hit Points	Damage per Attack
1	Jackal	7	½	2	1-2
2	Eagle	7	1	5	1-2/1-2/1
3	Baboon	7	1 + 1	6	1-4
4	Ostrich	7	3	15	1-4 or 2-8
5	Leopard	6	3 + 2	17	1-3/1-3/1-6 — 1-4/1-4
6	Jaguar	6	4 + 2	21	1-3/1-3/1-8 — 2-5/2-5
7	Buffalo	7	5	25	1-8/1-8
8	Tiger	6	5 + 5	30	2-5/2-5/1-10 — 2-8/2-8

Only 1 creature can be drawn forth at a time. It alone exists until it is slain or 1 turn has elapsed and it is ordered back into the *bag of tricks*. Another animal may then be brought forth, but it could be another just like the one which was drawn previously. Note that only one roll is made for type of *bag*, but type of creature is rolled for each time one is drawn forth. Up to 10 creatures maximum may be drawn from the bag each week.

Beaker of Plentiful Potions: This container resembles a jug or flask. It is a magical beaker with alchemical properties which compound from 2-5 doses of from 2-5 potions of any sort as initially determined by random selection. Different potion sorts are layered in the container, and each pouring takes 1 round and spills forth 1 dose of 1 potion type. Roll d4, +1, to find the number of potions the *beaker* contains. Roll for each potion contained so as to find what it is — *delusion* and *poison* are possible — and record type by order of occurrence. Duplication is possible. If the container holds only 2 potions it will dispense them 1 each per day, 3 times per week; if 3 are contained, it will dispense them 1 each per day, 2 times per week; and if 4 or 5 are contained it will pour each forth but 1 time per week. Once opened, the beaker will gradually lose the ability to produce potions. This reduction in ability results in the permanent loss of one potion type per month.

Boat, Folding: A *folding boat* will always be discovered as a small wooden "box" — about 1' long, ½' wide, and ½' deep. It will, of course, radiate magic if detection is possible. The "box" can contain other things. If a command word is given, the box will unfold itself to form a boat of 10' length, 4' width and 2' depth. A second (different) command word will cause it to unfold to a 24' long, 8' wide, and 6' deep ship. The former will have 1 pair of oars, an anchor, a mast, and lateen sail. The latter is decked, has single rowing seats, 5 sets of oars, a steering oar, anchor, a deck cabin, a mast, and square sail. The first can hold 3 or 4 persons comfortably, the second will carry 15 persons with ease. A third word of command will cause the boat/ship to fold itself into a box once again. You may have the words of command inscribed visibly or invisibly on the box, have them written elsewhere — perhaps on an item within the box, or you might simply have them lost and require a search (via *legend lore*, consulting a sage, physical search of the dungeon, etc.) to discover them.

Book of Exalted Deeds: This holy book is sacred to clerics of *good* alignment. Reading of the work will require 1 week, but upon completion the *good* cleric will gain 1 point of wisdom and experience points sufficient to place him or her exactly half way into their next level of experience. Clerics neither *good* nor *evil* will lose 20,000-80,000 experience points from perusal of the work (a negative x.p. total is possible, requiring *restoration* but not lowering level below 1st). *Evil* clerics will lose 1 full experience level, dropping to the lowest possible number of experience points possible to hold the level; they will furthermore have to *atone* by magical means or by offering up 50% of everything they gain for 2-5 adventures, losing the appropriate number of experience points as well, or gain no further experience. Fighters who handle or read the book will not be affected, although a *paladin* will feel it to be *good*. Magic-users who read it will suffer the loss of 1 point of intelligence unless they save versus magic; and if they do save they will lose from 2,000-20,000 experience points. A thief who handles or reads the work will sustain 5-30 hit points of damage and must save versus magic or lose 1 point of dexterity and have a 10%-60% chance of giving up his or her profession to become a *good* cleric if wisdom is 15 or higher. Assassins handling or reading the *book of exalted deeds* will take 5-40 hit points of damage and must save versus magic or commit suicide. Monks are not harmed by the work, nor can they understand it. Bards are treated as neutral clerics, experience point loss being from *bard* experience only. Note that except as indicated above, this writing cannot be distinguished by cover or scansion from *any* other magic book, libram, tome, etc. (This applies also to other magical writings detailed hereafter.) It must be perused. (This applies also to other magical writings detailed hereafter.) Once perused, the book vanishes, never to be seen again, nor can the same player character ever benefit from perusing the like a second time.

Book of Infinite Spells: This magical writing bestows spell use ability upon its possessor, but upon first reading the work any character not already able to use spells will suffer 5-20 hit points of damage and be *stunned* for 5-20 turns. Thereafter, he or she can examine the writing without further harm. The *book of infinite spells* contains from 23-30 (22 + d8) pages. The nature of each page must be determined by random die roll. Use the following table:

01-30	blank page
31-50	cleric spell
51-60	druid spell
61-95	magic-user spell
96-00	illusionist spell

If a spell is written on a page, roll d10 for all except magic-user spell, for which a d12 is rolled, to determine spell level. Results of 8-10 (or 10-12) indicate a d6 (d8 for magic-user spells) is to be rolled instead. When level is known, determine the particular spell by random means also. Record page contents secretly, and DO NOT REVEAL THIS INFORMATION TO THE HOLDER OF THE BOOK.

Once a page is turned it can never be flipped back, i.e. paging through the book is a one-way trip. When the last page is turned, the book vanishes. The owner of the *book of infinite spells* can cast the spell to which the book is opened, but once per day only, unless the spell is one which the character would normally be able to cast by reason of class and level, in which case the spell can be cast up to 4 times per day due to the book's magical powers. The book need *not* be in the actual presence of the owner in order to empower spell ability, so he or she can store it in a place of safety while adventuring and still cast spells by means of its power. Each time a spell is cast there is a chance the energy connected with its use will cause the page to magically turn (despite *all* precautions). The owner will know this and possibly even benefit from the turning by gaining access to a new spell. The chance of a page turning is as follows:

Spell-caster employing spells usable by his or her class
   and/or level 10%
Spell-caster using spell foreign to his or her class and/or level 20%
Non-spell caster using cleric spell 25%
Non-spell caster using magic-user spell 30%

Treat the spell use just as if a scroll were being employed, including time of casting, spell failure, etc.

Book of Vile Darkness: This work of ineffable *evil* is meat and drink to clerics of that alignment. To fully consume the contents requires 1 week of reading, but when such has been accomplished, the *evil* cleric will gain 1 point of wisdom and experience points sufficient to place him or her exactly half way into the next level of experience. Clerics neither *good* nor *evil* who read the book will either lose 30,000-120,000 experience points or become evil without benefit from the work; there is a 50% chance for either. *Good* clerics perusing the pages of the unspeakable *Book of Vile Darkness* will have to save versus poison or *die*; and if they do not die they must save versus magic or become *permanently insane*. In the latter event, even if the save is successful, the cleric loses 250,000 experience points, less 10,000 for each of his or her points of wisdom. Other characters of *good* alignment will take 5-30 hit points of damage from handling the tome and if they look inside there is an 80% chance a *night hag* (q.v.) will thereafter come to the character that night and attack. Non-evil *neutral* characters will take 5-20 hit points of damage from handling the book, and reading its pages will cause them to save versus poison or become *evil*, immediately seeking out an evil cleric to confirm their new alignment. (Cf. *Book of Exalted Deeds* for other details.)

Boots of Dancing: The magical *boots of dancing* will expand or contract to fit any foot size, from halfling to giant (just as other magic boots will do, of course). They radiate a dim magic if detection is used. They are indistinguishable from other magic boots, and until actual melee combat is engaged in they will function exactly as if they were one of the other 4 types of useful boots (see below). When in melee combat, or if the wearer is fleeing from the actuality of same, the *boots of dancing* will impede his or her movement, begin to tap and shuffle, heel and toe, or shuffle off to Buffalo, making the wearer behave exactly as if *Otto's Irresistible Dance* spell had been cast upon him or her (−4 from armor class rating, no saving throws possible, and no attacks possible). Only a *remove curse* spell will allow the boots to be removed once their true nature comes forth.

Boots of Elvenkind: These soft boots enable the wearer to move without sound of footfall in virtually any surroundings. Thus the wearer can walk across a patch of dry leaves or over a normally creaky wooden floor and make only a whisper of noise — say 95% chance of silence in the worst of conditions, 100% in the best.

Boots of Levitation: As other magical boots, these soft footgear will expand or contract to fit giant to halfling-sized feet. *Boots of levitation* allow the wearer, at will, to ascend or descend vertically. The speed of

ascent/descent is 20' per round (minute). There is no limitation on usage. The amount of weight the boots can levitate is randomly determined in 14 pound increments by rolling d20 and adding the result to a base of 280 pounds, i.e. a given pair of boots can *levitate* from 294 to 560 pounds of weight. Thus, an ogre could be wearing such boots, but its weight would be too great to *levitate*. (Cf. second level magic-user spell, *levitation*.)

Boots of Speed: These boots enable the wearer to run at the speed of a fast horse, viz. 24'' base movement speed. For every 10 pounds (100 g.p. equivalent) of weight over 200 pounds, the wearer is slowed 1'' in movement, so a 180 pound human with 60 pounds of gear would move at 20'' base movement rate, and if a sack of 500 gold pieces were being carried in addition, the movement rate would be slowed yet another 5''. For every hour of continuous fast movement, the wearer must rest 1 hour. No more than 8 hours of continuous fast movement are possible before the wearer *must* rest. *Boots of speed* give +2 to armor class value in combat situations where movement of this sort is possible.

Boots of Striding and Springing: The wearer of these magical boots has a base movement rate of 12'', regardless of size or weight. This speed can be maintained tirelessly for up to 12 hours per day, but thereafter the boots no longer function for 12 hours — assume they "recharge" for that period. In addition to the *striding* factor, these boots also have a *springing* factor. While "normal" paces for the individual wearing this type of footgear are 3' long, the boots also enable forward jumps of up to 30', backward leaps of 9', and vertical springs of 15'. If circumstances permit the use of such movement in combat, the wearer can effectively strike and spring away when he or she has the *initiative* during a melee round. However, such activity has a degree of danger, and there is a base 20% chance that the wearer of the boots will stumble and be stunned on the following round; adjust the 20% chance downwards by 3% for each point of dexterity above 12 of the wearer, i.e. 17% at 13 dexterity, 14% at 14, 11% at 15, 8% at 16, 5% at 17, and but 2% at 18 dexterity. In any event, the wearer increases armor class value by +1 due to the quickness of movement these boots imbue, so armor class 2 becomes 1, armor class 1 becomes 0, etc.

Bowl Commanding Water Elementals: This large container is usually fashioned from blue or green stone of semi-precious value such as malachite or lapis lazuli. Sometimes jade will be used. It is about 1' in diameter, half that deep, and relatively fragile. When the bowl is filled with water, fresh or salt, and certain words are spoken, an elemental of 12 hit dice will appear. The summoning words require 1 round to speak. Note that if salt water is used, the elemental will be stronger (+2 per hit die, maximum 8 h.p. per die, however). Control and similar information are given under *Elemental* in **ADVANCED DUNGEONS AND DRAGONS, MONSTER MANUAL**. (Cf. *bowl of watery death* below.)

Bowl of Watery Death: This device exactly resembles a *bowl commanding water elementals*, including color, design, magic radiation, etc. However, when it is filled with water, the magic-user must save versus magic or be shrunk to the size of a small and plunged into the center of the bowl. Note: if salt water is poured into the bowl the saving throw is at −2. The victim will drown in from 3-8 rounds, unless magic is used to save the individual, for he or she cannot be physically removed from the *bowl of watery death* except by magical means: *animal growth*, *enlarge*, or *wish* are the only spells which will free the victim, and restore normal size; a *growth* potion poured into the water will have the same effect; a *sweet water* potion will allow the victim another saving throw, i.e. a chance that the curse magic of the bowl works only briefly. If the victim drowns, death is permanent, no *resurrection* is possible, and even a *wish* will not work.

Bracers of Defense: These items appear to be some sort of wrist or arm guards. Their magic bestows an effective armor class equal to actually wearing armor and employing a shield. Of course, if armor is actually worn, the *bracers* will not be effective, but they do work in conjunction with other magical items of protection. The armor class the *bracers of defense* bestow is determined by random dicing on the table below:

	Armor Class
01-05	8
06-15	7
16-35	6
36-50	5
51-70	4
71-85	3
86-00	2

Bracers of Defenselessness: These items appear to be some sort of *bracers* of defense, and they will actually serve as one of the above types until the wearer is attacked in anger by a dangerous enemy. At that moment, the *bracers* will lower armor class to 10 and negate any and all other magical protections and dexterity bonuses. Thereafter the bracers can only be removed by means of a *remove curse* spell.

Brazier Commanding Fire Elementals: This device appears to be a normal container for holding burning coals unless magic is detected for. It enables a magic-user to summon an elemental of 12 hit dice strength from the *Elemental Plane of Fire*. A fire must be lit in the *brazier* — usually 1 round is required to do so. If sulphur is added the elemental will be of +1 on each hit die, i.e. 2-9 hit points per hit die. The fire elemental will appear as soon as the fire is burning and a command word is uttered. (See **MONSTER MANUAL** for other details.)

Brazier of Sleep Smoke: This device is exactly similar to the *brazier commanding fire elementals*. However, when a fire is started within it the burning will cause great clouds of magical smoke to pour forth in a cloud of 1″ radius from the brazier. All creatures within the cloud must save versus magic or fall into a deep sleep. At the same moment a fire elemental of 12 hit dice will appear and attack the nearest creature. Sleeping creatures can only be awakened by means of a *dispel magic* or *remove curse* spell.

Brooch of Shielding: The *brooch of shielding* appears to be a piece of silver or gold jewelry, usually (90%) without gems inset, which is meant to fasten a cloak or cape. It has the property, however, to absorb *magic missiles* of the sort generated by spell, wand, or other magic device. A *brooch* can absorb up to 101 hit points of *magic missile* damage before it melts and becomes useless. Its use can normally be determined only by means of a *detect magic* spell and then experimentation.

Broom of Animated Attack: Indistinguishable from a normal broom, except by means of detection of its magic, and completely identical to a *broom of flying* by all tests short of attempted use, the *broom of animated attack* is a very nasty item. If a command word (″fly″, ″soar″, etc.) is spoken, the *broom* will do a loop the loop with its hopeful rider, dumping him or her off on his or her head from 6′ to 9′ off the ground. The *broom* will then attack the stunned victim, swatting the face with the straw/twig end to blind and beating with the ″bald headed end″, the handle. Each such attack takes place twice per round, the *broom* attacking as if it were a 4 hit die monster. The straw end will cause blindness for 1 round if it hits. The other end causes 1-3 hit points of damage when it hits. The broom is armor class 7 and takes 18 hit points to destroy.

Broom of Flying: This magical broom is able to fly through the air at up to 30″ movement speed. The broom can carry 182 pounds at this rate, but every 14 additional pounds slows movement by 1″. The device can climb or dive at about 30 degrees. A command word must be used, the word to be determined by you as desired. The broom will travel alone to any destination named. It will come up to 30″ to its owner when he or she speaks the command word.

Bucknard's Everfull Purse: Appearing as nothing more than a leather pouch or small bag, this magical poke is most useful to its owner, for each morning it will duplicate certain coins — and possibly gems as well. When found, the *purse* will be full of coins. If totally emptied, and left so for more than a few minutes, the magic of the *purse* is lost, but if 1 of each type of coin is placed within the bag, the next morning 26 of each applicable type will be found inside. *Bucknard's Everfull Purse* can contain:

	C.P.	S.P.	E.P.	G.P.	P.P.	Gems*
01-50	—	26	26	26	—	—
51-90	26	—	26	—	26	—
91-00	26	—	26	—	—	26

* Base 10 g.p. gems which may increase to a maximum of 100 g.p. only.

Once the type of bag is first determined by roll, its abilities will not change.

(This item was designed to maintain spice, providing a constant source of funds without attracting undue attention to the bearer or necessitating chests of treasure.)

TABLE (III.E.) 2.

Candle of Invocation: *Candles of Invocation* are specially *blessed* and *prayered* tapers which are dedicated to the pantheon of gods of one of the nine alignments. The typical candle is not remarkable, but it will radiate

magic if such is detected, and good or evil will be radiated also if appropriate. Simply burning the candle will generate a favorable aura for the individual so doing if the candle's alignment matches that of the character's. If burned by a cleric of the same alignment, the *candle* temporarily increases the cleric's level of experience by 2, allowing him or her to cast additional spells, and even normally unavailable spells, as if he or she were of the higher level, but only so long as the taper is aflame. Any burning also allows the casting of a *gate* spell, the respondent being of the alignment of the *candle*, but the taper is immediately consumed in the process. Each candle will burn for 4 hours. It is possible to extinguish the candle as any other, but it can be placed in a lantern or otherwise sheltered to protect it from drafts and other things which could put it out, without affecting its magical properties.

Carpet of Flying: The size, carrying capacity and speed of a *carpet* are determined by use of the table below. Each *carpet* has its own command word to activate it, and each is then controlled by spoken directions. If the device is within voice range, the command word will activate it. These rugs are of oriental make and design. Each is very beautiful and durable. Note, however, that tears or other rents cannot be repaired without special weaving techniques which are generally known only in the East.

Dice	Size	Capacity	Speed
01-20	3′ × 5′	1 person	42″
21-55	4′ × 6′	2 persons	36″
56-80	5′ × 7′	3 persons	30″
81-00	6′ × 9′	4 persons	24″

Censer Controlling Air Elementals: This perforated golden vessel resembles any thurible found in places of worship. If filled with incense and lit, a command word need only be spoken to summon forth a 12 hit dice-sized air elemental which will appear on the following round. If *incense of meditation* is burned within this ½′ wide, 1′ high vessel, the air elemental will have +3 on each of its hit dice, and it will *willingly* obey the commands of its summoner. Note that if the *censer* is extinguished, the elemental will remain and turn on the summoner. (Cf. Elemental in **MONSTER MANUAL.**)

Censer of Summoning Hostile Air Elementals: This thurible is indistinguishable from other censers — magical or ordinary. It is cursed, so that if any incense is burned within it from 1 to 4 enraged air elementals will appear, 1 per round, from the *censer* and attack any and all creatures within sight. The *censer* will burn and cannot be extinguished until either the summoner or the elementals have been killed.

Chime of Opening: A *chime of opening* is a hollow mithral tube about 1′ long. When it is struck it sends forth magical vibrations which cause locks to open. Likewise lids, doors, valves, and portals will open when the *chime* is sounded. The device will function against normal bars, shackles, chains, bolts, etc. It also destroys the magic of a *hold portal* spell or even a *wizard lock* cast by a magic-user of less than 15th level. The *chime* must be pointed at the area of the item or gate which is to be loosed or opened. It is then struck, a clear chiming ring sounds (which may attract monsters), and in 1 round 1 of the functions of the device will be completed, i.e., a lock opened, a shackle loosed, a secret door opened, the lid of a chest lifted, etc. Note that if a chest is chained, padlocked, locked, and *wizard locked*, it will take 4 or 5 soundings of the *chime of opening* to get it open. A *silence* spell negates the power of the device. The *chime* has 20-80 (20 + d6 × 10) charges before it will crack and become useless.

Chime of Hunger: This device exactly resembles a *chime of opening*. When it is struck all creatures within 6″ are immediately struck with ravenous hunger. Characters will tear into their rations, ignoring everything else, and even dropping everything they are holding in order to eat. Creatures without food immediately available will rush to where the *chime of hunger* sounded and attack any creatures there in order to kill and eat them. All creatures must eat for at least 1 round, but they are then entitled to a saving throw vs. magic on each successive round until such is made, i.e. hunger is satisfied. *Note:* It is recommended that the *chime of hunger* operate as one of *opening* for several rounds of use before its curse be put into operation.

Cloak of Displacement: This item appears to be a normal cloak, but when it is worn by a character its magical properties distort and warp light waves. This *displacement* of light waves causes the wearer to appear to be from 1′ to 2′ from his or her actual position. Any attack by missile or melee strike which is aimed at the wearer will automatically miss the first time*. Thereafter the cloak affords +2 protection, i.e. 2 classes better on armor class, as well as +2 on saving throw dice versus attack forms directed at the wearer (such as *spells*, gaze weapon attacks, spitting and breath attacks, etc. which are aimed at the wearer of the *cloak of displacement*). Note that 75% of all *cloaks of displacement* are sized for humans or elves (persons 5′ to 6′ or so tall), and but 25% are sized for persons of about 4′ height (dwarves, gnomes, halflings).

> * This can apply to first attacks from multiple opponents *only* if the second and successive attackers were unable to observe the initial *displacement* miss.

Cloak of Elvenkind: A *cloak of elvenkind* is of a plain neutral gray which is indistinguishable from any sort of ordinary cloak of the same color. However, when it is worn, with the hood drawn up around the head, it enables the wearer to be nearly invisible, for the *cloak* has chameleon-like powers. In the outdoors the wearer of a *cloak of elvenkind* is almost totally invisible in natural surroundings, nearly so in other settings. Note that the wearer is easily seen if violently or hastily moving, regardless of the surroundings. The invisibility bestowed is:

Outdoors, natural surroundings
heavy growth 100%
light growth 99%
open fields 95%

Outdoors, other   .
rocky terrain 98%
buildings. 90%
brightly lit room 50%

Underground
torch/lantern light 95%
infravision 90%
light/continual light 50%

Fully 90% of these cloaks are sized for human to elven-sized persons. The other 10% are sized for smaller persons (4′ or so in height).

Cloak of the Manta Ray: This cloak appears to be made from leather. When it is donned it appears as a normal cloak until the wearer enters salt water, at which time the *cloak of the manta ray* adheres to the individual, and he or she appears nearly (90%) identical to a manta ray. The wearer is enabled to breath underwater and move as a manta ray — 18″, see **MONSTER MANUAL**. The wearer also has an armor class of at least 6, that of a manta ray, and other magical protections or magical armor will improve that armor value. Although the *cloak* does not enable the wearer to bite opponents as a manta ray does, the garment does have a tail spine which the wearer can use to strike at opponents behind him or her — damage is only 1-6 hit points, and there is no chance of stunning. This attack mode can be used in addition to other sorts, for the wearer can release his or her arms from the *cloak's* "wings" without sacrificing movement if so desired.

Cloak of Poisonousness: This particular cloak is usually of woolen-like material, although it can be leathern. It can be handled without harm, and it radiates magic. A *neutralize poison* spell will not affect it. As soon as the *cloak of poisonousness* is actually worn, the wearer will be stricken stone dead. The *cloak* can only be removed with a *remove curse*, which destroys the magical properties of the *cloak*. If a *neutralize poison* spell is then used, the person can possibly be revived by a *raise dead* or *resurrection* spell, but there is a –10% chance of success because of the poison. *After* its effects are known, a small label saying "Nessus Shirt Company" might be seen at your option.

Cloak of Protection: The various forms of this marvelous device all appear to be normal garments, whether made of cloth or leather. Each lends to its wearer benefits on armor class — each plus of the *cloak of protection* bettering armor class by 1 factor — and to saving throw — each plus being added to the wearer's saving throw dice rolls. Thus a +1 *cloak* would make armor class 10 (no armor) into armor class 9, and add +1 to saving throw dice rolls. To determine how powerful a given cloak is, use this table:

01-35	+1 cloak
36-65	+2 cloak
66-85	+3 cloak
86-95	+4 cloak
96-00	+5 cloak

Note that this device can be combined with other items, or worn with

leather armor. It cannot function in conjunction with any sort of magical armor, normal armor other than that of leather, or in conjunction with a shield of any sort.

Crystal Ball: This is the most common form of scrying device, a crystal sphere of about ½′ diameter. A magic-user can use the device to see over virtually any distance or into other planes of existence. The user of a *crystal ball* must know the subject which is to be viewed. Knowledge can be from personal acquaintance, possession of personal belongings, a likeness of the object, or accumulated information. Knowledge is the key to how successful location will be, not distance:

Subject is	Chance of Locating*
Personally well known	100%
Personally known slightly	85%
Pictured	50%
Part of in possession	50%
Garment in possession	25%
Well informed of	25%
Slightly informed of	20%
On another plane	–25%

* Unless masked by magic or psionics.

The chance of locating also dictates how long a magic-user will be able to view the subject, both with respect to length of period and frequency:

Chances of Locating*	Viewing Period and Frequency	
100% or more	1 hour,	3 times/day
99% to 90%	½ hour,	3 times/day
89% to 75%	½ hour,	2 times/day
74% to 50%	½ hour,	1 time/day
49% to 25%	¼ hour,	1 time/day
24% or less	1/6 hour,	1 time/day

* Unless masked by magic or psionics.

Viewing beyond the periods or frequencies noted will cause the magic-user to make a saving throw versus magic each round, and failure to make it will permanently lower the character's intelligence by 1 point and drive him or her *insane* until *healed*.

Certain spells cast upon the user of the *crystal ball* might improve his or her ability. They are: *comprehend languages, read magic, infravision, tongues*. Two spells can be cast *through* a *crystal ball*, with a 5% chance per level of experience of the magic-user of working correctly. The spells are: *detect magic, detect evil/good*.

Certain *crystal balls* have additional powers. To determine this, consult the table below:

01-50	crystal ball
51-75	crystal ball with *clairaudience*
76-90	crystal ball with *ESP*
91-00	crystal ball with *telepathy**

* Communication only.

The spell function of the device operates at 10th level.

Only creatures with intelligence of 12 or better have a chance of noticing the scrying. The base chance is determined by class.

Fighter	2%	Thief	6%
Paladin	6%	Assassin	5%
Ranger	4%	Monk	1%
		Bard	3%

For each factor of intelligence above 12 the creature has an additional arithmetically ascending cumulative chance beginning at 1%, i.e. 1%, 3%, 6%, 10%, 15%, 21%, at 13, 14, 15, 16, 17, and 18 intelligence. These creatures also have a cumulative chance of 1% per level of experience of detecting scrying. Treat monsters as one of above as is most applicable.

Check each round of scrying, and if the percentage or less is rolled, the subject is aware of being watched. If a spell-user (cleric, druid, magic-user, or illusionist) is being observed, use the **DETECTION OF INVISIBILITY** table on page 60 rather than the percentages above to determine whether the observation is detected, checking each round. A *dispel magic* will cause the *crystal ball* being used to cease functioning for 1 day. The various protections against *crystal ball* viewing will simply leave the device hazy and non-functioning.

(Note: You may allow scrying devices for clerics and druids; water basins and mirrors are suggested. Have them function as normal crystal balls.)

Crystal Hypnosis Ball: This cursed item type is indistinguishable from a normal crystal ball, and it radiates magic, but not evil, if detected for. Any magic-user attempting to use it will become hypnotized, and a telepathic suggestion will be implanted in his or her mind. The user of the device will believe that the desired object was viewed, but actually he or she became partially under the influence of a powerful magic-user, lich, or even some power/being from another plane. Each further use will bring the crystal ball gazer more under the influence of the creature, either as a servant, tool, or possession object. As referee, you must decide whether to make this a gradual or sudden affair according to the surroundings and circumstances peculiar to the finding of the crystal hypnosis ball and the character(s) locating it.

Cube of Force: A device of but about the size of a large die — perhaps ¾ of an inch across — the cube of force enables its possessor to put up a wall of force 1" per side around his or her person, and this cubic screen is impervious to the attack forms shown on the table below. The cube has 36 charges, and each day this energy is restored. The holder presses one face of the cube to activate or deactivate the field:

Cube Face	Charge Cost per Turn/Movement Rate	Effect
one	1/1"	keeps out gases, wind, etc.
two	2/8"	keeps out non-living matter
three	3/6"	keeps out living matter
four	4/4"	keeps out magic
five	6/3"	keeps out all things
six	0/normal	deactivates

When the force screen is up, the following attack forms cost extra charges from the cube in order to maintain the integrity of the screen. Note that these spells cannot be cast either into or out of the cube:

catapult-like missiles	1	flame strike	3
very hot normal fires	2	lightning bolt	4
horn of blasting	6	meteor swarm	8
delayed blast fireball	3	passwall	3
disintegrate	6	phase door	5
fireball	3	prismatic spray	7
fire storm	3	wall of fire	2

The cube of force can be of any hard mineral, ivory or bone.

Cube of Frost Resistance: This device resembles a cube of force. When the cube is activated it encloses an area of 1" per side, and the temperature within this area is always 65 degrees F. The field will absorb all cold-based attacks, i.e. cone of cold, ice storm, and even white dragon's breath. However, if the field is subjected to more than 50 hit points of cold in any turn (10 rounds) it collapses and cannot be renewed for 1 hour. If it receives over 100 hit points of damage in 1 turn the cube is destroyed. Note: cold below 0 degrees F. effectively inflicts 2 hit points of cold for every -10 degrees, so that the cube is at -2 at -1 to -10 degrees F., -4 at -11 to -20, etc. Thus, at -40 degrees F. the device can withstand only 42 hit points.

Cubic Gate: Another small cubic device, this item is fashioned from carnelian. The 6 sides of the cube are each keyed to a plane, 1 of which will always be the Prime Material, of course. The other 5 can be chosen by any means desired. If the side of the cubic gate is pressed but once, it opens a nexus to the appropriate plane, and there is a 10% chance per turn that something will come through it looking for food, fun, and/or trouble. If the side is pressed twice, the creature so doing, along with all creatures in a 5' radius will be drawn through the nexus to the other plane. It is impossible to open more than 1 nexial link at once.

Daern's Instant Fortress: This metal cube is of small size, but when activated it grows to form a metal tower 20' square and 30' high, with arrow slits on all sides and a machicolated battlement atop it, the metal extending 10' into the ground. It has a small door which will open only to the command of the owner of the fortress, knock spells notwithstanding. The adamantite walls of Daern's Instant Fortress are totally unaffected by normal weapons other than those of catapult type. The whole can take 200 points of damage before the tower collapses. Note that damage sustained is cumulative. The fortress cannot be repaired, although a wish will restore 10 points of damage sustained. It requires but 1 round to cause the fortress to spring up, but the person or persons nearby must be careful not to be

caught by its sudden growth, or else they will sustain 10-100 hit points of damage. The door will always be facing the owner of the device when it becomes a fortress, and it will open and close instantly at his command.

Decanter of Endless Water: This flask is quite ordinary looking, but if magic is detected it will radiate that property. The decanter has a stopper, and if this is removed, and the proper words spoken, it will pour forth a stream of fresh or salt water as ordered. There are separate command words for the amount as well as the type of water. Water can be made to come forth as follows:

Stream: pours out 1 gallon per round
Fountain: 5' long stream at 5 gallons per round
Geyser: 20' long stream at 30 gallons per round

The last shown application causes considerable back pressure, and the holder must be well braced or be knocked over. The force of the geyser will kill small animals and insects (mice, moles, small bats, etc.). The command word must be given to cease.

Deck of Many Things: A deck of many things (beneficial and baneful) usually is found contained within a box or leather pouch. Each deck contains a number of thin plaques or plates. These sheets are usually of ivory or vellum. Each is engraved and/or inscribed with glyphs, characters, and magical sigils. As soon as one of these sheets is drawn forth from the pack, its magic is bestowed upon the person who drew it, for better or worse. The character gaining a deck of many things may announce that only 1 will be drawn from the pack, or he or she may opt to draw forth 2, 3, or even 4, but the number must be announced prior to the first plaque withdrawn. Note that if the jester is drawn, the possessor of the deck may elect to draw 2 additional cards. Each time a plaque is taken from the deck it is replaced unless the draw is a jester or fool, in which case the plaque is discarded from the pack. The deck will contain either 13 or 22 plaques, 75%/25% chance. Additional plaques in a 22 card deck are indicated by an asterisk (*) before their names. To simulate the plaques you may use the normal playing card indicated:

Sun (KD)	Gain beneficial miscellaneous magic item and 50,000 experience points	
Moon (QD)	You are granted 1-4 wishes	
Star (JD)	Immediately gain 2 points on your major ability	
*Comet (2D)	Defeat the next monster you meet to gain 1 level	
Throne (KH)	Gain charisma of 18 and small keep	
Key (QH)	Gain a treasure map plus 1 magic weapon	
Knight (JH)	Gain the service of a 4th level fighter	
*Gem (2H)	Gain your choice of 20 jewelry or 50 gems	
The Void (KC)	Body functions, but soul is trapped elsewhere	
Flames (QC)	Enmity between you and a devil	
Skull (JC)	Defeat Death or be forever destroyed	
*Talons (2C)	All magic items you possess are torn from you	
Ruin (KS)	Immediately lose all wealth and real property	
Euryale (QS)	Minus 3 on all saving throws vs. petrification	
Rogue (JS)	One of your henchmen turns against you	
*Balance (2S)	Change alignment or be judged	
Jester (J)	Gain 10,000 experience points **or** 2 more draws from the deck	
*Fool (J with Trademark)	Lose 10,000 experience points; draw again	
*Vizier (AD)	Know the answer to your next dilemma	
*Idiot (AC)	Lose 1-4 points of intelligence, you may draw again	
*Fates (AH)	Avoid any situation you choose . . . once	
Donjon (AS)	You are imprisoned	

Upon drawing the last plaque possible, or immediately upon drawing the plaques in **bold face (The Void, Donjon)**, the deck disappears. The plaques are explained below:

Sun: Roll on the MISCELLANEOUS MAGIC TABLE (III.E., 1.-5.) until a useful item (other than artifacts or relics) is indicated. The player gets experience points for this as well.

Moon: This is best represented by a moonstone gem with the appropriate number of wishes shown as gleams therein. These wishes are the same as the ninth level magic-user spell (q.v.) and must be used in a number of turns equal to the number received.

Star: If the 2 points would place the character's score at 19, use 1 or both in any of the other abilities in this order: constitution, charisma, wisdom, dexterity, intelligence, strength.

Comet: The player must single-handedly defeat the next monster — singular or plural — of hostile nature or the benefit is lost. If successful, the character moves to the mid-point of the next experience level.

Throne: If charisma is 18 already, the individual still gains +25% on encounter and loyalty reactions. He or she becomes a real leader in people's eyes. The castle gained will be near to any stronghold already possessed.

Key: Roll a treasure map with +20% on the dice. The weapon with it must be one usable by the character, so use the table for SWORDS (III.G.), MISCELLANEOUS WEAPONS (III.H.), or RODS, et al. (III.D.) as needed.

Knight: The hero will join as the character's henchman and loyally serve until death. The hero has +1 per die (18 maximum) on each ability roll.

Gem: This indicates wealth. The jewelry will all be gold set with gems, the gems all of 1,000 g.p. base value. With this wealth should come experience points equal in value, but never more than sufficient for 1 level rise in experience.

The Void: This lightless black plaque spells instant disaster. The character's body functions, and he or she speaks like an automaton, but the psyche is trapped in a prison somewhere — in an object on a far planet or plane, possibly in the possession of a demon. A *wish* will not bring the character back, but the plane of entrapment might be revealed.

Flames: Hot anger, jealousy, envy, are but a few of the possible motivational forces for the enmity. The devil is usually of the *Greater* sort, possibly even an *Arch-devil*. The enmity can never be satisfied, save one or the other is slain.

Skull: A minor Death appears (AC −4; 33 hit points; strikes with a scythe for 2-16 hit points, never missing, always striking first in a round) and the character must fight it alone — if others help, they get minor Deaths to fight as well. If the character is slain he or she is slain *forever*. Treat the Death as undead with respect to spells. Cold or fire do not harm it, neither does electrical energy.

Talons: When this plaque is drawn each and every magic item owned or possessed by the character drawing are irrevocably *gone*. This happens instantly.

Ruin: As implied, when this plaque is drawn every bit of money (including all gems, jewelry, and like previous and valuable treasure and art) and all real property and buildings thereon currently owned are lost forever.

Euryale: The Medusa-like visage of this plaque brings a curse which only the Fates card or god-like beings can remove. The −3 is permanent otherwise.

Rogue: When this plaque is drawn, 1 of the character's henchmen will be totally alienated and forever hostile henceforward. If the character has no henchmen, the enmity of some powerful personage — community or religious — can be substituted. The hatred will be secret until the time is ripe for devastating effect.

Balance: As "weighed in the balance and found wanting", the character must change, and perform accordingly, to a radically different alignment, i.e. lawful-chaotic, good-evil, neutral-non-neutral. Failure brings judgment, and if there is substantial deviation from professed alignment, the character will be destroyed permanently.

Jester: This plaque actually makes either pack more beneficial if the experience point award is taken. It is *always* discarded when drawn, unlike all others except the *Fool*.

Fool: The payment and draw are mandatory!

Vizier: This plaque empowers the character drawing it with the ability to call upon supernatural wisdom to solve any single problem or answer fully any question whenever he or she so requests. Whether the information gained can be successfully acted upon is another question entirely.

Idiot: As indicated, the mongoloid countenance causes loss of 1-4 (d4) points of intelligence immediately. They are lost and cannot be

regained (although points can be restored by other means). The additional draw is optional.

Fates: This plaque enables the character to avoid even an instantaneous occurrence if so desired, for the fabric of reality is unraveled and respun, so to speak. Note that it does not allow something *to* happen, only *not to* take place. This reversal is for the individual character only, and the party must still endure the confrontation.

Donjon: This signifies *imprisonment* — either by spell or by some creature/being at your option. All gear and spells will be stripped from the victim in any case.

Drums of Deafening: This item is a pair of kettle drums, radiating magic if so detected, but otherwise unremarkable. If either is struck nothing happens, but if both are sounded together all creatures within 7″ are permanently *deaf* and will remain so until a *heal* spell or similar cure is used to restore shattered eardrums. Furthermore, those within 1″ of the drums will be stunned by the noise for from 2-8 rounds. Each drum is a hemisphere of about 1½′ diameter.

Drums of Panic: These kettle drums are unremarkable in appearance. If both of the pair are sounded, all creatures within 12″, save for a "safe zone" of 2″ radius from the *drums*, must make their saving throw versus magic or turn and move directly away from the sound for 1 full turn. Each turn thereafter, the panicked creatures may attempt to save versus magic again. Each failure brings another turn of movement away from the *drums of panic*. Movement is at fastest possible speed while fleeing in panic, and 3 rounds of rest are required for each 1 turn of fast movement after the saving throw is made. Creatures with intelligence of 2 make saving throws at −2, those with 1 or less save at −4. Each drum is a hemisphere of about 1½′ diameter.

Dust of Appearance: This fine powder appears much like any other dust unless a careful examination is conducted. The latter will reveal it to be more like a metal dust, but *very* fine and *very* light. One handful of this substance flung into the air will coat all objects, making them visible even if they are invisible, out of phase, astral, or ethereal. Note that the *dust* will also reveal *mirror images* and *projected images* for what they are, and it likewise negates the effects of *cloaks of displacement* or *elvenkind* or *robes of blending*. Appearance lasts for 2-20 turns. It is typically in small silk packets or hollow bone blow tubes. A packet can be shaken out to cover an area with a radius of 10′ from the user. A tube can be blown in a cone shape, 1′ wide at the start, 15′ at the end, and 20′ long. From 5 to 50 containers can be in one place.

Dust of Disappearance: This dust exactly resembles that of *appearance*, and it is typically found stored in the same manner and quantity. All things touched by it reflect and bend light of all sorts (infra-red and ultra-violet included) so as to become invisible to sight or virtually any other means of normal detection or even magical means such as *detect invisibility* spells, but not *dust of appearance*. Invisibility bestowed by the *dust* lasts for 2-20 turns, 11-20 if carefully sprinkled upon an object. Attack while thus invisible is possible, always by surprise if the opponent is unable to note invisible things and always at an armor class 4 places better while invisibility lasts. Note that unlike the *invisibility* spell, attack while using the *dust of disappearance* will not obviate the *invisibility*.

Dust of Sneezing and Choking: This fine dust appears to be either of the above types of magical powders. If spread, however, it will cause those within a 20′ radius to fall into fits of sneezing and coughing, those failing to save versus poison die immediately, those who do being disabled by the choking for 5-20 rounds.

Efreeti Bottle: This item is typically fashioned of brass or bronze, with a lead stopper bearing special seals. It not uncommonly has a thin stream of smoke issuing from it. There is a 10% chance that the efreeti will be insane and attack immediately upon being released. There is also a 10% chance that the efreeti of the bottle will only grant 3 *wishes*. The other 80% of the time, however, the inhabitant of the bottle will serve normally (see **MONSTER MANUAL**). When opened, the efreeti issues from the bottle in but 1 segment.

Eversmoking Bottle: This metal urn is identical to an *efreeti bottle*. It does nothing but smoke, however. The amount of smoke will be very great if the stopper is pulled out, pouring from the bottle and totally obscuring vision in a 50,000 cubic foot area in 1 round. The bottle, left unstoppered, will fill another 10,000 cubic feet of space with smoke each round until 120,000 cubic feet of space is fogged, and this area will continue to remain so smoked until the *eversmoking bottle* is *stoppered*. The *bottle* can only be resealed if a command word is known.

Eyes of Charming: This item consists of a pair of convex crystal lenses which fit over the user's eyes. When in place, the wearer is able to *charm persons* merely by meeting their gaze. Those failing to save versus magic are charmed as per the spell. One person per round can be thus looked at. Saving throws are at −2 if the wearer has both lenses, at +2 if he or she wears only 1 of a pair of *eyes of charming*.

Eyes of the Eagle: These optics are also of special crystal and fit over the eyes of the wearer. They give vision 100 times greater than normal at distances of 1′ or more, i.e. the wearer can see at 2,000′ what a person could normally see at 20′. Wearing only 1 of the cusps will cause the character to become dizzy, and in effect stunned, for 1 round. Thereafter, 1 eye must always be covered to avoid this vertigo.

Eyes of Minute Seeing: Appearing much the same as any other magical lenses, *eyes of minute seeing* enable the wearer to see 100 times better at distances of 1′ or less. Thus, tiny seams, minute marks, even the impression left from writing can be seen, thus secret compartments and hidden joints can be noted and the information acted upon. The effect of wearing but one of these crystals is the same as given for *eyes of the eagle*.

Eyes of Petrification: Totally indistinguishable from any other magical cusps, the effect of donning these lenses is instantaneous: the wearer is turned to stone. Note: 25% of these devices work as the gaze of a basilisk does, including reflection of the weapon turning the gazer to stone.

Note: Mixing eye types is certain to cause immediate insanity for 2-8 (2d4) turns.

TABLE (III.E.) 3.

Figurines of Wondrous Power: There are various *figurines*, but all have the following in common. Each is apparently a statuette of small size, but an inch or so high. When the *figurine* is tossed down and a command word spoken, however, it becomes a living creature which obeys and serves its owner. If any *figurine* is destroyed in its statuette form it is forever ruined, all magic is lost, and it has no power. If slain in animal-like form the *figurine* simply reverts to its statuette conformation and can be used again at a later time as long as the statuette is not broken. When *figurines of wondrous power* are indicated, roll on the table below to determine the type:

01-15	ebony fly
16-30	golden lions (pair)
31-40	ivory goats (trio)
41-55	marble elephant
56-65	obsidian steed
66-85	onyx dog
86-00	serpentine owl

Ebony Fly: At a word the small carving grows to the size of a pony. The *ebony fly* is armor class 4, has 4 + 4 hit dice, air maneuverability class C, and flies at 48″ movement rate without a rider, at 36″ carrying up to 210 pounds weight, and 24″ carrying from 211 to 350 pounds weight. The item can be used a maximum of 3 times per week, 12 hours per day. When 12 hours have expired, or in any event when the command word is spoken, the *ebony fly* shrinks to statuette size.

Golden Lions: A pair of *golden lions* are exceptionally useful as they become 2 normal adult male lions (armor class 5/6, 5 + 2 hit dice, and normal attack modes). If slain in combat, the lions cannot be brought back from statuette form for 1 full week; otherwise, they can be used once every day. They enlarge and shrink upon speaking the command word.

Ivory Goats: Each goat of this trio of statuettes looks slightly different, for each has a different function. These are:

1. *The Goat of Travelling:* This statuette provides a speedy and enduring mount of armor class 6, with 24 hit points and 2 attacks (horns) for 1-8 each (consider as 4 hit dice monster). It moves at 48″ bearing 280 pounds or less, and at −1″ for every additional 14 pounds of weight carried. The goat can travel a maximum of 1 day each week — continuously or in any combination of periods totalling 24 hours. At this point, or when the command word is

uttered, it returns to its small form for not less than 1 day before it can again be used.

2. *The Goat of Travail:* When commanded, this statuette becomes an enormous creature, larger than a bull, with sharp hooves (4-10/4-10), a vicious bite (2-8), and a pair of wicked horns of exceptional size (2-12/2-12). If it is charging to attack, it may only use its horns, but +6 damage is added to each hit on that round, i.e., 8-18 h.p. damage per horn. It is armor class 0, has 96 hit points, and attacks as a 16 hit dice monster. It can be called to life but once per month. It moves 24″.

3. *The Goat of Terror:* When called upon with the proper command word, this statuette becomes a destrier-like mount, 36″ movement, armor class 2, 48 hit points, and no attacks itself. However, its rider can employ the goat's horns as weapons, one horn as a +3 spear (lance), the other as a +6 sword. When ridden versus an opponent, the *goat of terror* radiates *terror* in a 3″ radius, and any opponent in this radius must make a saving throw versus magic or lose 50% of strength and suffer at least −3 on "to hit" dice rolls, all due to weakness caused by terror. When all opponents are slain, or upon the proper command, the *goat* returns to its statuette form. It can be used once every 2 weeks.

After 3 uses each of the *goats* loses its magical abilities forever.

Marble Elephant: These are the largest of the *figurines*, each statuette being about the size of a human hand. Upon utterance of the command word, a *marble elephant* can be caused to grow to the size and specifications of a true elephant or return to statuette form. The animal created from the statuette is fully obedient to its commander, serving as a beast of burden, mount, or attacking alone. The type of *marble elephant* obtained is determined as follows:

01-50	Asiatic (Elephant)
51-90	African (Loxodont)
91-93	Prehistoric (Mammoth)
94-00	Prehistoric (Mastodon)

Details of each type of creature are found in the **MONSTER MANUAL**. The statuette can be used a maximum of 24 hours at a time, 4 times per month.

Obsidian Steed: An *obsidian steed* appears as a small, nearly shapeless lump of black stone. Only careful inspection will reveal that it vaguely resembles some form of quadruped, and of course, if magic is detected for, the piece of rock which is the *steed* figurine will be noted as radiating some dweomer (magic). Upon speaking the command word, the near formless piece of obsidian becomes a true *nightmare*. It will allow itself to be ridden, but if the rider is of good alignment, it is 10% likely per use to carry its "master" to the floor of *Hades'* first layer and then return to its statuette form. See **MONSTER MANUAL** for details of the *nightmare*. The statuette can be used for a 24 hour period maximum, once per week. Note that when the *obsidian steed* becomes astral or ethereal its rider and gear likewise so become, thus travel to other planes is easily accomplished by means of this item.

Onyx Dog: When commanded, this statuette changes into a creature which has the same properties as a *war dog*, except that it is endowed with intelligence of 8-10, can communicate in the common tongue, and has exceptional olfactory and visual abilities. The olfactory power enables the *onyx dog* to scent the trail of a known creature 100% of the time if it is 1 hour or less old, −10% per hour thereafter, and subject to being thrown off by false trails, breaks, water, and masking or blocking substances or scents. The visual power enables the *onyx dog* to use 90′ range infravision, spotting hidden (such as in shadows) things 80% of the time, normally invisible things 65% of the time, and noting astral, ethereal, and out-of-phase things 50% of the time. For details, see DOG, WAR in the **MONSTER MANUAL**. An *onyx dog* can be used for up to 6 continuous hours, once per week. It obeys only its owner.

Serpentine Owl: A *serpentine owl* becomes a normal-sized horned owl (AC 7; 24″ move; 2-4 hit points; 1-2/1-2 hit points of damage when attacking) if its possessor so commands, or it can become a *giant owl* if its owner so requires. The latter usage, however, is limited to 3 times; thereafter the statuette loses all of its magical properties. The *normal-sized* form of the magical statuette moves with 95% silence, has infravision to 90′, can see in normal, above ground darkness as if it were full light, and twice as well as a human at that. Its hearing is so keen as to be able to detect a mouse moving at 60' distance; thus, silent movement chances are reduced 50% with respect to the *serpentine owl* in smaller form. Furthermore, it can and will communicate with its owner by telepathic means, informing of all it sees and hears according to its (low, 2-4) intelligence in normal-size. If commanded to giant-size, a *serpentine owl* is in all respects the same as a *giant owl*. For information see Owl, giant, in the **MONSTER MANUAL**. As with most other *figurines of wondrous power*, this one readily obeys all commands of its owner.

Flask of Curses: This item appears much the same as any beaker, bottle, container, decanter, flask, jug, etc. It has magical properties, but detection will not reveal the nature of the *flask of curses*. It often contains liquid substance too, or it may emit smoke. When the *flask* is first unstoppered, a *curse* of some sort will be visited upon the person or persons nearby (it will subsequently be harmless). The suggestions given for the *curse* reverse of the cleric *bless* spell, and those stated for typical *curses* found on a scroll are recommended for use here as well, or some monster can appear and attack all creatures in sight, etc.

Gauntlets of Dexterity: A pair of these gloves appears to be nothing more than light leather handwear of the everyday sort. Naturally, they radiate magic if so detected. They size themselves magically to fit any hand, from that of a huge human to that of a small halfling, when drawn on. A pair of *gauntlets of dexterity* increase overall dexterity by 4 points if at 6 or less, by 2 points if at 7-13, and by 1 point if dexterity is 14 or higher. Furthermore, wearing these gloves enables non-thief characters to *pick pockets* or *open locks* as if he or she were a 4th level thief; if worn by a thief they increase these abilities by adding 10% to the normal percentage chance for the character's level.

Gauntlets of Fumbling: These gauntlets may be of supple leather or heavy protective gloves suitable for use with armor of ring, scale, chain, etc. In the former instance these gauntlets will appear to be of *dexterity*, in the latter case of *ogre power*. They will perform according to every test just as if they were other *gauntlets*, but when an enemy is actively seeking to harm their wearer, or in some similar life and death situation, their curse is activated, and he or she will become very clumsy, with a 50% chance each round of dropping anything held in either hand — not from both singly. The *gauntlets* will also lower overall dexterity by 2 points Once the curse is activated, the gloves can only be removed by means of a *remove curse* spell or a *wish*.

Gauntlets of Ogre Power: A pair of *ogre power* gauntlets appear the same as typical handwear for armor. The wearer of these gloves, however, is imbued with 18/00 strength in his or her hands, arms, and shoulders. When striking with the hand or with a weapon hurled or held, the gauntlets add +3 to hit probability and +6 to damage inflicted when a hit is made. These gauntlets are particularly desirable when combined with a *girdle of giant strength* and a hurled weapon. They enlarge or shrink to fit human to halfling-sized hands.

Gauntlets of Swimming and Climbing: A pair of these gloves appear as normal lightweight handwear, but they are most useful magic items, and radiate their dweomer if a detection is attempted. The wearer can have hands of large (human) or small (halfling) size. He or she will be enabled to swim as fast as a triton (15") under water, and as fast as a merman (18") on the surface. Of course, these *gauntlets* do not empower the wearer to breathe water. These gloves also give the wearer a very strong and able gripping and holding ability with respect to climbing, so as to enable him or her to climb vertical or nearly vertical surfaces, upwards or downwards, with a 95% probability of not slipping and falling — and if the wearer is a thief the *gauntlets* increase success probability to 99.5%.

Gem of Brightness: This crystal appears to be nothing more than a gem in rather rough, long prismed shape. Upon utterance of the proper spell words, however, the crystal will emit bright light of 3 sorts. It can be caused to shed a pale light in a cone-shape 10' long, emanating from the *gem* to a radius of 2½' at the end of the beam. This does not discharge any of the energy of the device. Another command will cause the *gem of brightness* to send out a very bright ray of light of only 1' diameter but of 50' length, and any creature who is struck in the eyes by this beam will be dazzled for 1-4 rounds and unable to see. The creature struck is entitled to a saving throw versus magic to determine whether or not its eyes were shut or averted in time. This use of the *gem* expends 1 energy charge. The third manner in which the *gem* may be used is to flare in a blinding flash of light in a cone 30' long and 5' radius at its terminus. Although this glare lasts but a moment, all creatures within its area must save versus

magic or be blinded for 1-4 rounds and thereafter suffer a penalty of -1 to -4 on hit probability dice rolls due to permanent eye damage. This use expends 5 charges. Dazzling or blindness effect can be removed by a *cure blindness* spell; eye damage can be cured only by a *heal* spell. The *gem of brightness* has 50 charges and cannot be recharged. A *darkness* spell will drain 1 of its charges, or make it useless for 1 round, at the option of the *gem* owner. A *continual darkness* spell will cause it to be useless for 1 day, or expend 5 charges, at the option of the owner.

Gem of Seeing: One of these finely cut and polished stones is normally indistinguishable from a jewel of the ordinary sort, although a *detect magic* will reveal its dweomer. When gazed through, the *gem of seeing* enables the user to detect all hidden, illusionary, invisible, astral, ethereal, or out of phase things within viewing range. Peering through the crystal is time consuming and tedious. The viewing range of the *gem* is 30" for a cursory scan if only large, obvious objects are being sought, 10" if small things are to be seen. It requires 1 round to scan a 200' square area in a cursory manner, 2 rounds to view a 100' square area in a careful way. There is a 5% chance each time the *gem* is used that the viewer will see an hallucination, see something that is not there, or possibly see through some real thing as if it were an illusion.

Girdle of Femininity/Masculinity: This broad leather band appears to be a normal belt used commonly by all sorts of adventurers, but of course it is magical. If buckled on, it will *immediately* change the sex of its wearer to the opposite gender. Its magical curse fulfilled, the belt then loses all power. The original sex of the character cannot be restored by any normal means, although a *wish* might do so (50% chance), and a powerful being can alter the situation, i.e., it takes a god-like creature to set matters aright with certainty. 10% of these girdles actually remove *all* sex from the wearer.

Girdle of Giant Strength: This belt looks similar to those normal to adventuring. It is imbued with very powerful magic, of course, and when worn it increases the physical prowess of its wearer as follows:

Dice Roll	Type of Giant Strength & Rating		Bonuses		Open Doors*
			To Hit	Damage	
01-30	Hill	19	+3	+ 7	7 in 8 (3)
31-50	Stone	20	+3	+ 8	7 in 8 (3)
51-70	Frost	21	+4	+ 9	9 in 10 (4)
71-85	Fire	22	+4	+10	11 in 12 (4)
86-95	Cloud	23	+5	+11	11 in 12 (5)
96-00	Storm	24	+6	+12	19 in 20 (7 in 8)

* The number in parentheses is the number of chances out of 6 (8 for storm giant strength) for the character to be able to force open a locked, barred, magically held, or *wizard locked* door, but only one attempt ever (per door) may be made, and if it fails, no further attempts can succeed.

The wearer of the girdle is able to otherwise *hurl rocks* and *bend bars* as if he or she had imbibed a *potion of giant strength*. These abilities are:

		Rock Hurling			
Type	Weight Allowance	Range	Base Damage	Rock Wt.**	Bend Bars/ Lift Gates
Hill	+ 4,500	8"	1-6	140	50%
Stone	+ 5,000	16"	1-12	198	60%
Frost	+ 6,000	10"	1-8	156	70%
Fire	+ 7,500	12"	1-8	170	80%
Cloud	+ 9,000	14"	1-10	184	90%
Storm	+12,000	16"	1-12	212	100%

** Approximate average missile weight.

The strength gained is *not* cumulative with normal or magical strength bonuses except with regard to use in combination with *gauntlets of ogre power* and magic war hammers (q.v.).

Helm of Brilliance: When discovered, a *helm of brilliance* appears to be nothing more than an ordinary piece of armor for head protection, viz. a helmet, basinet, sallet, etc. of iron or steel. When worn, it functions only upon the utterance of a special command word. When so empowered the true nature of the *helm* is visible to all. The *helm* is armor of +2 value. It is of brilliant silver and polished steel, and set with 10 diamonds, 20 rubies, 30 fire opals, and 40 opals — each of large size and magicked — which perform as explained below. When struck by bright light the helm will scintillate and send forth reflective rays in all directions from its crown-like spikes set with gems. The jewels' functions are:

Diamond	*Prismatic spray* (as the seventh level illusionist spell)
Ruby	*Wall of fire* (as the fifth level druid spell)
Fire Opal	*Fireball* (as the third level magic-user spell)
Opal	*Light* (as the first level cleric spell)

Each gem can perform its spell-like power in but 1 segment, but each is usable only once. The *helm* may be thus used once per round. The level of the spell is doubled to obtain the level at which the spell was cast with respect to range, duration, and such considerations. Until all of its jewels are magically expended, a *helm of brilliance* also is capable of the following magical properties when activated:

1. It glows with a bluish light when undead are within 30', this light causing pain and 1-6 points of damage to all such creatures save skeletons and zombies.

2. The wearer may command any sword he or she wields to become a *sword of flame* (q.v.), this being additional to its other special properties, if any; 1 round of time is required to effect this fire.

3. The wearer may *produce flame* just as if he or she were a 5th level druid.

4. The wearer is protected just as if a double strength *fire resistance* ring were worn, but this protection cannot be augmented by further magical means.

Once all of its jewels have lost their magic, the *helm* loses all of its powers. The gems turn to worthless powder when this occurs. Removing a jewel destroys the gem. They may *not* be re-magicked.

If for any reason the wearer fails to make his or her saving throw versus a magical fire attack, he or she must attempt another saving throw for the helmet without magical additions. If this is failed, the remaining gems on the helm will all overload and detonate, causing in multiple whatever effects the gems would normally have.

Helm of Comprehending Languages and Reading Magic: Appearing as a normal war helmet, a *helm of comprehending languages and reading magic* enables its wearer to understand 90% of strange tongues and writings, 80% of magical writings. (Note these percentage figures apply to whether *all* or *none* of the speaking/writing or inscription is understandable. Understanding does not necessarily imply spell use.) This device is equal to a normal helmet of the type accompanying armor class 5.

Helm of Opposite Alignment: By appearance this metal hat is simply a typical helmet. By test, it will radiate an indeterminate dweomer. Once placed upon the head, however, its curse *immediately* takes place, and the alignment of the wearer is radically altered — good to evil, neutral to some absolute commitment (LE, LG, CE, CG) as radically different from former alignment as possible. Alteration in alignment is mental and, once effected, is desired by the individual whom the magic changed. Only a *wish*, or *alter reality*, can restore former alignment, and the affected individual will *not* make any attempt to return to former alignment. If a paladin is concerned, he or she must undergo a special *quest* and *atone* if the curse is to be obliterated. Note that once a *helm of opposite alignment* has functioned it loses all of its magical properties.

Helm of Telepathy: This sturdy metal helmet appears to be a normal piece of headgear, although it will radiate magic if this is detected for. The wearer of a *helm of telepathy* is able to determine the thoughts of creatures within a 6″ range, provided the wearer knows the language used by such creatures (the racial tongue will be used in thoughts in preference to the common, the common in preference to alignment languages), and there is not more than 3′ of solid stone, ¼′ of iron, or any solid sheeting of lead or gold between the wearer and the creatures. The thought pick-up is directional. Conscious effort must be made to pick up thoughts. The wearer may communicate by language with any creature within range if there is a mutually known speech, or emotions may be transmitted (empathy) so that a creature will receive the emotional message of the wearer. If the wearer of the *helm* desires to implant a *suggestion* (see the third level magic-user spell of that name under **CHARACTER SPELLS** in the **PLAYERS HANDBOOK**), he or she may attempt to do so as follows: For every 2 points of intelligence *greater* than the subject, the wearer is 5% more likely to be successful; but for every 1 point of intelligence *lower* than the subject, the probability decreases by 5%. Thus the subject creature receiving the *suggestion* gains a saving throw versus

magic with a –1 for every 2 points of intelligence lower than the telepathist, but +1 for every 1 point of intelligence *higher* than the wearer of the *helm*, and if intelligence is equal no adjustment is made when the saving throw is rolled. The *helm of telepathy* gives a +4 with respect to psionic related attacks (see **ATTACK MATRICES**). It increases total psionic strength by 40 points.

Helm of Teleportation: This is another helmet of normal appearance which will give off a magical aura if detected for. Any character wearing this device may *teleport* (q.v.) once per day, exactly as if he or she were a magic-user, i.e. the destination must be known, and a risk is involved. If a magic-user has access to this device, its full powers can be employed, for the wearer can then memorize a *teleportation* spell, and use the helm to refresh his or her memory so as to be able to repeat the spell up to 3 times upon objects or characters and still be able to personally *teleport* by means of the *helm*. As long as the magic-user retains the *teleportation* spell uncast, he or she can personally teleport up to 6 times before the memory of the spell is lost, and even then a usage of the *helm* remains as noted above.

Helm of Underwater Action: When this *helm* is viewed, it is indistinguishable from a normal helmet, but detection will reveal it as magical, and the possessor will be able to both see and breathe under water. Visual properties of the helm are activated when small lenses are drawn across the device from compartments on either side of the helmet. They allow the wearer to see 5 times farther than normal water and light conditions allow for normal human vision. (Note that weeds, obstructions, etc. will block vision in the usual manner.) If the command word is spoken, the *helm of underwater action* creates a globe of air around the wearer's head, and maintains it, until the command word is again spoken. Thus, the wearer can breathe freely.

Horn of Blasting: This magical horn appears as a normal trumpet, but it will reveal a dweomer if a detection for magic is cast upon it. It can be sounded as a normal horn, but if the correct word is spoken and the instrument then winded in the proper manner, it has the following effects:

1. A cone of sound, 12″ long and 3″ wide at the base, issues forth from the *horn* and all within it must save versus magic. Those saving are *stunned* for 1 round and *deafened* for 2. Those failing the saving throw sustain 1-10 hit points of damage, are *stunned* for 2 rounds and *deafened* for 4.

2. A wave of ultrasonic sound issues from the *horn* at the same time, a 1′ wide, 10″ long pulse, which causes a weakening of such materials as metal, stone, and wood, the weakening equal in effect to 3 times the damage caused by a hit from a missile hurled by a large catapult, i.e. 18 structural points, or sufficient to smash a drawbridge or flatten a normal cottage.

If a *horn of blasting* is winded magically more than once per day there is a 10% cumulative chance that it will explode itself and inflict 5-50 hit points of damage upon the person sounding it.

There are no charges upon a *horn*, but the device is subject to stresses as noted above, and each time it is used to magical effect there is a 2% cumulative chance of the instrument shivering itself. In the latter case, no damage is inflicted on the character blowing it.

Horn of Bubbles: This musical instrument will radiate magic if detected for. It appears as a normal horn, or possibly any one of the many magical ones. It will sound a note and call forth a mass of bubbles which completely surround and blind the individual who blew the horn for 2-20 rounds, but these bubbles will only appear in the presence of a creature actively seeking to slay the character who winded the *horn*, so their appearance might be delayed for a very short or extremely lengthy period.

Horn of Collapsing: The *horn* appears to be a normal musical instrument, perhaps a bugle or warning horn of some sort. If it is sounded without first speaking the proper rune, or 10% of the time in any event, the following will result:

Outside: A rain of fist-sized rocks will strike the individual sounding the horn, from 2-12 in number, each causing 1-6 hit points of damage.

Indoors: The ceiling overhead will collapse when the device is blown, so the character will take from 3-36 hit points of damage.

Underground: The area immediately above the character sounding the *horn* will fall upon him or her. The damage is 5-20 hit points base, multiplied by 1 factor for each 10' of height from which the material above drops (i.e., twice damage if a 20' ceiling, three times damage if a 30' ceiling, etc.).

Proper use of a *horn of collapsing* enables the character to sound it while it is pointed at the roof overhead from 30' to 60' beyond the user. The effect is to collapse a section of roof up to 20' wide and 20' long (10' radius from the central aiming point) which inflicts damage as noted above if *indoors* or *underground* only.

Horn of the Tritons: This device is a conch shell horn which can be blown but once per day, except by a triton who can sound it 3 times daily. A *horn of the tritons* can do any 1 of the following functions when properly blown:

1. Calm rough waters in a 1 mile radius (this has the effect of dispelling a water elemental or water weird);

2. Summon 5-20 hippocampi (1-2), 5-30 giant sea horses (3-5), or 1-10 sea lions (6) if the character is in a body of water wherein such creatures dwell (the creatures summoned will be friendly to and obey, to the best of their understanding, the character who sounded the *horn*); or

3. Panic marine creatures with animal, or lower, intelligence so as to cause them to flee unless each saves versus magic, and those who do save must take a –5 penalty on their ''to hit'' dice rolls for 3-18 turns (30-180 rounds).

Any sounding of a *horn of the tritons* can be heard by all tritons within a 1 league radius.

Horn of Valhalla: There are 4 varieties of this magical device. Each summons a number of berserkers from Valhalla to fight for the character who summoned them by blowing the horn. Each variety of *horn* can be blown but once every 7 days. These horns all appear to be normal instruments until their command word is discovered. The type *horn*, its powers, and who is able to employ it are shown below:

Die Roll	Type of Horn	Berserk Fighters Summoned	Usable By
1-8	Silver	4-10 2nd level	any class
9-15	Brass	3-9 3rd level	C, F, T
16-18	Bronze	2-8 4th level	C, F
19-20	Iron	2-5 5th level	F

Any character whose class is unable to employ a particular sort of a *horn of Valhalla* will be attacked by the berserk fighters summoned when the character winds the horn.

Fighters summoned are armor class 4, have 6 hit points per die, armed with sword and spear (50%), or battle axe and spear (50%). They gladly fight whomever the possessor of the horn commands, until they or their opponent(s) are slain, or 6 turns have elapsed, whichever occurs first.

Fully 50% of these *horns* are aligned and will summon only fighters of the *horn*'s alignment. A radical alignment difference will cause the *horn* blower to be attacked by the fighters.

Horseshoes of Speed: These iron shoes are magical and will not wear out. They consist of 4 normal-appearing horse shoes, but when affixed to any horse's hooves, they double the animal's speed. There is a 1% chance per 7 leagues travelled that 1 will drop off, and if this passes unnoticed, the horse's speed will drop to 150% normal rate. If 2 are lost, speed is normal.

Horseshoes of a Zephyr: These iron shoes can be affixed as normal horseshoes, and they allow a horse to travel without actually touching the ground, so water can be passed over or no tracks made on any sort of ground. The horse is able to move at normal speeds, and it will not tire for as long as 12 hours continuous riding per day when wearing these magical horseshoes.

Incense of Meditation: The small rectangular blocks of sweet-smelling *incense of meditation* are indistinguishable from non-magical incense until one is lit. When burning, the special fragrance and pearly-hued smoke of this special incense are recognizable by any cleric of 5th or higher level. When a cleric lights a block of the *incense of meditation* and spends 8 hours praying and meditating nearby, the *incense* will enable

him or her to gain full and best spell effects. Thus, *cure wounds* spells are always maximum, spell effects are of the broadest area possible, and saving throws against their effects are at –1, and when dead are brought back to life the cleric reduces their chance of *not* surviving by one-half (rounded down). When this item of magic is discovered, there will be from 2-8 pieces of incense. One piece burns for 8 hours; the effects remain for 24 hours.

Incense of Obsession: These strange blocks of incense exactly resemble *incense of meditation*. If set alight and meditation and prayer are conducted while the *incense of obsession* is nearby, its odor and smoke will cause the cleric to become totally confident that his or her spell ability is superior due to the magical incense. The cleric will be completely determined to use his or her spells at every opportunity, typically when not needed or when useless. Nonetheless, the cleric will remain obsessed with his or her abilities and spells until all are cast or 24 hours have elapsed. There are 2-8 pieces of this incense normally, each burning for 1 hour.

Ioun Stones: There are 14 sorts of useful *ioun stones*. These magical stones always float in the air and must be within 3' of their owner to be efficacious. The new possessor of the 'stones must hold each and then release it, so it takes up a circling orbit, whirling and trailing, circling at 1' to 3' radius of his or her head. Thereafter, they must be grasped or netted to separate them from their owner. The owner may voluntarily seize and stow the *stones* (at night, for example) to keep them safe. He or she would of course lose the benefits during that time. From 1-10 *ioun stones* will be found. Dice for the property of each *stone*, a duplication indicating a stone which is burned out and useless:

Dice Roll	Color of Stone	Shape	Use
1	pale blue	rhomboid	adds 1 point to strength (18 maximum)
2	scarlet & blue	sphere	adds 1 point to intelligence (18 maximum)
3	incandescent blue	sphere	adds 1 point to wisdom (18 maximum)
4	deep red	sphere	adds 1 point to dexterity (18 maximum)
5	pink	rhomboid	adds 1 point to constitution (18 maximum)
6	pink & green	sphere	adds 1 point to charisma (18 maximum)
7	pale green	prism	adds 1 level of experience
8	clear	spindle	sustains person without food or water
9	iridescent	spindle	sustains person without air
10	pearly white	spindle	regenerates 1 h.p. of damage/turn
11	pale lavender	ellipsoid	absorbs spells up to 4th level*
12	lavender & green	ellipsoid	absorbs spells up to 8th level**
13	vibrant purple	prism	stores 2-12 levels of spells
14	dusty rose	prism	gives +1 protection
15-20	dull gray	any	burned out, ''dead'' stone***

* After absorbing 10-40 spell levels the stone burns out and turns to dull gray, forever useless.

** After absorbing 20-80 spell levels the stone burns out and turns to dull gray, forever useless.

*** Adds 10 points to psionic strength total, 50 maximum points.

Whenever *ioun stones* are exposed to attack, they are treated as armor class –4 and take 10 hit points of damage to destroy. They save as if they were of hard metal, +3.

Instrument of the Bards: There are 7 magical instruments. Each can be fully utilized only by a bard, particularly a bard of at least as high a *college* as the instrument is named for, i.e. Fochlucan, Mac-Fuirmidh, Doss, etc. Bards of lower status, as well as other characters able to play such an *instrument*, will be able to use the device with only limited results. The 7 instruments are described below:

Fochlucan Bandore: If this small, 3-stringed instrument is played by a 1st level bard (*probationer*) or a non-bard, it has a 50% chance per round of playing to cast a *faerie fire* spell, but there is a 10% chance that the musician will be limned by the glow, if the spell is so cast, rather than the desired target. A bard of Fochlucan or higher college casts the *faerie fire* spell at base 50% per level of bard experience above 1st, reducing the reverse effect by 1% per level above 1st. Furthermore, the *bandore* also has the following song properties when properly played:

1. add 10% to the bard's *charm* percentage;
2. cast an *entangle* spell once per day;
3. cast a *shillelagh* spell once per day; and
4. enable the bard to *speak with animals* once per day.

If a 1st level bard attempts these powers, there is a 30% chance that they will work, but a 70% chance that the player will take 2-8 hit points of damage.

Mac-Fuirmidh Cittern: This lute-like instrument is 50% likely to deliver 3-12 hit points of damage to any non-bard or bard under 5th level who picks it up and attempts to play it. A 5th or higher level bard who uses the *cittern* has a 15% better chance of *charming* and can sing the following songs once per day which:

1. cast a *barkskin* spell;
2. *cure light wounds;* and
3. cast an *obscurement* spell.

Lower level bards cannot use the *cittern* even if they do not harm themselves (whether they take damage or not).

Doss Lute: This instrument is 60% likely to deliver 4-16 hit points of damage to any non-bard or bard under 8th level who picks it up and attempts to play it. An 8th or higher level bard who plays the *lute* has a 20% better chance of *charming* and can sing magical songs once per day which:

1. cast a *hold animal;*
2. *neutralize poison;* and
3. cast a *protection from fire* in a 10' radius.

Canaith Mandolin: The mandolin is 70% likely to cause 5-20 hit points of damage upon any non-bard or bard of under the 11th level who attempts to utilize its powers by playing it. An 11th or higher level bard is able to employ the instrument to add 25% to his or her *charming* ability and also to cast the following spells once per day:

1. *cure serious wounds;*
2. *dispel magic;* and
3. cast a *protection from lightning* in a 10' radius.

Cli Lyre: A Cli Lyre is 80% likely to cause 6-24 hit points of damage upon any non-bard or bard of less than the 14th level of experience who plays it. A 14th or higher level bard adds 30% to *charming* ability and can cast the following spells by singing and playing on the *Lyre,* once each per day:

1. *control winds;*
2. *transmute rock to mud;* and
3. create a *wall of fire.*

Anstruth Harp: This powerful instrument is 90% likely to cause 8-32 hit points of damage to any non-bard or bard of less than 17th level who attempts to strum it. In the hands of a 17th or higher level bard the *harp* adds 35% to *charming* abilities and can be played so as to cast the following spells, one each per day:

1. *cure critical wounds;*
2. create a *wall of thorns;* and
3. cast a *weather summoning.*

Ollamh Harp: If an *Ollamh Harp* is played by any non-bard or bard of under 20th level it will inflict 10-40 hit points of damage upon such an individual. When played by a bard of 20th or higher level, it adds 40% to his or her *charming* abilities and can cast one each of the following spells daily:

1. *confusion;*
2. *control weather;* and
3. *fire storm.*

General Properties Of All Bard Instruments:

Each and every instrument looks exactly alike due to powerful dweomers placed upon them.

Any character able to play one of these instruments can sing so as to do one of the following for as many turns as the order of the college, i.e. 1-7, a *magnus alumni* for 8 turns with any of the 7, once each per day:

1. put up a 10' radius *protection from evil;*
2. become *invisible* (although the strumming and singing can still be heard distantly, the exact location is impossible to discover unless detection of invisibility is possible);
3. *levitate;* and
4. *fly.*

Each ability of the instrument takes 5 segments to activate, and not less than 1 full round to complete.

If the bard's charming ability exceeds 100% with instrument bonus, the creature saving against the magic does so at −1 for every 5% above 100%, 3% or 4% being rounded to the next 5%, i.e. 3% = 5%, 8% = 10%, 13% = 15%, etc.

The type of instrument found is determined by the table below:

Die Roll	Instrument
1-5	Fochlucan Bandore
6-9	Mac-Fuirmidh Cittern
10-12	Doss Lute
13-15	Canaith Mandolin
16-17	Cli Lyre
18-19	Anstruth Harp
20	Ollamh Harp

Iron Flask: One of these special containers will typically be inlaid with runes of silver and stoppered by a brass plug bearing a seal of great dweomer set round with sigils, glyphs, and special symbols. When the user speaks a command, he or she can force any creature from another plane (daemon, demon, devil, elemental, etc.) *into* the container, provided the creature does not make its saving throw versus magic — after magic resistance, if any, is checked. Range is 6''. Only 1 creature at a time can be so contained. Loosing the stopper frees the captured creature; and if the individual loosing the plug knows the command word, the creature can be forced to serve for 1 turn (or to perform a *minor* service which takes up to 1 hour of time). If freed without command knowledge, dice for the creature's reaction . . . Any attempt to force the same creature into the *flask* a second time allows it +2 on its saving throw and makes it VERY angry and totally hostile. A discovered bottle can contain:

01-50	empty
51-54	air elemental
55-56	demon (type I-III)
57	demon (type IV-VI)
58-59	devil (lesser)
60	devil (greater)
61-65	djinni
66-69	earth elemental
70-72	efreeti
73-76	fire elemental
77-81	invisible stalker
82-83	mezzodaemon
84-85	night hag
86	nycadaemon
87-89	rakshasa
90-93	salamander
94-97	water elemental
98-99	wind walker
00	xorn

Javelin of Lightning: A *javelin of lightning* is considered equal to a +2 magic weapon, although it has neither "to hit" nor damage bonuses. It has a range of 9" and whenever it strikes, the *javelin* then becomes the head of a ½" wide, 3" long stroke of lightning. Any creature hit by the *javelin* suffers 1-6 hit points of damage, plus 20 hit points of electrical damage. Any other creatures in the path of the back stroke take either 20 or 10 hit points of damage. (Draw a straight line between point of impact 3" back in the direction of the character hurling it.) From 2-5 will be found. The *javelin* is consumed in the lightning discharge.

Javelin of Piercing: This weapon is not actually hurled, as when a command word is spoken, the *javelin of piercing* launches itself. Range is 6", all distances considered as *short* range. The javelin is +6 "to hit" and inflicts 7-12 hit points of damage. (Note this missile will fly horizontally, vertically, or any combination thereof to the full extent of its range.) From 2-8 will be found. The magic of the *javelin* is good for only 1 throw.

Jewel of Attacks: This gleaming gem radiates magic and appears to be a valuable item. It is cursed, however, and it brings both 100% more likelihood of encountering wandering monsters and 100% greater likelihood of pursuit when monsters are encountered and the party seeks to evade them by flight. Once picked up, the *jewel of attacks* will always magically return to its finder (secreting itself in pouch, bag, pack, pocket, etc.) until a *remove curse* spell or an *atonement* is cast upon him or her.

Jewel of Flawlessness: This magical gem appears to be a very fine stone of some sort, but if magic is detected for, its dweomer will be noted. When a *jewel of flawlessness* is placed with other gems, it increases the likelihood of their being more valuable by 100%, i.e., the chance for each stone going up in value increases from 1 in 10 to 2 in 10. The *jewel* has from 10-100 facets, and whenever a gem increases in value because of the magic of the *jewel of flawlessness* (a roll of 2 on d10), 1 of these facets disappears. When all are gone, the *jewel* is a spherical stone of no value.

Keoghtom's Ointment: This sovereign salve is useful for drawing poison, curing disease, or healing wounds. A jar of the unguent is small — perhaps three inches in diameter and one inch deep — but contains 5 applications. Placed upon a poisoned wound (or swallowed), it detoxifies any poison or disease. Rubbed on the body, the *ointment* heals 9-12 points of damage. 1-3 jars will commonly be found.

TABLE (III.E.) 4.

Libram of Gainful Conjuration: This mystic compilation contains much arcane knowledge for magic-users (including illusionists) of *neutral* (neutral, chaotic neutral, lawful neutral) alignment. If a character of this class and alignment spends a full week, cloistered and undisturbed, pondering its contents, he or she will gain experience points sufficient to place him or her exactly at the mid-point of the next higher level. When this occurs, the *libram* will disappear — totally gone — and that same character can never benefit again from reading such a work. Any non-neutral magic-user reading so much as a line of the *libram* will take 5-20 points of damage, be unconscious for a like number of turns, and must seek a cleric to *atone* in order to regain the ability to progress in experience (until doing so, he or she will gain no further experience). Any non-magic-user perusing the work will be required to save versus magic in order to avoid *insanity*. Those characters going *insane* must receive a *remove curse* and rest for 1 month or have a cleric *heal* them.

Libram of Ineffable Damnation: This work is exactly like the *Libram of Gainful Conjuration* except that it benefits *evil* magic-users, and non-evil characters of that class will *lose* 1 level of experience merely from looking inside of its brass-bound covers, in addition to the other ill effects of perusing but 1 line of its contents.

Libram of Silver Magic: This mystic text is the reverse of the *Libram of Ineffable Damnation*, greatly beneficial to *good* magic-users, most baneful to non-good ones. Like all magical works of this sort, it vanishes after 1 week of study, and the character having benefited from it can never be so aided again.

Lyre of Building: The enchantments placed upon this instrument make it indistinguishable from a normal one; and even if its magic is detected, it cannot be told from an *instrument of the bards* until it is played. If the proper chords are struck, the *lyre* will negate the effects of a *horn of blasting*, a *disintegrate* spell, or the effects of 6 rounds of an attack of an earth elemental — all as pertains to constructions. Such playing of these negatory chords can be done once per day. The *lyre* is also useful with

respect to actual building, of course. Once per week its strings can be strummed so as to produce chords which magically construct buildings, mines, tunnels, ditches, or whatever. The effect produced in but 3 turns of such playing is equal to the work of 100 men laboring for 3 days. If a false chord is struck, all effects of the *lyre* are 20% likely to be negated. A false chord is only 5% likely once the character knows the proper ones, but if disturbed by physical or mental attack while playing, the likelihood rises to 50%.

Manual of Bodily Health: As with all magical writings of this nature, the metal-bound *Manual of Bodily Health* appears to be an arcane, rare, but non-magical book. If a *detect magic* spell is cast upon it, the *manual* will radiate an aura of magic. Any single character who reads the work (24 hours of time over 3-5 days) will know how to increase his or her constitution by 1 point by following a regimen of special dietary intake and breathing exercises over a 1 month period. The book disappears immediately upon completion of its contents. The 1 point of constitution is gained only after the prescribed regimen is followed. In 3 months the knowledge of the secrets to bodily health will be forgotten. The knowledge cannot be articulated or recorded by the reader. The *manual* will not be useful to any character a second time, nor will other than a single character be able to benefit from it.

Manual of Gainful Exercise: This work is similar to the *Manual of Bodily Health*, but its reading and prescribed course of action will result in the addition of 1 point to the reader's strength.

Manual of Golems: This compilation is a treatise on the construction and animation of a golem. It contains all of the information and incantations necessary to make 1 of the 4 sorts of golems (cf. **ADVANCED DUNGEONS & DRAGONS, MONSTER MANUAL,** *Golem*). It will take a considerable amount of time, and be expensive as well, to construct and animate the golem. During this period, a single magic-user or cleric must have the *manual* at hand to study, and he or she must not be interrupted. The type of *manual* found is determined as noted below:

Die Roll	Type of Golem	Construction Time	G.P. Cost
1-5	Clay (C)	1 month	65,000
6-17	Flesh (M)	2 months	50,000
18	Iron (M)	4 months	100,000
19-20	Stone (M)	3 months	80,000

Once the golem is finished, the writing fades and the book is consumed in flames. When the ashes of the *manual* aré sprinkled upon the golem it becomes fully animated. It is assumed that the user of the manual is of 10th or higher level. For every level of experience under 10th there is a cumulative 10% chance that the golem will fall to pieces within 1 turn of completion of its construction due to the maker's imperfect understanding.

If a cleric reads a work for magic-users, he or she will lose 10,000-60,000 experience points. A magic-user reading a clerical work will lose 1 level of experience. Any other class of character will suffer 6-36 hit points of damage from opening the work.

Manual of Puissant Skill at Arms: This scholarly study contains expert advice and instruction regarding weapon use and various attack and defense modes. Any single fighter (including a bard, but *not* a paladin or ranger) who reads the *manual* and practices the skills described therein for 1 month will go up to the mid-point of the next higher level. The book disappears after it is read, and the knowledge therein will be forgotten within 3 months, so it must be acted upon with reasonable expedition. The fighter cannot articulate what he or she has read, nor can it be recorded in any fashion. A paladin or ranger will understand the work but it cannot benefit either class. Any cleric (including druid), thief (including assassin), or monk who handles/reads the *manual* will not understand it. If a magic-user (including an illusionist) so much as scans a few of its letters, he or she will be stunned for 1-6 turns and lose 10,000-60,000 experience points as the work is so opposed to the magic-using profession. Only one perusal of the work will benefit the same character.

Manual of Quickness of Action: The heavy covers and metal bindings of this compilation will not distinguish it from any of scores of semi-valuable, non-magical texts. This work contains certain secret formulae and prescriptions for unguents and exercises which enable a single reader to assimilate the text (3 days of uninterrupted study) and then practice the skills detailed therein. If this practice is faithfully done for 1 month, the character will gain 1 point of dexterity. While the *manual* will disappear immediately after reading, the contents will be remembered for 3 months (although the reader will *not* be able to articulate or otherwise record the information he or she retains). Only after the month of training will the dexterity bonus be gained. Further perusal of a similar text will not add further to the same character's dexterity.

Manual of Stealthy Pilfering: This guide to expertise at thievery is so learned and erudite that any single thief who reads it and then spends 1 month thereafter practicing the skills therein will gain experience points sufficient to place him or her at the mid-point of the next higher level. The text disappears after reading, but knowledge is retained for 3 months — as with other magical texts of this sort, the knowledge cannot be recorded or told of, however. Any additional reading of a like *manual'* is of no benefit to the same character. Assassins who read the work will gain but 5,000 additional experience points after the contents have been read and pondered for 1 week. Fighters, magic-users, and monks will not comprehend the work. Clerics, rangers, and paladins who read even a word of the book take 5-20 hit points of damage, are *stunned* for a like number of rounds, and if a saving throw versus magic is failed, they lose 5,000-20,000 experience points as well. In addition, such characters must *atone* within 1 day or lose 1 point of wisdom.

Mattock of the Titans: This huge digging tool is 10' long and weighs over 100 pounds. Any giant-sized creature with a strength of 20 or more can use it to loosen (or tumble) earth (or earthen ramparts) in a 100 cubic foot area in 1 turn. It will smash rock in a 20 cubic feet area in the same amount of time. If used as a weapon, it is +3 "to hit" and does 5-30 hit points of damage, exclusive of strength bonuses. (Cf. *girdle of giant strength*.)

Maul of the Titans: This huge mallet is 8' long and weighs over 150 pounds. Any giant-sized creature with strength of 21 or greater can employ it to drive piles of up to 2' diameter into normal earth at 4' per blow — 2 blows per round. The *maul* will smash to flinders an oaken door of up to 10' height by 4' width by 2 inch thickness in 1 blow — 2 if the door is heavily bound with iron. If used as a weapon it is +2 "to hit" and inflicts 10-40 hit points of damage, exclusive of strength bonuses.

Medallion of ESP: An *ESP Medallion* appears to be a normal neck chain — usually fashioned from bronze, copper, or nickel-silver — with pendant disc. The device enables the wearer to concentrate and pick up thoughts in a path 1' wide at the *medallion'* and broadening 2' every 10' from the device the magic reaches, up to an 11' maximum width at 50' (5''). It requires a full round for a character to so use the device. The *medallion* is prevented from functioning by stone of over 3' thickness, metal of over 1/6' thickness, or any continuous sheeting of lead, gold or platinum of any thickness greater than paint. The medallion malfunctions (with no result) on a die roll of 6 on d6, and the device must be checked each time it is used. The character using the device can pick up only the surface thoughts of creatures in the path of the ESP area. The general distance can be determined, but all thoughts will be understandable only if the user knows the language of the thinkers. If the creatures use no language, only the prevailing emotions can be felt — understood only with an *ESP-Empathy* device (see below). Note that undead and mindless golems have neither readable thoughts nor emotions. (See also **PSIONICS.**) The type of *medallion* found is determined below:

Die Roll	Medallion
1-15	30' range
16-18	30' range with empathy
19	60' range
20	90' range

Note that thoughts cannot be sent through any *medallion of ESP*.

Medallion of Thought Projection: This device is exactly like an *ESP Medallion* in every respect, even as to the range it functions at. However, in addition to picking up the thoughts of creatures, it broadcasts the thoughts of the user to the creatures in the path of the beam, thus alerting them. Note: it functions correctly, *without projecting thoughts*, on a roll of 6.

Mirror of Life Trapping: This crystal device is usually about 4 square feet in area, framed in metal, wood, etc. It is usable only by magic-users, although it can be affixed to a surface to operate alone by giving a command word. A *mirror'* has from 13 to 18 non-spatial/extra-dimensional compartments within it. Any creature coming within 30' of the device and looking at it so as to see its reflection must save versus magic or be *trapped* within the mirror in one of the cells. It is 100% probable that any creature not aware of the nature of the device will see its reflection, the probability dropping to 50% if the creature actively avoids so doing

and 20% if the creature is aware that the mirror traps life. When a creature is trapped, it is taken bodily into the *mirror'*. Size is not a factor, but automatons and non-living matter (including golems but excluding *intelligent* undead) are not trapped. The possessor of the mirror can call the reflection of any creature that is trapped within to the surface of the mirror, and the powerless creature can be conversed with. If mirror capacity is exceeded, 1 victim (random) will be set free in order to accommodate the latest one. If the mirror is broken, all victims are freed (usually to then attack the possessor of the device). Note that the possessor of a *mirror of life trapping* can speak a command word so as to free a trapped creature, but the cell of the creature must be known. Example: ''In the name of Zagig the Great I command the occupant of the 3rd cell to come forth!''

Mirror of Mental Prowess: This magical mirror resembles an ordinary one. The possessor, however, knowing the proper commands can cause it to perform as follows:

1. Read the thoughts of any creature reflected therein, even though these thoughts are in an unknown language;
2. Scry with it as if it were a *crystal ball* with *clairaudience*, but even being able to view into other planes if the viewer knows of them sufficiently;
3. It can be used as a portal to visit other places (possibly other planes, as well, at the DM's option) by first scrying them and then stepping through to the place pictured — an invisible area remains on the ''other side'', and those using the portal can return if the correct spot can be found. (Note that creatures being scried can step through also if the place is found by them!);
4. Once per week it will answer one short question, briefly, regarding a creature whose image is shown upon its surface.

The typical *mirror'* size is 5' X 2'.

Mirror of Opposition: This mirror exactly resembles a normal mirror. Any creature reflected in its surface will cause an exact duplicate to come into being, and this opposite will immediately attack. Note that the duplicate will have all items and powers of the original (including magic), but upon the defeat or destruction of either, the duplicate and his or her items disappear completely.

Necklace of Adaptation: This chain will resemble a medallion. The wearer will be able to ignore gases of all sorts which affect creatures through respiration, breathe underwater, or even exist in airless space for up to 7 days.

Necklace of Missiles: A device of this sort appears to be nothing but a cheap medallion or piece of valueless jewelry due to special enchantments placed upon it. If a character places it about his or her neck, however, that individual can see the *necklace* as it really is — golden missile globes depending from a golden chain. Each sphere is detachable only by the wearer. They can be easily hurled up to 7'' distance. When they arrive at the end of their trajectory they burst as a magical *fireball*. The number of missiles, and their respective hit dice of *fireball* damage, are determined on the table below:

Die Roll	Number of Missiles and Power in Hit Dice									
	11	10	9	8	7	6	5	4	3	2
1-4	—	--	—	—	—	—	1	—	2	—
5-8	—	—	—	—	—	1	—	2	—	2
9-12	—	—	—	—	1	—	2	—	4	—
13-16	—	—	—	1	—	2	—	2	—	4
17-18	—	—	1	—	2	—	2	—	2	—
19	—	1	—	2	—	2	—	4	—	—
20	1	—	2	—	2	—	2	—	2	—

For example, on a roll of 9-12 the necklace will possess 7 missiles — one 7-dice, two 5-dice, and four 3-dice fireballs.

The size will show that there is a difference in power between globes, but the number of dice and damage each causes cannot generally be known.

If the necklace is being worn or carried by a character who fails his or her saving throw versus a magical fire attack, the item must undergo a saving throw check as well. If it fails to save, all remaining missiles detonate simultaneously.

Necklace of Prayer Beads: A magical necklace of this sort appears to be a normal piece of non-valuable jewelry until it is placed about a character's neck. Even then, the true nature of the item will only be revealed if the wearer is a cleric (excluding druids and characters otherwise able to use spells of a clerical or druidic nature such as paladins and rangers). The *necklace of prayer beads* consists of 25-30 semi-precious (60%) and fancy (40%) stones. The wearer will be 25% more likely to successfully petition his or her deity to grant desired spells. There will also be 3-6 special beads (precious stones, gems of 1,000 g.p. base value) of the following sort (roll for each bead):

Die Roll	Results
1-5	BEAD OF ATONEMENT — as the 5th level spell of the same name
6-10	BEAD OF BLESSING — as the 1st level spell of the same name
11-15	BEAD OF CURING — *cures blindness, disease, or serious wounds* (as the appropriate spell does)
16-17	BEAD OF KARMA — allows the cleric to cast his or her spells as if he or she were 4 levels higher (with respect to range, duration, etc.)
18	BEAD OF SUMMONS — calls the cleric's deity (90% probability) to come to him or her in material form (but it had better be for a good reason!)
19-20	BEAD OF WIND WALKING — as the 7th level spell of the same name

Each special bead can be used but once per day. If the cleric summons his or her deity, the deity will take the *necklace* as the least punishment for vain purposes in so doing. The function of each bead is known only when the bead is grasped and a *commune* spell used. All powers of the special beads will be lost if they are removed from the necklace.

Necklace of Strangulation: Also covered by enchantments to completely mask its true nature, a *necklace of strangulation* can be discovered only when placed around a character's neck. The *necklace'* immediately constricts and cannot be removed short of an *alter reality, limited wish* or *wish* spell. The wearer will suffer 6 hit points of strangulation damage per round until the character is dead and the *necklace'* remains clasped until the character is a dry skeleton.

Net of Entrapment: This magical rope net is so strong as to defy strength under 20 and is equal to AC −10 with respect to blows aimed at cutting it. (Normal sawing attempts to cut it with dagger or sword will *not* succeed; it must be hacked at to sever a strand of its mesh.) Each net is 10' square and has ¼' mesh. It can be thrown 20' so as to cover and close upon opponents; each in its area must save versus magic to avoid being entrapped. It can be suspended from a ceiling (or generally overhead) and drop upon a command word. It can be laid upon the floor and likewise close upwards upon command. The *net* stretches so as to close over an area of up to a 5' cube in the latter case. It can be loosened by its possessor on command.

Net of Snaring: This net exactly resembles a *net of entrapment*, but it functions only underwater. There, it can be commanded to shoot forth up to 3" distance to trap a creature. It is otherwise the same as the former magical net.

Nolzur's Marvelous Pigments: These magical emulsions enable their possessor to create actual objects simply by depicting their form in 2 dimensions. The variegated *pigments* are applied by a stick tipped with bristles, hair, or fur. The emulsion flows from the application to form the desired object as the wielder concentrates on the desired image. One pot of *Nolzur's Marvelous Pigments* is sufficient to create a 1,000 cubic foot object by depicting it 2 dimensionally over a 100 square foot surface. Thus, a 10' × 10' × 10' pit, or a 10' × 10' × 10' room, or a large door with a passage behind it, etc. can be created by application of the *pigments*. Note that only normal, inanimate things can be so created — doors, pits, flowers, trees, cells, etc.; not monsters, people, golems, and the like. The pigments must be applied to a surface, i.e. a floor, wall, ceiling, door, etc. From 1-4 containers of *pigments* will be found, usually with a single instrument about 1' long with which to apply them. It takes 1 turn to depict an object with *pigments*. Objects of value depicted by *pigments* — precious metals, gems, jewelry, ivory, etc. — will *appear* valuable but will be tin, lead, paste gems, brass, bone, etc. Normal armor or weapons can, of course, be created.

Pearl of Power: This seemingly normal pearl of average size and coloration is a potent aid to a magic-user. Once a day, a *pearl of power* enables the possessor to recall any 1 spell as desired, even if the spell has already

been cast. Of course, the magic-user must have the spell to be remembered amongst those he or she most recently memorized. The power of the *pearl'* is determined below:

Die Roll	Level of Spell Recalled by Pearl
01-25	first
26-45	second
46-60	third
61-75	fourth
76-85	fifth
86-92	sixth
93-96	seventh
97-98	eighth
99	ninth
00	recalls 2 spells of 1st to 6th level (use d6)

1 in 20 of these *pearls* is of *opposite* effect, causing a spell to be forgotten. These pearls can be gotten rid of only by means of *exorcism* or a *wish!*

Pearl of Wisdom: Although it appears to be a normal pearl, a *pearl of wisdom* will cause a cleric to increase 1 point in wisdom if he or she retains the pearl for a 1 month period. The increase happens at the expiration of 30 days, but thereafter the pearl must be retained by the cleric and kept on his or her person, or the 1 point gain will be lost. Note that 1 in 20 of these magical pearls are cursed to work in reverse, but once the 1 point of wisdom is lost, the pearl turns to powder, and the loss is permanent barring some magical restoration means such as a *wish* or *Tome of Understanding.*

Periapt of Foul Rotting: This engraved gem is magicked so as to appear to be a gem of small value. If any character claims it as his or her own, he or she will contract a terrible rotting disease, a form of leprosy which can be removed only by application of a *remove curse* spell followed by a *cure disease* and then a *heal* or *limited wish* or *wish* spell. The rotting can also be countered by the crushing of a *periapt of health* and sprinkling of the dust thereof upon the afflicted character. Otherwise, the afflicted loses 1 point each of dexterity and constitution and charisma per week beginning 1 week after claiming the item, and when any score reaches 0, the character is dead. Each point lost due to the disease will be permanent regardless of subsequent removal of the affliction.

Periapt of Health: This gem appears exactly the same as a *periapt of foul rotting,* but the possessor will be immune from all diseases save that of the latter *periapt* so long as he or she has it on his or her person.

Periapt of Proof Against Poison: The *periapt of proof against poison* is indistinguishable from any of the other *periapts.* The character who has one of these magical gems is allowed a 10% saving throw per plus of *periapt* against poisons which normally disallow any such opportunity, a normal score for poisons which usually are at penalty, and a plus on all other poison saves:

Die Roll	Plus of Periapt
1-8	+1
9-14	+2
15-18	+3
19-20	+4

Periapt of Wound Closure: This magical stone looks exactly the same as the others of this ilk. The person possessing it will never need fear open, bleeding wounds, for the *periapt* prevents them. In addition, the *periapt* doubles the normal rate of healing, or allows normal healing of wounds which would not do so normally.

Phylactery of Faithfulness: There is no means to determine what function this device performs until it is worn. The wearer of a *phylactery of faithfulness* will be aware of any action or item which will adversely affect his or her alignment and standing with his or her deity prior to performing the action or becoming associated with such an item, if a prior moment is taken to contemplate the action. The *phylactery* must be worn normally by the cleric, of course.

Phylactery of Long Years: This device slows the aging process by one-quarter for as long as the cleric wears it. The reduction applies even to magical aging. Thus, if a cleric dons the *phylactery* at age 20, he or she will age 9 months every 12; so that in 12 chronological years, he or she will have aged but 9 and will physically be 29 rather than 32. 1 in 20 of these devices are cursed to operate in reverse.

Phylactery of Monstrous Attention: While this arm wrapping appears to be some sort of beneficial device, it actually draws the attention of supernatural creatures of exactly the opposite alignment of the cleric wearing it. This results in the cleric being plagued by powerful and hostile creatures whenever he or she is in an area where such creatures are or can appear. If the cleric is of 10th or higher level, the attention of his or her deity's most powerful enemy will be drawn, so as to cause this being to interfere directly. For example, a lawful good cleric attracts various demons and eventually the notice of Orcus or Demogorgon. Once donned, a *phylactery of monstrous attention* cannot be removed without an *exorcism* spell and then a quest must be performed to re-establish the cleric in his or her alignment.

Pipes of the Sewers: A set of these wooden pipes appear to be nothing extraordinary, but if the possessor learns the proper tune, he or she can attract from 10-60 (d6 × 10) giant rats (80%) or 30-180 (3d6 × 10) normal rats (20%) if either or both are within 40″. For each 5′ distance the rats have to travel there will be a 1 round delay. The piper must continue playing until the rats appear, and when they do so, they are 95% likely to obey the piper so long as he or she continues to play. If for any reason the piper ceases playing, the rats summoned will leave immediately. If they are again called it is 70% probable that they will come and obey, 30% likely that they will turn upon the piper. If the rats are under control of a creature such as a vampire, the piper's chance of taking over control is 30% per round of piping. Once control is assumed, there is a 70% chance of maintaining it if the other creature is actively seeking to reassert its control.

Portable Hole: A *portable hole* is a circle of magical cloth spun from the webs of a phase spider interwoven with strands of ether and beams of Astral Plane luminaries. When opened fully, a *portable hole* is 6′ in diameter, but it can be folded as small as a pocket handkerchief. When spread upon any surface, it causes an extra-dimensional hole 10′ deep to come into being. This hole can be "picked up" from inside or out by simply taking hold of the edges of the magical cloth and folding it up. Either way, the entrance disappears, but anything inside the "hole" remains. The only oxygen in the "hole" is that allowed by creation of the space, so creatures requiring the gas cannot remain inside for more than a turn or so without opening the space again by means of the magical cloth. The cloth does not accumulate weight even if its hole is filled with gold, for example. Each *portable hole* opens on its own particular non-dimensional space. If a *bag of holding* is placed within a *portable hole*, a rift to the Astral Plane is torn in the space, and the bag and the cloth are sucked into the void and forever lost. If a *portable hole* is placed within a *bag of holding*, it opens a *gate* to another plane, and the 'hole, bag' and any creatures within a 10′ radius are drawn to the plane, the *portable hole* and *bag of holding* being *destroyed* in the process.

Quaal's Feather Token: A *feather token* is a small magical device of various forms to suit a special need. These various tokens are listed below. Each is usable but once:

Die Roll	Tokens
1-4	ANCHOR — a *token* useful to moor a craft so as to render it immobile for 1 full day (or at any time prior upon command from the token's possessor).
5-7	BIRD — a *token* which can be used to drive off any sort of hostile avian creatures or as a vehicle of transportation equal to a roc of the largest size in all respects (1 day duration).
8-10	FAN — a *token* which forms a huge flapping fan which can cause a *strong breeze* (cf. **THE ADVENTURE, WATERBORNE ADVENTURES**) in an area large enough to propel one ship. This wind is not cumulative with existing wind speeds — if there is already a strong breeze blowing, this cannot be added to it to create a gale. It can, however, be used *against* it to create an area of relative calm or lesser winds (though this will not affect wave size in a storm, of course). The *fan* can be used up to eight hours a day. It will not function on land.
11-13	SWAN BOAT — a *token* which forms a huge swan-like boat capable of swimming at 24″ speed, and carrying 8 horses and gear or 32 men or any combination equal thereto (duration 1 day).
14-18	TREE — a *token* which causes a great oak to spring into being — 6′ diameter trunk, 60′ height, 40′ top diameter.

19-20	WHIP — a *token* which causes a huge leather whip to appear and be wielded against any opponent desired (+1 weapon, 9th level fighter "to hit" probability, 2-7 hit points damage plus save versus magic or be bound fast for 2-7 rounds) for up to 6 turns. (Cf. *Dancing Sword*.)

Other similar *tokens* may be added as desired.

TABLE (III.E.) 5.

Robe of the Archmagi: This normal-appearing garment can be *white* (45% — good alignment), *gray* (30% — neutral, but neither good nor evil, alignment), or *black* (25% — evil alignment). Its wearer gains the following powers:

1. It serves as armor equal to AC 5;
2. The *robe* confers a 5% magic resistance;
3. It adds +1 to saving throw scores; and
4. The robe reduces magic resistance and/or saving throws by 20%/−4 when the wearer casts any of the following spells: *charm monster, charm person, friends, hold monster, hold person, polymorph other, suggestion.*

Color of a *robe of the archmagi* is not determinable until donned by a magic-user. If a white *robe* is donned by an evil wizard, he or she will take 18-51 (11d4 + 7) hit points of damage and lose 18,000-51,000 experience points, and the reverse is true with respect to a black *robe* donned by a good aligned magic-user. An evil or good magic-user putting on a gray *robe*, or a neutral magic-user donning either a white or black *robe*, incurs 6-24 hit points damage, 6,000-24,000 experience points loss, and the wearer will be moved towards the alignment of the *robe* by its enchantments, i.e. he or she should be vocally urged to change alignment to that of the robe, and the magic-user will have to take steps to keep his or her old alignment pure.

Robe of Blending: This ordinary appearing robe *cannot* be detected by magical means. When it is put on, however, the wearer will detect a dweomer and know that the garment has very special properties. A *robe of blending* enables its wearer to appear to be part of a rock wall, a plant, a creature of another sort — whatever is appropriate. The coloration, form, and even odor are produced by the robe, although it will not make its wearer appear to be more than twice/one-half normal height, and it does not empower language/noise capabilities — either understanding or imitating. (In situations where several different forms are appropriate, the wearer is obliged to state which form he wishes the *robe* to camouflage him or her as.) Creatures with *exceptional* (15+) or better intelligence have a 1% per intelligence point chance of detecting something amiss when they are within 3″ of a *robe of blending,* and those creatures with *low* intelligence (5+) or better and 10 or more levels of experience or hit dice have a 1% per level or hit die chance of likewise noting something unusual about a robe-wearing character. (The latter is cumulative with the former chance for detection, so an 18 intelligence magic-user of 12th level has a 30% chance — 18% + 12% — of noting something amiss.) There must be an initial check per eligible creature, and successive checks should be made each turn thereafter, if the same creatures are within the 3″ range. All creatures acquainted with and friendly to the wearer will see him or her normally.

Robe of Eyes: This garment is most valuable (though it appears as a normal robe until it is put on), for its wearer is able to "see" in all directions at the same moment due to the scores of magical "eyes" which adorn the robe. The wearer is empowered with *infravisual* capability to 12″ range, *ultravisual* abilities, and the power to see *displaced* or *out of phase* objects and creatures in their actual positions. The *robe of eyes* sees *all* forms of invisible things within a 24″ normal vision range (or 12″ if infravision is being used). Of course, solid objects obstruct even the robe's powers of observation. While *invisibility, dust of disappearance, a robe of blending,* or even *improved invisibility* are not proof against observation, astral or ethereal things cannot be seen by means of this *robe*. *Illusions* and secret doors also cannot be seen, but creatures camouflaged or hidden in shadows are easily detected, so ambush or surprise of a character wearing a *robe of eyes* is impossible. Furthermore, the *robe* enables its wearer to *track* as if he or she were a 12th level ranger. A *light* spell thrown directly on a *robe of eyes* will blind it for 1-3 rounds, a *continual light* for 2-8 rounds.

Robe of Powerlessness: A robe of this nature appears to be a robe of another sort, and detection of any sort will discover nothing more than the fact that it has a magic aura. As soon as a character dons this garment, he or she drops to 3 intelligence, forgets all spells and magical knowledge, and becomes weak as well (3 strength). The *robe* can be removed easily, but in order to restore mind and body, the character must have a *remove curse* spell and then a *heal* spell placed upon his or her person.

Robe of Scintillating Colors: This garment appears quite normal, but a magic aura is detectable. Unless the wearer has an intelligence of 15 or higher and a wisdom of 13 or more, he or she will be unable to cause a *robe of scintillating colors* to function. If intelligence and wisdom are sufficient, the wearer can cause the garment to become a shifting pattern of incredible hues, color after color cascading from the upper part of the *robe* to the hem in sparkling rainbows of dazzling light. Although this effect sheds light in a 40' diameter sphere, it also has the powers of hypnotizing opponents and causing them to be unable to attack the wearer. It requires a full round for the wearer to cause the colors to begin "flowing" on the *robe*, but each round that they scintillate and move, any opponent not making its saving throw versus magic (or magic resistance check, then save) will stand transfixed for 2-5 rounds, hypnotized, and even when this effect wears off, additional saves must again be made in order to successfully attack. Furthermore, every round of continuous scintillation of the *robe* makes the wearer 5% more difficult to hit with missile attacks or hand-held or body weaponry (hands, fists, claws, fangs, horns, etc.) until a maximum of 25% (−5) is attained — 5 continuous rounds of the dazzling play of hues. After the initial round of concealment, the wearer is able to cast spells or engage in all forms of activity which do not require movement of more than 1" from his or her starting position. In non-combat situations, the *robe* will simply hypnotize creatures failing their saving throws versus magic for a period of 2-5 turns.

Robe of Useful Items: Although this appears to be an unremarkable item of apparel, if the *robe of useful items* is worn, the magic-user will note that it has small cloth patches in various shapes sewn onto it. The wearer, and *only* the wearer of the *robe*, can see, recognize, and detach any 1 of these patches in 1 round. Detaching a patch causes it to become an actual item as indicated below. A *robe* will always have 2 each of the following patches:

dagger	pole (10')
lantern (filled and lit)	rope (50' coil)
mirror (large)	sack (large)

Additionally, the *robe* will have 4-16 of the following items which must be diced for:

Dice Roll	Result
01-08	Bag of 100 gold pieces
09-15	Coffer (½' × ½' × 1'), silver (500 g.p. value)
16-22	Door, iron (up to 10' wide and 10' high and barred on 1 side — must be placed upright, will attach and hinge itself)
23-30	Gems, 10 of 100 gold piece value each
31-44	Ladder, wooden (24' long)
45-51	Mule (with saddle bags)
52-59	Pit (10 cubic feet), open
60-68	Potion of *extra healing*
69-75	Rowboat (12' long)
76-83	Scroll of 1 spell
84-90	War dogs, pair
91-96	Window (2' × 4' — up to 2' deep)
97-00	Roll twice more

Multiple items of the same kind are permissible. Once removed, any item may never be replaced.

Rope of Climbing: A 60' long *rope of climbing* is no thicker than a slender wand, weighs no more than 3 pounds, but is strong enough to support 3,000 pounds. Upon command the *rope* will snake forward, upward, downward, or any other direction at 10' per round and attach itself securely wherever desired. It will return or unfasten itself likewise. In any event, one end of the *rope* must be held by a character when it performs such actions. It can also be commanded to *knot* itself, and this will cause large knots to appear at 1' intervals along the rope; knotting shortens the rope to 50' length while so knotted.

Rope of Constriction: This *rope* exactly resembles a *rope of climbing* or *entanglement*, but as soon as it is commanded to perform some action, it lashes itself about the neck of the character holding it, and from 1-4 others

within 10' of the victim (each entitled to a saving throw versus magic) and strangles and crushes the life from each and every such victim. Each round it delivers 2-12 hit points of damage, and it will continue to constrict until a *dispel magic* is cast upon it. Note that any creature entwined by the *rope* cannot cast spells or otherwise free himself or herself by any means. This rope is AC −2 and takes 22 hit points to cut through; all hit points must be inflicted by the same creature (not the one entangled).

Rope of Entanglement: A *rope of entanglement* is exactly the same in appearance as any other magical rope. Upon command, the *rope* will lash forward 20', or upwards 10' to entangle and tie fast up to 8 man-sized creatures. (Figure 1 storm giant or fire giant = 2 frost or stone or hill giants = 3 ogres = 4 bugbears = 6 gnolls = 8 men = 10 elves = 12 dwarves = 16 gnomes or kobolds.) It takes but a single segment to strike, and another to entwine; the command requires 1 segment also, while the whole takes 3 segments to perform. The rope cannot be broken by sheer strength, it must be hit by an edged weapon. The *rope* is AC −2 and takes 22 hit points to cut through; all hit points must be inflicted by the same creature (not the one entangled). Damage under 22 hit points will repair itself in 6 turns. If a *rope of entanglement* is severed, it is destroyed.

Note: Any magical rope which is broken or severed will immediately lose its special properties.

Rug of Smothering: This finely woven carpet resembles a *carpet of flying* and will give off magical radiations if detected for. The character seating himself or herself upon it and giving a command will be surprised, however, as the *rug of smothering* will tightly roll itself around that individual and suffocate him or her in 3-6 rounds. The *rug* cannot be physically prevented from so wrapping itself, and the *rug* can be prevented from smothering its victim only by the casting of any one of the following spells: *alter reality, animate object, hold plant, wish*.

Rug of Welcome: A rug of this type appears exactly the same as a *carpet of flying*, and it performs the functions of one (6' × 9' size), but a *rug of welcome* has other powers in addition. Upon command it will function as a *rug of smothering*, entrapping any creature up to ogre-size which steps upon it. A *rug of welcome* will also elongate itself and stiffen to become as hard and strong as steel, the maximum length being 27' long at 2' width, to serve as a bridge, barricade, etc. In this latter form it is AC 0 and will take 100 hit points to destroy. Best of all, the possessor need only utter a word of command, and the *rug* will shrink to 1/12 size for easy storage and transportation.

Saw of Mighty Cutting: This notched adamantite blade is 12' long and over 1' wide. It requires 18/00 or greater strength to operate alone, or 2 persons of 17 or greater strength to work in tandem. The blade will slice through a 2' thick hardwood tree in 1 turn, a 4' thick trunk in 3 turns, or a 1' diameter tree in but 3 rounds. After 6 turns of cutting with the *saw*, the character or characters must rest for 6 turns before doing any further work.

Scarab of Death: This small brooch or pin of magical nature appears to be any one of the various amulets, brooches, or scarabs of beneficial sort. However, if it is held for more than 1 round or placed within a container (bag, pack, etc.) within 1' of a warm living body for 1 turn, it will change into a horrible burrowing beetle-like creature. The thing will then tear through any leather or cloth, burrow into flesh, and reach the victim's heart in a single round, causing death. It then returns to its *scarab* form. (Hard wood, ceramic, bone, ivory, or metal will prevent the monster from coming to life, if the *scarab* is secured within a container of such substance.)

Scarab of Enraging Enemies: When one of these devices is displayed and a command uttered, all intelligent hostile creatures within a 4" radius must save versus magic or become *enraged*. Those making the saving throw may perform normally; *enraged* enemies will fly into a berserk fury and attack the nearest creature (even their own comrades) — +1 "to hit", +2 on damage, −3 on their own armor class. The rage will last for 7-12 rounds, and during this period, the *enraged* creatures will continually attack without reason or fear, moving on to attack other creatures nearest them if initial opponents are slain. A *scarab* of this type contains from 19-24 charges.

Scarab of Insanity: This scarab is absolutely indistinguishable from any other amulet, brooch, or scarab. When displayed and a command word is spoken, all other creatures within a 2" radius must save versus magic at −2 (and −10% from any magic resistance as well). Those failing the save are completely *insane* for 9-12 rounds, unable to cast spells or use reasoning of any sort (treat as a *confusion* spell (q.v.) with no chance for acting in a non-confused manner). The *scarab* has 9-16 charges.

Scarab of Protection: This device appears to be any one of the various magical amulets, stones, etc. It gives off a faint dweomer, of course, and if it is held for 1 round by any character an inscription will appear on its surface letting the holder know it is a protective device. The possessor gains +1 on all saving throws versus magic, and if no save is normally possible, he or she gains one of 20, adjusted by any other magical protections which normally give bonuses to saving throw dice rolls. Thus, this device allows a save versus magic at base 20 against *magic missile* attacks, for example, and if the target also has +4 for magical armor and +1 for a *ring of protection*, any roll of 15 or better would indicate that the *missiles* did no damage. The *scarab* can additionally absorb up to 12 life energy level draining attacks (2 level drains count as 2 absorbings) or *death touches/death rays/fingers of death*. However, upon absorbing 12 such attacks the *scarab* turns to powder — totally destroyed. 1 in 20 of these *scarabs* are reversed cursed items, giving the possessor a –2 on his or her dice. However, 1 in 5 of these cursed items are actually +2 if the curse is removed by a cleric of 16 or higher level. In this latter case, the *scarab* will have absorption capability of 24 rather than 12.

Spade of Colossal Excavation: This digging tool is 8' long with a spade-like blade 2' wide and 3' long. Any fighter with 18 strength can use this magical shovel to dig great holes. 1 cubic yard of normal earth can be excavated in 1 round. Every 10 rounds, the user must rest for 5 rounds. Hard pan clay takes twice as long to dig, as does gravel. Loose soil takes only half as long.

Sphere of Annihilation: A *sphere of annihilation* is a globe of absolute blackness, a ball of nothingness 2' in diameter. A *sphere* is actually a hole in the continuity of the multiverse, a void. Any matter which comes in contact with a *sphere* is instantly sucked into the void, gone, utterly destroyed, *wishes* and similar magicks notwithstanding! A *sphere of annihilation* is basically static, resting in some spot just as if it were a normal hole. It can be caused to move, however, by mental effort, the brain waves of the individual concentrating on changing its position bending spatial fabrics so as to cause the hole to slide in some direction. Control range is 40' initially, 1''/level once control is established. Basic movement rate is 10' per round, modified as shown below. Concentration control is based on intelligence and level of experience — the higher the level the greater the mental power and discipline. For every 1 point of intelligence above 12, the magic-user adds 1%; for every 1 point over 15, he or she adds another 3%, i.e. 1% for each point from 13 to 15, and additional 3% for each point from 16-18 — a maximum of 12% bonus at 18 intelligence. The bonus applies to this table:

Level of Magic-User	Movement/ Round	Probability of Control per Round
up to 5th	8'	15%
6th-7th	9'	20%
8th-9th	10'	30%
10th-11th	11'	40%
12th-13th	12'	50%
14th-15th	13'	60%
16th-17th	14'	70%
18th-20th	15'	75%
21st & above	16'	80%

Any *attempt* to control the *sphere* will cause it to move, but if control is not established, the *sphere* will slide *towards* the magic-user attempting to do so, and it will continue so moving for 1-4 rounds or longer, if the magic-user is within 30' thereafter.

If 2 or more magic-users attempt to control a *sphere of annihilation*, the strongest (the one with the highest percentage chance to control the *sphere*) is checked first, then the next strongest, etc. Control chance is reduced 5% per person, cumulative, when 2 or more magic-users concentrate on the *sphere*, even if they are attempting the same thing (co-operating). If none are successful, the *sphere* will slip towards the strongest. Control *must* be checked each and every round.

Should a *gate* spell be cast upon a *sphere*, there is a 50% chance that the spell will destroy it, 35% that the spell will do nothing, and 15% that a gap will be torn in the spatial fabric, and everything in an 18'' radius will be catapulted into another plane or universe. If a *rod of cancellation* touches a *sphere*, the two will cause a tremendous explosion as they negate each other. Everything within a 6'' radius will sustain 30-120 (3d4 × 10) hit points of damage. A psionic using *probability travel* discipline when the *sphere* touches him or her will be able to do away with the sphere, and gain another major psionic power, if he or she succeeds in saving versus magic; failure indicates annihilation. (See *Talisman of the Sphere* hereafter.)

Stone of Controlling Earth Elementals: A stone of this nature is typically an oddly-shaped bit of extrusive rock, shaped and roughly polished. The possessor of such a stone needs but utter a single command word, and an earth elemental of 12 hit dice size will come to the summoner if earth is available, an 8 hit dice elemental if rough, unhewn stone is the summoning medium. (An earth elemental cannot be summoned from worked stone, but one can be from mud, clay, or even sand, although one from sand is an 8 dice monster.) The area of summoning for an earth elemental must be at least 4' square and have 4 cubic yards volume. The elemental will appear in 1-4 rounds. For details of elementals and their control see **ADVANCED DUNGEONS & DRAGONS, MONSTER MANUAL.** One elemental per day can be summoned by means of the *stone*.

Stone of Good Luck (Luckstone): This magical stone is typically a bit of rough polished agate or similar mineral. Its possessor gains a +1 (+5% where applicable) on all dice rolls involving factors such as saving, slipping, dodging, etc. — whenever a die or dice are rolled to find whether the character has an adverse happening befall or not. This luck does *not* affect "to hit" and damage dice or spell failure dice. Additionally, the *luckstone* gives the possessor a ±1%-10% (at owner's option) on rolls for determination of magic items or division of treasure. The *most* favorable results will always be gained with a *stone of good luck*.

Stone of Weight (Loadstone): This magical stone appears to be any one of the other sorts, and testing will not reveal its nature. However, as soon as the possessor of a *stone of weight* is in a situation where he or she is required to move quickly in order to avoid an enemy — combat or pursuit — the item causes a 50% reduction in movement, and even attacks are reduced to 50% normal rate. Furthermore, the stone *cannot* be gotten rid of by any means — throwing it away or smashing it notwithstanding — and it will always turn up somewhere on the character's person. If a *dispel evil* is cast upon a *loadstone*, the item will disappear and no longer haunt the individual.

Talisman of Pure Good: If a high priest or priestess possesses one of these mighty *talismans*, he or she has the power to cause an evil cleric to be swallowed up forever by a flaming crack which will open at the feet of the victim and precipitate him or her to the center of the earth. The wielder of the *talisman* **must** be good, and if he or she is not exceptionally pure in thought and deed, the evil cleric will gain a saving throw versus magic. A *talisman of pure good* has 7 charges. It cannot be recharged. If a neutral cleric touches one of these magic stones, he or she will take 7-28 hit points of damage; and if an evil cleric touches one he or she will take 12-48 hit points of damage. Non-clerics will not be affected by the device.

Talisman of the Sphere: This is a small adamantite loop and handle which will be useless in any but a magic-user's possession, and any other class touching a talisman of this sort will take 5-30 hit points of damage. When held by a magic-user concentrating on control of a *sphere of annihilation*, a *talisman of the sphere* doubles the intelligence bonus percentage for control, i.e. 2% per point of intelligence from 13-15, 6% per point of intelligence from 16-18. If control is established by the wielder of a *talisman*, he or she need check for continual control only every other round thereafter. If control is not established, the *sphere* will move towards the magic-user at maximum speed (16'/round). Note that a *wand of negation* will have no effect upon a *sphere of annihilation*, but if the wand is directed at the *talisman* it will negate its power of control so long as the wand is so directed.

Talisman of Ultimate Evil: This device exactly resembles a *talisman of pure good* and is exactly its opposite in all respects. It has 6 charges.

Talisman of Zagy: A *talisman* of this sort appears exactly the same as a *stone controlling earth elementals*. Its power is quite different, and these are dependent upon the charisma of the individual holding the *talisman*. Whenever a character touches a *Talisman of Zagy*, a reaction check is made as if the individual were meeting another creature. If a *hostile* reaction result is obtained, the device will act as a *stone of weight*, although discarding it or destroying it results only in 5-30 hit points of damage and the disappearance of the *talisman*. If a *neutral* reaction results, the *talisman* will remain with the character for 5-30 hours, or until a *wish* is made upon it, whichever first occurs, and it will then disappear. If a *friendly* reaction result is obtained, the character will find it impossible to be rid of the *talisman* for as many months as he or she has points of charisma. The device will grant 1 *wish* for every 6 points of the character's charisma; and it will also grow warm and throb whenever its possessor comes within 20' of a mechanical or magical trap. (If the *talisman* is not held, its warning heat and pulses will be of no avail.) Regardless of which reaction result is obtained, when its time period expires the *talisman* will disappear, but a base 10,000 g.p. gem (diamond) will remain in its stead.

Tome of Clear Thought: A work of this nature is indistinguishable from any normal book (cf. *Manual of Bodily Health*). Any single character who reads a *tome of clear thought* will be able to practice mental exercises which will increase his or her intelligence by 1 point. Reading a work of this nature takes 48 hours time over 6 days, and immediately thereafter the book disappears. The reader must begin a program of concentration and mental disciplines within 1 week of reading the *tome*. After 1 full month of such exercise, intelligence goes up. If psionics are employed in the campaign and the character is previously a non-psionic, another check may be allowed. The knowledge gained from reading the work can never be recorded or articulated. Any further perusal of a *tome of clear thought* will be of no benefit to the character.

Tome of Leadership and Influence: This leather and brass bound book is similar to a *tome of clear thought*; but upon completion of reading and practice of what was revealed therein, charisma is increased by 1 point.

Tome of Understanding: Identical to a *tome of clear thought*, this work increases wisdom by 1 point.

Trident of Fish Command: This three-tined fork atop a stout rod of 6' length appears to be a barbed military fork of some sort. However, its magical properties enable its wielder to cause all fish — including sharks and eels but excluding mollusks, crustaceans, amphibians, reptiles, mammals and similar sorts of non-piscine marine creatures — within a 6" radius to save versus magic (this uses one charge of the *trident*). Those which fail this throw are completely under empathic command, they will not attack the possessor of the *trident* nor any creature within 10' of him or her, and the wielder of the device can cause them to move in whatever direction is desired and convey messages of emotion, i.e. fear, hunger, anger, indifference, repletion, etc. Fish which make their saving throw are free of

empathic control, but they will not approach closer than 10' of the *trident*. Fish which school must be checked as a single entity. A *trident* of this type contains 17-20 charges. It is otherwise a +1 magic weapon.

Trident of Submission: A weapon of this nature appears unremarkable, exactly as any normal trident. The wielder of a *trident of submission* causes any opponent struck to save versus magic. If the opponent fails to save, it must check morale the next round *instead* of attacking; if morale is *good*, the opponent may act normally next round, but if it is *poor*, the opponent will cease fighting and surrender, overcome with a feeling of hopelessness. The duration of this hopelessness is 2-8 rounds. Thereafter the creature is normal once again. The *trident* has 17-20 charges. A *trident* of this type is a +1 magic weapon.

Trident of Warning: A weapon of this type enables its wielder to determine the location, depth, species, and number of hostile and/or hungry marine predators within 24". A *trident of warning* must be grasped and pointed in order for the person using it to gain such information, and it requires 1 round to so scan a 24" radius hemisphere. There are 19-24 charges in a *trident* of this type, each charge sufficient to last for 2 rounds of scanning. The weapon is otherwise a +2 magical arm.

Trident of Yearning: A *trident of yearning* looks exactly like any normal trident, and its dweomer is also indistinguishable from the magic aura of other enchanted weapons of this sort. Any character grasping this type of trident immediately conceives an overwhelming desire to immerse himself or herself in as great a depth of water as is possible. The unquenchable longing so generated causes the affected character to instantly proceed toward the largest/deepest body of water — in any event one that is sufficient to completely cover his or her person — and immerse himself or herself therein permanently. The character cannot loose his or her grip on the *trident*, and only a *water breathing* spell (after submersion) placed upon him or her, or use of a *wish* or *alter reality*, will enable the character to do so. The *trident* is otherwise a –2 cursed magical weapon. Note that this item does not confer the ability to breathe underwater.

Vacuous Grimoire: A book of this sort is totally impossible to tell from a normal one, although if a *detect magic* spell is cast, there will be a magical aura noted. Any character who opens the work and reads so much as a single glyph therein must make 2 saving throws versus magic. The first is to determine if 1 point of *intelligence* is lost or not, the second is to find if 2 points of *wisdom* are lost. Once opened and read, the *vacuous grimoire* remains, and it must be burned to be rid of it after first casting a *remove curse* spell. If the tome is placed with other books, its appearance will instantly alter to conform to one of the other works it is amongst.

Well of Many Worlds: This strange inter-dimensional device is exactly the same in appearance as a *portable hole*. Anything placed within it is immediately cast into another world — a parallel earth, another planet, or a different plane at your option or by random determination. If the *well* is moved, the random factor again comes into play. It can be picked up, folded, etc. just as a *portable hole*. Note that things from the world the *well* touches can come through the opening, just as easily as from the initiating place.

Wings of Flying: A pair of these magical wings appears to be nothing more than a plain cloak of old, black cloth. If the wearer speaks a command word, the cloak will turn into a pair of gigantic bat wings (20' span) and empower the wearer to fly as follows:

2 turns at 32" speed
4 turns at 18" speed
8 turns at 12" speed

Combinations are possible at the ratio above. After the maximum number of possible turns flying, the wearer must rest for 1 hour — sitting, lying down, or sleeping. Shorter periods of flight do not require full rest, but only relative quiet such as slow walking for 1 hour. Any flying of less than 1 turn duration does not require any rest. Note that regardless of the length of time spent flying the *wings* can be used but once per day. They will support up to 500 pounds weight.

TABLE (III.E.) SPECIAL

Notes Regarding Artifacts and Relics: Each *artifact* or *relic* is a singular thing of potent powers and possibly strange side effects as well. Regardless of how any of these items come into your campaign, only 1 of each may exist. As each is placed by you or found by player characters, you must draw a line through its listing on the table to indicate it can no longer be discovered randomly — if the dice indicate an item no longer available, you may substitute a clue as to its whereabouts or simply ignore the result so that no magic item is found at all.

Because of the unique nature of each *artifact* and *relic*, their powers are only partially described. You, the Dungeon Master, must at least decide what the major powers of each item are to be. This prevents players from gaining any knowledge of these items, even if they happen to own or read a copy of this volume, and it also makes each *artifact* and *relic* distinct from campaign to campaign.

Those *artifacts* and *relics* which you bring into play should be so carefully guarded by location and warding devices and monsters that recovery of any one is an undertaking of such magnitude that only very powerful characters, in concert, and after lengthy attempts have any chance whatsoever of attaining one. Naturally, each *artifact* and *relic* might have a body of rumors, tales, and other lore. Discovery of such information should not be by chance. Minor clues may be placed, but any extensive oral or written information must be sought out and obtained only after considerable expenditure of time and money, if at all.

Please note that you need not use any or all of the *artifacts* and/or *relics* here. If you prefer, you may rename those in your campaign to suit a particular mythos, or you may devise your own entirely. But any creation by you must be done so as to maintain the item in balance with the game as a whole — and this goes for assignment of powers with respect to any of these items, too! A super-weapon is certain to blast the whole campaign to smithereens, unless it is given proper limitations (and also a nemesis creature in some cases).

At the end of the descriptions of *artifacts* and *relics* are 5 tables which list the various powers and side effects of these items. Each item is described with only a few of its attributes, and its other characteristics are mentioned with respect to the number of each power or effect from the appropriate table, i.e. each item has several powers and/or effects you must select and record in your copy of this book. Players can know virtually nothing about any powers and effects of any *artifact* or *relic*. These must be discovered by them through experimentation by their characters, legends, *legend lore*, etc.

If a player refuses to risk his or her character when an item is discovered, preferring to allow some hireling or henchman to hazard the trial and error process necessary, the character given the item or ordered to determine its powers and effects will certainly do one of the following things:

1. If the character is *evil*, he or she will destroy, or at least escape from, the player character once the *artifact* or *relic* abilities are known to the character.
2. If the character is *neutral* and neither good nor evil otherwise, he or she will use the powers of the *artifact* or *relic* to dominate and control his or her former employer/master or mistress, destroying him or her if threatened.
3. If the character is *good*, he or she will realize that his or her employer/master or mistress acted in a most evil fashion by giving/forcing upon him or her the *artifact* or *relic*; so the character will use every wile to escape the player character and take the item along to give to his or her religious leaders or other suzerain. (And, of course, this character will *never* again associate with the player character in question.)

All hirelings and henchmen of a player character foisting off an *artifact* or *relic* in such manner will have a drop in loyalty of 10%-30% if the character having the item is permanently harmed or killed.

All *artifacts* and *relics* are of such power that they are virtually impervious to harm — magical or physical. Some predate the known gods, and others were formed by the gods. Typically, each can only be destroyed by a single means. A table after those of powers and effects gives a sampling of the various means suggested. Any character attempting to destroy an *artifact* or *relic* by disassembling its parts, removing a portion, or similarly defacing it must usually save versus magic at –5; failure equals death.

Many of these items tend to make their possessor reclusive, secretive, arrogant, and/or greedy. These effects are best to handle through manipulation of the player by means of powers, non-player characters, etc.

Finally, whatever befalls the possessor of an *artifact* or *relic*, or the effects

he or she causes by use of the *prime* powers (or even the *major* powers in some cases), is permanent and usually irreversible by the most powerful of spells — including *wishes*, for example — or even by deities. Exception: A deity who created the item, or one which can fully control it, may (at your option) be able to reverse effects of some powers.

Axe of the Dwarvish Lords: Legend relates that the greatest dwarf who ever lived, the first Dwarven King, forged this weapon in volcanic fires with the aid of a patron god. It passed from dwarven monarch to dwarven monarch until it was lost in the Invoked Devastation centuries gone. Rumors persist of the appearance of the *Axe* from time to time in various places, but it supposedly bears a curse. The blade of the *Axe* is equal to a *sword of sharpness*, and it is backed by a head equal to a +3 hammer. The handle extends or contracts upon command to equal a battle or hand axe (for throwing), and the *Axe* will return 30' to its thrower. The possessor has dwarven abilities of infravision, trap detection, etc. — double abilities if a dwarf. The possessor's life span is 50% longer than normal, but he or she becomes more and more dwarf-like with time, until eventually he or she exactly resembles one. The *Axe* has the following additional powers/effects:

2 × I: _____, _____
1 × II: _____
1 × III: _____
1 × IV: _____
1 × V: _____
1 × VI: _____

Baba Yaga's Hut: Ages ago the most powerful female mage ever known spent much of her power in the creation of a magical dwelling of superb character. When she passed to another plane, her hut disappeared and has only been rumored to have been seen once or twice since. Baba Yaga developed a small hut of ordinary appearance — a circular, thatched structure of 15' diameter and 10' high. To this dwelling are attached two powerful fowl legs 12' long, which appear to be stilts. Furthermore, the *Hut* has intelligence (*high*) and human senses, plus infravisual ability to 120' and ultravision. Inside, the *Hut* is a small palace — garden, fountains of water and wine, and 30 rooms on 3 floors, all lavishly and richly furnished! Despite the commodious interior, the bird legs can move *Baba Yaga's Hut* at up to 48" speed over swamp, 36" over rough or normal terrain, 12" over hills, through forests, etc. The *Hut* will obey commands from 1 person (the one first using a key phrase) and can come to a call from as far away as 1 league. Its legs deliver blows equal to those of a hill giant, 2 attacks per round, to any so rash as to come near without invitation or knowing the command phrase. The legs are armor class 2 and can take 48 hit points damage each, regenerating at 1 hit point/melee round. The walls of the *Hut* are the equivalent of 5' thick granite. The *Hut* has the following additional powers/effects:

4 × I: _____, _____, _____, _____
2 × II: _____, _____
1 × III: _____
1 × IV: _____
1 × V: _____
1 × VI: _____

Codex of the Infinite Planes: In the distant past the High Wizard Priest of the Isles of Woe (now sunken beneath the waters of the Nyr Dyv — see **THE WORLD OF GREYHAWK** from TSR) discovered this work and used its arcane powers to dominate the neighboring states, but legend also has it that these same powers eventually brought doom to the mage-priest and his tyrannical domain. It must be that somehow the *Codex* survived the inundation, for the archmage Tzunk scribed the following fragment prior to his strange disappearance:

"... and the two strong slaves lifted it [the *Codex*] from the back of the Beast. Thereupon I commanded the Brazen Portals to be brought low, and they were wrenched from their hinges and rang upon the stone. The Efreet howled in fear and fled when I caused the page to be read, and the Beast passed into the City of Brass. Now was I, Tzunk, Master of the Plane of Molten Skies. With sure hand I closed Yagrax's Tome [the *Codex*], dreading to —"

From the foregoing it is evident that the item is very large and of exceptional power. Any person reading its 99 damned pages is 99% certain to meet a terrible fate (1% cumulative chance per page). The *Codex's* other pages have the keys to instant physical transference to any one of the other planes and alternates of any world or universe. The work will destroy instantly any character under 11th level of experience who touches it, but those of 11th level or higher who make a saving throw versus magic can command the powers and effects of the *Codex*:

```
4 × I:   _____, _____, _____, _____
4 × II:  _____, _____, _____, _____
2 × III: _____, _____
2 × IV:  _____, _____
2 × V:   _____, _____
2 × VI:  _____, _____
```

Note: When activating powers and effects, base their coming into play upon the progress of the character's perusal of the *Codex*.

Crown of Might: According to tradition, great items of regalia were constructed for special servants of the deities of each alignment when the gods were contending amongst themselves. Who amongst them first conceived the idea is unknown. The champion of each ethic alignment — Evil, Good, Neutrality — was given a *crown*, an *orb*, and a *sceptre*. These items have been scattered and lost over the centuries of struggle since they first appeared. These 3 complete sets bestow great powers, but even mere possession of a *Crown of Might* gives a character of the same ethos great benefits (if a character of another alignment touches such an item he or she takes 5-30 hit points of damage and must save versus magic or be instantly killed). The alignment of a *Crown* is determined as follows:

```
01-06    Evil
07-14    Good
15-20    Neutrality
```

While being worn, the *Crown* raises its wearer's level of experience by 1 and confers the following additional powers/effects:

	Evil	**Good**	**Neutrality**
2 × I:	____, ____	____, ____	____, ____
1 × II:	____	____	____
1 × III:	____	____	____

Should a character wearing a *Crown* touch an *Orb of Might* (q.v.) or a *Sceptre of Might* of a different ethos, he or she takes damage and must save as noted above, and if the saving throw is successful, 1 malevolent power from Table IV. will affect him or her. However, if the *Orb* or *Sceptre* is of the same ethos, the following extra powers (and effects) are conferred upon the possessor:

2nd Item of Set	**Evil**	**Good**	**Neutrality**
1 × I:	_____	_____	_____
1 × II:	_____	_____	_____
3rd Item of Set			
1 × I:	_____	_____	_____
1 × II:	_____	_____	_____
1 × IV:	_____	_____	_____
1 × V:	_____	_____	_____
1 × VI:	_____	_____	_____

Note: Each of these items is so similar in appearance to the other that examination will reveal no difference, and detection magically will not reveal their ethic alignment. Each *Crown* is a slender diadem of gold set with 3 precious stones of great size so as to bring 50,000 or more gold pieces if openly sold.

Crystal of the Ebon Flame: The origin of this artifact is entirely unknown, as is its exact whereabouts. It is a beautifully formed, diamond-hard mineral the size of a hand. When it is touched, the *Crystal* sends forth rays of light and a black flame seems to leap and dance in the heart of the jewel. All creatures within 30' must save versus magic or be charmed as if by a *fire charm* spell. The possessor of the *Crystal* may draw upon its powers by gazing at the *Ebon Flame* at its center. These powers and effects are:

```
4 × I:   _____, _____, _____, _____
2 × II:  _____, _____
1 × III: _____
1 × IV:  _____
1 × V:   _____
1 × VI:  _____
```

Cup and Talisman of Al'Akbar: This pair of holy relics were given by the gods of the Paynims to their most exalted high priest of *lawful good* alignment in the days following the Invoked Devastation. It was lost to demihuman raiders and was last rumored to be somewhere in the Southeastern portion of the Bandit Kingdoms. The *Cup* is made of hammered gold, chased with silver filigree, and set with 12 great gems in electrum settings — a jewelry value of 75,000 or more gold pieces on the market. It does not radiate magic, but it has the following powers/effects:

```
4 × I:   _____, _____, _____, _____
1 × III: _____*
```

The *Talisman* is made of hammered platinum, a star of 8 points, chased with gold inlays, and with a small gem tipping each point. The star is hung from a chain of gold and electrum set with silver beading (8 sets of 3 beads each) — a jewelry value of 10,000 or more gold pieces. It does not radiate magic either, but has the following powers/effects:

```
2 × II:  _____, _____
1 × IV:  _____**
```

If a cleric, druid, paladin, or ranger possesses both, he or she may fill the cup with holy water and immerse the talisman into the fluid to create a potion once per week. The potion will be:

```
1-5      healing
6-10     extra healing
11-15    poison antidote balm
16-17    cure disease salve
18-19    remove curse ointment
20       raise dead balm
```

And the possessor gains the following powers/effects from both:

```
1 × V:   _____
1 × VI:  _____
```

* For *neutral* or *evil* characters only.

** For *evil* characters only.

Eye of Vecna: Seldom is the name of Vecna spoken except in hushed voice, and never within hearing of strangers, for legends say that the phantom of this once supreme lich still roams the Material Plane. It is certain that when Vecna finally met his doom, one eye and one hand survived. The *Eye of Vecna* is said to glow in the same manner as that of a feral creature. It appears to be an agate until it is placed in an empty eye socket of a living character. Once pressed in, it instantly and irrevocably grafts itself to the head, and it cannot be removed or harmed without slaying the character. The alignment of the character immediately becomes *neutral evil* and may *never* change. The *Eye* bestows both *infra-* and *ultravision* to its host, and gives the following additional powers/effects:

```
2 × I:   _____, _____
2 × II:  _____, _____
1 × IV:  _____
1 × V:   _____
```

The minor or major powers may be used without fear of harm, but use of the primary power causes a malevolent effect upon the host character.

The Hand of Vecna: The arch-lich Vecna supposedly imbued both his hand (left) and his eye (see the foregoing listing) with wondrous and horrible powers enabling them to persist long after his other remains mouldered away into dust (cf. *Eye of Vecna*). Tales say that the *Hand* appears to be a mummified extremity, a blackened and shriveled hand, possibly from a burned body. If the wrist portion is pressed against the stump of a forearm, it will instantly graft itself to the limb and become a functioning member with 18/00 strength in its grip (no "to hit" or damage bonuses). The *Hand* will eventually turn the alignment of the host character to *neutral evil* as explained hereafter.

The host character may use any minor power without fear, but as soon as a major power of the *Hand* is used, he or she awakes a spirit of great evil. (You, the DM, should then begin an insidious campaign of suggestion and urging towards evil on that character's part.) When a primary power is used, the host will instantly become *neutral evil* — very evil. The *Hand* can be severed from the host at any time before its powers are used with 100% certainty, but each major power use subtracts 1% from the probability, and each use of a primary power makes success 10% less likely. Whenever 100% subtraction has occurred there is no possibility of removing the *Hand*, and the character will know this.

To use any power, the fingers of the *Hand* must be extended, curled, or whatever in different combinations. The powers and effects are:

10 × I: _____, _____, _____, _____,
_____, _____, _____, _____, _____,
5 × II: _____, _____, _____, _____,
2 × III: _____, _____
2 × IV: _____, _____
2 × V: _____, _____
1 × VI: _____

Remember that NOTHING SHORT OF INTERVENTION FROM THE MOST POWERFUL OF GODS CAN ALTER THE EFFECTS OF VECNA'S HAND UPON ITS HOST, and it is urged that even the greatest of deities will be loath to attempt to undertake meddling with any host creature — so allow the effects to be irrevocable.

Note: Devise the combinations of finger/hand positions you have assigned to each power and record them, i.e. fist = ( ), thumb down = ( ), pointing little finger = ( ), etc. Keep this chart handy and make the host character use the positions to use a power of the *Hand*.

Heward's Mystical Organ: In the pages of the Fables of Burdock there is mention of a musical instrument of large size, an organ of such power that the mighty and terrible enchantments possible to cast by playing upon it are only hinted at. *Heward's Organ* has 77 great and small pipes, a console with many keys of black and white beneath 13 ivory stops, and 3 great foot pedals. The bellows which sends a rush of wind to the pipes is said to be worked by a conjured and chained air elemental of huge size. Each stop causes the pipes to sound in a different voice, while the keys vary the notes, of course. No one is certain what purpose the foot pedals serve. Despite the ravages of time which have silenced some of its pipes, and abuse and neglect which have supposedly made some keys and stops unworkable, the *Organ* can still work mighty magicks when properly played.

The would-be conjurer must be most careful, however, when attempting to work this relic/artifact, for pulling the wrong stops can cause the summoning of something undesired or the casting of the wrong type of spell. If the wrong keys are depressed — or the right ones are not — something called up might be unbound or the magic might backfire. Similarly, the alignment of the caster or manipulator of the *Organ* might be changed by improper playing.

After the powers and effects of the *Organ* have been determined by you, decide which stops and what key sequence/combinations will do what. (If you are conversant with musical notation, you can write tunes if you like, and make your players actually perform them on a piano or other instrument. Otherwise, pick some appropriate songs and give clues so that the player character can hum different ditties, i.e. "Fly Me to the Moon", "That Old Black Magic", "That Old Devil Moon", "You've Got Me in Between the Devil and the Deep Blue Sea", "The Monster Mash", etc.) The suggested powers and effects are:

7 × I: _____, _____, _____, _____,
_____, _____, _____,
7 × II: _____, _____, _____, _____,
_____, _____, _____
3 × III: _____, _____, _____
7 × IV: _____, _____, _____, _____,
_____, _____, _____
7 × V: _____, _____, _____, _____,
_____, _____, _____
3 × VI: _____, _____, _____

Remember that effects can be negated, reversed, changed, etc. by misplaying the *Organ*.

Horn of Change: This ancient artifact exactly resembles any of the more common magical horns such as a *horn of blasting*, a *horn of bubbles*, etc. If

---

it is winded 1 time, a power from Table I or an effect from Table III will occur. If the *Horn* is twice sounded, a power from Table II or an effect from Table VI will occur. If 3 blasts are given, a power from Table V or an effect from Table IV will occur. You must determine the probability of a power or effect. 75%/25% is suggested and then dice for a random result on the appropriate table. Results which are inappropriate should be ignored.

Invulnerable Coat of Arnd: The High Priest Arnd of Tdon is said to have been the original possessor of this relic. The *Coat* is a bright and shimmering shirt of fine and almost weightless chain links. It covers the upper arms, torso, and groin of any human-shaped wearer of from 3' to 8' height, and makes the wearer totally invulnerable to physical attacks with respect to covered areas and gives AC 5 protection to all other areas. In addition, the *Coat* adds +5 to saving throws as if it were +5 magic armor, protects its wearer from fire as if it were a *ring of fire resistance*, and acid, cold, and electrical attacks have no effect upon the wearer. Additionally, the *Invulnerable Coat of Arnd* has the following powers/effects:

3 × I: _____, _____, _____
2 × II: _____, _____
2 × III: _____, _____
1 × IV: _____
1 × V: _____
1 × VI: _____

Iron Flask of Tuerny the Merciless: This artifact is reported to be a small and heavy urn, easily carried in a pack or by hand despite its weight. The *Flask* is stoppered with a turnip-shaped plug, engraved and embossed with sigils, glyphs, and runes of power so as to contain the spirit therein. The possessor need but know 3 words to have the *Flask* function properly, i.e. the word of OPENING, the word of COMMAND, the word of CLOSING AND SEALING. *Tuerny's Flask* is rumored to imprison one of the following:

a greater devil
a groaning spirit
a major demon
a night hag
a nycadaemon

It is generally conceded that the Servant of the *Flask* can be loosed only to perform evil deeds, and it must always kill before it can be commanded to return to its prison. In addition to the Servant, the *Flask* has the following powers/effects:

3 × I: _____, _____, _____
1 × III: _____
1 × V: _____
1 × VI: _____

Jacinth of Inestimable Beauty: It is said that the finest corundum gem from the heart of the largest mountain was taken and fashioned by the gods themselves to form the *Jacinth of Inestimable Beauty*. This huge, priceless fiery orange jewel is indescribably beautiful and exquisitely cut in dozens of facets which shoot forth brilliant beams, and all who see it within 20' or less must save versus magic or be charmed by it. Legend relates that the *Jacinth* was possessed by the fabled Sultan Jehef Peh'reen for a time and then passed into the Land of Ket and southward into Keoland (see **THE WORLD OF GREYHAWK**), where all trace disappeared. When the possessor firmly grasps this lustrous orange gem, the following powers/effects are gained:

2 × I: _____, _____
2 × II: _____, _____
1 × III: _____
1 × IV: _____
1 × V: _____
1 × VI: _____

Johydee's Mask: The high priestess Johydee supposedly tricked the powers of evil into making this strange artifact and then wisely used it to overthrow their hold upon her nation. The *Mask* completely covers the wearer's face and enables him or her to assume the likeness of any human or human-like creature. It also prevents all forms of mind contact, detection or attack. *Johydee's Mask* is rumored to give the wearer total immunity to all gaze attacks (basilisk, catoblepas, medusa, etc.) and the following powers/effects:

2 × I: _____, _____
1 × II: _____
1 × VI: _____

Kuroth's Quill: There can be but little dispute that the master thief Kuroth was the most successful of his profession, and several sages attribute his performance to the acquisition of a writing instrument of unknown antiquity which now bears Kuroth's name. This *Quill* reportedly draws and writes infallibly upon command, depicting whatever its possessor sees or speaks accordingly. It also is supposed to be able to find treasure (as a *potion of treasure finding*) 1 time per month. These powers and effects are attributed to it as well:

```
2 × I:    _____, _____
1 × III:  _____
1 × IV:   _____
1 × VI:   _____
```

Mace of Cuthbert: This weapon is said to be that actually used by the Venerable Saint Cuthbert of the Cudgel when he demonstrated the folly of error to the unbeliever. Over the decades since then, holy relics of the Saint himself have been encased within the *Mace* to give this arm of *lawful good* a +5 bonus for both hitting and damage as well as *disruption* effects. Only clerics with 18 strength of lawful good alignment are able to wield this weapon and gain these other powers/effects:

```
3 × I:    _____, _____, _____
2 × II:   _____, _____
1 × VI:   _____
```

Machine of Lum the Mad: Perhaps this strange device was built by gods long forgotten and survived the eons since their passing, for it is incredibly ancient and of workmanship unlike anything known today. The *Machine* was used by Baron Lum to build an empire, but what has since become of this ponderous mechanism none can say. Legends report that it has 60 levers, 40 dials, and 20 switches (but only about one-half still function). Singly or in combination, these controls will generate all sorts of powers and effects.

The *Machine* is delicate, intricate, bulky and very heavy (5,500 pounds). It cannot be moved normally, and any serious jolt will set off and then destroy 1-4 functions of the artifact which can never be restored. It has a booth of a size suitable for 4 man-sized creatures (4' × 5' × 7') to stand inside, and if a creature or object is placed therein and the *Machine's* controls are worked, something might happen.

You must matrix the 60 levers, 40 dials, and 20 switches, showing which will perform functions. You may opt to include powers and/or effects of your own devising:

```
15 × I:   _____, _____, _____, _____, _____,
          _____, _____, _____, _____, _____,
          _____, _____, _____, _____, _____,
15 × II:  _____, _____, _____, _____, _____,
          _____, _____, _____, _____, _____,
          _____, _____, _____, _____, _____,
10 × III: _____, _____, _____, _____, _____,
          _____, _____, _____, _____, _____,
10 × IV:  _____, _____, _____, _____, _____,
          _____, _____, _____, _____, _____,
15 × V:   _____, _____, _____, _____, _____,
          _____, _____, _____, _____, _____,
          _____, _____, _____, _____, _____,
5 × VI:   _____, _____, _____, _____, _____
```

Mighty Servant of Leuk-O: Those who are most knowledgeable regarding ancient artifacts believe that this device is of the same manufacture as the *Machine of Lum*. The *Mighty Servant* of the famous General Leuk-O is a towering automaton of crystal, unknown metals, and strange fibrous material. It is over 9' tall, 6' deep, and some 4½' wide. Inside is a compartment suitable for holding 2 man-sized creatures, and there is space for 4-5 others to sit outside. If the possessor knows the proper command phrases, he or she can use the *Mighty Servant* as a transportation mode, magical attack device, or fighting machine. It is armor class −1 and can withstand 60 hit points of damage. Note all weapons do only 50% of normal damage (round down). The *Mighty Servant* regenerates (self-repairs) 2 points of damage per round. Its magic resistance is 100%. Acid, cold, fire, heat, vacuum, and/or water have no effect on the device. Electrical/lightning attacks cause only 20% normal damage (round down), even if the *Servant* fails the magic resistance check.

The *Mighty Servant* moves at a maximum speed of 3". After each 12 hours of operation it must rest (recharge) itself for 1 hour. Any intelligent viewer within 12" must save versus magic (+2 on the die roll) or flee in panic. It can attack but 1 time per round, and it has a base 15% chance to hit an opponent regardless of its armor class. Opponents with intelligence and a dexterity of 15 or better reduce the base chance to hit by 2½% per 1 point of dexterity above 14. A hit from the *Mighty Servant* causes 10-100 hit points of damage.

In addition, the *Mighty Servant of Leuk-O* has these powers/effects:

```
6 × I:    _____, _____, _____,
          _____, _____, _____,
6 × II:   _____, _____, _____,
          _____, _____, _____,
1 × III:  _____
2 × IV:   _____, _____
2 × VI:   _____, _____
```

Effects are triggered by major power use. The *Mighty Servant* will obey those humans who learn its secrets of automation and control.

Orb of Dragonkind: It is written that when certain of the good deities conspired to devise means to easily control the evil dragons plaguing mankind, demon servants of evil changed the magical forces involved so as to include all of dragonkind and then caused the *Orbs* fashioned to have inimical properties as well. In all, 8 globes of carven white jade were made, 1 each for each age in a dragon's life span. The smallest is but 3 inches in diameter, the largest is about 10 inches across. Each is covered with bas reliefs of entwined dragons of all sorts, the whole being of incredible hardness, and somehow imprisoning the very essence of all dragons. The 8 different *Orbs* are:

1. **Orb of the Hatchling:** The possessor of this device is empowered to *charm* any *very young* dragon. The Orb has an intelligence of 9 and an ego of 9, and if this combination equals or exceeds the combined intelligence and wisdom of its possessor, the *Orb* will control him or her and surely slay him or her. The *Orb* has these powers:

    ```
    3 × I:  _____, _____, _____
    ```

2. **Orb of the Wyrmkin:** The possessor of this device is empowered to *charm* any *young* dragon. The Orb has an intelligence of 10 and an ego of 10, and if this combination equals or exceeds the combined intelligence and wisdom of its possessor, the *Orb* will control him or her and cause the character's demise as speedily as possible. The *Orb* has these powers:

    ```
    2 × I:   _____, _____
    1 × II:  _____
    ```

3. **Orb of the Dragonette:** The possessor of this device is empowered to *charm* any *sub-adult* dragon. The Orb has an intelligence of 11 and an ego of 11, and if this combination equals or exceeds the combined intelligence and wisdom of its possessor, the *Orb* will control him or her and bring death as rapidly as possible to the individual. The *Orb* has these powers/effects:

    ```
    3 × I:   _____, _____, _____
    1 × II:  _____
    1 × III: _____
    ```

4. **Orb of the Dragon:** The possessor of this device is empowered to *charm* any *young adult* dragon. The Orb has an intelligence of 12 and an ego of 12, and if this combination equals or exceeds the combined intelligence and wisdom of its possessor, the *Orb* will control the character and cause his or her death as speedily as it can. The *Orb* has these powers/effects:

    ```
    4 × I:   _____, _____, _____, _____
    1 × II:  _____
    1 × III: _____
    ```

5. **Orb of the Great Serpent:** The possessor of this device is empowered to *charm* any *adult* dragon. It is otherwise the same as others of its ilk, with intelligence and ego of 13 each and has these powers/effects:

    ```
    3 × I:   _____, _____, _____
    2 × II:  _____, _____
    1 × III: _____
    1 × VI:  _____
    ```

6. **Orb of the Firedrake:** The possessor of this device is empowered to *charm* any *old* dragon. It is otherwise similar to its fellows, with an intelligence and ego of 14 each and has the following powers/effects:

3 × I: _____, _____, _____
3 × II: _____, _____, _____
2 × III: _____, _____
1 × VI: _____

7. **Orb of the Elder Wyrm:** The possessor of this device is empowered to *charm* any *very old* dragon. This *Orb* is the same as the others of its type, with intelligence and ego of 16 each and the following powers/effects:

4 × I: _____, _____, _____, _____
3 × II: _____, _____, _____
2 × III: _____, _____
1 × IV: _____
1 × V: _____
1 × VI: _____

8. **Orb of the Eternal Grand Dragon:** The possessor of this device is empowered to *charm* any *ancient* dragon. Furthermore, its possessor is given a +8 for any saving throws, attacks, and damage he or she makes when contending directly with either Tiamat or Bahamut. The *Orb* is similar to its lesser cousins, having 18 for both intelligence and ego, and the following powers/effects:

4 × I: _____, _____, _____, _____
3 × II: _____, _____, _____
2 × III: _____, _____
1 × IV: _____
2 × V: _____, _____
1 × VI: _____

Notes Regarding Orbs of Dragonkind: All of these *Orbs* have a strong component of evil, and a neutral or good character will have to save versus magic to resist *charming* a neutral/good dragon. *Charm* range is 5″ and requires 1 full round with the subject fully awake and aware of the character. Because of the original purpose, only *evil* dragons are automatically charmed, *neutral* dragons save at −4 on their dice, *good* dragons at −2. *Charmed* characters can be considered as possessing 50% of their normal wisdom with respect to an *Orb of Dragonkind*. Any possessor with *feeblemind* affecting him or her, or insane, will have 3 intelligence, or 50% of normal, respectively. The *Orb* can control only an active and awake mind. Destruction of a character will typically be by sacrifice to a dragon, if one is at hand, otherwise by the most sure and expeditious method.

Orb of Might: For the legendary source of the 3 *Orbs of Might*, see the foregoing *Crown of Might*. Each *Orb* has an *ethic alignment* determined as follows:

01-06	Evil
07-14	Good
15-20	Neutrality

If a character of another ethos touches an *Orb* different from his or hers, a saving throw versus magic must be made to avoid death and from 4-24 hit points of damage will be taken if the save is successful. If the character so touching an *Orb* also possesses a *Crown* and/or *Sceptre*, surviving the saving throw versus magic will invoke a malevolent effect from Table IV. Each *Orb* is of platinum, encrusted with gems, and topped with a device of precious metals and stones, so as to be worth 100,000 or more gold pieces on the open market. Each *Orb* is equal to a *Gem of Brightness* and also has the following powers/effects:

	Evil	**Good**	**Neutrality**
2 × I:	_____, _____	_____, _____	_____, _____
1 × III:	_____	_____	_____

For additional powers in combination with other items of regalia, see *Crown of Might*.

Queen Ehlissa's Marvelous Nightingale: The origin of this artifact is unknown, although the Mage Mordenkainen is reported to have asserted that the *Nightingale* was made by Xagy and the goddess of volcanic activity, Joramy, some 17 centuries ago. Queen Ehlissa bent all to her will with the enchantments of the device, and throughout her reign of several centuries the *Nightingale* never escaped its confinement. This bejeweled songbird seems to actually spring to life when its mechanism is activated. The creature is held within a fine mesh of golden wires, much like the cage of a real bird, and when set in motion the *Nightingale* opens its glittering wings, hops to the highest perch in the cage and performs. It is rumored that the eyes of this artifact can shoot forth scintillating rays of brilliant color, each color having a different effect; its songs likewise are able to work magical wonders, and if the rays and songs are directed in combination highly powerful spells are supposedly woven. It is known that the device throws forth a protective sphere, preventing detection or magical (or psionic) intrusion in a 30′ radius. Those within this sphere are reported to neither hunger nor thirst as long as they remain within. The *Marvelous Nightingale* also has these powers and effects:

4 × I: _____, _____, _____, _____
2 × II: _____, _____
1 × III: _____
1 × IV: _____
1 × V: _____
1 × VI: _____

Recorder of Ye'Cind: This most magical wind instrument needs no musician to play upon it, for the *Recorder* itself can play the most complicated of airs upon command. It will always sound an alarm if anything belonging to its possessor (including itself) is stolen while within 30′ of it, and the *Recorder* is able to give information through music to its possessor by playing certain tunes and songs with clue words in their lyrics if the character desires information of what has taken place within 30′ of the instrument. It is also rumored that the device can communicate other information, as well as cast certain spells, by means of its notes. Its other powers and effects are:

5 × I: _____, _____, _____, _____, _____
2 × II: _____, _____
1 × III: _____
1 × IV: _____
1 × V: _____
1 × VI: _____

Ring of Gaxx: This piece of jewelry is of totally alien origin, for while its loop appears to be of platinum and its stone a very fine spinel, examination by the most astute dwarf or expert jeweler will discover the workmanship to be unique and the gem of unknown type. The *Ring of Gaxx* must be placed on a finger in order to discover its powers. Its wearer can turn the nine-faceted gem set in the *Ring*, and each facing of the gem gives a different power/effect when it is faced towards the top (the finger end) of the ring. Note, however, that the stone will turn by itself whenever the *Ring* is taken off, put on, or its wearer is asleep. Therefore, each day the ring is used, a random facet facing *must* be determined (secretly by the DM) and discovered by the wearer. Of course, once all powers/effects are known to the possessor, knowledge of a single facet facing should enable him or her to determine the order of the other facets and make desired settings. It is absolutely impossible to mark either the ring or the gem stone in any way, so random determination and discovery is totally unavoidable — even a *wish* will not help determine which facet is which. The *Ring* has the following powers/effects:

3 × I: _____, _____, _____
2 × II: _____, _____
1 × III: _____
1 × IV: _____
1 × V: _____
1 × VI: _____

Rod of Seven Parts: The Wind Dukes of Aaqa are the legendary creators of this artifact. It is said that they constructed the *Rod* to use in the great battle of Pesh where Chaos and Law contended. There, the *Rod* was shattered, and its parts scattered, but the enchantments of the item were such that nothing could actually destroy it, so if its sections are recovered and put together *in the correct order*, the possessor will wield a weapon of surpassing power. The 7 parts of the *Rod* are slightly different, the first being the largest in length and diameter, the seventh being the smallest. No single part has any power or effect alone. Singly each appears to be a short bar or baton, except the seventh which looks much the same as a short metal wand. The first part of the *Rod* will give its possessor a feeling as to which *direction* the second part lies in — but only when the character thinks of the section as a fraction of a whole magic item. If the second, third, etc. parts are discovered prior to the first, second, etc., the section will lead only to the next higher numbered, not a lower one. If an out-of-order section is placed against another part of the *Rod* (first — third, second — sixth, whatever), the higher numbered piece will teleport away in a random direction from 100 to 1,000 miles away. When fully assembled, the *Rod of Seven Parts* is almost 5' long.

As soon as three joining sections are fitted together, the possessor is unable to let go of the *Rod* as long as he or she lives, until all parts are joined. The powers of each part of the *Rod* are cumulative whenever joined, but the *full* powers shown work only when *all* parts of the artifact are joined. Although the *Rod* cannot be disassembled by its possessor, each time a prime power is used, there is a 1 in 20 (5%) chance that the whole will fly into its component pieces and teleport 100-1200 miles away in random directions.

Assembly Powers and Effects
Parts 1-2 — 1 × III: _____
Parts 2-3 — 1 × I: _____
Parts 3-4 — 1 × I: _____
Parts 4-5 — 1 × IV: _____
Parts 5-6 — 1 × II: _____
Parts 6-7 — 1 × VI: _____

Complete Rod Powers and Effects
1 × I: _____
1 × II: _____
2 × III: _____
2 × V: _____
1 × VI: _____

If the *Rod* is not assembled in order, the powers/effects are *not* cumulative; only the power or effect of the last piece joined will be active, all prior parts being negated. Note that as stated earlier, if the first section is joined to the second, the second to the third, etc., powers/effects are cumulative, and when the entire *Rod* is assembled, the additional *full powers and effects* are gained.

Sceptre of Might: For the legendary source of the 3 *Sceptres of Might,* see the foregoing section on *Crown of Might.* Each *Sceptre* has an *ethic alignment* as follows:

1-6   Evil
7-14   Good
15-20   Neutrality

The effects of handling a *Sceptre* of an ethos not a character's own are the same as those of a *Crown.* Each *Sceptre* is wrought of bronze inlaid with silver and many fine gems, with a huge precious stone tipping its 2' length, giving the item a value of 150,000 or more gold pieces on the open market. Each *Sceptre* functions as a *Rod of Beguiling* and has the following powers and effects:

	Evil	**Good**	**Neutrality**
1 × I:	_____	_____	_____
1 × II:	_____	_____	_____
1 × VI:	_____	_____	_____

For additional powers in combination with a *Crown* or *Orb* of the same ethic alignment, see *Crown of Might.*

Sword of Kas: There is recorded this additional information regarding the lich, Vecna: "When Vecna grew in power he appointed a most evil and ruthless lieutenant to serve as his bodyguard and right hand. This henchman was the lord, Kas, and for him Vecna found a weapon of potency, a long and thin flatchet of dull gray metal; a sword of unsurpassed hardness with sharp point, keen edges, and magical properties. For a long, long time Kas faithfully served the lich, but as his power grew, so did his hubris, for his *Sword* was constantly urging him on, saying that Kas was now greater than Vecna himself, and with the might of the *Sword* to aid and direct him, Kas could rule in Vecna's stead. Legend says that the destruction of Vecna was by Kas and his *Sword,* but at the same time Vecna wrought his rebellious lieutenant's doom, and the world was made brighter thereby."

Although the powers and effects of the *Sword* are only hinted at, there can be little doubt that Kas became the most renowned swordsman of his age because of it. It is a +6 *defender,* doing double damage against all creatures which are from a plane other than the Prime Material (but only normal damage when on any plane other than the Prime Material). This

short sword is highly evil and chaotic in alignment, and with its 15 intelligence and 19 ego, it will certainly attempt to control whomever takes it as his or her own. The *Sword of Kas* has these powers and effects:

5 × I: _____, _____, _____, _____, _____
2 × II: _____, _____
1 × III: _____
2 × IV: _____, _____
2 × V: _____, _____
1 × VI: _____

The Teeth of Dahlver-Nar: If any cleric was more powerful than the renowned Dahlver-Nar, histories do not tell us. The gods themselves gave special powers to him, and these have passed on to others by means of the great relics of Dahlver-Nar, his teeth. Each of the *Teeth* has some power, and if one character manages to gain a full quarter, half, or all of them, other grand benefits accrue. In order to gain the power of one of these *teeth,* however, the character must place it into his or her mouth, where it will graft itself in the place of a like missing tooth. The *teeth* can never be removed once so emplaced, short of the demise of the possessor. Their powers/effects are:

Tooth #		Tooth #	
1) 1 × I:	_____	17) 1 × I:	_____
2) 1 × II:	_____	18) 1 × I:	_____
3) 1 × III:	_____	19) 1 × I:	_____
4) 1 × I:	_____	20) 1 × I:	_____
5) 1 × I:	_____	21) 1 × IV:	_____
6) 1 × I:	_____	22) 1 × I:	_____
7) 1 × VI:	_____	23) 1 × I:	_____
8) 1 × I:	_____	24) 1 × II:	_____
9) 1 × III:	_____	25) 1 × I:	_____
10) 1 × I:	_____	26) 1 × III:	_____
11) 1 × I:	_____	27) 1 × I:	_____
12) 1 × I:	_____	28) 1 × II:	_____
13) 1 × I:	_____	29) 1 × III:	_____
14) 1 × VI:	_____	30) 1 × I:	_____
15) 1 × I:	_____	31) 1 × I:	_____
16) 1 × II:	_____	32) 1 × I:	_____

Set of
1-8) 1 × II:	_____	1 × VI:	_____
9-16) 1 × II:	_____	1 × IV:	_____
17-24) 1 × II:	_____	1 × III:	_____
25-32) 1 × II:	_____	1 × III:	_____

Set of
1-16) 1 × V: _____
17-32) 1 × V: _____

1-32) 1 × V: _____

Powers/effects are cumulative.

Throne of the Gods: It is said that somewhere there is carven from the heart of a majestic mountain a massive stone chair, inlaid with mosaics of ivory and precious metals and set about with gems, a throne upon which certain gods actually sat when they walked the world. The *Throne* supposedly is within a great cavern, a part of the mountain's core, so as to be immobile and immovable. Anyone daring to seat himself or herself upon this chair is subject to the effects, and may gain benefits from the *Throne's* magic. It is certain, according to fables, that the character will gain a magic item, but in doing so he or she will also be subject to malevolent effect. The same character cannot again gain any magic item, but he or she can have the *Throne* affect him or her if the proper words and gestures are known and followed. The powers/effects of the *Throne of the Gods* are:

3 × I: _____, _____, _____
3 × II: _____, _____, _____
2 × III: _____, _____
2 × IV: _____, _____
2 × V: _____, _____
2 × VI: _____, _____

As DM you should determine which power or effect will be activated when the character seated on the *Throne* grasps either arm, both, or none and utters a command or asks that the *Throne* give him or her its power.

Wand of Orcus: This ghastly weapon is the property of the demon prince, Orcus, but at times it is said that he will allow his *Wand* to pass into the Prime Material Plane in order to wreak chaos and evil upon all living things there. (See **ADVANCED DUNGEONS & DRAGONS, MONSTER MANUAL,** Demon, Orcus, for information regarding both Orcus and his *Wand*.) The wielder of the *Wand* does not have the full death-dealing power of the device, the victim of its blow having a saving throw versus magic to avoid death or annihilation (gods, godlings, demon lords, greater devils, saints, and demi-gods are *not* affected at all, of course). However, the *Wand of Orcus* confers these other powers/effects upon the user:

    4 × I: _____, _____, _____, _____
    2 × II: _____, _____
    2 × III: _____, _____
    1 × IV: _____
    1 × VI: _____

ARTIFACTS AND RELICS POWERS/EFFECTS TABLES

   I. Minor Benign Powers
  II. Major Benign Powers
 III. Minor Malevolent Effects
  IV. Major Malevolent Effects
   V. Prime Powers
  VI. Side Effects

TABLE I: MINOR BENIGN POWERS

A. Adds 1 point to possessor's major attribute
B. *Animate dead* (1 figure) (by touch) — 7 times/week
C. *Audible glamer* upon command — 3 times/day
D. *Bless* (by touch)
E. *Clairaudience* (when touched to the ear)
F. *Clairvoyance* (when touched to the eyes)
G. *Color spray* — 3 times/day
H. *Comprehend languages* when held
I. *Create food and water* — 1 time/day
J. *Cure light wounds* — 7 times/week
K. *Darkness* (5', 10', or 15' radius) — 3 times/day
L. *Detect charm* — 3 times/day
M. *Detect evil/good* when held or ordered
N. *Detect invisibility* when held and ordered
O. *Detect magic* — 3 times/day
P. *ESP* (30', 40', 50', or 60' range) — 3 times/day
Q. *Feather fall* when grasped and ordered
R. *Find traps* — 3 times/day
S. *Fly* when held and ordered — 1 time/day
T. *Hypnotic pattern* (when moved) — 3 times/day
U. *Infravision* when held or worn
V. *Invisibility* (improved) — 3 times/day
W. *Know alignment* when held and ordered — 1 time/day
X. *Levitate* when held and ordered — 3 times/day
Y. *Light* — 7 times/week
Z. *Mind blank* — 3 times/day
AA. *Obscurement* — 1 time/day
BB. *Pass without trace* — 1 time/day
CC. Possessor immune to disease
DD. Possessor immune to fear
EE. Possessor immune to gas of any type
FF. Possessor need neither eat nor drink for up to 1 week
GG. *Protection +2* when held or worn
HH. *Remove fear* by touch
II. *Sanctuary* when held or worn — 1 time/day
JJ. *Shield*, when held or worn, upon command — 3 times/day
KK. *Speak with animals* — 3 times/day
LL. *Speak with dead* — 1 time/day
MM. *Speak with plants* — 7 times/week
NN. *Tongues* when held or worn and commanded
OO. *Ultravision* when held or worn
PP. *Ventriloquism* upon command — 3 times/day
QQ. *Water breathing* upon command
RR. *Water walking* ability
SS. Wearer immune to *charm* or *hold* spells
TT. Wearer immune to *magic missiles*
UU. *Web* — 1 time/day
VV. *Wizard lock* — 7 times/week
WW. *Write* — 1 time/day
XX. *Zombie animation* — 1 time/week

TABLE II: MAJOR BENIGN POWERS

A. *Animal summoning* (II or III) — 2 times/day
B. *Animate object* upon command — 1 time/day
C. +2 to armor class of possessor or AC 0, whichever is better
D. *Cause serious wounds* by touch
E. *Charm monster* — 2 times/day
F. *Charm person* — 7 times/week
G. *Cone of cold* (9-12 dice) — 2 times/day
H. *Confusion* — 1 time/day
I. *Cure blindness* by touch
J. *Cure disease* by touch
K. *Dimension door* — 2 times/day
L. *Disintegrate* — 1 time/day
M. *Dispel illusion* upon command — 2 times/day
N. *Dispel magic* upon command — 2 times/day
O. Double movement speed (on foot)
P. *Emotion* — 2 times/day
Q. *Exorcise* — 1 time/month
R. *Fear* by touch or gaze
S. *Fireball* (9-12 dice) — 2 times/day
T. *Fire shield* — 2 times/day
U. *Giant strength* (determine type) for 2 turns — 2 times/day
V. *Haste* — 1 time/day
W. *Heal* — 1 time/day
X. *Hold animal* — 1 time/day
Y. *Hold monster* — 1 time/day
Z. *Hold person* — 1 time/day
AA. *Lightning bolt* (9-12 dice) — 2 times/day
BB. *Minor globe of invulnerability* — 1 time/day
CC. *Paralyzation* by touch
DD. *Passwall* — 2 times/day
EE. *Phantasmal killer* — 1 time/day
FF. *Polymorph self* — 7 times/week
GG. *Regenerate* 2 h.p./turn (but not if killed)
HH. *Remove curse* by touch — 7 times/week
II. *Slow* — 1 time/day
JJ. *Speak with monster* — 2 times/day
KK. *Stone to flesh* — 2 times/day
LL. *Suggestion* — 2 times/day
MM. *Telekinesis* (1,000-6,000 g.p. weight) — 2 times/day
NN. *Teleport* (no error) — 2 times/day
OO. *Transmute rock to mud* — 2 times/day
PP. *True seeing* — 1 time/day
QQ. *Turn wood* — 1 time/day
RR. *Wall of fire* — 2 times/day
SS. *Wall of ice* — 2 times/day
TT. *Wall of thorns* — 2 times/day
UU. Weapon damage is +2 hit points
VV. *Wind walk* — 1 time/day
WW. *Wizard eye* — 2 times/day
XX. *Word of recall* — 1 time/day
YY. *X-ray vision* — 2 times/day

TABLE III: MINOR MALEVOLENT EFFECTS

A. Acne on possessor's face
B. Blindness for 1-4 rounds when first used against an enemy
C. Body odor noticeable at 10' distance
D. Deafness for 1-4 turns when first used against an enemy
E. Gems or jewelry found never increase in value
F. Holy water within 10' of item becomes polluted
G. Lose 1-4 points of charisma for 1-4 days when major power used
H. Possessor loses interest in sex
I. Possessor has satyriasis
J. Possessor's hair turns white
K. Saving throws versus magic are at –1
L. Saving throws versus poison are at –2
M. Sense of smell lost for 2-8 hours when first used against an enemy
N. Small fires (torches, *et al.*) extinguished when major power used
O. Small items of wood rot from possessor's touch (any item up to normal door size, 1-7 days time)
P. Touch of possessor kills green plants
Q. User causes hostility towards himself in all mammals within 6''
R. User must eat and drink 6 times the normal amount due to the item's drain upon him or her
S. User's sex changes
T. Wart appears on possessor's nose

U. Weight gain of 10-40 pounds
V. Weight loss of 5-30 pounds
W. Yearning for item forces possessor to never be away from it for more than 1 day if at all possible
X. Yelling becomes necessary to invoke spells with verbal components

Notes Regarding Minor Malevolent Effects:

These powers should be inflicted upon the possessor of the item after he or she has had the artifact or relic for a period of time (1-4 weeks) or after using major powers of the item.

TABLE IV: MAJOR MALEVOLENT EFFECTS

A. Body rot is 10% cumulative likely whenever a primary power is used, and part of the body is lost permanently
B. Capricious alignment change each time a primary power is used
C. Geas/quest placed upon possessor
D. Item contains the life force of another person, and after a set number of uses, the possessor's life force is drawn into it and the former soul released
E. Item has power to affect its possessor when a primary power is used if the character has not followed the alignment or purposes of the artifact/relic
F. Item is a prison for a powerful being; and there is a 1%-4% cumulative chance per usage that it will break free, kill the possessor's soul, and, using his or her body, proceed to slay all associates and henchmen of this character
G. Item is itself a living, sentient being forced to serve; but each usage of a primary power gives a 1%-3% cumulative possibility that the spell will be broken and the being will:

    1) change the possessor into a like artifact/relic
    2) geas/quest the possessor to perform a mission of its choosing
    3) kill the possessor
    4) mentally enslave the possessor for a period of 2-8 weeks

H. Item is powerless against and hates 1-3 species of creatures, and when within 10″ of any such creatures it forces its possessor to attack
I. Item releases a gas which renders all creatures, including wielder, within 20′ powerless to move for 5-20 rounds
J. Lose 1 point of charisma permanently
K. Lose 1 point of constitution permanently
L. Lose 1 point of dexterity permanently
M. Lose 1 point from hit points permanently
N. Lose 1 point of intelligence permanently
O. Lose 1 point of strength permanently
P. Lose 1 point of wisdom permanently
Q. Magic drained from the most powerful magic item (other than an artifact or relic) within 20′ of user
R. Reverse alignment permanently
S. Sacrifice a certain animal to activate item for 1 day
T. Sacrifice a human or player character to activate item for 1 day
U. Sacrifice 10,000-60,000 g.p. worth of gems and/or jewelry to activate item for 1 day
V. User becomes berserk and attacks creatures within 20′ randomly (check each round) for 5-20 rounds
W. User goes insane for 1-4 days
X. User grows ¼′ taller each time primary power is used
Y. User instantly killed (but may be raised or resurrected)
Z. User loses 1 level of experience
AA. User receives 2-20 hit points damage
BB. User receives 5-30 hit points damage
CC. User required to slay a certain type of creature to activate item, and slaying another set type will de-activate item
DD. User shrinks ¼′ each time primary power is used
EE. User transformed into a very powerful but minor being from another plane (demon, devil, godling) by creator of item and is carried off to serve this new master (start a new character)
FF. User withers and ages 3-30 years each time the primary power is used, eventually turning the possessor into a deathless withered zombie guardian of the item
GG. Utterance of a spell causes complete loss of voice for one day
HH. Yearning to be worshipped is uncontrollable; those failing to bow and scrape to the artifact's possessor will be subject to instant attack.

Notes Regarding Major Malevolent Effects:

Malevolent powers operate whenever a major or primary power of the

artifact or relic is used, unless operation occurs after a pre-determined (but low) number of uneventful usages of a major or primary power, as stated above (item description or Table). Effects can be successive and cumulative.

Body rot affects extremities — toes, fingers, ears, nose, lips, eyelids, hands, feet, arms, legs, head in that order — 1 member per operation. Nothing can prevent the loss or restore the member.

Geas/quest fulfillment enables the possessor to act freely until primary power use once again operates this power.

Life force freeing and associated entrapment of the possessor's soul will likewise free the life force of a player character (and restore his or her body) if and when another character so uses the item.

Where creature types are called for, select powerful types which would be logically connected to the item, usually foes of its creator or alignment or purpose.

Aging 3-30 years is done by race life expectancy:

    1) 3 years for half-orcs
    2) 4 years for humans
    3) 7 years for halflings
    4) 12 years for half-elves
    5) 20 years for gnomes
    6) 25 years for dwarves
    7) 30 years for elves

The aging *cannot* be reversed.

TABLE V: PRIME POWERS

A. All of possessor's ability totals permanently raised 2 points each upon pronouncement of a command word (18 maximum)
B. All of possessor's ability totals raised to 18 each upon pronouncement of a command word
C. Bones/exoskeleton/cartilage of opponent turned to jelly — 1 time/day
D. Cacodemon-like power summons a demon lord, arch-devil, or nycadaemon — 1 time/month
E. Creeping doom callable — 1 time/day
F. Death ray equal to a finger of death with no saving throw — 1 time/day
G. Death spell power of 110%-200% effectiveness with respect to number of levels affected — 1 time/day
H. Gate spell power, 100% effective — 1 time/day
I. Imprisonment spell power — 1 time/week
J. Magical resistance of 50%-75% for possessor upon command word — 1 time/day
K. Major attribute permanently raised to 19 upon command word
L. Meteor swarm — 1 time/day
M. Monster summoning VIII — 2 times/day
N. Plane shift — 1 time/day
O. Polymorph any object — 1 time/day
P. Power word blind/kill/stun — 1 time/day
Q. Premonition of death or serious harm to possessor
R. Prismatic spray — 1 time/day
S. Restoration — 1 time/day
T. Resurrection — 7 times/week
U. Shades — 2 times/day
V. Shape change — 2 times/day
W. Spell absorption, 19-24 levels — 1 time/week
X. Summon 1 of each type of elemental, 16 hit dice each, no need for control — 1 time/week
Y. Summon djinn or efreet lord (8 h.p./die, +2 "to hit" and +4 damage) for 1 day of service — 1 time/week
Z. Super sleep spell affects double the number of creatures plus up to 2 5th or 6th and 1 7th or 8th level creature
AA. Temporal stasis, no saving throw, upon touch — 1 time/month
BB. The item enables the possessor to legend lore, commune, or contact higher plane (7th-10th) — 1 time/week
CC. Time stop of twice normal duration — 1 time/week
DD. Total fire/heat resistance for all creatures within 20′ of the item
EE. Total immunity from all forms of mental and psionic attacks
FF. Total immunity from all forms of cold
GG. Trap the soul with 90% effectiveness — 1 time/month
HH. User can cast combination spells (if a spell caster) as follows (d4):

    1) 1st and 2nd level spells simultaneously
    2) 2nd and 3rd level spells simultaneously
    3) 3rd and 4th level spells simultaneously
    4) 1st, 2nd, and 3rd level spells simultaneously

II.   *Vanish* — 2 times/day
JJ.   *Vision* — 1 time/day
KK. *Wish* — 1 time/day
LL.   Youth restored to creature touched — 1 time/month

TABLE VI: SIDE EFFECTS

A.   Alignment of possessor permanently changed to that of item
B.   Charisma of possessor reduced to 3 as long as item is owned
C.   *Fear* reaction possible in any creature within 20' of the item whenever a major or primary power is used; all, including possessor, must save versus magic or flee in panic
D.   *Fumble* reaction possible (as C. above)
E.   Greed and covetousness reaction in all intelligent creatures viewing the item; save versus magic or attack possessor and steal the item — associates are only 25% likely to have to check; henchmen check loyalty first, failure then requires saving throw as above
F.   Lycanthropy inflicted upon the possessor, type according to alignment of item, change to animal form involuntary and 50% likely (1 check only) whenever confronted and attacked by an enemy
G.   Treasure within 5' radius of mineral nature (metal or gems) of non-magical type is reduced by 20%-80% as the item consumes it to sustain its power
H.   User becomes ethereal whenever any major or primary power of the item is activated, and there is a 5% cumulative chance that he or she will thereafter become ethereal whenever a stress (combat, life-or-death, difficult problem involving user's decision) situation exists; the ethereal state lasts until stress is removed
I.   User becomes fantastically strong (18/00 — 19 if 18/00 already) but very clumsy; so dexterity is reduced by as many points as strength was increased, and so no "to hit" bonuses are allowed for strength, and a −2 for clumsiness is given instead; furthermore, the individual must be checked as if he or she has a *fumble* spell cast upon him or her whenever any item is handled or spell is to be cast by the user
J.   User cannot touch or be touched by any (even magical) metal; metal simply passes through his or her body as if it did not exist and has no effect
K.   User has a poison touch which requires that humans and man-sized humanoids (but not undead) save versus poison whenever touched
L.   User has limited omniscience and may request the DM to answer 1 question per game day (answer is given with limitations set by DM's discretion, with overall campaign factors and knowledge of player vs. player character overriding considerations)
M.   User has short-duration super charismatic effect upon creatures of the same basic alignment — evil, good, neutral (chaotic, lawful, true) — so that they will willingly join and serve the character for 1-4, 2-8, or 3-12 turns (depending upon how exact the alignment match is); thereafter the effect of the dweomer wears off and the creature(s) will no longer serve due to realization of the enchantment and fear of it (and hostility is possible)
N.   Whenever any power of the item is used, temperature within a 6" radius is raised 20°-50° F. for 2-8 turns (moves with item)
O.   Whenever the major or prime power of the item is used, temperature within a 6" radius is lowered 20°-80° F. for 2-12 turns (moves with item)
P.   Whenever the prime power is used the possessor must save versus magic or lose 1 level of experience
Q.   Whenever the prime power is used, those creatures friendly to the user within 20', excluding the user, will sustain 5-20 hit points of damage
R.   Whenever this item is used as a weapon to strike an enemy, it does double normal damage to the opponent but the wielder takes (normal) damage just as if he or she had been struck by the item

POSSIBLE DESTRUCTION MEANS FOR ARTIFACTS/RELICS

Artifacts and relics are virtually impervious to magical and physical harm and each may only be "destroyed" by a single legendary means. Frequently, the supposed "destruction" is actually a form of nullification or containment of the artifact/relic, but results in the neutralization of its powers for vast periods of time. The following table suggests various means that might apply to the destruction of an artifact/relic and is open to additions and alterations by the DM. No artifact/relic should have the

same nemesis as another; though the means may be the same, the specifics should vary. It should be kept in mind that the means of destruction are as rare and nearly unattainable as are the artifacts/relics themselves. Actively seeking the destruction of an artifact/relic is tedious, demanding, and fraught with great perils to body and soul, and the chances of surviving the destruction of the artifact/relic are minute without the grace of the gods.

The way to destroy a particular artifact/relic is to:

1. Melt it down in the fiery furnace, pit, mountain, forge, crucible or kiln in which it was created.

2. Drop it into or bury it beneath (1) the Well of Time, (2) the Abyss, (3) the Earth Wound, (4) Adonais' Deep, (5) the Spring of Eternity, (6) Marion's Trench, (7) the Living Stone, (8) Mountain of Thunder, (9) 100 adult red dragon skulls, (10) the Tree of the Universe.

3. Cause it to be devoured by (1) Cerebus, (2) a Lernaean Hydra, (3) a Titan, (4) an ancient Dragon Turtle.

4. Cause it to be broken against/by or crushed by (1) Talos, a triple iron golem, (2) the Gates of Hell, (3) the Cornerstone of the World, (4) Artur's Dolmen, (5) the Juggernaut of the Endless Labyrinth, (6) the heel of a god, (7) the Clashing Rocks, (8) the foot of a humble ant.

5. Expose it to the penetrating light and flame of (1) the Ray of Eternal Shrinking, (2) the Sun, (3) Truth: that which is pure will become Light, that which is impure will surely wither.

6. Cause it to be steeped in either the encephalic fluids of the brain of Bahamut (the platinum dragon), or in the black and foul blood from the heart of Tiamat, the chromatic dragon.

7. Cause it to be seared by the odious flames of Geryon's destroyed soul or disintegrated in the putrid ichor of Juiblex's deliquescing flesh.

8. Sprinkle it with/baptize it in the (1) Well of Life, (2) River Styx, (3) River of Flame, (4) River Lethe (the river of forgetfulness).

Legended items and regions should be placed by the DM in his or her own milieu in isolated locales — preferably warded by mighty mythical and magical guardians (e.g., the serpent which guarded the golden fleece).

ARMOR AND SHIELD (III.F.)

As Dungeon Master you must be fully conversant with the armor gradation system. Because prior game forms worked from a high base number (9) upwards, I have opted to follow the same progression herein for the sake of continuity and familiarity. As a shield is the single common factor, it must be given a +1 factor, i.e. be 1 class (5%) better than *no* armor, but listed before the diverse armor types, in order to allow its inclusion as a constant (without over-valuing it). For each +1 of armor, regardless of the type of armor, the wearer moves upwards (toward or beyond AC 2 to 1, 0, −1, −2, etc.). Thus, chain mail +1 is chain mail (AC 5) 1 category better (AC 4), while a shield +1 is equal to armor class 8 — or 2 places better than the armor worn by its inclusion, rather than but 1 (+1 for bearing shield, +1 for the magical bonus of the shield).

For game purposes *all* magical armor should be considered as being virtually weightless — equal to normal clothing, let us assume. This gives characters so clad a base movement speed equal to an unarmored man. Magic shields, however, weigh the same as a normal shield of the same size.

Armor of +3 bonus is of special meteorite iron steel, +4 is mithral alloyed steel, +5 is adamantite alloyed steel.

Special items are described below:

Leather armor +1 is usable by those characters permitted to wear this form of armor.

Plate Mail of Etherealness is seemingly normal +5 armor, but if a command word is spoken, the suit enables its wearer and all non-living items he or she wears and carries to become ethereal, just as if *oil of etherealness* (q.v.) had been used. While in the ethereal state the wearer cannot attack material creatures. A *phase door* spell will negate the ethereal state and prevent the armor from again so functioning for 1 day. There are 20 charges placed upon *plate mail of etherealness*, and, once used, they cannot be replaced or recharged. Furthermore, every 5 uses reduces the class of the armor by 1, so if 5 charges are used to become ethereal the armor is +4, if 10 are used it is +3, +2 if 15 are used, and only +1 if all 20 are exhausted.

Plate Mail of Vulnerability appears to every test to be magical +1, +2, or +3 armor, but it is actually -2, -3, or -4 cursed plate mail, whose great vulnerability will not be apparent until an enemy successfully strikes a blow in anger with desire and intent to kill its wearer. *The armor will fall to pieces whenever an opponent strikes the wearer with an unmodified "to hit" score of 20.*

Shield, large, +1, +4 versus missiles is a typical large shield, but it is four times more effective against hand hurled and mechanically propelled missiles of all sorts. More importantly, the shield has a 20% chance of negating *magic missile* attacks (from a frontal position, of course).

Shield -1, missile attracter not only makes the bearer equivalent to a shieldless person, it also attracts missiles of all sorts to itself, so double or treble the bearer's chances of being selected by random die rolling according to the size of the party he or she is in. This cursed shield is not distinguishable from a useful magical shield.

Note: If you are unfamiliar with medieval armor types, you might find Charles ffoulkes' ARMOUR AND WEAPONS (Oxford 1909) a short and useful text. The armor types I have selected are fitted into a *game* system. Here is what they subsume: LEATHER ARMOR is cuir bouli, consisting of coat, leggings, boots, and gauntlets. STUDDED LEATHER adds protective plates set in the leather and an extra layer of protection at shoulder area. RING MAIL is leather armor sewn with closely set iron rings. SCALE MAIL is a suit of leather armor set with small overlapping iron plates. CHAIN MAIL needs no explanation. BANDED MAIL is horizontal strips of articulated armor plates worn over a suit of chain mail. SPLINT MAIL is a coat of vertical plates of armor sandwiched within the layers of the garment and worn over chain. PLATE MAIL is a set of pieces of plate (shoulder, breast, back, elbow, groin/hips, legs) worn over chain mail. *Plate armor* is a late development and is not considered, i.e. the full suit of solid plate used c. 1500 is not an armor type used, but the reader should be aware that this form of protection was *lighter* and more mobile than plate mail! It is also two or three times more costly . . .

SWORDS (III.G.)

All magic swords receive their stated bonus both for purposes of hitting (as a bonus to the "to hit" die) and for damage (as +1, +2, +3, etc. addition to hit points of damage scored). The special features of listed swords are described below. Thereafter, considerations of *unusual* aspects of swords are listed, i.e. intelligence, abilities, powers, purpose, alignment, languages, and ego. Finally, the effects of *unusual* swords are dealt with. Note that few swords will have any *unusual* aspects.

All +5 *Holy Avenger* swords are lawful good. All *Swords of Sharpness* are of chaotic alignment. All *Vorpal Weapons* are lawfully aligned.

Most swords (and all daggers) of magical nature shed light when drawn from their scabbard (see ADVANCED DUNGEONS & DRAGONS, PLAYERS HANDBOOK, THE ADVENTURE, Light). The sole exceptions are the *Flame Tongue, Frost Brand, Holy Avenger, Life Stealing,* and *Sharpness* swords, and these will be dealt with individually.

Whenever a sword has some unknown quality — such as the wishes in a *Luck Blade* or a sword with *unusual* aspects, you should prepare a special 3 X 5 index card on it and keep the information handy whenever the possessor of the weapon is playing.

Sword +1, +2 vs. magic-using and enchanted creatures, gives its +1 bonus always, +2 when employed against magic-users, monsters which can cast spells, *conjured, created, gated,* or *summoned* creatures. Note that the +2 would *not* operate against a creature magically empowered by some item to cast spells — such as a *ring of spell storing.*

Sword +1, +3 vs. lycanthropes and shape changers, gives its +3 against *were* creatures, those able to assume the form of another creature (such as a vampire or a druid), or any creature under the influence of a *polymorph* or *shape change* spell.

Sword +1, +3 vs. regenerating creatures, will give the +3 bonus to its

wielder even when the regenerating creature does so because of a magical device — such as a *ring of regeneration.*

Sword +1, +4 vs. reptiles, gives the +4 against such creatures as dinosaurs, dragons, hydras, lizards, snakes, wyverns, etc.

Sword +1, Flame Tongue, +2 vs. regenerating creatures, +3 vs. cold-using, inflammable, or avian creatures, +4 vs. undead, sheds light only when its possessor speaks a command word or phrase, and this flame illuminates the area as brightly as a torch. Note that the flame from this sword easily ignites oil, burns webs, or sets fire to paper, parchment, dry wood, etc. Cold-using creatures are those whose attack mode involves cold (ice toads, white dragons, winter wolves, yeti, etc.)

Sword +1, Luck Blade, gives its possessor +1 on all saving throws and will have from 2-5 wishes (you must keep a secret note of the number and their use) determined by d4 +1.

Sword +2, Giant Slayer, has a +3 bonus versus any giant, ettin, ogre mage, or titan. Against any of the true giants (hill, stone, frost, fire, cloud, storm) the sword does *double damage,* i.e. 2-24 + 3 or 5-27.

Sword +2, Dragon Slayer, has a +4 against any sort of true dragon and against 1 sort it will do *triple damage,* i.e. 3-36 + 4 or 7-40. Note that an *unusual* sword with intelligence and alignment will *not* be made to slay dragons of the same alignment. Determine dragon type by random roll, excluding the singular ones (Bahamut and Tiamat):

black (CE)	gold (LG)
blue (LE)	green (LE)
brass (CG)	red (CE)
bronze (LG)	silver (LG)
copper (CG)	white (CE)

Sword +2, Nine Lives Stealer, will always perform as a +2 weapon, but it also has the power to draw the life force from an opponent, and it can do so only a total of 9 times before the ability is lost. A natural 20 must be scored on the wielder's "to hit" die roll for the sword to function. The opponent is entitled to a saving throw versus magic in such case, and if it is successful the sword does *not* function, no charge is used, and normal damage is determined.

Sword +3, Frost Brand, +6 vs. fire-using/dwelling creatures, bestows the +6 bonus in a self-explanatory manner. The weapon does not shed any light, except when the air temperature is below 0° F, but it does give special benefits against fire, for its wielder is protected as if he or she were wearing a *ring of fire resistance* and whenever it is thrust into fires it has a 50% chance of extinguishing them in a 10' radius — including a *wall of fire* but excluding a *fireball, meteor swarm,* or *flame strike.*

Sword +4, Defender, gives its wielder the option of using all, some, or none of the +4 bonus in defense against any opponent using a hand held weapon such as a dagger, mace, spear (not hurled), sword, etc. For example, the wielder can on the 1st round of battle opt to use the sword as +2 and save the other 2 bonus factors to be added on to his or her armor class. This can be done each round.

Sword, +5, Holy Avenger, is a *holy sword.* In the hands of any character other than a paladin, it will perform only as a +2 sword. In the hands of a paladin, however, it creates a magic resistance of 50% in a 5' radius, *dispels magic* in a 5' radius at the level of magic use equal to the experience level of the paladin, and inflicts +10 hit points of bonus damage upon chaotic evil opponents. (Cf. also ADVANCED DUNGEONS & DRAGONS, PLAYERS HANDBOOK, CHARACTER CLASSES, The Paladin.)

Sword of Dancing is progressively and doubly dangerous. On the 1st round of melee it is +1, on the 2nd +2, on the 3rd +3, and on the 4th it is +4, but it then drops to +1 on the 5th round and again goes upwards. After 4 rounds of melee its wielder can opt to allow it to "dance". "Dancing" consists of loosing the sword on any round when its bonus is +1. The sword then fights at the same level of experience as its wielder, doing so for 4 rounds. Thereafter, it must again be grasped, as it returns to its wielder, i.e. it is loosed to "dance" for 4 rounds, going from +1 to +4, and must be again held by its wielder at a +1 stage and physically used for 4 successive rounds of melee combat. When "dancing", the sword will leave its owner's hand and may be up to 3" distant, and at the end of its 4th round of solo combat it will move to its possessor's hand automatically. Note that when "dancing" the sword cannot be physically hit, although certain magic attacks such as a *fireball, lightning bolt,* or *transmute metal to wood* could affect it. Finally, remember that the *dancing sword* fights alone at the same level (and class) of its possessor — if a 4th level fighter, the sword fights alone exactly the same; if a 7th level thief is the wielder, the sword will so fight when "dancing". Thus relieved of his or her weapon for 4 melee rounds, the possessor may act in virtually any manner desired, as dictated by circumstances, and so long as he or she remains within 3" or less of the sword (otherwise it falls "lifeless" to the ground and is a +1 weapon when again grasped). The possessor can rest, discharge missiles, draw another weapon and engage in hand-to-hand combat, etc.

Sword of Wounding is a sword of only +1 bonus, but any hit it makes cannot be healed by regeneration, and the opponent so wounded loses 1 additional hit point per round for each wound inflicted by the sword on the round after such a wound is received. Thus, an opponent hit for 4 points of damage on the 1st melee round will automatically lose 1 additional hit point on the 2nd and each successive round of combat. Loss of 1 point stops only when the creature so wounded bandages its wound or after 10 melee rounds (1 turn). Damage from a *sword of wounding* can be healed only by normal means (rest and time) — never by potion, spell, or other magical means short of a *wish*. Note that successive wounds will damage in the same manner as the first.

Sword of Life Stealing is a +2 weapon which will eliminate 1 level of experience (or hit die) and its accompanying hit die and abilities when it strikes any opponent with a score of a natural 20 on the "to hit" die roll. This function is exactly the same as the life energy level draining ability of certain *undead* creatures. The sword wielder will gain as many hit points as an opponent loses to this function of the weapon, subject to the limit of his or her maximum number of hit points predetermined by rolling hit dice, i.e. only a character who has somehow suffered loss of hit points can benefit from the function.

Sword of Sharpness is a weapon which is treated as +3 or better for purposes of who or what can be hit by it, even though it gets only +1 bonus "to hit" and on damage inflicted. Its power is great, however, for on a very high "to hit" die roll as shown below it will sever an extremity — arm, leg, neck, tail, tentacle, whatever — determined by random dice roll:

Opponent is	Modified score to sever*
normal/armored	19-21
larger than man-sized	20-21
solid metal or stone	21

A *sword of sharpness* will respond to its wielder's desire with respect to the light it sheds — none, a 5' circle of dim illumination, a 15' light, or a 30' radius glow equal to a *light* spell.

    * Considers only the sword's bonus of +1.

Sword, Vorpal Weapon, is similar but superior to a *sword of sharpness*. A *vorpal weapon* is +3 "to hit" and for damage bonus. When a score on the "to hit" die as shown below is made, it will sever the neck/head of its opponent:

Opponent is	Modified score to sever*
normal/armored	20-23
larger than man-sized	21-23
solid metal or stone	22-23

    * Considers only the sword's bonus of +3.

The DM will note that there are many creatures that cannot suffer decapitation due to lack or mutability of form. There are also certain creatures that may have heads but will not necessarily be killed by decapitation (among these are dopplegangers, elementals, and golems).

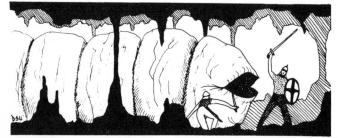

Sword +1, cursed, performs in all respects as a +1 weapon, but when its wielder is faced by an enemy the sword will weld itself to the character's hand and force him or her to fight until the enemy or the wielder is slain. Thereafter, the possessor can loose, but never rid himself or herself of the cursed sword. No matter what is done, it will appear in his or her hand whenever an opponent is faced. To be free of the weapon, the character must have a cleric *exorcise* it.

Sword -2, cursed, is a sword which gives off a magical aura and performs well against targets in practice, but when it is used against an opponent in combat it lowers hit probability by -2 for its user, although only by careful observation can this lowering of probability be detected; all damage scored is likewise reduced by 2 hit points, but never below a 1 in any event. The sword will always force the character to employ it against enemies, teleporting to the character's hand. It can be gotten rid of only by means of *limited wish, wish,* or *alter reality*.

Sword, Cursed Berserking performs by every test, save that of the heat of battle, as a +2 magic sword of some sort. However, in actual battle its wielder will go berserk, attacking the nearest creature and continuing to fight until dead or until no living thing remains within 6" of him or her. The sword has a +2 bonus and otherwise acts as a +1 cursed sword. The possessor of a *Cursed Beserking Sword* can be rid of it only if it is *exorcised* or *wished* away.

Unusual Swords:

The tables hereafter are used to determine if a sword is *unusual*; and if it is so, what intelligence, alignment, etc. it has.

Table I.: Sword Intelligence and Capabilities

Dice Roll	Intelligence	Capabilities	Communication
01-75	none	none	none
76-83	12	1 primary ability	semi-empathy*
84-89	13	2 primary abilities	empathy
90-94	14	2 primary abilities	speech**
95-97	15	3 primary abilities	speech**
98-99	16	3 primary abilities†	speech**
00	17	3 primary abilities†† plus 1 extraordinary power	speech and telepathy***

    * The possessor will receive some signal (a throb, tingle, etc.) and feel urges when its ability functions.

   ** The sword will speak its alignment language plus 1 or more other tongues as indicated on a table hereafter.

  *** The sword can use either communication mode at will, with language use as any speaking sword.

    † The sword can also read languages/maps of any non-magical sort.

   †† The sword can read languages as well as magical writings.

Table 2.: Sword Alignment

Any sword with intelligence will have an alignment. Note that certain swords — *Holy Avenger, Sharpness, Vorpal* (q.q.v.) — have alignment restrictions. All cursed swords are absolutely *neutral*.

Dice Roll	Alignment of Sword
01-05	chaotic good
06-15	chaotic neutral*
16-20	chaotic evil
21-25	neutral evil*
26-30	lawful evil
31-55	lawful good
56-60	lawful neutral*
61-80	neutral (absolute)
81-00	neutral good*

    * The sword can also be used by any character whose alignment corresponds to the *non-neutral* alignment portion of the weapon's alignment, i.e. *chaotic* or *evil* or *good* or *lawful*. Thus *any chaotic* character can use a sword with *chaotic neutral* alignment.

Note: Any character whose alignment does not correspond to that of the sword, except as noted by the asterisk above, will sustain hit points of damage equal to the number of *ego points* (see hereafter) of the sword each and every time the character touches any portion of the sword unless the sword is in the grasp or possession of a character whose alignment is compatible with the weapon.

Table 3.: Sword Primary Abilities

Dice Roll	Ability
01-11	detect "elevator"/shifting rooms/walls in a 1″ radius
12-22	detect sloping passages in a 1″ radius
23-33	detect traps of large size in a 1″ radius
34-44	detect evil/good in a 1″ radius
45-55	detect precious metals, kind, and amount in a 2″ radius
56-66	detect gems, kind, and number in a ½″ radius
67-77	detect magic in a 1″ radius
78-82	detect secret doors in a ½″ radius
83-87	detect invisible objects in a 1″ radius
88-92	locate object in a 12″ radius
93-98	roll twice on this table ignoring scores of 93 to 00
99-00	roll on the Extraordinary Power Table instead

If the same ability is rolled twice or more, range of the power is double or triple, etc.

All abilities function only when the sword is held, drawn, and the possessor is concentrating on the desired result. A sword can do only one function at a time, and thus can fight or detect but one thing at a time.

Table 4.: Sword Extraordinary Powers

Dice Roll	Power*
01-07	*charm person* on contact — 3 times/day
08-15	*clairaudience*, 3″ range — 3 times/day, 1 round per use
16-22	*clairvoyance*, 3″ range — 3 times/day, 1 round per use
23-28	determine directions and depth — 2 times/day
29-34	*ESP*, 3″ range — 3 times/day, 1 round per use
35-41	*flying*, 12″/turn — 1 hour/day
42-47	*heal* — 1 time/day
48-54	*illusion*, 12″ range — 2 times/day, as the *wand*
55-61	*levitation*, 1 turn duration — 3 times/day, at 6th level of magic use ability
62-67	*strength* — 1 time/day (upon wielder only)
68-75	*telekinesis*, 2,500 g.p. wt. maximum — 2 times/day, 1 round each use
76-81	*telepathy*, 6″ range — 2 times/day
82-88	*teleportation* — 1 time/day, 6,000 g.p. wt. maximum, 2 segments to activate
89-94	*X-ray vision*, 4″ range — 2 times/day, 1 turn per use
95-97	roll twice on this table ignoring scores of 95-97
98-99	character may choose 1 power from this table
00	character may choose 1 power from this table, and then roll for a Special Purpose

* Saving throws apply as usual

If the same power is rolled twice, the uses/day are doubled, etc.

Powers function only when the sword is held and drawn and the possessor is concentrating upon the desired effect. Most powers will require that the character stop and concentrate for a full round.

Table 5.: Special Purpose Swords

A.: Purposes

Dice Roll	Purpose
01-10	defeat/slay diametrically opposed alignment*
11-20	kill clerics
21-30	kill fighters
31-40	kill magic-users
41-50	kill thieves
51-55	kill bards/monks
56-65	overthrow law and/or chaos
66-75	slay good and/or evil
76-00	slay non-human monsters

* The purpose of the *true neutral* version of this sword is to *preserve the balance* (cf. **ALIGNMENT**) by defeating/slaying powerful beings of the extreme alignments (LG, LE, CG, CE).

Purpose must suit the type and alignment of the sword in question. Killing is always restricted to evil when the sword is of good alignment. Swords dedicated to *slaying monsters* will *always* be either *good* and slay *neutral* or *evil* monsters or *evil* which will slay *neutral* or *good* monsters.

B.: Special Purpose Power

Dice Roll	Power
01-10	*blindness** for 2-12 rounds
11-20	*confusion** for 2-12 rounds
21-25	*disintegrate**
26-55	*fear** for 1-4 rounds
56-65	*insanity** for 1-4 rounds
66-80	*paralysis** for 1-4 rounds
81-00	+2 on all saving throws, −1 on each die of damage sustained

* Upon scoring a hit with the weapon unless the opponent makes a saving throw versus magic.

The power will operate only in pursuit of the special purpose.

Table 6.: Non-Alignment Languages Spoken by Sword

Dice Roll	Number of Languages
01-40	1
41-70	2
71-85	3
86-95	4
96-99	5
00	6, or the result of 2 additional rolls ignoring a score of 00, whichever is the greater

See the section on **LANGUAGE DETERMINATION** under **PERSONAE OF NON-PLAYER CHARACTERS** for a listing of many of the possible tongues which can be spoken by a sword. You should select languages which will suit the type of sword and its abilities.

Table 7.: Sword Ego

Only after all aspects of a sword have been determined and recorded can the ego rating of a sword be found. Ego, along with intelligence, will be a factor with regard to the dominance of sword over character, as detailed hereafter:

Attribute of Sword	Ego Points
each + of sword*	1
each primary ability**	1
each extraordinary power**	2
special purpose	5
each language spoken***	½
telepathic ability	2
reading languages ability	1
reading magic ability	2

* Thus, a +1 sword is 1 ego point, but if it has another (higher) plus, these are also counted, i.e. a +1 *Flame Tongue* has a maximum plus of 4, so it is +1/+4 for 5 ego points. In addition, swords which have no extra pluses but extra powers (*Holy Avenger, Sharpness,* etc.) add double their + rating for ego.

** If double ability, double ego points.

*** Round upwards.

Swords Versus Characters

When a sword possesses *unusual* characteristics, it has a personality which is rated by combining its intelligence and ego scores. The sword will, of course, be absolutely true to its alignment, and if the character who possesses the sword is not, *personality conflict* will result, i.e. sword versus character. Similarly, any sword with an ego of 19 or higher will always consider itself superior to any character, and a *personality conflict* will result if the possessor does not always agree with the sword's dictums.

The personality strength of a character is: INTELLIGENCE + CHARISMA + LEVEL OF EXPERIENCE. Note *level* is reduced by 1 for every group of hit points of damage taken equal to the character's average number of points per hit die for total levels of experience (rangers, for example, getting 2 dice at 1st level). Example: A fighter of 7th level has 53 hit points: 53 ÷ 7 = 7.6 — for every 8 points of damage he or she takes, his or her personality strength will be lowered by 1.

Whenever *personality conflict* occurs, the sword will resist the character's desires and demand concessions such as:

1. removal of associates, henchmen, hirelings, or creatures of alignment or personality distasteful to the sword
2. the character divesting himself or herself of all other magic weapons
3. obedience from the character so that the sword can lead the expedition for its purposes
4. immediate seeking out and slaying of creatures hateful to the sword
5. encrustation of gems on pommel, hilt, scabbard, baldric, or belt and a special container for its safekeeping likewise of precious substances
6. magical protections and devices to protect it from molestation when not in use
7. that the character pay it handsomely for all abilities and powers the sword is called upon to exercise in behalf of its possessor
8. that the character always take it along on all occasions
9. that the character relinquish the sword in favor of a more suitable person due to alignment differences and/or conduct

At any time that the personality score of a sword exceeds the personality score of the character who possesses it, the sword will dominate its possessor, and it can force any or all of the above demands or actually cause any of the following actions:

1. force its possessor into combat
2. refuse to strike opponents
3. strike at its wielder or his or her associates
4. force its possessor to surrender to an opponent
5. cause itself to drop from the character's grasp

Naturally, such actions are unlikely where the character-sword alignment and purposes are harmonious. However, the sword might well wish to have a lesser character possess it so as to easily command him or her, or a higher level possessor so as to better accomplish its goals.

All magic swords with personalities will desire to play an important role in the success of activities, particularly combat. Likewise, they are rivals, even if of the exact same alignment, and they will be aware of the presence of any similar weapon within 60', and try the best to lead a possessor into missing or destroying the rival unless this is totally inimical to its nature, i.e. a *Holy Avenger* would certainly not allow destruction of any other lawful good sword and might encourage discovery of same — even at the risk of having to face grim odds to do so . . .

Swords of this nature will never be totally controlled or silenced by the characters who possess them, even though they may be heavily outweighed by *personality* force. They may be powerless to force their demands, but they will be in there plugging. Even a humble +1 sword of *unusual* nature can be a vocal martyr, denigrating its own abilities and asking that the character only give it the chance to shatter itself against some hated enemy, etc.

N.B. Most players will be unwilling to play swords with personalities as the personalities dictate. It is incumbent upon the DM to ensure that the role of the sword is played to the hilt, with the DM assuming the persona of the sword if necessary.

MISCELLANEOUS WEAPONS (III.H.)

The various items listed generally have their bonus applied to both "to hit" and damage dice, whether it is +1, +2, +3, or +4. Any miscellaneous weapon which is not totally self-explanatory is detailed in one of the special paragraphs below:

Magic arrows which miss their target are 50% likely to be broken or otherwise rendered useless. All which hit are destroyed.

Arrow of Slaying is a +3 arrow with some unusual characteristics — a shaft of some special material, feathers of some rare creature, a head of strange design, a rune carved on the nock, etc. — which will distinguish it as fell against some creature type. If the arrow is employed against the kind of creature it has been enchanted to slay, the missile will kill it instantly if it hits the target creature. The following list comprises only a portion of the possible kinds of these arrows:

1) arachnids	9) elementals	17) monks
2) avians	10) fighters	18) paladins
3) bards	11) giants	19) rangers
4) clerics	12) golems	20) reptiles
5) demons	13) illusionists	21) sea monsters
6) devils	14) ki-rin	22) thieves
7) dragons	15) magic-users	23) titans
8) druids	16) mammals	24) undead

Develop your own types and modify and/or limit the foregoing as fits your campaign.

Axes (hand, not battle) can be thrown up to 3" with the hit probability bonus, but no damage bonus.

Axe +2, throwing, is a hand axe which can be thrown up to 6" at the same hit probability as if it were swung by the character, and the standard damage bonus.

Bow +1 gives +1 "to hit" and +1 damage potential to arrows fired from it. If magic arrows are used, the bonus is the total of the bow's and the arrows'. The type of bow found should be based on the circumstances of your campaign, i.e. composite, short, long, etc. according to the nature of the area.

Crossbow of accuracy, +3, gives a +3 bonus to its missiles and all ranges are considered *short*. 10% of these weapons will be heavy crossbows.

Crossbow of Distance has double range in all categories. 10% of these weapons will be heavy crossbows. It is otherwise +1 "to hit" and for damage.

Crossbow of speed allows its possessor to double the rate of fire normal for the weapon. If it is grasped, the *crossbow of speed* will automatically cock itself. In *surprise* situations it is of no help, but in *complete surprise* situations the held *crossbow* will enable its user to fire in the 2nd segment portion. Otherwise, it allows first fire in any melee round, and end of round fire also, when applicable. 10% of these weapons are heavy crossbows. The weapon has a +1 bonus.

Dagger of Venom appears to be a standard +1 type of dagger, but its hilt holds a hidden store of poison. Any hit on a score of 20 injects fatal poison into the opponent unless a saving throw versus poison is successful. The *dagger of venom* holds 6 doses of poison, and more can be poured within when less than that amount is within the hilt. (Use of this weapon by good — particularly lawful good — characters must be carefully monitored.)

Hammer +3, dwarven thrower appears to be a standard +2 hammer; but, if in the hands of a dwarven fighter, and a special command word is spoken, its full potential is realized. The +3 bonus is gained and the following characteristics: The hammer has a 6" range and it will return to its wielder's hand in much the same manner as a boomerang would. It has +3 bonus "to hit" and on damage. When so hurled, the *hammer* does double damage against all opponents save giants (including ogres, ogre magi, trolls and ettins), against which it causes triple damage (plus bonus of 3).

Hammer of Thunderbolts appears to be a regular hammer of largish size and extra weight. It will be too imbalanced, somehow, to wield properly in combat, unless the character has 18/01 or better strength and a height of over 6'. The *hammer* then functions as +3 and gains double damage dice on any hit. If the wielder wears any *girdle of giant strength* and *gauntlets of ogre power* in addition, he or she may properly wield the weapon if the *hammer's* true name is known. When swung or hurled it gains a +5, double damage dice, all *girdle* and *gauntlets* bonuses, and strikes dead any giant* upon which it scores a hit. When hurled and successfully hitting, a great noise as if a clap of thunder broke overhead will resound, *stunning* all creatures within 3″ for 1 round. Throwing range is 1″ + ½″/point of strength bonus for the *gauntlets* and *girdle,* i.e. 6 + 7 to 12 = 13 to 18 × ½″ = 6½″, 7″, 7½″, 8″, 8½″, 9″. (Thor would throw the hammer about double the above ranges . . .). The *hammer of thunderbolts* is very difficult to hurl, so only 1 throw every other round can be made, and after 5 throws within the space of any 2 turn period, the wielder *must* rest for 1 turn.

* Depending on your campaign, you might wish to limit the effect to exclude storm giants and include ogres, ogre magi, trolls, ettins, and clay, flesh, and stone golems.

Hammers can be hurled just as hand axes are.

Mace of Disruption appears to be a +1 mace, but it has a *neutral good* alignment, and any *evil* character touching it will take 5-20 points of damage due to the powerful enchantments laid upon the weapon. If a *mace of disruption* strikes any undead creature or evil creature from one of the lower planes it functions similarly to a cleric turning undead (see **ATTACK MATRICES**). The *mace* causes such creatures to roll on matrix III., **MATRIX FOR CLERICS AFFECTING UNDEAD,** as if the wielder were 12th level, and if the creature struck scores equal to or below the number shown, it is disrupted and slain. Thus, skeletons, zombies, ghouls, shadows, and wights are instantly blasted out of existence, as are ghasts and even wraiths; and mummies have only a 20% chance, spectres 35%, vampires 50%, ghosts 65%, liches 80%, and other affected evil creatures 95% chance of saving. Even if these saving throws are effective, the *mace of disruption* scores double damage upon opponents of this sort, i.e., 2 × bonus and 2 × dice.

Scimitar +2 is optionally treated the same as a magic sword — especially if your campaign is Asian in flavor or the activity area borders near such a nation. The possibilities are then rolled as follows:

01-45	scimitar +1
46-65	scimitar +2
66-80	scimitar +3
81-90	scimitar +4
91-95	scimitar +5
96-98	scimitar of wounding
99-00	scimitar of sharpness

Then roll for *unusual* characteristics as usual.

Sling of seeking +2 gives its user a +2 bonus for both "to hit" and damage dice, but missiles from such a weapon are only regarded as +1 with respect to determination of whether or not certain creatures are affected by the weapon, i.e. a special defense of "+2 or better weapon to hit" means the creature is impervious to normal missiles from this sling.

Spears can be used as hand or missile weapons. In the latter employment they might be broken by any creature with 18/00 or greater strength or against or by one that is massive, i.e. cave bear, hippo, rhino, etc. Intelligent creatures will be 70% likely to use the hurled spear against the hurler if struck by the weapon, 25% likely to break it (the spear must save versus crushing blow). Unintelligent creatures will be 25% likely to break it (save as above).

Spear, Cursed Backbiter, is to all tests a magic spear with a +1 bonus (or at your option +2 or +3). Even when it is used in combat against a deadly enemy it will possibly perform properly, but each time it is used in melee in anger against a foe, there is a 5% (1 in 20) cumulative chance that it will function against its wielder, and once so functioning it cannot be loosed without a *remove curse* spell. When functioning, the spear will curl to strike its wielder in the back, having a hit probability which negates any shield and/or dexterity bonuses to armor class, and doing normal damage. Backbiting includes hurling, but if the wielder has hurled the spear, he or she is, of course, loosed from grasping it; the damage done to the hurler will be double, however.

Trident (military fork) +3 is a short-hafted weapon about 6′ length overall. Upon command, the middle tine of the *trident* will retract into the pole while the shaft of the weapon lengthens to 9′, thus creating a military fork with a short center spike. The changing of the form of the weapon from trident to fork or vice versa requires 1 round.

APPENDICES

APPENDIX A: RANDOM DUNGEON GENERATION

When you need help in designing a dungeon — whether it is a level in your main dungeon or a labyrinth discovered elsewhere — the following random generation system has proven itself to be useful. It must be noted that the system requires time, but it can be used directly in conjunction with actual play.

The upper level above the dungeon in which adventures are to take place should be completely planned out, and it is a good idea to use the outdoor encounter matrix to see what lives where (a staircase discovered later just might lead right into the midst of whatever it is). The stairway down to the first level of the dungeon should be situated in the approximate middle of the upper ruins (or whatever you have as upper works).

The first level of the dungeon is always begun with a room; that is, the stairway down leads to a room, so you might go immediately to TABLE V. and follow the procedure indicated or use one of the following "starter" areas. Always begin a level in the middle of the sheet of graph paper.

Keep a side record of all monsters, treasures, tricks/traps, and whatever — a normal dungeon matrix.

Discretion must prevail at all times. For example: if you have decided that a level is to be but one sheet of paper in size, and the die result calls for something which goes beyond an edge, amend the result by rolling until you obtain something which will fit with your predetermined limits. Common sense will serve. If a room won't fit, a smaller one must serve, and any room or chamber which is called for can be otherwise drawn to suit what you believe to be its best positioning.

START AREAS FOR RANDOM DUNGEON

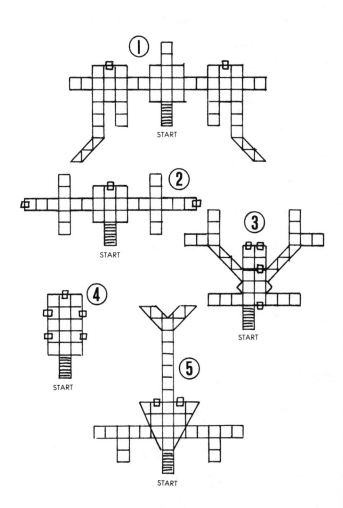

TABLE I.: PERIODIC CHECK (d20)

Die	Result
1-2	Continue straight — check again in 60' (this table)
3-5	Door (see TABLE II.)
6-10	Side Passage (see TABLE III.) — check again in 30' (this table)
11-13	Passage Turns (see TABLE IV., check width on TABLE III.) — check again in 30' (this table)
14-16	Chamber (see TABLE V.) — check 30' after leaving (this table)
17	Stairs (see TABLE VI.)
18	Dead End (walls left, right, and ahead can be checked for Secret Doors, see TABLE V.D., footnote)
19	Trick/Trap (see TABLE VII.), passage continues — check again in 30' (this table)
20	Wandering Monster, check again immediately to see what lies ahead so direction of monster's approach can be determined.

TABLE II.: DOORS* (d20)

Location of Door:		Space Beyond Door Is:	
Die	Result	Die	Result
1-6	Left	1-4	Parallel passage**, or 10' x 10' room if door is straight ahead
7-12	Right	5-8	Passage straight ahead
13-20	Ahead	9	Passage 45 degrees ahead/behind***
		10	Passage 45 degrees behind/ahead***
		11-18	Room (go to TABLE V.)
		19-20	Chamber (go to TABLE V.)

Always check width of passage
(TABLE III. A.)

  * Check again immediately on TABLE I. unless door is straight ahead; if another door is not indicated, then ignore the result and check again 30' past the door. If a room or chamber is beyond a door, go to TABLE V.

  ** Extends 30' in both directions.

  *** The direction will be appropriate to existing circumstances, but use the direction before the slash in preference to the other.

TABLE III.: SIDE PASSAGES (d20)

Die	Result
1-2	left 90 degrees
3-4	right 90 degrees
5	left 45 degrees ahead
6	right 45 degrees ahead
7	left 45 degrees behind (left 135 degrees)
8	right 45 degrees behind (right 135 degrees)
9	left curve 45 degrees ahead
10	right curve 45 degrees ahead
11-13	passage "T"s
14-15	passage "Y"s
16-19	four-way intersection
20	passage "X"s (if present passage is horizontal or vertical it forms a fifth passage into the "X")

TABLE III. A.: PASSAGE WIDTH (d20)

Die	Result
1-12	10'
13-16	20'
17	30'
18	5'
19-20	SPECIAL PASSAGE (TABLE III. B. below)

TABLE III. B.: SPECIAL PASSAGE (d20)

Die	Result
1-4	40', columns down center
5-7	40', double row of columns
8-10	50', double row of columns
11-12	50', columns 10' right and left support 10' wide upper galleries 20' above*
13-15	10' stream**
16-17	20' river***
18	40' river***
19	60' river***
20	20', chasm****

  * Stairs up to gallery will be at end of passage (1-15) or at beginning (16-20). In the former case if a stairway is indicated in or adjacent to the passage it will replace the end stairs 50% (1-10) of the time and supplement 50% (11-20) of the time.

  ** Streams bisect the passage. They will be bridged 75% (1-15) of the time and be an obstacle 25% (16-20) of the time.

  *** Rivers bisect the passage. They will be bridged 50% (1-10) of the time, have a boat 25% (11-15) of the time (50% chance for either bank), and be an obstacle 25% of the time.

  **** Chasms bisect the passage. They are 150' to 200' deep. They will be bridged 50% (1-10) of the time, have a jumping place 5'-10' wide 25% (11-15) of the time, and be an obstacle 25% (16-20) of the time.

TABLE IV.: TURNS (d20)

Die	Result (check on width of passage on TABLE III. A.)
1-8	left 90 degrees
9	left 45 degrees ahead
10	left 45 degrees behind (left 135 degrees)
11-18	right 90 degrees
19	right 45 degrees ahead
20	right 45 degrees behind (right 135 degrees)

TABLE V.: CHAMBERS AND ROOMS SHAPE AND SIZE (d20)
(Roll for Shape, Size, and Exits; then Contents, Treasure, and how the latter is contained, if applicable.)

Die	Chamber Shape and Area	Room Shape and Area
1-2	Square, 20' x 20'	Square, 10' x 10'
3-4	Square, 20' x 20'	Square, 20' x 20'
5-6	Square, 30' x 30'	Square, 30' x 30'
7-8	Square, 40' x 40'	Square, 40' x 40'
9-10	Rectangular, 20' x 30'	Rectangular, 10' x 20'
11-13	Rectangular, 20' x 30'	Rectangular, 20' x 30'
14-15	Rectangular, 30' x 50'	Rectangular, 20' x 40'
16-17	Rectangular, 40' x 60'	Rectangular, 30' x 40'
18-20	Unusual shape and size — see sub-tables below	

TABLE V. A.: UNUSUAL SHAPE (Roll Separately for Size) (d20)

Die	Shape
1-5	Circular*
6-8	Triangular
9-11	Trapezoidal
12-13	Odd-shaped**
14-15	Oval
16-17	Hexagonal
18-19	Octagonal
20	Cave

  * 1-5 has pool (see TABLE VIII. A. and C. if appropriate), 6-7 has well, 8-10 has shaft, and 11-20 is normal.

  ** Draw what shape you desire or what will fit the map — it is a special shape if desired.

TABLE V. B.: UNUSUAL SIZE (d20)

Die	Size
1-3	about 500 sq. ft.
4-6	about 900 sq. ft.
7-8	about 1,300 sq. ft.
9-10	about 2,000 sq. ft.
11-12	about 2,700 sq. ft.
13-14	about 3,400 sq. ft.
15-20	roll again and add result to 9-10 above (if another 15-20 repeat the process, doubling 9-10 above, and so on)

TABLE V. C.: NUMBER OF EXITS (d20)

Die	Room Area	Number of Exits
1-3	up to 600'	1
1-3	over 600'	2
4-6	up to 600'	2
4-6	over 600'	3
7-9	up to 600'	3
7-9	over 600'	4
10-12	up to 1200'	0*
10-12	over 1200'	1
13-15	up to 1600'	0*
13-15	over 1600'	1
16-18	any size	1-4 (d4)
19-20	any size	1 — door in chamber, passage in room

* Check once per 10' for secret doors (see TABLE V. D., footnote).

TABLE V. D.: EXIT LOCATION (d20)

Die*	Location
1-7	opposite wall
8-12	left wall
13-17	right wall
18-20	same wall

* If a passage or door is indicated in a wall where the space immediately beyond the wall has already been mapped, then the exit is either a secret door (1-5) or a one-way door (6-10) or it is in the opposite direction (11-20).

TABLE V. E.: EXIT DIRECTION (d20)

Die	Direction (if a Door use TABLE II instead) — check for width on TABLE III.A.
1-16	straight ahead
17-18	45 degrees left/right*
19-20	45 degrees right/left*

* The exit will be appropriate to existing circumstances, but use the direction before the slash in preference to the other.

TABLE V. F.: CHAMBER OR ROOM CONTENTS (d20)

Die	Contents
1-12	Empty
13-14	Monster only (determine on appropriate table from **APPENDIX C: RANDOM MONSTER ENCOUNTERS, Dungeon Encounter Matrix**).
15-17	Monster and treasure (see TABLE V.G. below)
18	Special*, or contains stairway up 1 level (1-5), up 2 levels (7-8), down 1 level (9-14), down 2 levels (15-19), or down 3 levels — 2 flights of stairs and a slanting passageway (20).
19	Trick/Trap (see TABLE VII.)
20	Treasure (see TABLE V.G.)

* Determine by balance of level or put in what you desire; otherwise put in stairs as indicated.

TABLE V. G.: TREASURE* (d%)

Die	Without Monster	With Monster
01-25	1,000 copper pieces/level	Take two rolls on "Without Monster" Table, add 10% to the total of each roll.
26-50	1,000 silver pieces/level	
51-65	750 electrum pieces/level	
66-80	250 gold pieces/level	
81-90	100 platinum pieces/level	
91-94	1-4 gems/level	
95-97	1 piece jewelry/level	
98-00	Magic (roll once on Magic Items Table)	

* See also TABLES V. H. and I. or J.

TABLE V. H.: TREASURE IS CONTAINED IN* (d20)

Die	Result
1-2	Bags
3-4	Sacks
5-6	Small Coffers
7-8	Chests
9-10	Huge Chests
11-12	Pottery Jars
13-14	Metal Urns
15-16	Stone Containers
17-18	Iron Trunks
19-20	Loose

* Go to TABLE V. I. on a roll of 1-8, TABLE V. J. on a 9-20 to determine protection if desired.

TABLE V. I.: TREASURE IS GUARDED BY (d20)

Die	Result
1-2	Contact poison on container
3-4	Contact poison on treasure
5-6	Poisoned needles in lock
7	Poisoned needles in handles
8	Spring darts firing from front of container
9	Spring darts firing up from top of container
10	Spring darts firing up from inside bottom of container
11-12	Blade scything across inside
13	Poisonous insects or reptiles living inside container
14	Gas released by opening container
15	Trapdoor opening in front of container
16	Trapdoor opening 6' in front of container
17	Stone block dropping in front of the container
18	Spears released from walls when container opened
19	*Explosive runes*
20	*Symbol*

TABLE V. J.: TREASURE IS HIDDEN BY/IN (d20)

Die	Result
1-3	*Invisibility*
4-5	*Illusion* (to change or hide appearance)
6	Secret space under container
7-8	Secret compartment in container
9	Inside ordinary item in plain view
10	Disguised to appear as something else
11	Under a heap of trash/dung
12-13	Under a loose stone in the floor
14-15	Behind a loose stone in the wall
16-20	In a secret room nearby

TABLE VI.: STAIRS (d20)

Die	Result (roll on TABLE I. upon ascending/descending).
1-5	Down 1 level*
6	Down 2 levels**
7	Down 3 levels***
8	Up 1 level
9	Up dead end (1 in 6 chance to chute down 2 levels)
10	Down dead end (1 in 6 chance to chute down 1 level)
11	Chimney up 1 level, passage continues, check again in 30'
12	Chimney up 2 levels, passage continues, check again in 30'
13	Chimney down 2 levels, passage continues, check again in 30'
14-16	Trap door down 1 level, passage continues, check again in 30'
17	Trap door down 2 levels, passage continues, check again in 30'
18-20	Up 1 then down 2 (total down 1), chamber at end (roll on TABLE V.)

   * 1 in 20 has a door which closes egress for the day.
   ** 2 in 20 has a door which closes egress for the day.
   *** 3 in 20 has a door which closes egress for the day.
   N.B. Check for such doors only after descending steps if playing solo!

TABLE VII.: TRICK/TRAP (d20)

Die	Result
1-5	Secret Door **unless** unlocated: Non-elf locates 3 in 20, elf locates 5 in 20, magical device locates 18 in 20 (then see TABLE II.). Unlocated secret doors **go to die 6, 7 below.**
6-7	Pit, 10' deep, 3 in 6 to fall in.
8	Pit, 10' deep with spikes, 3 in 6 to fall in.
9	20' x 20' elevator room (party has entered door directly ahead and is in room), descends 1 level and will not ascend for 30 turns.
10	As 9. above, but room descends 2 levels.
11	As 9. above, but room descends 2-5 levels — 1 upon entering and 1 additional level each time an unsuccessful attempt at door opening is made, or until it descends as far as it can. This will not ascend for 60 turns.
12	Wall 10' behind slides across passage blocking it for from 40-60 turns.
13	Oil (equal to one flask) pours on random person from hole in ceiling, followed by flaming cinder (2-12 h.p. damage unless successful save vs. magic is made, which indicates only 1-3 h.p. damage).
14	Pit, 10' deep, 3 in 6 to fall in, pit walls move together to crush victim(s) in 2-5 rounds.
15	Arrow trap, 1-3 arrows, 1 in 20 is poisoned.
16	Spear trap, 1-3 spears, 1 in 20 is poisoned.
17	Gas; party has detected it, but must breathe it to continue along corridor, as it covers 60' ahead. Mark map accordingly regardless of turning back or not. (See TABLE VII. A.)
18	Door falls outward causing 1-10 hit points, or stone falls from ceiling causing 2-20 hit points of damage to each person failing his saving throw versus petrification.
19	Illusionary wall concealing 8. (pit) above (1-6), 20. (chute) below (7-10) or chamber with monster and treasure (11-20) (see TABLE V.).
20	Chute down 1 level (cannot be ascended in any manner).

TABLE VII. A.: GAS SUB-TABLE (d20)

Die	Result
1-7	Only effect is to obscure vision when passing through.
8-9	Blinds for 1-6 turns after passing through.
10-12	Fear: run back 120' feet unless saving throw versus magic is made.
13	Sleep: party sound asleep for 2-12 turns (as *sleep* spell).

14-18	Strength: adds 1-6 points of strength (as *strength* spell) to all fighters in party for 1 to 10 hours.
19	Sickness: return to surface immediately.
20	Poison: killed unless saving throw versus poison is made.

CAVES AND CAVERNS FOR LOWEST LEVELS: You may wish to have "roughhewn" and natural tunnels in lower levels, and where rooms and chambers are indicated substitute Caves and Caverns. Exits are as above.

TABLE VIII.: CAVES AND CAVERNS (d20)

Die	Result
1-5	Cave about 40' x 60'
6-7	Cave about 50' x 75'
8-9	Double Cave: 20' x 30', 60' x 60'
10-11	Double Cave: 35' x 50', 80' x 90'*
12-14	Cavern about 95' x 125'*
15-16	Cavern about 120' x 150'
17-18	Cavern about 150' $\times$ 200'*
19-20	Mammoth cavern about 250'-300' $\times$ 350'-400'**

   * Roll to see if pool therein (see TABLE VIII.A.).
   ** Roll to see if lake therein (see TABLE VIII.B.).

TABLE VIII. A.: POOLS (d20)

Die	Result
1-8	No pool
9-10	Pool, no monster
11-12	Pool, monster
13-18	Pool, monster & treasure
19-20	Magical pool*

   * See TABLE VIII. C.

TABLE VIII. B.: LAKES (d20)

Die	Result
1-10	No lake
11-15	Lake, no monsters
16-18	Lake, monsters*
19-20	Enchanted lake**

   * Determine monster and treasure from appropriate encounter matrix.
   ** Enchanted lake leads any who manage to cross it to another dimension, special temple, etc. (if special map is available, otherwise treat as lake with monsters), 90% chance that monster will guard lake.

TABLE VIII. C.: MAGIC POOLS* (d20)

Die	Result
1-8	Turns gold to platinum (1-11) or lead (12-20), one time only.
9-15	Will, on a one-time only basis, add (1-3) or subtract (4-6) from one characteristic of all who stand within it:

        1 = strength   4 = dexterity
        2 = intelligence   5 = constitution
        3 = wisdom   6 = charisma
        (add or subtract from 1-3 points, checking for each character as to addition or subtraction, characteristic, and amount).

16-17	Talking pool which will grant 1 *wish* to characters of its alignment and damage others from 1-20 points. *Wish* can be withheld for up to 1 day. Pool's alignment is: lawful good 1-6, lawful evil 7-9, chaotic good 10-12, chaotic evil 13-17, neutral 18-20.
18-20	Transporter pool: 1-7, back to surface; 8-12, elsewhere on level; 13-16, 1 level down; 17-20, 100 miles away for outdoor adventure.

   * In order to find out what they are, characters must enter the magic pools.

RANDOM DUNGEON GENERATION FOR SOLO PLAY

The random dungeon generation system is easily adaptable to solitary play. Locate the entrance to the dungeon, and then select one of the random dungeon starting areas given here, locating it in the middle of the graph paper.

Monsters: Inhabitants of the dungeon are determined from the **DUNGEON ENCOUNTER MATRIX.** For special areas you can have a friend or correspondent send you sealed information.

Listening at Doors: Use a 12-sided die, and if a 1 is rolled, there **is** a monster (with or without treasure). Procedure is then normal, but surprise is possible only on the monster's part.

ESP and Other Detection Devices: Use a 6-sided die, a 1 indicating a monster which will be known — roll it out, ignoring any undead or other non-thinking monsters. Check other rooms, chambers, etc. normally and for any monster which can not be indicated by the *ESP* or detection device *surprise* is only possible on a roll of 1 on an 8-sided die.

APPENDIX B: RANDOM WILDERNESS TERRAIN

If a wilderness expedition moves into an area where no detailed map has been prepared in advance, the random terrain determination system below can be utilized with relative ease for a 1 space = 1 mile, or larger, scale. In using it, however, common sense must prevail. For example, if the expedition is in the north country the forest will be pine or possibly scrub, while in tropical regions it will be jungle. Similarly, if a pond is indicated in two successive spaces, the two should be treated as one larger body of water. The Dungeon Master must also feel free to add to the random terrain as he sees fit in order to develop a reasonable configuration. In any event, the DM must draw in rivers, large lakes, seas, oceans, and islands as these features cannot easily be generated by a random method.

As the party enters each space, generate a random number from 1 to 20. Find the type of terrain the party is currently on by reading across the page, then read down the column until you find the line where the random number generated falls, and simply move left to determine the terrain that predominates in the new space.

If a pond is indicated, the terrain it is in is the same as that of the previous space.

If a depression is indicated, the referee must decide as to its nature and extent. Generally, the terrain it is in must be the same as the previous space. A depression in a marsh is some form of lake.

Note: Glens in forests, paths/tracks, and streams can be included as desired. Paths/tracks and streams must lead to/from unmapped spaces, of course.

Terrain Guide:

Plain: tundra, steppe, savanna, prairie, heath, moor, downs, meadow

Scrub: brush, veldt, bush, thickets, brackens

Forest: woods, jungle, groves and copses (light forest)

Rough: badlands

Desert: barrens, waste, flat, snowfield

Hills: ridges, bluffs, dunes

Mountains: mesas, glacier, tors

Marsh: fen, slough, swamp, bog, mire, quagmire, morass

Pond: pools, tarn, lake

Depression: gorge, rift, valley, canyon

	Plain	Scrub	Forest	Rough	Desert	Hills	Mountains	Marsh
Plain	1-11	1-3	1	1-2	1-3	1	1	1-2
Scrub	12	4-11	2-4	3-4	4-5	2-3	2	3-4
Forest*	13	12-13	5-14	5	—	4-5	3	5-6
Rough	14	14	15	6-8	6-8	6-7	4-5	7
Desert	15	15	—	9-10	9-14	8	6	—
Hills**	16	16	16	11-15	15	9-14	7-10	8
Mountains***	17	17	17	16-17	16-17	15-16	11-18	—
Marsh	18	18	18	18	18	17	—	9-15
Pond	19	19	19	19	19	18-19	19	16-19
Depression	20	20	20	20	20	20	20	20

* 1 in 10 also includes **hills.**
** 1 in 10 also includes **forest.**
*** 1 in 20 have a **pass** which leads through the range.

INHABITATION

Check each space for the possibility of inhabitation. Use random numbers 01 to 00.

Type of Settlement			Population
Single Dwelling		01-03	1-12
Thorp		04-05	20-80
Hamlet		06-07	100-400
Village		08-09	600-900
Town		10	1,500-6,500
City		11	10,000-60,000
Castle		12-14	*
Ruins		15-16	
Roll again	Village	01-30	
	City	31-60	
	Shrine	61-85	
	Tomb	86-00	
Uninhabited		17-00	

*See **Castle Tables,** APPENDIX C, pp. 182-183

APPENDIX C: RANDOM MONSTER ENCOUNTERS

The procedures and tables for determining random monster encounters during the course of a campaign are given here. The state of **ADVANCED DUNGEONS & DRAGONS** is such that new and different creatures are being devised regularly and often, so that by-and-large, the only monsters which are included are those in **MONSTER MANUAL**. Two notable exceptions to this are those the *mezzodaemon* and *nycadaemon* which are found in the **AD&D** module D3, **VAULT OF THE DROW** (TSR Games, Inc.). If you do not have this module, simply ignore results calling for these monsters and roll again. It is quite possible that at some future time a new edition of this work will be updated to include all of the recognized **AD&D** monsters. You may do this for yourself now — and include your own favorite creatures at the same time — by finding the experience points value of such monsters and equating them to those already found herein. Determine the frequency (*common, uncommon,* etc.) of the new creatures, and then include them on the appropriate tables by adding them after comparable monsters already shown. Be careful not to upset the probability balance.

Dungeon random monster levels are determined as follows:

I	up to 20 X.P.	VI	501-1,000 X.P.
II	21-50 X.P.	VII	1,001-3,000 X.P.
III	51-150 X.P.	VIII	3,001-5,500 X.P.
IV	151-250 X.P.	IX	5,501-10,000 X.P.
V	251-500 X.P.	X	over 10,000 X.P.

Random monster tables are included for the following types of encounters:

DUNGEON ENCOUNTERS
— Dungeon Random Monster Level Determination Matrix
— Monster Levels One-Ten
— Human Subtable
— Character Subtable
— Dragon Subtables (by monster level)

UNDERWATER ENCOUNTERS
— Underwater Encounters In Fresh Water (Shallow, Deep)
— Underwater Encounters In Salt Water (Shallow, Deep)

ASTRAL & ETHEREAL ENCOUNTERS
— Psychic Wind
— Ether Cyclone
— Astral Encounter Table
— Ethereal Encounter Table

PSIONIC ENCOUNTERS
— Psionic Encounter Table
— Human Subtable Modifiers

OUTDOOR RANDOM MONSTER ENCOUNTERS
— Patrols (Inhabited Areas)
— Outdoor Random Monster Encounter Tables
— Arctic Conditions
— Sub-Arctic Conditions
— Temperate And Sub-Tropical Conditions, Uninhabited/Wilderness Areas
— Subtables: Demi-Human, Dragon, Frog, Giant, Humanoid, Lycanthrope, Men, Snake, Sphinx, Spider, Undead

— Temperate And Sub-Tropical Conditions, Inhabited And/Or Patrolled Areas
— Temperate Conditions, Faerie And Sylvan Settings
— Pleistocene Conditions
— Sub-Tropical To Tropical Conditions, Prehistoric Settings, Age Of Dinosaurs
— Tropical And Near-Tropical Conditions, Uninhabited/Wilderness Areas
— Sphinx Subtable

WATERBORNE RANDOM MONSTER ENCOUNTERS
— Fresh Water, Small Body Of Water
— Fresh Water, Large Body Of Water
— Salt Water, Shallow Waters, Coastal Waters, Small Inland Seas
— Salt Water, Deep Waters
— Dinosaur Subtable

AIRBORNE RANDOM MONSTER ENCOUNTERS

Procedure: When a random encounter is indicated by the periodic check, and you do not have an encounter table specially devised for the area, roll a d20. Cross-index the level of the dungeon (or whatever is equivalent to it) with the die result and read up to find which **DUNGEON RANDOM MONSTER TABLE** (by Roman numeral monster level, I to X) to consult to find the type of monster encountered. Once the table is found, dice will discover at random which monster has been encountered and in what numbers.

MONSTER ENCOUNTERED ADJUSTMENT FOR RELATIVE DUNGEON LEVEL

The *Numbers* column assumes that the encounter will take place on the level which is equivalent to the level assigned to the particular monster (cf. **DUNGEON RANDOM MONSTER LEVEL DETERMINATION MATRIX**). In order to adjust for the more difficult conditions on lower levels of the dungeon, and the relatively easier ones above, use the following rules:

Lesser monsters on lower levels have their numbers augmented by a like number of the same sort of creatures for each level of the dungeon beneath that of the assigned level of the monster type encountered. Example: First level monsters on the 2nd level of a dungeon will be twice as numerous as the *Numbers* variable indicates, i.e. 2-8 giant ants, rather than 1-4, if they are encountered on the 2nd level (or its equivalent) of a dungeon. The same is true for second level monsters encountered on the 3rd dungeon level, third level monsters on the 4th dungeon level, etc. *There are two exceptions to this rule:*

1. Characters are increased by level of experience rather than by numbers encountered, as indicated in the **DUNGEON RANDOM MONSTER TABLE Notes.**

2. Ninth and tenth level monsters are typically given attendant monsters, rather than greater numbers, in lower dungeon levels, i.e., a demon prince encountered on the 11th dungeon level might have a single type I demon attendant, while on the 15th level of the dungeon the same demon prince might have 5 such lesser demons or a pair of type III escorts.

Greater monsters on higher levels will have their numbers reduced by 1 for each level of the dungeon above their assigned level, subject to a minimum number of 1. Example: 1-3 shadows are normally encountered on the 4th level of the dungeon; as shadows are fourth level monsters, a max-

DUNGEON RANDOM MONSTER LEVEL DETERMINATION MATRIX (d20)

Equivalent Level Of The Dungeon	I	II	III	IV	V	VI	VII	VIII	IX	X
				Monster Level Table Which Must Be Consulted						
1st	1-16	17-19	20	—	—	—	—	—	—	—
2nd-3rd	1-12	13-16	17-18	19	20	—	—	—	—	—
4th	1-5	6-10	11-16	17-18	19	20	—	—	—	—
5th	1-3	4-6	7-12	13-16	17-18	19	20	—	—	—
6th	1-2	3-4	5-6	7-12	13-16	17-18	19	20	—	—
7th	1	2-3	4-5	6-10	11-14	15-16	17-18	19	20	—
8th	1	2	3-4	5-7	8-10	11-14	15-16	17-18	19	20
9th	1	2	3	4-5	6-8	9-12	13-15	16-17	18-19	20
10th-11th	1	2	3	4	5-6	7-9	10-12	13-16	17-19	20
12th-13th	1	2	3	4	5	6-7	8-9	10-12	13-18	19-20
14th-15th	1	2	3	4	5	6	7-8	9-11	12-17	18-20
16th & down	1	2	3	4	5	6	7	8-10	11-16	17-20

imum of 2 can be encountered on the 3rd dungeon level, and but 1 on the 2nd level. (Fourth level monsters cannot be encountered on the 1st level of the dungeon.) Hydras, for instance, will have fewer heads, while creatures with attendants will have fewer or none at all on the lesser-numbered levels.

DUNGEON RANDOM MONSTER TABLES

MONSTER LEVEL I

Dice Score	Creature Encountered	Numbers
01-02	Ant, giant	1-4
03-04	Badger*	1-4
05-14	Beetle, fire	1-4
15	Demon, manes	1-4
16-17	Dwarf	4-14
18	Ear seeker	1
19	Elf	3-11
20-21	Gnome	5-15
22-26	Goblin	6-15
27-28	Halfling**	9-16
29-33	Hobgoblin	2-8
34-48	Human — see **Human Subtable** below	
49-54	Kobold	6-18
55-66	Orc	7-12
67-70	Piercer	1-3
71-83	Rat, giant	5-20
84-85	Rot grub	1-3
86-96	Shrieker	1-2
97-98	Skeleton	1-4
99-00	Zombie	1-3

* Not encountered below the 2nd level; treat as a roll of 29-33 (hobgoblin) thereafter.

** Not encountered below the 4th level; treat as a roll of 71-83 (Rat, giant) thereafter.

Monster Level I: Human Subtable

Dice Score	Creature Encountered	Numbers
01-25	Bandit*	5-15
26-30	Berserker*	3-9
31-45	Brigand*	5-15
46-00	Character — see **Character Subtable** below	

* Upper level leaders and sub-leaders are *not* with groups numbering under 30, and at only 50% of normal level (rounded up) for groups under 60. As a general rule, you may wish to exclude all of these encounters on levels below whatever point you find them to be unlikely.

Character Subtable (Used For Encounters On All Dungeon Levels)

Dice Score	Character Type	Maximum Number Per Party
01-17	CLERIC	3
18-20	Druid	2
21-60	FIGHTER	5
61-62	Paladin	2
63-65	Ranger	2
66-86	MAGIC-USER	3
87-88	Illusionist	1
89-98	THIEF	4
99	Assassin	2
00	MONK OR BARD	1 or 1

Number Of Characters In Party: There will always be from 2-5 characters in a character group, with men-at-arms or henchmen to round the party out to 9. Roll d4, and add 1 to the result in order to find the number of characters, then dice on the **Character Subtable** to find the profession of each, ignoring rolls which are contradictory (a paladin and an assassin, for instance) or exceed the maximum number of a character class possible in any given party. The number of characters subtracted from 9 gives the number of men-at-arms or henchmen accompanying the characters.

Level Of Characters: The level of each character will be equal to that of the level of the dungeon or the level of monster, whichever is greater, through the 4th level. Thereafter it will be between 7th and 12th, determined by a roll of d6 +6, and adjusted as follows: If the total is higher than the level of the dungeon, reduce it by −1. If it is lower than the

level of the dungeon, adjust it upwards by +1, but not to exceed 12 levels unless the dungeon level is 16th or deeper.

Level Of Others With Characters: Men-at-arms will only accompany characters encountered on the 1st, 2nd, or 3rd level of the dungeon. On the 4th or deeper level, all others will be henchmen. The profession of henchmen is discovered by dicing on the **Character Subtable**, again ignoring incompatible results, i.e. a paladin as the henchman of a thief, a ranger of less than 8th level with any henchman, etc. Each character should be paired with one or more henchmen, in rotation, until the entire party totals nine members. Each henchman will have a level equal to one-third that of his or her master, rounded down in all cases where fractions are below one-half, and plus 1 level per 3 levels of the master's experience level where the character's level is above 8th. For example, a 5th level magic-user would have a 2nd level henchman, as one-third of 5 is 1.7; at 9th level the character's henchman would be 3 + 3 (one third of 9 plus 1 level for every 3 levels of experience of the master equals 3 + 3) or 6th level. Bonus for the level of the character master is only in whole numbers, all fractions being dropped, i.e. at 11th level there is still only a bonus of 3, but at 12th there is a bonus of 4.

Character And Henchman Abilities & Alignment: This information must be generated individually, per group, using the **PERSONAE OF NON-PLAYER CHARACTERS** section of the rules. Alternately, you may wish to obtain prepared lists of such characters, or generate such lists yourself in advance, and select therefrom. *Men-At-Arms* will need only hit points, of course. Alignments must be compatible!

Character And Henchman Equipment: Arms, armor, and equipment typical to a party of dungeon adventurers may be assumed. That is, characters at 1st level will have scale or chain armor (if applicable to their professions), standard weapons, and only minimal gear. At second level plate mail will be typical, weapons profuse, and gear very complete (much oil, holy/unholy water, silver mirrors, etc.). Consider men-at-arms to have only lower value armor and few weapons, i.e. studded leather, crossbow and dagger, or (at best) scale mail, shield, spear, sword (long) and back pack.

Character Spells: Select cleric spells according to those which you believe most suited to the party as a whole. Do likewise with magic-user spells, following limitations of known spells. Henchmen with spell ability should be similarly supplied with spells selected by the DM.

Party Magic Items: In order to simulate a party of adventurers, it is absolutely necessary that characters and henchmen have and employ some magic devices. While it is possible to give such parties the whole gamut of items listed, it is suggested that you use the following lists and select according to the following rule:

Individual is 1st level — 10% chance: 1 item from Table I.
Individual is 2nd level — 20% chance: 2 items from Table I.
Individual is 3rd level — 30% chance: 2 items from Table I;
           10% chance: 1 item from Table II.
Individual is 4th level — 40% chance: 2 items from Table I;
           20% chance: 1 item from Table II.
Individual is 5th level — 50% chance: 2 items from Table I;
           30% chance: 1 item from Table II.
Individual is 6th level — 60% chance: 3 items from Table I;
           40% chance: 2 items from Table II.
Individual is 7th level — 70% chance: 3 items from Table I;
           50% chance: 2 items from Table II;
           10% chance: 1 item from Table III.
Individual is 8th level — 80% chance: 3 items from Table I;
           60% chance: 2 items from Table II;
           20% chance: 1 item from Table III.
Individual is 9th level — 90% chance: 3 items from Table I;
           70% chance: 2 items from Table II;
           30% chance: 1 item from Table III.
Individual is 10th level — 3 items from Table I;
           80% chance: 2 items from Table II;
           40% chance: 1 item from Table III.
Individual is 11th level — 3 items from Table I;
           90% chance: 2 items from Table II;
           50% chance: 1 item from Table III;
           10% chance: 1 item from Table IV.
Individual is 12th level — 3 items from Table I;
           2 items from Table II;
           60% chance: 1 item from Table III;
           20% chance: 1 item from Table IV.

Individual is 13th level — 3 items from Table I;
2 items from Table II;
1 item from Table III;
60% chance: 1 item from Table IV.

It is suggested that you personally select appropriate items, using random determination only when any item would be suitable to the particular individual. Note that some items are groups or multiples.

Magic Item Tables For Character Encounters

TABLE I

Die	Item (d20)
1	2 POTIONS: *climbing, flying*
2	2 POTIONS: *extra-healing, polymorph (self)*
3	2 POTIONS: *fire resistance, speed*
4	2 POTIONS: *healing, giant strength*
5	2 POTIONS: *heroism, invulnerability*
6	2 POTIONS: *human control, levitation*
7	2 POTIONS: *super-heroism, animal control*
8	1 SCROLL: 1 Spell, level 1-6
9	1 SCROLL: 2 Spells, level 1-4
10	1 SCROLL: *protection from magic*
11	1 RING: *mammal control*
12	1 RING: *protection* +1
13	1 ARMOR: *leather* +1
14	1 SHIELD: +1
15	1 SWORD: +1 (no special abilities)
16	10 ARROWS: +1
17	4 BOLTS: +2
18	1 DAGGER: +1 (or +2) *et al.*
19	1 JAVELIN +2
20	1 MACE +1

TABLE II

Die	Item (d8, d6)
1	1 SCROLL: 3 Spells, level 2-9 or 2-7
2	2 RINGS: *fire resistance, invisibility*
3	1 RING: *protection* +3
4	1 STAFF: *striking*
5	1 WAND: *illusion*
6	1 WAND: *negation*
7	1 *bracers of defense, armor class 4*
8	1 *brooch of shielding*
9	1 *cloak of elvenkind*
10	1 *dust of appearance*
11	1 FIGURINE OF WONDROUS POWER: *serpentine owl*
12	3 *javelins of lightning*
13	1 set: *chainmail* +1, *shield* +2
14	1 ARMOR: *splint mail* +4
15	1 SWORD: +3 (no special abilities)
16	2 WEAPONS: *crossbow of speed,* +2 *hammer*

TABLE III

Die	Item (d8, d6)
1	1 RING: *spell storing*
2	1 ROD: *cancellation*
3	1 STAFF: *serpent — python or adder*
4	1 *bag of tricks*
5	1 *boots of speed*
6	1 *boots of striding and leaping*
7	1 *cloak of displacement*
8	1 *gauntlets of ogre power*
9	1 *pipe of the sewers*
10	1 *robe of blending*
11	2 ROPES: *climbing, entanglement*
12	1 set: *plate mail* +3, *shield* +2
13	1 SHIELD: +5
14	1 SWORD: +4, *defender*
15	1 *mace* +3
16	1 *spear* +3

TABLE IV

Die	Item (d12)
1	1 RING: *djinni summoning*
2	1 RING: *spell turning*
3	1 ROD: *smiting*
4	1 WAND: *fire*
5	1 *cube of force*
6	1 *eyes of charming*
7	1 *horn of valhalla*
8	1 *robe of scintillating colors*
9	1 *talisman* of either *ultimate evil* or *pure good*
10	1 set: *plate mail* +4, *shield* +3
11	1 SWORD: *wounding*
12	1 *arrow of slaying* (select character type)

General Notes: Substitute freely, following the examples given. Remember that characters will be prone to use all items if hostilities commence. Also remember that if the characters are defeated, some of these items will be brought into your campaign. BE CAREFUL in handling groups.

Race And Multi-Class: It is suggested that non-human characters and henchmen be about 20% of the total. If the profession of the character or henchman is very limited or impossible for the race, use it, or its closest approximation, as one of two or three classes of the individual. About 50% of non-humans will have two professions, about 25% of those will have three. Race and probability of multi-profession is shown below:

Dice Score	Race Of Individual	% Of Multi-Class
01-25	Dwarf	15%
26-50	Elf	85%
51-60	Gnome	25%
61-85	Half-elf	85%
86-95	Halfling	10%
96-00	Half-Orc	50%

Level Of Multi-Classed Individuals: Determine level for a single profession, add 2, and divide by 2, dropping fractions below one-half. For a triple class, add three, divide by three, and drop fractions below one-half. If one class is thereby exceeded, take one-half the excess levels and assign them to the other. In a triple-classed individual, divide excess levels and assign to the two remaining classes.

Confrontation: When the party of adventurers meets a party of characters and henchmen/men-at-arms, be certain that you consider relative aggressiveness and alignments. A character party feeling itself weak in relation to the adventurers encountered will certainly attempt to avoid, negotiate, or use wit and guile to bluff their way out of actual combat. They will be prepared for whatever happens, however, unless surprised. Check reaction if negotiations occur. CHARACTER PARTIES WILL NEVER JOIN WITH ADVENTURERS UNLESS YOU PERSONALLY CAN OBTAIN MORE BENEFIT FOR THE FORMER FROM SOME FORM OF CO-OPERATION. This typically indicates little or no gain, or possibly loss, for the player party. Do not check morale for the character party, but place yourself in their position, just as if you personally were the player to whom each and every individual in the group belonged. In short, play them as if they were player-characters! If the confrontation is going against the group, use means to right it in their favor, or break off, whichever is the most likely to bring the greatest benefit. If adventurers are bested, the character party will not necessarily kill them — to strip and abandon, hold for ransom, and imprison for sacrifice later are but three possible alternatives to instant slaughter.

It is strongly suggested that if you use these tables for random encounters you prepare character groups ahead of time, determining all information for as many such groups as time permits. Likewise, do the same for character groups encountered astrally or ethereally (see **ASTRAL & ETHEREAL ENCOUNTER TABLES, ** note). Whenever an encounter with any such group occurs, you then need but turn to the prepared information, use the first group, and when the encounter is over, that party is crossed off. This procedure assures that undue time will not be wasted during actual play, and that you will have had time to properly prepare and know the encountered group.

MONSTER LEVEL II

Dice Score	Creature Encountered	Numbers
01	Badger, giant*	1-4
02-16	Centipede, giant	3-13
17-27	Character — see **Character Subtable**	
28-29	Devil, lemure	2-5
30-31	Gas spore	1-2
32-38	Gnoll	4-10
39-46	Piercer	1-4
47-58	Rat, giant	6-24
59-60	Rot grub	1-4
61-72	Shrieker	1-3
73-77	Stirge	5-15
78-87	Toad, giant	1-4
88-00	Troglodyte	2-8

* Not encountered below the 3rd level; treat as a roll of 32-38 (Gnoll) thereafter.

MONSTER LEVEL III

Dice Score	Creature Encountered	Numbers
01-10	Beetle, boring	1-3
11-20	Bugbear	2-7
21-30	Character — see **Character Subtable**	
31-32	Dragon — see **Dragon Subtable** below	1
33-34	Fungi, violet	1-3
35-40	Gelatinous cube	1
41-45	Ghoul	1-4
46-50	Lizard, giant	1-3
51-54	Lycanthrope, wererat	2-5
55-60	Ochre jelly	1
61-72	Ogre	1-3
73-74	Piercer	2-5
75	Rot grub	1-4
76-77	Shrieker	2-5
78-84	Spider, huge	1-3
85-93	Spider, large	2-5
94-95	Tick, giant	1-3
96-00	Weasel, giant	1-4

Dragon Subtable

Dice Score	Dragon Type	Age Category (Hit Points/Die)
01-28	Black	very young (1)
29-62	Brass	very young (1)
63-00	White	very young (1)

Determine the number of hit dice for a dragon as normal.

MONSTER LEVEL IV

Dice Score	Creature Encountered	Numbers
01-08	Ape, carnivorous	1-3
09-14	Blink dog	2-5
15-22	Character — see **Character Subtable**	
23-24	Dragon — see **Dragon Subtable** below	1
25-30	Gargoyle	1-2
31-36	Ghast	1-4
37-40	Gray ooze	1
41-44	Hell hound	1-2
45-47	Hydra, 5 or 6 heads	1
48	Hydra, pyro-, 5 heads	1
49-62	Lycanthrope, werewolf	1-2
63-75	Mold, yellow	—
76-78	Owlbear	1-2
79	Rust monster	1
80-82	Shadow	1-3
83-90	Snake, giant, constrictor	1
91-94	Su-monster	1-2
95-96	Toad, ice	1
97-00	Toad, poisonous	1-3

Dragon Subtable

Dice Score	Dragon Type	Age Category (Hit Points/Die)
01-09	Black	young/sub-adult (2/3)
10-20	Blue	very young/young (1/2)
21-30	Brass	young/sub-adult (2/3)
31-37	Bronze	very young/young (1/2)
38-50	Copper	very young/young (1/2)
51-54	Gold	very young/young (1/2)
55-70	Green	very young/young (1/2)
71-80	Red	very young/young (1/2)
81-88	Silver	very young/young (1/2)
89-00	White	young/sub-adult (2/3)

Determine the number of hit dice for a dragon as normal.

MONSTER LEVEL V

Dice Score	Creature Encountered	Numbers
01-08	Character — see **Character Subtable**	
09-15	Cockatrice	1-2
16-18	Displacer beast	1-2
19-22	Doppleganger	1-3
23-24	Dragon — see **Dragon Subtable**	1
25-26	Hydra, 7 heads	1
27	Hydra, pyro-, 6 heads	1
28	Imp	1-2
29-31	Leucrotta	1-2
32-50	Lizard, subterranean	1-3
51-52	Lycanthrope, wereboar	1-3
53-60	Minotaur	1-3
61-64	Mold, yellow	—
65	Quasit	1
66-67	Rust Monster	1
68-70	Shrieker	2-5
71-72	Slithering Tracker	1
73-74	Snake, giant, amphisbaena	1
75-82	Snake, giant, poisonous	1
83-86	Snake, giant, spitting	1
87-00	Spider, giant	1-2

Dragon Subtable

Dice Score	Dragon Type	Age Category (Hit Points/Die)
01-08	Black	young adult/adult (4/5)
09-20	Blue	sub-adult/young adult (3/4)
21-30	Brass	young adult/adult (4/5)
31-37	Bronze	sub-adult/young adult (3/4)
38-50	Copper	sub-adult/young adult (3/4)
51-54	Gold	sub-adult/young adult (3/4)
55-70	Green	sub-adult/young adult (3/4)
71-80	Red	sub-adult/young adult (3/4)
81-88	Silver	sub-adult/young adult (3/4)
89-00	White	young adult/adult (4/5)

Determine the number of hit dice for a dragon as normal.

MONSTER LEVEL VI

Dice Score	Creature Encountered	Numbers
01-03	Basilisk	1
04-10	Carrion crawler	1-2
11-16	Character — see **Character Subtable**	
17	Devil, erinyes	1-2
18-19	Djinni	1
20-21	Dragon — see **Dragon Subtable** below	1
22-25	Green slime	---
26-28	Hydra, 8-9 heads	1
29-32	Jackalwere	1-2
33-36	Lammasu	1-3
37-38	Lycanthrope, werebear	1
39-41	Lycanthrope, weretiger	1-2
42-50	Manticore	1-2
51-55	Medusa	1
56	Mold, brown	---
57-58	Mold, yellow	---
59-60	Ogre magi	1-2
61-68	Otyugh	1
69-70	Rakshasa	1
71-73	Salamander	1-2
74-77	Spider, phase	1-3
78-88	Troll	1-3
89-93	Wight	1-4
94-95	Wind walker	1-2
96-98	Wraith	1-2
99-00	Wyvern	1

Dragon Subtable

Dice Score	Dragon Type	Age Category (Hit Points/Die)
01-08	Black	old (6)
09-19	Blue	adult (5)
20-29	Brass	old (6)
30-36	Bronze	adult (5)
37-48	Copper	adult (5)
49-52	Gold	adult (5)
53-65	Green	adult (5)
66-78	Red	adult (5)
79-87	Silver	adult (5)
88-00	White	old (6)

Determine the number of hit dice for a dragon as normal.

MONSTER LEVEL VII

Dice Score	Creature Encountered	Numbers
01-05	Black pudding	1
06-10	Character — see **Character Subtable**	
11-14	Chimera	1-2
15	Demon, succubus	1
16	Demon, type I	1
17	Demon, type II	1
18	Demon, type III	1
19	Devil, barbed	1
20	Devil, bone	1
21	Devil, horned	1
22-23	Dragon — see **Dragon Subtable** below	1
24	Efreeti	1
25-26	Elemental*	1
27-30	Ettin	1-2
31-35	Giant, hill or stone	1-3
36-38	Giant, fire or frost	1-2
39	Golem, flesh	1
40-41	Gorgon	1
42-43	Groaning spirit	1
44-46	Hydra, 10-12 heads	1
47	Hydra, pyro-, 7-9 heads	1
48-49	Intellect devourer	1
50	Invisible stalker	1
51-52	Lamia	1-2
53-56	Lizard, fire	1-3
57-59	Lurker above	1
60	Mezzodaemon	1
61-63	Mimic	1
64-65	Mind flayer	1-2

66-69	Mummy	1-2
70	Naga, spirit	1-2
71-73	Neo-otyugh	1
74	Night hag	1-2
75-78	Roper	1-2
79-82	Shambling mound	1-2
83-86	Shedu	1-2
87	Slug, giant	1
88-91	Spectre	1
92-93	Trapper	1
94-95	Umber hulk	1
96-97	Will-o-wisp	1-3
98-00	Xorn	1-3

* Choose, or use equal probabilities as applicable.

Dragon Subtable

Dice Score	Dragon Type	Age Category (Hit Points/Die)
01-10	Black	very old (7)
11-21	Blue	old (6)
22-29	Brass	very old (7)
30-36	Bronze	old (6)
37-48	Copper	old (6)
49-52	Gold	old (6)
53-66	Green	old (6)
67-80	Red	old (6)
81-87	Silver	old (6)
88-00	White	very old (7)

Determine the number of hit dice for a dragon as normal.

MONSTER LEVEL VIII

Dice Score	Creature Encountered	Numbers
01	Aerial servant	1
02-06	Character — see **Character Subtable**	
07	Demon, type IV	1
08	Demon, type V	1
09	Demon, type VI	1
10	Devil, ice	1
11-12	Dragon — see **Dragon Subtable** below	1
13-17	Ghost	1
18-21	Giant, cloud	1-2
22-23	Golem, clay	1
24-26	Hydra, 13-16 heads	1
27	Hydra, pyro-, 12 heads	1
28-29	Intellect devourer	1-2
30-35	Lurker above	1
36-41	Mold, brown	---
42-43	Mold, yellow	---
44-47	Mind flayer	1-4
48-50	Naga, guardian	1-2
51-56	Neo-otyugh	1
57-64	Purple worm	1
65-69	Rust monster	1
70-73	Slug, giant	1
74-78	Trapper	1
79-86	Vampire	1
87-92	Will-o-wisp	2-5
93-00	Xorn	2-5

Dragon Subtable

Dice Score	Dragon Type	Age Category (Hit Points/Die)
01-13	Black	ancient (8)
14-24	Blue	very old (7)
25-31	Brass	ancient (8)
32-35	Bronze	very old (7)
36-43	Copper	very old (7)
44-47	Gold	very old (7)
48-62	Green	very old (7)
63-78	Red	very old (7)
79-82	Silver	very old (7)
83-00	White	ancient (8)

Determine the number of hit dice for a dragon as normal.

MONSTER LEVEL IX

Dice Score	Creature Encountered	Numbers
01-09	Character — see **Character Subtable**	
10-12	Devil, pit fiend	1
13-15	Dragon — see **Dragon Subtable** below	1-2
16-21	Giant, storm	1-2
22-23	Golem, stone	1
24-30	Hydra, 17-20 heads	1
31-33	Hydra, pyro-, 12 heads	1
34-40	Mold, brown	1
41-50	Mold, yellow	1
51-52	Nycadaemon	1
53-64	Purple worm	1
65-67	Rust monster	1
68-69	Titan, lesser	1
70-73	Titan, minor	1
74-80	Umber Hulk	1-4
81-83	Vampire*	1
84-93	Will-o-wisp	2-5
94-00	Xorn	2-9

* Former cleric, with full powers, of 7th - 10th level.

Dragon Subtable

Dice Score	Dragon Type	Age Category (Hit Points/Die)
01-10	Black,2	ancient & old (8 & 6)
11-22	Blue	ancient (8)
23-31	Brass, 2	ancient & old (8 & 6)
32-34	Bronze	ancient (8)
35-42	Copper	ancient (8)
43-46	Gold	ancient (8)
47-62	Green	ancient (8)
63-78	Red	ancient (8)
79-82	Silver	ancient (8)
83-00	White, 2	ancient & very old (8 & 7)

Determine the number of hit dice for a dragon as normal.

MONSTER LEVEL X

Dice Score	Creature Encountered	Numbers
01-12	Beholder	1
13-20	Character — see **Character Subtable**	
21-28	Demon, prince*	1
29-30	Devil, arch-*	1
31-40	Dragon — see **Dragon Subtable** below	1-2
41-50	Golem, iron	1
51-60	Lich	1
61-70	Titan, elder	1
71-80	Vampire**	1
81-00	NO ENCOUNTER	

* Select one or find randomly.

** Former magic-user, with full powers, of 9th - 12th level.

Dragon Subtable

Dice Score	Dragon Type	Age Category (Hit Points/Die)
01-20	Blue, 2	ancient & very old (8 & 7)
21-26	Bronze,2	ancient & very old (8 & 7)
27-33	Copper,2	ancient & very old (8 & 7)
34-35	Chromatic	(Tiamat)
36-40	Gold,2	ancient & old (8 & 6)
41-60	Green, 2	ancient & very old (8 & 7)
61-63	Platinum	(Bahamut)
64-94	Red, 2	ancient & old (8 & 6)
95-00	Silver, 2	ancient & old (8 & 6)

Determine the number of hit dice for a dragon as normal.

UNDERWATER RANDOM MONSTER ENCOUNTERS

Underwater encounters are divided into those which occur in fresh water and those in salt water (seas and oceans). Each division is further broken down by depth — shallow and deep water encounters. In fresh water, shallow water encounters occur at 50' or less depth (where the vision is relatively easy). In salt water, shallow water encounters occur to twice that depth, i.e., 100'. As a reminder, the maximum depth for shallow water encounters is shown in parentheses after the designation. The numbers of monsters encountered are those shown in **MONSTER MANUAL.**

When a random monster encounter is indicated, go to the appropriate portion of the table and roll percentile dice. Read down the *Dice Score* column until the total of the dice is found, then read right to find the creature encountered. Inappropriate encounters should be ignored and a new number generated in order to gain a reasonable result. Number of creatures encountered should be appropriate to the strength of the encountering party.

UNDERWATER ENCOUNTERS IN FRESH WATER

Shallow Water Encounters (to 50')

Dice Score	Creature Encountered
01-06	Beaver, giant*
07-10	Crayfish, giant
11-18	Crocodile**
19-20	Crocodile, giant**
21-23	Dinosaur** — see **Dinosaur Subtable**
24-26	Eel, electric**
27-32	Frog, giant
33-34	Frog, giant, killer
35	Frog, giant, poisonous
36-40	Gar, giant
41-42	Green slime*
43-47	Hippocampus
48-52	Hippopotamus**
53-56	Koalinth (hobgoblin)
57-58	Kopoacinth (gargoyle)
59-60	Lacedon (ghoul)
61-65	Lamprey*
66-71	Leech, giant
72-76	Lizard man
77	Naga, water
78-81	Nixie*
82	Nymph
83-87	Otter, giant
88-90	Pike, giant
91-94	Spider, giant, water
95-99	Turtle, giant, snapping,
00	Water weird

Deep Water Encounters (below 50')

Dice Score	Creature Encountered
01	Beaver, giant*
02-06	Beetle, giant, water
07-09	Crayfish, giant
10-14	Crocodile, giant**
15-20	Dinosaur** — see **Dinosaur Subtable**
21	Dragon turtle
22-25	Eel, electric**
26-32	Gar, giant
33-34	Giant, storm
35-36	Hippocampus
37-38	Koalinth (hobgoblin)
39-43	Kopoacinth (gargoyle)
44-47	Lacedon (ghoul)
48-55	Lamprey, giant*
56-60	Lizard man
61-63	Mottled (purple) worm
64	Naga, water
65-70	Nixie
71-76	Otter, giant
77-86	Pike, giant
87-95	Spider, giant, water
96-99	Turtle, giant, snapping,
00	Water weird

* Result possible only in cool waters, otherwise roll again.

** Result possible only in warm (sub-tropical and tropical) waters, otherwise roll again.

UNDERWATER ENCOUNTERS IN LARGE BODIES OF SALT WATER

Shallow Water Encounters (to 100')

Dice Score	Creature Encountered
01-02	Barracuda
03-05	Crab, giant
06	Crayfish (lobster), giant
07-08	Dinosaur — see **Dinosaur Subtable**
09-12	Dolphin
13	Eel, giant
14-17	Eel, weed
18-19	Elf, aquatic
20-21	Eye, floating
22	Giant, storm
23-26	Hippocampus
27-28	Ixitxachitl
29-34	Koalinth (hobgoblin)
35-36	Kopoacinth (gargoyle)
37-38	Lacedon (ghoul)
39-41	Locathah
42-43	Masher
44-46	Merman
47	Nymph
48-49	Ochre jelly
50-51	Octopus, giant
52-54	Portuguese man-o-war, giant
55-56	Ray, manta
57-58	Ray, pungi
59-60	Ray, sting
61-65	Sahuagin
66	Sea hag
67-72	Sea horse
73-78	Sea lion
79-81	Shark
82	Shark, giant
83	Snake, sea
84	Squid, giant
85-87	Strangle weed
88-90	Triton
91	Turtle, giant, sea

92	Whale, carnivorous, large
93	Whale, carnivorous, medium
94-96	Whale, carnivorous, small
97	Whale, large
98	Whale, medium
99-00	Whale, small

Deep Water Encounters (below 100')

Dice Score	Creature Encountered
01-03	Crayfish (lobster), giant
04-05	Crocodile, giant (salt water)
06-12	Dinosaur — see **Dinosaur Subtable**
13-20	Dolphin
21	Dragon Turtle
22-23	Eel, giant
24	Eye of the deep
25	Giant, storm
26-30	Hippocampus
31-33	Ixitxachitl
34-35	Koalinth (hobgoblin)
36-38	Kopoacinth (gargoyle)
39-40	Lacedon (ghoul)
41-42	Lamprey, giant
43-44	Locathah
45	Masher
46-50	Merman
51-52	Morkoth
53-54	Octopus, giant
55-57	Ray, manta
58-61	Sahuagin
62-63	Sea hag
64-68	Sea horse
69-73	Sea lion
74-78	Shark, giant
79-80	Snake, sea
81-82	Squid, giant
83-85	Triton
86	Turtle, giant, sea
87-88	Whale, carnivorous, large
89-90	Whale, carnivorous, medium
91-92	Whale, carnivorous, small
93-95	Whale, large
96-98	Whale, medium
99-00	Whale, small

Darlene
3-79

ASTRAL & ETHEREAL ENCOUNTERS

Encounters occur 1 in 20; check at the beginning, midpoint, and end of the journey. If an encounter is indicated (usually 20 on the die), consult the appropriate table and roll percentile dice. Read to the right on the table to find the creature encountered and the number encountered. Evasion is possible only if the adventurers are able to move more quickly than the monster encountered.

Psychic Wind & Ether Cyclone

While you can threaten the dire effects of the *Psychic Wind* and the *Ether Cyclone*, these devices cannot be fully employed unless you have developed extensive information on the various planes, or else you have obtained commercial offerings on the subject. Becoming lost or injured is always possible, of course, and this is detailed below:

Chance For Wind Or Cyclone Blowing: The chance of a delayed or disrupted journey is 5% per plane crossed (including alternate worlds) or solar system travelled to. Effects of these forces are shown prior to the encounter tables.

ASTRALLY PROJECTED: PSYCHIC WIND

Dice Score	Effect Of Wind
1-12	Slows travel only, incurs 1 additional check for random encounter.
13-16	Blows off course, and party is lost for 2-20 days' time, then must return to starting place.
17-19	Blows off course so that party arrives at a different destination as determined by random method.
20	Storm blows, and unless a saving throw versus magic is made, the silver cord is broken, and the party is killed. If a save is successful, the party is lost for 4-40 days and must return to the starting place thereafter.

Note: If *astral projection* does not involve a silver cord attachment, then the party concerned is both lost and arrives at a different destination when struck by a *psychic storm wind*.

ETHEREAL: ETHER CYCLONE

Dice Score	Effect Of Cyclone
1-10	Blows so as to move party in random direction at 120' per round, and if travelling is involved, party is slowed so as to incur 1 additional encounter check.
11-15	Blows to a different plane than that the party is on or desires to travel to; usual encounter checks must be made.
16-18	Blows so as to cause party to be lost for 5-60 days, and when no longer lost the party will arrive at a different plane as determined by random means.
19-20	Storm cyclone causes party to be lost for 10-120 days, and unless saving throw versus magic is made, the party is blown to the Astral Plane. If a save is successful, then party will still arrive at a randomly determined plane touched by the ether.

ASTRAL & ETHEREAL ENCOUNTER TABLES

Astral Encounter Table

Dice Score	Creature Encountered	Numbers
01-04	Aerial servant	1
05-10	Basilisk*	1-2
11-13	Cockatrice*	1-4
14-16	Demon, major	1
17-22	Demon, minor	1-3
23	Demon, prince	1
24	Devil, arch-	1
25-28	Devil, greater-	1
29-37	Devil, lesser-	1-3
38	Dragon, chromatic	1
39	Dragon, platinum	1
40-41	Gorgon*	1-2
42-46	Human traveller — see **Human Subtable****	
47-49	Intellect devourer	1-2
50-55	Invisible stalker	1-3
56-61	Ki-rin	1
62-63	Medusa*	1-2
64-71	Night hag	1-4
72-74	Nightmare	1-4
75-79	Rakshasa	1-3
80-91	Shedu	2-5
92	Titan, elder	1
93-97	Titan, lesser	1
98-00	Titan, major	1

* See below next table.

** See below next table.

Ethereal Encounter Table

Dice Score	Creature Encountered	Numbers
01-05	Aerial servant	1
06-10	Basilisk*	1-2
11-13	Cockatrice*	1-4
14-18	Couatl	1-4
19-26	Djinni	1-6
27	Dragon, chromatic	1
28	Dragon, platinum	1
29-30	Efreeti	1-3
31-37	Elemental, air	1
38-39	Elemental, earth	1
40-41	Elemental, fire	1
42	Elemental, water	1
43-48	Ghost	1
49-50	Gorgon*	1-2
51-52	Groaning spirit	1-2
53-57	Human traveller — see **Human Subtable**	
58-59	Intellect devourer	1-2
60-62	Invisible stalker	1-3
63-68	Ki-rin	1
69-76	Lammasu	2-8
77-78	Medusa*	1-2
79-80	Nightmare	1-4
81-82	Salamander	2-5
83-87	Spider, phase	1-6
88-94	Thought eaters	1-3
95-97	Wind walkers	2-5
98-00	Xorn	3-6

* These creatures' perceptions extend into the astral and ethereal planes (as do their magical attack forms), but they do not actually travel therein. Their possible appearance applies only to situations in which the encounter allows effect to extend from the Prime Material Plane; otherwise, ignore the encounter result and roll again.

** The **Human Subtable** used for **DUNGEON RANDOM MONSTER ENCOUNTERS** is used, with the following modifications: Party size will be only 1-6. No limits to the number of characters of one class apply. There will always be 1 cleric; if 2 or more in the party, there will also be a minimum of 1 magic-user. Character level will be:

CLERIC	9th - 18th
Druid	7th - 14th
FIGHTER	8th - 15th
Paladin	7th - 16th
Ranger	7th - 16th
MAGIC-USER	11th - 20th
Illusionist	10th - 17th
THIEF	9th - 16th
Assassin	10th - 15th
MONK	8th - 17th
BARD†	11th - 18th

† 7th or 8th level fighter ability, 6th to 9th level (d4 for determination) thief ability.

PSIONIC ENCOUNTERS

If you opt to include psionic powers in your campaign, then certain random encounters will be with psionically-empowered creatures. Check for random encounters as is normal, but if the player party has used psionic powers during the last turn, or spells resembling psionic powers during the last round, then the chance for a psionic encounter will be 1 in 4 if an encounter is otherwise indicated. After checking for a random encounter, roll d4 to find if the encounter is psionic. If the second table is positive, go to the **PSIONIC ENCOUNTER TABLE** and check thereon to find what creature is involved. The encounter otherwise occurs as normal, although certain creatures will not be detected by the party.

Spells Resembling Psionic Powers

astral spell	enlarge	levitation
augury	ESP	plane shift
blink	feather fall	polymorph (any)
charm (any)	feign death	remove curse
clairaudience	heal	shape change
clairvoyance	heat metal	stone tell
cure (any)	hypnotism	tele- (any)
detect (any)	invisibility (any)	temporal stasis
dimension door	know alignment	

Note: Magic items performing these powers, or those which duplicate psionic abilities may be included as spell functions resembling psionic operations.

PSIONIC ENCOUNTER TABLE

Dice Score	Creature Encountered	Numbers
01-05	Brain mole	1-3
06-12	Cerebral parasite	3-12
13-15	Couatl	1-4
16-18	Demon, major*	1-2
19-24	Demon, minor*	1-4
25-26	Demon, prince*	1
27-28	Devil, arch-*	1
29-34	Devil, greater-*	1-2
35-38	Gray ooze	1-3
39-48	Intellect devourer	1-2
49-51	Ki-rin	1
52-56	Lich	1
57-62	Men (human psionic)**	—
63-69	Mind flayer	1-4
70-72	Mold, yellow	—
73-82	Shedu	2-8
83-92	Su-monster	1-12
93-98	Titan	1-2
99-00	Triton (1-3 of total are psionic)	10-60

* Dice for type or select.

** See **DUNGEON RANDOM MONSTER TABLE, Character Subtable.**

Roll until an appropriate encounter occurs, ignoring inappropriate results (or optionally considering it as *no encounter*).

OUTDOOR RANDOM MONSTER ENCOUNTERS

Outdoor encounters are divided into two sets of tables, one for areas which are inhabited and patrolled, the other for uninhabited wilderness areas.

Inhabited areas are always assumed to be patrolled. WHEN AN ENCOUNTER IN SUCH AN AREA IS INDICATED, ROLL d20; 5 IN 20 ARE ENCOUNTERS WITH A PATROL. Patrols are detailed hereafter. It is assumed that you will have all communities and fortresses indicated in inhabited areas. If not, use the random terrain indicator for such, ignoring *ruins* if you choose.

Uninhabited areas will occasionally have *fortresses*. Whenever an encounter is indicated, roll d20; 1 in 20 is an encounter which discovers such a stronghold. These are also detailed hereafter. If you are not using the random terrain method for discovery of ruins, check by rolling percentile dice on that table nonetheless. Check only when an encounter is

indicated, however. If ruins are indicated, then the encounter will occur there, and if the monster is not appropriate to the setting, check the *rough terrain* column to find a result.

Patrols:

Patrols will be of a racial composition appropriate to the area. Patrols will always be mounted unless there are extenuating circumstances such as terrain or a nation which shuns mounts. Leaders will ride warhorses.

Patrols will be commanded by a fighter (or ranger, where applicable) of from 6th to 8th level, with a lieutenant of from 4th to 5th level, and a serjeant of 2nd or 3rd level. There will be from 3 to 4 1st level men and from 13 to 24 soldiers (men-at-arms) forming the main body. Armor and arms will be plate mail, shield, lance, flail, and long sword for all fighters of 1st level and above. Soldiers will typically have chain or scale mail, shield, bow or light crossbow, and a hand weapon. Accompanying each patrol will be a cleric (40%) of 6th or 7th level or a magic-user (60%) of 5th to 8th level. For magic-items of a patrol, see **Character Subtable, Party Magic Items,** of DUNGEON RANDOM MONSTER TABLES.

It is suggested that you personalize and prepare about a dozen or so standard patrol groups which you can then use repeatedly when needed.

Fortresses:

Uninhabited areas are not all wilderness. There will be small settlements and a few strongholds scattered about. If the roll of d20 indicates that there is a fortress in the area, the party will be within visual range of the construction — ½ to 5 miles depending upon terrain considerations. The castle type, the master of the stronghold, his or her forces, and the castle's awareness of the party of adventurers are treated below.

CASTLE TABLE I: SIZE CLASS AND TYPE

Dice Roll	Size Class	Type
01-10	Small	Small shell keep
11-25	Small	Tower
26-35	Small	Moat house or friary
36-45	Medium	Large shell keep
46-65	Medium	Small walled castle with keep
66-80	Medium	Medium walled castle with keep
81-88	Large	Concentric castle
89-95	Large	Large walled castle with keep
96-00	Large	Fortress complex

For details of castle types see **CONSTRUCTION AND SIEGE ENGINES.**

Once the size and type of castle discovered has been determined, the inhabitants are found.

CASTLE TABLE II: INHABITANTS

Dice Roll	Castle Size	Inhabitants
01-45	Small	Totally deserted
46-60	Small	Deserted (monster therein)*
61-70	Small	Humans
71-00	Small	Character-types
01-30	Medium	Totally deserted
31-50	Medium	Deserted (monster therein)*
51-65	Medium	Humans
66-00	Medium	Character-types
01-15	Large	Totally deserted
16-40	Large	Deserted (monster therein)*
41-60	Large	Humans
61-00	Large	Character-types

* Roll on the appropriate **OUTDOOR ENCOUNTER TABLE,** ignoring any rolls which indicate men.

Notes on Castle Table II:

Totally deserted indicates the construction is in disrepair and upon close inspection appears empty.

Deserted castles appear as totally deserted ones, even upon close inspection, but entry into the construction will discover the monster.

Humans means that the place is occupied by bandits, brigands, etc. Determine this as follows:

CASTLE SUB-TABLE II. A.:

Dice Roll	Humans are:
01-25	Bandits
26-85	Brigands
86-97	Berserkers
98-00	Dervishes

Numbers and other details of these humans are given in the **MONSTER MANUAL** under the heading of **MEN**.

Character-types refers to the basic and sub-classes of characters:

CASTLE SUB-TABLE II.B.:

Dice Score	Master's Class And Level	
01-18	CLERIC	9th-12th
19-20	Druid	12th-13th
21-65	FIGHTER	9th-12th
66	Paladin	9th-10th
67-68	Ranger	10th-13th
69-80	MAGIC-USER	11th-14th
81-85	Illusionist*	10th-13th
86-93	THIEF	10th-14th
94-96	Assassin	14th
94-99	MONK**	9th-12th
00	BARD	23rd

* Illusionists' strongholds will often be covered by an *illusion* to appear as a mound of rock, a ruined place or a huge castle.

** Monks' strongholds will usually be monasteries, resembling a type of enlarged moat house, having fewer of the defensive constructions of a typical castle — but being nonetheless formidable.

For magic items possessed by the stronghold's master, as well as for discovering the level of his or her henchmen, use the **Character Subtable** of the **DUNGEON RANDOM MONSTER TABLES**. There will be from 2-5 henchmen found within a fortress. Certain character types will have special followers, and these will be found there also. However, except for the clerical profession, these followers will not serve as the main castle garrison. These men-at-arms will be:

    9-12 heavy horse, splint mail & shield, lance, long sword, mace
    9-16 light horse, studded leather, light crossbow, long sword
    13-24 men-at-arms, scale mail, shield, spear, hand axe
    7-12 men-at-arms, scale mail, heavy crossbow, morning star

Cavalry will be stabled and fight on the walls when necessary. Each of the above units will be led by a fighter of 3rd or 4th level with normal chances for magic items. Leaders are in addition to the figures shown.

Fortresses will be stocked with food, water, and supplies of arms and missiles. Each will have artillery and sufficient crew to operate each engine as follows:

Fortress Type	Ballistae Scorpions	Light Catapults	Oil Cauldrons
Moat house	2	-	1
Tower	1	-	1
Shell keep	-	1	2
Small castle	1	1	2
Small concentric castle	2	1	4
Medium castle	2	2	5
Medium concentric castle	4	2	6
Large castle	4	4	8

To determine if the occupants of the stronghold are aware of the party of adventurers, roll a surprise die for the latter, and if they are surprised, then the fortress occupants know they are there — if surprise is 2 or greater, the occupants are actually outside the place and within normal surprise distance of the party of adventurers. Otherwise, the adventurers have not been detected, and they may opt to pass the place by or go and investigate it.

The reactions of the castle or other type of stronghold to the adventurer party are discovered as normally done. Friendly or hostile reactions will be dictated by the culture and society of the area. For instance, if you have the area as a typical medieval European fantasy one, a friendly reaction will result in the host party welcoming the adventurers, feting them, and offering an escort to the borders of their territory when they choose to leave (but meanwhile entertaining them royally with hunts, drinking bouts, etc.) A neutral reaction would be refusal to allow them into the place without facing one or more of their fighters in some form of non-lethal combat (such as jousting), and taking armor and weapons from them if they lose; or it could as well be a demand for a toll to pass through, meanwhile keeping the castle gates shut tight. A hostile reaction could be feigning good fellowship, getting the adventurers drunk, and then stripping them and imprisoning them for ransom; or it could result in immediate attack. You must decide.

OUTDOOR RANDOM MONSTER ENCOUNTER TABLES

Arctic Conditions

Creature Type	Predominant Terrain		
	Plain	Rough*	Mountains
Bear, brown[a]	01-10	01-09	01-07
Dragon, white	11-12	10-12	08-15
Giant, frost	13-15	13-15	16-20
Herd animal	16-55	16-55	21-55
Men, tribesmen	56-65	56-60	56-60
Owl, giant	66-70	61-70	61-70
Remorhaz	71-72	71-75	71-72
Snake, giant, constrictor[b]	73-74	76-80	73-75
Toad, ice	75-80	81-83	76-80
Wolf	81-90	84-91	81-86
Wolf, winter	91-95	92-95	87-90
Yeti	96-00	96-00	91-00

* Includes ruins (cities, temples, fortresses) within up to five miles of the party.

[a] This is treated the same as a brown bear, but it is a white-coated polar bear.

[b] This is treated the same as a giant constrictor, but it is a white, furred, snake.

Monsters in *italic* type are 75% likely to be encountered while they are airborne.

Sub-Arctic Conditions

Creature Type	Plain	Scrub	Forest	Predominant Terrain			Marsh
				Rough*	Hills	Mountains	
Bear, brown	—	01-05	01-10	01-05	01-05	—	—
Bear, cave	—	—	11-15	06-10	06-10	—	—
Dragon, white	01-05	06-10	—	11-15	11-15	01-15	—
Giant, frost	06-10	11-15	16-20	16-20	16-20	16-30	01-05
Gnoll	11-15	16-20	21-25	21-25	21-25	31-35	06-20
Hell hound	—	—	26-27	26-27	26-27	36-40	—
Herd animal	16-40	21-40	28-38	28-40	28-50	41-60	21-50
Lynx, giant	—	—	39-45	—	—	—	—
Mammoth	41-45	41-50	46-50	—	—	—	—
Mastadon	46-55	51-55	51-55	—	—	—	—
Men, tribesmen	56-65	56-65	56-65	41-50	51-60	—	51-55
*Owl, giant***	66-70	66-70	66-70	51-55	61-65	61-65	56-65
Ram, giant	—	—	—	56-60	66-70	66-70	66-75
Rat, giant	—	—	71-75	61-65	—	—	76-85
Remorhaz	—	—	—	66-67	—	71-75	—
Rhino, woolly	71-80	71-80	—	—	71-75	—	—
Tiger	81-90	81-90	76-80	68-75	76-80	—	—
Toad, ice	—	—	—	—	—	—	86-90
Troll	—	—	81-85	76-80	81-85	76-85	91-00
Wolf	91-00	91-00	86-95	81-90	86-92	86-92	—
Wolf, winter	—	—	—	—	—	—	—
Wolverine	—	—	—	—	93-94	93-95	—
Wolverine, giant	—	—	96-98	91-96	95-96	—	—
Yeti	—	—	—	99-00	99-00	96-00	—

* Includes ruins within up to five miles of the party.

** Night only, except in forest and not airborne (25%).

Temperate And Sub-Tropical Conditions

Uninhabited/Wilderness Areas

Creature Type	Plain	Scrub	Forest	Predominant Terrain				Marsh
				Rough*	Desert	Hills	Mountains	
Ant, giant	01	01	01	01	—	01	—	—
Badger	—	—	02	02-03	—	—	—	—
Badger, giant	—	—	—	04	—	—	—	—
Bear, brown	02	02	03-04	05	—	02-03	01-02	—
Beaver, giant	—	—	—	—	—	—	—	01
Beetle, bombardier	—	—	05	—	—	—	—	—
Beetle, stag	—	—	06	—	—	—	—	—
Beholder	—	—	—	—	—	—	—	02
Blink dog	03	03	07	06	01	04	03	—
Boar, wild	04	04-05	08	07	—	—	—	—
Bugbear	05	06	09	08	—	05-08	04-05	—
Bull/Cattle, wild	06-09	07-08	10	—	—	09	—	—
Catoblepas	—	—	—	—	—	—	—	03-05
Demi-human[a]	10	09	11	09	—	10-20	06-07	—
Displacer beast	—	—	12	10	—	—	08	06
Dog, wild	11-12	10	13	11	02-05	21-22	09	—
Dragon[b]	13-14	11	14	12	06-07	23-24	10-11	07
Dragonne	—	—	—	13	08	—	12	—
Eagle, giant	15	—	15	14	09	25	13-14	08
Frog[c]	—	—	—	—	—	—	—	09-15
Gargoyle	—	—	—	—	—	—	15-16	16
Giant[d]	17-18	12-13	16	15-16	—	26-27	17-28	—
Goat, giant	—	—	—	17	—	28-30	29	—
Griffon	19	14	17	18	10-11	31-32	30	—
Herd animal	20-25	15-20	18-20	19-20	12	33-35	—	—
Hippogriff	26-27	21-22	21-22	21-22	13-14	36-37	31-32	—
Horse, wild	28-30	23-25	23-25	23-25	15-19	38-39	—	—
Humanoid[e]	31-33	26-32	26-30	26-30	20-28	40-50	33-40	17-30
Jackal**	34-38	33-34	—	—	—	—	—	—
Ki-rin/Lammasu/Shedu	39	35	31	31	29-30	51	41	31
Leprechaun/Brownie	—	—	32	—	—	52-53	—	—
Leucrotta	—	—	—	32-33	—	—	42	32
Lion	40-49	36-40	33-35	34-35	31-40	54-55	—	—
Lizard, giant	—	—	36	36-37	41-44	—	—	33-36
Lycanthrope[f]	50	—	37-38	38-39	—	56-58	43-45	—
Lynx, giant	—	—	39-40	—	—	—	—	—
Men[g]	51-70	41-60	41-50	40-50	45-69	59-70	46-60	37-52
Ogre***	71-74	61-65	51-55	51-55	—	71-75	61-65	—
Owl, giant	75	66	56-58	56	70	76	66	53
Owlbear	—	—	59-60	—	—	—	—	54

				Predominant Terrain				
Creature Type	Plain	Scrub	Forest	Rough*	Desert	Hills	Mountains	Marsh
Pegasus	76-77	67	—	57	71-74	77	67	—
Porcupine/Skunk	—	68-69	61-63	58	—	78	—	—
Pseudo-dragon	—	70	64-65	—	—	—	—	—
Shambling mound	—	—	66	—	—	—	—	55-58
Snake[h]	78	71	67-68	59-60	75-79	79	68	59-72
Sphinx[i]	—	—	69-70	61-63	80-89	80-81	69-72	73-78
Spider[j]	79-80	72-80	71-73	64-65	90-93	82-83	—	—
Stag	81	81-85	74-76	66	—	84-87	—	—
Tick, giant	—	86	77-78	—	—	—	—	—
Toad, giant	82	87	79	67	—	88	—	79-83
Treant	—	—	80-84	—	—	—	—	—
Troll	83-84	88	85	68-75	—	89	73-78	84-86
Undead*	—	—	86-87	76-80	—	90-91	79-83	87-92
Wasp, giant	85-86	89	88	81-82	94-95	92	—	93-94
Weasel, giant	87	90-91	89	83-84	—	93	84-86	95-96
Will-o-wisp	—	—	90	85-86	—	—	87-92	97-00
Wind walker	—	—	—	—	—	—	93-94	—
Wolf	88-97	92-97	91-97	87-97	96-00	94-98	95-96	—
Wolf, worg	98-00	98-00	98-00	98-00	—	99-00	97-00	—

* Includes ruins within up to five miles of the party.

** 10% of these encounters will be with *jackalwere*.

*** 10% of these encounters will be with *ogre magi*.

[a] Demi-Human Subtable

Demi-Human	Plain	Scrub	Forest	Rough	Hills	Mountains
Dwarf	01-05	01-05	01-05	01-10	01-20	01-70
Elf	06-70	06-60	06-70	11-15	21-30	71-75
Gnome	71-80	61-80	71-95	16-85	31-70	76-95
Halfling	81-00	81-00	96-00	86-00	71-00	96-00

[b] Dragon Subtable (base 50% chance of encounter while creature airborne)

Dragon Type	Plain	Scrub	Forest	Rough	Desert	Hills	Mountains	Marsh
Black	01-02	01-02	01-16	01-30	01-02	01-06	01-04	01-50
Blue	03-04	03-04	17-18	31-32	03-20	07-10	05-15	51-52
Brass	05-06	05-06	19-20	33-40	21-65	11-20	16-17	53-54
Bronze	07-08	07-08	21-22	41-45	66-67	21-25	18-25	55-56
Chimera	09-10	09-10	24-30	46-50	68-70	26-35	26-30	57-58
Copper	11-12	11-14	31-35	51-55	71-80	36-45	31-40	59-60
Gold	13-28	15-16	36-40	56-57	81-82	46-50	41-45	61-62
Green	29-30	17-36	41-80	58-59	83-84	51-52	46-47	63-75
Red	31-32	37-38	81-82	60-64	85-88	53-60	48-60	76-77
White	33-34	39-40	83-84	65-66	89-90	61-65	61-95	78-79
Wyvern	35-00	41-00	85-00	67-00	91-00	66-00	96-00	80-00

[c] Frog Subtable

Frog Type	Marsh
Giant	01-70
Killer	71-80
Poisonous	81-00

[d] Giant Subtable

Giant Type	Plain	Scrub	Forest	Rough	Hills	Mountains
Cloud	01-02	01-02	01-02	01-02	01-03	01-15
Ettin	03-04	03-05	03-10	03-10	04-10	16-20
Fire	05-06	06-07	11-12	11-20	11-15	21-30
Frost	07-08	08-09	13-14	21-25	16-20	31-45
Hill	09-95	10-94	15-93	26-85	21-81	46-50
Stone	96-98	95-98	94-98	86-98	81-98	51-90
Storm	99	99	99	99	99	91-98
Titan	00	00	00	00	00	99-00

[e] Humanoid Subtable

Humanoid	Plain	Scrub	Forest	Rough	Hills	Mountains	Marsh
Gnoll	01-05	01-10	01-10	01-20	01-25	01-15	01-25
Goblin	06-10	11-15	11-20	21-30	26-50	16-50	26-35
Hobgoblin	11-15	16-50	21-30	31-50	51-75	51-65	36-75
Kobold	—	51-80	31-80	51-55	—	—	—
Orc	16-00	81-00	81-00	56-00	76-00	66-00	76-00

j **Lycanthrope Subtable**

Lycanthrope	Plain	Forest	Rough	Hills	Mountains
Werebear	01-02	01-10	01-02	01-02	01-75
Wereboar	03-25	11-70	03-15	03-15	—
Wererat	26-30	—	16-90	16-20	76-80
Weretiger	31-40	71-90	—	21-30	81-90
Werewolf	41-00	91-00	91-00	31-00	91-00

g **Men Subtable**

Men Type	Plain	Scrub	Forest	Rough	Desert	Hills	Mountains	Marsh
Bandit	01-05	01-10	01-10	01-10	01-05	01-10	01-05	01-05
Berserker	06-07	11-12	—	11-12	—	11-12	06-10	—
Brigand	08-10	13-15	11-15	06-10	06-10	13-20	11-20	06-10
Character	see special note hereafter pertaining to **Characters** — 10% in all cases							
Dervish	21-22	26-27	—	26-27	21-50	31-40	31-35	—
Merchant	23-60	28-60	26-40	28-50	51-75	41-65	36-50	21-35
Nomad	61-90	61-80	—	51-60	76-95	66-80	—	—
Pilgrim	91-95	81-85	41-45	61-80	96-00	81-90	51-65	36-30
Tribesman	96-00	86-00	46-00	81-00	—	91-00	66-00	31-00

h **Snake Subtable**

Snake Type	Plain	Scrub	Forest	Rough	Desert	Hills	Mountains	Marsh
Amphisbaena	01-10	01-05	—	—	01-15	01-05	—	—
Constrictor	—	06-10	01-65	01-05	—	06-10	—	01-70
Poisonous	11-80	11-80	66-95	06-95	16-90	11-90	01-90	71-00
Spitting	81-00	81-00	96-00	96-00	91-00	91-00	91-00	—

i **Sphinx Subtable**

Sphinx Type	Forest	Rough	Desert	Hills	Mountains	Marsh
Andro-	01-05	01-10	01-40	01-10	01-15	01-05
Crio-	06-75	11-30	41-50	11-70	16-35	06-55
Gyno-	76-80	31-50	51-90	71-80	36-55	56-65
Hieraco-	81-00	51-00	91-00	81-00	56-00	66-00

j **Spider Subtable**

Spider Type	Plain	Scrub	Forest	Rough	Desert	Hills
Giant	—	—	01-55	—	—	—
Huge	01-15	01-25	56-75	01-20	—	01-20
Large	16-00	26-00	76-80	21-00	01-00	21-00
Phase	—	—	81-00	—	—	—

k **Undead Subtable**

Undead Type	Forest	Rough	Hills	Mountains	Marsh
Ghast	01-10	01-15	01-10	01-10	01-15
Ghost	11-12	16-20	11-12	11-13	16-18
Ghoul	13-55	21-55	13-35	14-30	19-75
Lich	56	56-60	36-40	31-35	—
Mummy	—	61-70	41-55	36-40	—
Shadow	57-70	71-84	56-61	41-50	76-81
Spectre	71-79	85-87	62-64	51-60	82-91
Vampire	80-89	88-89	65-74	61-75	92-93
Wight	90-96	90-98	75-97	76-94	—
Wraith	97-00	99-00	98-00	95-00	94-00

Special Note Regarding Characters Encountered In Uninhabited/Wilderness Areas: It is suggested that you use typical parties of dungeon characters for such encounters (90% will be mounted, warhorses where applicable, 10% afoot). Character level will range from 7th through 10th, with henchmen of approximately one-half (round up) character level. Mounted fighters will have lances, those afoot will have spears.

Temperate And Sub-Tropical Conditions

Inhabited And/Or Patrolled Areas

Creature Type	Plain	Scrub	Forest	Predominant Terrain Rough*	Desert	Hills	Mountains	Marsh
Anhkheg	01-02	01	01-02	—	—	01	—	—
Ant, giant	03-05	02	03-04	01-02	—	02	—	—
Bear, black	—	03-04	05-07	03-04	—	—	01-02	01-05
Beetle, bombardier	06	05	08-09	—	—	03	—	—
Beetle, stag	07	06	10-11	—	—	—	—	—
Boar, wild	08-10	07-08	12-14	05-06	—	04-05	—	06-08
Bulette	11	09	—	—	—	06	—	—
Dwarf	—	—	—	07-08	—	07-08	03-15	—

	Predominant Terrain							
Creature Type	Plain	Scrub	Forest	Rough*	Desert	Hills	Mountains	Marsh
Elf	12	10-11	15-18	—	—	09-10	—	—
Ghast	—	—	—	09-10*	—	—	—	—
Ghost	—	—	—	11*	—	—	—	—
Ghoul	—	—	—	12-14*	—	—	—	09-10
Giant, hill	13	12	19	15-16	—	11-15	16-17	—
Gnoll	14-15	13	20	17-18	01-03	16-17	18-19	11-13
Gnome	16	—	21-22	19-20	—	18-21	20-21	—
Goblin	17-18	—	23	21-22	—	22-23	22-24	—
Groaning spirit	19	14	—	—	—	24	—	14
Halfling	20-21	15	24	—	—	25-27	—	—
Hobgoblin	22	16-17	25	23	—	28	25-26	15
Leprechaun	23	—	—	—	—	29-30	—	—
Lycanthrope, -bear	—	—	26	—	—	—	27	—
Lycanthrope, -boar	—	18-19	27	—	—	—	—	—
Lycanthrope, -rat	—	20	—	24-25	—	—	—	16
Lycanthrope, -tiger	24	21	28	—	—	—	—	—
Lycanthrope, -wolf	25-26	—	29	26	—	31	28-29	17
Manticore	27	22	—	27	04-07	32	30	18-19
Men, bandit	28-32	23-27	30-32	28-32	08-12	33-36	31-32	20-22
Men, berserker	33-34	28-29	33-35	33-34	13-14	37-38	33-34	23-24
Men, brigand	35-38	30-34	36-40	35-39	15-19	39-44	35-39	25-29
Men, dervish	39-40	35-36	41-42	40-44	20-30	45-46	40-41	—
Men, merchant	41-68	37-56	43-55	45-55	31-56	47-60	42-51	—
Men, nomad	69-70	57-58	—	56-57	57-76	61-62	—	—
Men, pilgrim	71-80	59-69	56-60	58-63	77-84	63-67	52-59	30-31
Ogre	81-83	70-76	61-70	64-69	—	68-75	60-67	32-40
Orc	84-87	77-86	71-82	70-82	85-94	76-85	68-80	41-60
Rat, giant	88-89	87-89	83-85	83-85	—	86-88	—	61-75
Skunk, giant	90-91	90-91	86-91	86-87	—	89-90	—	—
Vampire	92	—	92	—	95	—	81-87	76-80
Will-o-wisp	—	—	—	88-89	—	—	88-89	81-00
Wolf	93-00	92-00	93-00	90-00	96-00	91-00	90-00	—

* Includes ruins (cities, temples, fortresses, etc.) within up to five miles of the party.

Temperate Conditions

Faerie And Sylvan Settings

Creature Type	Plain	Forest	Hills	Mountains
Ape, carnivorous	—	01-03	—	01-02
Basilisk	—	04	01	03
Bear, brown	—	05-08	02-03	04-08
Boar, wild, giant	01-02	09-11	04-05	—
Brownie	—	13	06-08	—
Bull, wild	03-08	14-15	09-10	—
Centaur	09-12	16	11-14	—
Chimera	13-14	17	15-16	09-14
Cockatrice	—	18	—	15
Dryad	—	19	—	—
Dwarf	—	—	17-18	16-22
Elf	15	20-22	19-22	23
Ettin	16-18	23	23	24-26
Gnome	—	24-25	24-27	27-28
Gorgon	19-21	26	28	29
Griffon	22-25	27	29-30	30-31
Harpy	26	—	31	32-33
Hippogriff	27-30	—	32-33	34-36
Leopard	31-32	28-31	34	37
Lion, mountain	—	—	35	38-39
Manticore	33-36	32-33	36-37	40
Men, bandit	37-38	34-38	38-39	41
Men, dervish	39-41	39	40-41	42
Men, pilgrim	42-46	40-41	42-43	43-44
Men, tribesmen	47-51	42-44	44-46	45
Ogre	52-59	45-47	47-48	46-50
Pegasus	60-65	—	49	51-55
Peryton	66-69	48-50	50-51	56-58
Pixie	70-76	51-55	52-53	—
Satyr	77	56-65	54-55	—
Sprite	78-79	66-70	56-57	—
Stag, giant	80-81	71-75	58-60	59-60
Stirge	82-83	76-78	61-65	61-65
Su-monster	—	79-85	—	—
Sylph	84-86	86	66-70	66-70
Troll	87-88	87-88	71-75	71-85
Unicorn	89-90	89-96	76-80	—
Wolf	91-00	97-00	81-00	86-00

Pleistocene Conditions

				Predominant Terrain			
Creature Type	Plain	Scrub	Forest	Rough	Hills	Mountains	Marsh
Axe beak	01-05	01-02	—				
Baluchitherium	06-10	03-07	01-05	—	—	—	—
Bear, cave		—	06-07	01-05	01-05	01-20	—
Boar, wild, giant	11-13	08-12	08-12	06-09	06-10	—	—
Bull	14-16	13-14	13-14		11-13	—	—
Camel	—	15-17	15-17	—		—	—
Cattle, wild	17-21	18-20	18-19	10-11	14-16	—	—
Crocodile, giant	—	21-23**	—	12-15**	—	—	01-20
Flightless bird	22-26	24-25	—	16-25	17-20		21-70
Herd animal	27-50	26-50	20-50	26-65	21-50	—	71-90
Hyena, giant	51-55	51-55		66-75	51-55	21-50	
Irish deer	—	—	51-55		56-60	51-60	—
Lion, spotted	56-57	56-57	56-60	76-85	61-65	61-70	
Mammoth	58-65	58-65	61-65	—	66-70	—	—
Mastadon	66-70	66-70	66-70	—	71-75	—	—
Men, cavemen	—	—	71-75	86-90	76-80	71-90	91-98***
Rhino, wooly	71-75	71-75			81-85	—	—
Stag, giant	76-80	76-80	76-80		86-90	—	—
Snake, giant, constrictor	—	—	81-82	—			99-00
Tiger, sabre-tooth	81-87	81-90	83-90	—	91-92	—	
Titanothere	88-95	91-95	—	—	—	—	—
Weasel, giant*	96-98	96-98	91-95	—	93-95	—	—
Wolf, dire	99-00	99-00	96-00	91-00	96-00	91-00	—

* Simulates a class of early carnivores — describe the creature as "cat-like", but with short legs and long body.

** If water is also nearby; otherwise treat as cattle, wild.

*** Simulates "shovel-toothed" proboscidia.

Sub-Tropical To Tropical Conditions

Prehistoric Settings, Age Of Dinosaurs

Dinosaur Type	Plain	Scrub	Forest	Marsh
Anatosaurus	01-10	01-06	01-08	01-12
Ankylosaurus	11-12	07-10	—	—
Antrodemus	—	11-12	09-14	—
Apatosaurus	13†	13†	15-19†	13-18
Brachiosaurus	14†	14†	20†	19-23
Camarasaurus	15	15-17	21-23	24-28
Ceratosaurus	—	18-22	24-28	—
Cetiosaurus	16†	23†	29†	29-34
Crocodile, giant	—	—	—	35-40
Diplodocus	17†	24†	30†	41-48
Gorgosaurus	18-20	25-28	—	—
Iguanadon/Lambeosaurus	21-40	29-35	31-40	49-56
Lizard, giant	—	—	41-45	57-60
Lizard, minotaur	41-42	—	—	61-63
Megalosaurus	—	—	46-50	—
Monoclonius	43-46	36-41	—	—
Miscellaneous Small-Medium Reptiles*	47-53	42-47	51-55	64-65
Nothosaurus**	—	—	—	66-71
Paleoscincus	—	—	56-63	72-76
Pentaceratops	54-67	48-54	—	—
Plateosaurus	—	55-60	64-80	—
Pterodactyl, small*	68-69	61-62	—	77-82
Pteranodon	70-76	63-67	—	83-89
Snake, giant, constrictor	—	68-69	81-85	90-00
Stegosaurus	—	70-82	86-95	—
Styracosaurus	77-79	83-87	—	—
Teratosaurus	80-82	88-89	96-00	—
Triceratops	83-92	90-95	—	—
Tyrannosaurus Rex	93-00	96-00	—	—

† If water body is nearby; otherwise roll again.

* Basically small or inoffensive creatures which can not be immediately distinguished as such by onlookers.

** The nothosaurus is to be treated as a megalosaurus in all respects save habitat and movement, the latter being 6"//12".

The creatures listed above are not all from the same geological period, but they provide a highly interesting mixture for adventuring. Feel free to devise your own encounter matrix for Jurassic, Triassic, or other period with non-aberrant creatures.

Tropical And Near-Tropical Conditions

Uninhabited/Wilderness Areas

Creature Type	Plain	Scrub	Forest	Predominant Terrain Rough*	Desert	Hills	Mountains	Marsh
Ant, giant	01-02	01-02	01-02	01-02	—	01-02	—	—
Ape	—	—	03-05	—	—	—	—	—
Baboon	—	03-05	06	03-07	01-04	—	01-03	—
Bear, black	—	—	07-09	08-09	—	—	04-06	—
Beetle, rhinoceros	—	—	10-12	—	—	—	—	—
Boar, warthog	03-05	06-08	—	10-13	—	—	—	—
Buffalo	06-10	09-12	—	14-15	—	03-07	—	01-10
Camel	—	—	—	—	05-11	—	—	—
Centipede, giant	—	—	13-16	—	12-14	—	—	—
Couatl	—	—	17-18	—	—	—	—	—
Crocodile	—	—	—	—	—	—	—	11-35
Elephant	—	13-16	19-24	—	—	08-10	—	—
Elephant, loxodont	—	17-20	25-30	—	—	—	—	—
Flightless bird	11-16	21-22	—	—	—	—	—	—
Herd animal	17-35	23-35	31-33	16-18	15-16	11-20	07-10	—
Hippopotamus	—	—	—	—	—	—	—	36-50
Hyena	36-40	36-40	—	19-25	—	21-25	—	—
Jackal	41-44	41-44	—	26-29	17-24	26-29	—	—
Jackalwere	45	45	—	30	25	30	—	—
Jaguar	—	—	34-38	—	—	—	—	—
Lamia	—	—	39-40	31-35	26-28	—	—	—
Lammasu/Shedu	—	46	—	36-38	29-35	31-32	11-15	—
Leech, giant	—	—	—	—	—	—	—	51-60
Leopard	—	47-50	41-47	39-40	36-37	—	16-20	—
Lion	46-55	51-55	48-50	—	38-40	33-38	—	—
Lizard, minotaur	—	—	—	41-45	—	—	—	—
Lycanthrope, -tiger	—	—	51-52	—	—	39-40	21-22	—
Men, bandit**	56-59	56-59	53-56	46-48	41-45	41-45	23-28	—
Men, dervish	60	—	—	49-50	46-55	46-47	29-30	—
Men, merchant	61-68	60-65	—	51-53	56-65	48-55	31-35	—
Men, nomad	69-70	—	—	54-60	66-81	56-63	—	—
Men, pilgrim	—	—	—	61-68	82-83	64-68	36-38	—
Men, tribesman	—	66-71	57-60	69-72	—	69-74	39-50	61-73
Naga, guardian	—	—	—	73-74	—	75	51-53	—
Naga, spirit	—	—	—	75-76	—	76-78	54-55	74-75
Rakshasa	—	—	—	77-80	—	79-80	56-60	—
Rhinoceros	71-80	72-77	—	—	—	—	—	—
Roc	81-85	78-84	—	81-83	—	81-85	61-70	—
Scorpion, giant	86-90	85-86	61-64	84-85	84-89	—	—	—
Snake, amphisbaena	91-92	—	—	—	90-91	—	—	—
Snake, constricting	—	—	65-70	—	—	—	—	76-80
Snake, poisonous	—	87-92	71-74	86-88	92-93	—	71-75	81-85
Snake, spitting	93-95	—	75-76	89-90	94-95	86-87	—	—
Spectre	—	—	—	91-93	—	—	—	—
Sphinx^a	—	—	—	94-95	96-00	88-90	76-80	—
Spider, giant	—	—	77-80	—	—	—	—	—
Spider, huge	—	—	81-86	—	—	—	—	—
Spider, large	—	93-95	—	—	—	—	—	86-89
Tiger	—	—	87-95	—	—	91-95	81-90	—
Toad, giant	—	—	96-98	—	—	—	—	90-96
Toad, giant, poisonous	—	—	99-00	—	—	—	—	97-00
Wolf/Wild dog	96-00	96-00	—	96-00	—	96-00	91-00	—

* Includes ruins within up to five miles of the party.

** Slavers.

^aSphinx Subtable

01-10	Androsphinx
11-40	Criosphinx
41-70	Gynosphinx
71-00	Hieracosphinx

WATERBORNE ENCOUNTERS

Fresh Water

Encounter occurs 1 in 20, check morning, evening, and midnight. Un-intelligent monsters will be 75% likely to be driven off by flaming oil near-by, 90% if actually burned by it. Large amounts of food will be 50% likely to end encounters.

Salt Water

Encounter occurs 1 in 20, check dawn and noon in coastal and shallow waters, check only once during daylight (usually noon) in deep water. Burning oil works as noted above for fresh water encounters, as will food.

WATERBORNE RANDOM MONSTER ENCOUNTERS

FRESH WATER

Small Body Of Water

Dice Score	Creature Encountered
01-15	Beaver, giant*
16-30	Crocodile**
31-40	Hippopotamus**
41-60	Lizard man
61-65	Nixie*
66-70	Nymph
71-85	Otter, giant
86-98	Turtle, snapping, giant
99-00	Water weird

Large Body Of Water

Dice Score	Creature Encountered
01-02	Beaver, giant*
03-04	Crayfish, giant
05-06	Crocodile**
07-10	Crocodile, giant**
11-15	Dinosaur — see **Dinosaur Subtable**
16-21	Gar, giant
22-23	Hippopotamus**
24-26	Koalinth (hobgoblin)
27-28	Kopoacinth (gargoyle)
29	Lacedon (ghoul)
30-33	Lizard man
34-48	Man, buccaneer (or warship)
49-78	Man, merchant
79-84	Man, pirate
85	Naga, water
86-90	Nixie*
91-93	Otter, giant
94-97	Pike, giant
98-99	Turtle, snapping, giant
00	Water weird

* Result possible only in cool waters, otherwise roll again.

** Result possible only in warm waters, otherwise roll again.

Small bodies of water include large ponds, fens, small lakes to medium-sized ones, and rivers other than major ones which can carry large shipping.

Large bodies of water include large lakes, great lakes, and major rivers.

SALT WATER

Shallow Waters, Coastal Waters, Small Inland Seas

Dice Score	Creature Encountered
01-02	Crocodile, giant**
03-10	Dinosaur — see **Dinosaur Subtable**
11-17	Dolphin
18	Dragon turtle
19-20	Elf, Aquatic
21	Ixitxachitl
22-23	Koalinth (hobgoblin)
24	Kopoacinth (gargoyle)
25	Lacedon (ghoul)
26	Locathah
27-35	Man, buccaneer (warship)
36-63	Man, merchant
64-67	Man, pirate
68-70	Man, pirate (tribesman with small craft)
71-73	Merman
74	Nymph
75	Octopus, giant
76-80	Sahuagin
81-83	Shark, giant
84-86	Snake, sea
87-89	Triton
90	Turtle, giant, sea
91-96	Whale, carnivorous, small
97-00	Whale, small

Deep Waters

Dice Score	Creature Encountered
01-05	Dinosaur — see **Dinosaur Subtable**
06-13	Dolphin
14	Dragon turtle
15-16	Man, buccaneer (warship)
17-25	Man, merchant
26-27	Man, pirate
28-35	Merman
36-40	Octopus, giant
41-45	Sahuagin
46-50	Shark, giant
51-53	Snake, sea
54-55	Squid, giant
56-65	Triton
66-68	Turtle, giant, sea
69-72	Whale, carnivorous, large
73-78	Whale, carnivorous, medium
79-85	Whale, carnivorous, small
86-90	Whale, large
91-95	Whale, medium
96-00	Whale, small

Dinosaur Subtable

Dice Score	Creature Encountered
01-15	Archelon ischyras
16-35	Dinicthys*
36-55	Elasmosaurus**
56-75	Mosasaurus**
76-00	Plesiosaurus**

* Encountered only in deep water, otherwise roll again.

** If encounter occurs in fresh water, it must be in a relatively warm clime (sub-tropical), otherwise roll again.

AIRBORNE RANDOM MONSTER ENCOUNTERS

When the party is travelling by means of flying, simply use the appropriate **OUTDOOR RANDOM MONSTER ENCOUNTERS** table. Check at every opportunity (four times in the daylight, twice if flying at night also, or four times if flying at night only), but an encounter occurs only if the creature indicated is able to fly or is actually flying.

CITY/TOWN ENCOUNTERS

The prime city or cities/town or towns in a campaign will usually have pre-determined denizens and many encounters will be set according to facts thus developed. All sections of these prime inhabited areas will not be matrixed, and all other cities/towns will be basically undeveloped. For all such areas the CITY/TOWN ENCOUNTER MATRIX is useful.

All encounters must be in their appropriate areas. A ghost will not be encountered in the main square of a city, rats in a palace, etc. If the roll indicates an improbable encounter, just ignore it, and no encounter has taken place. Check for encounters every three turns as normally, or otherwise as desired.

Disguise all encounters by using vagueness and similarity.

CITY/TOWN ENCOUNTERS MATRIX

Daytime Dice Roll	Nighttime Dice Roll	Result
01	01-03	Assassin*
02	04-05	Bandit
03-12	06-08	Beggar
13	09-10	Brigand
14-18	11	City guard*
19-21	12	City official
22-23	13-21	City watchman
24-25	22	Cleric*
—	23	Demon or Nycadaemon (60%/40%)
—	24	Devil or Mezzodaemon (50%/50%)
—	25	Doppleganger
26	26	Druid*
27	27-31	Drunk
28-29	32-33	Fighter*
30-33	34-35	Gentleman
—	36	Ghast or Ghoul (30%/70%)
—	37	Ghost
34	38-42	Giant rats
35-39	43	Goodwife
40-41	44-50	Harlot
42	51	Illusionist*
43-50	52	Laborer or Peddler (50%/50%)
51	53	Magic-user*
52-55	54-58	Mercenary
56-62	59-60	Merchant
63	61	Monk or Bard (60%/40%)
—	62	Night hag
64-65	63-64	Noble
66	65	Paladin
67-69	66	Pilgrim
70	67	Press Gang
71-72	68-71	Rake
—	72	Rakshasa
73	73	Ranger*
74-78	74-80	Ruffian**
—	81	Shadow
—	82	Spectre
79-82	83-88	Thief*
83-97	89-90	Tradesman
98	91-93	Wererat
99	94	Weretiger
00	95-96	Werewolf
—	97	Wight
—	98	Will-o-wisp
—	99	Wraith
—	00	Vampire or Lich (75%/25%)

* Check to see if race is human or demi-human:

01-08	Dwarven	16-23	Half-elven	31-00	Human
09-13	Elven	24-25	Halfling		
14-15	Gnomish	26-30	Half-orc		

** If desired, 1 in 4 can be half-orc or of humanoid race (goblin, hobgoblin, kobold, orc).

CITY/TOWN ENCOUNTERS EXPLANATIONS

Assassin encounters are dependent upon the locale. Normally 1-3 assassins will be encountered, but near the Thieves' Quarter the encounter could be with many assassins — at the guild, for instance. Assassins will typically ignore passers-by or act as thieves, but are as likely to slay first and steal afterwards as to simply pick a pocket or two.

Bandit encounters in daylight hours will simply be a case of a nondescript group being seen — the bandits will perhaps be watching the encountered party as a future prospect. Nighttime encounters will typically be with 3-12 bandits with 1 or more leaders.

Beggar encounters are with but 1 (or possibly 2) person(s) (young or old; maimed, diseased, or whole; religious or otherwise; male or female) beseeching alms. There is a chance that a beggar will be a thief (q.v.). A beggar has a slight chance (1% to 8%) of knowing information of interest to the character encountering him or her, but payment must be made. Any gratuity or gift given to a beggar will immediately attract the attention of

other beggars nearby (0-9 others will be near).

Brigand encounters are the same as bandit encounters.

City guard encounters are with 2-16 mercenary soldiers in the employ of the city as gate and wall guards or in a police function. There will always be 1 higher level leader — 2 if more than 8 guards, 3 if more than 12 — in addition to the 0 level guardsmen. Leaders are of 2nd to 5th level fighting ability. They will question suspicious persons, arrest law breakers, etc. In addition, the guard party will always be accompanied by a magic-user of 1st to 4th level who is indentured for 1 year for some service rendered to him or her by the city which was not repayable in some other manner (bad debts, resurrection, infraction of city rules, non-payment of taxes, etc.).

City official encounters will be with some minor bureaucrat such as a tax collector, customs officer, guard or watch lieutenant, deputy bailiff, or assistant magistrate. A 10% chance for an encounter with a major official exists, however, such as meeting a steward, alderman, justice, guard or watch captain, chamberlain, or magistrate. Major officials will have 2-8 city guards with them, as detailed above. Officials will resent unwarranted intrusion, but they will speak with persons regarding important matters. Any official will have 1-4 fighters as personal guards (d4 to determine individual level).

City watchman encounters are with squads of the watch (5 men plus a 1st-3rd level sergeant during daylight; double numbers, plus a 4th or 5th level lieutenant at night). These squads will always be accompanied by a cleric of 2nd to 5th level indentured to the city as magic-users are to the city guard (q.v.). They will generally act as do city guards, and at night these patrols will be ready to aid attacked persons and arrest lawbreakers.

Cleric encounters will be with a cleric 6th to 11th level (d6 + 5). There will be 0-5 lesser clerics (d4 for level) with the major character. Alignments can be rolled for or dictated by area or race. Encountered clerics will typically try to convert the party, ask for contributions, or try to dupe the party into becoming sacrificial victims.

Demon or Devil encounters must be carefully restricted, and they may be ignored entirely if desirable. For example, near an evil temple there may well be a demon or devil, a succubus may be roaming at night, a wizard may have conjured a demon, etc. Treat these encounters as highly special. Only 1 demon or devil will be encountered.

Doppleganger encounters will normally take place only near deserted places where there are entrances to the underworld, ruins, and the like. The number of dopplegangers encountered will be 3-6 (d4 + 2).

Druid encounters will be with a druid of 6th to 11th level (d6 + 5) with 0-3 lesser druids (d4 for level) 50% of the time and 1-4 fighters (d6 for level) 50% of the time. Druids will generally shun conversation with the encountering party.

Drunk encounters are typically with 1-4 tipsy revelers or wine-sodden bums (50% chance for either). In the former case the type of character(s) found drunk should be diced for:

01-02	Assassin	28-29	Druid	74-80	Merchant
03-10	Bandit	30-38	Fighter	81-82	Noble
11-18	Brigand	39-45	Gentleman	83-90	Rake
19-20	City guard	46-48	Illusionist	91-95	Ruffian
21-22	City official	49-63	Laborer	96-97	Thief
23-25	City watchman	64-65	Magic-user	98-00	Tradesman
26-27	Cleric	66-73	Mercenary		

When an encounter with a drunk occurs, reaction for the latter will dictate what is said to the party. The drunk character(s) will become sober on a roll of 10% or less (out of 100%) if threatened, check each turn or melee round. (See **Effects of Alcohol and Drugs** in the **DAMAGE** subsection of **COMBAT**.)

Fighter encounters will be with a 6th to 12th level fighter (2d4 + 4) accompanied by 0-3 henchmen (d4 for level).

Gentleman encounters are with a foppish dandy and 1-4 sycophants 40% of the time, a gentlewoman 20% of the time, and 40% of the time with well-dressed fighter-types of 7th to 10th level (d4 + 6) with 1-4 friends of the same abilities. Any rude remarks will give offense, of course. Fops will seek revenge by causing trouble for the party with officials, gentlewomen will send a champion, fighters will challenge the offenders.

Ghast encounters must be near charnel houses, graveyards, and the like. The number encountered will be 2-8.

Ghost encounters are treated in a fashion similar to ghast encounters, but of course a locale or two can be haunted. One ghost will be encountered.

Ghoul encounters are treated the same as ghast encounters, except 4-16 will be encountered.

Giant rats are encountered throughout any inhabited place, using their own tunneled warrens, sewers, cellars, etc. In daylight such encounters will take place only in dim alleys or dark buildings and similar places. The number encountered will be 2-8 in daylight, 4-24 at night.

Goodwife encounters are with a single woman, often indistinguishable from any other type of female (such as a magic-user, harlot, etc.). Any offensive treatment or seeming threat will be likely to cause the woman to scream for help, accusing the offending party of any number of crimes, i.e. assault, rape, theft, or murder. 20% of goodwives know interesting gossip.

Harlot encounters can be with brazen strumpets or haughty courtesans, thus making it difficult for the party to distinguish each encounter for what it is. (In fact, the encounter could be with a dancer only prostituting herself as it pleases her, an elderly madam, or even a pimp.) In addition to the offering of the usual fare, the harlot is 30% likely to know valuable information, 15% likely to make something up in order to gain a reward, and 20% likely to be, or work with, a thief. You may find it useful to use the sub-table below to see which sort of harlot encounter takes place:

01-10	Slovenly trull	76-85	Expensive doxy
11-25	Brazen strumpet	86-90	Haughty courtesan
26-35	Cheap trollop	91-92	Aged madam
36-50	Typical streetwalker	93-94	Wealthy procuress
51-65	Saucy tart	95-98	Sly pimp
66-75	Wanton wench	99-00	Rich panderer

An expensive doxy will resemble a gentlewoman, a haughty courtesan a noblewoman, the other harlots might be mistaken for goodwives, and so forth.

Illusionist encounters will be with an illusionist of 7th to 10th level (d4 + 6) with 0-3 apprentice illusionists (d4 for level) 50% of the time or 1-3 fighter guards (d6 for level) 50% of the time. The illusionist typically wishes to be left alone.

Laborer encounters are with a group of 3-12 non-descript persons loitering or on their way to or from work. These fellows will be rough customers in a brawl. There is a 10% chance for each to be a levy in the city watch, with commensurate friends and knowledge.

Magic-user encounters will be with a magic-user of 7th to 12th level (d6 + 6) and 1-4 henchmen — 45% apprentice magic-users (d6 for level), 30% fighter guards (d4 + 3 for level), 25% for a mixture of the two, providing 2 or 4 henchmen are in the magic-user's company. As with illusionists, magic-users wish to mind their own affairs and like others to do likewise.

Mercenary encounters are with 3-12 non-descript men. There will be a 1st level fighter for every 3 level 0 mercenaries and a 2nd to 5th level leader (d4 + 1) if there are 10 or more mercenaries encountered. There is a 70% likelihood that they are already in the employ of someone. Otherwise, normal reaction dice are used.

Merchant encounters are with 1-3 purveyors or factors in the daytime, but at night there will be 2-8 mercenary guards with the merchant(s) if the encounter is in a dangerous sector. Guards will be 0 level, with one leader of 1st to 4th level (d4 for level). A merchant will fear robbery, but is 10% likely to have useful knowledge for a price. 10% of merchants encountered will be rich, thus indistinguishable from an important city official or noble.

Monk encounters will be with a single monk of 7th to 10th level (d4 + 6). The monk might appear as a beggar or other character. The business of the monk is typically that of travelling from point A to point B. Reaction is determined by standard test.

Night hag encounters are treated similar to demon and devil encounters, i.e. the area must suit the encounter. From 1 to 2 night hags will be encountered.

Noble encounters are with a nobleman and retainers 75% of the time and with a noblewoman 25% of the time. A noble will have 1-4 guards of 1st-4th level fighting ability, 1-2 servants, and there is a 75% likelihood that a noblewoman will have a sedan chair, carriers and linkboys (at night). Noblemen can easily be mistaken for important city officials or very rich merchants; noblewomen can likewise be mistaken for a courtesan or procuress. Any insult will be taken seriously. Nobles are 50% likely to be fighters (80%) or clerics (20%) of 5th to 12th level (d8 + 4).

Paladin encounters will be with a paladin of 6th to 9th level (d4 + 5). The paladin will be indistinguishable from any other fighter.

Pilgrim encounters are with 3-12 persons bent upon a journey to some religious or quasi-religious site. The alignment of pilgrims is variable, but that of a group is always homogeneous. For every 4 pilgrims there will be 1 of unusual type (cleric, fighter, etc.). See **ADVANCED DUNGEONS & DRAGONS, MONSTER MANUAL** for exact probability of each character type if desired. As pilgrims are non-descript, it is quite probable that they can be confused with other groups (bandits, laborers, and so on).

Press gang encounters will involve 2-16 burly sailors or soldiers armed with swords but wielding clubs. Gang members will be 1st level, with one leader of level 2-5 (d4 + 1). Outnumbered or incapacitated characters may be "shanghaied" into the local navy or militia.

Rake encounters are with 2-5 young gentlemen fighters of 5th to 10th level (d6 + 4). The rakes will always be aggressive, rude, and sarcastic. There is a 25% chance they will be drunk.

Rakshasa encounters are treated the same as demon or devil encounters, i.e. the area must suit the encounter. From 1-3 will be encountered.

Ranger encounters will be with a ranger of 7th to 10th level (d4 + 6). The ranger will be indistinguishable from any other fighter.

Ruffian encounters will be with from 7 to 12 (d6 + 6) fellows of shabby appearance and mean disposition. They will be armed with clubs and daggers, fighting at 2nd level ability and having 2 dice (d8) for hits. There is a 5% chance per ruffian encountered that an assassin of 5th to 8th level (d4 + 4) will be with the group. All weapons will be concealed.

Shadow encounters are treated the same as those of demon and devil, except that there is a small likelihood of shadows being encountered in any deserted place. From 2-8 shadows will be encountered.

Spectre encounters are treated in the same fashion as those with a ghost. From 1-3 spectres will be encountered.

Thief encounters will be with an 8th to 11th level thief (d4 + 7) with 0 to 2 apprentices of 1st to 4th level. If there is but 1 thief, he or she will be an adventurer, merely stopping for a short time in the city/town. Other thieves encountered will be on guild business, or "working", or both.

Tradesman encounters are with from 2 to 8 non-descript tradesmen (smiths, coopers, etc.) on their way to or from their work. They are greatly valued citizens and generally friendly with city guards and watch.

Wererat encounters will be with from 2 to 5 of the creatures. In daylight, it is 90% likely that the wererats will be in human form, at night it is 50% likely they will be in human form, 50% for giant rat form. Wererats can be any type of human, if desired (see **SWORDS OF LANKHMAR** by Fritz Leiber). They will intelligently try to set up, ambush, or otherwise react to the encountering party.

Weretiger encounters will be with 1 or 2 weretigers. All day, and 90% of the night, encounters will be with creatures in their human form. The weretiger(s) will be 90% likely to be temporary residents of the city/town and on some errand rather than seeking to prey upon passers-by.

Werewolf encounters are with 2-5 werewolves. All day, and 50% of the night, encounters will be with creatures in their human form. The werewolves will generally be seeking prey, although there is a 20% chance that they will be on some special errand and ignore the encountered party.

Wight encounters are the same as ghast encounters, except that 2-5 wights will be encountered.

Will-o-wisp encounters are the same as ghost encounters, except 1-2 will-o-wisps can be encountered.

GREEN GRIFFON

EMIRIKOL
THE CHAOTIC

D.A.T.

Wraith encounters are treated the same as ghost encounters, except that 1-4 wraiths can be encountered.

Vampire encounters are the same as ghost encounters, but the vampire ranges nearly anywhere in the city/town in human, bat, or gaseous form. They are always seeking new victims.

Magic Possessed by Encountered Creatures

All 1st or higher level characters encountered in a city/town may possess one or more magic items on his or her person at the time of encounter. Of course, as they **will** employ the item(s), this should be determined before interaction takes place between the party and the encountered. The power of the item must be commensurate with the level of the possessor.

CHANCE PER LEVEL FOR MAGIC ITEM

Item	Assassin, Fighter, Thief, etc.	Cleric, Druid	Magic-User	Monk
Sword	10%	—	—	—
Misc. Weapon	5%	10%	5%	5%
Armor &/or Shield	10%	10%	—	—
Protection Device*	2%	2%	10%	2%
Potion	3%	5%	10%	—
Scroll	1%	5%	10%	—
Ring	5%	5%	5%	5%
Wand, Rod, or Staff	—	5%	5%	—
Misc. Magic	5%	5%	5%	5%

* Protection devices are determined using the table below:

Dice Roll	Result
01-25	+1 *Ring of Protection*
26-30	+2 *Ring of Protection*
31	+3 *Ring of Protection*
32	*Amulet of Life Protection*
33-55	*Bracers of Defense, Armor Class 6*
56-70	*Bracers of Defense, Armor Class 4*
71-75	*Bracers of Defense, Armor Class 2*
76-82	*Cloak of Displacement*
83-95	*Cloak of Protection, +1*
96-99	*Cloak of Protection, +2*
00	*Cloak of Protection, +3*

Note: Any item generated must be appropriate to the character and usable. Any duplications are disregarded; for example, a magic-user with a protection device, a *cloak of displacement*, for whom a miscellaneous magic item is also determined can not have another such cloak.

APPENDIX D: RANDOM GENERATION OF CREATURES FROM THE LOWER PLANES

At times it might be useful to have an unrecognizable creature of evil from the planes of the Abyss, Tarterus, Hades, Gehenna, or Hell. It is no great matter to sit down and design a fairly interesting one given an hour or so, but time or desire lacking, the following will enable you to create one or several such monsters in but a few minutes. The format is straight from the **AD&D MONSTER MANUAL** for ease of recording and handling the creature(s) developed.

FREQUENCY: *Common, uncommon, or rare (d6: 1, 2-3, 4-6)*
NO. APPEARING: *1 to 2-8 (circumstances must dictate)*
ARMOR CLASS: *0 to −3 (d4)*
MOVE: *6'', 9'', 12'', 15'', or 18'' (d8, 6-8 = roll d4 for move and creature also has swimming or flying ability; roll d6, 1-2 = swimming, 3-6 = flying, and as a rule these speeds will be greater than land move speed add 1-4 3'' increments as you see fit or by random determination using d4)*
HIT DICE: *7 to 10 (d4 + 6, roll a second d4, and on a 4 the creature has 1-4 additional hit points per hit die, as determined by another roll of the d4)*
% IN LAIR: *(circumstances must dictate)*
TREASURE TYPE: *low value if any (circumstances must dictate)*
NO. OF ATTACKS: *See APPEARANCE TABLE below*
DAMAGE/ATTACK: *See ATTACK TABLE below*
SPECIAL ATTACKS: *See SPECIAL ATTACKS TABLE below*

SPECIAL DEFENSES: *See SPECIAL DEFENSES TABLE below*
MAGIC RESISTANCE: *5% per hit die (to vary use d6, 1 = −5%, 2 = −10%, 3 = +5%, 4 = +10%, 5 = +15%, and 6 = STANDARD magic resistance)*
INTELLIGENCE: *Low, average, very, or high (d4)*
ALIGNMENT: *According to plane of origin*
SIZE: *S, M, or L (d8, 1 = S, 2-4 = M, 5-8 = L)*
PSIONIC ABILITY: *Nil (90%) or 96 - 115 (d20 + 95)*
    Attack/Defense Modes: A-D (d4) /F-H (d6, 1-2 = F, 3-4 = F and G, 5-6 = F, G, and H)

Appearance Table:

HEAD	HEAD ADORNMENT
1. bat-like	1. antlers
2. bird-like*	2. crest or peak
3. crocodilian	3. horns (1-4)
4. horse-like	4. knobs
5. human-like	5. ridge(s)
6. monkey-like	6. ruff
7. snake-like	7. spines
8. weasel-like	8. none

OVERALL VISAGE	EARS
1. gibbering - drooling	1. dog-like
2. glaring - menacing	2. elephant-like
3. rotting	3. human, tiny
4. skeletal	4. human, huge
5. twitching - moving	5. trumpet-like
6. wrinkled - seamed	6. none

EYE COLOR	EYES (d6, 1 = 1, 2-4 = 2, 5-6 = 3-4)
1. amber	1. small, multi-faceted
2. black	2. small, slitted
3. blue	3. swivel-socketed
4. green	4. stalked
5. metallic	5. huge, flat
6. orange-red	6. huge, protruding

NOSE (if necessary)	MOUTH (d6, 1 = tiny, 2-3 = average, 4-6 = huge)
1. flat, misshapen	1. fanged
2. huge, bulbous	2. mandibled**
3. slits only	3. sucker-like**
4. snouted	4. toothed, small or ridged
5. tiny	5. toothed, large
6. trunk-like	6. tushed

BODY ATTRIBUTES (d6, 1-4 = bipedal, 5-6 = quadrupedal, et al.)

Bipedal Torso	Quadrupedal or Other Torso
1. ape-like	1. amoeba-like
2. bear-like	2. bison-like
3. bird-like	3. cat-like
4. human-like	4. crab-like
5. pig-like	5. horse-like
6. rat-like	6. insect-like
	7. serpent-like or reptilian
	8. spider-like

General Characteristics (roll twice)	
1. fat	1. broad
2. long	2. muscled
3. short	3. narrow
4. thin	4. rubbery

Tail (d6, 1-4 = tail)	Body Odor
1. barbed**	1. bloody
2. dog-like	2. fishy
3. goat-like	3. fecal
4. horse-like	4. gangrenous
5. lion-like	5. moldy
6. pig-like	6. sweaty
7. prehensile	7. urine
8. stingered**	8. vomit

Skin
1. bald/smooth
2. furred
3. hairy/bristled
4. leathery/leprous
5. scaled
6. slimy
7. warted/bumpy
8. wrinkled/folded

Predominant Color
1. blackish
2. bluish
3. brownish
4. grayish - whitish
5. greenish
6. orangy
7. pinkish
8. purplish
9. reddish
10. yellowish - tannish

Back
1. humped/hunched
2. maned
3. normal
4. spiked/spined/ridged

Wings, if Any
1. bat-like
2. bird-like
3. insect-like
4. membranous or fan-like

ARMS (2 or 4 if bipedal; 2,4, or 6 if otherwise)

1. animal-like
2. human-like
3. insect-like
4. tentacles

HANDS (d6, 1-3 = all alike, 4-6 = different)

1. clawed
2. human-nailed
3. pincered
4. taloned
5. tentacle-fingered
6. withered and bony

LEGS AND FEET (as applicable)

1. clawed
2. hooved
3. human-like
4. insect-like
5. snake-like
6. suctioned
7. taloned
8. webbed (all swimmers)

*1. duck-like
2. hawk-like
3. owl-like
4. pelican-like
5. stork-like
6. turkey-like

**Optionally poisoned (or 4 in 6)
1. +1 on save
2. normal
3. -1 on save
4. -2 on save
5. insanity for 1-4 rounds
6. weakness; 1 point per hit die permanently lost

A bit of imaginative creation is helpful in using the tables above. For example, if the creature's body is amoeba-like, you might well decide to give it scores of tiny, bubbling sucker mouths over its entire body, and omit any mouth on the head; of course, body covering would have to be adjusted accordingly, and appendages selected to suit the monster. Likewise, you should feel at ease adding to or amending the tables as you desire in order to arrive at still more diverse and unexpected lower planes creatures. (Cf. THE DRAGON #20, Vol. III, No. 6: "Demonology Made Easy", by Gregory Rihn. This excellent article gives some interesting thoughts on variant creatures of the evil planes!) When you have the form and appearance of the creature, determine strength, if necessary, and then attack capabilities.

Strength	"To Hit"	Damage
01 - 25 = 17	+1	+1
26 - 45 = 18	+1	+2
46 - 60 = 18 (01-50)	+1	+3
61 - 70 = 18 (51-75)	+2	+3
71 - 80 = 18 (76-90)	+2	+4
81 - 90 = 18 (91-99)	+2	+5
91 - 95 = 18 (00)	+3	+6
96 - 98 = 19	+3	+7
99 - 00 = 20	+3	+8

ATTACK TABLE
antlers or horns = 1 attack each, damage 1-2 to 2-8
mouth = 1 attack each, damage from 1 to 3-12
tail = special attacks only, damage from 1 to 1-6
hands = 1 attack each possible if no weapon use, strength bonus applicable if used as clubbing weapon, damage from base 1-2 to 2-12
feet = 1 attack each if applicable (flyer, leaper, etc.), damage from 1-2 to 3-12

Damage amount is determined by overall size of creature, with strength bonuses where applicable, and the size and type of body weaponry, i.e. a huge creature with clawed hands would get damage ratings of at least 2-8 per hit. Constriction or hugging damage would be commensurate with a known creature of the same approximate size. Incidental spine-type damage is best kept relatively low — 1-3, 1-4, or 1-6 range. Special effects from these attack forms — poison, energy drain, heat, cold, electrical discharge, paralysis, or whatever — should be kept to a minimum.

Special attacks and **special defenses** can't be dealt with in as much detail as would be desirable in a work of unlimited length. The tables below will suggest various magical attack/defense forms, and the DM is urged to add others of his own creation as appropriate to the plane and the creature.

SPECIAL ATTACKS (1-3)

1. ability drain
2. energy drain (cold)
3. gaseous discharge or missile discharge
4. heat generation
5. life level drain
6. spell-like abilities
7. spell use
8. summon/gate

Spell-like and **spell use abilities** should be based upon intelligence level and relative strength in hit dice. Compare daemons, demons, devils, and night hags. From 1-2 spells and a like number of spell-like abilities is sufficient for lesser creatures, while the more powerful and intelligent will get a total of 2-5 each, some being of higher level (telekinesis, teleportation, etc.).

SPECIAL DEFENSES (1-4)

1. acid immunity
2. cold immunity
3. electrical immunity
4. fire immunity
5. gas immunity
6. metal immunity
7. poison immunity
8. regeneration
9. spell immunity
10. weapon immunity

Immunities above four are possible only if the general class (demons, devils, etc.) has more. **Metal** immunity can pertain to iron, silver, steel, or any other, including combinations, but excluding magical weaponry. **Regeneration** base is 1 hit point per turn, with exceptional creatures having a maximum of 1 per round. **Spell** immunity must be limited to 1-4 pre-determined spells. **Weapon** immunity refers to creatures hit only by magical weapons of a certain value, i.e. +1, +2, etc.

OTHER ABILITIES

1. audial superiority
2. surprise capability
3. visual superiority

Audial or visual superiority will tend to negate surprise and enable detection of creatures through sound or vision. Surprise capability relates to special movement ability and possibly other factors. Visual superiority refers to infravisual and ultravisual capabilities.

To avoid having nothing more than different mixtures of the same old ingredients, be certain that you put a bit of personal creativity into each monster. A list of new and different factors should be started, perhaps in the margin, and then fresh ideas added as they come. When a monster is devised, cross off the unique features from the marginal list.

APPENDIX E: ALPHABETICAL RECAPITULATION OF MONSTERS (With Experience Point Values)

Monster	Size	To Hit A.C. 0	Armor Class	Hit Dice	No. of Attacks	Damage Per Attack	Special Attacks	Special Defenses	Intelligence	X.P. Value
aerial servant	L	7	3	16	1	8-32	surprise on 1-4	magic weapon to hit	semi-	5250 + 20/hp
ankheg	L	16/15/14/13	2/4	3-8	1	3-18 + 1-4	squirt acid, 8-32	nil	non-	390 + hp value
ant, giant	S	16	3	2(3)	1(2)	1-6 (2-8/3-12)	(sting)	nil	animal	20 + 2/hp (40 + 3/hp)
ape	M	15	6	4 + 1	3	1-3/1-3/1-6	rending (1-6)	nil	low	130 + 5/hp
ape, carnivorous	L	15	6	5	3	1-4/1-4/1-8	rending (1-8)	surprise only on a 1	low+	170 + 5/hp
axe beak	L	16	6	3	3	1-3/1-3/2-8	nil	nil	animal	35 + 3/hp
baboon	S	18	7	1 + 1	1	1-4 (2-5)	nil	climbing	low-	20 + 2/hp
badger	S	18	4	1 + 2	3	1-2/1-2/1-3	nil	nil	semi-	20 + 2/hp
badger, giant	M	16	4	3	3	1-3/1-3/1-6	nil	nil	semi-	35 + 3/hp
baluchitherium	L	8	5	14	2	5-20/5-20	nil	nil	semi-	4200 + 18/hp
barracuda	S-L	19 or 16	6	1-3	1	2-8	nil	nil	non-	20 + 2/hp
basilisk	M	13	4	6 + 1	1	1-10	gaze petrifies	nil	animal	1000 + 8/hp
bear, black	M	16	7	3 + 3	3	1-3/1-3/1-6	hug (2-8)	nil	semi-	85 + 4/hp
bear, brown	L	15	6	5 + 5	3	1-6/1-6/1-8	hug (2-12)	nil	semi-	300 + 6/hp
bear, cave	L	13	6	6 + 6	3	1-8/1-8/1-12	hug (2-16)	nil	semi-	475 + 8/hp
beaver, giant	M	15	6	4	1	4-16	nil	nil	low-average	60 + 4/hp
beetle, giant—										
bombardier	M	16	4	2 + 2	1	2-12	acid cloud	firing cloud	non-	105 + 3/hp
boring	L	15	3	5	1	5-20	nil	nil	animal	90 + 5/hp
fire	S	18	4	1 + 2	1	2-8	nil	nil	non-	20 + 2/hp
rhinoceros	L	9	2	12	2	3-18/2-16	nil	nil	non-	2150 + 16/hp
stag	L	13	3	7	3	4-16/1-10/1-10	nil	nil	non-	400 + 8/hp
water	L	15	3	4	1	3-18	nil	nil	non-	85 + 4/hp
beholder	L	10/9/8/7	0/2/7	45-75 hp	1	2-8	magic	anti-magic	exceptional	12900 + 20/hp
black pudding	S-L	10	6	10	1	3-24	dissolves wood & metal	blows, cold, lightning useless	non-	1350 + 14/hp
blink dog	M	15	5	4	1	1-6	rear attack 75%	teleport away	average	170 + 5/hp
boar, giant	L	13	6	7	1	3-18	nil	nil	animal	225 + 8/hp

Monster	Size	To Hit A.C. 0	Armor Class	Hit Dice	No. of Attacks	Damage Per Attack	Special Attacks	Special Defenses	Intelligence	X.P. Value
boar, wild	M	16	7	3 + 3	1	3-12	nil	nil	semi-	85 + 4/hp
boar, warthog	M	16	7	3	2	2-8/2-8	nil	nil	animal	35 + 3/hp
brain mole	S	—	9	1 hp	nil	nil	psionic	nil	animal	31
brownie	S	20	3	½	1	1-3	magic use	saving throws, no surprise	high	65 + 1/hp
buffalo	L	15	7	5	2	1-8/1-8	charge (3-18/1-4)	head AC 3	semi-	350 + 8/hp
bugbear	L	16	5	3 + 1	1	2-8 or by weapon	surprise on 1-3	nil	low-average	135 + 4/hp
bulette	L	12	-2/4/6	9	3	4-48/3-18/3-18	8' jump	nil	animal	2300 + 12/hp
bull	L	15	7	4	2	1-6/1-6	charge (3-12 + 1-4)	nil	semi-	85 + 4/hp
camel, wild	L	16	7	3	1	1-4	spitting	nil	animal to semi-	35 + 3/hp
carrion crawler	L	16	3/7	3 + 1	8	special	paralysis	nil	non-	580 + 4/hp
catoblepas	L	13	7	6 + 2	1	1-6 + stun	gaze = death, stun	nil	semi-	700 + 8/hp
cattle, wild	L	19/16/15	7	1 to 4	1	1-4	stampede	nil	semi-	35 + 2/hp
centaur	L	15	5 (4)	4	2	1-6/1-6	human weapon	nil	low-average	85 + 4/hp
centipede, giant	S	20	9	¼	1	nil	poison	nil	non-	30 + 1/hp
cerebral parasite	S	—	—	—	—	—	infest psionics	killed only by cure disease	non-	nil
chimera	L	12	6/5/2	9	6	1-3/1-3/1-4/ 1-4/2-8/3-12	breath weapon (3-24)	nil	semi-	1000 + 12/hp
cockatrice	S	15	6	5	1	1-3	touch petrifies	nil	animal	315 + 5/hp
couatl	M	12	5	9	2	1-3/2-8	poison, magic use	become ethereal	genius	2400 + 12/hp
crab, giant	L	16	3	3	2	2-8/2-8	nil	nil	non-	35 + 3/hp
crayfish, giant	L	15	4	4 + 4	2	2-12/1-12	nil	nil	non-	90 + 5/hp
crocodile, normal	L	16	5	3	2	2-8/1-12	nil	nil	animal	60 + 4/hp
crocodile, giant	L	13	4	7	2	3-18/2-20	nil	nil	animal	400 + 8/hp
demon—										
Demogorgon	L	7	-8	200 hp	3	1-6/1-6/special	energy drain, rotting, hypnosis, beguiling, insanity, magic use, psionics	hit only by +2 or better weapon, magic resistance (95%)	supra-genius	74,000[a]
Juiblex	L	7	-7	88 hp	1	4-40	spew ochre-slime, magic use, psionics	hit only by +2 or better weapon, magic resistance (65%)	genius	47,280[a]

[a] For destroying material form only — if actually killed permanently multiply x.p. figure by 10.

Monster	Size	To Hit A.C. 0	Armor Class	Hit Dice	No. of Attacks	Damage Per Attack	Special Attacks	Special Defenses	Intelligence	X.P. Value
manes	S	19	7	1	3	1-2/1-2/1-4	nil	hit only by +1 or better weapon, resistant to spells as undead	semi-	18 + 1/hp
Orcus	L	7 (1[b])	6	120 hp	2	2-8 + special with tail/hand 1-4/ or fist 3-13/ or wpn. +8	poison (-4 on save), death wand, magic use, psionics	hit only by +3 or better weapon, magic resistance (85%)	supra-genius	63,900[a]
succubus	M	13	0	6	2	1-3/1-3	energy drain, magic use, psionics	hit only by magic weapons, magic resistance (70%)	exceptional	2100 + 6/hp
type I (vrock)	L	12	0	8	5	1-4/1-4/1-8/1-8/1-6	magic use	magic resistance (50%)	low	1275 + 10/hp
type II (hezrou)	L	12	-2	9	3	1-3/1-3/4-16	magic use, psionics	magic resistance (55%)	low	2000 + 12/hp
type III (glabrezu)	L	10	-4	10	5	2-12/2-12/1-3/1-3/2-5	magic use, psionics	magic resistance (60%)	average	2400 + 14/hp
type IV (Bilwhr, Johud, Nalfeshnee)	L	8[c]	-1	11	3	1-4/1-4/2-8	magic use, psionics	hit only by +2 or better weapon, magic resistance (65%)	very	3000 + 16/hp
type V (Aishapra, Kevokulli, Marilith, Rehnaremme)	L	12	-7/-5	7 + 7	7	2-8 + 6 various weapons	magic use, psionics	hit only by magic weapons, magic resistance (80%)	high	3000 + 12/hp
type VI (Alzoll, Balor, Errtu, Ndulu, Ter-soth, Wendonai)	L	12	-2	8 + 8	1	2-13	whip & immolate (2-12/3-18 or 4-24), magic use, psionics	hit only by magic weapons, magic resistance (75%)	high	3600 + 12/hp
Yeenoghu	L	7	-5	100 hp	1	flail = 3-18 plus special	paralyzation & confusion with flail, magic use, psionics	hit only by magic weapons, magic resistance (80%), regenerates 3 hp/hr.	exceptional	54500[a]
devil—										
Asmodeus	L	7	-7	199 hp	1	4-14	rod, magic use, psionics	hit only by +3 weapons, magic resistance (90%)	supra-genius	70,965[a]
Baalzebul	L	7	-5	166 hp	1	2-12 + special	poison, magic use, psionics	hit only by +3 weapons, magic resistance (85%)	genius	61,410[a]
barbed	M	12	0	8	3	2-8/2-8/3-12	fear, magic use	never surprised, magic resistance (35%)	very	1425 + 10/hp

[a] For destroying material form only — if actually killed permanently multiply x.p. figure by 10.

[b] Shows effect of +6 to hit if weapon is used.

[c] Number is adjusted for +2 bonus to hit.

198

Monster	Size	To Hit A.C. 0	Armor Class	Hit Dice	No. of Attacks	Damage Per Attack	Special Attacks	Special Defenses	Intelligence	X.P. Value
bone	L	12	−1	9	1	3-12	bone hook, tail (2-8 + 1-4 strength points lost), magic use	magic resistance (40%)	very	2800 + 12/hp
Dispater	M	7	−2	144 hp	1	4-24	rod, magic use, psionics	hit only by +2 weapons, magic resistance (80%)	genius	48,040ª
erinyes	M	13	2	6 + 6	1	2-8	pain poison, rope of entanglement, magic use	magic resistance (30%)	average	875 + 8/hp
Geryon	L	7	−3	133 hp	3	3-18/3-18/2-8	poison, horn of minotaur summoning (5-20), magic use, psionics	hit only by +2 weapons, magic resistance (75%)	exceptional	47,975ª
horned	L	13	−5	5 + 5	4 or +1 weapon	1-4/1-4/2-5/1-3 or 1-3	tail, spell use, psionics, spec. wpn. fork (2-12) or whip (1-4 + stun)	hit only by magic weapons, magic resistance (50%)	high	1320 + 6/hp
ice	L	10	−4	11	4	1-4/1-4/2-8/3-12	weapon, magic use, psionics	hit only by +2 weapon, regeneration, magic resistance (55%)	high	4400 + 16/hp
lemure	M	16	7	3	1	1-3	nil	regeneration, spell immunity, (charm, sleep, etc.)	semi-	65 + 3/hp
pit fiend	L	9	−3	13	2	5-8/7-12	tail (2-8), magic use, psionics	hit only by +2 weapons, regeneration, magic resistance (65%)	exceptional	7900 + 18/hp

ª For destroying material form only — if actually killed permanently multiply x.p. figure by 10.

dinosaurª —

Monster	Size	To Hit A.C. 0	Armor Class	Hit Dice	No. of Attacks	Damage Per Attack	Special Attacks	Special Defenses	Intelligence	X.P. Value
anatosaurus	L	9	5	12	1	1-4	nil	nil	non-	1300 + 16/hp
ankylosaurus	L	12	0	9	1	3-18	nil	nil	non-	900 + 12/hp
antrodemus	L	8	5	15	3	1-4/1-4/6-24	nil	nil	non-	2400 + 20/hp
apatosaurus	L	7	5	30	1	3-18	step on (4-40)	nil	non-	5000 + 35/hp
archelon ischyras	L	13	3	7	1	3-12	nil	nil	non-	225 + 8/hp
brachiosaurus	L	7	5	36	1	5-20	step on (8-80)	nil	non-	5000 + 35/hp
camarasaurus	L	7	6	20	1	3-12	step on (3-30)	nil	non-	4000 + 30/hp
ceratosaurus	L	12	5	8	3	1-6/1-6/4-16	nil	nil	non-	600 + 12/hp
cetiosaurus	L	7	6	24	1	3-18	step on (4-40)	nil	non-	5000 + 35/hp
dinichtys	L	10	7	10	1	5-20	swallowing whole	nil	non-	1500 + 14/hp

ª Dinosaur stampede kills smaller creatures; marine beasts upset craft to get at prey.

Monster	Size	To Hit A.C. 0	Armor Class	Hit Dice	No. of Attacks	Damage Per Attack	Special Attacks	Special Defenses	Intelligence	X.P. Value
diplodocus	L	7	6	24	1	3-18	step on (3-30)	nil	non-	5000 + 35/hp
elasmosaurus	L	8	7	15	1	4-24	nil	nil	non-	2400 + 20/hp
gorgosaurus	L	9	5	13	3	1-3/1-3/7-28	nil	nil	non-	1800 + 18/hp
iguanadon	L	13	4	6	3	1-3/1-3/2-8	nil	nil	non-	150 + 6/hp
lambeosaurus	L	9	6	12	1	2-12	nil	nil	non-	1300 + 16/hp
megalosaurus	L	9	5	12	1	3-18	nil	nil	non-	1300 + 16/hp
monoclonius	L	12	3/4	8	1	2-16	charge/trample (2-16)	nil	non-	550 + 8/hp
mosasaurus	L	9	7	12	1	4-32	nil	nil	non-	1300 + 18/hp
paleoscincus	L	12	-3	9	1	2-12	nil	biting inflicts 3-12 hp on attacker	non-	1300 + 12/hp
pentaceratops	L	9	2/6	12	3	1-6/1-10/1-10	charge/trample (2-20)	nil	non-	1300 + 18/hp
plateosaurus	L	12	5	8	nil	nil	nil	nil	non-	375 + 10/hp
plesiosaurus	L	7	7	20	1	5-20	flippers in water (2-12/2-12)	nil	non-	4000 + 30/hp
pteranodon	L	16	7	3 + 3	1	2-8	nil	nil	non-	85 + 4/hp
stegosaurus	L	7	2/5	18	1	5-20	nil	nil	non-	3000 + 25/hp
styracosaurus	L	10	2/4	10	1	2-16	charge/trample (2-16)	biting inflicts 1-6 to 3-18 hp	non-	1950 + 14/hp
teratosaurus	L	10	5	10	3	1-3/1-3/3-18	nil	nil	non-	900 + 14/hp
triceratops	L	7	2/6	16	3	1-8/1-12/1-12	charge/trample (2-24)	nil	non-	4000 + 20/hp
tyrannosaurus Rex	L	7	5	18	3	1-6/1-6/5-40	swallowing whole	nil	non-	6550 + 25/hp

ª Dinosaur stampede kills smaller creatures; marine beasts upset craft to get at prey.

Monster	Size	To Hit A.C. 0	Armor Class	Hit Dice	No. of Attacks	Damage Per Attack	Special Attacks	Special Defenses	Intelligence	X.P. Value
displacer beast	L	13	4	6	2	2-8/2-8	nil	-2 on opponent's "to hit" dice, +2 on own saving throws	semi-	475 + 8/hp
djinni	L	13	4	7 + 3	1	2-16	whirlwind, magic use	nil	average-high	725 + 5/hp
dog, war	M	16	6	2 + 2	1	2-8	nil	nil	semi-	35 + 3/hp
dog, wild	S	18	7	1 + 1	1	1-4	nil	nil	semi-	20 + 2/hp
dolphin	M	16	5	2 + 2	1	2-8	nil	save as 4th level fighter	very	65 + 3/hp
doppleganger	M	15	5	4	1	1-12	mutable form, surprise	ESP, immune to sleep and charm, save as 10th level ftr.	very	330 + 4/hp

Monster	Size	To Hit A.C. 0	Armor Class	Hit Dice	No. of Attacks	Damage Per Attack	Special Attacks	Special Defenses	Intelligence	X.P. Value
dragon—										
black	L	13/12	3	6-8	3	1-4/1-4/3-18	breath weapon, magic use	nil	average	**
blue	L	12/10	2	8-10	3	1-6/1-6/3-24	breath weapon, magic use	nil	very	**
brass	L	13/12	2	6-8	3	1-4/1-4/4-16	breath weapon, magic use	nil	high	**
bronze	L	12/10	0	8-10	3	1-6/1-6/4-24	breath weapon, magic use	nil	exceptional	**
chromatic	L	7	0	128 hp	6	2-16/3-18/2-20/ 3-24/3-30/1-6	poison sting, breath weapons, magic use	nil	genius	63580[a]
copper	L	13/12	1	7-9	3	1-4/1-4/5-20	breath weapon, magic use	nil	high	**
gold	L	10/9	-2	10-12	3	1-8/1-8/3-36	breath weapon, magic use	nil	genius	**
green	L	13/12	2	7-9	3	1-6/1-6/2-20	breath weapon, magic use	nil	average-very	**
platinum	L	7	-3	168 hp	3	2-12/2-12/6-48	breath weapon, magic use	nil	supra-genius	58080[a]
red	L	12/10	-1	9-11	3	1-8/1-8/3-30	breath weapon, magic use	nil	exceptional	**
silver	L	12/10	-1	9-11	3	1-6/1-6/5-30	breath weapon, magic use	nil	exceptional	**
white	L	15/13	3	5-7	3	1-4/1-4/2-16	breath weapon, magic use	nil	average-low	**
dragonne	L	12	6/2	9	3	1-8/1-8/3-18	roar	nil	low	1400 + 14/hp
dragon turtle	L	9/8	0	12-14	3	2-12/2-12/4-32	breath weapon, capsizing	nil	very	7300 + 18/hp
dryad	M	16	9	2	1	(dagger)	charm person	magic use	high	105 + 3/hp
eagle, giant	M	15	7	4	3	1-6/1-6/2-12	diving (+4 to hit, 2-12 × 2)	eyesight	average	150 + 4/hp
ear seeker	S	20	9	1 hp	1	special	burrowing into ear to brain	nil	non-	nil
eel —										
electric	M	16	9	2	1	1-3	jolt (1, 2 or 3D8)	nil	non-	65 + 2/hp
giant	M	15	6	5	1	3-18	nil	nil	non-	49 + 1/hp
weed	S	20	8	1-1	1	1	poison	camouflage	non-	150 + 6/hp
efreeti	L	10	2	10	1	3-24	magic use	resists fire damage	very	1950 + 14/hp
elemental —										
air	L	12/9/7	2	8/12/16	1	2-20	whirlwind	hit only by +2 weapons	low	2850 + 15/hp
earth	L	12/9/7	2	8/12/16	1	4-32	nil	hit only by +2 weapons	low	2850 + 15/hp

[a] For destroying material plane form only — if actually killed permanently multiply x.p. figure by 10.

** Variables preclude a fixed number.

Monster	Size	To Hit A.C. 0	Armor Class	Hit Dice	No. of Attacks	Damage Per Attack	Special Attacks	Special Defenses	Intelligence	X.P. Value
fire	L	12/9/7	2	8/12/16	1	3-24	burn inflammables	hit only by +2 weapons	low	2850 + 15/hp
water	L	12/9/7	2	8/12/16	1	5-30	nil	hit only by +2 weapons	low	2850 + 15/hp
elephant—										
elephant	L	10	6	10	5	2-12 (×5)	nil	nil	semi-	1500 + 14/hp
loxodont	L	10	6	11	5	2-16 (×2)/2-12 (×3)	nil	nil	semi-	2125 + 16/hp
ettin	L	10	3	10	2	2-16/3-18	nil	surprised only on a 1	low	1950 + 14/hp
eye, floating	S	20	9	½	nil	nil	hypnotism	nil	non-	30 + 1/hp
eye of the deep	L	10/9	5	10-12	3	2-8/2-8/1-6	stunning, magic use	nil	very	3700 + 16/hp
flightless bird	M	19/16	7	1-3	1 or 1	1-4 or 2-8	nil	nil	animal	**
frog—										
giant	S-L	19/16	7	1-3	1	1-3 or 1-6 or 2-8	surprise (1-4), jump, tongue	nil	non-	45 + 3/hp
killer	S	16	8	1+4	3	1-2/1-2/2-5	surprise (1-4), jump	nil	non-	36 + 2/hp
poisonous	S	19	8	1	1	1	poison	nil	non-	35 + 1/hp
fungi, violet	S-M	16	7	3	1-4	special	rotting poison	nil	non-	135 + 4/hp
gar, giant	L	12	3	8	1	5-20	swallow whole	nil	non-	550 + 10/hp
gargoyle[d]	M	15	5	4+4	4	1-3/1-3/1-6/1-4	nil	only hit by magic weapons	low	165 + 5/hp
gas spore	L	20	9	1 hp	1	special	touch = infestation	explosion (6-36)	non-	33
gelatinous cube	L	15	8	4	1	2-8	paralyzation, surprise on 1-3	immunity to some attacks	non-	150 + 4/hp
ghast	M	15	4	4	3	1-4/1-4/1-8	nausea, paralyzation	immune to sleep and charm	very	190 + 4/hp
ghost	M	10	0(8)	10	1	special	age 10 years & panic, age 10-40 years per touch, magic jar	ethereal vs. weapons & spells	high	4050 + 14/hp
ghoul[d]	M	16	6	2	3	1-3/1-3/1-6	paralyzation	immune to sleep and charm	low	65 + 2/hp

[d] Includes marine varieties as well.

** Variables preclude a fixed number.

Monster	Size	To Hit A.C. 0	Armor Class	Hit Dice	No. of Attacks	Damage Per Attack	Special Attacks	Special Defenses	Intelligence	X.P. Value
giant—										
cloud	L	9	2	12+2-7	1	6-36	hurl rocks (2-24)	surprised only on a 1	average-very	4250+16/hp
fire	L	10/9	3	11+2-5	1	5-30	hurl rocks (2-20)	impervious to fire	average-low	2700+16/hp
frost	L	10	4	10+1-4	1	4-24	hurl rocks (2-20)	impervious to cold	average-low	2250+14/hp
hill	L	12	4	8+1-2	1	2-16	hurl rocks (2-16)	nil	low	1400+12/hp
stone	L	12	0	9+1-3	1	3-18	hurl rocks (3-30)	camouflage	average	1800+14/hp
storm	L	8/7	1	15+2-7	1	7-42	magic use (can also hurl rocks for 3-36 hp)	impervious to electricity	exceptional	5850+20/hp
gnoll	L	16(15)	5(+)***	2(+)***	1	2-8 or weapon	nil	nil	low-average	28+2/hp
goat, giant	L	16	7	3+1	1	2-16	charge (+4 to hit, 6-20)	nil	semi-	85+4/hp
goblin	S	20(18/16)***	6(+)***	1-1	1	1-6 or weapon	nil (missile weapons)	nil	average	10+1/hp
golem—										
clay	L	10	7	50 hp	1	3-30	haste	immunity to sharp weapons and most magic	non-	3600
flesh	L	12	9	40 hp	2	2-16/2-16	nil	hit only by magic weapons, immunity to most spells	semi-	2380
iron	L	7	3	80 hp	1	4-40	poison gas	hit only by +3 weapons, immunity to most spells	non-	14,550
stone	L	9	5	60 hp	1	3-24	slow spell	hit only by +2 magic weapons, immunity to most spells	non-	8950
gorgon	L	12	2	8	1	2-12	breath weapon	nil	animal	1750+10/hp
gray ooze	M-L	16	8	3+3	1	2-16	corrosive properties, possible psionics	immunity to most spells	animal	200+5/hp
green slime	S	16	9	2	nil	nil	infect flesh, corrosive properties	immunity to most weapons and spells	non-	610+2/hp
griffon	L	13	3	7	3	1-4/1-4/2-16	nil	nil	semi-	375+10/hp
groaning spirit	M	13	0	7	1	1-8	death groan, fear	hit only by magic weapons, some spell immunity, magic resistance (50%)	exceptional	2450+10/hp
harpy	M	16	7	3	3	1-3/1-3/1-6	singing & charm	nil	low	145+3/hp

*** For guards and leaders.

203

Monster	Size	To Hit A.C. 0	Armor Class	Hit Dice	No. of Attacks	Damage Per Attack	Special Attacks	Special Defenses	Intelligence	X.P. Value
hell hound	M	15/13	4	4-7	1	1-10	breath (1 hp/hd), surprise on 1-4	surprised only on 1, see invisible (50%)	low	250 + 8/hp
herd animal	S-L	**	8-7	1-5	**	**	stampede	nil	animal	**
hippocampus	L	15	5	4	1	1-4	nil	nil	average	60 + 4/hp
hippogriff	L	16	5	3 + 3	3	1-6/1-6/1-10	nil	nil	semi-	60 + 4/hp
hippopotomus	L	12	6	8	1	2-12 or 3-18	upset river craft	nil	animal	375 + 6/hp
hobgoblin^a	M	18(16/15)***	5(+)***	1 + 1	1	1-8 or weapon	nil (missile weapons)	nil	average	20 + 2/hp

^a Includes marine variety.

Monster	Size	To Hit A.C. 0	Armor Class	Hit Dice	No. of Attacks	Damage Per Attack	Special Attacks	Special Defenses	Intelligence	X.P. Value
homonculous	S	16	6	2	1	1-3	bite causes sleep	saves at level of its creator	very	81 + 2/hp
hydra —	L	see below	5	see below	see below	see below	1-4 attacks on same opponent	all heads must be killed to slay	semi-	see below
5 heads		15		5	5	1-6				165 + 5/hp
6 heads		13		6	6	1-6				250 + 6/hp
7 heads		13		7	7	1-8				400 + 8/hp
8 heads		12		8	8	1-8				650 + 10/hp
9 heads		12		9	9	1-8				1000 + 12/hp
10 heads		10		10	10	1-8				1500 + 14/hp
11 heads		10		11	11	1-10				2150 + 16/hp
12 heads		9		12	12	1-10				2850 + 16/hp
13 heads		9		13	13	1-10				3000 + 18/hp
14 heads		8		14	14	1-12				3950 + 18/hp
15 heads		8		15	15	1-12				4000 + 20/hp
16 heads		7		16	16	2-12				5250 + 20/hp

hydra, Lernaean — as above according to final number of heads.

hydra, pyro — as above plus amounts shown below:

Monster	Size	To Hit A.C. 0	Armor Class	Hit Dice	No. of Attacks	Damage Per Attack	Special Attacks	Special Defenses	Intelligence	X.P. Value
5 heads		15	5	5	5	1-6	1-4 attacks on same opponent, breath weapon (1-8/head except 11 & 12 dice monsters who gain 1-10/head)	all heads must be killed to slay		+500

** Variables preclude a fixed number.

*** For guards and leaders.

204

Monster	Size	To Hit A.C. 0	Armor Class	Hit Dice	No. of Attacks	Damage Per Attack	Special Attacks	Special Defenses	Intelligence	X.P. Value
6 heads		13		6	6	1-6				+700
7 heads		13		7	7	1-8				+825
8 heads		12		8	8	1-8				+1200
9 heads		12		9	9	1-8				+1600
10 heads		10		10	10	1-8				+1800
11 heads		10		11	11	1-10				+2550
12 heads		9		12	12	1-10				+3400
hyena	M	16	7	3	1	2-8	nil	nil	animal	35 + 3/hp
hyena, giant	L	15	7	5	1	3-12	nil	nil	semi-	90 + 5/hp
imp	S	16	2	2 + 2	1	1-4	poison, magic use	hit only by magic weapons, regeneration, magic resistance (25%), immunity to some magic, save at 7 hit dice	average	275 + 3/hp
intellect devourer	M	13	4	6 + 6	4	1-4 (×4)	hide in shadows, psionics	immunity to most weapons & magic	very	1510 + 8/hp
invisible stalker	L	12	3	8	1	4-16	surprise 1-5	invisibility (–2 on opponent "to hit" dice)	high	1090 + 10/hp
irish deer	L	15	7	4	1 (2)	2-12 (2-12)	nil	nil	animal	60 + 4/hp
ixitxachitl	M	18ᵉ	6	1 + 1(+)	1	3-12	cleric spell use	nil	average-high	28 + 2/hpᵉ
, vampire	M	16ᵉ	6	2 + 2(+)	1	3-12	energy level drain, spell use	regenerate (3/round)	average-high	290 + 3/hp

ᵉ This is for those without extra hit dice or spell use; adjust the numbers accordingly for such monsters.

Monster	Size	To Hit A.C. 0	Armor Class	Hit Dice	No. of Attacks	Damage Per Attack	Special Attacks	Special Defenses	Intelligence	X.P. Value
jackal	S	20	7	½	1	1-2	nil	nil	semi-	5 + 1/hp
jackalwere	S(M)	15	4	4	1	2-8	sleep gaze affects any level not saving	hit only by iron or magic weapons	very	800 + 4/hp
jaguar	L	15	6	4 + 1	3	1-3/1-3/1-8	rear claws (2-5/2-5)	surprised on 1 only	semi-	205 + 5/hp
ki-rin	L	9	–5	12	3	2-8/2-8/3-18	magic use, psionics	magic resistance (90%)	supra-genius	8500 + 16/hp
kobold	S	20	7 (6)	½	1	1-4 (1-6) or weapon	nil	nil	average-low	5 + 1/hp
lamia	M	12	3	9	1	1-4	touch drains 1 point of wisdom, spell use	nil	high	1700 + 12/hp

Monster	Size	To Hit A.C. 0	Armor Class	Hit Dice	No. of Attacks	Damage Per Attack	Special Attacks	Special Defenses	Intelligence	X.P. Value
lammasu	L	12	6	7 + 7	2	1-6/1-6	spell use	protection from evil	genius	850 + 10/hp
lamprey, normal	S	18	7	1 + 2	1	1-2	blood drain	nil	non-	28 + 2/hp
lamprey, giant	M	15	6	5	1	1-6	blood drain	nil	non-	165 + 5/hp
larva	M	19	7	1	1	2-5	nil	nil	low	10 + 1/hp
leech, giant	S-M	19/16/15	9	1-4	1	1-4	drain blood, anesthesia, disease	nil	non-	160 + 4/hp
leopard	M	16	6	3 + 2	3	1-3/1-3/1-6	rear claws (1-4/1-4)	surprised on 1 only	semi-	150 + 4/hp
leprechaun	S	—	8	2-5 hp	nil	nil	magic use	never surprised	exceptional	80 + 1/hp
leucrotta	L	13	4	6 + 1	1	3-18	voice imitation	back kicks (1-6/1-6)	average	475 + 8/hp
lich	M	10	0	11+	1	1-10 + special	paralyzation, fear, spell use, (psionics)	magic weapons only can hit, immunity to some magic	supra-genius	10500 + 16/hp
lion	L	15	5/6	5 + 2	3	1-4/1-4/1-10	rear claws (2-7/2-7)	surprised on 1 only	semi-	300 + 6/hp
mountain	M	16	6	3 + 1	3	1-3/1-3/1-6	rear claws (1-4/1-4)	surprised on 1 only	semi-	110 + 4/hp
spotted	L	13	5/6	6 + 2	3	1-4/1-4/1-12	rear claws (2-8/2-8)	surprised on 1 only	semi-	300 + 6/hp
lizard —										
fire	L	10	3	10	3	1-8/1-8/2-16	fire puff	immune to fire	animal	1350 + 14/hp
giant	L	16	5	3 + 1	1	1-8	die 20 indicates double damage (2-16)	nil	non-	125 + 4/hp
minotaur	L	12	5	8	3	2-12/2-12/3-18	surprise on 1-4, bite and hold fast on a 20	nil	non-	875 + 10/hp
subterranean	L	13	5	6	1	2-12	able to move on walls and ceilings, 20 equals double damage (4-24)	nil	non-	350 + 6/hp
lizard man	M	16	5 (4)	2 + 1	3	1-2/1-2/1-8 (or weapon)	(missile weapons)	nil	low-average	35(50) + 3/hp
locathah	M	****	6	2	1	weapon	nil	nil	very	20 + 2/hp
lurker above	L	10	6	10	1	1-6	surprise on 1-4, smother prey in 2-5 rounds	nil	non-	1500 + 14/hp
lycanthrope —										
werebear	L	13	2	7 + 3	3	1-3/1-3/2-8	hug (2-16)	hit only by silver or magic weapons	exceptional	825 + 10/hp

Monster	Size	To Hit A.C. 0	Armor Class	Hit Dice	No. of Attacks	Damage Per Attack	Special Attacks	Special Defenses	Intelligence	X.P. Value
wereboar	L	15	4	5 + 2	1	2-12	nil	hit only by silver or magic weapons	average	275 + 6/hp
wererat	S-M	16	6	3 + 1	1	1-8 (sword)	surprise on 1-4	hit only by silver or magic weapons	very	150 + 4/hp
weretiger	L	13	3	6 + 2	3	1-4/1-4/1-12	rear claws (2-5/2-5)	hit only by silver or magic weapons	average	525 + 8/hp
werewolf	M	15	5	4 + 3	1	2-8	surprise on 1-3	hit only by silver or magic weapons	average	205 + 5/hp
lynx, giant	M	16	6	2 + 2	3	1-2/1-2/1-4	rear claws (1-3/1-3) surprise 1-5	hide (90%), detect traps (75%)	very	120 + 3/hp
mammoth	L	9	5	13	5	3-18/3-18/2-16/2-12/2-12	nil	nil	semi-	3000 + 18/hp
manticore	L	13	4	6 + 3	3	1-3/1-3/1-8	tail spikes	nil	low	525 + 8/hp
mastodon	L	9	6	12	5	2-16/2-16/2-12 2-12/2-12	nil	nil	semi-	2000 + 16/hp
medusa	M	13	5	6	1	1-4	gaze petrifies, hair of asps poisons	nil	very	725 + 6/hp
men	M	**	**	**	**	**	**	**	**	**
merman	M	18	7	1 + 1	1	by weapon	nil	nil	avg.-very	20 + 2/hp
mimic	L	13/12/10	7	7-10	1	3-12	glue, surprise	camouflage	semi- to average	1300 + 12/hp 1000 + 10/hp
mind flayer	M	12	5	8 + 4	4	2 hp each	mind blast, psionics, tentacle hit slays in 1-4 rounds	nil	genius	1800 + 12/hp
minotaur	L	13	6	6 + 3	2	2-8 or 1-4/ by weapon	nil	surprised on a 1 only	low	400 + 8/hp
mold	*****	*****	*****	*****	*****	*****	*****	*****	*****	*****
morkoth	M	13	3	7	1	1-10	hypnosis, charm	spell reflection	exceptional	1050 + 8/hp
mummy	M	13	3	6 + 3	1	1-12	fear, paralyzation, disease	hit only by magic weapons (or fire or holy water) at reduced damage, immunity to some magic	low	1150 + 8/hp
naga —										
guardian	L	10/9	3	11-12	2	1-6/2-8	poison bite, spit poison, spell use	nil	exceptional	3550 + 16/hp
spirit	L	12/10	4	9-10	1	1-3	poison bite, spell use, gaze charms	nil	high	2700 + 14/hp

** Variable preclude a fixed number.
***** Monster not rateable.

Monster	Size	To Hit A.C. 0	Armor Class	Hit Dice	No. of Attacks	Damage Per Attack	Special Attacks	Special Defenses	Intelligence	X.P. Value
water	M	13/12	5	7-8	1	1-4	poison bite, spell use	nil	very	1325 + 10/hp
neo-otyugh	L	12/10/9	0	9-12	3	2-12/2-12/1-3	disease	never surprised	avg.-very	1500 + 15/hp
night hag	M	12	9	8	1	2-12	sleep magic, spell use	hit only by iron, silver or +3 weapons, immunity to some magic	exceptional	1750 + 10/hp
nightmare	L	13	-4	6 + 6	3	2-8/4-10/4-10	nil	smoke cloud (-2 on opponent "to hit" and damage)	high	600 + 8/hp
nixie	S	20	7	½	1	by weapon	charm	magic resistance (25%)	very	32 + 1/hp
nymph	M	—	9	3	nil	nil	sight causes blindness/death, spell use	magic resistance (50%)	exceptional	350 + 3/hp
ochre jelly	M	13	8	6	1	3-12	nil	immune to lightning	non-	150 + 6/hp
octopus	L	12	7	8	7	1-4 (×6)/2-12	constriction	nil	animal	550 + 10/hp
ogre	L	15	5	4 + 1	1	1-10 or by weapon	nil	nil	low	90 + 5/hp
leader	L	13	4	30-33 hp	1	2-12 or by weapon	nil	nil	low-average	225 + 8/hp
chieftain	L	13	3	34-37 hp	1	4-14 or by weapon	nil	nil	average	225 + 8/hp
ogre magi	L	15	4	5 + 2	1	1-12	magic & spell use	regeneration	avg. to excep.	900 + 6/hp
chieftain	L	12	4	5 + 2 + 2 die	1	3-14	magic & spell use	regeneration	avg. to excep.	1300 + 10/hp
orc	M	19	6	1	1	1-6 or by weapon	nil	nil	low-average	10 + 1/hp
guard or subchief	M	16	4	11 hp	1	2-7 or by weapon	nil	nil	average	20 + 2/hp
bodyguard or chief	M	16	4	13-16 hp	1	2-8 or by weapon	nil	nil	high-average	20 + 2/hp
otter, giant	L	15	5	5	1	3-18	nil	nil	semi-	90 + 5/hp
otyugh	M-L	13/12	3	6-8	3	1-8/1-8/2-5	disease	never surprised	low-average	700 + 8/hp
owl, giant	M	15	6	4	3	2-8/2-8/2-5	surprise on 1-5	nil	very	150 + 4/hp
owlbear	L	15	5	5 + 2	3	1-6/1-6/2-12	hug (2-16) with paw hit of 18	nil	low	225 + 8/hp
pegasus	L	15	6	4	3	1-8/1-8/1-3	nil	nil	average	60 + 4/hp
peryton	M	15	7	4	1	4-16	nil	hit only by magic weapons	average	150 + 4/hp
piercer —										
largest	M	15	3	4	1	4-24	all are 95% likely to attack by surprise	nil	non-	60 + 4/hp

Monster	Size	To Hit A.C. 0	Armor Class	Hit Dice	No. of Attacks	Damage Per Attack	Special Attacks	Special Defenses	Intelligence	X.P. Value
large	S	16	3	3	1	3-18	surprise on 1-4	nil	non-	35 + 3/hp
medium	S	16	3	2	1	2-12		nil	non-	20 + 2/hp
small	S	19	3	1	1	1-6		nil	non-	10 + 1/hp
pike, giant	L	15	5	4	1	4-16	surprise on 1-4	nil	non-	85 + 4/hp
pixie	S	20	5	½	1	by weapon	special arrows, spell use, magic	magic resistance (25%), invisibility, (−4 on opponent's "to hit" dice)	exceptional	105 + 1/hp
porcupine, giant	L	13	5	6	1	2-8	shoot quills (1-8 for 1-4 hp each)	quills (1-4 per attack upon)	animal	350 + 6/hp
portuguese man-o-war	S-L	19/16/15	9	1-4	1	1-10	paralyzation	transparent (90% undetectable)	non-	185 + 4/hp
pseudo-dragon	S	16	2	2	1	1-3	poison sting (+4 to hit), see invisible	chameleon power, magic resistance (35%)	average	200 + 2/hp
purple worm	L	8	6	15	1 & 1	2-24/2-8	swallow whole, poison sting	nil	non-	4900 + 20/hp
quasit	S	16	2	3	3	1-2/1-2/1-4	attack poison causes dexterity loss (1/hit), spell use	regenerate, magic use & partial immunity to spells, magic resistant (25%), save as 7 dice monster, hit only by magic weapons	low	325 + 3/hp
rakshasa	M	13	−4	7	3	1-3/1-3/2-5	illusion, spell use	hit only by magic weapons, not affected by spells under 8th level	very	925 + 8/hp
ram, giant	L	15	6	4	1	2-12	charge (4-24)	nil	animal	85 + 4/hp
rat, giant	S	20	7	½	1	1-3	disease	nil	semi-	7 + 1/hp
ray —										
manta	L	12/10	6	8-11	1 & 1	3-12/2-20	swallow whole, paralyzation	nil	non-	1200 + 16/hp
pungi	L	15	7	4	1-12	1-4 each	poison, concealment	nil	non-	410 + 4/hp
sting	S	19	7	1	1	1-3	poison	nil	non-	90 + 1/hp
remorhaz	L	**	2/4/0	7-14	1	6-36	swallow whole	glowing back heat melts non-magic weapons	animal	1700 + 16/hp

** Variables preclude a fixed number.

209

Monster	Size	To Hit A.C. 0	Armor Class	Hit Dice	No. of Attacks	Damage Per Attack	Special Attacks	Special Defenses	Intelligence	X.P. Value
rhinoceros	L	12	6	8-9	1	2-8 or 2-12	charge (4-16 or 4-24)	nil	animal	900 + 12/hp
wooly	L	10	5	10	1	2-12	charge (4-24)	nil	animal	1350 + 14/hp
roc	L	7	4	18	2 or 1	3-18/3-18 or 4-24	nil	nil	animal	5000 + 25/hp
roper	L	10/9	0	10-12	1	5-20	6 poisonous strands cause weakness	magic resistance (80%), disguise ability	exceptional	2750 + 16/hp
rot grub	S	—	9	1 hp	nil	nil	burrow into flesh	nil	non-	nil
rust monster	M	15	2	5	nil	nil	destroy metal	hit on monster destroys metal	animal	185 + 4/hp
sahuagin	M (L)	16	5	2 + 2	1 or 3 or 5	by weapon or 1-2/1-2/1-4/1-4	possible spell use, weapons	sight and hearing keenness	high	35 + 3/hp
baron/noble	L	13	3	6 + 6					exceptional	350 + 8/hp
chieftain	L	15	4	4 + 4					very	130 + 5/hp
cleric	M-L	16	5	2-6					very	**
guard/lieutenant	L	16	5	3 + 3					very	85 + 4/hp
king	L	10	1	10 + 10		triple damage			genius	1350 + 14/hp
mutant	L	16	4	2 + 4	2 or 5 or 7	by weapons or 1-2 (×4)/1-4/1-4/1-4			high	50 + 3/hp
prince	L	12	3	8 + 8		double damage			genius	600 + 12/hp
salamander	M	12	5/3	7 + 7	2	by weapon/2-12, constrict/2-12	heat (1-6)	hit only by magic weapons, heat and limited spell immunity	high	825 + 10/hp
satyr	M	15	5	5	1	2-8	magical weapons, magic pipes	surprised on a 1 only, 90% undetectable, magic resistance (50%)	very	280 + 5/hp (+300 if piper)
scorpion, giant	M	13	3	5 + 5	3	1-10/1-10/1-4	poison sting	nil	non-	650 + 6/hp
sea hag	M	16	7	3	1	dagger	weakness, death gaze	magic resistance (50%)	average	600 + 3/hp
sea horse	L	16/15	7	2-4	1	1-4 or 2-5 or 2-8	nil	nil	semi-	20 + 4/hp
sea lion	L	13	5/3	6	3	1-6/1-6/2-12	nil	nil	semi-	150 + 6/hp
shadow	M	16	7	3 + 3	1	2-5	drain strength	hit only by magic weapons, 90% undetectable	low	255 + 4/hp

** Variables preclude a fixed number.

210

Monster	Size	To Hit A.C. 0	Armor Class	Hit Dice	No. of Attacks	Damage Per Attack	Special Attacks	Special Defenses	Intelligence	X.P. Value
shambling mound	L	12/10	0	8-11	2	2-16/2-16	suffocation	partial magic and spell immunity	low	1800 + 10/hp
shark	M-L	**	6	3-8	1	2-5 or 2-8 or 3-12	nil	nil	non-	**
giant	L	**	5	10-15	1	4-16 or 5-20 or 6-24	swallow whole	nil	nil	**
shedu	L	10	4	9 + 9	2	1-6/1-6	psionics	ethereal, magic resistance (25%)	exceptional	1950 + 14/hp
shrieker	S-L	—	7	3	nil	nil	nil	noise	non-	5 + 1/hp
skeleton	M	19	7	1	1	1-6	nil	sharp weapons score half damage only	non-	14 + 1/hp
skunk, giant	M	15	7	5	1	1-6	squirt musk	squirt musk	animal	165 + 5/hp
slithering tracker	S	15	5	5	nil	nil	paralyzation	95% undetectable	average	280 + 5/hp
slug, giant	L	9	8	12	1	1-12	spit acid	not harmed by blunt weapons	non-	2000 + 16/hp
snake, giant —										
amphisbaena	M	13	3	6	2	1-3/1-3	poison	not harmed by cold	animal	475 + 6/hp
constrictor	L	13	5	6 + 1	2	1-4/2-8	continuing constriction	nil	animal	225 + 8/hp
poisonous	L	15	5	4 + 2	1	1-3	poison (3-18 even if save)	nil	animal	390 + 5/hp
sea	L	12/10	5	8-10	2	1-6/3-18	poison & constriction	nil	animal	1000 + 12/hp
spitting	M	15	5	4 + 2	1	1-3	poison & poison spit	nil	animal	390 + 5/hp
spectre	M	13	2	7 + 3	1	1-8	energy drain (2 levels)	hit only by magic weapons, partial magic and spell resistance	high	1650 + 10/hp
sphinx —										
andro-	L	9	-2	12	2	2-12/2-12	spell use, roar	nil	exceptional	2850 + 16/hp
crio-	L	10	0	10	3	2-8/2-8/3-18	nil	nil	average	1350 + 14/hp
gyno-	L	12	-1	8	2	2-8/2-8	spell use	nil	genius	1550 + 10/hp
hieraco-	L	12	1	9	3	2-8/2-8/1-10	nil	nil	low	600 + 12/hp
spider —										
giant	L	15	4	4 + 4	1	2-8	webs, poison	nil	low	315 + 5/hp

** Variables preclude a fixed number.

211

Monster	Size	To Hit A.C. 0	Armor Class	Hit Dice	No. of Attacks	Damage Per Attack	Special Attacks	Special Defenses	Intelligence	X.P. Value
huge	M	16	6	2+2	1	1-6	surprise on 1-5, poison	nil	animal	145 + 3/hp
large	S	18	8	1+1	1	1	poison	nil	non-	65 + 2/hp
phase	L	15	7	5+5	1	1-6	webs, poison	phasing out	low	700 + 6/hp
water	M	16	5	3+3	1	1-4	poison	nil	semi-	190 + 4/hp
sprite	S	19	6	1	1	by weapon	sleep arrows	invisibility, 75% undetectable otherwise	very	80 + 1/hp
squid, giant	L	9	7/3	12	9	1-6 (×8)/5-20	constriction (2-12)	tentacle hits, ink	non-	2000 + 16/hp
stag	L	16	7	3	1 or 2	2-8 or 1-3/1-3	nil	nil	animal	35 + 3/hp
stag, giant	L	15	7	5	1 or 2	4-16 or 1-4/1-4	nil	nil	animal	90 + 5/hp
stirge	S	18	8	1+1	1	1-3	attack as 4 hit dice monster, drain blood (1-4)	nil	animal	36 + 2/hp
strangle weed	S	16/15	6	2-4	1	special	constriction	nil	animal	35 + 3/hp
su-monster	M	13	6	5+5	5	1-4 (×4)/2-8	psionics	nil	average	225 + 6/hp
sylph	M	—	9	3	nil	nil	spell use, magic	invisibility, magic resistance (50%)	exceptional	325 + 3/hp
thought eater	S	—	9	3	nil	nil	devour mental energy	ethereal	non-	255 + 3/hp
tick, giant	S	16/15	3	2-4	1	1-4	blood drain (1-6), disease	nil	non-	105 + 2/hp
tiger	L	13	6	5+5	3	2-5/2-5/1-10	rear claws (2-8/2-8)	surprised on a 1 only	semi-	225 + 6/hp
sabre-tooth	L	11	6	7+2	3	2-5/2-5/2-12	rear claws (2-8/2-8)	surprised on a 1 only	animal	550 + 10/hp
titan	L	7	2 to -3	17-22	1		spell use, psionics	invisibility, etherealness	genius to supra-genius	7000 + 25/hp
lesser			2	17		7-42				7000 + 25/hp
lesser			1	18		7-42				7000 + 25/hp
major			0	19		7-42				9000 + 30/hp
major			-1	20		7-42				9000 + 30/hp
elder			-2	21		8-48				11000 + 35/hp
elder			-3	22		8-48				11000 + 35/hp
titanothere	L	9	6	12		2-16	charge (4-32), trample (2-12/2-12)	nil	animal	2000 + 16/hp
toad, giant	M	16	6	2+4	1	2-8	hop	nil	animal	50 + 3/hp

Monster	Size	To Hit A.C. 0	Armor Class	Hit Dice	No. of Attacks	Damage Per Attack	Special Attacks	Special Defenses	Intelligence	X.P. Value
toad, ice	L	15	4	5	1	3-12	cold radiation	nil	average	205 + 5/hp
toad, poisonous	M	16	7	2	1	2-5	poison	nil	animal	155 + 2/hp
trapper	L	9	3	12	1	4 + A.C.	95% undetectable, smothers in 6 rounds, trapped cannot use weapons	partial immunity to cold and fire	high	2850 + 16/hp
treant	L		0	7-12	2		control 1 or 2 trees	never surprised	very	
"shrubling"		13/12		7-8		2-16/2-16				1200 + 10/hp
mature		12/10		9-10		3-18/3-18				1950 + 14/hp
"moss trunk"		10/9		11-12		4-24/4-24				2850 + 16/hp
triton	M	16	5	3	1	by weapon	spell use, magic, psionics	magic resistance (90%)	high & up	105 + 3/hp
leaders	M	**	4 or better	4-9	1	by weapon	spell use, magic, psionics	magic resistance (90%)	high & up	**
troglodyte	M	16	5	2	3 or 1	1-3/1-3/2-5 or by weapon	revulsion odor, missiles, surprise on 1-4	chameleon power	low	36 + 2/hp
chief leader		13	5 or 4	6						300 + 6/hp
major leader		13	5	4						110 + 4/hp
minor leader/guard		16	5	3						65 + 3/hp
female		18	5	1 + 1						28 + 2/hp
troll	L	13	4	6 + 6	3	5-8/5-8/2-12	nil	surprised on a 1 only, regeneration (+3/r)	low	525 + 8/hp
turtle, giant —										
sea	L	8	2/5	15	1	4-16	nil	nil	non-	900 + 10/hp
snapping	L	10	0/5	10	1	6-24	surprise on 1-4, shoot neck	nil	non-	1950 + 14/hp
umber hulk	L	12	2	8 + 8	3	3-12/3-12/2-10	gaze confuses	nil	average	1300 + 12/hp
unicorn	L	15	2	4 + 4	3	1-6/1-6/1-12	charge (2-24), surprise on 1-5	immune to poison, senses enemies at 24", teleport, saves as 11th level magic-user	average	400 + 5/hp
vampire	M	12	1	8 + 3	1	5-10	energy drain (2 levels), charm	hit only by magic weapons, regenerates, gaseous form, limited immunity to magical attacks/poison/paralyzation	exceptional	3800 + 12/hp

** Variables preclude a fixed number.

213

Monster	Size	To Hit A.C. 0	Armor Class	Hit Dice	No. of Attacks	Damage Per Attack	Special Attacks	Special Defenses	Intelligence	X.P. Value
wasp, giant	M	15	4	4	2	2-8/1-4	poison	nil	non-	320 + 4/hp
water weird	L	16	6	3 + 3	nil	nil	drag into water, take over water elementals	general immunity to weapons and magic	very	370 + 4/hp
weasel, giant	M	16	6	3 + 3	1	2-12	drain blood (2-12/r)	nil	animal	125 + 4/hp
whale	L		4				smash with tail for d8 damage equal to half hit dice of whale, sperm whales swallow whole	nil	low	**
black		7		18-23	1	3-24 or 4-32				
humpback		7		26-33	1	4-32 or 4-40				
killer		9/8		12-15	1	6-24 to 10-40				
right		7		20-26	1	2-16 or 3-24				
sperm		7		29-36	1	10-40 to 15-60				
white (beluga)		9		12-13	1	5-20				
wight	M	15	5	4 + 3	1	1-4	energy drain	nil	average	540 + 5/hp
will-o-wisp	S	12	-8	9	1	2-16	nil	invisibility, general immunity to spells	exceptional	1200 + 12/hp
wind walker	L	13	7	6 + 3	1	3-18	nil	telepathic, ethereal, limited immunity to spells, magic	very	575 + 8/hp
wolf	S	16	7	2 + 2	1	2-5	(howling)	nil	semi-	35 + 3/hp
dire	M	16	6	3 + 3	1	2-8	(howling)	nil	semi-	60 + 4/hp
winter	L	15	5	5	1	2-8	frost breath	not harmed by cold	average	245 + 5/hp
worg	L	15	6	4 + 4	1	2-8	(howling)	nil	low	90 + 5/hp
wolverine	S	16	5	3	3	1-4/1-4/2-5	musk, exceptional intelligence in combat	nil	semi-	125 + 3/hp
giant	M	15	4	4 + 4	3	2-5/2-5/2-8	musk, exceptional intelligence in combat	nil	semi-	205 + 5/hp

** Variables preclude a fixed number.

214

Monster	Size	To Hit A.C. 0	Armor Class	Hit Dice	No. of Attacks	Damage Per Attack	Special Attacks	Special Defenses	Intelligence	X.P. Value
wraith	M	15	4	5 + 3	1	1-6	energy drain	hit only by silver/ magic weapons, limited immunity to spells/magic/ poison/paralysis	very	575 + 6/hp
wyvern	L	12	3	7 + 7	2	2-16/1-6	poison	nil	low	925 + 10/hp
xorn	M	12	-2	7 + 7	4	1-3 (×3)/6-24	surprise on 1-5	molecular adjustment, immunity to most spells and magic	average	1275 + 10/hp
yeti	L	15	6	4 + 4	2	1-6/1-6	squeeze (2-16), paralyzation	near invisibility, immunity to cold	average	435 + 5/hp
zombie	M	16	8	2	1	1-8	nil	some spell immunity	non-	20 + 2/hp

APPENDIX F: GAMBLING

This pastime is common in all taverns, inns, and just about any barracks. You may, of course, make up any games for wagering purposes you wish. Here are some few for those of you who are unfamiliar with basic dice games. Cards are too involved to go into here except as noted.

Dice Games:

Craps: The shooter wins on a first roll (2d6) of 7 or 11, or loses on 2, 3, or 12. Otherwise the shooter rolls until the number first rolled is rolled a second time — a win — or a 7 is rolled — a loss. Shooters bet before rolling, as others may. Side bets may be made thereafter as applicable, if there are takers. (The fancy line play of modern casinos is ignored.) Dice pass clockwise to next player when the shooter loses.

Horse: The first roller is determined by whatever means is desired. 5d6 are used, 6 high, 1 low. Lowest to highest hands are: pair, two pair, three of a kind, straight (1-5 or 2-6), full house (triplet and pair), four of a kind, five of a kind. The first roller may elect to roll once or twice. If only once, all other players may roll only once to beat him or her. If two rolls are made, the roller may retain none, one, two, three, or four of the dice of the first toss, rolling the remainder. Winner becomes the "boss" — first roller.

Knucklebones: Again, this is a crap-type game, but the object is to score the highest total. A variant allows a second roll of the dice by the first shooter, retaining none or one of them, if he or she so desires, but then all other players are entitled to do the same. Winner rolls first.

Slot Variant: Use 3d6, one roll only, the wager being made prior to the roll. The table below is weighted in favor of the "house". You may, of course, devise your own tables:

6-6-1	PAYS	2-1	1 =	LEMON
6-6-2		3-1	2 =	ORANGE
6-6-3		4-1	3 =	BAR
6-6-4		5-1	4 =	BELL
6-6-5		6-1	5 =	PLUM
1-1-1		4-1	6 =	CHERRIES
2-2-2		8-1		
3-3-3		10-1		
4-4-4		12-1		
5-5-5		24-1 (little jackpot)		
6-6-6		36-1 (big jackpot)		

Zowie Slot Variant: Use 3d8 instead of 3d6. The odds on any given combination are changed from 1:216 to 1:512. Payoffs are as follows:

6-6-1	PAYS	2-1	1 =	LEMON
6-6-2		4-1	2 =	ORANGE
6-6-3		6-1	3 =	BAR
6-6-4		8-1	4 =	BELL
6-6-5		10-1	5 =	PLUM
6-6-7		12-1	6 =	CHERRIES
6-6-8		15-1	7 =	ANCHOR
1-1-1		8-1	8 =	CROWN
2-2-2		12-1		
3-3-3		14-1		
4-4-4		16-1		
5-5-5		20-1		
6-6-6		24-1		
7-7-7		50-1 (jackpot)		
8-8-8		100-1 (zowie jackpot)		

Dice Racing: Use a checker board. Four players maximum place their tokens on alternate rows. The object is to move the token to the end of the board, sideways one, and then back on the adjacent file to the first row. A roll of d6 determines the number of spaces each player moves. Wagers are to be made prior to commencement of game.

In Between: Roll 3d20 — 2 white and 1 of a different color. The player must roll in between the 2 white dice with the colored die. Equaling a number is a loss. If the 2 white dice equal each other, the loss is automatic. Odds are always 5:2 before dice are cast. Note: A crooked house might paint 11 sides of a die black and only 9 red.

Card Games:

Twenty-One: A 52 card deck is used, each player betting against the "house" dealer (the DM). Two cards are dealt to each player and the dealer. Players in turn elect to take additional cards up to a total of five. Hands totalling over 21 automatically lose, hands of five cards under 22 automatically win double their wager (exception: dealer).

The object is to come as close to 21 as possible. Ties go to the "house". Aces count either 1 or 11 at the holding player's option, face cards count as 10, and numbered cards are as marked. Players get first two cards down; others are dealt face up. Dealer gets second card face up. Dealer must take a hit (additional card) on any total under 17, and cannot take a card on any total of 17 or better. (This rule is not per Hoyle.) Dealer gets cards last, bets are made after the first two cards are dealt around. If a player has a natural pair he or she may elect to "go double", flipping them up, asking for two additional face down cards (one for each face up card), and betting on each hand. The "house" always retains the deal.

High-Low: Each player gets two cards face down. Prior to dealing some stake is placed in the pot. After looking at the cards, each player turns one up, and the player with the highest up card bets. (A three raise limit is suggested.) Each player has the option of changing his or her up or down card for a fresh one from the deck. This takes place three times going around the table, with a betting interval after each round. A 2 is low, an ACE is high. The object is to have the highest hand (a pair on down) to a 2-3 (lowest possible hand, followed by 2-4, 3-4, 2-5, 3-5, 4-5, 2-6, 3-6, 4-6, 5-6, 2-7, and so forth). High and low hands split the pot equally, odd money going to high.

Other gambling games can be devised on principles of colors, shapes, position or whatever.

APPENDIX G: TRAPS

TRAP LIST (d%)

01-05	Arrow trap	53-54	Gas, weakness
06	Arrow trap, poisoned	55-56	Jaw trap
07	Ball trap	57	Lightning bolt
08-09	Caltrops	58-59	Pendulum, ball or blade
10	Caltrops, poisoned	60-63	Pit
11	Ceiling block falls	64-65	Pit, locking
12	Ceiling collapses	66-67	Pit, locking & flooding
13	Ceiling lowers	68-70	Pit, with spikes
14-16	Chute	71-72	Pit, with poisoned spikes
17-18	Door, falling	73-77	Passage, blocked by
19-23	Door, one way		falling bars
24-30	Door, resisting	78-79	Passage, closed by
31	Door, specific		stone block
32	Door, spring	80	Room, elevator
33	Floor, collapsing	81	Room, flooding
34	Floor, illusionary	82	Room, sliding
35-36	Gas, blinding	83-84	Scything blade
37-38	Gas, corroding	85-87	Spear trap
39-40	Gas, fear	88	Spear trap, poisoned
41-42	Gas, nausea	89	Stairs, collapsing
43-46	Gas, obscuring	90-91	Teleporter
47-48	Gas, poison	92	Vent, acid
49-50	Gas, sleep	93-94	Vent, fire
51-52	Gas, slowing	95-00	Vent, gas

APPENDIX H: TRICKS

As with traps, there are nearly endless numbers of tricks which can be devised and used in the campaign. Most experienced Dungeon Masters will probably already have a proud repertoire of clever and innovative (not to mention unique and astounding) artifices, deceptions, conundrums, and sundry tricks which will put to shame the humble offering which follows. Nonetheless, this enumeration might serve for those who have not yet had the experience and seasoning necessary to invent more clever devices to bring consternation to overbold and incautious characters. Even if you are fairly conversant with the idea of tricks in the dungeon, check the lists anyway, for you might find one or two useful ideas there.

The first list is *features* commonly found in a dungeon. Thereafter is a longer list of *attributes*. Select a feature or several, as desired. Assign one or more attributes to each feature, or combination thereof, in order to develop an interesting trick which will challenge the players and yet not

be too difficult for the level of experience of their characters. When you come to an appropriate spot in your dungeon (or elsewhere for that matter), enliven the place with the addition of a few tricky attributes to an otherwise unremarkable or now ordinary feature.

FEATURES

ALTAR	MACHINE
ARCH	MONSTER
CEILING	PASSAGE
CONTAINER (barrel, jar, vase, etc.)	PEDESTAL
DOME	PILLAR OR COLUMN
DOOR	PIT
DOOR, SECRET	POOL
FIRE	ROOM
FIREPLACE	STAIRWAY
FORCE FIELD	STATUE
FOUNTAIN	TAPESTRY
FRESCO, MOSAIC, OR PAINTING	VEGETATION
FURNISHINGS	WALL
IDOL	WELL
ILLUSION	

ATTRIBUTES

AGES	MOVES/ROLLS
ANIMATED	ONE-WAY
ANTI-MAGIC	PIVOTS TWO POSSIBLE WAYS
APPEARING/DISAPPEARING	POINTS
ASKS	POISON
ATTACKS	POLYMORPHING
CHANGES - ALIGNMENT	RANDOMLY ACTS
- ATTRIBUTE	RELEASES - COINS
- CLASS	- COUNTERFEIT
- MINDS FROM BODY	- GEMS/JEWELRY
TO BODY	- MAGIC ITEM
- SEX	- MAP
COMBINATION	RESISTING - GENERAL
COLLAPSING	- SPECIFIC
DIRECTS	RISING/SINKING
DISINTEGRATES	SUGGESTS
DISTORTED - WIDTH/LENGTH	SUSPENDS ANIMATION
- HEIGHT/DEPTH	TAKES/STEALS
ENLARGES/REDUCES	TALKS - INTELLIGENTLY/NORMALLY
ENRAGES	- NONSENSE
ELECTRICAL SHOCK - IF METALLIC	- POETRY & RHYMES
- MAGICAL	- SINGING
FALSE	- SPELL CASTING
FLESH TO STONE	- YELLS/SCREAMS
FRUIT	SHIFTING
GASEOUS	SHOOTS
GEASES	SLIDING
GRAVITY - GREATER	SLOPING
- LESSER	SPINNING
- NIL	SYMBIOTIC
- VARYING	TELEPORTS
GREED-PRODUCING	WISH FULFILLMENT
INTELLIGENT	WISH FULFILLMENT, REVERSAL
INVISIBLE	

The following examples of tricks are offered as a guide only. Vary such tricks in order to avoid the possibility of player knowledge.

ALTAR: Touching this feature without uttering the name of the deity to which it is dedicated will alternately do the following: *age* the character 10 years, *animate* his or her weapons for 4 rounds and cause them to attack their owner (cf. *Sword of Dancing*), or cause *cancellation* (as the rod) to drain his or her most powerful magic item of all of its dweomer. If the deity's name is uttered when the altar is touched, then characters of neutral alignment will have a *wish* granted if it is made within the turn; characters of other alignment will have a *geas* laid upon them to go and slay a monster who is inimical to the deity, but upon successful completion of this duty they too will be granted a *wish*.

ARCH: This feature will exist when the party first enters the place, but thereafter it will appear and disappear on a random basis on a 1 in 20 chance for either. It will alternately do one of the following: *change sex, enlarge/reduce* to giant/brownie size (assuming man size upon entry), or *teleport* the individual to an area where gems grow on plants. Those within the arch when it disappears are trapped until it reappears again, and exiting does not cause any of its functions to operate.

CONTAINER: This is a jar which is alternately a *polymorphed* black pudding which the touch of a character will dispel to its normal form, or an obsidian vase of the finest workmanship which is worth 5,000 gold pieces. If a *polymorph* spell is cast upon the jar form, or a *dispel magic* is cast upon the vase form, then the vase will become a normal item of great worth. Otherwise, each time it is touched there are equal chances for either form to exist.

DOOR, SECRET: This *pivoting* stone portal will always swing open to the left, giving egress to an area guarded by a basilisk. However, if a second hidden stud is found (1% chance), then it will pivot to the right and allow entry to a chamber containing a magical fountain.

FOUNTAIN: This feature is a beautiful work of onyx and jet black stone. A grinning gargoyle and a lovely nymph are depicted, the former with an open mouth, the latter with a pitcher. As soon as the party enters, the gargoyle will ask a riddle, and if it is not answered it will spray poison upon the group (save or dead). If answered, the nymph will then recite a poem which is a clue to a special treasure.

MONSTER: The shriekers found in the area have a heavy growth of yellow mold upon them and if they are struck, the spores will spread in their usual poisonous cloud. These creatures totally surround a pedestal.

PEDESTAL: This short, thick cylinder has six knobs in the shape of flowers. Atop the pedestal lies a strangely wrought crown, but it is untouchable due to a *force field*. Turning the knobs will 1) lower one *attribute* of the character by 1 point, 2) give a *magical shock* for 5-50 hit points, 3) turn the character to *gaseous* form, 4) deliver a scroll upon which is a clue as to how to lower the force field, 5) turn the character permanently *invisible*, and 6) open a trap door in the floor which drops all in the room down a chute to a level far beneath the place.

From these examples, you will note that nearly endless combinations are possible even without your own ideas for additions — and these will surely come. There can be monsters hidden by *illusion*, illusional monsters, symbiotic monsters, monsters in combined pairs or trios or whatever, parts of the dungeon which are distorted, invisible, shifting, slanting, spinning, and so on. For some further examples of tricks in the campaign you might wish to consult **DUNGEONS & DRAGONS,** Volume 3, **The Underworld & Wilderness Adventures,** and **GREYHAWK,** Supplement I.

APPENDIX I : DUNGEON DRESSING (MISCELLANEOUS ITEMS AND POINTS OF SEMI-INTEREST FOR CORRIDORS AND UNPOPULATED AREAS OR TO ROUND OUT OTHERWISE DRAB PLACES)

Air Currents:

01-05	breeze, slight
06-10	breeze, slight, damp
11-12	breeze, gusting
13-18	cold current
19-20	downdraft, slight
21-22	downdraft, strong
23-69	still
70-75	still, very chill
76-85	still, warm (or hot)
86-87	updraft, slight
88-89	updraft, strong
90-93	wind, strong
94-95	wind, strong, gusting
96-00	wind, strong, moaning

Odors:

01-03	acrid smell
04-05	chlorine smell
06-39	dank, mouldy smell
40-49	earthy smell
50-57	manure smell
58-61	metallic smell
62-65	ozone smell
66-70	putrid smell
71-75	rotting vegetation smell
76-77	salty, wet smell
78-82	smoky smell
83-89	stale, fetid smell
90-95	sulphurous smell
96-00	urine smell

Air:

01-70	clear
71-80	foggy (or steamy)
81-88	foggy near floor (or steamy)
89-90	hazy (dust)
91-98	hazy (smoke)
99-00	misted

Note air and odor information in level keys. If random determination is used, be sure that some logic prevails in the overall scheme.

General:

01	arrow, broken	61	leather boot
02-04	ashes	62-64	leaves (dry) & twigs
05-06	bones	65-68	mold (common)
07	bottle, broken	69	pick handle
08	chain, corroded	70	pole, broken (5⅔')
09	club, splintered	71	pottery shards
10-19	cobwebs	72-73	rags
20	coin, copper (bent)	74	rope, rotten
21-22	cracks, ceiling	75-76	rubble & dirt
23-24	cracks, floor	77	sack, torn
25-26	cracks, wall	78	slimy coating, ceiling
27	dagger hilt	79	slimy coating, floor
28-29	dampness, ceiling	80	slimy coating, wall
30-33	dampness, wall	81	spike, rusted
34-40	dripping	82-83	sticks
41	dried blood	84	stones, small
42-44	dung	85	straw
45-49	dust	86	sword blade, broken
50	flask, cracked	87	teeth/fangs, scattered
51	food scraps	88	torch stub
52	fungi, common	89	wall scratchings
53-55	guano	90-91	water, small puddle
56	hair/fur bits	92-93	water, large puddle
57	hammer head, cracked	94-95	water, trickle
58	helmet, badly dented	96	wax drippings
59	iron bar, bent, rusted	97	wax blob (candle stub)
60	javelin head, blunt	98-00	wood pieces, rotting

Distribute these items randomly by choice or by dice roll, or place them as desired. An interval of 60' or more between each placement is suggested.

Unexplained Sounds and Weird Noises:

01-05	bang, slam	50-53	knocking
06	bellow (ing)	54-55	laughter
07	bong	56-57	moaning
08	buzzing	58-60	murmuring
09-10	chanting	61	music
11	chiming	62	rattling
12	chirping	63	ringing
13	clanking	64	roar(ing)
14	clashing	65-68	rustling
15	clicking	69-72	scratching/scrabbling
16	coughing	73-74	scream(ing)
17-18	creaking	75-77	scuttling
19	drumming	78	shuffling
20-23	footsteps (ahead)	79-80	slithering
24-26	footsteps (approaching)	81	snapping
27-29	footsteps (behind)	82	sneezing
30-31	footsteps (receding)	83	sobbing
32-33	footsteps (side)	84	splashing
34-35	giggling (faint)	85	splintering
36	gong	86-87	squeaking
37-39	grating	88	squealing
40-41	groaning	89-90	tapping
42	grunting	91-92	thud
43-44	hissing	93-94	thumping
45	hooting	95	tinkling
46	horn/trumpet sounding	96	twanging
47	howling	97	whining
48	humming	98	whispering
49	jingling	99-00	whistling

Select noises as desired. Locate in 20'-40' areas for detection. Have at least 120' intervals between each.

Furnishing and Appointments, General

01	altar	50	hogshead
02	armchair	51	idol (largish)
03	armoire	52	keg
04	arras	53	loom
05	bag	54	mat
06	barrel	55	mattress
07-08	bed	56	pail
09	bench	57	painting
10	blanket	58-60	pallet
11	box (large)	61	pedestal
12	brazier & charcoal	62-64	pegs
13	bucket	65	pillow
14	buffet	66	pipe (large cask)
15	bunks	67	quilt
16	butt (large barrel)	68-70	rug (small-medium)
17	cabinet	71	rushes
18	candelabrum	72	sack
19	carpet (largish)	73	sconce, wall
20	cask	74	screen
21	chandelier	75	sheet
22	charcoal	76-77	shelf
23-24	chair	78	shrine
25	chair, padded	79	sideboard
26	chair, padded, arm	80	sofa
27	chest, large	81	staff, normal
28	chest, medium	82	stand
29	chest of drawers	83	statue
30	closet (wardrobe)	84	stool, high
31	coal	85	stool, normal
32-33	couch	86	table, large
34	crate	87	table, long
35	cresset	88	table, low
36	cupboard	89	table, round
37	cushion	90	table, small
38	dais	91	table, trestle
39	desk	92	tapestry
40-42	fireplace & wood	93	throne
43	fireplace with mantle	94	trunk
44	firkin	95	tub
45	fountain	96	tun
46	fresco	97	urn
47	grindstone	98	wall basin and font
48	hamper	99	wood billets
49	hassock	00	workbench

Use this list to select furnishings. Random use is suggested only for rounding out the furnishings of an area.

Religious Articles and Furnishings:

01-05	altar	56-58	offertory container
06-08	bell(s)	59	paintings/frescoes
09-11	brazier(s)	60-61	pews
12	candelabra	62	pipes (musical)
13-14	candles	63	prayer rug
15	candlesticks	64	pulpit
16	cassocks	65	rail
17	chime(s)	66-67	robes
18-19	cloth (altar)	68-69	sanctuary
20-23	columns/pillars	70-71	screen
24	curtain/tapestry	72-76	shrine
25	drum	77	side chair(s)
26-27	font	78-79	stand
28-29	gong	80-82	statue(s)
30-35	holy/unholy symbol(s)	83	throne
36-37	holy/unholy writings	84-85	thurible
38-43	idol(s)	86-88	tripod
44-48	incense burner(s)	89-90	vestry
49	kneeling bench	91-97	vestments
50-53	lamp(s)	98-99	votive light
54	lectern	00	whistle
55	mosaics		

Select from the above list. Use random determination only to round out or fill in.

Torture Chamber Furnishings:

01-02	bastinadoes	49-50	pillory
03	bell (huge)	51-54	pincers
04-06	bench	55-56	pliers
07-10	boots (iron)	57-58	pot (huge)
11-15	branding irons	59-66	rack
16-20	brazier	67-68	ropes
21-22	cage	69	stocks
23-26	chains	70-71	stool
27	chair with straps	72-75	strappado
28	clamps	76-78	straw
29-31	cressets	79-80	table
32	fetters	81	thongs
33-35	fire pit	82-85	thumb screws
36	grill	86-88	torches
37-38	hooks	89-90	"U" rack
39-43	iron maiden	91	vice
44	knives	92-93	well
45	manacles	94-96	wheel
46	oubliette (pit)	97-00	whips
47-48	oil (barrel of)		

Use this list to select from. Random selection by dice roll is useful only to fill in.

Magic-User Furnishings:

01-03	alembic	54	magic circle
04-05	balance & weights	55	mortar & pestle
06-09	beaker	56	pan
10	bellows	57-58	parchment
11	bladder	59	pentacle
12-13	bottle	60	pentagram
14-16	book	61	phial
17	bowl	62	pipette
18	box	63	pot
19-22	brazier	64	prism
23	cage	65	quill
24-25	caldron	66-68	retort
26	candle	69	rod, mixing/stirring
27	candlestick	70-71	scroll
28	carafe	72	scroll tube
29-30	chalk	73	sheet
31	crucible	74	skin
32	cruet	75	skull
33	crystal ball	76	spatula
34	decanter	77	spoon, measuring
35	desk	78	stand
36	dish	79	stool
37-38	flask	80	stuffed animal
39	funnel	81	tank (container)
40	furnace	82	tongs
41-44	herbs	83	tripod
45	horn	84	tube (container)
46	hourglass	85-86	tube (piping)
47-48	jar	87	tweezers
49	jug	88-90	vial
50	kettle	91	waterclock
51	ladle	92	wire
52	lamp	93-00	workbench
53	lens (concave, convex, etc.)		

General Description of Container Contents:

01-03	ash	49-56	liquid
04-06	bark	57-58	lump(s)
07-09	bone	59-61	oily
10-14	chunks	62-65	paste
15-17	cinders	66-68	pellets
18-22	crystals	69-81	powder
23-26	dust	82-83	semi-liquid
27-28	fibers	84-85	skin/hide
29-31	gelatin	86-87	splinters
32-33	globes	88-89	stalks
34-37	grains	90-92	strands
38-40	greasy	93-95	strips
41-43	husks	96-00	viscous
44-48	leaves		

Use these lists for direct selection. Random determination is useful only for adding items and in odd situations.

Miscellaneous Utensils and Personal Items:

01	awl	51	oil fuel
02	bandages	52	oil, scented
03	basin	53	pan
04-05	basket	54	parchment
06	beater	55	pitcher
07	book	56	pipe, musical
08-09	bottle	57	pipe, smoking
10	bowl	58	plate
11	box (small)	59	platter
12-13	brush	60	pot
14	candle	61	pouch
15	candle snuffer	62	puff
16	candlestick	63	quill
17	cane (walking stick)	64	razor
18	case	65	rope
19	casket (small)	66	salve
20	chopper	67	saucer
21	coffer	68	scraper
22	cologne	69	scroll
23	comb	70	shaker
24	cup	71	sifter
25	decanter	72	soap
26	dipper	73	spigot
27	dish	74	spoon
28	earspoon	75	stopper
29	ewer	76	statuette/figurine
30	flagon	77	strainer
31	flask	78	tankard
32	food	79	thongs
33	fork	80	thread
34	grater	81-84	tinderbox (with flint & steel)
35	grinder	85-86	towel
36	hourglass	87	tray
37	jack (container)	88	trivet
38	jar	89	tureen
39	jug	90-91	twine
40	kettle	92	unguent
41	knife	93	vase
42	knucklebones	94	vial
43	ladle	95	wallet
44-45	lamp/lantern	96	washcloth
46	masher	97	whetstone
47	mirror	98	wig
48	mug	99	wool
49	needle(s)	00	yarn
50	oil, cooking (or fuel)		

Use this list to select miscellaneous items in an area. Random use is suggested only to fill in after selection.

Clothing and Footwear:

01-02	apron	47-48	kirtle
03-04	belt	49-50	leggings
05	blouse	51-54	linen (drawers)
06-08	boots	55-58	linen (undershirt)
09	buskins	59	mantle
10-11	cap	60	pantaloons
12-13	cape	61-62	petticoat
14-16	cloak	63-66	pouch/purse
17-18	coat	67-70	robe
19	coif	71-74	sandals
20	doublet	75-76	scarf
21-22	dress	77	shawl
23-24	frock/pinafore	78-79	shift
25-26	gauntlets	80-83	slippers
27-28	girdle	84-86	smock
29	gloves	87-89	stockings
30-31	gown	90	surcoat
32-34	hat	91	toga
35	habit	92-94	trousers
36-39	hood	95-96	tunic
40-41	hose	97	veil
42-43	jerkin	98	vest
44	jupon	99	wallet
45-46	kerchief	00	wrapper

Select from this list for wardrobe items. Use random determination only to round out or find an odd article.

Jewelry and Items Typically Bejewelled:

01-02	anklet	41-45	earring
03-06	arm band	46-47	fob
07-09	belt	48-52	goblet
10-12	box (small)	53-54	headband (fillet)
13-16	bracelet	55-57	idol
17-19	brooch	58-59	locket
20-21	buckle	60-62	medal
22-25	chain	63-68	medallion
26	chalice	69-75	necklace
27	choker	76-78	pendant
28-30	clasp	79-83	pin
31-32	coffer	84	orb
33	collar	85-93	ring
34-35	comb	94	sceptre
36	coronet	95-96	seal
37	crown	97-99	statuette
38-39	decanter	00	tiara
40	diadem		

Use the list to select jewelry or to identify items of treasure if jewelry is indicated.

Food & Drink:

01-02	ale	39-42	mead
03	apricots	43-46	meal (grain)
04-05	apples	47-56	meat*
06	beans	57	milk
07-10	beer	58	muffins
11	berries	59	mushrooms
12	biscuits	60-62	nuts*
13	brandy	63-64	onions
14-18	bread	65	pastries
19	broth	66	peaches
20	butter	67	pears
21	cakes	68	peas
22-24	cheese*	69	pickles
25	cookies	70	pie
26	eggs	71	plums
27	fish*	72-74	porridge
28	fish, shell*	75	prunes
29-30	fowl*	76	pudding
31	grapes	77	raisins
32	greens*	78-80	soup
33	gruel	81-82	stew
34	honey	83	sweetmeats
35	jam	84-87	tea
36	jelly	88-89	tubers/roots*
37	leeks	90-95	water
38	lentils	96-00	wine

Condiments & Seasonings:

01-15	garlic	56-58	pepper
16-50	herbs**	59-85	salt
51-55	mustard	86-00	vinegar

* In the interest of space, the varieties of these items have been omitted, for they are generally well-known and can be enumerated by the DM with little or no difficulty.

** A listing of herbs and associated vegetable matter is given elsewhere in this book. The listing gives the purported uses for herbs with regard to healing, magic, poisons, etc., but it can be used to enumerate herbs used for cooking purposes.

Use the lists above for the stocking of kitchens, store rooms, etc. Random selection is suggested only to round out an already stocked area.

CHAMBER, ROOM, AND OTHER SPACE LIST

ANTECHAMBER	KITCHEN
ARMORY	LABORATORY
AUDIENCE-	LIBRARY
AVIARY	LOUNGE
BANQUET-	MEDITATION
BARRACKS	OBSERVATORY
BATH	OFFICE
BEDROOM/BOUDIOR	PANTRY
BESTIARY	PEN/PRISON
CELL	PRIVY/SECRET-
CHANTRY	RECEPTION-
CHAPEL	REFECTORY
CISTERN	ROBING ROOM
CLASS-	SALON
CLOSET	SHRINE
CONJURING-	SITTING ROOM
CORRIDOR	SMITHY
COURT	SOLAR
CRYPT	STABLE
DINING-	STORAGE
DIVINATION-	STRONGROOM/VAULT
DORMITORY	STUDY
DRESSING ROOM	TEMPLE
ENTRY-/VESTIBULE	THRONE ROOM
GALLERY	TORTURE CHAMBER
GAME ROOM	TRAINING/EXERCISE-
GUARDROOM	TROPHY ROOM/MUSEUM
HALL	WAITING ROOM
HALL, GREAT	WATER CLOSET/TOILET
HALLWAY	WELL
HAREM/SERAGLIO	WORKROOM
KENNEL	WORKSHOP

APPENDIX J: HERBS, SPICES AND MEDICINAL VEGETABLES

There are hundreds of different vegetable flavorings and seasonings which were or are reputed to have medicinal and/or magic properties. It is not within the scope of this work to detail all of these herbs and spices, particularly as regards their description, habitat, and the many uses claimed for most. An alphabetical listing with one or two comments on each is presented. The dedicated herbologist will have to pursue his or her research in scholarly texts.

Plant And/Or Special Part:	Uses And/Or Powers:
abcess root (sweet root)	respiratory disorders
acacia (Gum Arabic)	tissue repair
aconite (monkshood, wolfsbane, friar's cap., etc.)	sedative/drives off werewolves
acorn	tissue hardening
adder's tongue	emetic, emollient
adrue	anti-vomiting, sedative
agar-agar (jelly)	anti-inflammation, nutrient
agaric	astringent, purgative
agrimony (cocklebur, stickwort)	muscle toner, diuretic
alder	anti-inflammation, tonic
alkanet root	emollient, antiseptic, wormer
all-heal (wound-wort)	antiseptic, anti-spasmodic
almond milk/powder	nutrient/emollient
aloe (bitter aloe)	bites, burns, laxative, tonic/insect repellent
amaranth (red cockscomb, love-lies-bleeding)	astringent, anti-hemorrhaging
ammoniacum (Persian Gum)	stimulant, respiratory aid
angelica	lungs, liver, spleen, vision, hearing
anise	antacid, digestion, coughing
arbutus (mayflower)	astringent, bladder infection
areca nut (betel nut)	astringent, tape wormer
arenaria rubra (sandwort)	diuretic, urinary diseases
arrach (goosefoot)	sedative (nervous tension or hysteria in particular)
artichoke juice	jaundice curative
asafetida (gum asafetida, devil's dung, food of the gods)	aphrodisiac, brain and nervous stimulant, tonic, many more
asarabacca (hazelwort, wild nard)	emetic, purgative
ash (bark and leaves of)	laxative, anti-inflammation, fever
asparagus juice/root	sedative, heart problems/anti-oxalic acid
avens (colewort, herb bennet)	astringent, anti-hemorrhaging, anti-weakness, tonic, more
bael	anti-inflammation, ulcers
balm (sweet balm) leaves	calms nerves, fevers
balm of gilead	nutrient, organ stimulant (general)
balmony (bitter herb, snake head)	tissue builder and strengthener, liver ailments, wormer
barley	nutrient (recuperative)
basil	nervous disorders
bay leaf	?
beet	organic cleanser
belladonna (deadly nightshade, dwale, black cherry root)	diuretic, sedative, pain reliever, anti-opiate, circulation stimulant, poison/lycanthropy cure
benne (sesam, sesame)	respiratory disorders, eye infections, more
benzoin (gum benzoin)	expectorant, stimulant, anti-septic, wounds and sores
berberis	fevers
beth root (lamb's quarters)	astringent, coughs, tonic, anti-hemorrhaging, more
bilberry (huckleberry, hurtleberry, whortleberry)	anti-thirst, dropsy, typhoid, more
birch (white birch)	intestines and stomach, venereal diseases, skin conditions
birthwort	circulatory stimulant
bistort (adderwort)	astringent
bittersweet (felonwort, scarlet berry, woody nightshade)	abcesses, lymph infections, swelling and inflammation
blackberry (dewberry)	astringent, tonic, dysentary
black currant	diuretic, antiseptic, blood purifier
black willow (pussy willow) bark	astringent, antiseptic
blueberry — see bilberry	
blue flag (flag lily, poison flag, water flag, water lily)	diuretic, cathartic, blood purifier (vs. poison), wound healing, venereal disease, much more
blue mallow (common mallow)	coughs, colds
boneset (thoughtwort)	fevers, tonic, skin diseases
borage	coughs, lung infections
box leaves	tonic, blood purifier
bryony	paralysis, bruises
bugle	gastrointestinal disorders, hemorrhaging
burdock	laxative, tuberculosis, more
butterbur	fevers, urinary complaints
cabbage juice	ulcer and stomach treatment
calotopis (mudar bark)	skin leprosy, elephantiasis, more
camphor (gum camphor)	bruises, sprains, chills, fevers, cardiac stimulant
caraway	antacid, aids digestion
cardamom	?
carrot juice and seeds	tonic for improved health
castor oil bush	purgative, cathartic
catnip	colds, fevers, anti-spasmodic, hysteria
cayenne	stimulant
celery	liver functions, tonic, stimulant
chamomile	nervous conditions, ear and tooth aches
chaulmoogra oil	fevers, sedative, skin eruptions
cherry gum	respiratory infections/food substitute
chervil	?
chives	colds, general diseases/evil eye
cinnamon	disinfectant, nausea, preservative
cleavers (goosegrass)	fevers, circulation, blood purifier, wounds, liver disease
clover	tonic
cloves	anesthetic, circulation, germicide, disinfectant
comfrey root (healing herb)	colds, respiratory conditions, wounds, bone fractures, gangrene, much, much more
coriander	tonic
couchgrass	bladder and urinary infections
cucumber	inflammation

cumin seed	stimulant
dandelion	diuretic, purgative, tonic
digitalis (dead men's bells, fairy bells, fairy cap, fairy fingers, foxglove, etc.)	heart stimulant, tonic, kidney treatment (poison)
dill	nausea
ergot (rye smut)	hemorrhaging, venereal diseases
eyebright	astringent, eye infections
fennel	digestion, weight control, muscle tone, reflexes, vision, much, much more
fenugreek	stimulant
fig	demulcent
figwort (scrofula plant, throatwort)	abcesses, wounds, pain killer
fireweed	astringent, anti-spasmodic
fluellin	astringent, tissue strengthener
garden burnet	?
garlic	coughs, colds, blood purifier, detoxifier, kills parasites/wards off vampires
gelsemium (wild woodbine)	sedative, nerve tonic, fevers, more
gentian (bitter root, felwort)	tonic, fevers, anti-venom
geranium (sweet geranium)	alkalizer
ginger	stimulant, colds, cramps
ginseng	glandular stimulant, vision, dizziness, headaches, weakness
goat's rue	diuretic, wormer (vermifuge)
grape juice	blood fortifier
hartstongue	cough, liver, spleen, bladder
hawthorn	heart, arteries
hedge mustard	throat, lungs
hellebore	heart tonic (rootlets are poison)
honeysuckle	liver, spleen, respiratory disorders
horehound, white	coughs, pulmonary diseases, anti-venom
horehound, black	stimulant, wormer, hemorrhaging
horseradish	tonic, antiseptic, wormer
hyssop	respiratory ailments, jaundice, blood purifier, tonic, cuts and wounds, more
ipecac	dysentery, mouth infections, more
irish moss	coughs, scalds, burns
jambul seed	blood purifier, diabetes
jewel weed (balsam weed, pale touch-me-not)	diuretic, kidneys, skin growths, fungus, infections, liver
juniper berry	aphrodisiac, stimulant, disinfectant, venereal disease, more
jurubera	anemia
kelp (seawrack)	thyroid, heart, arteries, much more
larkspur (knight's spur)	external parasites
leek	same as chives
lily-of-the-valley	heart tonic
lotus	?
lucerne (alfalfa)	strength
lycopodium (common club moss, fox tail, lamb's tail)	wounds, lungs, kidneys, more
mace	stimulant
marigold	fevers, varicosities, eyes, heart
marjoram	meloncholia, dizziness, brain disorders, toothaches
masterwort	stimulates organs, anti-spasmodic, more
mistletoe	convulsions, hysteria, narcotic, tonic, typhoid fever, heart
muira-puama	aphrodisiac
mustard	emetic, counter-irritant, colds, fevers
nutmeg	nausea, vomiting, diarrhea
nux vomica (poison nut)	stimulant, debility tonic
onion	poultice, colds (as chives)
oregano	germicide, pain killer
paprika	stimulant, poultice
parsley	blood purifier
parsnip	fevers
peach seed	fevers, blood tonic
pepper, black	sprains, neuritis
peppermint	?
pitcher plant	small pox preventative and cure, stomach, liver, kidneys
plantain (ripple grass, waybread)	minor wounds, stings, rashes
pomegranate	nerve sedative, wormer
poppy	?
pumpkin seed	virility, organ tonic
quince	eye disease, dysentery, skin disorders
radish	blood purifier, liver
raspberry	fevers, tonic
rhubarb	astringent, cathartic
rose	colds, fevers
rosemary	germicide, muscle tonic/drives off evil spirits
saffron	scarlet fever, measles, respiratory infections
sage	tonic, wounds
sarsaparilla (china root, spikenard)	system balance, blood purifier, venereal disease, many more
scopolis	nerve and muscle sedative, pain killer, coughs
scullcap (madweed)	nervous disorders, rabies
senna	purgative
spearmint	?
strawberry	vision, swelling and inflammation
summer savory	blood purifier, palsy
tamarind	infection, gangrene
tansy	tonic, narcotic, wormer
tarragon	?
tea	poison antidote
thyme	antiseptic, blood purifer
turmeric	?
turnip	mouth disease, throat
watercress	blood tonic (anemia)
white bryony (mandragora)	cathartic, respiratory diseases, heart, kidneys

It is suggested that you use the above list as a guide to which herbs, spices, or vegetable you will require for various magical effects desired from potions, scroll inks, and other magic items. You may add to or delete from the list as you desire. Reputed folk uses are not detailed with respect to magic in most cases, as this decision is the purview of the DM.

APPENDIX K: DESCRIBING MAGICAL SUBSTANCES

Some Dungeon Masters have difficulty describing the contents of potion bottles, magical elixirs, and like liquid substances. The lists below give the appearances of liquids, colors, tastes, and smells. In combination with **APPENDIX I: DUNGEON DRESSING** (q.v.) or by itself, these various descriptive words will serve the DM in good stead when preparing level keys or when "winging it".

Appearance/Consistency:
bubbling
cloudy
effervescent
fuming
oily
smoky

syrupy
vaporous
viscous
watery

Transparency:
clear (transparent)
flecked (transparent and other)
layered (color or transparency)
luminous (determine transparency)
opaline (glowing)
phosphorescent (determine transparency)
rainbowed (transparent)
ribboned (determine transparency)
translucent
variegated (determine colors)

Taste and/or Odor:

acidic	herbal	salty
bilious	honeyed	soothing/sugary
bitter	lemony	sour
burning/biting	meaty	spicy
buttery	metallic	sweet
dusty	milky	tart
earthy	musty	vinegary
fiery	oniony	watery
fishy	peppery	
greasy	perfumy	

Colors:

METALLIC	WHITE	GRAY	BROWN	BLACK
brassy	bone	dove	chocolate	ebony
bronze	colorless	dun	ecru	inky
coppery	ivory	neutral	fawn	pitchy
gold	pearl		mahogany	sable
silvery		RED	tan	sooty
steely	YELLOW	carmine	terra cotta	
	amber	cerise		ORANGE
VIOLET	buff	cherry	GREEN	apricot
fuchsia	citrine	cinnabar	aquamarine	flame
heliotrope	cream	coral	emerald	golden
lake	fallow	crimson	olive	salmon
lavender	flaxen	madder		tawny
lilac	ochre	maroon	BLUE	
magenta	peach	pink	azure	
mauve	saffron	rose	cerulean	
plum	straw	ruby	indigo	
puce		russet	sapphire	
purple		rust	turquoise	
		sanguine	ultramarine	
		scarlet		
		vermilion		

APPENDIX L: CONJURED ANIMALS

When the conjuring cleric or illusionist states the number of hit dice of the animals he or she will summon, consult the appropriate section of the table hereafter. Note that the variation includes fractions of hit points, and these must be charged off against the total conjurable by the spell-caster. Where several possibilities exist, a number for random selection has been assigned, for the cleric or illusionist cannot specify what sort of animal he or she will summon.

CONJURED ANIMALS TABLE

Hit Dice Category	Dice Score	Animal Type	Hit Dice Cost
1	01-15	Baboon	1¼
	16-45	Dog, wild	1¼
	46-55	Flightless Bird	½
	56-65	Jackal	½
	66-00	Rat, giant	½
2	01-25	Badger	1½
	26-35	Flightless bird	2
	36-60	Herd animal	2
	61-00	Horse, wild	2
3	01-05	Axe beak	3
	06-10	Badger, giant	3
	11-15	Boar, warthog	3
	16-20	Camel	3
	21-30	Cattle, wild	2½
	31-40	Dog, war	2½
	41-45	Flightless bird	3
	46-55	Goat, giant	3¼
	56-65	Hyena	3
	66-75	Lion, mountain	3¼
	76-80	Lynx, giant	2½
	81-85	Mule	3
	86-90	Stag	3
	91-95	Wolf	2½
	96-00	Wolverine	3
4	01-05	Ape	4¼
	06-15	Bear, black	3¾
	16-20	Beaver, giant	4
	21-30	Boar, wild	3¾
	31-40	Bull	4
	41-45	Eagle, giant	4
	46-50	Irish deer	4
	51-55	Jaguar	4¼
	56-60	Leopard	3½
	61-65	Owl, giant	4
	66-75	Ram, giant	4
	76-85	Weasel, giant	3¾
	86-00	Wolf, dire	3¾

5	01-10	Ape, carnivorous	5
	11-25	Buffalo	5
	26-35	Hyena, giant	5
	36-50	Otter, giant	5
	51-70	Skunk, giant	5
	71-85	Stag, giant	5
	86-00	Wolverine, giant	5
6	01-40	Bear, brown	6¼
	41-60	Lion	5½
	61-80	Porcupine, giant	6
	81-00	Tiger	6¼
7	01-65	Boar, giant	7
	66-00	Lion, spotted	6½
8	01-30	Bear, cave	7½
	31-70	Hippopotamus	8
	71-00	Tiger, sabre-tooth	7½
9		Rhinoceros	8½
10	01-60	Elephant	10
	61-00	Rhinoceros, wooly	10
11		Elephant (loxodont)	11
12	01-60	Mastodon	12
	61-00	Titanothere	°12
13		Mammoth	13
		Whale (small)	13
14		Baluchitherium	14
		Whale (small)	14
15 & up		Whales only, to a maximum of 36 hit dice cost	

If in or on water, only the appropriate sorts of animals can be called, i.e., swimmers and flying ones, where applicable.

APPENDIX M: SUMMONED MONSTERS

When a *monster summoning* spell is cast, consult the tables below to ascertain what sort of creature appears. Each table is presented according to the level of the spell. If the summoner is evil, the monster in parentheses may be used.

Monster Summoning I

Dice Score	Monster Summoned
01-10	Demon, manes
11-25	Goblin (Dwarf)
26-40	Hobgoblin (Elf)
41-55	Kobold (Halfling)
56-70	Orc (Gnome)
71-00	Rat, giant

Monster Summoning II

Dice Score	Monster Summoned
01-15	Centipede, giant
16-25	Devil, lemure
26-45	Gnoll
46-60	Stirge
61-75	Toad, giant
76-00	Troglodyte

Monster Summoning III

Dice Score	Monster Summoned
01-07	Beetle, boring
08-17	Bugbear
18-25	Gelatinous cube
26-32	Ghoul
33-40	Lizard, giant
41-47	Lycanthrope, wererat
48-57	Ochre jelly
58-67	Ogre
68-75	Spider, huge
76-85	Spider, large
86-95	Tick, giant
96-00	Weasel, giant

Monster Summoning IV

Dice Score	Monster Summoned
01-07	Ape, carnivorous
08-15	Gargoyle (blink dog)
16-25	Ghast
26-35	Gray ooze
36-42	Hell hound
43-50	Hydra, 5 heads
51-58	Lycanthrope, werewolf
59-67	Owlbear
68-76	Shadow
77-86	Snake, giant, constrictor
87-93	Toad, ice
94-00	Toad, poisonous

Monster Summoning V

Dice Score	Monster Summoned
01-07	Cockatrice
08-17	Displacer beast
18-26	Doppleganger
27-36	Hydra, 7 heads
37-45	Leucrotta
46-55	Lizard, subterranean
56-63	Lycanthrope, wereboar
64-72	Minotaur
73-78	Snake, giant, amphisbaena
79-85	Snake, giant, poisonous
86-90	Snake, giant, spitting
91-00	Spider, giant

Monster Summoning VI

Dice Score	Monster Summoned
01-06	Carrion crawler
07-12	Devil, erinyes
13-19	Hydra, 8 heads
20-26	Jackalwere (lammasu)
27-31	Lycanthrope, weretiger (werebear)
32-38	Manticore
39-43	Ogre magi
44-51	Otyugh
52-56	Rakshasa
57-63	Salamander
64-68	Spider, phase
69-78	Troll
79-84	Wight
85-88	Wind walker
89-92	Wraith
93-00	Wyvern

Monster Summoning VII

Dice Score	Monster Summoned
01-03	Chimera (couatl)
04-06	Demon, succubus
07-09	Demon, type I
10-12	Demon, type II
13-15	Demon, type III
16-18	Devil, barbed
19-21	Devil, bone
22-23	Devil, horned
24-26	Ettin
27-29	Giant, fire
30-32	Giant, frost
33-35	Giant, hill
36-38	Giant, stone
39-41	Gorgon
42-43	Groaning spirit
44-46	Hydra, 10 heads
47-49	Hydra, pyro-, 8 heads
50-52	Intellect devourer
53-55	Invisible stalker
56-58	Lamia
59-61	Lizard, fire
62-64	Mind flayer
65-67	Mummy
68-70	Naga, spirit
71-73	Neo-otyugh
74-76	Night hag
77-79	Roper (shedu)
80-82	Shambling mound
83-85	Slug, giant
86-88	Spectre
89-91	Sphinx, hieraco- (andro-)
92-94	Umber hulk
95-97	Will-o-wisp
98-00	Xorn

Remember that it is always within your purview to not only select what monster is summoned but to appoint the numbers as well, where applicable. Thus you may select to have rats come to a first level *summoning*, but because they are relatively weak you might also allow a maximum number to appear. The major drawback to personal selection is that players might view it as personal bias on the part of the DM — whether pro or con. It is quite obvious that there are superior and inferior monsters on each list, and as a general rule it might be better to allow random selection sans "interference from the gods".

When a *monster summoning* spell is cast while upon a body of water or underwater, use the following tables to ascertain what sort of creature appears. Note that there are separate tables for fresh and salt water.

Monster Summoning I

Dice Score	Monster Summoned
	Fresh
01-67	Koalinth (hobgoblin)
68-00	Nixie
	Salt
01-50	Koalinth (hobgoblin)
51-00	Merman

Monster Summoning II

Dice Score	Monster Summoned
	Fresh
01-00	Lizard man
	Salt
01-33	Ixitxachitl
34-00	Locathah

Monster Summoning III

Dice Score	Monster Summoning
	Fresh
01-33	Crab, giant
34-00	Lacedon (ghoul)
	Salt
01-50	Lacedon (ghoul)
51-00	Sahuagin

Monster Summoning IV

Dice Score	Monster Summoned
	Fresh
01-33	Beetle, water, giant
34-50	Crayfish, giant
51-67	Kopoacinth (gargoyle)
68-00	Spider, water, giant
	Salt
01-40	Kopoacinth (gargoyle)
41-80	Lobster (crayfish), giant
81-00	Triton

Monster Summoning V

Dice Score	Monster Summoned
	Fresh
01-80	Crocodile, giant
81-00	Water weird
	Salt
01-50	Crocodile, giant
51-70	Sea hag
71-90	Sea lion
91-00	Water weird

Monster Summoning VI

Dice Score	Monster Summoned
	Fresh or Salt
01-33	Octopus, giant
34-00	Snake, sea, giant

Monster Summoning VII

Dice Score	Monster Summoned
	Fresh
01-20	Morkoth
21-00	Naga, water
	Salt
01-15	Morkoth
16-70	Ray, manta
71-00	Squid, giant

APPENDIX N: INSPIRATIONAL AND EDUCATIONAL READING

Inspiration for all of the fantasy work I have done stems directly from the love my father showed when I was a tad, for he spent many hours telling me stories he made up as he went along, tales of cloaked old men who could grant wishes, of magic rings and enchanted swords, or wicked sorcerors and dauntless swordsmen. Then too, countless hundreds of comic books went down, and the long-gone EC ones certainly had their effect. Science fiction, fantasy, and horror movies were a big influence. In fact, all of us tend to get ample helpings of fantasy when we are very young, from fairy tales such as those written by the Brothers Grimm and Andrew Lang. This often leads to reading books of mythology, paging through bestiaries, and consultation of compilations of the myths of various lands and peoples. Upon such a base I built my interest in fantasy, being an avid reader of all science fiction and fantasy literature since 1950. The following authors were of particular inspiration to me. In some cases I cite specific works, in others, I simply recommend all their fantasy writing to you. From such sources, as well as just about any other imaginative writing or screenplay you will be able to pluck kernels from which grow the fruits of exciting campaigns. Good reading!

Inspirational Reading:

Anderson, Poul. THREE HEARTS AND THREE LIONS; THE HIGH CRUSADE; THE BROKEN SWORD
Bellairs, John. THE FACE IN THE FROST
Brackett, Leigh.
Brown, Fredric.
Burroughs, Edgar Rice. "Pellucidar" Series; Mars Series; Venus Series
Carter, Lin. "World's End" Series
de Camp, L. Sprague. LEST DARKNESS FALL; FALLIBLE FIEND; *et al.*
de Camp & Pratt. "Harold Shea" Series; CARNELIAN CUBE
Derleth, August.
Dunsany, Lord.
Farmer, P. J. "The World of the Tiers" Series; *et al.*
Fox, Gardner. "Kothar" Series; "Kyrik" Series; *et al.*
Howard, R. E. "Conan" Series
Lanier, Sterling. HIERO'S JOURNEY
Leiber, Fritz. "Fafhrd & Gray Mouser" Series; *et al.*
Lovecraft, H. P.
Merritt, A. CREEP, SHADOW, CREEP; MOON POOL; DWELLERS IN THE MIRAGE; *et al.*
Moorcock, Michael. STORMBRINGER; STEALER OF SOULS; "Hawkmoon" Series (esp. the first three books)
Norton, Andre.
Offutt, Andrew J., editor SWORDS AGAINST DARKNESS III.
Pratt, Fletcher, BLUE STAR; *et al.*
Saberhagen, Fred. CHANGELING EARTH; *et al.*
St. Clair, Margaret. THE SHADOW PEOPLE; SIGN OF THE LABRYS
Tolkien, J. R. R. THE HOBBIT; "Ring Trilogy"
Vance, Jack. THE EYES OF THE OVERWORLD; THE DYING EARTH; *et al.*
Weinbaum, Stanley.
Wellman, Manly Wade.
Williamson, Jack.
Zelazny, Roger. JACK OF SHADOWS; "Amber" Series; *et al.*

The most immediate influences upon **AD&D** were probably de Camp & Pratt, REH, Fritz Leiber, Jack Vance, HPL, and A. Merritt; but all of the above authors, as well as many not listed, certainly helped to shape the form of the game. For this reason, and for the hours of reading enjoyment, I heartily recommend the works of these fine authors to you.

APPENDIX O: ENCUMBRANCE OF STANDARD ITEMS

Item	Encumbrance in gold pieces
Backpack	20
Belt	3
Belt pouch, large	10
small	5
Book, large metal-bound	200
Boots, hard	60
soft	30
Bottles, flagons	60
Bow, composite long	80
composite short	50
long	100
short	50
Caltrop	50
Candle	5
Chest, large solid iron	1,000-5,000
small solid iron	200-500
small wooden	100-250
large wooden	500-1,500
Clothes (1 set)	30
Cord, 10'	2
Crossbow, heavy	80
light	50
Crystal ball, base and wrapping	150
Flask, empty	7
full	20
Gem	1-5
Grapnel	100
Hand tool	10
Helm	45
Helm, great	100
Holy water, potion bottles	25
Horn	50
Jewelry, large	50
small	1-5
Lantern	60
Mirror	5
Musical instrument*	350
Pole, 10'	100
Purse	1
Quiver	30
Rations, iron	75
standard	200
Robe or cloak, folded	50
worn	25
Rod	60
Rope, 50'	75
Sack, large	20
small	5
Saddle, light horse	250
heavy horse	500
Saddlebag	150
Saddle blanket (pad)	20
Scroll case, bone or ivory	50
leather	25
Spike	10
Staff	100
Tapestry (very small to huge)	50-1,000+
Tinderbox	2
Torch	25
Wand, bone or ivory case	60
box	80
leather case	30
Waterskin or wineskin, empty	5
full	50

* Musical instruments include only large and bulky instruments such as lutes and drums.

The maximum weight a normal-strength person can carry and still move is 1500 g.p. (150#).

Certain items are not included when figuring encumbrance. These include:

material components (unless large and bulky).
any helm but great helm, if the character has any armor.
one set of clothing.
thieves' picks and tools.

Many other things will be bought or found, but it is impossible to list them all here. The encumbrance of most items not on this list may be inferred by comparison with objects similar to them; thus a *decanter of endless water* will encumber as much as a bottle or flagon. In some cases no equivalent may be found on the table; such instances require the judge to decide.

Many people looking at the table will say, "But a scroll doesn't weigh two pounds!" The encumbrance figure should not be taken as the weight of the object — it is the *combined weight* and *relative bulkiness* of the item. These factors together will determine how much a figure can carry.

As an example, Dimwall the magic-user and Drudge the fighter have prepared for a dungeon expedition. Dimwall, besides his normal clothing, has strapped on a belt with a large pouch on it. Into this and his robe, he tucks his material components (minimal encumbrance). He also places in his pouch a potion bottle, a mirror, some garlic and belladonna, and his tinderbox. At his right side hangs a dagger and sheath and four more daggers are on a bandolier slung across his chest. Over all these belts, he puts his backpack. In his pack goes a hand axe (for chopping, not fighting), 3 flasks of oil, a candle, 3 small sacks, 1 large sack, and 7 torches. Lashed in a bundle to the pack is 50' of rope. At his left side, hanging from his belt, are a leather scroll case and his purse, filled with 20 gold pieces. He holds a staff in his right hand and a torch in his left. He is now ready to travel, with a total encumbrance of 689 g.p.

Meanwhile, his companion, Drudge, has strapped on his splint armor. He wears 2 belts around his waist; his longsword hangs from one. On the other belt he places his quiver with 40 bolts, a cocking hook, and a dagger. He slips on his backpack, already loaded with 10 spikes, one week's iron rations, and a flask of oil. To the bottom of the pack he has strapped 50' of rope. Hanging on the rear of the pack is his heavy crossbow. Around his neck he wears a holy symbol. Finally, he straps his large shield on his left arm, fits his helmet, and takes his lantern, ready to go with a total encumbrance of 1117 g.p.

During their adventures, Dimwall and Drudge find 800 gold pieces in a troll's treasure horde. Dimwall can carry 400 gold pieces in his large sack and another 300 gold pieces in his small sacks. Dimwall leaves his torches and staff, since he must have his hands free. Then he fastens a small sack to his belt and, using two hands, carries the large sack over his shoulder. Drudge eats part of his iron rations and throws the rest away, along with his spikes and oil. He places the remaining bags in the bottom of his pack and then pours the loose coins on top of them. Encumbrance for Dimwall is now 889 gold pieces and 1222 gold pieces for Drudge.

As they leave, Dimwall and Drudge meet the troll. There is little time to react, so Drudge must quickly drop his lantern (possibly putting it out) and attack. As he does this, Dimwall must drop the large sack (probably scattering coins about), unsling his pack, and start digging for his oil. By the time he finds it, the troll may have killed them both!

APPENDIX P: CREATING A PARTY ON THE SPUR OF THE MOMENT

There are times — often if you attend many conventions — when you will have a group of players desiring to adventure in your campaign who have no suitable characters with which to do so. You might want only low, medium or high level characters for the particular scenario you have in mind, and regardless of level it is certain that you will not wish to have ultra-powerful (considering character level) or strange magic items in the group. It therefore becomes necessary to have the party generate special characters on the spot, and this takes up valuable playing time. In order to reduce this to a minimum, the following system, one which I have developed perforce from DMing many conventions, is suggested:

Abilities: Players roll 4d6, discard the low die, and arrange the scores as they like.

Race & Class: After generating ability stats, each player selects the race and class of his or her character as desired, making adjustments accordingly.

225

Alignment: Make certain that the alignments allowed to participants are not so diverse as to cause a breakdown in the game due to player quarrels. You may require players to select from two or three compatible alignment types if you think best — such as neutral, neutral good, and lawful neutral, for example.

Level: For low level, you might use random dice to find out if players are levels 1-2, 1-3, 2-4; medium range might be 5-7, 5-8, or 7-9; upper range is typically 8-10, 8-11, or 9-12. *Multi-class* races are best handled by adding 1 level per profession to the level generated, and then dividing the total by the number of classes involved, counting all fractions as whole numbers.

Standard Equipment: Assuming that these are not 1st level characters, you will probably find it best to allow them to take whatever is desired, reminding them that they can only carry so much, and then quickly checking the character sheets before the start of the adventure. Whatever restrictions you decide to place upon standard items is, of course, your own business. Technologically impossible items, and items that you deem unlikely to be used can always be refused to the party.

Magic Items: If the party is assumed to have been adventuring for some time, however brief, then it is probable that one or more of their number would have acquired certain magic items. In order to reflect this likelihood, use the following tables for the various classes of adventurers, as applicable to your group:

PROTECTIVE ITEMS TABLE

Character Class	Per Level Chance For Shield, Armor, Etc. (Typically +1)						
	Shield	Plate	Banded	Chain	Leather	Ring of Protection	Bracers*
CLERIC	10%	5%**	6%**	8%**	—	2%	—
Druid	—	—	—	—	8%	5%	—
FIGHTER	10%	6%**	8%**	10%**	—	—	—
Paladin	10%	6%**	8%**	10%**	—	—	—
Ranger	8%	5%**	7%**	15%**	—	—	—
MAGIC-USER	—	—	—	—	—	15%	4%
Illusionist	—	—	—	—	—	15%	4%
THIEF	—	—	—	—	10%	4%	—
Assassin	8%	—	—	—	10%	3%	—

* Bracers of AC 6 value.

** Only one sort of armor may be tried for, so the character must make a decision as to what type before the odds are computed and the percentile dice are rolled.

Multiply level by percentage chance to determine odds; then roll percentile dice, and if the score is equal to or less than the percentage chance, the character has the item. There is a 1% chance per level of experience of the character that any item will be above average — +2, or bracers of AC 5, for example. If the chance for having the item was greater than 90%, add the percentage above 90% to the chance for the item to be above average. If the resulting roll indicates an above-average item, then see if it goes up to +3, or bracers of AC 4, on a straight 1% per level of experience chance. *Example:* Gonzo the 9th level ranger discovers that he has magic chain mail, having opted to take a sure thing with a 135% chance. Gonzo's level (9) plus the percentage chance above 90% (45%) are added together to find the chance for +2 chain — 9% + 45% = 54%. Percentile dice are rolled, and the result is 51, so Gonzo has at least +2 chain. A third check is made, and it is discovered that he has just +2 as the dice roll was 99.

Chances for +2 or +3 weapons are the same as for protective items. You may alternately give special features to swords instead of further pluses, i.e., +1 sword *Flame Tongue*, or +2 sword, *Giant Slayer*. Add a crossbow *of speed* to +2 bolts if a +3 is indicated, otherwise double their number only.

SCROLLS TABLE

Character Class	Per Level Chance For Having Scroll	Type Of Scroll (And Spell Level)		
		Protection	1 Spell*	3 Spells**
CLERIC	8%	no	1-3	1-4
Druid	7%	yes	1-3	1-4
FIGHTER	6%	yes	—	—
Paladin	4%	yes	—	—
Ranger	5%	yes	—	—
MAGIC-USER	15%	no	1-4	1-6
Illusionist	12%	no	1-3	1-4
THIEF***	6%	yes	1-3	1-4
Assassin***	3%	yes	1-3	—

* Determine randomly, but only normally useful spells for the sort of adventure undertaken.

** Normally given only if no other types of scrolls are in the possession of the character; otherwise as above.

*** Only one scroll type available. If spell scroll, they will be magic-user spells; otherwise as above.

WEAPONS TABLE

Character Class	Per Level Chance For Weapon (Typically +1)						
	Dagger	Sword*	Mace	Battle Axe	Spear	Bow	15 Bolts +2
CLERIC	—	—	12%	—	—	—	—
Druid	10%	7%	—	—	10%	—	—
FIGHTER	10%	10%**	—	7%**	8%**	1%	10%**
Paladin	10%	10%**	—	10%**	10%**	—	—
Ranger	10%	9%**	—	9%**	8%**	5%	10%**
MAGIC-USER	15%	—	—	—	—	—	—
Illusionist	15%	—	—	—	—	—	—
THIEF	12%	11%	—	—	—	—	—
Assassin	10%	5%**	—	5%**	5%**	—	1%
MONK	5%	—	—	—	2%	—	—

* Scimitar in the case of druids; short swords for characters less than 5' tall, long swords in all other cases, except the character may opt for a short sword if desired.

** As with protective items, only one category of weapons of this type may be had, so before finding odds the player must state which his or her character wishes to go for.

POTIONS TABLE

Character Class	Per Level Chance For Having Potion	Maximum No. Of Potions	Possible Potion Types
CLERIC	6%	1	1. Climbing
Druid	11%	2	2. Diminution
FIGHTER	8%	1	3. Extra-healing
Paladin	6%	1	4. Fire Resistance
Ranger	7%	1	5. Flying
MAGIC-USER	10%	3	6. Gaseous Form
Illusionist	10%	2	7. Growth
THIEF	9%	2	8. Healing
Assassin	5%	1	9. Invisibility
			0. Polymorph Self

You may allow characters to have whatever potion(s) suit them, or you can dice to find them at random. Any character with a score of 100% or more for having a potion MUST be allowed to select their own, as this reflects the fact that such characters would have supplies of them available to choose from.

MISCELLANEOUS ITEMS

If the party is generally above 5th level and going into a hazardous area, or if the party is generally above 8th level, then you might determine it advantageous to award from one to four miscellaneous items according to the following list. Large groups are less likely to need such items. Higher level characters are more likely to have them despite numbers. Selection can be by you or by the party, as you deem best. You may add or delete items as desired, but remember that those shown are chosen to maintain a low key of power.

1. Feather falling ring
2. Warmth ring
3. Water walking ring
4. Wand of negation
5. Wand of wonder
6. Bag of holding (500 pound capacity)

7. Boat, folding (small rowboat)
8. Brooch of shielding
9. Cloak and boots of elvenkind
10. Javelin of lightning, pair
11. Javelin of piercing, pair
12. Necklace of adaptation
13. Robe of useful items — SEE BELOW
14. Rope of climbing
15. Trident of warning
16. Wings of flying or boots of levitation

Items On A Robe Of Useful Items (Select 7-12)

BONFIRE, small
CASK, 1-3 = water, 4-5 = wine, 6 = brandy (3 gallon capacity)
CALTROPS, six
CROWBAR, 4' tempered iron
DAGGER, silver
DOG, WAR
DOOR, standard size, oak with iron bindings and bar
GEM, 100 gold piece value
LADDER, 12' long
LANTERN, bullseye
MALLET & STAKES
MEAT, haunch of roast mutton, venison, etc.
MONEY, stack of 50 silver coins
MULE, pack
OAK TREE, 30' high, large
OWL, GIANT
PICK, standard digging
POLE, 10'
ROOSTER
ROPE, 50' coil
SHOVEL
TORCH, flaming
WASP NEST, normal, about 200 wasps

When you are thoroughly familiar with this system, you will be able to ready a party of players for an adventure with a minimum amount of time and effort on your part, and do so with relative assurance that they will be about right for the area they will adventure in.

GLOSSARY

Ability Scores — Numerical ratings ranging from 3-18 for a character's strength, intelligence, wisdom, constitution, dexterity, and charisma.

AD&D — **ADVANCED DUNGEONS & DRAGONS**TM.

Alignment — A general description of a character's behaviorial and ethical tendencies named by a combination of Law, Neutrality, or Chaos with Good, Neutrality, or Evil.

Armor Class — A number representing the relative protection from harm the character will enjoy. This includes type of armor, dexterity bonuses or penalties, magical protections, etc.

Artifact — A magical item of tremendous power, fabricated in the distant past.

Astral — Pertaining to or within the Astral Plane (see **PHB**, p. 120). *Not the same as ethereal* (q.v.).

Bolt — 1. Missile from a crossbow. 2. Bar locking a door. 3. Streak of lightning. 4. To flee.

Breath Weapon — Special attack of certain creatures like dragons, chimerae, etc. causing any of several different effects. For saving throw purposes the "Breath Weapon" category excludes *petrification* and *polymorph* results, which have their own category.

Campaign — General term referring to one DM's adventures as a whole rather than individually. An ongoing series of games based upon a created milieu.

Cf. — Compare.

Charm — A magical form of minor mind control.

Class — Refers to an adventurer's profession: fighter, cleric, thief, etc.

c.p. (Also **cp**) — Copper piece(s), a monetary unit worth 1/200 of a gold piece.

Damage — The number of hit points or structural points that have been inflicted on the being or structure.

Death — This occurs when a creature's hit points reach 0 (or optionally, –10). Most dead characters can be *resurrected*, although destruction of the body (among other factors) will prevent this.

Death Magic — *Death rays*, *Fingers of Death*, and other magicks which will kill a victim which fails its saving throw.

Deities — Any of the god-like beings of myth and legend the DM desires which may be included in the campaign.

Demi-humans — Refers to anthropomorphic, generally non-hostile (towards man) creatures that may be played as characters: elves, dwarves, halflings, etc.

DM — Dungeon Master, the referee of **ADVANCED DUNGEONS & DRAGONS**TM.

Dungeon — A generic term for any castle, location, or ruin that serves as the site of an underground adventure.

Dweomer — From dweomercraeft, the art (craeft) of magic (dweomer).

e.g. — For example.

Encounter — An unexpected confrontation with a monster, another party, etc.

Encumbrance — Generally, the weight and bulkiness of a particular adventurer's possessions (armor, weapons, equipment, etc.).

e.p. (Also **ep**) — Electrum piece(s), a monetary unit of a naturally occurring silver-gold alloy worth ½ of a gold piece.

et al. — And others.

Ethereal — Pertaining to or within the Ethereal Plane (see **PHB**, p. 120). Not the same as astral (q.v.).

Exceptional Strength — Strength exceeding 18, usually designated as 18/x, where x is a value between 01 and 00 (100) inclusive.

Experience — The reward (expressed in points, or x.p.) for slaying monsters, winning treasure, and playing the character role. The more experience a character has, the better his or her fighting ability, saving throws, etc.

Feet — Where the term "feet" or the mark ′ is used (e.g., 30 feet or 30′), the distance referred to is usually actual feet with reference to the character (q.q.v. **Inches**, also **PHB**, p. 39).

Followers — A loyal group of associates garnered by a character at a certain level.

g.p. (Also **gp**) — Gold piece(s), the standard monetary unit; 10 g.p. = 1 pound, each g.p. weighing 1.6 avoir. oz. Sometimes used as a unit of weight/encumbrance.

Henchman — A low-level non-player character whose loyalty is to one member of the party rather than the party itself.

Hireling — A non-player character hired to accompany a party on an adventure, or employed for some other temporary purpose.

Hit Dice — The number of dice rolled to determine the creature's hit points.

Hit Points — The number of points of damage a creature can sustain before death (or optionally, coma), reflecting the creature's physical endurance, fighting experience, skill, or luck.

Holy/Unholy Water — Water which has been specially prepared by a cleric. Useful as a weapon against undead or to slow the effects of poison.

Humanoid — Refers to anthropomorphic, generally hostile creatures: orcs, goblins, hobgoblins, kobolds, etc.

i.e. — That is.

Inches — One inch = 10 feet on the indoor (dungeon) scale; one inch = 10 yards on the outdoor scale (See **PHB**, p. 39).

Initiative — The means of determining the order of actions of opposing individuals or groups. By means of initiative the order in which blows are struck in combat (or other actions are undertaken) is determined.

Invisibility — A manner of hiding from normal visual means. This does not make someone soundless or odorless.

League — For game purposes a league equals approximately 3 miles.

Level — 1. The relative depth and/or degree of difficulty of one floor of a dungeon. 2. The degree of difficulty and power of a spell. 3. The degree of proficiency and experience a character has in his or her profession. 4. A measure of how "tough" a monster is.

Lycanthrope — Any of the shape-changing man-beasts of legend (werewolves, weretigers, etc.).

Magic — Anything which cannot be explained by the science of the milieu. Any weapon or item which has a bonus (+1, +2, etc.) is considered a magic item.

Magic Resistance — The percentage chance of any spell absolutely failing in the monster's presence. It is based on the spell being cast by an 11th level magic-user, and must be adjusted upwards by 5% for each level the caster is below 11th or downwards by 5% for each level the caster is above 11th. Thus a magic resistance of 95% means that a 10th level magic-user has no possibility of affecting the monster with a spell, while a 12th level MU has a 10% chance. Even if a spell does take effect on a magic-resistant creature, the creature is then entitled to normal saving throws.

Melee — Combat with hand-held weapons between more than two figures. This is distinguished from list combat, which is between two opponents, and missile (q.v.) combat, which is at a distance and involves thrown or propelled weapons.

Mezzodaemon — A monster encountered in **AD&D MODULE D3, VAULT OF THE DROW.** Ignore it if its statistics are unavailable to you.

Milieu — An unique game setting embodying numerous possible variables in its creation, i.e. the "world" in which adventures take place.

Miniature — A small lead or plastic figure which serves as a visual aid in **AD&D**.

Missile — Any weapon which is hurled or propelled towards a target; this includes arrows, spears, catapult boulders, and sling bullets, as well as anything else flung at a target (flasks of oil, vials of holy water, etc.).

Monster — For game purposes, any potentially threatening creature encountered, man or beast.

Monty Haul — A campaign (or the DM running it) in which greatly excessive amounts of treasure and/or experience are given out.

MU (Also **M-U**) — Magic-user.

Natural 20 — When a 20-sided die is rolled and a ''20'' appears. This is distinguished from a *result* of 20, which could be a lower roll augmented by ability and magical bonuses.

N.B. — Note well.

NPC (Also **N-PC**) — Non-player character.

Nycadaemon — A monster encountered in **AD&D MODULE D3, VAULT OF THE DROW.** Ignore it if its statistics are unavailable to you.

Party — A group of adventurers.

PC — Player character.

Persona — The role or identity of the character the player is portraying.

Petrification (Also **petrifaction**) — The rapid turning to stone of some object or being by magical means such as a basilisk's gaze, etc.

Philter — A magical draught or potion.

Phylactery — An arm wrapping with a container holding religious writings, thus a form of amulet or charm.

Planes — Other realms of existence, some of which interconnect with the Prime Material Plane, the normal milieu setting (see **PHB**, p. 120).

Poison — Refers to both toxic man-made substances and venom from poisonous creatures.

Pole Arm — A hafted weapon, other than a spear or staff, with a length of 5' or more.

Polymorph — The physical alteration by magical means of the shape of a creature.

p.p. (Also **pp**) — Platinum piece(s), a monetary unit. Each p.p. is worth 5 g.p.

Psionics — Mental combat, possible only by very intelligent beings and some monsters. Psionics also encompasses certain other special mental abilities, such as *telekinesis*. See **PHB, APPENDIX I.**

Q.E.D. — Which was to be demonstrated.

q.v. (Also **q.q.v.**) — Which see; something that is also referenced.

Random Generation — Determining at random something from a list of several possibilities, usually by rolling dice.

Relic — A magical holy item of great power, usually extremely old.

Research — In addition to its normal meaning, the work involved when a MU or alchemist is involved in preparing new spells, enchanting items, etc.

Resurrection — The revival of a character after its death by magical means.

Round (Also **melee round**) — A unit of time in **AD&D** equal to 1 minute. Each round is composed of 10 *segments,* and 10 rounds constitute a *turn.*

Saving Throw — A die roll which is used in adverse circumstances to determine the efficacy of a spell, whether a character fell into a pit or not, whether a character escaped a dragon's breath, etc.

Scrying — Viewing a person or thing through mystical means.

Segment — The smallest unit of time in **AD&D**; each segment is 6 seconds long. 10 segments comprise a *round* (q.v.).

s.p. (Also **sp**) — Silver piece(s), a monetary unit. 20 s.p. = 1 gold piece.

Structural Points — The amount of damage a structure can sustain before it gives way.

Surprise — Both parties in an encounter must check to see if either or both are *surprised,* which may result in a loss of *initiative* (q.v.).

To Hit — That number which must be matched or beaten by a 20-sided die roll in order to inflict damage on an opponent.

Trap — Any of several mechanical or magical devices which may be triggered by adventurers, usually causing damage to one or more of them. Examples are pits, pits with spikes, poison needle traps on treasure chests, etc.

Treasure — A general term meaning anything of value which may be acquired by adventuring.

Trick — Any device or machination which is more likely to be solved by wits rather than force. Tricks do not necessarily involve physical harm to the characters; examples are rooms which rotate or descend to confuse mappers, statues which perform random actions, slanting passageways which take the party unknowingly to a deeper level, etc.

Turn — A unit of time in **AD&D**, equal to 10 minutes. Each turn consists of 10 *rounds* (q.v.), and each round is comprised of 10 *segments* (q.v.).

Turning Undead — A process by which a cleric attempts to use his or her holy power to *turn* (force to retreat), *influence, destroy,* or *damn* encountered creatures of the undead (q.v.) class.

Undead — A class of malevolent, soulless monsters which are neither truly dead nor alive, including skeletons, vampires, ghosts, zombies, ghouls, *et al.*

vis-a-vis — Face-to-face; compared with.

viz. — That is; namely.

Wandering Monster — General term for any encounter not previously keyed by the DM; usually refers to the periodic check for monsters in dungeons.

x.p. — Experience points.

AFTERWORD

IT IS THE SPIRIT OF THE GAME, NOT THE LETTER OF THE RULES, WHICH IS IMPORTANT. NEVER HOLD TO THE LETTER WRITTEN, NOR ALLOW SOME BARRACKS ROOM LAWYER TO FORCE QUOTATIONS FROM THE RULE BOOK UPON YOU, IF IT GOES AGAINST THE OBVIOUS INTENT OF THE GAME. AS YOU HEW THE LINE WITH RESPECT TO CONFORMITY TO MAJOR SYSTEMS AND UNIFORMITY OF PLAY IN GENERAL, ALSO BE CERTAIN THE GAME IS MASTERED BY YOU AND NOT BY YOUR PLAYERS. WITHIN THE BROAD PARAMETERS GIVEN IN THE **ADVANCED DUNGEONS & DRAGONS VOLUMES,** YOU ARE CREATOR AND FINAL ARBITER. BY ORDERING THINGS AS THEY SHOULD BE, THE GAME AS A WHOLE FIRST, YOUR CAMPAIGN NEXT, AND YOUR PARTICIPANTS THEREAFTER, YOU WILL BE PLAYING **ADVANCED DUNGEONS & DRAGONS** AS IT WAS MEANT TO BE. MAY YOU FIND AS MUCH PLEASURE IN SO DOING AS THE REST OF US DO!

INDEX

This is a combined index for both the **DUNGEON MASTERS GUIDE** and the **ADVANCED DUNGEONS AND DRAGONS PLAYERS HANDBOOK,** included to provide a handy reference to those areas most often consulted by the AD&D DM and player. (It is not designed to be a totally exhaustive listing.) **DMG** page numbers are always listed first and in **boldface.** Page numbers for listings in the **PHB** are in regular type, and follow those in boldface (where simultaneous listings occur.).

ADVANCED D&D is an entire family of related game products comprising several hardbound volumes, playing aid items, and accessories. **AD&D** is only a part of the larger line of TSR Games. TSR products are available at fine book, game, hobby, and department stores nationwide. If you are unable to locate desired items, write to us at the address below and inquire as to the name of your nearest TSR dealer. A listing of all TSR products is also available upon request.

The ADVANCED DUNGEONS & DRAGONS™ Game Family

PLAYERS HANDBOOK. This hardbound volume contains everything the player needs to know in AD&D. It contains complete information on characters, levels, equipment, spells, and more.

MONSTER MANUAL. A hardbound compendium of the creatures inhabiting the AD&D fantasy world. Over 350 descriptions of monsters, from Aerial Servant to Zombie, profusely illustrated.

THE WORLD OF GREYHAWK. This work provides a complete campaign milieu in which to base adventures and characters, place dungeons, etc. Two large full-color maps, a folder, and a 32-page booklet full of ready-made historical and geographical information. Approved for use with Advanced D&D.

DUNGEON MASTERS SCREEN. Actually two laminated reference screens, one for normal combat, saving throws, and other oft-needed information, and another for psionic combat. With full color illustrations.

PLAYER CHARACTER RECORD SHEETS
PERMANENT CHARACTER FOLDER AND ADVENTURE RECORD SHEETS
NON-PLAYER CHARACTER RECORD SHEETS

These three products are designed for various types of character record keeping, and are made for the convenience of player and Dungeon Master alike. All are three-hole drilled for easy notebook storage.

THE ROGUES GALLERY. An aid for the harried Dungeon Master, this booklet contains hundreds of ready-made non-player characters, as well as caravans, bandit groups, dungeon parties, and more.

MODULES

Every AD&D module is a ready-to-play adventure setting, populated with appropriate monsters, treasures, tricks, and traps, and including maps, background information, and histories. Though each individual module is designed to stand on its own, several series are specially made to form a connected progression of adventures.

G1: STEADING OF THE HILL GIANT CHIEF
G2: GLACIAL RIFT OF THE FROST GIANT JARL
G3: HALL OF THE FIRE GIANT KING

D1: DESCENT INTO THE DEPTHS OF THE EARTH
D2: SHRINE OF THE KUO-TOA
D3: VAULT OF THE DROW

S1: TOMB OF HORRORS
S2: WHITE PLUME MOUNTAIN

T1: VILLAGE OF HOMMLET

C1: HIDDEN SHRINE OF TAMOACHAN

ENCUMBRANCE OF STANDARD ITEMS

Item	Encumbrance in gold pieces
Backpack	20
Belt	3
Belt pouch, large	10
small	5
Book, large metal-bound	200
Boots, hard	60
soft	30
Bottles, flagons	60
Bow, composite long	80
composite short	50
long	100
short	50
Caltrop	50
Candle	5
Chest, large solid iron	1,000-5,000
small solid iron	200-500
small wooden	100-250
large wooden	500-1,500
Clothes (1 set)	30
Cord, 10'	2
Crossbow, heavy	80
light	50
Crystal ball, base and wrapping	150
Flask, empty	7
full	20
Gem	1-5
Grapnel	100
Hand tool	10
Helm	45
Helm, great	100
Holy water, potion bottles	25
Horn	50
Jewelry, large	50
small	1-5
Lantern	60
Mirror	5
Musical instrument*	350
Pole, 10'	100
Purse	1
Quiver	30
Rutions, iron	75
standard	200
Robe or cloak, folded	50
worn	25
Rod	60
Rope, 50'	75
Sack, large	20
small	5
Saddle, light horse	250
heavy horse	500
Saddlebag	150
Saddle blanket (pad)	20
Scroll case, bone or ivory	50
leather	25
Spike	10
Staff	100
Tapestry (very small to huge)	50-1,000+
Tinderbox	2
Torch	25
Wand, bone or ivory case	60
box	80
leather case	30
Waterskin or wineskin, empty	5
full	50

Armor Type	Bulk	Weight*	Base Movement
BANDED	bulky	35#+	9"
CHAIN	fairly	30#+	9"
CHAIN, ELFIN	non-	15#	12"
LEATHER	non-	15#	12"
PADDED	fairly	10#	9"
PLATE (MAIL)	bulky	45#	6"
RING	fairly	25#	9"
SCALE	fairly	40#	6"
SHIELD, LARGE	bulky	10#	—
SHIELD, SMALL	non-	5#	—
SHIELD, SMALL, WOOD	non-	3#	—
SPLINT	bulky	40#	6"
STUDDED (LEATHER)	fairly	20#	9"

*Assumes human-size.

STANDARD HIRELINGS TABLE OF DAILY AND MONTHLY COSTS

Occupation	Daily Cost	Monthly Cost*
bearer/porter	1 s.p.	1 g.p.
carpenter	3 s.p.	2 g.p.**
leather worker	2 s.p.	30 s.p.**
limner	10 s.p.	10 g.p.
linkboy	1 s.p.	1 g.p.
mason	4 s.p.	3 g.p.
pack handler	2 s.p.	30 s.p.
tailor	2 s.p.	30 s.p.**
teamster	5 s.p.	5 g.p.
valet/lackey	3 s.p.	50 s.p.

*Monthly rate assumes that quarters are provided for the hireling, and that these quarters contain a bed and like necessities.

**Additional cost is 10% of the normal price of items fashioned by the hireling.

EXPERT HIRELINGS TABLE OF MONTHLY COSTS IN GOLD PIECES

Occupation or Profession	Cost
alchemist	300
armorer	100*
blacksmith	30
engineer-architect	100*
engineer-artillerist	150
engineer-sapper/miner	150
jeweler-gemcutter	100*
mercenary soldier —	
archer (longbow)	4
archer (shortbow)	2
artillerist	5
captain	special
crossbowman	2
footman, heavy	2
footman, light	1
footman, pikeman	3
hobilar, heavy	3
hobilar, light	2
horseman, archer	6
horseman, crossbowman	4
horseman, heavy	6
horseman, light	3
horseman, medium	4
lieutenant	special
sapper/miner	4
serjeant	special
slinger	3
sage	special
scribe	15
ship crew	special
ship master	special
spy	special
steward/castellan	special
weapon maker	100*

*Cost does not include all remuneration or special fees. Add 10% of the usual cost of items handled or made by these hirelings on a per job basis, i.e. an armorer makes a suit of plate mail which has a normal cost of 400 gold pieces, so 10% of that sum (40 g.p.) is added to the costs of maintaining the blacksmith.

DUNGEON MASTERS GUIDE

(This page is perforated for easy removal and reference.)

MORALE

Morale Checks Made When

Faced by obviously superior force*	check each round
25% of party** eliminated or slain	check at +5%
Leader unconscious	check at +10%
50%+ of party** eliminated or slain	check at +15%
Leader slain or deserts	check at +30%

* Such as in melee when one force is hitting twice as often as the other.

** Or individual taking this much personal wound damage.

Other Morale Check Modifiers

Each enemy deserting	−5%
Each enemy slain	−10%
Inflicting casualties without receiving any	−20%
Each friend killed	+10%
Taking casualties without receiving any	+10%
Each friend deserting	+15%
Outnumbered & outclassed by 3 or more to 1	+20%

MORALE FAILURE

1% to 15%	fall back, fighting
16% to 30%	disengage-retreat
31% to 50%	flee in panic
51% or greater	surrender

TYPICAL LOYALTY, OBEDIENCE, AND MORALE CHECK SITUATIONS

Situation	Failure Result
offered bribe	co-operates
ordered to testify against liege	agrees
has a chance to steal goods	steals
left alone in possible danger	deserts
abandoned	deserts
ordered into possible danger	refuses
ordered to perform heroic act	refuses
ordered to perform heroic and dangerous act	refuses
ordered to rescue party member(s)	refuses
ordered to rescue liege	refuses
in combat with possibly dangerous foe	runs away
liege incapacitated or slain	runs away
offered surrender terms	surrenders
surrounded by superior foe	surrenders
ordered to use up or diminish own magic item	refuses

NORMAL LOYALTY BASE: 50%, +/− charisma adjustment

LOYALTY OF HENCHMEN AND ALLIED CREATURES

Adjusted Loyalty Score	Loyalty
Less than 01	None — will attempt to kill, capture, harm, or desert at first possible opportunity
01-25	Disloyal — will always seek own advantage regardless of circumstances
26-50	Little — will seek own advantage at first sign of weakness
51-75	Fair — will support cause if no great risk is involved
76-00	Loyal — will always attempt to further the ends of the liege, even at great risk
Greater than 00	Fanatical — will serve unquestioningly and lay down own life if necessary without hesitation

LOYALTY BASE MODIFIERS:

Length Of Enlistment or Association*

	Modifer
less than 1 month	− 5%
less than 1 year	0%
1 to 5 years	+10%
more than 5 years	+25%

*This includes time between service or length of time that the player character has been generally known and familiar to the figure(s) in question.

Enlistment Or Association

	Modifier
associated non-player character	−10%
captured and enlisted	−15%
henchman	+5%
hired mercenary	0%
hired mercenary, short term	− 5%
slave	−30%

Training Or Status Level

	Modifier
untrained or peasant	−25%
little training, levied troops	−15%
newly recruited regulars	− 5%
trained regulars	+10%
elite, sub-officers, minor officials/expert hireling	+20%
guards, officers, or major officials/henchmen	+30%

Pay Or Treasure Shared

	Modifier
none	−20%
partial, late, or unfair	−10%
average	0%
above average, choice shares	+5%
exceptional, bonuses, gift items*	+10%

*Typically magic items if a henchman is concerned

Discipline/Activity

	Modifier
none/one	−10%
lax/little	− 5%
firm and harsh/occasional	0%
firm and fair/often	+10%

General Treatment By Liege

	Modifier
inhuman and heartless	−25%
cruel and domineering	−10%*
indifferent and uncaring or variable	− 5%
just and invariable	+10%
just, kind, and invariable	+15%

*Applies only when the liege is not present, is incapacitated or dead; if the liege is near and in power, minuses are treated as pluses — otherwise treat as 0% adjustment (fear).

Racial Preference For -

	Liege	Associated Group
antipathy	−5%	−10%
good will	+10%	+5%
hatred	−20%	−15%
neutral	0%	0%
preferred	+20%	+15%
tolerance	0%	− 5%

Alignment Factors

Alignment Is	Liege	Associated Group
1 place removed	0%	0%
2 places removed	−15%	− 5%
3 places removed	−35%	−20%

Examples: lawful evil - lawful neutral = 1 place removed
lawful evil - lawful good = 2 places removed
lawful evil - chaotic good = 3 places removed

Alignment of Liege

	Modifier
lawful good	+15%
lawful neutral	+10%
lawful evil	+5%
neutral good	0%
neutral	0%
chaotic good	− 5%
chaotic neutral	−10%
neutral evil	−15%
chaotic evil	−20%

Situation Modifiers

	Modifier
liege dead or surrounded and outnumbered	−25%
liege hors de combat	−15%
each henchman dead or hors de combat	− 5%
each hit die or level dead, friendly	− 3%
each hit die or level alive, enemy	− 1%
each hit die or level dead, enemy	+1%
each hit die or level alive, friendly	+2%
each henchman present, in sight, alive	+5%
liege present, in sight, alive	+15%